The highest temperature ever recorded in Death Valley was 134°F.

140°F
130°F
120°F
110°F
100°F
90°F
80°F
70°F
60°F
50°F
40°F
30°F
20°F
10°F
0°F

134°F

The highest and lowest temperatures both occurred in 1913.

15°F

The lowest temperature recorded in Death Valley was 15°F.

# CALIFORNIA
# HSP Math

## Harcourt
### SCHOOL PUBLISHERS

Visit *The Learning Site!*
**www.harcourtschool.com**

CALIFORNIA HSP Math

*Mathematics Content Standards for California Public Schools* reproduced by permission, California Department of Education, CDE Press, 1430 N Street, Suite 3207, Sacramento, CA 95814

Printed in the United States of America

ISBN 13: 978-0-15-354172-8
ISBN 10: 0-15-354172-5

3 4 5 6 7 8 9 10  751  16 15 14 13 12 11 10 09 08

## Mathematics Advisor

**David Singer**
Professor of Mathematics
Case Western Reserve University
Cleveland, Ohio

## Senior Authors

**Evan M. Maletsky**
Professor Emeritus
Montclair State University
Upper Montclair, New Jersey

**Joyce McLeod**
Visiting Professor, Retired
Rollins College
Winter Park, Florida

## Authors

**Angela G. Andrews**
Assistant Professor,
    Math Education
National-Louis University
Lisle, Illinois

**Juli K. Dixon**
Associate Professor of
    Mathematics Education
University of Central Florida
Orlando, Florida

**Vicki Newman**
Classroom Teacher
McGaugh Elementary School
Los Alamitos Unified
    School District
Seal Beach, California

**Robin C. Scarcella**
Professor and Director
Program of Academic English
    and ESL
University of California, Irvine
Irvine, California

**Tom Roby**
Associate Professor of Mathematics
Director, Quantitative
    Learning Center
University of Connecticut
Storrs, Connecticut

**Jennie M. Bennett**
Mathematics Teacher
Houston Independent
    School District
Houston, Texas

**Lynda Luckie**
Director, K–12 Mathematics
Gwinnett County Public Schools
Suwanee, Georgia

**Karen S. Norwood**
Associate Professor of
    Mathematics Education
North Carolina State University
Raleigh, North Carolina

**Janet K. Scheer**
Executive Director
Create-A-Vision
Foster City, California

**David G. Wright**
Professor
Department of Mathematics
Brigham Young University
Provo, Utah

## Program Consultants and Specialists

**Russell Gersten**
Director, Instructional
    Research Group
Long Beach, California
Professor Emeritus of
    Special Education
University of Oregon
Eugene, Oregon

**Michael DiSpezio**
Writer and On-Air Host,
    JASON Project
North Falmouth, Massachusetts

**Tyrone Howard**
Assistant Professor,
    UCLA Graduate School
    of Education
    Information Studies
University of California
    at Los Angeles
Los Angeles, California

**Lydia Song**
Program Specialist, Mathematics
Orange County Department
    of Education
Costa Mesa, California

**Rebecca Valbuena**
Language Development Specialist
Stanton Elementary School
Glendora, California

**MATH ON LOCATION**

Photos from
The Futures Channel
with California
Chapter Projects and
**VOCABULARY
POWER** ........ 1

**READ Math
WORKSHOP** ...... 45

**WRITE Math
WORKSHOP** ...... 17

**GO ONLINE** Technology

Harcourt Mega Math: Chapter 1, p. 10; Chapter 2, p. 40; Chapter 3, p. 71; Chapter 4, p. 91; Extra Practice: Chapter 1, p. 26; Chapter 2, p. 58; Chapter 3, p. 82; Chapter 4, p. 106
The Harcourt Learning Site:
www.harcourtschool.com
Multimedia Math Glossary:
www.harcourtschool.com/hspmath

The World Almanac for Kids

Counting
Votes ........ 112

# Rational Numbers and Integer Operations

 Math on Location . . . . . . . . . . . . . . . . . . . . . . . . . . . . 115

### MATH ON LOCATION

Photos from The Futures Channel with California Chapter Projects and **VOCABULARY POWER** ....... 115

**READ Math WORKSHOP** ..... 129

**WRITE Math WORKSHOP** ..... 185

**GO ONLINE** — Technology

Harcourt Mega Math: Chapter 6, p. 146; Chapter 7, p. 171; Extra Practice: Chapter 5, p. 134; Chapter 6, p. 162; Chapter 7, p. 188
The Harcourt Learning Site: www.harcourtschool.com
Multimedia Math Glossary: www.harcourtschool.com/hspmath

The World Almanac for Kids

Highs and Lows in California..... 194

# UNIT 3

# Statistics and Graphing

 Math on Location . . . . . . . . . . . . . . . . . . . . . . . . . . . 197

# 10 Graph Data 242

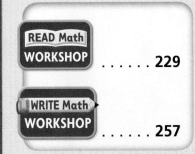

**MATH ON LOCATION**

Photos from
The Futures Channel
with California
Chapter Projects and
**VOCABULARY
POWER** . . . . . . . **197**

READ Math
WORKSHOP . . . . . . **229**

WRITE Math
WORKSHOP . . . . . . **257**

GO ONLINE — Technology

Harcourt Mega Math: Extra
Practice: Chapter 10, p. 260
The Harcourt Learning Site:
www.harcourtschool.com
Multimedia Math Glossary:
www.harcourtschool.com/
hspmath

The World Almanac
for Kids

Population
Trends . . . . . . . **266**

# UNIT 4

# Algebra: Expressions and Equations

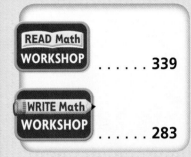

# UNIT 5

# Geometry: Two-Dimensional Figures

# 17 Circles 416

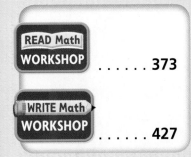
GO ONLINE     Technology

Harcourt Mega Math: Chapter
15, p. 380; Chapter 16, p. 394;
Extra Practice: Chapter 15,
p. 384; Chapter 16, p. 410
The Harcourt Learning Site:
www.harcourtschool.com
Multimedia Math Glossary:
www.harcourtschool.com/
hspmath

The World Almanac
for Kids

California
Architecture. . . 436

# Ratio, Proportion, and Percent

## 20 Percent and Change 490

**MATH ON LOCATION**

Photos from The Futures Channel with California Chapter Projects and **VOCABULARY POWER** . . . . . . . **439**

READ Math WORKSHOP . . . . . . **475**

WRITE Math WORKSHOP . . . . . . **451**

 **Technology**

Harcourt Mega Math: Chapter 19, p. 470; Chapter 20, p. 502; Extra Practice: Chapter 19, p. 484; Chapter 20, p. 510
The Harcourt Learning Site: www.harcourtschool.com
Multimedia Math Glossary: www.harcourtschool.com/hspmath

The World Almanac for Kids

Solar Power—Energy for the Future? **516**

# 22 Probability of Compound Events 542

**MATH ON LOCATION**

Photos from
The Futures Channel
with California
Chapter Projects and
**VOCABULARY
POWER** . . . . . . . 519

**WRITE Math
WORKSHOP** . . . . . . . 525

**GO
ONLINE** — Technology

Harcourt Mega Math: Chapter
21, p. 524; Extra Practice:
Chapter 21, p. 536
The Harcourt Learning Site:
www.harcourtschool.com
Multimedia Math Glossary:
www.harcourtschool.com/
hspmath

The World Almanac
for Kids

Board
Games . . . . . . . 564

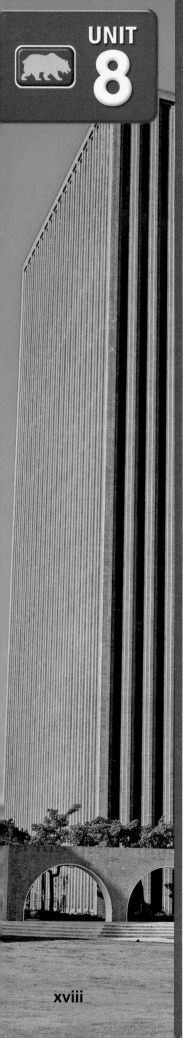

# UNIT 8

# Perimeter, Area, and Volume

# 24 Surface Area and Volume 594

## 🐻 Student Handbook

**MATH ON LOCATION**

Photos from
The Futures Channel
with California
Chapter Projects and
**VOCABULARY
POWER** . . . . . . . 567

**READ Math
WORKSHOP** . . . . . . 583

 Technology

Harcourt Mega Math: Chapter
23, p. 582; Chapter 24, p. 602;
Extra Practice: Chapter 23,
p. 588; Chapter 24, p. 612
The Harcourt Learning Site:
www.harcourtschool.com
Multimedia Math Glossary:
www.harcourtschool.com/
hspmath

🐻

The World Almanac
for Kids

Sand
Castles . . . . . . . 618

# TALK, READ, and WRITE
## About Math

Mathematics is a language of numbers, words, and symbols.

This year you will learn ways to communicate about math as you **talk, read,** and **write** about what you are learning.

The double line graph shows the average monthly maximum and minimum temperatures for the Yosemite Valley in Yosemite National Park.

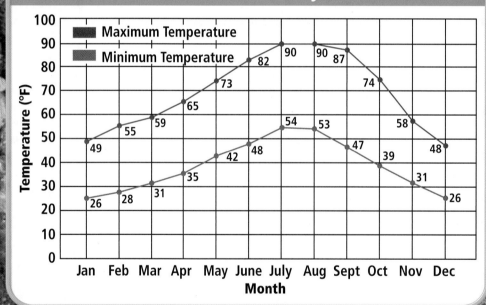

**Average Maximum and Minimum Temperatures for Yosemite Valley**

**TALK Math**

**Talk** about the double-line graph.

1. What do the words *average, maximum,* and *minimum* in the title tell you about the data?

2. What are the scale and the interval for the graph?

3. Why does the graph have a key at the top?

4. What can you infer by looking at the lines on the graph?

**Read** the data on the double-line graph.

5. Which month has the lowest maximum temperature?

6. Which months have the highest maximum temperatures?

7. Which two months have the greatest difference between their minimum temperatures?

8. Which two months have a difference of 10°F between their maximum temperatures?

WRITE Math ▶

**Write** a problem about the double-line graph.

This year you will write many problems. When you see **Pose a Problem**, you look at a problem on the page and use it to write your own problem.

In your problem you can
- change the numbers or some of the information.
- exchange the known and unknown information.
- write an open-ended problem that can have more than one correct answer.

These problems are examples of ways you can pose your own problem. Solve each problem.

**Problem**  What is the range of the average maximum monthly temperatures in Yosemite Valley?

● **Change the Numbers or Information**
   What is the range of the average minimum monthly temperatures in Yosemite Valley?

● **Exchange the Known and Unknown Information**
   The range of the average monthly temperatures is 42°F. Is that the range of the average maximum or the average minimum monthly temperatures?

● **Open-Ended**
   Which months have a range of between 35°F and 44°F in their average maximum and minimum temperatures?

**Pose a Problem**  Choose one of the three ways to write a new problem. Use the information in the double-line graph.

# Number Theory, Fraction Concepts, and Operations

# Math on Location

▲ Careful measuring of ingredients using fractions and mixed numbers results in delicious foods.

▲ Herb rolls are cut from dough and placed on baking trays in rows of equal numbers.

▲ Meals that are ready to serve are artfully arranged and decorated with flowers.

# VOCABULARY POWER

## TALK Math

What math is shown in the **Math on Location** photographs? How can you use fractions when cooking and baking?

## READ Math

**REVIEW VOCABULARY** You learned the words below when you learned about fractions. How do these words relate to **Math on Location**?

**equivalent fractions** fractions that name the same amount or part

**mixed number** a number represented by a whole number and a fraction

**multiple** the product of a given whole number and another whole number

## WRITE Math

Copy and complete the circle maps like the ones below. Use what you know about fractions to answer the questions.

### Equivalent Fractions

What do you know about equivalent fractions? What experience have you had that taught you about equivalent fractions?

$\frac{2}{4}$   $\frac{3}{6}$

$\left(\frac{1}{2}\right)$

$\frac{4}{8}$   $\frac{5}{10}$

$\frac{6}{12}$

$\left(\frac{1}{3}\right)$

**Technology**
Multimedia Math Glossary link at
**www.harcourtschool.com/hspmath**

# 1

# Number Theory and Fraction Concepts

**The Big Idea** The study of number theory builds understanding of factors and multiples; fractions and mixed numbers can be expressed in equivalent forms and can be compared and ordered.

## CALIFORNIA FAST FACT

The Altamont Pass wind farm in Northern California has more than 6,000 wind turbines of various sizes, the largest concentration of wind turbines in the world.

## Investigate

Suppose you are a researcher investigating energy production in California. What combinations of two to four types of energy sources would allow California to meet at least $\frac{3}{5}$ of its energy production needs?

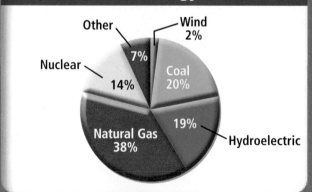

**2005 California Energy Production**

- Other 7%
- Wind 2%
- Coal 20%
- Nuclear 14%
- Natural Gas 38%
- Hydroelectric 19%

**GO ONLINE**

**Technology**
Student pages are available in the Student eBook.

# Show What You Know

Check your understanding of important skills
needed for success in Chapter 1.

▶ **Compare and Order Whole Numbers to 100,000**

**Compare. Write <, >, or =.**

1. 11,000 ● 11,050
2. 21,034 ● 22,345
3. 45,687 ● 45,238
4. 14,329 ● 14,329
5. 60,806 ● 68,600
6. 12,000 ● 1,200

**Order the numbers from greatest to least.**

7. 47,899; 48,799; 48,797
8. 40,133; 43,100; 14,330
9. 78,311; 78,300; 78,310
10. 94,586; 92,801; 99,934

▶ **Model Fractions**

Write a fraction for the shaded part.

11.
12.

13.
14.

# VOCABULARY POWER

**CHAPTER VOCABULARY**

composite number
factor
greatest common divisor (GCD)
greatest common factor (GCF)
least common multiple (LCM)
multiple
percent
prime factorization
prime number
simplest form

**WARM-UP WORDS**

**multiple** the product of a given whole number and another whole number

**factor** a number that is multiplied by another number to find a product

**prime number** a whole number greater than 1 whose only factors are 1 and itself

# LESSON 1

# Multiples and Factors

**OBJECTIVE:** Use patterns in multiples and factors to solve problems and identify prime and composite factors.

## Quick Review

1. 7 × 4
2. 8 × 3
3. 9 × 6
4. 5 × 4
5. 12 × 5

## Vocabulary

multiple          prime number

factor            composite number

## Learn

**PROBLEM** At a 40-mi bike-a-thon, there is a drink station at every fourth mi marker and a snack station at every sixth mile marker. At which mile markers will both drinks and snacks be available?

You can find the common multiples of 4 and 6 to solve this problem. A **multiple** of a whole number is the product of a given whole number and another whole number. Common multiples are numbers that are multiples of two or more numbers.

### Example 1  Find the common multiples of 4 and 6 that are less than or equal to 40.

> Multiples of 4: 4, 8, 12, 16, 20, 24, 28, 32, 36, 40
>
> Multiples of 6: 6, 12, 18, 24, 30, 36
>
> The common multiples of 4 and 6 are 12, 24, and 36.

So, both drinks and snacks will be available at mile markers 12, 24, and 36.

• Explain any patterns you see in the multiples of 4 and 6.

A **factor** is a number that is multiplied by another number to find a product. Common factors are numbers that are factors of two or more numbers.

### Example 2  Find the common factors of 24 and 32.

> Factors of 24: 1, 2, 3, 4, 6, 8, 12, 24          Factors of 32: 1, 2, 4, 8, 16, 32

So, the common factors of 24 and 32 are 1, 2, 4, and 8.

All whole numbers greater than 1 are either prime or composite numbers. A **prime number** is a whole number greater than 1 whose only factors are 1 and itself. A **composite number** is a whole number greater than 1 that has more than two factors.

> **Math Idea**
>
> The whole numbers 0 and 1 are neither prime nor composite.

### Example 3  Find the factors of each number. Tell whether the number is prime, composite, or neither.

**Ⓐ** 12

Factors of 12: 1, 2, 3, 4, 6, 12
12 is composite.

**Ⓑ** 29

Factors of 29: 1, 29
29 is prime.

**Ⓒ** 1

1 has only one factor, 1, so it is neither prime nor composite.

 **O⊓ NS 2.4** Determine the least common multiple and the greatest common divisor of whole numbers; use them to solve problems with fractions (e.g., to find a common denominator to add two fractions or to find the reduced form for a fraction). *also* **MR 2.4, MR 2.5, MR 3.0, MR 3.2, MR 3.3**

1. List the multiples of 6 and 9 that are less than 60. Then list the common multiples of 6 and 9.

**Write the first three common multiples.**

2. 8, 12　　　　3. 4, 5　　　　4. 5, 12　　　　5. 2, 4, 12　　　　✓6. 3, 4, 8

**Write the common factors.**

7. 12, 2　　　　8. 6, 7　　　　9. 36, 40　　　　10. 6, 12, 24　　　　✓11. 3, 5, 15

12. **TALK Math** Explain 2 is the only even prime number.

## Independent Practice and Problem Solving

**Write the first three common multiples.**

13. 4, 9　　　　14. 10, 14　　　　15. 8, 18　　　　16. 3, 8, 16　　　　17. 2, 4, 7

**Write the common factors.**

18. 25, 70　　　　19. 15, 30　　　　20. 50, 70　　　　21. 32, 45　　　　22. 24, 42

23. 4, 6, 16　　　　24. 18, 45, 72　　　　25. 8, 30, 46　　　　26. 7, 18, 21　　　　27. 4, 28, 36

**Tell whether the number is prime, composite, or neither.**

28. 98　　　　29. 61　　　　30. 0　　　　31. 37　　　　32. 82　　　　33. 1

**Algebra Find the unknown factor.**

34. $75 = \blacksquare \times 15$　　　35. $110 = 5 \times \blacksquare \times 11$　　　36. $42 = 2 \times \blacksquare \times 7$　　　37. $48 = \blacksquare \times 3 \times 4$

38. Mr. Tran's class has 12 boys and 18 girls. He will divide the whole class into groups so that all groups have the same number of boys and all have the same number of girls. What groups are possible?

39. What number is less than 30 and has exactly eight factors?

40. Write 65 as the product of two prime numbers.

41. **Reasoning** Will the product of two prime numbers be prime or composite? **Explain.**

42. **WRITE Math** The product of 9 and 6 is 54. Explain how to find what multiple of 3 results in a product of 54 when multiplied by 3.

## Achieving the Standards

43. What is the product of 0.8 and 120?
(Grade 5 ⊙━━ NS 2.1)

44. If $n = 79$, what is the value of $103 - n$?
(Grade 5 ⊙━━ AF 1.2)

45. What is the quotient of 8.25 divided by 5?
(Grade 5 ⊙━━ NS 2.1)

46. **Test Prep** Which of the following is a common multiple of 6 and 8?

　　A 18　　　　B 24　　　　C 40　　　　D 42

 **Extra Practice** on page 26, Set A

# 2 Greatest Common Factor

**OBJECTIVE:** Find the greatest common factor of two or more numbers, and use it to solve problems.

## Learn

**PROBLEM** Patsy and her mom want to plant 36 red petunias and 42 white petunias in equal rows in a rectangular garden. If they plant the same color of petunia throughout a row, what is the greatest number of petunias they can plant in each row?

You can solve the problem by using a list to find the greatest common factor of 36 and 42.

The **greatest common factor,** or **GCF,** is the greatest factor that two or more numbers have in common. Since factors are divisors of a number, the greatest common factor can also be called the **greatest common divisor,** or **GCD.**

| Factors of 36: 1, 2, 3, 4, 6, 9, 12, 18, 36 | Think: The common factors are 1, 2, 3, and 6. |
| Factors of 42: 1, 2, 3, 6, 7, 14, 21, 42 | The GCF of 36 and 42 is 6. |

So, the greatest number of petunias they can plant in each row is 6.

The **prime factorization** of a number is the number written as the product of its prime factors. For example, you know that $12 = 4 \times 3$. Using only prime numbers, $12 = 2 \times 2 \times 3$. So, the prime factorization of 12 is $2 \times 2 \times 3$.

You can use prime factorization or a ladder diagram to find the GCF of two or more numbers.

**ERROR ALERT**

When you list factors of a number, no factor can be greater than the number itself.

| **ONE WAY** Use the prime factorization to find the GCF of 8, 12, and 20. | **ANOTHER WAY** Use a ladder diagram to find the GCF of 12, 18, and 48. |
|---|---|
| $8 = 2 \times 2 \times 2$  Use only prime numbers. <br> $12 = 2 \times 2 \times 3$  Write the prime factorization <br> $20 = 2 \times 2 \times 5$  of each number. <br><br> $2 \times 2 = 4$  List the common prime factors and find their product. | $\begin{array}{c|ccc} 2 & 12 & 18 & 48 \\ 3 & 6 & 9 & 24 \\ & 2 & 3 & 8 \end{array}$  Divide each number by a common factor of the numbers. Keep dividing until the numbers have no common factors. <br><br> $2 \times 3 = 6$  Find the product of the divisors. |

So, the GCF of 8, 12, and 20 is 4.          So, the GCF of 12, 18, and 48 is 6.

• Steve used a ladder diagram to find the GCF of 36 and 48. He divided by 3 and then by 4. Would the GCF change if he chose two different common factors? Explain and give an example.

 **O⌐П NS 2.4** Determine the least common multiple and the greatest common divisor of whole numbers; use them to solve problems with fractions (e.g., to find a common denominator to add two fractions or to find the reduced form for a fraction). also **MR 2.4, MR 2.5, MR 3.2**

1. Complete the prime factorization to find the GCF of 12 and 28.

    Factors of 12: $2 \times \blacksquare \times 3$        Factors of 28: $2 \times 2 \times \blacksquare$        GCF: $2 \times \blacksquare = \blacksquare$

**Find the GCF.**

2. 18, 24        3. 50, 75        ✓4. 45, 81        5. 6, 9, 18        ✓6. 6, 10, 12

7. **TALK Math** **Explain** how to use prime factorization to find the GCF of 8 and 52.

## Independent Practice and Problem Solving

**Find the GCF.**

| | | | | |
|---|---|---|---|---|
| 8. 26, 28 | 9. 12, 40 | 10. 96, 120 | 11. 14, 21 | 12. 9, 16 |
| 13. 42, 96 | 14. 21, 56 | 15. 9, 48 | 16. 15, 28 | 17. 16, 35 |
| 18. 16, 32, 48 | 19. 3, 9, 18 | 20. 20, 50, 70 | 21. 32, 36, 45 | 22. 4, 12, 20 |

**Find two pairs of numbers that satisfy each statement.**

23. The GCF is 8.        24. The GCF is 6.        25. The GCF is 12.        26. The GCF is 15.

27. Kevin's class is selling boxes of plants. Each box will have one type of plant and all boxes will have the same number of plants. If there are 60 begonias, 48 geraniums, and 96 marigolds, what is the greatest number of plants the class can put in each box?

**For 28–29, use the information below.**

A class at Walker Elementary will receive 24 pens, 16 rulers, 32 pencils, and 12 notebooks for a school project. Each student that receives supplies will get the same number of each item as every other student gets.

28. What is the greatest number of students that can receive supplies if every item is used?

29. If there were 20 more rulers and 16 more pencils, what could be the greatest number of students that would receive supplies if every item were used?

30. **WRITE Math** Give an example to support this statement: "The GCF of a number and one of its multiples is the number itself."

## Achieving the Standards

31. What is the product of 56 and 0.053?
    (Grade 5 O┱ NS 2.1)

32. What factors of 16 are also factors of 64?
    (O┱ NS 2.4, p. 4)

33. 682 − 48.9 (Grade 5 O┱ NS 2.1)

34. **Test Prep** Which of the following is the greatest common divisor of 56 and 49?

    A 2                    C 7

    B 4                    D 9

# 3 Equivalent Fractions and Simplest Form

**OBJECTIVE:** Identify and write equivalent fractions, and write fractions in simplest form.

## Quick Review

Find the GCF.

1. 8, 12          2. 21, 28
3. 9, 30          4. 32, 60
5. 20, 45

## Vocabulary

**equivalent fractions**

**simplest form**

## Learn

**PROBLEM** A recipe for oatmeal cookies calls for $\frac{3}{4}$ cup of brown sugar. Daniel misplaced his $\frac{3}{4}$-cup and $\frac{1}{4}$-cup measuring cups, so he will use his $\frac{1}{8}$-cup measuring cup. How many times does he need to fill the $\frac{1}{8}$-cup measuring cup with brown sugar to make the oatmeal cookies?

**Equivalent fractions** are fractions that name the same amount or part. You can model equivalent fractions to find how many eighths are equivalent to $\frac{3}{4}$.

### Activity

**Materials** ■ fraction bars

- Begin with three $\frac{1}{4}$ fraction bars.

- Place $\frac{1}{8}$ fraction bars along the three $\frac{1}{4}$ bars until the lengths are equal.

- How many $\frac{1}{8}$ bars are there?

The model shows that $\frac{3}{4} = \frac{6}{8}$. So, Daniel needs to fill the $\frac{1}{8}$-cup measuring cup six times.

- Use fraction bars. How many twelfths are equivalent to $\frac{3}{4}$?

  Complete. $\frac{3}{4} = \frac{\blacksquare}{12}$

> **READ Math**
>
> You can read $\frac{3}{4} = \frac{6}{8}$ as three fourths is equivalent to six eighths.

Another way to find an equivalent fraction is to multiply or divide. You can multiply the numerator and denominator by the same number, other than 0 or 1. You can also divide a numerator and denominator by a common factor greater than 1.

### Example 1 Complete.

**Ⓐ** $\frac{1}{6} = \frac{\blacksquare}{12}$

To get the denominator 12, multiply the denominator by 2.

$\frac{1 \times 2}{6 \times 2} = \frac{2}{12}$   To keep the fraction's value the same, also multiply the numerator by 2.

**Ⓑ** $\frac{4}{12} = \frac{\blacksquare}{3}$

To get the denominator 3, divide the denominator by 4.

$\frac{4 \div 4}{12 \div 4} = \frac{1}{3}$   To keep the fraction's value the same, also divide the numerator by 4.

- Look at Examples A and B. Which operation results in a fraction with more parts than the original fraction? Explain how you know this.

**O━┓ NS 1.0** Students compare and order positive and negative fractions, decimals, and mixed numbers. Students solve problems involving fractions, ratios, proportions, and percentages: *also* **O━┓ NS 2.1,** **O━┓ NS 2.4, MR 2.4, MR 2.5, MR 3.2**

# Simplest Form

A fraction is in **simplest form** when the only common factor of the numerator and denominator is 1.

$\frac{17}{24}$ **is** in simplest form because the only common factor of 17 and 24 is 1.

$\frac{18}{24}$ **is not** in simplest form because 18 and 24 have the common factor 6.

## Example 2  Write $\frac{24}{36}$ in simplest form.

**ONE WAY**  Use common factors.

24: 1, 2, 3, 4, 6, 8, 12, 24
36: 1, 2, 3, 4, 6, 9, 12, 18, 36
*Find the common factors of 24 and 36.*

$\frac{24}{36} = \frac{24 \div 6}{36 \div 6} = \frac{4}{6}$  *Divide the numerator and denominator by a common factor other than 1.*

$\frac{4}{6} = \frac{4 \div 2}{6 \div 2} = \frac{2}{3}$  *Repeat until the fraction is in simplest form.*

**ANOTHER WAY**  Use a ladder diagram.

$\begin{array}{r|c} 2 & 24/36 \\ 2 & 12/18 \\ 3 & 6/9 \\ \hline & 2/3 \end{array}$  *Divide the numerator and denominator by a prime common factor. Repeat until they have no common factors other than 1.*

$\frac{24}{36} = \frac{2}{3}$  *The new numerator is 2 and the new denominator is 3.*

So, $\frac{2}{3}$ is the simplest form of $\frac{24}{36}$.

You can find a fraction in simplest form in just one step if you divide by the greatest common factor (GCF).

## Example 3  Write the fraction in simplest form.

**A** $\frac{18}{24}$

18: 1, 2, 3, 6, 9, 18      *Find the GCF.*
24: 1, 2, 3, 4, 6, 8, 12, 24
GCF = 6

$\frac{18}{24} = \frac{18 \div 6}{24 \div 6} = \frac{3}{4}$  *Divide the numerator and denominator by 6.*

So, $\frac{3}{4}$ is the simplest form of $\frac{18}{24}$.

**B** $\frac{20}{64}$

20: 1, 2, 4, 5, 10, 20      *Find the GCF.*
64: 1, 2, 4, 8, 16, 32, 64
GCF = 4

$\frac{20}{64} = \frac{20 \div 4}{64 \div 4} = \frac{5}{16}$  *Divide the numerator and denominator by 4.*

So, $\frac{5}{16}$ is the simplest form of $\frac{20}{64}$.

## Guided Practice

1. Look at the model. Count to find how many twelfths are equivalent to $\frac{3}{4}$. Complete: $\frac{3}{4} = \frac{\blacksquare}{12}$.

| $\frac{1}{4}$ | $\frac{1}{4}$ | $\frac{1}{4}$ |
|---|---|---|

$\frac{1}{12}$ $\frac{1}{12}$ $\frac{1}{12}$ $\frac{1}{12}$ $\frac{1}{12}$ $\frac{1}{12}$ $\frac{1}{12}$ $\frac{1}{12}$ $\frac{1}{12}$

**Complete.**

2. $\frac{3}{5} = \frac{\blacksquare}{10}$

3. $\frac{5}{6} = \frac{\blacksquare}{24}$

4. $\frac{6}{8} = \frac{\blacksquare}{4}$

5. $\frac{2}{10} = \frac{\blacksquare}{80}$

6. $\frac{25}{40} = \frac{\blacksquare}{8}$

7. $\frac{8}{12} = \frac{\blacksquare}{36}$

**Write the fraction in simplest form.**

8. $\frac{70}{75}$

9. $\frac{9}{12}$

10. $\frac{6}{28}$

11. $\frac{44}{121}$

12. $\frac{15}{27}$

✓13. $\frac{18}{54}$

14. **TALK Math** Explain how to find a fraction equivalent to $\frac{12}{15}$.

## Independent Practice and Problem Solving

**Complete.**

15. $\frac{12}{18} = \frac{\blacksquare}{3}$

16. $\frac{15}{51} = \frac{5}{\blacksquare}$

17. $\frac{3}{20} = \frac{24}{\blacksquare}$

18. $\frac{7}{8} = \frac{\blacksquare}{72}$

19. $\frac{\blacksquare}{49} = \frac{4}{7}$

20. $\frac{15}{55} = \frac{\blacksquare}{11}$

21. $\frac{3}{\blacksquare} = \frac{18}{24}$

22. $\frac{7}{8} = \frac{\blacksquare}{32}$

23. $\frac{\blacksquare}{3} = \frac{9}{1}$

24. $\frac{66}{75} = \frac{\blacksquare}{25}$

25. $\frac{\blacksquare}{6} = \frac{42}{84}$

26. $\frac{2}{\blacksquare} = \frac{6}{57}$

**Write the fraction in simplest form.**

27. $\frac{24}{42}$

28. $\frac{18}{30}$

29. $\frac{4}{10}$

30. $\frac{48}{32}$

31. $\frac{45}{20}$

32. $\frac{50}{60}$

33. $\frac{10}{65}$

34. $\frac{8}{62}$

35. $\frac{4^2}{128}$

36. $\frac{3^2}{36}$

37. $\frac{2^3}{4^2}$

38. $\frac{5^2}{10^2}$

**Reasoning** For 39–42, write *always, sometimes,* or *never* for each statement.

39. The denominator of an equivalent fraction is less than the denominator of the original fraction.

40. The denominator of an equivalent fraction is a multiple of the denominator of the original fraction.

41. The numerator of a fraction in simplest form is greater than the numerator of an equivalent fraction that is not in simplest form.

42. An equivalent fraction can be written for any fraction.

**USE DATA** For 43–45, use the graph.

43. Which household water use can be written as $\frac{4}{25}$ in simplest form?

44. The fraction for shower use is $\frac{17}{100}$. Is this fraction in simplest form? If not, write it in simplest form. Explain your answer.

45. The fractions of which household water uses can be written as equivalent fractions with a denominator of 50?

46. Margie has 25 green, 36 yellow, 10 blue, and 29 red marbles. Write a fraction in simplest form to show what part of the marbles in her collection are blue or green.

47. **WRITE Math** What's the Question? Bob has 8 red apples, 6 green apples, and 4 yellow apples. The answer is $\frac{4}{9}$ of the apples.

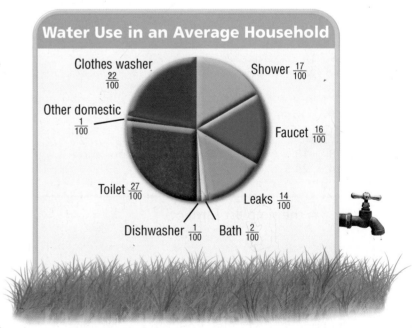

**Water Use in an Average Household**

Clothes washer $\frac{22}{100}$

Shower $\frac{17}{100}$

Other domestic $\frac{1}{100}$

Faucet $\frac{16}{100}$

Toilet $\frac{27}{100}$

Leaks $\frac{14}{100}$

Dishwasher $\frac{1}{100}$

Bath $\frac{2}{100}$

**CD ROM** **Technology** — Use Harcourt Mega Math, Fraction Action, *Fraction Flare Up*, Levels D and E.

Extra Practice on page 26 Set C

**48.** Norberto earned $13.25 mowing the yard. A jump rope costs $6.95. How much money will Norberto have left after buying the jump rope? (Grade 5 ⊶ NS 2.1)

**49.** Find the value of the algebraic expression $m - 12$ for $m = 51$. (Grade 5 ⊶ AF 1.2)

**50.** Write a fraction for the shaded part. (Grade 5 ⊶ NS 1.5)

**51. Test Prep** Jade saves $\frac{9}{15}$ of her earnings each week. Which of the following is an equivalent fraction for $\frac{9}{15}$?

**A** $\frac{1}{5}$   **B** $\frac{18}{45}$   **C** $\frac{3}{5}$   **D** $\frac{5}{3}$

**52. Test Prep** A cake is cut into 16 pieces. Four pieces are eaten. Which fraction represents, in simplest form, the amount of cake that is left?

**A** $\frac{12}{16}$   **B** $\frac{3}{4}$   **C** $\frac{1}{3}$   **D** $\frac{4}{16}$

---

## MATH POWER · Problem Solving and Reasoning

**REASONING** You can use your knowledge of number relationships and equivalent fractions to find unknown numbers.

**Remember**

A variable is a letter or symbol that can stand for one or more numbers. The letters and symbols $x$, $y$, $a$, $b$, and ■ are examples of variables.

**Example** What are the values of $a$ and $b$ for $\frac{4}{5} = \frac{a}{b}$?

**Clue 1:** Both $a$ and $b$ are greater than 10 and less than 20.

Based on Clue 1, $a$ and $b$ can be 11, 12, 13, 14, 15, 16, 17, 18, or 19.

**Clue 2:** Both $a$ and $b$ are multiples of 3.

Based on Clues 1 and 2, $a$ and $b$ can be 12, 15, or 18.

Since $\frac{a}{b}$ has to be equivalent to $\frac{4}{5}$, then $a$ is 12 and $b$ is 15.

**Use the clues to find the values of $a$ and $b$.**

**1.** $\frac{3}{10} = \frac{a}{b}$

**Clue 1:** The sum of the digits of $a$ is 9.

**Clue 2:** $a$ and $b$ are two-digit numbers that are less than 65.

**2.** $\frac{4}{a} = \frac{b}{6}$

**Clue 1:** $a$ is a multiple of 3 that is less than 30.

**Clue 2:** $b$ is a prime number.

**3.** $\frac{5}{7} = \frac{a}{b}$

**Clue 1:** $a$ and $b$ are even numbers that are greater than 10 and less than 30.

**Clue 2:** The sum of $a$ and $b$ is 48.

**4.** $\frac{a}{9} = \frac{16}{b}$

**Clue 1:** The factors of $b$ are 1, 2, 3, 4, 6, 9, 18, and 36.

**Clue 2:** $a$ and $b$ are multiples of 4.

# Fractions and Mixed Numbers

**OBJECTIVE:** Write fractions as mixed numbers and mixed numbers as fractions.

## Quick Review

Write the fraction in simplest form.

1. $\frac{21}{27}$    2. $\frac{24}{40}$    3. $\frac{33}{77}$

4. $\frac{27}{36}$    5. $\frac{72}{84}$

## Vocabulary

mixed number

## Learn

**PROBLEM** A **mixed number,** such as $2\frac{1}{4}$, is a number represented by a whole number greater than 0 and a fraction between 0 and 1. A mixed number can be renamed as a fraction greater than one. Fractions greater than one, such as $\frac{6}{5}$, are sometimes called "improper fractions."

**Example 1** Write $2\frac{1}{4}$ as a fraction.

**ONE WAY**   Use a diagram.

Count the shaded fourths. There are nine fourths, or $\frac{9}{4}$.

**ANOTHER WAY**   Use multiplication and addition.

$$2\frac{1}{4} = \frac{(4 \times 2)}{4} + \frac{1}{4} = \frac{8+1}{4} = \frac{9}{4}$$

Multiply the denominator of the fraction part by the whole number part. Then add the numerator. This sum is the new numerator. Use the same denominator.

So, $2\frac{1}{4} = \frac{9}{4}$.

You can use division to write a fraction greater than 1 as a mixed number or a whole number.

**Example 2** Write $\frac{26}{10}$ as a mixed number in simplest form.

$$\begin{array}{r} 2 \text{ r}6 \\ 10\overline{)26} \\ -20 \\ \hline 6 \end{array}$$

Since $\frac{26}{10}$ can be read as 26 divided by 10, divide the numerator by the denominator.

Use the remainder as the numerator and the divisor as the denominator. Write the fraction in simplest form.

So, $\frac{26}{10} = 2\frac{6}{10} = 2\frac{3}{5}$.

## Guided Practice

1. Look at the model. Write the modeled number as a mixed number and as a fraction. Then write each in words.

**Write the mixed number as a fraction.**

2. $6\frac{1}{3}$     3. $1\frac{3}{4}$     4. $3\frac{2}{5}$     5. $1\frac{7}{16}$     6. $5\frac{1}{2}$     7. $2\frac{1}{8}$

**NS 2.0** Students calculate and solve problems involving addition, subtraction, multiplication, and division: *also* MR 2.4, MR 2.5, MR 3.2

**Write the fraction as a mixed number in simplest form or as a whole number.**

8. $\frac{14}{5}$     9. $\frac{45}{10}$     10. $\frac{56}{8}$     11. $\frac{19}{6}$     12. $\frac{64}{16}$     ✓13. $\frac{55}{20}$

14. **TALK Math** Explain how to use the remainder and divisor when using division to write a fraction as a mixed number.

## Independent Practice and Problem Solving

**Write the mixed number as a fraction.**

15. $4\frac{5}{8}$     16. $7\frac{2}{3}$     17. $5\frac{5}{6}$     18. $11\frac{1}{4}$     19. $12\frac{4}{5}$     20. $3\frac{7}{10}$

21. $2\frac{1}{2}$     22. $8\frac{3}{5}$     23. $5\frac{3}{10}$     24. $6\frac{3}{8}$     25. $3\frac{3}{4}$     26. $2\frac{1}{2}$

**Write the fraction as a mixed number in simplest form or as a whole number.**

27. $\frac{17}{3}$     28. $\frac{44}{8}$     29. $\frac{45}{12}$     30. $\frac{41}{18}$     31. $\frac{65}{5}$     32. $\frac{85}{25}$

33. $\frac{32}{7}$     34. $\frac{60}{4}$     35. $\frac{34}{4}$     36. $\frac{66}{8}$     37. $\frac{23}{3}$     38. $\frac{39}{6}$

39. **≡FAST FACT** In a total lunar eclipse, the earth blocks all direct sunlight from reaching the moon. The longest total lunar eclipse in the next 90 years will take place in 2018 and last $1\frac{11}{15}$ hr. Write $1\frac{11}{15}$ as a fraction, and use the fraction to find how many minutes the eclipse will last.

40. The longest total lunar eclipse since 1900 occurred in 2000 and lasted 107 min. Write 107 min in hours as a fraction and a mixed number.

41. **WRITE Math** What's the Error? Greg renamed $2\frac{5}{7}$ as $\frac{17}{7}$. Describe his error and write the correct answer.

**USE DATA** For 42–43, use the recipe.

42. Lee has only a $\frac{1}{4}$-cup measuring cup to make a peach smoothie refresher. Write the amount of each ingredient, except banana, as a fraction in fourths.

43. Suppose Lee has only a $\frac{1}{8}$-cup measuring cup. Write the amount of peach slices as a fraction in eighths.

Peach Smoothie Refresher
$1\frac{3}{4}$ cups apple juice
1 cup frozen yogurt
$\frac{1}{2}$ banana
1 cup peach yogurt
$1\frac{1}{2}$ cups frozen peach slices

 ## Achieving the Standards

44. What is the greatest common divisor of 12 and 24? (O━┓ NS 2.4, p. 6)

45. Write a mixed number for the shaded part.
    (Grade 5 O━┓ NS 1.5)

46. What is the perimeter of a square with sides that measure 5 inches long? (Grade 5 MG 1.4)

47. **Test Prep** John bought $3\frac{3}{4}$ pounds of mixed nuts and divided them into $\frac{1}{8}$-pound servings. How many servings of mixed nuts did he make?

    **A** 8     **B** 15     **C** 24     **D** 30

**Extra Practice** on page 26, Set D

# 5 Least Common Multiple

OBJECTIVE: Find the least common multiple of two or more numbers, and use it to solve problems.

## Quick Review

Write the first 4 multiples of each number.

1. 4     2. 6     3. 12

4. 8     5. 15

## Vocabulary

**least common multiple (LCM)**

## Learn

**PROBLEM** For a school cookout, each of the 20 parent volunteers needs a large serving tray and a serving spoon. Trays come in sets of 8 and spoons come in sets of 12. What is the least number of trays and spoons the school should buy to have the same number of trays as spoons and have enough for the parent volunteers?

You can solve the problem by finding the **least common multiple, or LCM,** of 8 and 12. The LCM is the smallest number, other than 0, that is a common multiple of two or more numbers.

**ONE WAY**   **Use a list.**

> Multiples of 8: 8, 16, 24, 32, 40, 48, 56, 64, 72, 80, …
>
> Multiples of 12: 12, 24, 36, 48, 60, 72, …

The first three common multiples are 24, 48, and 72. The least common multiple, or LCM, is 24.

**ANOTHER WAY**   **Use prime factorization.**

> $8 = 2 \times 2 \times 2 = 2^3$     Write the prime factorization of each number.
>
> $12 = 2 \times 2 \times 3 = 2^2 \times 3$
>
> $2^3 \times 3 = 24$     Write each factor the greatest number of times it appears in any prime factorization. Multiply.

So, the least number of trays and spoons the school should buy is 24.

- **What if** trays came in sets of 6 and spoons came in sets of 12? What would be the least number of trays and spoons the school should buy?

- Use prime factorization to find the LCM of 16 and 24.

**Remember**
An exponent shows how many times a number called the base is used as a factor. In $2^3 = 2 \times 2 \times 2$, the exponent 3 shows that the base 2 is used as a factor three times.

## Example 1 Find pairs of numbers with an LCM of 20.

> You can solve the problem by using the LCM and one of its factors. Factors of 20: 1, 2, 4, 5, 10, 20
>
> Possible number pairs:   1, 20     2, 20     4, 20     5, 20     10, 20

- What other pairs of numbers have an LCM of 20?

NS 2.4 Determine the least common multiple and the greatest common divisor of whole numbers; use them to solve problems with fractions (e.g., to find a common denominator to add two fractions or to find the reduced form for a fraction). *also* MR 2.4, MR 2.5, MR 3.2

# LCM of Three Numbers

You can use similar methods to find the LCM of three numbers.

**ONE WAY** Use a list to find the LCM of 10, 14, and 70.

Multiples of 10: 10, 20, 30, 40, 50, 60, 70, 80, 90, 100, 110, 120, 130, 140, …

Multiples of 14: 14, 28, 42, 56, 70, 84, 98, 112, 126, 140, …

Multiples of 70: 70, 140, …

So, the LCM of 10, 14, and 70 is 70.

**ANOTHER WAY** Use prime factorization to find the LCM of 6, 9, and 15.

$6 = 2 \times 3$

$9 = 3 \times 3$          Write the prime factorization of each number.

$15 = 3 \times 5$

$2 \times 3 \times 3 \times 5 = 90$     Write each factor the greatest number of times it appears in any prime factorization. Multiply.

So, the LCM of 6, 9, and 15 is 90.

**Example 2** Find three numbers with an LCM of 36.

36: 1, 2, 3, 4, 6, 9, 12, 18, 36          List the factors of 36.

| 1, 2, 36 | 2, 9, 36 | 3, 4, 36 | First, use the LCM, 36, and any two factors. Possible sets are given. |

| 2, 4, 9 | 4, 6, 9 | 9, 12, 18 | Then, find other sets of three factors |
| 4, 9, 12 | 6, 12, 18 | 12, 18, 36 | of 36 that have an LCM of 36. Possible sets are given. |

## Guided Practice

**1.** List the first six multiples of 12 and 18. Circle the common multiples. Then find the least common multiple.

**Write the LCM of the numbers.**

**2.** 9, 12          **3.** 4, 30          **4.** 5, 25          **5.** 3, 5, 15          ✓**6.** 2, 3, 4

**Write two numbers with the given LCM.**

**7.** 15          **8.** 16          **9.** 44          **10.** 100          ✓**11.** 56

**12.** **TALK Math** **Explain** how each of these number pairs is related to its LCM, 24: 12, 24; 3, 8; and 6, 8.

**Write the LCM of the numbers.**

**13.** 15, 25          **14.** 8, 14          **15.** 8, 15          **16.** 11, 22          **17.** 4, 18

**18.** 3, 12, 15          **19.** 10, 16, 20          **20.** 4, 36, 54          **21.** 2, 7, 10          **22.** 27, 3, 6

**Write two numbers with the given LCM.**

**23.** 40          **24.** 39          **25.** 24          **26.** 30          **27.** 22

**Write three numbers with the given LCM.**

**28.** 10          **29.** 20          **30.** 18          **31.** 28          **32.** 45

**USE DATA** For 33–34, use the graph.

**33.** Marcus bought equal numbers of bottles of orange, apple, and cranberry juice for the school cookout. What is the least number of each that Marcus could have bought to have the same number of bottles of each juice with none left over?

**34.** What if Marcus buys equal numbers of bottles of two types of juice? Will he buy more bottles of juice if he chooses orange and apple, cranberry and orange, or apple and cranberry? How many bottles of each juice will he buy? **Explain** your reasoning.

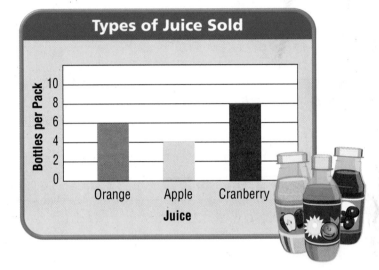

**35.** The LCM of two numbers is 18. The GCF of the numbers is 3. What are the possible numbers?

**36.** The LCM of two numbers is 40. The GCF of the numbers is 4. What are the possible numbers?

**37. Pose a Problem** Look back at Problem 35. Write a similar problem by changing the LCM and the GCF.

**38.** **WRITE Math** Liam says that the LCM of two different prime numbers is their product. **Explain** whether or not he is correct.

### Achieving the Standards

**39.** Round 12.082 to the nearest tenth. (Grade 5 NS 1.1)

**40.** What are two equivalent fractions for $\frac{12}{15}$? (O—ⁿ NS 2.4, p. 8)

**41. Test Prep** What is the least common multiple of 12 and 18?

    **A** 6          **C** 36

    **B** 30          **D** 120

**42.** What are two common multiples of 4, 10, and 12? (O—ⁿ NS 2.4, p. 4)

**43. Test Prep** The LCM of 3 numbers is 90. One number is 15. Which could be the other two numbers?

    **A** 6, 8          **C** 2, 10

    **B** 18, 30          **D** 30, 50

# Write to Explain

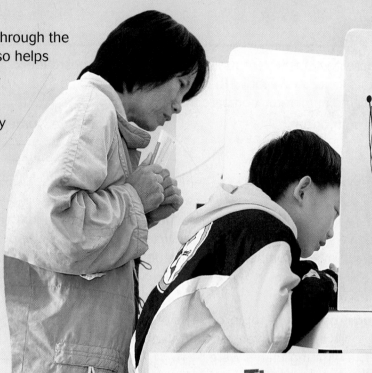

Writing an explanation helps you think through the steps you took to solve a problem. It also helps you understand a math concept or skill.

A governor is elected every 4 years. A United States Senator is elected every 6 years. If a senator and a governor are elected in the same year, how soon can the senator and the governor run for reelection in the same year?

The least common multiple of 4 and 6 is the least number of years it will be before the senator and the governor can run for reelection in the same year. Read Liz's explanation of her solution.

---

First, find the common factors of 4 and 6.

4: 1, 2, 4     The common factors are 1 and 2.

6: 1, 2, 3, 6     The greatest common factor is 2.

Next, multiply the number of years a governor serves by the number of years a senator serves.

$$4 \times 6 = 24$$

Finally, divide the product by the greatest common factor to find the least common multiple.

$$24 \div 2 = 12$$

So, in 12 years, the senator and the governor can run for reelection during the same year.

## Tips

**Tips to Writing an Explanation**
- Tell what the problem is in the first sentence.
- Use transition words such as *first*, *next*, and *finally* to show the order of your steps.
- Use correct math terms.
- Show all computations.
- State the solution to the problem in the last sentence of your explanation.

---

**Problem Solving** Write an explanation to show how to solve each problem.

1. Diane is hanging red, white, and blue lights for an election party. Red lights are in packages of 6, white lights in packages of 8, and blue lights in packages of 3. She plans to hang an equal number of each color. What is the least number of lights of each color she must buy? How many packages of each color should she buy?

2. Kirk has 12 posters and 36 sample ballots for the school election. He is making packages, all with the same number of posters and sample ballots. What is the greatest number of packages he can make without any items left over? How many of each item will be in each package?

# 6 Compare and Order

OBJECTIVE: Compare and order fractions and mixed numbers.

## Learn

To compare fractions with the same denominator, compare the numerators, since each part is the same size. To compare fractions with the same numerator, compare the denominators.

**Same Denominator**

$\frac{2}{3}$  Two of three equal parts is greater than one of three equal parts. So, $\frac{2}{3} > \frac{1}{3}$.

$\frac{1}{3}$

**Same Numerator**

$\frac{2}{3}$  Two of three equal parts is greater than two of five equal parts. So, $\frac{2}{3} > \frac{2}{5}$.

$\frac{2}{5}$

To compare mixed numbers, compare the whole numbers and then the fractions. You can use common multiples to compare and order fractions and mixed numbers with unlike denominators.

## Example 1

California is one of the top producers of sunflowers. At a festival, prizes were given for the tallest sunflower plants. The winning plants were $5\frac{1}{2}$ ft, $5\frac{2}{3}$ ft, and $5\frac{5}{8}$ ft tall. Order the plant heights from least to greatest.

> The whole numbers are the same, so compare the fractions. Write equivalent fractions with the same denominator and then compare the numerators.
>
> $5\frac{1}{2} = 5\frac{12}{24}$    $5\frac{2}{3} = 5\frac{16}{24}$    $5\frac{5}{8} = 5\frac{15}{24}$    Think: 24 is a common multiple of 2, 3, and 8.

Since $5\frac{12}{24} < 5\frac{15}{24} < 5\frac{16}{24}$, the order of the plant heights from least to greatest is $5\frac{1}{2}$ ft, $5\frac{5}{8}$ ft, $5\frac{2}{3}$ ft.

You can also use a number line to compare and order fractions.

## Example 2  Order $\frac{1}{2}$, $\frac{2}{5}$, and $\frac{7}{10}$ from greatest to least.

> Locate the numbers on the number line. $\frac{7}{10}$ is to the right of $\frac{1}{2}$, and $\frac{1}{2}$ is to the right of $\frac{2}{5}$.
>
> $$0 \quad \frac{1}{10} \quad \frac{1}{5} \quad \frac{3}{10} \quad \frac{2}{5} \quad \frac{1}{2} \quad \frac{3}{5} \quad \frac{7}{10} \quad \frac{4}{5} \quad \frac{9}{10} \quad 1$$

So, the order from greatest to least is $\frac{7}{10}$, $\frac{1}{2}$, $\frac{2}{5}$.

**Math Idea**

Values increase as you move to the right on the number line. Values decrease as you move to the left.

▲ A sunflower grown in the Netherlands set the record for being the tallest in the world. It measured 25 ft 5 in.

1. Use the fraction models to see which part is greater. Then compare $\frac{2}{5}$ and $\frac{2}{8}$, using $<$, $>$, or $=$.

**Compare. Write $<$, $>$, or $=$.**

2. $\frac{4}{5}$ ⬤ $\frac{4}{9}$

3. $\frac{5}{8}$ ⬤ $\frac{7}{8}$

4. $1\frac{4}{12}$ ⬤ $1\frac{3}{8}$

✓5. $1\frac{5}{6}$ ⬤ $\frac{7}{6}$

✓6. $\frac{28}{42}$ ⬤ $\frac{4}{6}$

7. **TALK Math** Explain how to use the number line to order $\frac{2}{3}$, $\frac{1}{2}$, and $\frac{11}{12}$ from greatest to least.

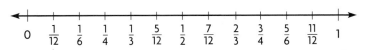

## Independent Practice and Problem Solving

**Compare. Write $<$, $>$, or $=$.**

8. $\frac{1}{2}$ ⬤ $\frac{11}{12}$

9. $\frac{7}{15}$ ⬤ $\frac{7}{10}$

10. $\frac{7}{9}$ ⬤ $\frac{4}{9}$

11. $7\frac{1}{3}$ ⬤ $6\frac{2}{3}$

12. $1\frac{2}{5}$ ⬤ $1\frac{1}{3}$

**Order from greatest to least.**

13. $\frac{5}{7}$, $\frac{5}{6}$, $\frac{5}{12}$

14. $\frac{4}{7}$, $\frac{4}{10}$, $\frac{4}{5}$

15. $1\frac{3}{4}$, $\frac{5}{7}$, $1\frac{3}{5}$

16. $3\frac{7}{10}$, $3\frac{1}{6}$, $3\frac{2}{5}$

17. $\frac{3}{7}$, $\frac{5}{6}$, $\frac{2}{3}$

18. $\frac{1}{2}$, $\frac{2}{9}$, $\frac{11}{18}$

19. $1\frac{7}{8}$, $\frac{6}{7}$, $1\frac{9}{10}$

20. $5\frac{5}{8}$, $5\frac{7}{10}$, $5\frac{3}{4}$

21. Last week, Malia and José each bought 2 lb of sunflower seeds. Malia has $1\frac{1}{3}$ lb left, and José has $1\frac{2}{5}$ lb left. Who ate more sunflower seeds?

22. **Reasoning** Find a fraction that is between $\frac{3}{4}$ and $\frac{5}{6}$.

23. **WRITE Math** Explain how to find which number is less, $\frac{4}{5}$ or $\frac{5}{6}$. Then show the comparison by using symbols.

## Achieving the Standards

24. Which is less, $24 \times 3$ or $23 \times 4$? (Grade 5 NS 1.0)

25. If $n = 3$, what is the value of $5 \times (n - 3)$?
    (Grade 5 O━ AF 1.2)

26. What is the greatest common divisor of 66, 36, and 18? (O━ NS 2.4, p. 6)

27. **Test Prep** Which number makes the expression $\frac{2}{3} < ⬤ < 1\frac{1}{8}$ true?

    A $\frac{11}{20}$

    B $\frac{7}{9}$

    C $1\frac{1}{3}$

    D $1\frac{1}{5}$

**Extra Practice** on page 27, Set F

# Cross-Multiply to Compare Fractions

OBJECTIVE: Compare fractions using cross-multiplication.

## Learn

**PROBLEM** Lisa is a gymnast. She works on the balance beam for $\frac{4}{9}$ of her practice time on Monday and $\frac{3}{5}$ of her practice time on Wednesday. On which day does Lisa practice the balance beam for a greater fraction of practice time?

You can cross-multiply to compare $\frac{4}{9}$ and $\frac{3}{5}$.

### Example 1

$$\frac{4}{9} \times \frac{3}{5}$$

Multiply the numerator of each fraction by the denominator of the other fraction. Start with the numerator on the left.

$4 \times 5 \qquad 3 \times 9$  Compare the products.

$20 \ < \ 27$  The relationship between the fractions is the same as the relationship between the products.

So $\frac{4}{9} < \frac{3}{5}$.

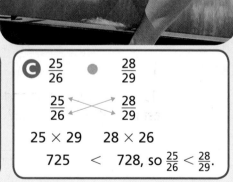

So, Lisa practices the balance beam for a greater fraction of practice time on Wednesday.

Cross-multiplication works because 20 and 27 are the numerators when you write equivalent fractions for $\frac{4}{9}$ and $\frac{3}{5}$ using the product of the denominators as the common denominator.

$$\frac{4}{9} = \frac{4 \times 5}{9 \times 5} = \frac{20}{45} \qquad \frac{3}{5} = \frac{3 \times 9}{5 \times 9} = \frac{27}{45}$$

### More Examples  Compare. Write <, >, or =.

**A** $\frac{8}{9} \bullet \frac{14}{19}$

$\frac{8}{9} \times \frac{14}{19}$

$8 \times 19 \quad 14 \times 9$

$152 \ > \ 126$, so $\frac{8}{9} > \frac{14}{19}$.

**B** $\frac{34}{51} \bullet \frac{2}{3}$

$\frac{34}{51} \times \frac{2}{3}$

$34 \times 3 \quad 2 \times 51$

$102 \ = \ 102$, so $\frac{34}{51} = \frac{2}{3}$.

**C** $\frac{25}{26} \bullet \frac{28}{29}$

$\frac{25}{26} \times \frac{28}{29}$

$25 \times 29 \quad 28 \times 26$

$725 \ < \ 728$, so $\frac{25}{26} < \frac{28}{29}$.

• **What if** $\frac{14}{19}$ in Example A were changed to $\frac{96}{108}$? Would the comparison change? Explain.

○━┓ NS 1.0 Students compare and order positive and negative fractions, decimals, and mixed numbers. Students solve problems involving fractions, ratios, proportions, and percentages: *also* ○━┓ NS 1.1, MR 2.4, MR 2.5, MR 3.2

1. Complete to compare.

$\frac{1}{2} \times\!\!\!\!\!\times \frac{5}{9}$  $1 \times \blacksquare < \blacksquare \times 2$    $\blacksquare < 10$, so $\blacksquare < \blacksquare$.

Compare. Use <, >, or =.

2. $\frac{5}{8} \bullet \frac{4}{10}$

3. $\frac{4}{5} \bullet \frac{5}{6}$

4. $\frac{3}{4} \bullet \frac{15}{20}$

✓5. $\frac{8}{9} \bullet \frac{48}{54}$

✓6. $\frac{3}{5} \bullet \frac{7}{12}$

7. **TALK Math** Maria compared the products $9 \times 12 \blacksquare 7 \times 14$. **Explain** what fractions she could have been comparing.

## Independent Practice and Problem Solving

Compare. Use <, >, or =.

8. $\frac{4}{5} \bullet \frac{2}{3}$

9. $\frac{4}{5} \bullet \frac{5}{6}$

10. $\frac{7}{9} \bullet \frac{9}{10}$

11. $\frac{3}{4} \bullet \frac{11}{12}$

12. $\frac{7}{12} \bullet \frac{7}{10}$

13. $\frac{6}{16} \bullet \frac{3}{8}$

14. $\frac{11}{12} \bullet \frac{9}{10}$

15. $\frac{14}{23} \bullet \frac{9}{22}$

16. $\frac{8}{11} \bullet \frac{15}{17}$

17. $\frac{5}{7} \bullet \frac{9}{11}$

**USE DATA** For 18–21, use the table and cross-multiplication.

18. Alex was successful in 7 of 8 total attempts on Saturday. How does that compare with his success on Friday?

19. Did Alex improve from Monday to Tuesday? **Explain.**

20. Did Alex improve between Tuesday and Friday? **Explain**

21. **WRITE Math** Between which two days did Alex not improve? **Explain.**

| Alex's Tumbling Practice | | | | | |
|---|---|---|---|---|---|
| Day | M | T | W | Th | F |
| Successes | 3 | 5 | 7 | 8 | 13 |
| Attempts | 8 | 10 | 10 | 12 | 16 |

22. Compare $\frac{7}{8}$ and $\frac{2}{3}$. Then place the numbers on a number line and label them.

## Achieving the Standards

23. A triangle has angles of 95° and 46°. What is the measure of the third angle?

    (Grade 5 O━┓ MG 2.2)

24. How much greater is 7.865 than 0.603?

    (Grade 5 O━┓ NS 2.1)

25. If $n = 8$, what is the value of $(22 + n) - 4$?

    (Grade 5 O━┓ AF 1.2)

26. Which comparison is true?

    A $\frac{4}{7} > \frac{2}{3}$

    B $\frac{7}{12} < \frac{3}{4}$

    C $\frac{8}{35} < \frac{3}{24}$

    D $\frac{5}{6} > \frac{9}{10}$

**Extra Practice** on page 27, Set G

# Problem Solving Workshop
# Skill: Identify Relationships

OBJECTIVE: Solve problems by using the skill *identify relationships*.

## Read to Understand

**PROBLEM** Pat and Selina made the table shown below to identify relationships among a pair of numbers, their greatest common factor, and their least common multiple. What relationships are shown?

| a | b | a × b | GCF | LCM | GCF × LCM |
|---|---|-------|-----|-----|-----------|
| 3 | 4 | 12 | 1 | 12 | 12 |
| 4 | 6 | 24 | 2 | 12 | 24 |
| 3 | 6 | 18 | 3 | 6 | 18 |
| 8 | 24 | 192 | 8 | 24 | 192 |
| 7 | 3 | 21 | 1 | 21 | 21 |
| 15 | 9 | 135 | 3 | 45 | 135 |
| 54 | 9 | 486 | 9 | 54 | 486 |

Look at the number pairs, and describe the relationships.

| Number Pair | Relationship |
|-------------|--------------|
| Find the row with 3 and 6. The number 6 is a multiple of 3. What is the relationship between the LCM and the numbers? | When one number is a multiple of the other, the LCM is the greater number. |
| Find the row with 3 and 4. The GCF of the numbers is 1. What is the relationship between the LCM and the product of the numbers? | When the GCF is 1, the LCM is the product of the numbers. |
| Find the row with 8 and 24. The greater number is the LCM. What is the relationship between the GCF and the numbers? | When the LCM is the greater number, the GCF is the lesser number. |

## Think and Discuss

**Use the relationships shown above to help you solve the problems.**

**a.** Look at the table. Which other pairs of numbers has the same relationship as 3 and 6? How can you find the LCM of each pair of numbers?

**b.** The GCF of 14 and 17 is 1. How can you find the LCM?

**c.** The LCM of 5 and 10 is 10. How can you find the GCF?

○━┓ NS 2.4 Determine the least common multiple and the greatest common divisor of whole numbers; use them to solve problems with fractions (e.g., to find a common denominator to add two fractions or to find the reduced form for a fraction). *also* MR 1.0, MR 1.1, MR 2.0, MR 2.4, MR 2.5, MR 3.0, MR 3.1, MR 3.2, MR 3.3

1. James and Rico want to see if there is a relationship between two prime numbers and their LCM. They made a table to help them. What relationship do you see?

| a | b | LCM |
|---|---|---|
| 2 | 3 | 6 |
| 2 | 5 | 10 |
| 3 | 5 | 15 |
| 3 | 7 | 21 |
| 5 | 7 | 35 |
| 13 | 11 | 143 |

**First,** look at each number pair and its LCM.

**Then,** decide if there is a relationship.

2. **What if** there are three prime numbers? What relationship is there between the numbers and their LCM? Explain.

3. What relationship is there between the sum of two even numbers and the sum of two odd numbers? **Explain** and give an example.

## Mixed Applications

4. A relationship exists among the composite numbers 4, 16, 36, 81, 100, and 144. Identify the relationship and write two other numbers that have the same relationship.

5. How are the product of two even numbers and the product of an even number and an odd number related? Are the product of two even numbers and the product of two odd numbers related in the same way? Explain and give an example.

**For 6–9, use the table.**

6. How many of which stamp can you buy to spend exactly $20?

7. How many of which two stamps can you buy to spend exactly $7?

8. How many of which two stamps can you buy to spend exactly $49?

9. What is the least number of Mount McKinley and Acadia National Park stamps that you can buy if you want to spend the same amount on each type of stamp?

### Commemorative Stamps

| Name | Face Value | Date Issued | Place |
|---|---|---|---|
| Acadia National Park | $0.60 | 5/30/01 | Bar Harbor, ME |
| California Statehood | $0.33 | 9/8/00 | Sacramento, CA |
| Mt. McKinley | $0.80 | 4/17/01 | Fairbanks, AK |
| Niagara Falls | $0.48 | 5/12/99 | Niagara Falls, NY |
| Ohio Statehood | $0.37 | 3/1/03 | Chillicothe, OH |

# 9 Fractions, Decimals, and Percents

**OBJECTIVE:** Convert fractions to decimals and percents, decimals to fractions and percents, and percents to fractions and decimals.

**Quick Review**

Write in word form.

1. 0.65     2. $\frac{7}{100}$     3. 0.03

4. $\frac{36}{100}$     5. 0.40

**Vocabulary**

percent

## Learn

**PROBLEM** A class took a survey of girls' names. Thirty percent of the class chose Kayla as the favorite. Write 30% as a fraction and as a decimal.

**Percent** means "per hundred" or "hundredths." The symbol used to write a percent is %. You can use a grid with 100 squares to model percents.

### HANDS ON

### Activity

**Materials** ■ decimal models

Thirty percent means 30 of 100, or $\frac{30}{100}$.

Shade 30 squares of 100 squares.

The model for 30% shows 30 of 100 equal parts shaded. It represents $\frac{30}{100}$ and 0.30.

So, 30% can be written as $\frac{30}{100}$, or 0.30.

• Model 18%. Then write 18% as a fraction and as a decimal.

You can use place value and equivalent fractions to write a fraction or decimal as a percent.

### Example

**A** Write 0.17 as a fraction and as a percent.

Use place value to write the decimal as a fraction.

0.17          Think: 0.17 is seventeen hundredths.

$0.17 = \frac{17}{100}$     Percent means "out of 100."

So, $0.17 = \frac{17}{100} = 17\%$.

**B** Write $\frac{3}{4}$ as a decimal and as a percent.

Write an equivalent fraction with 100 as the denominator.

$\frac{3}{4} = \frac{3 \times 25}{4 \times 25} = \frac{75}{100}$     Think: $\frac{75}{100}$ is seventy-five hundredths.

Use place value and the meaning of percent.

$\frac{75}{100} = 0.75 = 75\%$

So, $\frac{3}{4} = 0.75 = 75\%$.

• Explain how to write $\frac{1}{5}$ as a decimal and as a percent.

**NS 1.1** Compare and order positive and negative fractions, decimals, and mixed numbers and place them on a number line. *also* **NS 1.0, NS 2.4, MR 2.4, MR 2.5, MR 3.2**

**Complete.**

1. The model shows ■ of ■ equal parts are shaded.

   The model represents the fraction ■, the decimal ■, and ■%.

**Copy and complete. Write each fraction in simplest form.**

| | Fraction | Decimal | Percent |
|---|---|---|---|
| **2.** | ■ | ■ | 63% |
| **4.** | $\frac{3}{100}$ | ■ | ■ |

| | Fraction | Decimal | Percent |
|---|---|---|---|
| **3.** | ■ | 0.05 | ■ |
| **5.** | $\frac{4}{5}$ | ■ | ■ |

6. **TALK Math** Explain how to write $\frac{7}{20}$ as a percent.

## Independent Practice and Problem Solving

**Copy and complete. Write each fraction in simplest form.**

| | Fraction | Decimal | Percent |
|---|---|---|---|
| **7.** | $\frac{7}{10}$ | ■ | ■ |
| **9.** | ■ | 0.10 | ■ |
| **11.** | ■ | ■ | 9% |

| | Fraction | Decimal | Percent |
|---|---|---|---|
| **8.** | $\frac{45}{100}$ | ■ | ■ |
| **10.** | ■ | ■ | 76 |
| **12.** | ■ | 0.38 | ■ |

**USE DATA For 13–15, use the table.**

13. Which name was popular with $\frac{19}{50}$ of the people surveyed?

14. Which name was popular with 0.3 of the people surveyed?

15. Use decimals and < or > to compare the choices for Puff and Rascal.

16. There are 16 boys and 9 girls in J.T.'s class. Blue is the favorite color of 5 boys and 6 girls. Blue is the favorite color of what percent of the class? Explain.

**Favorite Kitten Names**

| Name | Puff | Ginger | Rascal |
|---|---|---|---|
| Votes | 38% | 30% | 32% |

17. **WRITE Math** One third of the students in a class said they had no middle name. Is that fraction more than or less than 30%? Explain.

### Achieving the Standards

18. Round 3.1264 to the nearest thousandth.
    (Grade 5 NS 1.1)

19. Write a percent for the shaded part. (Grade 5 ⚬━ NS 1.2)

20. What are the first five multiples of 9?
    (⚬━ NS 2.4, p. 4)

21. **Test Prep** Rod got 24 out of 30 questions correct on a math test. What percent of the questions did he get correct?

    **A** 20%    **B** 30%    **C** 80%    **D** 90%

# Extra Practice

## Set A  Write the first three common multiples. (pp. 4–5)

**1.** 4, 6    **2.** 3, 8    **3.** 7, 14    **4.** 3, 4, 12    **5.** 4, 5, 8

### Write the common factors.

**6.** 20, 40    **7.** 7, 17    **8.** 32, 40    **9.** 16, 32, 64    **10.** 5, 10, 35

### Tell whether the number is prime, composite, or neither.

**11.** 51    **12.** 42    **13.** 19    **14.** 0    **15.** 29

## Set B  Find the GCF. (pp. 6–7)

**1.** 16, 24    **2.** 8, 16    **3.** 18, 54    **4.** 4, 14    **5.** 84, 108

**6.** 15, 36    **7.** 18, 42    **8.** 24, 84    **9.** 21, 56    **10.** 15, 70

**11.** Mary has 16 roses and 12 lilies to put in vases. If she places the same number of roses and lilies in each vase, what is the largest number of vases she will need if she uses every flower?

**12.** What is the largest number of party bags Bill can make using 20 party favors and 16 balloons if each bag gets the same number of favors and balloons and he uses every item?

## Set C  Complete. (pp. 8-11)

**1.** $\frac{1}{4} = \frac{\blacksquare}{12}$    **2.** $\frac{12}{14} = \frac{6}{\blacksquare}$    **3.** $\frac{5}{7} = \frac{\blacksquare}{21}$    **4.** $\frac{3}{4} = \frac{\blacksquare}{16}$    **5.** $\frac{5}{25} = \frac{1}{\blacksquare}$

**6.** $\frac{\blacksquare}{13} = \frac{18}{26}$    **7.** $\frac{4}{\blacksquare} = \frac{8}{20}$    **8.** $\frac{7}{14} = \frac{1}{\blacksquare}$    **9.** $\frac{24}{30} = \frac{\blacksquare}{15}$    **10.** $\frac{4}{\blacksquare} = \frac{1}{4}$

### Write the fraction in simplest form.

**11.** $\frac{6}{9}$    **12.** $\frac{16}{30}$    **13.** $\frac{6}{10}$    **14.** $\frac{18}{36}$    **15.** $\frac{3}{5}$

## Set D  Write the mixed number as a fraction. (pp. 12–13)

**1.** $4\frac{3}{4}$    **2.** $7\frac{1}{5}$    **3.** $12\frac{2}{3}$    **4.** $5\frac{7}{10}$    **5.** $3\frac{1}{2}$    **6.** $2\frac{5}{8}$

**7.** $6\frac{3}{7}$    **8.** $2\frac{1}{3}$    **9.** $5\frac{4}{5}$    **10.** $7\frac{3}{10}$    **11.** $8\frac{1}{4}$    **12.** $7\frac{2}{3}$

### Write the fraction as a mixed number in simplest form or as a whole number.

**13.** $\frac{19}{3}$    **14.** $\frac{47}{8}$    **15.** $\frac{54}{9}$    **16.** $\frac{23}{4}$    **17.** $\frac{45}{7}$    **18.** $\frac{69}{8}$

**19.** $\frac{58}{4}$    **20.** $\frac{32}{8}$    **21.** $\frac{121}{11}$    **22.** $\frac{112}{6}$    **23.** $\frac{57}{5}$    **24.** $\frac{31}{18}$

**25.** Phil spent 2 hr 7 min repairing his skateboard. Write that amount of time as a mixed number and as a fraction.

**26.** Mary rides the bus $2\frac{1}{4}$ mi to school each morning. Write that distance as a fraction.

**CD ROM** **Technology**
Use Harcourt Mega Math, Fraction Action, *Number Line Mine*, Levels F, H.

## Set E  Write the LCM of the numbers. (pp. 14–17)

**1.** 4, 6     **2.** 7, 14     **3.** 10, 15     **4.** 3, 4     **5.** 6, 24

**6.** 12, 18, 36     **7.** 6, 12, 18     **8.** 10, 16, 20     **9.** 3, 7, 21     **10.** 10, 18, 72

**11.** 7, 5     **12.** 9, 6, 4     **13.** 8, 18     **14.** 15, 12     **15.** 6, 8, 48

**16.** The LCM of two numbers is 16. The GCF of the numbers is 4. What are the numbers?

**17.** The LCM of two numbers is 40. The GCF of the numbers is 20. What are the numbers?

## Set F  Compare. Use <, >, or =. (pp. 18–19)

**1.** $\frac{5}{8}$ ⬤ $\frac{5}{9}$     **2.** $\frac{3}{5}$ ⬤ $\frac{4}{5}$     **3.** $\frac{3}{4}$ ⬤ $\frac{3}{5}$     **4.** $\frac{21}{56}$ ⬤ $\frac{7}{8}$     **5.** $\frac{15}{16}$ ⬤ $\frac{12}{13}$

**6.** $2\frac{5}{6}$ ⬤ $2\frac{1}{12}$     **7.** $3\frac{7}{10}$ ⬤ $3\frac{3}{4}$     **8.** $1\frac{4}{9}$ ⬤ $1\frac{4}{7}$     **9.** $2\frac{2}{9}$ ⬤ $2\frac{4}{15}$     **10.** $1\frac{13}{16}$ ⬤ $1\frac{3}{4}$

### Order from greatest to least.

**11.** $\frac{4}{6}, \frac{4}{5}, \frac{4}{8}$     **12.** $1\frac{3}{5}, \frac{3}{4}, 1\frac{1}{4}$     **13.** $\frac{3}{7}, \frac{3}{6}, \frac{3}{4}$     **14.** $1\frac{6}{7}, \frac{7}{8}, 1\frac{3}{10}$

**15.** $\frac{3}{8}, \frac{3}{7}, \frac{3}{6}$     **16.** $\frac{1}{3}, \frac{2}{7}, \frac{12}{16}$     **17.** $3\frac{1}{2}, 3\frac{1}{4}, 3\frac{1}{6}$     **18.** $4\frac{7}{8}, 4\frac{1}{4}, 4\frac{3}{5}$

## Set G  Compare. Use <, >, or =. (pp. 20–21)

**1.** $\frac{2}{3}$ ⬤ $\frac{2}{5}$     **2.** $\frac{2}{3}$ ⬤ $\frac{4}{5}$     **3.** $\frac{8}{9}$ ⬤ $\frac{7}{8}$     **4.** $\frac{1}{4}$ ⬤ $\frac{2}{6}$     **5.** $\frac{1}{4}$ ⬤ $\frac{25}{100}$

**6.** $\frac{5}{6}$ ⬤ $\frac{8}{10}$     **7.** $\frac{13}{22}$ ⬤ $\frac{6}{21}$     **8.** $\frac{7}{10}$ ⬤ $\frac{12}{16}$     **9.** $\frac{4}{6}$ ⬤ $\frac{8}{12}$     **10.** $\frac{7}{8}$ ⬤ $\frac{20}{24}$

**11.** $\frac{4}{5}$ ⬤ $\frac{8}{9}$     **12.** $\frac{1}{4}$ ⬤ $\frac{1}{5}$     **13.** $\frac{10}{12}$ ⬤ $\frac{5}{6}$     **14.** $\frac{5}{8}$ ⬤ $\frac{4}{6}$     **15.** $\frac{7}{12}$ ⬤ $\frac{3}{5}$

## Set H  Copy and complete. Write each fraction in simplest form. (pp. 24–25)

| | Fraction | Decimal | Percent |
|---|---|---|---|
| **1.** | ▦ | 0.20 | ▦ |
| **3.** | $\frac{3}{4}$ | ▦ | ▦ |
| **5.** | ▦ | 0.55 | ▦ |
| **7.** | ▦ | ▦ | 42% |

| | Fraction | Decimal | Percent |
|---|---|---|---|
| **2.** | ▦ | ▦ | 23% |
| **4.** | ▦ | ▦ | 6% |
| **6.** | ▦ | 0.89 | ▦ |
| **8.** | $\frac{3}{5}$ | ▦ | ▦ |

**9.** Jill answered 23 out of 25 questions on a science test correctly. What percentage of the questions did she answer correctly?

**10.** At Mayberry School, 15% of the students are members of the marching band. What is 15% written as a fraction in simplest form?

# Chapter 1 Review/Test

## Check Vocabulary and Concepts

**Choose the best term from the box.**

1. A whole number greater than 1 whose only factors are 1 and itself, is called a ___?___. (O—¬ NS 2.4, p. 4)

2. The number 3 is the ___?___ of the numbers 6 and 15. (O—¬ NS 2.4, p. 6)

3. The factors of 6 are 1, 2, 3, and 6. The number 6 is a ___?___ because it is a whole number greater than 1 that has more than two factors. (O—¬ NS 2.4, p. 4)

## Check Skills

**Find the GCF and LCM of each set of numbers.** (O—¬ NS 2.4, pp. 6–7, 14–17)

4. 3, 4
5. 8, 64
6. 15, 18
7. 9, 12, 18
8. 10, 20, 50

**Write each mixed number as a fraction. Write each fraction as a mixed number in simplest form or as a whole number.** (O—¬ NS 2.0, pp. 12–13)

9. $6\frac{1}{3}$
10. $\frac{14}{5}$
11. $\frac{35}{9}$
12. $10\frac{3}{4}$
13. $4\frac{2}{7}$

**Compare. Write <, >, or =.** (O—¬ NS 1.0, O—¬ NS 2.4, pp. 18–19, 20–21)

14. $\frac{3}{8}$ ● $\frac{2}{3}$
15. $\frac{4}{7}$ ● $\frac{6}{7}$
16. $\frac{1}{4}$ ● $\frac{1}{5}$
17. $5\frac{5}{6}$ ● $6\frac{1}{6}$
18. $4\frac{1}{2}$ ● $3\frac{3}{4}$

**Copy and complete. Write each fraction in simplest form.** (O—¬ NS 1.0, O—¬ NS 2.4, pp. 10–11, 24–25)

|  | Fraction | Decimal | Percent |
|---|---|---|---|
| 19. | ■ | 0.44 | ■ |
| 21. | $\frac{3}{10}$ | ■ | ■ |

|  | Fraction | Decimal | Percent |
|---|---|---|---|
| 20. | ■ | ■ | 62% |
| 22. | $\frac{23}{100}$ | ■ | ■ |

## Check Problem Solving

**Solve.** (O—¬ NS 2.4, MR 1.1, pp. 22–23)

23. Mark found that a relationship exists between the composite numbers 6 and 24. Identify the relationship and write two other numbers that have the same relationship.

24. Raul wrote the numbers 12 and 18 on the board. He found that the LCM of 12 and 18 is 36. What is the GCF of the pair of numbers?

25. **WRITE Math** Amber wrote the prime numbers 3 and 11. She says that when the GCF of two numbers is 1, the LCM is the quotient of the numbers. Is Amber correct? **Explain.**

# Enrich • Perfect, Abundant, and Deficient Numbers

# Perfect or Not Perfect?

Numbers can be classified as abundant, deficient, or perfect. The classification of a number depends on the sum of the number's proper divisors. The **proper divisors** of a number are the factors of a number, excluding the number itself.

The sum of the proper divisors of an **abundant number** is greater than the number itself. The sum of the proper divisors of a **deficient number** is less than the number itself. The sum of the proper divisors of a **perfect number** is equal to the number itself.

Classify 18 by looking at the sum of its proper divisors.

Step 1: 1, 2, 3, 6, 9

Step 2: $1 + 2 + 3 + 6 + 9 = 21$

## Example

Classify the numbers 18, 21, and 6 as abundant, deficient, or perfect.

|  | | 18 | 21 | 6 |
|---|---|---|---|---|
| **Step 1** | Write the proper divisors of the number. | 1, 2, 3, 6, 9 | 1, 3, 7 | 1, 2, 3 |
| **Step 2** | Find the sum of the proper divisors. | 21 | 11 | 6 |
| **Step 3** | Compare the sum and the number. | $21 > 18$ | $11 < 21$ | $6 = 6$ |
| **Step 4** | Classify the number. | abundant | deficient | perfect |

So, 18 is an abundant number, 21 is a deficient number, and 6 is a perfect number.

## Try It

Classify each number as abundant, deficient, or perfect.

**1.** 29      **2.** 30      **3.** 28      **4.** 17      **5.** 64      **6.** 24

**7.** 51      **8.** 48      **9.** 12      **10.** 40      **11.** 53      **12.** 496

**13.** Emil wrote the prime numbers 31 and 13 on a piece of paper. What do you notice about the prime numbers 31 and 13? **Explain**.

**14. Reasoning** The first odd abundant number is between 800 and 1,000. If its prime factors are 3, 5, and 7, what is the number?

**WRITE Math** Explain why the product of 2 and any perfect number will always be an abundant number.

# Achieving the Standards
 Chapter 1

## Number Sense

**1.** Which list of numbers is ordered from *least* to *greatest*? (O⟶ NS 1.1)

  **A** $\frac{1}{3}$, 0.3, 0.03, $3\frac{1}{3}$

  **B** $3\frac{1}{3}$, 0.3, 0.03, $\frac{1}{3}$

  **C** 0.03, 0.3, $\frac{1}{3}$, $3\frac{1}{3}$

  **D** 0.03, $\frac{1}{3}$, 0.3, $3\frac{1}{3}$

**2.** Which point shows the location of $\frac{5}{2}$ on the number line? (O⟶ NS 1.1)

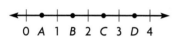

  0  A  1  B  2  C  3  D  4

  **A** point A

  **B** point B

  **C** point C

  **D** point D

**3.** $3^4 =$     (Grade 5 NS 1.3)

  **A** $4 \times 4 \times 4$

  **B** $4 + 4 + 4$

  **C** $3 + 3 + 3 + 3$

  **D** $3 \times 3 \times 3 \times 3$

**4.** $12.4 \times 2.3 =$ ■ (Grade 5 O⟶ NS 2.1)

  **A** 27.52

  **B** 27.72

  **C** 28.52

  **D** 28.72

**5.** **WRITE Math** Explain how to write $\frac{3}{8}$ as a percent. (Grade 5 O⟶ NS 1.2)

## Algebra and Functions

**6.** What is the value of $6 \times n - 4$ for $n = 5$? (Grade 5 O⟶ AF 1.2)

  **A** 6

  **B** 12

  **C** 13

  **D** 26

**7.** Which equation could have been used to make this function table? (Grade 5 O⟶ AF 1.5)

| x | y |
|---|---|
| 13 | 7 |
| 34 | 28 |
| 51 | 45 |
| 60 | 54 |

  **A** $y = \frac{x}{4}$     **C** $y = x - 6$

  **B** $y = 4x$     **D** $y = x + 6$

**8.** What value for $n$ makes the following equation true? (Grade 5 AF 1.3)

  $$9 \times 35 = (9 \times 30) + (9 \times n)$$

  **A** 5     **C** 30

  **B** 9     **D** 35

**9.** Which expression represents the product of $c$ and 12? (Grade 5 O⟶ AF 1.2)

  **A** $12 + c$

  **B** $12c$

  **C** $12 \div c$

  **D** $12 - c$

**10.** **WRITE Math** Explain how to find the value of the expression $x - 10$ for $x = 12$. (Grade 5 O⟶ AF 1.2)

# Measurement and Geometry

**Test Tip** **Eliminate choices.**

See item 11. You can eliminate choices that are the same size or smaller than the area of triangle *UWX*. The parallelogram *UVWX* is clearly larger than the triangle *UWX*.

**11.** In the figure below, *UVWX* is a parallelogram.

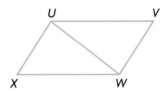

If the area of triangle *UWX* is 12 square centimeters, what is the area of parallelogram *UVWX*? (Grade 5 ○━π MG 1.1)

**A** 6 square centimeters

**B** 12 square centimeters

**C** 18 square centimeters

**D** 24 square centimeters

**12.** What is the measure of angle *x* in the figure below? (Grade 5 ○━π MG 2.2)

**A** 20°          **C** 118°

**B** 110°         **D** 180°

**13.** **WRITE Math** ▶ Billy says that two acute angles can have a sum of 180°. Is he correct? **Explain** why or why not. (Grade 5 ○━π MG 2.1)

# Statistics, Data Analysis, and Probability

**14.** Mrs. Hooper recorded the attendance at five concert performances in the table below.

| Concert Attendance | |
|---|---|
| **Performance** | **Number of People** |
| Monday | 125 |
| Tuesday | 234 |
| Wednesday | 190 |
| Thursday | 305 |
| Friday | 331 |

What is the median of the data? (Grade 5 SDAP 1.1)

**A** 125          **C** 234

**B** 190          **D** 237

**15.** Samantha scored the following point totals in 7 dart games: 72, 84, 84, 95, 104, 132, and 145. What is the mode of the data? (Grade 5 SDAP 1.1)

**A** 72          **C** 95

**B** 84          **D** There is no mode.

**16.** A scientist recorded the number of insects caught in a trap each day for five days. What is the mean of the data? (Grade 5 SDAP 1.1)

12, 14, 10, 16, 13

**A** 4          **C** 13

**B** 6          **D** 14

**17.** **WRITE Math** ▶ **Explain** how it is possible to have a data set with no mode. (Grade 5 SDAP 1.1)

# 2 Add and Subtract Fractions

**The Big Idea** Addition and subtraction of fractions and mixed numbers is based on understanding equivalent fractions.

## Investigate

Suppose you are a park ranger at Yosemite National Park. If a visitor wants to hike between 9 mi and 11 mi in one day, what combinations of two or more trails could you suggest they hike?

### Yosemite National Park Trails

| Trail | Distance (in mi) |
|---|---|
| Four Mile Trail to Glacier Point | $9\frac{3}{5}$ |
| Lower Yosemite Fall | $\frac{1}{2}$ |
| Panorama | $8\frac{1}{2}$ |
| Upper Yosemite Fall | $7\frac{2}{10}$ |
| Vernal Fall | $1\frac{3}{5}$ |

**CALIFORNIA FAST FACT**

Yosemite National Park, in the central Sierra Nevada of California, contains thousands of lakes and ponds, 1,600 mi of streams, and 800 mi of hiking trails.

**GO ONLINE**

**Technology**
Student pages are available in the Student eBook.

Check your understanding of important skills
needed for success in Chapter 2.

▶ **Equivalent Fractions**

Complete.

1. $\frac{2}{7} = \frac{\blacksquare}{14}$   2. $\frac{1}{8} = \frac{\blacksquare}{24}$   3. $\frac{1}{\blacksquare} = \frac{3}{24}$   4. $\frac{1}{6} = \frac{5}{\blacksquare}$   5. $\frac{\blacksquare}{6} = \frac{2}{12}$

6. $\frac{2}{\blacksquare} = \frac{20}{100}$   7. $\frac{9}{36} = \frac{1}{\blacksquare}$   8. $\frac{\blacksquare}{36} = \frac{1}{2}$   9. $\frac{\blacksquare}{15} = \frac{1}{3}$   10. $\frac{\blacksquare}{4} = \frac{11}{44}$

▶ **Simplest Form**

Write the fraction in simplest form.

11. $\frac{3}{6}$   12. $\frac{4}{32}$   13. $\frac{5}{15}$   14. $\frac{2}{10}$   15. $\frac{9}{27}$

16. $\frac{4}{6}$   17. $\frac{6}{10}$   18. $\frac{2}{40}$   19. $\frac{5}{75}$   20. $\frac{4}{16}$

▶ **Add and Subtract Like Fractions**

Find the sum or difference. Write the answer in simplest form.

21. $\frac{11}{20} - \frac{9}{20}$   22. $\frac{3}{8} + \frac{1}{8}$   23. $\frac{14}{15} + \frac{1}{15}$   24. $\frac{3}{4} - \frac{2}{4}$   25. $\frac{5}{8} - \frac{3}{8}$

26. $\frac{9}{12} + \frac{1}{12}$   27. $\frac{9}{10} - \frac{2}{10}$   28. $\frac{9}{20} + \frac{5}{20}$   29. $\frac{3}{5} - \frac{1}{5}$   30. $\frac{1}{7} + \frac{1}{7}$

# VOCABULARY POWER

**CHAPTER VOCABULARY**

benchmark
least common denominator
  (LCD)
unlike fractions

**WARM-UP WORDS**

**benchmark**  a familiar number used as a point
of reference

**unlike fractions**  fractions with different denominators

**least common denominator (LCD)**  the least common
multiple of two or more denominators

**LESSON 1**

# Estimate Sums and Differences

**OBJECTIVE:** Estimate sums and differences of fractions and mixed numbers.

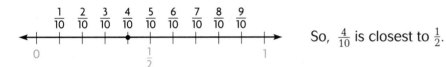

## Quick Review

Lily made three jumps in a long-jump contest. She jumped $3\frac{1}{2}$ ft, $3\frac{2}{5}$ ft, and $3\frac{5}{6}$ ft. Order the distances from least to greatest.

## Vocabulary

**benchmark**

## Learn

Rounding fractions can help you to estimate sums and differences. A **benchmark** is a reference point on a number line that is useful for rounding fractions. Look at the number line. Is $\frac{4}{10}$ closest to $0$, $\frac{1}{2}$, or $1$?

$$\frac{1}{10} \quad \frac{2}{10} \quad \frac{3}{10} \quad \frac{4}{10} \quad \frac{5}{10} \quad \frac{6}{10} \quad \frac{7}{10} \quad \frac{8}{10} \quad \frac{9}{10}$$

$$0 \qquad\qquad \frac{1}{2} \qquad\qquad 1$$

So, $\frac{4}{10}$ is closest to $\frac{1}{2}$.

Also, you can compare the numerator to the denominator.

| $\frac{2}{16} \quad \frac{1}{7}$ | $\frac{9}{16} \quad \frac{5}{11}$ | $\frac{9}{10} \quad \frac{15}{16}$ |
|---|---|---|
| Each numerator is much less than half the denominator, so the fractions are close to 0. | Each numerator is about half the denominator, so the fractions are close to $\frac{1}{2}$. | Each numerator is about the same as the denominator, so the fractions are close to 1. |

**PROBLEM** Suppose that in a Special Olympics marathon, the lead runner is $\frac{1}{8}$ mi ahead of the second-place runner, and the second-place runner is $\frac{15}{16}$ mi ahead of the third-place runner. About how far apart are the lead runner and the third-place runner?

**Estimate.** $\frac{1}{8} + \frac{15}{16}$

| | | |
|---|---|---|
| $\frac{1}{8} \rightarrow$ | $0$ | $\frac{1}{8}$ is between 0 and $\frac{1}{2}$, but closer to 0. |
| $+\frac{15}{16} \rightarrow$ | $+1$ | $\frac{15}{16}$ is between $\frac{1}{2}$ and 1, but closer to 1. |
| | $1$ | |

So, the lead runner is about 1 mi ahead of the third-place runner.

### Example 1  Estimate. $\frac{7}{8} - \frac{4}{5}$

| | | |
|---|---|---|
| $\frac{7}{8} \rightarrow$ | $1$ | The numerators are both about the same as the |
| $-\frac{4}{5} \rightarrow$ | $-1$ | denominators—round both fractions to 1. |
| | $0$ | |

So, $\frac{7}{8} - \frac{4}{5}$ is about 0.

157

NS 2.1 Solve problems involving addition, subtraction, multiplication, and division of positive fractions and explain why a particular operation was used for a given situation. *also* NS 2.0, MR 2.4, MR 2.5, MR 3.2

# Mixed Numbers

To estimate sums and differences of mixed numbers, compare each mixed number to the nearest whole number or to the nearest $\frac{1}{2}$.

**Example 2** A marathon runner has a goal to run 20 mi during the first week of training. On Sunday, she ran $8\frac{1}{5}$ mi. On Tuesday, she ran $6\frac{7}{10}$ mi. About how many more miles does she need to run that week to meet her goal?

**Estimate.** $20 - \left(8\frac{1}{5} + 6\frac{7}{10}\right)$

$20 - \left(8\frac{1}{5} + 6\frac{7}{10}\right)$    $8\frac{1}{5}$ is close to 8, and $6\frac{7}{10}$ is close to 7.

$20 - \left(8 + 7\right)$    Add.

$20 - 15 = 5$    Subtract.

So, she needs to run about 5 more miles.

> **Remember**
> A mixed number is represented by a whole number and a fraction. $8\frac{3}{5}$ is a mixed number.

Some situations may require an overestimate or underestimate for the answer. To overestimate the sum of two or more fractions, round all of the fractions up. To underestimate the sum of two or more fractions, round all of the fractions down.

**Example 3** A figure skater likes to listen to music while he trains. He only has 12 more minutes of memory on his MP3 player. He wants to download 3 songs of $3\frac{2}{10}$ min, $2\frac{3}{4}$ min, and $4\frac{2}{3}$ min. Will all three songs fit on his MP3 player?

**Estimate.** $3\frac{2}{10} + 2\frac{3}{4} + 4\frac{2}{3}$

To decide whether all three songs will fit, find an overestimate.

$$
\begin{array}{lll}
3\frac{2}{10} & \rightarrow & 3\frac{1}{2} \\
2\frac{3}{4} & \rightarrow & 3 \\
+ 4\frac{2}{3} & \rightarrow & + 5 \\
\hline
& & 11\frac{1}{2}
\end{array}
$$

$3\frac{2}{10}$ rounds up to $3\frac{1}{2}$.
$2\frac{3}{4}$ rounds up to 3.
$4\frac{2}{3}$ rounds up to 5.

$11\frac{1}{2} < 12$. So, all three songs will fit on his MP3 player.

## Guided Practice

1. Use the number line to tell whether $\frac{1}{3}$ is closest to 0, $\frac{1}{2}$, or 1. Write *close to 0, close to $\frac{1}{2}$,* or *close to 1.*

0    $\frac{1}{12}$   $\frac{1}{6}$   $\frac{1}{4}$   $\frac{1}{3}$   $\frac{5}{12}$   $\frac{1}{2}$   $\frac{7}{12}$   $\frac{2}{3}$   $\frac{3}{4}$   $\frac{5}{6}$   $\frac{11}{12}$   1

**Estimate the sum or difference.**

2. $\frac{6}{7} + \frac{11}{12}$    3. $\frac{3}{5} - \frac{1}{9}$    ✓4. $9\frac{2}{15} - 3\frac{7}{8}$    ✓5. $5\frac{7}{12} + 1\frac{3}{8}$

6. **TALK Math** Explain how to use benchmarks to estimate $4\frac{1}{9} + 4\frac{4}{5}$.

## Independent Practice and Problem Solving

Use the number line to tell whether the fraction is closest to 0, $\frac{1}{2}$, or 1. Write *close to 0, close to $\frac{1}{2}$,* or *close to 1.*

0 $\frac{1}{12}$ $\frac{1}{6}$ $\frac{1}{4}$ $\frac{1}{3}$ $\frac{5}{12}$ $\frac{1}{2}$ $\frac{7}{12}$ $\frac{2}{3}$ $\frac{3}{4}$ $\frac{5}{6}$ $\frac{11}{12}$ 1

7. $\frac{7}{12}$    8. $\frac{1}{6}$    9. $\frac{5}{12}$    10. $\frac{5}{6}$

**Estimate the sum or difference.**

11. $\frac{6}{11} - \frac{1}{6}$    12. $\frac{1}{5} + \frac{8}{9}$    13. $\frac{6}{13} - \frac{4}{9}$    14. $\frac{9}{10} + \frac{1}{5} + \frac{3}{7}$

15. $8\frac{1}{5} + 9\frac{5}{8}$    16. $10\frac{1}{5} - 9\frac{4}{7}$    17. $7\frac{9}{10} - 5\frac{5}{8}$    18. $16\frac{1}{8} + 13\frac{8}{9} + 3\frac{4}{5}$

**Estimate to compare. Write $<$ or $>$ for each ⬤.**

19. $\frac{5}{8} + \frac{7}{12}$ ⬤ 2    20. $4\frac{9}{10} - 3\frac{2}{7}$ ⬤ 1    21. $12\frac{3}{5} + 4\frac{4}{9}$ ⬤ 15    22. $4\frac{1}{12} + 5\frac{1}{6}$ ⬤ 10

**For 23–24, tell whether an *overestimate* or an *underestimate* is needed. Solve.**

23. Pam is making a winner's plaque for a relay competition. She needs to cut wood trim to edge a rectangular plaque that has a length of $7\frac{2}{5}$ in. and a width of $4\frac{7}{8}$ in. Estimate the length of the piece of wood she should purchase.

24. Ray wants his combined triple jump distance to be at least 20 ft. His three jumps measure $6\frac{2}{3}$ ft, $5\frac{1}{9}$ ft, and $8\frac{5}{8}$ ft. Estimate his combined triple-jump distance. Did Ray meet his goal?

**USE DATA For 25–28, use the graph.**

25. Jan and her friends go to the pool several times each week to train in four different swimming styles. Estimate the total number of hours Jan swims in one week.

26. About how many more hours does Ben swim freestyle and backstroke than Darren?

27. Andrea trains for butterfly for $4\frac{1}{5}$ hr each week. About how many more hours does she swim butterfly than Jan does?

28. **WRITE Math** Ben says he trains for freestyle for a greater amount of time than both Jan and Darren combined. Is this true? Explain.

| Average Weekly Training Time (hr) | | | |
|---|---|---|---|
| | Freestyle | Backstroke | Breaststroke | Butterfly |
| Jan | $5\frac{2}{3}$ | $4\frac{1}{6}$ | $3\frac{2}{3}$ | $2\frac{5}{12}$ |
| Darren | $4\frac{5}{6}$ | $5\frac{1}{12}$ | $2\frac{1}{5}$ | $3\frac{4}{5}$ |
| Ben | $8\frac{9}{10}$ | $8\frac{9}{10}$ | $4\frac{8}{15}$ | $3\frac{2}{5}$ |

**29.** What is the greatest common divisor of 65 and 91? (○━┑ NS 2.4, p. 6)

**30.** What are the first five multiples of the number 14? (○━┑ NS 2.4, p. 4)

**31.** Write $\frac{6}{8}$ in simplest form. (○━┑ NS 2.4, p. 8)

**32. Test Prep** Antonio needs to buy 15 pounds of chicken for a dinner party. He bought three packages: $2\frac{1}{4}$ pounds, $4\frac{6}{7}$ pounds, and $5\frac{2}{3}$ pounds. About how many more pounds does Antonio need to buy?

   **A** 2 pounds      **C** 6 pounds

   **B** 4 pounds      **D** 8 pounds

**33. Test Prep** Dr. Driben needs to complete Milo's vet record. What is her estimation of Milo's new weight?

> **Milo's vet record**
> Prior weight: $15\frac{1}{8}$ lb  Weight lost: $2\frac{3}{4}$ lb
> New weight estimation: ■

   **A** about $2\frac{3}{4}$ pounds

   **B** about 10 pounds

   **C** about 12 pounds

   **D** about 18 pounds

 **Problem Solving and Reasoning**

**NUMBER SENSE** You can round fractions and mixed numbers to find a range to estimate a sum or difference.

Estimate. $8\frac{3}{4} + 4\frac{3}{8}$

Since $8\frac{3}{4}$ is halfway between $8\frac{1}{2}$ and 9, find two estimates for the difference.

**Estimate 1**

$8\frac{3}{4} + 4\frac{3}{8}$     $8\frac{3}{4}$ is close to $8\frac{1}{2}$ and $4\frac{3}{8}$ is close to 4.
$\downarrow$   $\downarrow$
$8\frac{1}{2} + 4 = 12\frac{1}{2}$    Add.

**Estimate 2**

$8\frac{3}{4} + 4\frac{3}{8}$     $8\frac{3}{4}$ is close to 9, and $4\frac{3}{8}$ is close to $4\frac{1}{2}$.
$\downarrow$   $\downarrow$
$9 + 4\frac{1}{2} = 13\frac{1}{2}$    Add.

The estimates are $12\frac{1}{2}$ and $13\frac{1}{2}$.

So, 13, which is halfway between $12\frac{1}{2}$ and $13\frac{1}{2}$, is a good estimate of $8\frac{3}{4} + 4\frac{3}{8}$.

**Use a range to estimate each sum or difference.**

  **1.** $9\frac{5}{6} + 2\frac{2}{8}$        **2.** $11\frac{3}{5} + 4\frac{7}{8}$        **3.** $9 - 4\frac{1}{8}$        **4.** $8\frac{1}{2} - 2\frac{1}{8}$

# 2 Add and Subtract Fractions

**OBJECTIVE:** Find sums and differences of fractions with unlike denominators.

## Quick Review

**Complete.**

1. $\frac{9}{\blacksquare} = \frac{3}{4}$    2. $\frac{10}{15} = \frac{\blacksquare}{3}$

3. $\frac{\blacksquare}{36} = \frac{2}{9}$    4. $\frac{16}{28} = \frac{4}{\blacksquare}$

5. $\frac{12}{54} = \frac{\blacksquare}{9}$

## Vocabulary

unlike fractions

least common denominator (LCD)

## Learn

**PROBLEM** The human body is made of approximately $\frac{3}{5}$ oxygen, $\frac{1}{5}$ carbon, and $\frac{1}{10}$ hydrogen. Find the fraction of the human body that is made up of these elements.

**Unlike fractions** are fractions with different denominators. You can add and subtract unlike fractions with the help of fraction bars.

### Activity 1

**Materials** ■ fraction bars

**Add.** $\frac{3}{5} + \frac{1}{5} + \frac{1}{10}$   Estimate. $1 + 0 + 0 = 1$

**Step 1**

First, use mental math to find $\frac{3}{5} + \frac{1}{5}$.

$$\frac{3}{5} + \frac{1}{5} = \frac{4}{5}$$

Then, use fraction bars to model $\frac{4}{5} + \frac{1}{10}$.

| $\frac{1}{5}$ | $\frac{1}{5}$ | $\frac{1}{5}$ | $\frac{1}{5}$ | $\frac{1}{10}$ |

**Step 2**

Last, find which fraction bars fit exactly across $\frac{4}{5}$ and $\frac{1}{10}$.

| $\frac{1}{5}$ | $\frac{1}{5}$ | $\frac{1}{5}$ | $\frac{1}{5}$ | $\frac{1}{10}$ |

| $\frac{1}{10}$ | $\frac{1}{10}$ | $\frac{1}{10}$ | $\frac{1}{10}$ | $\frac{1}{10}$ | $\frac{1}{10}$ | $\frac{1}{10}$ | $\frac{1}{10}$ | $\frac{1}{10}$ |

$$\frac{4}{5} + \frac{1}{10} = \frac{8}{10} + \frac{1}{10} = \frac{9}{10}$$

Since $\frac{9}{10}$ is close to the estimate of 1, the answer is reasonable.

So, $\frac{9}{10}$ of the human body is made up of oxygen, carbon, and hydrogen.

When subtracting a fraction from a whole number, rename the whole number.

### Activity 2

**Materials** ■ fraction bars

**Subtract.** $1 - \frac{3}{8}$   Estimate. $1 - \frac{1}{2} = \frac{1}{2}$

| $\frac{1}{8}$ | $\frac{1}{8}$ | $\frac{1}{8}$ | $\frac{1}{8}$ | $\frac{1}{8}$ | $\frac{1}{8}$ | $\frac{1}{8}$ | $\frac{1}{8}$ |

Rename 1 whole using eight $\frac{1}{8}$ bars. Subtract $\frac{3}{8}$.

$$1 - \frac{3}{8} = \frac{8}{8} - \frac{3}{8} = \frac{5}{8}$$

Since $\frac{5}{8}$ is close to the estimate of $\frac{1}{2}$, the answer is reasonable. So, $1 - \frac{3}{8} = \frac{5}{8}$.

NS 2.1 Solve problems involving addition, subtraction, multiplication, and division of positive fractions and explain why a particular operation was used for a given situation. *also* ⊶ NS 2.0, ⊶ NS 2.4, MR 2.1, MR 2.4, MR 2.5, MR 3.2

# Using Common Denominators

To add or subtract unlike fractions without using models, find equivalent fractions. Equivalent fractions can be written by using a common denominator or the **least common denominator (LCD)**. The LCD is the least common multiple (LCM) of two or more denominators.

**Example 1** Use a common denominator to find $\frac{5}{6} + \frac{4}{9}$.

Estimate. $\frac{5}{6}$ is close to 1, and $\frac{4}{9}$ is close to $\frac{1}{2}$. $1 + \frac{1}{2} = 1\frac{1}{2}$

**Step 1**

$$\frac{5}{6} = \frac{5 \times 9}{6 \times 9} = \frac{45}{54}$$
$$+\frac{4}{9} = \frac{4 \times 6}{9 \times 6} = +\frac{24}{54}$$

Multiply 6 and 9 to find a common denominator, 54. Use the common denominator to write equivalent fractions.

**Step 2**

$$\frac{5}{6} = \frac{45}{54}$$
$$+\frac{4}{9} = +\frac{24}{54}$$
$$\frac{69}{54}, \text{ or } 1\frac{5}{18}$$

Add the numerators. Write the sum over the denominator.

Write the answer as a fraction or as a mixed number.

Compare the answer to your estimate. Since $1\frac{5}{18}$ is close to the estimate of $1\frac{1}{2}$, the answer is reasonable.

So, $\frac{5}{6} + \frac{4}{9} = 1\frac{5}{18}$.

**ERROR ALERT**

Multiply both the numerator and the denominator by the same factor to find an equivalent fraction.

**Example 2** Use the LCD to find $\frac{7}{12} - \frac{1}{3}$.

Estimate. $\frac{7}{12}$ is close to $\frac{1}{2}$, and $\frac{1}{3}$ is close to 0. $\frac{1}{2} - 0 = \frac{1}{2}$

**Step 1**

$$\frac{7}{12} = \frac{7}{12}$$
$$-\frac{1}{3} = \frac{1 \times 4}{3 \times 4} = -\frac{4}{12}$$

The LCD of $\frac{7}{12}$ and $\frac{1}{3}$ is 12. Multiply to write equivalent fractions using the LCD.

**Step 2**

$$\frac{7}{12} = \frac{7}{12}$$
$$-\frac{1}{3} = -\frac{4}{12}$$
$$\frac{3}{12} = \frac{1}{4}$$

Subtract the numerators.

Write the difference over the denominator. Write the answer in simplest form.

Compare the answer to your estimate. Since $\frac{1}{4}$ is close to the estimate of $\frac{1}{2}$, the answer is reasonable.

So, $\frac{7}{12} - \frac{1}{3} = \frac{1}{4}$.

You can also use this key sequence on a calculator.

7 [n] 12 [−] 1 [n] 3 [Enter =]    $\frac{\frac{N}{D} \to \frac{n}{d}}{\frac{7}{12} - \frac{1}{3} = \frac{3}{12}}$

To write the answer in simplest form, continue pressing the [Simp] and [Enter =] keys as long as $\frac{N}{D} \to \frac{n}{d}$ shows in the display.

     $\frac{3}{12} \blacktriangleright S \quad \frac{1}{4}$

**1.** Use the fraction bars to find $\frac{1}{4} + \frac{2}{3}$.

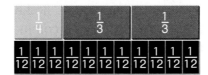

**Use a common denominator to write the problem using equivalent fractions.**

**2.** $\frac{5}{8} + \frac{1}{6}$

**3.** $\frac{5}{6} + \frac{1}{2}$

**4.** $\frac{6}{7} - \frac{1}{2}$

**5.** $\frac{7}{9} - \frac{2}{3}$

**6.** $\frac{2}{3} + \frac{5}{12}$

**Estimate. Then write the sum or difference in simplest form.**

**7.** $\frac{2}{3} + \frac{1}{12}$

**8.** $\frac{11}{18} - \frac{3}{18}$

**9.** $\frac{4}{15} + \frac{2}{5}$

**10.** $\frac{7}{16} + \frac{3}{4}$

**11.** $\frac{3}{4} - \frac{5}{12}$

**12.** **TALK Math** Explain how to find $\frac{1}{8} + \frac{5}{6}$.

## Independent Practice and Problem Solving

**Use a common denominator to write the problem using equivalent fractions.**

**13.** $\frac{5}{8} + \frac{1}{4}$

**14.** $\frac{4}{11} - \frac{8}{22}$

**15.** $\frac{7}{16} + \frac{3}{8}$

**16.** $\frac{4}{9} + \frac{1}{5}$

**17.** $\frac{11}{20} - \frac{1}{3}$

**18.** $\frac{2}{5} + \frac{1}{6}$

**19.** $\frac{6}{7} - \frac{1}{3}$

**20.** $1 - \frac{1}{15}$

**21.** $\frac{1}{2} + \frac{3}{14}$

**22.** $\frac{2}{3} + \frac{1}{5}$

**Estimate. Then write the sum or difference in simplest form.**

**23.** $\frac{7}{9} + \frac{1}{2}$

**24.** $\frac{4}{5} - \frac{1}{15}$

**25.** $\frac{3}{8} - \frac{1}{10}$

**26.** $\frac{1}{2} + \frac{1}{3}$

**27.** $\frac{4}{5} - \frac{2}{5}$

**28.** $\frac{2}{3} - \frac{1}{4}$

**29.** $\frac{6}{10} - \frac{4}{15}$

**30.** $\frac{6}{25} + \frac{3}{10}$

**31.** $\frac{11}{20} + \frac{2}{5} + \frac{1}{2}$

**32.** $\frac{1}{4} + \frac{1}{3} + \frac{1}{2}$

**33.** What is the sum of $\frac{2}{7}$ and $\frac{1}{2}$?

**34.** How much less than $\frac{1}{4}$ is $\frac{1}{6}$?

**35.** How much longer than $\frac{3}{4}$ mi is $\frac{7}{8}$ mi?

**36.** What is the total of $\frac{5}{6}$ and $\frac{5}{12}$?

**Algebra** Use mental math to solve. Write the answer in simplest form.

**37.** $n + \frac{1}{8} = \frac{7}{8}$

**38.** $y - \frac{1}{6} = \frac{1}{6}$

**39.** $m + \frac{1}{3} = \frac{2}{3}$

**40.** $z - \frac{1}{9} = \frac{6}{9}$

**For 41–43, use the diagram at the right.**

**41.** Find the sum of the fractions that are inside the triangle but outside the square.

**42.** Find the sum of the fractions outside the triangle but inside the square.

**43.** Find the difference of the fractions inside both the triangle and the square.

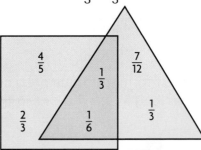

**Technology**
Use Harcourt Mega Math, Fraction Action, *Fraction Flare Up,* Levels G–K.

**44.** What fraction of sedimentary rock is not limestone?

**45.** **Pose a Problem** Look back at Problem 44 and write and solve a similar problem.

**46.** **≡FAST FACT** Geologists classify rocks in three main groups: igneous, metamorphic, and sedimentary. The earth's crust is about $\frac{13}{20}$ igneous rock, $\frac{1}{4}$ metamorphic rock, and $\frac{1}{10}$ sedimentary rock. About what fraction of earth's crust is igneous or metamorphic rock?

**47.** **WRITE Math** Explain how to use the LCD to find the sum of $\frac{1}{4}$ and $\frac{5}{6}$ in simplest form.

| Type of Sedimentary Rock | | | |
|---|---|---|---|
| Type | Shale | Sandstone | Limestone |
| Fraction of Sedimentary Rock | $\frac{3}{5}$ | $\frac{1}{4}$ | $\frac{3}{20}$ |

## Achieving the Standards

**48.** Order $\frac{5}{8}$, $\frac{1}{2}$, $\frac{3}{4}$ from least to greatest. (O⌐ NS 1.1, p. 18)

**49.** Lonnie needs $\frac{4}{5}$ yard of blue fabric and $\frac{1}{4}$ yard of red fabric for a project. About how much fabric does Lonnie need? (O⌐ NS 2.4, p. 34)

**50.** What is the least common multiple of 14 and 35? (O⌐ NS 2.4, p. 14)

**51.** **Test Prep** What is the sum, in simplest form, of $\frac{9}{16} + \frac{14}{16} + \frac{12}{16}$?

**A** $\frac{9}{16}$    **B** $\frac{37}{16}$    **C** $\frac{14}{16}$    **D** $2\frac{3}{16}$

**52.** **Test Prep** What is the difference, in simplest form, of $\frac{7}{12} - \frac{3}{10}$?

**A** $\frac{8}{15}$    **B** $\frac{9}{20}$    **C** $\frac{17}{60}$    **D** $\frac{53}{60}$

# MATH POWER
## Problem Solving and Reasoning

**ALGEBRA** Number patterns follow rules. If you know a rule for a pattern, you can use it to find the next number. Look at the pattern. $\frac{5}{6}$, $1\frac{1}{3}$, $1\frac{5}{6}$, $2\frac{1}{3}$, ▪. Find the next number in the pattern.

| **Step 1** Find a possible rule. | **Step 2** Use the rule to find the next number. |
|---|---|
| Since the numbers increase, try addition. Try add $\frac{1}{2}$. $\frac{5}{6} + \frac{1}{2} = 1\frac{1}{3}$   $1\frac{1}{3} + \frac{1}{2} = 1\frac{5}{6}$   $1\frac{5}{6} + \frac{1}{2} = 2\frac{1}{3}$ A possible rule is **add $\frac{1}{2}$**. | $2\frac{1}{3} + \frac{1}{2} = 2\frac{5}{6}$ |

So, $2\frac{5}{6}$ is the next number in the pattern.

**Write a possible rule. Find the next fraction in the pattern.**

**1.** $\frac{1}{12}$, $\frac{1}{3}$, $\frac{7}{12}$, $\frac{10}{12}$, ▪

**2.** 5, $4\frac{1}{4}$, $3\frac{1}{2}$, $2\frac{3}{4}$, ▪

**3.** $1\frac{2}{3}$, $1\frac{5}{6}$, 2, $2\frac{1}{6}$, ▪

# 3 Add and Subtract Mixed Numbers

OBJECTIVE: Find sums and differences of mixed numbers.

## Quick Review

**Find the sum or difference in simplest form.**

1. $\frac{3}{4} + \frac{1}{12}$

2. $\frac{5}{12} + \frac{2}{3} + \frac{5}{6}$

3. $\frac{7}{10} - \frac{1}{5}$

4. $\frac{3}{4} - \frac{1}{12}$

5. $\frac{1}{4} + \frac{1}{3} + \frac{5}{12}$

## Learn

**PROBLEM** At a local amusement park, Valerie spent $2\frac{1}{4}$ min on one roller coaster and $1\frac{3}{8}$ min on another. What is the total amount of time she spent on the roller coasters?

**Add.** $2\frac{1}{4} + 1\frac{3}{8}$    Estimate. $2 + 1\frac{1}{2} = 3\frac{1}{2}$

**ONE WAY** Draw a diagram.

Show $2\frac{1}{4} + 1\frac{3}{8}$.

| 1 |
| 1 | $\frac{1}{4}$ |
| 1 | $\frac{1}{8}$ $\frac{1}{8}$ $\frac{1}{8}$ |
| 1 |
| 1 | $\frac{1}{4}$ $\frac{1}{8}$ $\frac{1}{8}$ $\frac{1}{8}$ |
| 1 |

Combine whole numbers. Combine fractions. 8 is a common multiple of 4 and 8. Draw eighths under $\frac{1}{4}$ and $\frac{3}{8}$.

$2 + 1 = 3$          $\frac{2}{8} + \frac{3}{8} = \frac{5}{8}$    Add fractions.
                                                   Add whole numbers.

So, Valerie spent $3\frac{5}{8}$ min on the roller coasters.

**ANOTHER WAY** Use a common denominator.

**Add.** $3\frac{2}{3} + 2\frac{3}{4}$

$3\frac{2}{3} = 3\frac{8}{12}$

$+ 2\frac{3}{4} = 2\frac{9}{12}$

$\overline{\quad\quad 5\frac{17}{12} = 5 + 1\frac{5}{12} = 6\frac{5}{12}}$

Write equivalent fractions, using the LCD, 12. Add fractions. Add whole numbers.

Rename the fraction as a mixed number. Rewrite the sum.

So, $3\frac{2}{3} + 2\frac{3}{4} = 6\frac{5}{12}$.

You can also use this key sequence on a calculator.

3  2  3  2  3  4 **Enter**    $\boxed{3\frac{2}{3} + 2\frac{3}{4} = \quad 6\frac{5}{12}}$

  NS 2.1 Solve problems involving addition, subtraction, multiplication, and division of positive fractions and explain why a particular operation was used for a given situation. also 🔑 NS 2.0, 🔑 NS 2.4, MR 2.1, MR 2.2, MR 2.4, MR 2.5, MR 3.0, MR 3.2, MR 3.3

# Subtract Mixed Numbers

The Kingda Ka, in New Jersey, is the tallest and fastest roller coaster in the world. It reaches the bottom of the longest drop in $3\frac{1}{2}$ sec. The Xcelerator roller coaster, in California, has a drop time of $2\frac{3}{10}$ sec. What is the difference in the drop times?

**Subtract.** $3\frac{1}{2} - 2\frac{3}{10}$

**ONE WAY** Draw a diagram.

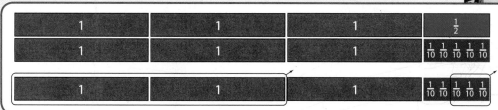

Draw $3\frac{1}{2}$.

10 is a common multiple of 2 and 10. Draw tenths under the $\frac{1}{2}$.

Subtract $2\frac{3}{10}$ from $3\frac{1}{2}$.

$3\frac{1}{2} - 2\frac{3}{10} = 1\frac{2}{10}$, or $1\frac{1}{5}$. So, the difference in the times is $1\frac{1}{5}$ sec.

- Explain why you used subtraction to solve this problem.

**ANOTHER WAY** Use the LCD to find $4\frac{4}{5} - 2\frac{1}{4}$.

Estimate. $4\frac{4}{5}$ is close to 5, and $2\frac{1}{4}$ is close to 2. So, the difference is about 3.

$$4\frac{4}{5} = 4\frac{16}{20}$$ Write equivalent fractions using the LCD, 20.

$$-2\frac{1}{4} = -2\frac{5}{20}$$ Subtract fractions.

$$2\frac{11}{20}$$ Subtract whole numbers.

The answer is reasonable because it is close to the estimate of 3.

So, $4\frac{4}{5} - 2\frac{1}{4} = 2\frac{11}{20}$.

## Guided Practice

1. Copy the diagram shown. Then use your diagram to record and find the difference.

**Draw a diagram to show the sum or difference. Then write the answer in simplest form.**

2. $1\frac{5}{6} + 2\frac{1}{3}$   3. $2\frac{2}{5} + 3\frac{1}{10}$   4. $3\frac{4}{12} - 3\frac{1}{3}$   5. $3\frac{1}{3} - 2\frac{1}{4}$   ✓6. $5\frac{4}{5} - 3\frac{3}{10}$

**Estimate. Then write the sum or difference in simplest form.**

7. $8\frac{7}{8} - 2\frac{1}{8}$   8. $3\frac{7}{8} + 3\frac{1}{2}$   9. $10\frac{9}{20} + 8\frac{3}{4}$   10. $8\frac{1}{3} - 1\frac{2}{15}$   ✓11. $4\frac{1}{6} + 3\frac{1}{4}$

12. **TALK Math** Explain how to find $4\frac{5}{8} - 2\frac{1}{4}$.

**Draw a diagram to show the sum or difference. Then write the answer in simplest form.**

**13.** $4\frac{1}{2} - 2\frac{1}{5}$     **14.** $9\frac{5}{6} - 1\frac{1}{3}$     **15.** $3\frac{5}{12} + \frac{1}{3}$     **16.** $2\frac{4}{7} - 1\frac{1}{2}$     **17.** $1\frac{1}{3} + 2\frac{1}{6}$

**Estimate. Then write the sum or difference in simplest form.**

**18.** $16\frac{3}{4} - 5\frac{1}{3}$     **19.** $30\frac{5}{6} - 21\frac{2}{3}$     **20.** $25\frac{7}{18} + 15\frac{1}{6}$     **21.** $10\frac{9}{20} + 8\frac{3}{4}$     **22.** $4\frac{1}{2} + 3\frac{4}{5}$

**23.** $12\frac{2}{3} + 6\frac{3}{4}$     **24.** $7\frac{5}{6} - 4\frac{1}{5}$     **25.** $8\frac{3}{8} + 2\frac{1}{3}$     **26.** $4\frac{7}{10} - 1\frac{2}{5}$     **27.** $5\frac{1}{2} - 2\frac{1}{6}$

**28.** What is the sum of $4\frac{1}{2}$ and $7\frac{1}{6}$?       **29.** What is the sum of $6\frac{5}{6}$ and $4\frac{5}{6}$?

**30.** How much greater is $10\frac{3}{4}$ than $8\frac{2}{3}$?       **31.** How much greater is $12\frac{7}{12}$ than $9\frac{1}{3}$?

★**Algebra** **Find the unknown number, and identify which property of addition you used.**

**32.** $5\frac{1}{2} + \blacksquare = 3\frac{1}{4} + 5\frac{1}{2}$     **33.** $7\frac{1}{8} + 0 = \blacksquare$     **34.** $1\frac{1}{6} + (1\frac{1}{5} + 1\frac{1}{4}) = (1\frac{1}{6} + \blacksquare) + 1\frac{1}{4}$

**USE DATA** For 35–37, use the table.

**35.** How much faster is the Zaturn roller coaster than the Stealth? **Explain.**

**36.** **Reasoning** Which 2 roller coasters have the least difference in maximum speed?

**37.** **WRITE Math** **What's the Error?** Clinton says that Thunder Dolphin is faster than Zaturn by $\frac{4}{10}$ mi per hr. Describe his error and find the correct answer.

**Roller Coaster Speeds**

| Roller Coaster | Maximum Speed (mi per hr) |
|---|---|
| Silver Star | $78\frac{9}{10}$ |
| Stealth | $79\frac{1}{2}$ |
| Beast | $64\frac{4}{5}$ |
| Thunder Dolphin | $80\frac{8}{10}$ |
| Zaturn | $80\frac{4}{5}$ |

## Achieving the Standards

**38.** What is the least common multiple of the numbers 2 and 3? (○━ NS 2.4, p. 14)

**39.** List the first three multiples common to the numerator and denominator in $\frac{3}{5}$. (○━ NS 2.4, p. 4)

**40.** **Test Prep** There are $16\frac{3}{4}$ yards of fabric on a bolt. If $4\frac{2}{3}$ yards are used, how much is left?

   **A** 10 yards       **C** $12\frac{1}{4}$ yards

   **B** $12\frac{1}{12}$ yards     **D** $21\frac{5}{12}$ yards

**41.** Allen used $\frac{2}{3}$ cup of grape juice plus $\frac{3}{4}$ cup of apple juice to make fruit punch. About how many cups of fruit punch did he make? (○━ NS 2.0, p. 34)

**42.** **Test Prep** A butcher sold two packages of meat weighing $1\frac{2}{3}$ pounds and $5\frac{3}{4}$ pounds. What was the total weight of the meat?

   **A** 4 pounds       **C** $5\frac{3}{4}$ pounds

   **B** $4\frac{1}{3}$ pounds     **D** $7\frac{5}{12}$ pounds

# Attack the Track

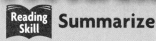 **Summarize**

An amusement park in Los Angeles, California, offers guests a variety of rides. TATSU, a 62-mi per hr rollercoaster, has been entertaining riders with 3,602 feet of twisting track since it opened in May 2006. TATSU, meaning "flying beast," consists of 3 trains of 8 cars each. Riders sit 4 to a row, and each train can hold 32 riders.

The operators of TATSU record the number of riders on each train during its run. During one run, the operators reported that $7\frac{1}{4}$ of the cars in the first train and $5\frac{1}{2}$ of the cars in the second train were filled. On the third train, they reported that $6\frac{1}{2}$ of the cars were filled. How many more cars were filled in the first train than in the third train?

When you summarize, you restate the most important information in a shortened form to understand what you have read.

**Summary:** There are 3 trains, with eight cars per train. Riders sit 4 to a row in each car. A total of $7\frac{1}{4}$ of the cars were filled on the first train, $5\frac{1}{2}$ of the cars were filled on the second train, and $6\frac{1}{2}$ of the cars were filled on the third train.

**Problem Solving Summarize the information to solve the problems.**

1. Solve the problem above.

2. One of the park's most popular wooden roller coasters is the Psyclone. It has one train with 6 cars. The train's 24 riders are arranged in 2 rows of 2 riders each. Viper, another of the park's coasters, was once the world's largest looping roller coaster. Viper consists of one train with 7 cars, each car holding 4 riders. During a count by the operators at both roller coasters, $4\frac{1}{4}$ of the cars were filled on Viper and $5\frac{1}{2}$ of the cars were filled on Psyclone. How many cars were filled on both the Psyclone and Viper during the count? Solve the problem.

# 4 Model Subtraction with Renaming

OBJECTIVE: Use fraction bars to rename and subtract mixed numbers.

**Quick Review**

Find the LCM for each set of numbers.

1. 9, 12          2. 8, 12
3. 5, 6           4. 4, 5
5. 12, 18, 72

## Investigate

**Materials** ■ fraction bars

Fraction bars can be used to help you subtract mixed numbers from whole numbers.

**A** Use fraction bars to find $3 - 1\frac{2}{3}$. Model 3 by using three whole bars.

| 1 |
| 1 |
| 1 |

**B** Since you are subtracting thirds, model 3 in another way by renaming one of the whole bars with three $\frac{1}{3}$ bars.

| 1 |
| 1 |
| $\frac{1}{3}$ | $\frac{1}{3}$ | $\frac{1}{3}$ |

**C** Subtract $1\frac{2}{3}$. Write the answer in simplest form.

| 1 |
| 1 |
| $\frac{1}{3}$ | $\frac{1}{3}$ | $\frac{1}{3}$ |

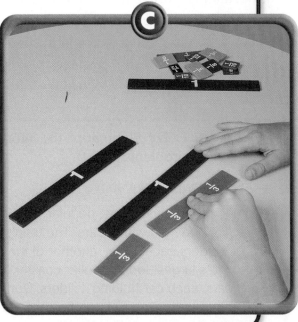

## Draw Conclusions

1. Explain how the 3 wholes were renamed.

2. In Step B, why did 3 have to be renamed as $2\frac{3}{3}$?

3. Are there other ways to rename 3? Explain.

4. **Application** Use steps like the ones above to find $5 - 2\frac{1}{6}$.

○━┱ NS 2.0 Students calculate and solve problems involving addition, subtraction, multiplication, and division: *also* NS 2.1, ○━┱ NS 2.4, MR 2.0, MR 2.1, MR 2.4, MR 2.5, MR 3.2, MR 3.3

# Connect

Fraction bars can also be used to subtract two mixed numbers.

## Activity

**Materials** ■ fraction bars

Find $2\frac{1}{4} - 1\frac{3}{8}$.

- Use fraction bars to model $2\frac{1}{4}$.

$\leftarrow 2\frac{1}{4}$

- Since you are subtracting eighths, think of the LCD for $\frac{1}{4}$ and $\frac{3}{8}$. Change fourths to eighths.

$\leftarrow 2\frac{2}{8}$

- Can you subtract $1\frac{3}{8}$ from either of these models?

- Here is another way to model $2\frac{1}{4}$. Subtract $1\frac{3}{8}$ from $1\frac{10}{8}$.

  What is $2\frac{1}{4} - 1\frac{3}{8}$?

$\leftarrow 1\frac{10}{8}$

So, $2\frac{1}{4} - 1\frac{3}{8} = \frac{7}{8}$.

**TALK Math**

Explain why renaming is necessary to find $5\frac{1}{9} - 2\frac{5}{9}$. Then solve.

# Practice

**Find the difference. The models show the renaming needed.**

1. $2 - 1\frac{1}{5}$
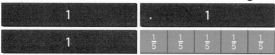

2. $3\frac{1}{3} - 2\frac{2}{3}$

**Use fraction bars to find the difference. Write the answer in simplest form.**

3. $6 - 2\frac{3}{4}$

4. $5 - 1\frac{1}{2}$

5. $3 - 1\frac{9}{10}$

6. $4 - 1\frac{1}{4}$

7. $5\frac{1}{10} - 4\frac{7}{10}$

8. $4\frac{1}{6} - 1\frac{5}{6}$

9. $6\frac{2}{6} - 5\frac{5}{6}$

10. $4\frac{1}{8} - 3\frac{5}{8}$

11. **WRITE Math** **What's the Error?** Jan solved $10\frac{1}{4} - 6\frac{3}{4}$ by renaming. Describe her error and find the correct answer.

$$10\frac{5}{4} - 6\frac{3}{4} = 4\frac{1}{2}$$

# 5 Record Subtraction with Renaming

**OBJECTIVE:** Rename to find the difference of two mixed numbers.

## Learn

You can use a diagram or the LCD to find the difference of two mixed numbers.

**ONE WAY** Draw a diagram.

Find $2\frac{1}{2} - 1\frac{5}{6}$.

$$2\frac{1}{2} = 2\frac{3}{6}$$
$$-1\frac{5}{6} = -1\frac{5}{6}$$

Write an equivalent fraction using the LCD.

| 1 | 1 | $\frac{1}{6}$ $\frac{1}{6}$ $\frac{1}{6}$ |

$$2\frac{1}{2} = 2\frac{3}{6} = 1\frac{9}{6}$$
$$-1\frac{5}{6} = -1\frac{5}{6} = -1\frac{5}{6}$$

Since $\frac{5}{6} > \frac{3}{6}$, rename $2\frac{3}{6}$ as $1\frac{9}{6}$.

| 1 | $\frac{1}{6}$ $\frac{1}{6}$ $\frac{1}{6}$ $\frac{1}{6}$ $\frac{1}{6}$ $\frac{1}{6}$ $\frac{1}{6}$ $\frac{1}{6}$ $\frac{1}{6}$ |

$$1\frac{9}{6}$$
$$-1\frac{5}{6}$$

Subtract, and then simplify.

$$\frac{4}{6}, \text{ or } \frac{2}{3}$$

So, $2\frac{1}{2} - 1\frac{5}{6} = \frac{4}{6}$, or $\frac{2}{3}$.

**Math Idea**

Renaming a mixed number decreases the whole-number part by 1 and increases the fraction part by 1.

**ANOTHER WAY** Use the LCD to find $8\frac{1}{3} - 4\frac{7}{12}$.

Estimate. $8\frac{1}{2} - 4\frac{1}{2} = 4$.

| Step 1 | Step 2 |
|---|---|
| $8\frac{1}{3} = 8\frac{4}{12}$ <br> $-4\frac{7}{12} = -4\frac{7}{12}$ <br><br> The LCD of $\frac{1}{3}$ and $\frac{7}{12}$ is 12. Write equivalent fractions using the LCD. | $8\frac{1}{3} = 8\frac{4}{12} = 7\frac{16}{12}$ <br> $-4\frac{7}{12} = -4\frac{7}{12} = -4\frac{7}{12}$ <br><br> $3\frac{9}{12}$, or $3\frac{3}{4}$    $\frac{7}{12}$ is greater than $\frac{4}{12}$, so rename $8\frac{4}{12}$. <br> $8\frac{4}{12} = 7 + \frac{12}{12} + \frac{4}{12} = 7\frac{16}{12}$. <br> Subtract, and then simplify. |

The answer is reasonable because it is close to the estimate of 4.

So, $8\frac{1}{3} - 4\frac{7}{12} = 3\frac{3}{4}$.

1. Copy and complete to rename $2\frac{2}{3}$ as $1\frac{5}{3}$.  $2\frac{2}{3} = 1 + \blacksquare + \blacksquare = 1\frac{5}{3}$

**Estimate. Then write the difference in simplest form.**

2. $4\frac{3}{8} - 2\frac{5}{8}$   3. $1\frac{3}{4} - \frac{7}{8}$   4. $12\frac{1}{9} - 7\frac{1}{3}$   ✅5. $4\frac{1}{2} - 3\frac{4}{5}$   ✅6. $9\frac{1}{6} - 2\frac{3}{4}$

7. **TALK Math** Explain how to using renaming to find $3\frac{1}{9} - 2\frac{1}{3}$.

## Independent Practice and Problem Solving

**Estimate. Then write the difference in simplest form.**

8. $2\frac{1}{5} - 1\frac{4}{5}$   9. $3\frac{2}{3} - 1\frac{11}{12}$   10. $4\frac{1}{4} - 2\frac{1}{3}$   11. $11\frac{1}{9} - 3\frac{2}{3}$   12. $6 - 3\frac{1}{2}$

13. $7 - 5\frac{2}{3}$   14. $7\frac{5}{9} - 2\frac{5}{6}$   15. $1\frac{1}{5} - \frac{1}{2}$   16. $4\frac{3}{8} - 3\frac{1}{2}$   17. $13\frac{1}{6} - 3\frac{4}{5}$

18. What is the difference between $12\frac{2}{5}$ and $5\frac{3}{4}$?   19. How much greater is $6\frac{1}{7}$ than $1\frac{11}{14}$?

⭐**Algebra** Find the value of the expression, in simplest form, for $c = 2\frac{7}{10}$.

20. $4\frac{3}{5} + c$   21. $5\frac{1}{2} - c$   22. $4\frac{3}{5} - c$   23. $5\frac{1}{2} + c$

**USE DATA For 24–26, use the table.**

24. What is the difference in wall heights at Adventure Land and Rock-a-Wall?

25. Which company's rock wall height is $2\frac{3}{4}$ ft shorter than Rock-a-Wall's?

26. **Pose a Problem** Look back at Problem 24. Write a similar subtraction problem that involves Climbing Nation. Then solve your problem.

| Rock-Climbing Walls | | | | |
|---|---|---|---|---|
| Company | Adventure Land | Rock-a-Wall | Climbing Nation | Scale-a-Wall |
| Wall Height (ft) | $27\frac{2}{3}$ | $30\frac{1}{4}$ | $32$ | $27\frac{1}{2}$ |

27. **WRITE Math** Why do you write equivalent fractions before you rename? Can you rename before you write equivalent fractions? Explain.

## Achieving the Standards

28. Tom poured $2\frac{1}{4}$ pounds of sand on his icy driveway. How much does he have left from his 5-pound bag? (O▬┓ NS 2.0, p. 42)

29. Write $5\frac{1}{2}$ as a fraction. (Grade 5 O▬┓ NS 1.5)

30. Maria used $\frac{1}{3}$ yard of purple fabric and $\frac{1}{6}$ yard of yellow fabric. How much fabric in all did she use? (O▬┓ NS 2.0, p. 38)

31. **Test Prep** Tricia usually works $38\frac{1}{3}$ hours a week. Last week, she was absent $6\frac{3}{4}$ hours. How many hours did she work?

**A** $31\frac{7}{12}$ hours   **C** $32\frac{4}{7}$ hours

**B** $32\frac{1}{3}$ hours   **D** $44\frac{7}{12}$ hours

**Extra Practice** on page 58, Set D

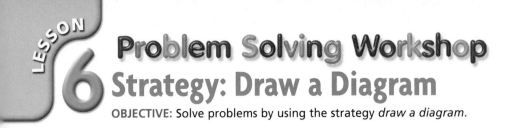

# Problem Solving Workshop
## Strategy: Draw a Diagram

**OBJECTIVE:** Solve problems by using the strategy *draw a diagram*.

## Learn the Strategy

Drawing a diagram can help you better understand a problem and can help you see the solution. You can use different types of diagrams to help solve different types of problems.

### A diagram can show position.

Fatima won the women's long jump competition by jumping 16 ft. Mia came in second place by jumping 14 ft, and Jenny came in third place by jumping 13 ft.

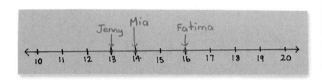

### A diagram can show direction.

Todd walked 4 blocks south and then 4 blocks east. He then continued 6 blocks north to reach the library.

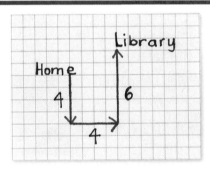

### A diagram can show size.

Scott donated 2 large boxes of food to the food drive. The first box weighed 3 lb more than twice the weight of the second box. Together the boxes weighed 33 lb.

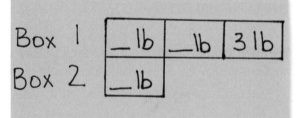

**TALK Math**

What types of problems can be solved by using the *draw a diagram* strategy?

To use the strategy *draw a diagram*, carefully read the information or follow the directions given in the problem. Keep the diagram simple. Label each part to show what it represents.

⭘━┓ NS 2.0 Students calculate and solve problems involving addition, subtraction, multiplication, and division; *also* NS 2.1, ⭘━┓ NS 2.4, MR 1.0, MR 2.0, MR 2.4, MR 2.5, MR 2.7, MR 3.0, MR 3.1, MR 3.2, MR 3.3

# Use the Strategy

**PROBLEM** Suppose the California Animal Rescue Center of Sonoma County decides to build a rectangular dog run that measures 33 ft by $16\frac{1}{2}$ ft. Steel posts will be inserted every $5\frac{1}{2}$ ft along the perimeter. There will be one post at each corner, and all posts will be 6 ft tall. How many steel posts will be needed?

## Read to Understand

- Identify the details.
- What details will you use?
- Are there any details you will not use? If so, what?

## Plan

- What strategy can you use to solve this problem?

  You can draw a diagram to help you solve the problem.

## Solve

- How can you use the strategy to solve the problem?

  Draw a rectangle to represent the dog run. Place marks along the perimeter of the rectangle to represent the posts.

  Count the number of marks you placed around the rectangle. Each corner should only have one mark.

  So, 18 steel posts will be needed.

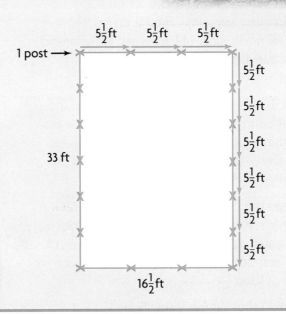

## Check

- How can you check your answer?

## Guided Problem Solving

Read to
Understand

Plan

Solve

Check

1. Suppose the veterinarians decide to divide the dog run shown on page 51 to have an area just for miniature dogs. This new section will be $10\frac{1}{4}$ ft by $16\frac{1}{2}$ ft. Find the dimensions of the dog run used for the other dogs.

   **First,** draw a diagram of the entire dog run.

   **Next,** subtract the length of the new section from the length of the entire dog run.

   **Last,** write the dimensions of the area for other dogs.

2. What if the length of the miniature dog section was $5\frac{1}{2}$ ft longer? What would be the length of the dog run used for the other dogs?

3. Two new dogs are placed in the dog run. Rover weighs $2\frac{1}{2}$ lb more than twice the weight of Jada. Together the dogs weigh 100 lb. What is the weight of each dog?

## Problem Solving Strategy Practice

**Draw a diagram to solve.**

4. The rescue center's van drove $7\frac{1}{2}$ mi south to collect donated supplies. Then it drove $3\frac{1}{2}$ mi east, $4\frac{1}{3}$ mi north, and $11\frac{1}{2}$ mi west. How far did the van travel before it crossed its own path?

5. A pet store donated a total of 72 cans of dog and cat food. There were 4 more than three times as many cans of dog food as cat food. How many cans of dog food did the pet store donate?

6. Sandy's cat was one of the top four cats at the show, but Sandy's cat did not place better than Carl's. Brian's cat placed below both Mia's and Sandy's. Carl's cat placed two spots ahead of Brian's. Whose cat won the show?

7. Mac took his dog to the park on March 1 and every third day after that. Mac took his dog for a jog with him on March 2 and every fourth day after that. What is the first date that Mac took his dog to the park and took her for a jog with him?

8. Dillon uses the table at the right to keep track of how much food to give to the dogs at the rescue center. Which dog did he give the most food? Which dogs did he give between $3\frac{1}{2}$ c and $4\frac{1}{4}$ c of food?

9. Look at the table on the right. Two of the dogs eat a total of $8\frac{1}{8}$ c of food at a feeding. If one dog eats $1\frac{1}{8}$ c more than the other at a feeding, how much does each dog eat?

| Daily Amount of Dry Food | |
| --- | --- |
| **Name** | **Cups of Food** |
| Chestnut | $4\frac{1}{8}$ |
| Blanca | $3\frac{1}{4}$ |
| Orson | $4\frac{3}{8}$ |
| Max | $3\frac{3}{4}$ |

Choose a
STRATEGY

Draw a Diagram or Picture
Make a Model or Act it Out
Make an organized List
Find a Pattern
Make a Table or Graph
Predict and Test
Work Backward
Solve a Simpler Problem
Write an Equation
Use Logical Reasoning

## Mixed Strategy Practice

**10.** A 50-lb bag of dog food contains meat protein, vitamins, and cereal. In the 50-lb bag, meat protein makes up $19\frac{3}{4}$ lb and vitamins make up $18\frac{7}{8}$ lb. How many pounds of cereal are in the food?

**11.** A puppy weighed $1\frac{3}{4}$ lb at birth. Each day of the first week it gained $\frac{1}{8}$ lb. What did the puppy weigh after one week?

**12.** Each week, Jennifer saves $\frac{2}{3}$ of her allowance and spends $\frac{1}{5}$ of it on toys for her new puppy. What fraction of her allowance is left?

**13. Pose a Problem** Look back at Problem 12. Write a similar problem by changing the amount that Jennifer saves of her allowance.

**14. Open-Ended** Suppose you want to build a fenced rectangular play area for your new puppy. Make a plan for the play area, using $24\frac{1}{2}$ ft of fencing. Draw a diagram of your play area and label the measure of each side.

**15.** WRITE Math ► **Explain** what operation you used to solve Problem 10.

### CHALLENGE YOURSELF

For the long-jump event at the Doggie Olympics, the lengths of a dog's three jumps are added together for a final distance. For 16–17, use the table.

| Doggie Olympics Long-Jump | | | |
|---|---|---|---|
| Dog | Jump 1 (ft) | Jump 2 (ft) | Jump 3 (ft) |
| Shadow | $3\frac{1}{2}$ | $3\frac{1}{3}$ | $4\frac{1}{12}$ |
| Luke | $4\frac{1}{6}$ | $3\frac{3}{4}$ | $3\frac{5}{6}$ |

**16.** After the second round of jumps, Maisy was only $\frac{1}{4}$ ft behind Luke. She finished with a final distance $\frac{1}{3}$ ft greater than Luke's. How long was Maisy's last jump?

**17.** Hunter's last jump was $3\frac{3}{4}$ ft, and he tied Shadow's final distance. Hunter's first jump was $\frac{1}{2}$ ft longer than his second. How long was Hunter's second jump?

# LESSON 7 Practice Addition and Subtraction

**OBJECTIVE:** Add and subtract fractions and mixed numbers.

## Learn

**PROBLEM** Members of the Diaz family spent their vacation cross-country skiing in Medford, Wisconsin. They chose the Beaver Creek trails, which have a total distance of 4 mi. Yesterday, they skied the $\frac{7}{10}$-mi Tamarack Trail. Today, they skied the $\frac{3}{5}$-mi Pine Trail. If the family members plan to ski all the Beaver Creek trails, how many more miles do they have left to ski?

You can subtract the distance they have skied from the total distance.

**Example 1** Find $4 - (\frac{7}{10} + \frac{3}{5})$.

Estimate. Both $\frac{7}{10}$ and $\frac{3}{5}$ are close to $\frac{1}{2}$. So, the difference is about $4 - (\frac{1}{2} + \frac{1}{2})$, or 3.

Add to find the distance skied so far.

$$\frac{7}{10} = \frac{7}{10}$$
$$+\frac{3}{5} = \frac{6}{10}$$
$$\frac{13}{10}, \text{ or } 1\frac{3}{10}$$

Write equivalent fractions, using the LCD, 10.

Rename the fraction as a mixed number in simplest form.

Subtract to find the distance left to ski.

$$4 = 3\frac{10}{10}$$
$$-1\frac{3}{10} = 1\frac{3}{10}$$
$$2\frac{7}{10}$$

Since you are subtracting tenths, rename 4 as $3\frac{10}{10}$.
Subtract fractions. Subtract whole numbers.

The answer is reasonable because it is close to the estimate of 3.

So, the Diaz family members have $2\frac{7}{10}$ mi left to ski.

- **What if** Tamarack Trail was $1\frac{3}{10}$ mi long? How would you expect this to change the answer?

54

NS 2.0 Students calculate and solve problems involving addition, subtraction, multiplication, and division; also NS 1.0, NS 2.1, NS 2.4, MR 2.1, MR 2.4, MR 2.5, MR 3.0, MR 3.2, MR 3.3

## Example 2

What is the difference in the average annual snowfall amounts for Salt Lake City and La Crosse?

**Subtract.** $58\frac{3}{5} - 42\frac{9}{10}$

**Estimate.** $58\frac{1}{2} - 43 = 15\frac{1}{2}$

| Snowfall Amounts | |
|---|---|
| Location | Snow (in.) |
| Detroit, MI | $43\frac{1}{2}$ |
| Duluth, MN | $84\frac{3}{10}$ |
| Salt Lake City, UT | $58\frac{3}{5}$ |
| La Crosse, WI | $42\frac{9}{10}$ |

$$58\frac{3}{5} = 58\frac{6}{10}$$
$$-42\frac{9}{10} = -42\frac{9}{10}$$

The LCD of $\frac{3}{5}$ and $\frac{9}{10}$ is 10.

Write equivalent fractions, using the LCD, 10.

$$58\frac{3}{5} = 58\frac{6}{10} = 57\frac{16}{10}$$
$$-42\frac{9}{10} = -42\frac{9}{10} = -42\frac{9}{10}$$
$$15\frac{7}{10}$$

Since $\frac{9}{10}$ is greater than $\frac{6}{10}$, rename $58\frac{6}{10}$.
$58\frac{6}{10} = 57 + \frac{10}{10} + \frac{6}{10} = 57\frac{16}{10}$.

Subtract the fractions. Subtract the whole numbers.

The answer is reasonable because $15\frac{7}{10}$ is close to the estimate, $15\frac{1}{2}$.

So, the difference in the snowfall amounts is $15\frac{7}{10}$ in.

**Remember**
Use renaming when the numerator of the fraction being subtracted is greater than the numerator of the fraction being subtracted from.

## More Examples

**(A)** Find $6\frac{1}{2} + 11\frac{7}{16} + 4\frac{7}{8}$.

$$6\frac{1}{2} = 6\frac{8}{16}$$
$$11\frac{7}{16} = 11\frac{7}{16}$$
$$+4\frac{7}{8} = +4\frac{14}{16}$$
$$21\frac{29}{16} = 22\frac{13}{16}$$

Write equivalent fractions, using the LCD, 16.

Add. Rename $21\frac{29}{16}$ as $22\frac{13}{16}$.

So, $6\frac{1}{2} + 11\frac{7}{16} + 4\frac{7}{8} = 22\frac{13}{16}$.

**(B)** Find $12\frac{1}{5} - 7\frac{1}{7}$.

$$12\frac{1}{5} = 12\frac{7}{35}$$
$$-7\frac{1}{7} = -7\frac{5}{35}$$
$$5\frac{2}{35}$$

Write equivalent fractions, using the LCD, 35.

Subtract.

So, $12\frac{1}{5} - 7\frac{1}{7} = 5\frac{2}{35}$.

## Guided Practice

1. Copy and complete the problem. Then find the difference.

$$6\frac{1}{21} = \blacksquare\frac{22}{21}$$
$$-\frac{1}{3} = \frac{7}{\blacksquare}$$

**Estimate. Then write the sum or difference in simplest form.**

2. $\frac{3}{16}$
$+\frac{5}{8}$
_____

3. $\frac{3}{4}$
$+\frac{2}{3}$
_____

4. $\frac{4}{5}$
$-\frac{3}{20}$
_____

✓5. $\frac{7}{8}$
$-\frac{1}{6}$
_____

6. $3 - (2\frac{1}{6} + \frac{1}{3})$

7. $10\frac{5}{18} + 8\frac{5}{6}$

8. $5\frac{1}{12} - \frac{1}{4}$

✓9. $3 - 2\frac{1}{6}$

10. **TALK Math** **Explain** how you know whether renaming is needed to subtract a fraction or mixed number.

## Independent Practice and Problem Solving

**Estimate. Then write the sum or difference in simplest form.**

11. $\frac{3}{10}$
$+\frac{1}{5}$
_____

12. $\frac{9}{16}$
$-\frac{1}{4}$
_____

13. $\frac{1}{2}$
$+\frac{1}{7}$
_____

14. $\frac{7}{9}$
$-\frac{2}{3}$
_____

15. $4\frac{1}{4}$
$+2\frac{5}{6}$
_____

16. $3$
$-1\frac{3}{4}$
_____

17. $6\frac{2}{5}$
$+9\frac{7}{10}$
_____

18. $8\frac{2}{3}$
$-3\frac{4}{5}$
_____

19. $4\frac{3}{4} + 2\frac{7}{20}$

20. $2\frac{1}{6} + 1\frac{1}{2}$

21. $2\frac{1}{5} - 1\frac{1}{20}$

22. $2\frac{3}{5} + 5\frac{3}{8}$

23. $7 - 2\frac{3}{5}$

24. $8 - \left(1\frac{1}{4} + \frac{5}{6}\right)$

25. $\frac{3}{5} + \frac{1}{3} + \frac{4}{15}$

26. $6\frac{1}{3} + 2\frac{1}{2} + \frac{1}{4}$

27. What number is $\frac{5}{7}$ less than $3\frac{1}{2}$?

28. How much greater than $2\frac{1}{2}$ is $3\frac{5}{12}$?

29. **Reasoning** Erin chose a mixed number, added $\frac{1}{8}$, subtracted $\frac{7}{8}$, and added $\frac{1}{3}$ more than $\frac{3}{4}$. The final number was $2\frac{3}{4}$. What was Erin's number?

⭐ **Algebra** **Find a possible rule for each pattern. Use the rule to write the next two numbers in the pattern.**

30. $9, 7\frac{3}{4}, 6\frac{1}{2}, 5\frac{1}{4},$ ▇, ▇

31. $5\frac{3}{8}, 6\frac{3}{4}, 8\frac{1}{8}, 9\frac{1}{2},$ ▇, ▇

**Solve. Then explain how you solved the problem.**

32. Danielle spends $3\frac{1}{3}$ hr skiing downhill on Saturday and $4\frac{3}{5}$ hr skiing cross-country on Sunday. How many hours did she spend skiing on the two days?

33. Liam skied $4\frac{1}{3}$ mi on a cross-country trail that ends at a ski lodge. After he skied the first $2\frac{7}{8}$ mi, he passed a farm. How far from the lodge is the farm?

34. Ben and Jack ski a trail that is $1\frac{5}{6}$ mi long. They skied $\frac{2}{3}$ mi before lunch and $\frac{3}{4}$ mi after lunch. How many more miles do they have left to ski?

35. Damon skied $3\frac{1}{4}$ mi, walked $2\frac{1}{8}$ mi, and rode $3\frac{1}{6}$ mi on a snowmobile. How far in all did he travel?

**Extra Practice** on page 58, Set E

36. Mr. Diaz skied two trails. He skied a total of $\frac{9}{10}$ mi. Which two trails did he ski?

37. **WRITE Math** **What's the Question?** The answer is that Aspen Trail is longer by $\frac{1}{4}$ mi.

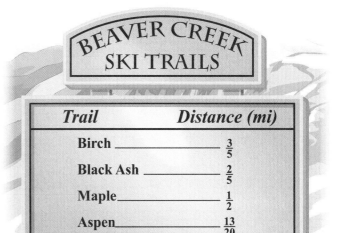

**BEAVER CREEK SKI TRAILS**

| Trail | Distance (mi) |
|---|---|
| Birch | $\frac{3}{5}$ |
| Black Ash | $\frac{2}{5}$ |
| Maple | $\frac{1}{2}$ |
| Aspen | $\frac{13}{20}$ |

## Achieving the Standards

38. On a coordinate grid, how would the point 3 units above the origin and 2 units to the left be written as an (x,y) ordered pair?

(Grade 5 **O━┓** AF 1.4)

39. **Test Prep** Ben ran $6\frac{3}{4}$ miles on Monday and $3\frac{1}{2}$ miles on Sunday. How many miles did Ben run in the two days?

   **A** 8 miles     **C** $10\frac{1}{4}$ miles

   **B** $9\frac{1}{2}$ miles     **D** 12 miles

40. If a box $\frac{1}{3}$ foot tall is placed on top of a box $\frac{3}{4}$ foot tall, about how tall are the boxes when stacked? (NS 2.1, p. 34)

41. Find $\frac{2}{3} + \frac{2}{3} + \frac{2}{3}$. (NS 2.1, p. 38)

42. **Test Prep** Find the missing number.

$$9 = 8\frac{\blacksquare}{7}$$

   **A** 6     **C** 8

   **B** 7     **D** 9

## Problem Solving connects to Social Studies

Ancient Romans wrote fractions in words rather than by using numerals. For example, the fraction two sevenths would have been represented as *duae septimae*.

However, when ancient Romans needed to do calculations with fractions, they would use the *uncia*, which represented $\frac{1}{12}$ of anything. The table shows the ancient Roman representations for some common fractions.

**Use the table of Roman names of fractions to solve.**

1. Antavius plowed a *triens* of his field in the morning and another *quadrans* of the field in the afternoon. How many *uncia* does he have left to plow?

2. Lucia spilled an *uncia* of the water from the pitcher carrying it from the well. She used a *quadrans* of the pitcher to make soup. How many *uncia* of the pitcher did Lucia have left?

| Fraction | Roman Name |
|---|---|
| $\frac{1}{12}$ | uncia |
| $\frac{1}{6}$ | sextans |
| $\frac{1}{4}$ | quadrans |
| $\frac{1}{3}$ | triens |
| $\frac{1}{2}$ | semis |

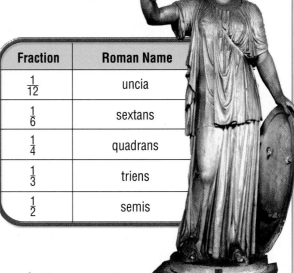

▲ **Minerva, goddess of wisdom**

# Extra Practice

## Set A  Estimate the sum or difference. (pp. 34–37)

1. $\frac{5}{12} + \frac{4}{9}$

2. $\frac{4}{7} - \frac{3}{8}$

3. $\frac{4}{9} - \frac{1}{5}$

4. $\frac{2}{3} + \frac{1}{9} + \frac{4}{5}$

5. $10\frac{4}{5} - 8\frac{1}{11}$

6. $6\frac{8}{9} - 3\frac{1}{3}$

7. $3\frac{1}{6} + 5\frac{5}{7}$

8. $15\frac{1}{3} + 13\frac{1}{9} + 4\frac{4}{5}$

## Set B  Use a common denominator to write the problem using equivalent fractions. (pp. 38–41)

1. $\frac{2}{3} + \frac{1}{4}$

2. $\frac{2}{5} - \frac{1}{15}$

3. $\frac{5}{8} - \frac{1}{5}$

4. $\frac{1}{4} + \frac{1}{6}$

5. $\frac{3}{4} - \frac{2}{5}$

6. $\frac{1}{2} + \frac{3}{5}$

7. $\frac{9}{10} + \frac{1}{3}$

8. $\frac{6}{7} - \frac{1}{4}$

9. $\frac{3}{5} + \frac{1}{4}$

10. $1 - \frac{1}{6}$

## Set C  Estimate. Then write the sum or difference in simplest form. (pp. 42–45)

1. $12\frac{1}{3} - 7\frac{1}{5}$

2. $5\frac{5}{6} - 3\frac{1}{3}$

3. $32\frac{5}{18} + 4\frac{5}{6}$

4. $9\frac{7}{20} + 5\frac{1}{4}$

5. $3\frac{3}{4} + 7\frac{4}{5}$

6. $5\frac{5}{6} - 3\frac{1}{2}$

7. $12\frac{1}{3} - 9\frac{1}{4}$

8. $5\frac{5}{8} + 3\frac{1}{2}$

9. $3\frac{1}{2} + 2\frac{1}{9}$

10. $14\frac{5}{7} - 3\frac{3}{14}$

11. Kathy's one puppy weighs $9\frac{5}{6}$ lb, and the other weighs $7\frac{1}{3}$ lb. How much do they weigh together?

12. Chris cut lengths of rope that were $6\frac{3}{4}$ ft and $3\frac{2}{3}$ ft long. How much longer was the longer piece of rope?

## Set D  Estimate. Then write the difference in simplest form. (pp. 48–49)

1. $3\frac{1}{4} - 2\frac{3}{4}$

2. $2\frac{2}{3} - 1\frac{5}{6}$

3. $5\frac{1}{5} - 3\frac{1}{4}$

4. $10\frac{1}{8} - 4\frac{3}{4}$

5. $5 - 2\frac{3}{4}$

6. $8 - 4\frac{1}{3}$

7. $5\frac{1}{6} - 4\frac{2}{5}$

8. $1\frac{1}{6} - \frac{2}{3}$

9. $3\frac{3}{8} - 2\frac{1}{2}$

10. $8\frac{1}{3} - 3\frac{5}{6}$

## Set E  Estimate. Then write the sum or difference in simplest form. (pp. 54–57)

1. $\frac{1}{10} + \frac{1}{3}$

2. $\frac{13}{16} - \frac{3}{4}$

3. $8\frac{5}{8} - 4\frac{1}{4}$

4. $10 - 3\frac{2}{5}$

5. $\frac{2}{5} + \frac{2}{3} + \frac{7}{15}$

6. $\frac{11}{12} - \frac{2}{5}$

7. $5\frac{3}{4} + 6\frac{5}{6}$

8. $4\frac{1}{10} - 3\frac{3}{5}$

9. $6\frac{3}{16} - 2\frac{3}{8}$

10. $4\frac{3}{8} + 2\frac{1}{4} + \frac{5}{12}$

11. The plumber used $2\frac{1}{2}$ ft of copper pipe, and then another $\frac{3}{4}$ ft. How much pipe did he use in all?

12. Jess baled 14 bales of hay, and Adam baled $10\frac{1}{6}$ bales of hay. How much more hay did Jess bale than Adam?

# TWO'S THE TICKET

**Players**
2 players

**Materials**
- Number cards
- Watch or timer

## How to Play

- Players determine who will be Player 1 and who will be Player 2.

- Players shuffle the number cards and place them faceup in a 6-by-6 array.

- Player 1 has 30 seconds to select two or more cards that have a sum of 2.

- If Player 1 correctly makes a sum of 2, one point is awarded for each card he or she used and the cards are placed in a discard pile.

- If Player 1 does not make a sum of 2, play passes to Player 2. The cards are put back in place.

- Play alternates until no cards remain that can make a sum of 2.

- The player with more points at the end of the game wins.

## Check Vocabulary and Concepts

**Choose the best term from the box.**

> **VOCABULARY**
> benchmark
> least common
> denominator (LCD)
> unlike fractions

1. Equivalent fractions can be written using a ___?___. (NS 2.1, p. 39)

2. A ___?___ is a reference point on a number line that is useful when rounding fractions. (NS 2.1, p. 34)

## Check Skills

**Estimate the sum or difference.** (NS 2.1, pp. 34–37)

3. $\frac{1}{9} + \frac{8}{11}$

4. $\frac{7}{15} - \frac{3}{5}$

5. $\frac{6}{7} + \frac{1}{8}$

6. $4\frac{11}{12} - 2\frac{5}{8}$

7. $7\frac{1}{8} - 6\frac{4}{7}$

8. $10\frac{1}{16} + 1\frac{7}{8}$

9. $\frac{11}{12} + \frac{3}{7} + \frac{1}{9}$

10. $3\frac{4}{5} + 7\frac{7}{8} + 1\frac{1}{9}$

**Use a common denominator to write the problem using equivalent fractions.** (NS 2.1, pp. 38–41)

11. $\frac{3}{8} + \frac{3}{4}$

12. $\frac{5}{13} - \frac{3}{26}$

13. $\frac{1}{3} + \frac{4}{9}$

14. $\frac{4}{5} - \frac{2}{15}$

15. $\frac{5}{7} + \frac{1}{2}$

16. $\frac{3}{4} + \frac{1}{5}$

17. $\frac{5}{6} - \frac{1}{4}$

18. $\frac{13}{20} - \frac{1}{3}$

19. $\frac{4}{9} - \frac{1}{5}$

20. $\frac{1}{2} + \frac{1}{3}$

**Estimate. Then write the sum or difference in simplest form.**

(O—■ NS 2.0, NS 2.1, pp. 38–41, 42–45, 46–47, 48–49, 54–57)

21. $\frac{2}{5} - \frac{3}{10}$

22. $\frac{3}{4} + \frac{2}{3}$

23. $\frac{2}{9} + \frac{1}{3}$

24. $\frac{4}{7} - \frac{1}{2}$

25. $2\frac{2}{5} - 1\frac{2}{5}$

26. $7\frac{5}{12} + 3\frac{1}{6}$

27. $10\frac{3}{4} - 8\frac{1}{3}$

28. $4\frac{1}{2} - 2\frac{2}{3}$

29. $3\frac{1}{3} - 2\frac{3}{4}$

30. $2\frac{2}{3} + 4\frac{3}{8} + \frac{1}{2}$

## Check Problem Solving

**Solve.** (O—■ NS 2.0, MR 2.0, pp. 50–53)

31. Yuri walks $1\frac{1}{2}$ mi south, $2\frac{1}{4}$ mi west, $\frac{3}{8}$ mi north, 1 mi east, and $1\frac{1}{8}$ mile north. How far and in what direction should he go to get home by the shortest route?

32. Marla builds a rectangular pen for her pig. The pen is $13\frac{1}{2}$ ft long and 9 ft wide. Wooden posts are to be inserted every $4\frac{1}{2}$ ft around the perimeter with one post at each corner. How many posts will she need?

33. **WRITE Math** As they walk along a straight road together, John is $15\frac{1}{2}$ ft in front of a point that is $12\frac{3}{4}$ ft behind Mary. Where is Mary in relation to John? **Explain** by drawing a diagram.

**GO** Technology Use *Online Assessment.*

# Enrich • Unit Fractions
# The Egyptian Way

**Unit fractions**, introduced by ancient Egyptians, are fractions that have 1 as their numerator and a nonzero whole number as their denominator. Ancient Egyptians used sums of unit fractions to represent all non-unit fractions.

A fraction written as a sum of different unit fractions is called an **Egyptian fraction**. Every fraction can be written as a sum of unit fractions. Each sum can be written in an unlimited number of ways.

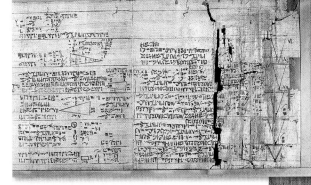

▲ Henry Rhind bought this papyrus scroll in Egypt in 1858. The papyrus is permanently housed in the British Museum in London, England.

## Discover

Write $\frac{5}{6}$ as the sum of unit fractions.

**Step 1**

$\frac{5}{6} > \frac{1}{2}$, so subtract $\frac{1}{2}$.    Find the greatest unit fraction that can be subtracted from $\frac{5}{6}$.

**Step 2**

$\frac{5}{6} - \frac{1}{2} = \frac{5}{6} - \frac{3}{6}$    Subtract. Repeat the process until the difference is a unit fraction.

$= \frac{2}{6}$, or $\frac{1}{3}$

> **Remember**
> The greatest possible unit fraction is $\frac{1}{2}$.
> $\frac{1}{2} > \frac{1}{3} > \frac{1}{4} > \frac{1}{5} \cdots$

So, $\frac{5}{6}$ can be written as $\frac{1}{2} + \frac{1}{3}$.

- Show that $\frac{1}{3}$ can be written as $\frac{1}{4} + \frac{1}{12}$ and $\frac{1}{4}$ can be written as $\frac{1}{5} + \frac{1}{20}$.
- Show that $\frac{5}{6}$ can be written as $\frac{1}{2} + \frac{1}{4} + \frac{1}{12}$ or as $\frac{1}{2} + \frac{1}{5} + \frac{1}{12} + \frac{1}{20}$.

## Translate

Write each fraction as the sum of unit fractions.

1. $\frac{8}{15}$    2. $\frac{4}{9}$    3. $\frac{9}{14}$

4. $\frac{10}{21}$    5. $\frac{4}{3}$    6. $\frac{7}{24}$

## Report Your Findings

**WRITE Math** Explain how to write $\frac{3}{8}$ as the sum of unit fractions.

## Number Sense

**1.** What is the greatest common factor of 64, 48, and 128? (O—¬ NS 2.4)

   **A** 4

   **B** 8

   **C** 12

   **D** 16

**2.** $\frac{5}{6} + \frac{1}{9} =$    (O—¬ NS 2.4)

   **A** $\frac{5}{54}$

   **B** $\frac{1}{3}$

   **C** $\frac{17}{36}$

   **D** $\frac{17}{18}$

**3.** Mrs. Rodriguez's class spent $\frac{1}{4}$ of the day on science and $\frac{1}{3}$ of the day on spelling. What fraction of the day did the class spend on other subjects? (NS 2.1)

   **A** $\frac{1}{12}$

   **B** $\frac{5}{12}$

   **C** $\frac{1}{2}$

   **D** $\frac{7}{12}$

**4.** What is the least common multiple of 6, 8, and 12? (O—¬ NS 2.4)

   **A** 36

   **B** 24

   **C** 12

   **D** 2

**5.** **WRITE Math** ▶ Find $\frac{3}{4} + 1\frac{2}{3}$. **Explain** how you found your answer. (O—¬ NS 2.0)

## Algebra and Functions

**6.** Which situation could be described by the expression $v + 3\frac{1}{4}$? (Grade 5 O—¬ AF 1.2)

   **A** Gabe rode his bike $3\frac{1}{4}$ miles yesterday, and $v$ miles fewer today.

   **B** Gabe rode his bike $3\frac{1}{4}$ miles yesterday, and $v$ times as far today.

   **C** Gabe rode his bike $v$ miles yesterday, and $3\frac{1}{4}$ miles farther today.

   **D** Gabe rode his bike $v$ miles yesterday, and $3\frac{1}{4}$ miles fewer today.

**7.** The map below shows the locations of 4 different trees.

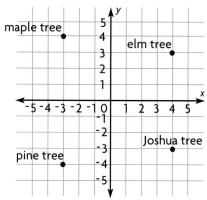

Which tree is at $(^-3,4)$? (Grade 5 O—¬ AF 1.4)

   **A** maple tree

   **B** pine tree

   **C** elm tree

   **D** Joshua tree

**8.** **WRITE Math** ▶ If $z = 10$, what is the value of $3z - 13$? **Explain** how you found your answer. (Grade 5 O—¬ AF 1.2)

## Measurement and Geometry

9. In the figure below, *ABCD* is a rectangle.

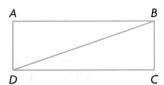

   If the area of triangle *ABD* is 24 square feet, what is the area of *ABCD*? (Grade 5 O—¬ MG 1.1)

   **A** 12 square feet    **C** 36 square feet

   **B** 24 square feet    **D** 48 square feet

10. What is the surface area of the box formed by the pattern below? (Grade 5 O—¬ MG 1.2)

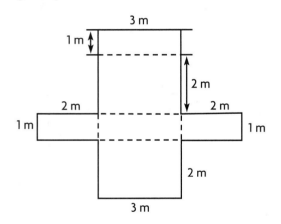

   **A** 6 square meters    **C** 18 square meters

   **B** 12 square meters    **D** 22 square meters

**Test Tip**   **Look for important words.**

See item 11. The key words are *right triangle*. What do you know about the measure of one of the angles of a right triangle?

11. **WRITE Math** ▶ Your teacher tells you that one angle of a right triangle measures 30°. **Explain** how you would find the measures of the other two angles. (Grade 5 O—¬ MG 2.2)

## Statistics, Data Analysis, and Probability

12. The graph shows the numbers of meteors that Robert counted during four nights.

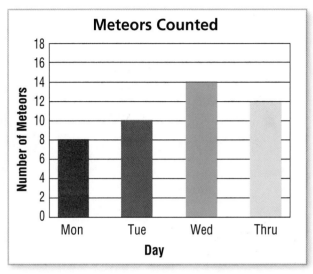

   Robert counted 6 fewer meteors on Friday than he did on Wednesday. How many meteors did he count on Friday?

   (Grade 5 SDAP 1.0)

   **A** 2             **C** 6

   **B** 4             **D** 8

13. Barb received the following scores on her math tests.

   $$88, 97, 82, 91, 92$$

   What is the median of these scores?

   (Grade 5 SDAP 1.1)

   **A** 9             **C** 90

   **B** 88            **D** 91

14. **WRITE Math** ▶ **Sense or Nonsense?** Kevin says that the ordered pairs (2,4) and (⁻1,⁻4) are the same distance from the *x*-axis. Is he correct? If so, explain why.

   (Grade 5 O—¬ SDAP 1.4)

# 3 Multiply Fractions

**The Big Idea** Multiplication of fractions involves finding part of a part of a whole.

## CALIFORNIA FAST FACT

An adult killer whale at SeaWorld in San Diego receives between 140 and 240 lb of food per day, in a balanced, high-quality diet that includes several species of fish.

## Investigate

Suppose you are a marine biologist studying killer whale calves. The table shows the average daily weight gains of three calves for a year. Choose one calf and explain how to determine its average weekly weight gain and its average monthly weight gain.

| Average Daily Weight Gain of Killer Whale Calves | |
|---|---|
| **Calf** | **Average Gain** |
| Sheba | $2\frac{3}{4}$ lb |
| Charlie | $2\frac{1}{2}$ lb |
| Barbie | $2\frac{1}{3}$ lb |

**GO ONLINE**

**Technology**
Student pages are available in the Student eBook.

**Check your understanding of important skills needed for success in Chapter 3.**

▶ **Fractions and Mixed Numbers**

Write the fraction as a mixed number.

1. $\frac{10}{6}$      2. $\frac{7}{5}$      3. $\frac{13}{4}$      4. $\frac{42}{15}$      5. $\frac{32}{9}$

Write the mixed number as a fraction.

6. $2\frac{5}{16}$      7. $1\frac{1}{6}$      8. $5\frac{3}{4}$      9. $3\frac{5}{9}$      10. $14\frac{1}{2}$

▶ **Greatest Common Factor**

Find the GCF of the set of numbers.

11. 10, 24      12. 24, 36      13. 9, 35      14. 4, 16      15. 10, 16, 48

▶ **Round Fractions and Mixed Numbers**

Write whether the fraction is closest to 0, $\frac{1}{2}$, or 1.

16. $\frac{1}{16}$      17. $\frac{5}{9}$      18. $\frac{7}{8}$      19. $\frac{15}{32}$      20. $\frac{14}{16}$

Round the mixed number to the nearest whole number.

21. $2\frac{5}{6}$      22. $14\frac{1}{10}$      23. $5\frac{3}{5}$      24. $1\frac{1}{9}$      25. $32\frac{7}{16}$

# VOCABULARY POWER

**CHAPTER VOCABULARY**

greatest common factor (GCF)
mixed number
simplest form

**WARM-UP WORDS**

**greatest common factor (GCF)** the greatest factor that two or more numbers have in common

**mixed number** a number represented by a whole number and a fraction

**simplest form** the form in which the numerator and denominator of a fraction have no common factors other than 1

# 1 Model Multiplication

OBJECTIVE: Model multiplication of fractions.

 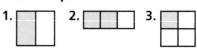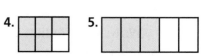
## Investigate

**Materials** ■ paper ■ colored pencils

You can make a model to find a fractional part of a fraction.

**A** Find $\frac{3}{4}$ of $\frac{2}{3}$, or $\frac{3}{4} \times \frac{2}{3}$. Draw a rectangle. Draw vertical lines to divide the rectangle into 3 equal parts. Then shade 2 parts to show $\frac{2}{3}$.

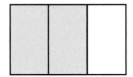

**B** Draw 3 horizontal lines through the rectangle to divide it into 12 equal parts. Shade $\frac{3}{4}$ of the shaded region. The parts that are shaded twice represent $\frac{3}{4}$ of $\frac{2}{3}$, or $\frac{3}{4} \times \frac{2}{3}$.

**C** What fraction of the whole is $\frac{3}{4}$ of $\frac{2}{3}$? Record your answer.

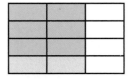

**D** Make a model to find $\frac{1}{4} \times \frac{1}{2}$. Record your answer.

## Draw Conclusions

1. Explain how your models show $\frac{3}{4} \times \frac{2}{3}$ and $\frac{1}{4} \times \frac{1}{2}$.

2. Compare your models and products with those of other classmates. What can you conclude?

3. **Analysis** Suppose two positive fractions less than 1 are multiplied. Is the product greater than or less than the two fractions that were multiplied?

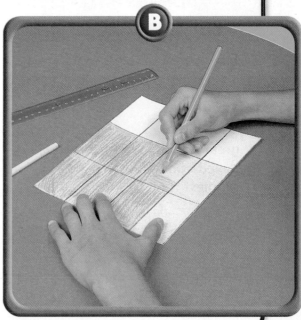

NS 2.2 Explain the meaning of multiplication and division of positive fractions and perform the calculations (e.g., $\frac{5}{8} \div \frac{15}{16} = \frac{5}{8} \times \frac{16}{15} = \frac{2}{3}$). *also* O━┓ NS 2.0, NS 2.1, O━┓ NS 2.4, MR 2.0, MR 2.4, MR 2.5, MR 3.2

You can use fraction bars to multiply some fractions.

**Example 1** Make a model to find $\frac{1}{3} \times \frac{9}{10}$.

| Step 1 | Step 2 | Step 3 |
|---|---|---|
| Use fraction bars to show $\frac{9}{10}$.  $\frac{9}{10}$ | Divide $\frac{9}{10}$ into 3 equal groups.  $\frac{9}{10}$ | Take 1 group of three $\frac{1}{10}$ bars.  $\frac{3}{10}$ |

So, $\frac{1}{3} \times \frac{9}{10} = \frac{3}{10}$.

**Example 2** Make a model to find $\frac{1}{4} \times \frac{8}{10}$.

| Step 1 | Step 2 | Step 3 |
|---|---|---|
| Use fraction bars to show $\frac{8}{10}$.  $\frac{8}{10}$ | Divide $\frac{8}{10}$ into 4 equal groups.  $\frac{8}{10}$ | Take 1 group of two $\frac{1}{10}$ bars.  $\frac{2}{10}$ |

**TALK Math**
Explain whether the model in Example 1 can be used to find $\frac{1}{2} \times \frac{9}{10}$.

So, $\frac{1}{4} \times \frac{8}{10} = \frac{2}{10}$, or $\frac{1}{5}$.

**Practice**

**Draw a picture or make a model to find the product.**

1. $\frac{1}{4} \times \frac{1}{3}$    2. $\frac{4}{5} \times \frac{3}{4}$    3. $\frac{3}{5} \times \frac{2}{3}$    ✅4. $\frac{1}{3} \times \frac{3}{4}$

5. $\frac{2}{3} \times \frac{2}{5}$    6. $\frac{1}{5} \times \frac{3}{8}$    7. $\frac{1}{4} \times \frac{8}{12}$    ✅8. $\frac{2}{3} \times \frac{9}{10}$

**Write a number sentence that the model represents.**

9.     10. 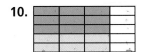    11.     12.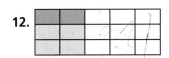

13. Sheila knows that $\frac{3}{4}$ of her classmates bought lunch in the cafeteria on Friday. Of those who bought lunch, $\frac{1}{3}$ bought tuna subs. Make a model to find what part of her classmates bought tuna subs in the cafeteria on Friday.

14. Robert spent $\frac{5}{6}$ hr doing his homework. He spent $\frac{1}{2}$ of that time working on math problems. Make a model to find what part of an hour he spent working on math problems.

15. **WRITE Math** Explain how to draw a picture or make a model to find $\frac{1}{2} \times \frac{1}{4}$.

# Record Multiplication

**OBJECTIVE:** Record multiplication of fractions.

## Learn

**PROBLEM** Students are making adobe bricks for a California history project. Of the total bricks, $\frac{2}{3}$ dry without cracking. Of those bricks, $\frac{1}{4}$ are two inches thick. What fraction of all the bricks have no cracks and are two inches thick?

**Example 1** Find $\frac{1}{4} \times \frac{2}{3}$.

**ONE WAY** Make a model.

Of the 4 × 3, or 12 parts, 1 × 2, or 2 parts are shaded twice. So $\frac{2}{12}$ of the model is shaded twice.

$\frac{1}{4} \times \frac{2}{3} = \frac{2}{12}$, or $\frac{1}{6}$

Write the product in simplest form.

**ANOTHER WAY** Use paper and pencil.

$\frac{1}{4} \times \frac{2}{3} = \frac{1 \times 2}{4 \times 3} = \frac{2}{12}$

Multiply the numerators.
Multiply the denominators.

$\frac{2}{12} = \frac{1}{6}$

Write the product in simplest form.

So, $\frac{1}{6}$ of all the bricks have no cracks and are two inches thick.

You can use common factors to simplify before multiply.

**Example 2** Find $\frac{1}{6} \times \frac{9}{10}$. **Simplify before multiplying.**

$\frac{1}{6} \times \frac{9}{10}$  ← The GCF of 6 and 9 is 3.

Look for a numerator and denominator with common factors. Find the GCF.

$\frac{1}{\underset{2}{\cancel{6}}} \times \frac{\overset{3}{\cancel{9}}}{10} = \frac{1 \times 3}{2 \times 10} = \frac{3}{20}$

Divide 6 and 9 by the GCF, 3. Multiply.

So, $\frac{1}{6} \times \frac{9}{10} = \frac{3}{20}$.

• Suppose you did not simplify before multiplying. Would you get the same product? **Explain.**

NS 2.2 Explain the meaning of multiplication and division of positive fractions and perform the calculations (e.g., $\frac{5}{8} \div \frac{15}{16} = \frac{5}{8} \times \frac{16}{15} = \frac{2}{3}$). *also* ○━┓ NS 2.0, NS 2.1, ○━┓ NS 2.4, MR 2.4, MR 2.5, MR 3.2

1. Use the model to find the product $\frac{1}{3} \times \frac{4}{5}$.

**Find the product. Write it in simplest form.**

2. $\frac{1}{4} \times \frac{3}{8}$    3. $\frac{1}{2} \times \frac{1}{6}$    4. $\frac{4}{5} \times \frac{1}{2}$    ✓5. $\frac{2}{3} \times \frac{4}{7}$    ✓6. $\frac{3}{5} \times \frac{1}{3}$

7. $\frac{3}{5} \times \frac{5}{7}$    8. $\frac{1}{2} \times \frac{5}{8}$    9. $\frac{4}{5} \times \frac{3}{4}$    10. $\frac{3}{5} \times \frac{5}{9}$    11. $\frac{4}{9} \times \frac{1}{4}$

12. **TALK Math** Explain how to simplify before multiplying to find $\frac{5}{6} \times \frac{1}{15}$.

## Independent Practice and Problem Solving

**Find the product. Write it in simplest form.**

13. $\frac{1}{3} \times \frac{2}{3}$    14. $\frac{2}{5} \times \frac{3}{4}$    15. $\frac{5}{6} \times \frac{1}{2}$    16. $\frac{1}{3} \times \frac{4}{9}$    17. $\frac{1}{4} \times \frac{4}{5}$

18. $\frac{3}{4} \times \frac{1}{2}$    19. $\frac{2}{3} \times \frac{5}{8}$    20. $\frac{5}{7} \times \frac{3}{10}$    21. $\frac{5}{8} \times \frac{4}{25}$    22. $\frac{3}{5} \times \frac{5}{6}$

23. $\frac{7}{8} \times \frac{4}{21}$    24. $\frac{4}{15} \times \frac{5}{7}$    25. $\frac{3}{16} \times \frac{4}{9}$    26. $\frac{3}{4} \times \frac{16}{15}$    27. $\frac{6}{25} \times \frac{7}{12}$

**Compare. Write <, >, or =.**

28. $\frac{5}{6} \times \frac{2}{3}$ ● $\frac{3}{5}$    29. $\frac{3}{4} \times \frac{2}{3}$ ● $\frac{1}{2}$    30. $\frac{3}{8} \times \frac{7}{9}$ ● $\frac{4}{7} \times \frac{3}{4}$    31. $\frac{4}{5} \times \frac{5}{12}$ ● $\frac{1}{3} \times \frac{15}{16}$

32. **≡FAST FACT** Many of the oldest buildings still standing in California are made of adobe bricks. In one adobe wall, $\frac{3}{8}$ of the bricks are damaged. Of those bricks, $\frac{3}{4}$ can be repaired. What fraction of the bricks in the wall can be repaired?

33. Alice is given money to restore historical sites. She uses $\frac{4}{5}$ of the money to restore a 19th-century building in Santa Clara Valley. She uses $\frac{3}{14}$ of that money restoring the living quarters. What fraction of the total money did she spend restoring the living quarters?

34. Jim and Ty work together to paint a wall. Jim paints $\frac{2}{3}$ of the wall. Ty paints $\frac{1}{2}$ of the remaining wall. What fraction of the entire wall did Ty paint?

35. **WRITE Math** Ken cleans his room for $\frac{5}{6}$ hr. He dusts $\frac{1}{2}$ of this time. Liz spends $\frac{1}{2}$ hr dusting her room. Who spends more time dusting? **Explain** without multiplying.

## Achieving the Standards

36. What is the GCD of 16 and 24? (O━┓ NS 2.4, p. 6)

37. What is the mean value of the data set 17, 18, 21, 14, and 15? (Grade 5 SDAP 1.1)

38. Find the measure of an angle in a triangle if the other angles are 52° and 25°.
(Grade 5 O━┓ MG 2.2)

39. **Test Prep** Find the product of $\frac{3}{10}$ and $\frac{2}{9}$.

A $\frac{1}{15}$    C $\frac{3}{30}$

B $\frac{2}{11}$    D $\frac{17}{30}$

# 3 Multiply Whole Numbers and Fractions

**OBJECTIVE:** Multiply whole numbers and fractions.

## Learn

**PROBLEM** Puddingstone Reservoir Path is a bike trail in the Los Angeles area. Rebecca planned an 8-mi route with a scheduled stop for a picnic after she rides $\frac{7}{10}$ of the way. How many miles will she ride before she stops for a picnic?

**Quick Review**

Write as a mixed number in simplest form.

1. $\frac{20}{12}$  2. $\frac{9}{2}$

3. $\frac{56}{13}$  4. $\frac{51}{24}$

5. $\frac{27}{4}$

### Example 1

Find $\frac{7}{10} \times 8$.  Estimate. $\frac{1}{2} \times 8 = 4$

$\frac{7}{10} \times 8 = \frac{7}{10} \times \frac{8}{1}$     Write the whole number as a fraction.

$= \frac{7}{\underset{5}{10}} \times \frac{\overset{4}{8}}{1}$     Divide 8 and 10 by the GCF, 2.

$= \frac{7 \times 4}{5 \times 1}$     Multiply.

$= \frac{28}{5}$, or $5\frac{3}{5}$     Write the answer as a fraction or a mixed number in simplest form.

Since $5\frac{3}{5}$ is close to the estimate of 4, the product is reasonable.

So, Rebecca will ride $5\frac{3}{5}$ mi before she stops for a picnic.

### Example 2 Find $20 \times \frac{2}{5}$. Write it in simplest form.

$20 \times \frac{2}{5} = \frac{20}{1} \times \frac{2}{5}$     Write the whole number as a fraction.

$= \frac{\overset{4}{20}}{1} \times \frac{2}{\underset{1}{5}}$     Divide 20 and 5 by the GCF, 5.

$= \frac{4 \times 2}{1 \times 1}$     Multiply.

$= \frac{8}{1}$, or 8     Write the product as a whole number.

• How does multiplying a whole number by a fraction less than 1 compare to multiplying two whole numbers? Explain.

**NS 2.0** Students calculate and solve problems involving addition, subtraction, multiplication, and division: *also* **NS 2.1, NS 2.2, NS 2.4, MR 2.1, MR 2.4, MR 2.5, MR 3.0, MR 3.2**

1. Copy and complete to find $4 \times \frac{2}{3}$.     $4 \times \frac{2}{3} = \frac{4}{1} \times \frac{2}{3} = \frac{4 \times 2}{1 \times 3} = \frac{\blacksquare}{\blacksquare}$, or $\blacksquare$

**Find the product. Write it in simplest form.**

2. $6 \times \frac{4}{9}$     3. $\frac{1}{2} \times 17$     4. $\frac{2}{3} \times 25$     ✓5. $8 \times \frac{1}{5}$     ✓6. $\frac{3}{4} \times 6$

7. **TALK Math** Explain how to write a whole number as a fraction.

## Independent Practice and Problem Solving

**Find the product. Write it in simplest form.**

8. $\frac{5}{8} \times 6$     9. $20 \times \frac{1}{6}$     10. $9 \times \frac{4}{5}$     11. $\frac{4}{7} \times 30$     12. $\frac{3}{10} \times 14$

**Compare. Write <, >, or =.**

13. $6 \times \frac{2}{3} \, \bullet \, \frac{3}{8} \times 7$     14. $\frac{3}{4} \times 20 \, \bullet \, \frac{5}{8} \times 24$     15. $7 \times \frac{5}{6} \, \bullet \, 9 \times \frac{3}{5}$     16. $\frac{1}{3} \times 4 \, \bullet \, \frac{5}{7} \times 3$

**Algebra** Find the missing numerator or denominator.

17. $4 \times \frac{1}{3} = 1\frac{\blacksquare}{3}$     18. $9 \times \frac{1}{2} = 4\frac{1}{\blacksquare}$     19. $2 \times \frac{\blacksquare}{4} = 1\frac{1}{2}$     20. $2 \times \frac{6}{\blacksquare} = 1\frac{5}{7}$

**USE DATA For 21–22, use the table.**

21. After riding $\frac{3}{8}$ of the Legg Lake Park route, Tim's bike got a flat tire. After fixing his tire, how many more miles did Tim have to ride to finish the route?

22. **Reasoning** Tim rode $\frac{4}{5}$ of his route and then stopped for a snack. At that point he had $2\frac{2}{5}$ mi left. Which route was he riding?

23. **WRITE Math** What's the Question? Yan bikes $\frac{3}{4}$ of the distance Jeff bikes in one week. Jeff biked 32 mi last week. The answer is 24 mi.

**Tim's Bike Trips**

| Route | Distance (mi) |
|---|---|
| San Gabriel River | 12 |
| Legg Lake Park | 4 |
| Rio Hondo to ocean | 28 |

## Achieving the Standards

24. What is the greatest common divisor of 75 and 20? (O⊓ NS 2.4, p. 6)

25. Lynn had test scores 85, 70, 85, 85, and 90. Of the mean, median, and mode of her scores, which value is least? (Grade 5 SDAP 1.1)

26. What is the volume of a cube that has a side length of 2 yards? (Grade 5 O⊓ MG 1.3)

27. **Test Prep** A class has 27 students. Last week, $\frac{7}{9}$ of them went on a field trip. How many students went on the field trip?

   **A** 7 students     **C** 16 students

   **B** 9 students     **D** 21 students

**Technology**
Use Harcourt Mega Math, Fraction
Action, *Number Line Mine,* Level L.

Extra Practice on page 82, Set B

## LESSON 4 — Multiply Fractions

**OBJECTIVE:** Find the product of fractions.

### Learn

**PROBLEM** A school survey found that $\frac{21}{25}$ of the students have pets. Of the students who have pets, $\frac{4}{7}$ have dogs. What fraction of the students have dogs?

#### Example 1

Find $\frac{4}{7} \times \frac{21}{25}$.    Estimate. $\frac{1}{2} \times 1 = \frac{1}{2}$

$\frac{4}{7} \times \frac{21}{25}$ — Look for a numerator and denominator with a common factor. Find the GCF.

$\frac{4}{7} \times \frac{\overset{3}{21}}{25} = \frac{4 \times 3}{1 \times 25} = \frac{12}{25}$ — Divide 21 and 7 by the GCF, 7. Multiply.

Since $\frac{12}{25}$ is close to the estimate of $\frac{1}{2}$, the product is reasonable.

So, $\frac{12}{25}$ of the students have dogs.

### More Examples

**A  Whole number and a fraction**

$10 \times \frac{7}{9} = \frac{10}{1} \times \frac{7}{9}$    Write the whole number as a fraction.

$= \frac{10 \times 7}{1 \times 9}$

$= \frac{70}{9}$, or $7\frac{7}{9}$    Multiply.

**B  Three fractions**

$\frac{5}{14} \times \frac{3}{10} \times \frac{7}{9}$    Look for numerators and denominators with common factors. Find the GCFs.

$\frac{\overset{1}{5}}{14} \times \frac{\overset{1}{3}}{\underset{2}{10}} \times \frac{\overset{1}{7}}{\underset{3}{9}}$    Divide 5 and 10 by the GCF, 5. Divide 3 and 9 by the GCF, 3. Divide 7 and 14 by the GCF, 7.

$\frac{1 \times 1 \times 1}{2 \times 2 \times 3} = \frac{1}{12}$    Multiply.

• Explain how to find $\frac{5}{6} \times 7 \times \frac{3}{14}$ by simplifying before multiplying.

### Guided Practice

1. Copy and complete to find $\frac{15}{16} \times \frac{2}{3}$.    $\frac{15}{16} \times \frac{2}{3} = \frac{\overset{5}{15}}{\underset{8}{16}} \times \frac{\overset{1}{2}}{\underset{1}{3}} = \frac{\blacksquare \times 1}{\blacksquare \times 1} = \frac{\blacksquare}{\blacksquare}$

**NS 2.0** Students calculate and solve problems involving addition, subtraction, multiplication, and division; *also* NS 2.1, NS 2.2, **NS 2.4**, MR 2.1, MR 2.4, MR 2.5, MR 3.2

**Find the product. Write it in simplest form.**

**2.** $\frac{3}{5} \times \frac{4}{9}$  **3.** $\frac{2}{3} \times 36$  **4.** $\frac{4}{5} \times 2 \times \frac{5}{6}$  ✔**5.** $\frac{3}{5} \times 30$  ✔**6.** $\frac{12}{13} \times \frac{26}{33}$

**7.** [TALK Math] Explain how to find the product of two fractions.

## Independent Practice and Problem Solving

**Find the product. Write it in simplest form.**

**8.** $\frac{7}{12} \times \frac{8}{9}$  **9.** $\frac{2}{5} \times \frac{7}{9}$  **10.** $\frac{16}{25} \times \frac{5}{8}$  **11.** $45 \times \frac{4}{9}$  **12.** $\frac{3}{7} \times 14 \times \frac{1}{6}$

**13.** $\frac{14}{25} \times \frac{5}{7}$  **14.** $\frac{4}{5} \times \frac{6}{7}$  **15.** $\frac{7}{8} \times \frac{9}{10}$  **16.** $15 \times \frac{4}{5}$  **17.** $\frac{2}{3} \times 12 \times \frac{1}{4}$

**Compare. Write <, >, or =.**

**18.** $\frac{3}{8} \times \frac{2}{3} \bullet \frac{1}{8}$  **19.** $\frac{3}{5} \times 20 \bullet \frac{4}{7} \times 21$  **20.** $\frac{9}{10} \times \frac{5}{6} \bullet 1$  **21.** $\frac{1}{3} \times \frac{3}{8} \bullet \frac{5}{7} \times \frac{7}{10}$

⭐**Algebra** Find the missing numerator or denominator.

**22.** $\frac{3}{4} \times \frac{1}{3} = \frac{1}{\blacksquare}$  **23.** $10 \times \frac{1}{\blacksquare} = 5$  **24.** $\frac{8}{9} \times \frac{\blacksquare}{4} = \frac{2}{3}$  **25.** $\frac{14}{17} \times \frac{6}{\blacksquare} = \frac{12}{17}$

**USE DATA** For 26–28, use the table.

**26.** In the best trick category, $\frac{3}{8}$ of the pets entered are cats. Of these, $\frac{1}{3}$ are calico cats. How many calico cats are entered in the best trick category?

**27.** **Reasoning** One half of the pets entered in this category are dogs. Of these dogs, $\frac{1}{6}$, or 5 dogs, have long ears. What is the category?

**28.** In the looks like owner category, $\frac{8}{15}$ are cats and $\frac{2}{5}$ are dogs. How many more cats are there than dogs in this category?

**29.** [WRITE Math] Explain how to multiply $\frac{3}{8} \times \frac{4}{5} \times \frac{1}{3}$. Then find the product.

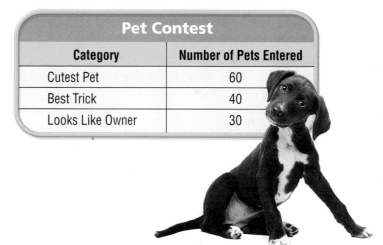

| Pet Contest | |
|---|---|
| **Category** | **Number of Pets Entered** |
| Cutest Pet | 60 |
| Best Trick | 40 |
| Looks Like Owner | 30 |

## Achieving the Standards

**30.** What is the greatest common divisor of 24 and 18? (O━┓ NS 2.4, p.6)

**31.** If $y = 9$, what is the value of $\frac{3}{4} \times \frac{2}{y}$?
(Grade O━┓ 5 AF 1.2)

**32.** What is the median value of the data set 5, 9, 17, 14, 12, and 10? (Grade 5 SDAP 1.1)

**33.** **Test Prep** What is the product of $\frac{4}{5}$ and $\frac{5}{6}$?

**A** $\frac{2}{3}$  **C** $\frac{9}{11}$

**B** $\frac{24}{30}$  **D** $1\frac{1}{24}$

Extra Practice on page 82, Set C

# 5 Multiply Fractions and Mixed Numbers

OBJECTIVE: Multiply fractions and mixed numbers.

## Quick Review

Write the missing numerator.

1. $2\frac{1}{3} = \frac{\blacksquare}{3}$    2. $5\frac{2}{5} = \frac{\blacksquare}{5}$

3. $1\frac{7}{16} = \frac{\blacksquare}{16}$    4. $7\frac{9}{10} = \frac{\blacksquare}{10}$

5. $6\frac{5}{7} = \frac{\blacksquare}{7}$

## Learn

**PROBLEM** Kim used $1\frac{2}{3}$ lb of clay to make a vase. Li used $\frac{1}{4}$ as much clay to make a bowl. How many pounds of clay did Li use?

You can use rectangles to model $\frac{1}{4} \times 1\frac{2}{3}$.

### Activity

**Step 1**

Draw 2 rectangles and divide each into thirds vertically. Shade 1 whole rectangle and $\frac{2}{3}$ of the other rectangle to show $1\frac{2}{3}$, or $\frac{5}{3}$.

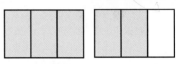

**Step 2**

Divide the rectangles into fourths horizontally. Each rectangle is now divided into twelfths.

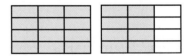

**Step 3**

Shade $\frac{1}{4}$ of the shaded parts of each rectangle. The parts that are shaded twice show the product. $\frac{1}{4} \times 1\frac{2}{3} = \frac{5}{12}$

So, Li used $\frac{5}{12}$ lb of clay.

You can simplify before multiplying a fraction and a mixed number or a whole number and a mixed number.

**ERROR ALERT**

When finding products, be sure to write mixed numbers as fractions before trying to simplify.

## Examples  Find the product. Write it in simplest form.

**A** $\frac{5}{6} \times 2\frac{2}{5}$

$\frac{5}{6} \times 2\frac{2}{5} = \frac{5}{6} \times \frac{12}{5}$    Write the mixed number as a fraction.

$\overset{1}{\underset{1}{\frac{5}{6}}} \times \overset{2}{\underset{1}{\frac{12}{5}}} = \frac{2}{1}$, or 2    Simplify. Multiply.

So, $\frac{5}{6} \times 2\frac{2}{5} = 2$.

**B** $8 \times 1\frac{3}{10}$

$8 \times 1\frac{3}{10} = \frac{8}{1} \times \frac{13}{10}$    Write both factors as fractions.

$\overset{4}{\frac{8}{1}} \times \frac{13}{\underset{5}{10}} = \frac{52}{5}$, or $10\frac{2}{5}$    Simplify. Multiply.

So, $8 \times 1\frac{3}{10} = 10\frac{2}{5}$.

- Explain whether the product of a whole number and a mixed number is greater than, less than, or equal to the whole number.

74

**O‑π NS 2.2** Explain the meaning of multiplication and division of positive fractions and perform the calculations (e.g., $\frac{5}{8} \div \frac{15}{16} = \frac{5}{8} \times \frac{16}{15} = \frac{2}{3}$). *also* **O‑π NS 2.0, NS 2.1, O‑π NS 2.4, MR 2.1, MR 2.4, MR 2.5, MR 3.2**

**1.** Use the model to find $\frac{1}{2} \times 2\frac{1}{4}$.

**Find the product. Write it in simplest form.**

**2.** $3\frac{3}{5} \times \frac{5}{6}$   **3.** $4 \times 2\frac{1}{3}$   **4.** $\frac{2}{3} \times 6\frac{3}{4}$   **⊘5.** $\frac{7}{12} \times 2\frac{2}{9}$   **⊘6.** $2\frac{5}{8} \times 2$

## Independent Practice and Problem Solving

**7.** **TALK Math** How is multiplying a fraction and a mixed number like multiplying two fractions? **Explain.**

**Find the product. Write it in simplest form.**

**8.** $\frac{1}{2} \times 7\frac{3}{7}$   **9.** $2\frac{4}{5} \times \frac{3}{10}$   **10.** $\frac{18}{25} \times 5$   **11.** $5\frac{1}{6} \times \frac{6}{11}$   **12.** $\frac{6}{7} \times 1\frac{7}{8}$

**13.** $12 \times 2\frac{1}{4}$   **14.** $4\frac{2}{5} \times 3$   **15.** $1\frac{2}{3} \times \frac{3}{4}$   **16.** $5\frac{1}{2} \times 6$   **17.** $4\frac{1}{2} \times 3$

**Compare. Write <, >, or =.**

**18.** $\frac{2}{9} \times 1\frac{1}{2}$ ● $\frac{1}{9} \times 2\frac{1}{4}$   **19.** $1\frac{1}{2} \times 3$ ● $2\frac{1}{4} \times 2$   **20.** $2\frac{5}{8} \times \frac{10}{21}$ ● $2\frac{1}{4} \times \frac{1}{2}$   **21.** $2\frac{3}{4} \times 4$ ● $10 \times 1\frac{1}{10}$

**22.** $8\frac{1}{2} \times \frac{1}{4}$ ● $8\frac{1}{4} \times \frac{1}{3}$   **23.** $3 \times 5\frac{1}{6}$ ● $5 \times 3\frac{1}{5}$   **24.** $1\frac{2}{3} \times 2$ ● $\frac{2}{3} \times 4\frac{3}{4}$   **25.** $7 \times 1\frac{2}{7}$ ● $\frac{6}{7} \times 12\frac{1}{2}$

**26.** Rob had $1\frac{1}{2}$ lb of clay. He used $\frac{2}{3}$ of the clay to make a sculpture. How much clay was left after Rob made his sculpture?

**27.** Amy is making cups out of clay. Each cup requires $4\frac{3}{8}$ oz of clay. How many ounces of clay will she need to make 4 cups?

**28.** **Pose a Problem** Look back at Exercise 27. Write a new problem by changing the number of cups Amy is making. Have a classmate solve the problem.

**29.** **WRITE Math** Without multiplying, tell whether the product $1\frac{1}{25} \times 25$ is less than or greater than 25. **Explain** your reasoning.

## Achieving the Standards

**30.** What is $\frac{4}{9} + 2\frac{5}{6}$? (NS 2.1, p. 42)

**31.** If $z = 5$, what is the value of $\frac{15}{4} \times \frac{2}{z}$?
(Grade 5 O━┱ AF 1.2)

**32.** What is the area of a parallelogram with a base of 12 inches and a height of 10 inches?
(Grade 5 O━┱ MG 1.1)

**33.** **Test Prep** Glenda has $2\frac{1}{4}$ cups of sugar. She put $\frac{1}{3}$ of the sugar in a bowl. How much sugar did she put in the bowl?

**A** $\frac{2}{3}$ cup

**B** $\frac{3}{4}$ cup

**C** $1\frac{1}{3}$ cups

**D** $1\frac{1}{12}$ cups

LESSON

# 6 Multiply Mixed Numbers

OBJECTIVE: Find the product of mixed numbers.

## Learn

**PROBLEM** Mr. Davis used $12\frac{2}{3}$ rolls of wallpaper to decorate her house. If one roll contains $5\frac{1}{4}$ m², how many square meters of wallpaper did he use?

To find the total amount of wallpaper Mr. Davis used, multiply the number of rolls by the amount of wallpaper in each roll.

### Example 1

**Find $12\frac{2}{3} \times 5\frac{1}{4}$.**     **Estimate. $13 \times 5 = 65$**

$$12\frac{2}{3} \times 5\frac{1}{4} = \frac{38}{3} \times \frac{21}{4}$$

Write the mixed numbers as fractions.

$$= \frac{\overset{19}{\cancel{38}}}{\underset{1}{\cancel{3}}} \times \frac{\overset{7}{\cancel{21}}}{\underset{2}{\cancel{4}}}$$

Divide 21 and 3 by the GCF, 3. Divide 38 and 4 by the GCF, 2. Multiply.

$$= \frac{133}{2}, \text{ or } 66\frac{1}{2}$$

The product is reasonable since $66\frac{1}{2}$ m² is close to the estimate of 65 m².

So, Mr. Davis used $66\frac{1}{2}$ m² of wallpaper.

**Example 2** Some paint comes in $\frac{5}{6}$-oz tubes. Carol used $4\frac{1}{5}$ tubes of paint to stencil the walls in her room. How much paint did she use?

**Find $4\frac{1}{5} \times \frac{5}{6}$.**     **Estimate. $4 \times 1 = 4$**

$$4\frac{1}{5} \times \frac{5}{6} = \frac{21}{5} \times \frac{5}{6}$$

Write the mixed number as a fraction.

$$= \frac{\overset{7}{\cancel{21}}}{\underset{1}{\cancel{5}}} \times \frac{\overset{1}{\cancel{5}}}{\underset{2}{\cancel{6}}}$$

Divide 21 and 6 by the GCF, 3. Divide 5 and 5 by the GCF, 5. Multiply.

$$= \frac{7}{2}, \text{ or } 3\frac{1}{2}$$

The product is reasonable since $3\frac{1}{2}$ oz is close to the estimate of 4 oz.

So, Carol used $3\frac{1}{2}$ oz of paint.

**Remember**
When rounding fractions to estimate, round to 0, $\frac{1}{2}$, or 1. When rounding mixed numbers, round to the nearest whole number.

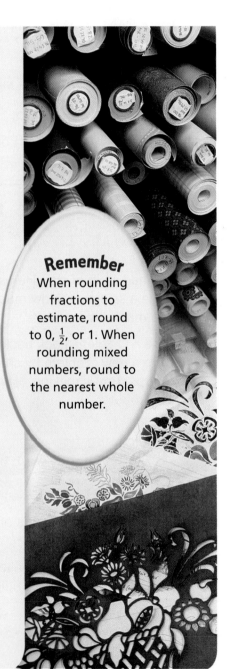

NS 2.0 Students calculate and solve problems involving addition, subtraction, multiplication, and division. *also* NS 2.1, NS 2.2, NS 2.4, MR 2.1, MR 2.2, MR 2.4, MR 2.5, MR 3.0, MR 3.2, MR 3.3

**Example 3** Cindy made curtains for 4 windows in her room. She used $4\frac{7}{8}$ yd of fabric for each window. How much fabric did she use?

**Find $4\frac{7}{8} \times 4$.**     **Estimate. $5 \times 4 = 20$**

$$4\frac{7}{8} \times 4 = \frac{39}{8} \times \frac{4}{1}$$     Write the mixed number and the whole number as fractions.

$$= \frac{39}{\overset{2}{8}} \times \frac{\overset{1}{4}}{1}$$     Divide 4 and 8 by the GCF, 4. Multiply.

$$= \frac{39}{2}, \text{ or } 19\frac{1}{2}$$

The product is reasonable since $19\frac{1}{2}$ is close to the estimate of 20.

So, Cindy used $19\frac{1}{2}$ yd of fabric.

• **What if** Cindy's room had 5 windows? How much fabric would she use?

You can multiply three or more mixed numbers, fractions, and whole numbers.

**Example 4** Find $\frac{8}{9} \times 2\frac{1}{7} \times 14$.     **Estimate. $1 \times 2 \times 14 = 28$**

$$\frac{8}{9} \times 2\frac{1}{7} \times 14 = \frac{8}{9} \times \frac{15}{7} \times \frac{14}{1}$$     Write the mixed number and the whole number as fractions.

$$= \frac{8}{\overset{3}{9}} \times \frac{\overset{5}{15}}{\overset{1}{7}} \times \frac{\overset{2}{14}}{1}$$     Divide 15 and 9 by the GCF, 3. Divide 14 and 7 by the GCF, 7.

$$= \frac{8 \times 5 \times 2}{3 \times 1 \times 1} = \frac{80}{3}, \text{ or } 26\frac{2}{3}$$     Multiply.

The product is reasonable, since $26\frac{2}{3}$ is close to the estimate of 28.

So, $\frac{8}{9} \times 2\frac{1}{7} \times 14 = 26\frac{2}{3}$.

• Find the product $6 \times \frac{7}{16} \times 3\frac{1}{10}$. Estimate. Then compare the product to the estimate for reasonableness.

## Guided Practice

1. Copy and complete to find $6\frac{3}{4} \times 3\frac{1}{3}$.     $6\frac{3}{4} \times 3\frac{1}{3} = \frac{\blacksquare}{4} \times \frac{\blacksquare}{3} = \frac{\blacksquare}{\blacksquare} = \blacksquare$

**Find the product. Write it in simplest form.**

2. $2\frac{1}{4} \times 10\frac{2}{3}$

3. $2\frac{4}{5} \times \frac{1}{2}$

4. $3 \times 4\frac{1}{6}$

5. $7\frac{1}{5} \times 1\frac{3}{5}$

6. $4 \times 3\frac{5}{6}$

**Compare. Write <, >, or = for each ●.**

**7.** $\frac{2}{3} \times 2\frac{2}{5}$ ● $1\frac{1}{3} \times 2\frac{1}{4}$     **8.** $5\frac{3}{4} \times 2$ ● $12\frac{1}{2} \times \frac{4}{5}$     **9.** $4 \times 3\frac{1}{2}$ ● $3 \times 4\frac{2}{3}$     **10.** $2\frac{1}{7} \times 3\frac{2}{5}$ ● $3\frac{4}{7} \times 2$

**11.** ( TALK Math ) When you multiply two mixed numbers, is the product less than or greater than each factor? Explain.

## Independent Practice and Problem Solving

**Find the product. Write it in simplest form.**

**12.** $40\frac{1}{2} \times 1\frac{5}{6}$     **13.** $\frac{2}{3} \times 36\frac{1}{2}$     **14.** $3\frac{5}{18} \times 12$     **15.** $1\frac{11}{15} \times 1\frac{2}{3}$     **16.** $2\frac{2}{9} \times 1\frac{1}{10} \times \frac{3}{5}$

**17.** $12\frac{3}{4} \times 2\frac{2}{3}$     **18.** $4\frac{2}{5} \times 1\frac{1}{3}$     **19.** $2\frac{3}{5} \times 10$     **20.** $3\frac{7}{12} \times \frac{4}{5}$     **21.** $3\frac{1}{5} \times \frac{5}{6} \times \frac{3}{10}$

**22.** $8 \times 2\frac{1}{4}$     **23.** $2\frac{5}{8} \times 1\frac{3}{4}$     **24.** $3\frac{5}{6} \times 1\frac{1}{2}$     **25.** $4\frac{4}{5} \times 3\frac{2}{3}$     **26.** $5\frac{1}{2} \times \frac{2}{3} \times 1\frac{1}{4}$

**Compare. Write <, >, or = for each ●.**

**27.** $1\frac{1}{7} \times 2\frac{1}{4}$ ● $1\frac{5}{7} \times 1\frac{1}{2}$     **28.** $7\frac{1}{2} \times 1\frac{1}{3}$ ● $20\frac{2}{3} \times \frac{1}{2}$     **29.** $3 \times 2\frac{5}{6}$ ● $1\frac{1}{2} \times 5\frac{2}{3}$     **30.** $2\frac{1}{4} \times 1\frac{1}{3}$ ● $\frac{1}{3} \times 4\frac{1}{2}$

⭐ **Algebra** Use mental math to solve.

**31.** $1\frac{1}{2} \times \blacksquare = \frac{3}{4}$     **32.** $3\frac{6}{7} \times \blacksquare = 1\frac{2}{7}$     **33.** $2\frac{1}{8} \times \blacksquare = 8\frac{1}{2}$     **34.** $1\frac{1}{5} \times \blacksquare = \frac{4}{5}$     **35.** $6\frac{2}{5} \times \blacksquare = 3\frac{1}{5}$

**USE DATA** For 36–38, use the table.

**36.** Mr. Gomez used $4\frac{1}{5}$ rolls of the striped wallpaper for the family room. How many square meters of wallpaper did he use?

**37.** Karen started with $7\frac{1}{2}$ rolls of wallpaper of the same pattern. After she used $\frac{1}{2}$ of the wallpaper, she had $22\frac{1}{2}$ m² of wallpaper left over. Which pattern did she use?

| Wallpaper Patterns | | | |
|---|---|---|---|
| Pattern | striped | flowered | checkered |
| Amount per Roll (in m²) | $3\frac{1}{3}$ | 6 | $\frac{5}{8}$ |

**38.** Lee Ann wants to use two different wallpaper patterns to cover a wall. She needs at least 15 m² but no more than 16 m². List two different combinations she could use. Include the number of rolls of each type of wallpaper needed.

**39.** **Reasoning** Use each of the following numbers once to form a multiplication number sentence: $4, \frac{2}{3}, 5, 1\frac{1}{5}$.

**40.** Bruce ate $\frac{1}{3}$ of a $3\frac{3}{4}$-oz chocolate bar. Describe two different ways to find how many ounces of chocolate are left. Then solve.

**41.** ( WRITE Math ) **What's the Error?** David tried to find the product $5 \times 3\frac{1}{5}$ as shown on the right. Describe his error and find the correct answer.

$$5 \times 3\frac{1}{5} = \frac{\cancel{5}^{1}}{1} \times \frac{9}{\cancel{5}_{1}} = \frac{1 \times 9}{1 \times 1} = \frac{9}{1}, \text{ or } 9$$

( Extra Practice ) on page 82, Set E

42. List $5\frac{5}{8}$, $5\frac{3}{4}$, and $5\frac{9}{16}$ in order from least to greatest. (○ーП NS 1.1, p. 18)

43. What is the surface area of a cube with a side length of 2 inches? (Grade 5 ○ーП MG 1.2)

44. **Test Prep** What is the product of $3\frac{1}{8}$ and $2\frac{4}{5}$ written in simplest form?

   **A** $8\frac{3}{4}$   **B** $8\frac{6}{8}$   **C** $12\frac{1}{2}$   **D** 15

45. If $n = 5$, what is the value of $\frac{n}{7} \times 1\frac{3}{10}$? (Grade 5 ○ーП AF 1.2)

46. **Test Prep** Chris bought 6 bags of rice. If each bag weighs $1\frac{3}{4}$ pounds, how many pounds of rice did Chris buy?

   **A** $4\frac{3}{4}$ pounds   **C** $8\frac{1}{2}$ pounds

   **B** $6\frac{3}{4}$ pounds   **D** $10\frac{1}{2}$ pounds

## Problem Solving connects to Visual Arts

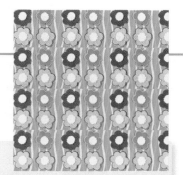

Some artists print multiple copies of the same image on a single canvas. For instance, Andy Warhol is known for his use of repeating images, from soup cans to celebrity portraits.

Terri prints copies of her collage, influenced by Andy Warhol, in rows and columns to form a rectangular grid. Each image measures $3\frac{3}{4}$ in. per side. If she fits $3\frac{1}{3}$ images across and 4 images down a single canvas, what are the width and height of the canvas?

**Step 1**

Multiply $3\frac{3}{4}$ by $3\frac{1}{3}$ to find the width.

$3\frac{3}{4} \times 3\frac{1}{3} = \frac{15}{4} \times \frac{10}{3}$   Write each mixed number as a fraction.

$= \frac{\overset{5}{\cancel{15}}}{\underset{2}{\cancel{4}}} \times \frac{\overset{5}{\cancel{10}}}{\underset{1}{\cancel{3}}}$   Simplify. Multiply.

$= \frac{25}{2}$, or $12\frac{1}{2}$

**Step 2**

Multiply $3\frac{3}{4}$ by 4 to find the height.

$3\frac{3}{4} \times 4 = \frac{15}{4} \times \frac{4}{1}$   Write the mixed number and whole number as fractions.

$= \frac{15}{\underset{1}{\cancel{4}}} \times \frac{\overset{1}{\cancel{4}}}{1}$   Simplify. Multiply.

$= \frac{15}{1}$, or 15

So, the width is $12\frac{1}{2}$ in. and the height is 15 in.

**Find the width and height of the canvas based on the dimensions of one square image that are given above.**

1. 6 images across, $7\frac{1}{3}$ images down

2. $8\frac{2}{5}$ images across, $\frac{4}{5}$ image down

3. $4\frac{2}{3}$ images across, 8 images down

4. $1\frac{7}{8}$ images across, $3\frac{7}{9}$ images down

# Problem Solving Workshop
## Skill: Estimate or Find an Actual Answer

**OBJECTIVE:** Decide when to estimate and when to find an actual answer.

## Use the Skill

**PROBLEM** For Victor's birthday party, his dad needs 80 oz of ground turkey to make burgers. The ground turkey is in packages weighing 6 oz, 9 oz, $24\frac{1}{2}$ oz, and $31\frac{1}{2}$ oz. Is there enough?

Sometimes an estimate is all you need to answer a problem. Other times, you need an actual answer.

To find out if there is enough turkey, Victor can estimate the total ounces of turkey in the packages.

$6 + 9 + 24 + 31 = 70$, or 70 oz

To estimate, round each fraction down.

70 oz < 80 oz

So, there is not enough turkey.

## Think and Discuss

**Decide whether you need an estimate or an actual answer. Solve.**

a. Victor's friend Joe will bring 3 jars of pickles to the party. Each jar weighs $1\frac{15}{16}$ lb. About how many pounds of pickles will Joe bring?

b. Victor's aunt will bring 7 bags of pretzels to the party. Each bag weighs $7\frac{7}{8}$ oz. Approximately how many ounces of pretzels will she bring?

c. Kelly uses 1 cup of red peppers, $\frac{1}{4}$ cup of green peppers, $\frac{1}{2}$ cup of onions, and cucumbers to make relish. She wants to make a total of 1 qt of relish. How many cups of cucumbers does she need? (1 qt = 4 cups)

**NS 2.0** Students calculate and solve problems involving addition, subtraction, multiplication, and division. *also* **NS 2.1, NS 2.4, MR 1.0, MR 2.0, MR 2.1, MR 2.2, MR 2.4, MR 2.5, MR 2.6, MR 3.0, MR 3.1, MR 3.2, MR 3.3**

1. Victor's mom expects 10 cups of potato salad to be eaten at the party. Would four bowls of potato salad containing 3 cups, $4\frac{1}{2}$ cups, $2\frac{1}{4}$ cups, and $3\frac{1}{4}$ cups be enough?

   **First,** decide whether an estimate or an actual answer is needed.

   **Then,** either estimate or find the actual amount of potato salad the four bowls would hold in all.

   **Finally,** compare the amount of potato salad that the bowls would hold to the amount needed. Would there be enough?

2. **What if** Victor's mom expects 16 cups of potato salad to be eaten? Is an estimate or actual answer needed? Would there be enough potato salad? Explain.

3. Victor's father pays $12.87 for banners and $3.10 for balloons. He pays with a $20 bill. How much change should he receive?

## Mixed Applications

**USE DATA** For 4–6, use the table.

4. Lee wants to include at least 8 min of video clips on a DVD he plans to make as a present. Are the five tourist video clips long enough? Should he estimate or find an actual answer? Explain.

5. Lucinda makes a music video using the Desert View Tower video clip. She repeats the video clip $2\frac{1}{2}$ times to make the music video the length she wants. How long is the music video?

6. Ana makes a video exactly 5 min long about unusual tourist attractions in California. If she includes the clip about the building shaped like a shoe, which other clip does she include?

7. **WRITE Math** **Sense or Nonsense** A stereo system is on sale at Tim's Toys for $\frac{1}{5}$ off the regular price. At Eli's Electronics, the system is on sale for 25% off the regular price. Johnny plans to purchase the system at Eli's Electronics. Does Johnny's decision make sense? **Explain.** yes

8. Liz uses 32 roses and 72 tulips to make bouquets. All bouquets should have the same number of roses and all should have the same number of tulips. What is the greatest number of bouquets she can make without any flowers left over? How many of each flower will be in each bouquet?

| Unusual Tourist Attraction Video Clips ||
| Unusual Tourist Attraction | Length of Clip (min) |
| --- | --- |
| World's Largest Thermometer Baker, California | $2\frac{1}{2}$ |
| World's Longest-Burning Light Bulb Livermore, California | $1\frac{7}{8}$ |
| Building Shaped Like a Shoe Bakersfield, California | $3\frac{1}{8}$ |
| Desert View Tower Jacumba, California | $1\frac{1}{5}$ |
| Old Faithful Geyser of California Calistoga, California | $2\frac{1}{3}$ |

# Extra Practice

1. $\frac{5}{8} \times \frac{3}{5}$
2. $\frac{2}{3} \times \frac{1}{6}$
3. $\frac{3}{8} \times \frac{2}{5}$
4. $\frac{1}{4} \times \frac{1}{5}$
5. $\frac{3}{25} \times \frac{1}{3}$

6. $\frac{7}{12} \times \frac{21}{49}$
7. $\frac{5}{8} \times \frac{2}{3}$
8. $\frac{7}{15} \times \frac{3}{14}$
9. $\frac{5}{6} \times \frac{11}{12}$
10. $\frac{1}{2} \times \frac{4}{9}$

11. Karen and Minni worked together to rake a yard. Karen raked $\frac{3}{5}$ of the yard. Then Minni raked $\frac{3}{4}$ of the yard that was left. What fraction of the yard did Minni rake?

12. Roberto used $\frac{1}{4}$ of his savings for the garden to replant the Main Street garden. He spent $\frac{5}{12}$ of that money buying new plants. What fraction of his savings for the garden did he spend buying new plants?

**Set B** Find the product. Write it in simplest form. (pp. 70–71)

1. $5 \times \frac{3}{4}$
2. $\frac{1}{9} \times 36$
3. $8 \times \frac{3}{5}$
4. $\frac{2}{3} \times 2$
5. $\frac{3}{5} \times 20$

6. $3 \times \frac{7}{9}$
7. $\frac{2}{3} \times 6$
8. $\frac{5}{8} \times 4$
9. $15 \times \frac{1}{3}$
10. $\frac{7}{9} \times 27$

**Set C** Find the product. Write it in simplest form. (pp. 72–73)

1. $\frac{2}{3} \times \frac{1}{8}$
2. $8 \times \frac{5}{6}$
3. $12 \times \frac{3}{4}$
4. $\frac{5}{9} \times \frac{8}{9}$
5. $\frac{3}{8} \times \frac{9}{10}$

6. $\frac{3}{10} \times 25$
7. $\frac{11}{12} \times \frac{6}{7}$
8. $\frac{7}{8} \times 30$
9. $\frac{11}{12} \times \frac{6}{7} \times \frac{7}{9}$
10. $\frac{9}{10} \times \frac{1}{6} \times \frac{10}{3}$

**Set D** Find the product. Write it in simplest form. (pp. 74–75)

1. $\frac{1}{4} \times 1\frac{5}{6}$
2. $7\frac{1}{12} \times 4$
3. $2\frac{3}{7} \times \frac{5}{6}$
4. $2\frac{1}{6} \times \frac{2}{3}$
5. $4\frac{2}{3} \times \frac{5}{7}$

6. $\frac{7}{10} \times 4\frac{1}{4}$
7. $5 \times 2\frac{2}{3}$
8. $4\frac{2}{9} \times \frac{1}{2}$
9. $3 \times 2\frac{4}{5}$
10. $\frac{4}{5} \times 3\frac{1}{2}$

11. Marisol had $2\frac{2}{3}$ bales of hay. She used $\frac{1}{2}$ of the hay to feed her horse. How much hay was left after Marisol fed her horse?

12. David had $4\frac{1}{2}$ cups of flour. He put $\frac{3}{4}$ of the flour into a mixing bowl. How many cups of flour did he put in the bowl?

**Set E** Find the product. Write it in simplest form. (pp. 76–79)

1. $2\frac{1}{2} \times 3\frac{1}{4}$
2. $1\frac{5}{7} \times 3\frac{3}{4}$
3. $\frac{4}{5} \times 30\frac{1}{2}$
4. $1\frac{11}{15} \times 1\frac{1}{6}$
5. $6\frac{4}{9} \times 3\frac{3}{4}$

6. $15 \times 2\frac{7}{12}$
7. $2\frac{4}{5} \times 6\frac{1}{6}$
8. $2\frac{1}{3} \times 3\frac{4}{5}$
9. $1\frac{1}{2} \times 2\frac{1}{6} \times 3\frac{3}{4}$
10. $2\frac{1}{2} \times 2\frac{1}{4} \times 2\frac{1}{3}$

**Technology**
Use Harcourt Mega Math, Fraction Action, *Fraction Flare Up*, Level O.

# Fraction Frenzy

**Get Ready!**
2 players

**Get Set!**
- 8-sided polyhedron labeled 1–8
- 2 different coins
- Fraction Frenzy game sheets (4 per player)

FINISH

START

**Play!**

■ Players choose their coins and place them on START. Each player takes four game sheets.

■ Players take turns tossing the polyhedron and recording the resulting number in one of the empty boxes of Game 1 until all boxes are filled. Fractions greater than 1 are allowed.

■ Each player finds the product of his or her numbers. The player with the greater product moves his or her coin one space clockwise.

■ Play continues, using a different game on the game sheets. The first player to reach FINISH wins.

 # Chapter 3 Review/Test

## Check Concepts

1. Make a model to find $\frac{1}{3} \times \frac{1}{4}$. (NS 2.2, pp. 66–67)

2. Explain the steps you would use to find $6 \times \frac{2}{5}$. (O⊸ NS 2.0, pp. 70–71)

3. Explain how to simplify $\frac{3}{4} \times 2\frac{2}{3}$ before multiplying. (O⊸ NS 2.0, pp. 74–75)

## Check Skills

**Find the product. Write it in simplest form.**
(O⊸ NS 2.0, NS 2.2, pp. 68–69, 70–71, 72–73, 74–75, 76–79)

4. $\frac{3}{7} \times \frac{1}{2}$

5. $\frac{4}{5} \times \frac{2}{3}$

6. $\frac{1}{8} \times \frac{4}{15}$

7. $\frac{5}{8} \times \frac{5}{6}$

8. $12 \times \frac{5}{6}$

9. $20 \times \frac{5}{7}$

10. $\frac{3}{10} \times 16$

11. $\frac{5}{6} \times 24$

12. $\frac{5}{6} \times 12 \times \frac{1}{5}$

13. $4 \times \frac{1}{6} \times 12$

14. $6\frac{1}{4} \times \frac{1}{5}$

15. $\frac{8}{9} \times 1\frac{1}{4}$

16. $3\frac{2}{7} \times 2\frac{1}{3}$

17. $2\frac{1}{4} \times 20\frac{2}{3}$

18. $2\frac{2}{5} \times 1\frac{1}{10} \times \frac{3}{4}$

19. $3\frac{1}{3} \times 1\frac{2}{5} \times 1\frac{1}{3}$

20. $\frac{5}{6} \times 18 \times \frac{3}{10}$

21. $3\frac{1}{4} \times \frac{7}{8}$

22. $2\frac{3}{5} \times 1\frac{1}{4}$

23. $2\frac{1}{6} \times 12 \times \frac{3}{4}$

**Compare. Write $<$, $>$, or $=$.** (O⊸ NS 2.0, pp. 70–71, 72–73, 74–75, 76–79)

24. $\frac{2}{3} \times \frac{2}{5} \bullet \frac{1}{3}$

25. $\frac{1}{3} \times 30 \bullet \frac{1}{4} \times 20$

26. $1\frac{2}{3} \times \frac{2}{5} \bullet 1$

27. $\frac{2}{3} \times 12 \bullet 9$

28. $\frac{2}{5} \times 1\frac{1}{6} \bullet \frac{2}{9} \times 2\frac{1}{3}$

29. $2\frac{5}{6} \times 2 \bullet 5\frac{1}{6} \times 1$

30. $4 \times 1\frac{1}{5} \bullet 2 \times 2\frac{1}{10}$

31. $1\frac{2}{3} \times \frac{3}{4} \bullet 1\frac{1}{4}$

32. $6\frac{1}{2} \times \frac{1}{4} \bullet 6\frac{1}{4} \times \frac{1}{3}$

33. $1\frac{1}{5} \times 2\frac{1}{3} \bullet 1\frac{4}{5} \times 1\frac{1}{2}$

34. $3\frac{2}{3} \times 2\frac{1}{2} \bullet 1\frac{1}{5} \times 5\frac{1}{2}$

35. $3\frac{1}{5} \times 1\frac{1}{2} \bullet \frac{1}{4} \times 5\frac{2}{3}$

36. $3\frac{3}{5} \times \frac{1}{3} \bullet 1\frac{1}{5}$

37. $1 \bullet 2\frac{1}{3} \times \frac{2}{5}$

38. $3\frac{4}{5} \times 2\frac{1}{4} \bullet 2\frac{1}{6} \times 3\frac{1}{3}$

## Check Problem Solving

**Solve.** (O⊸ NS 2.0, MR 2.0, pp. 80–81)

39. Monique expects each of the 16 people at the picnic to eat a $\frac{1}{3}$-lb hamburger. Will five packages of ground beef weighing 6 oz, 12 oz, $12\frac{3}{4}$ oz, $32\frac{1}{4}$ oz, and $18\frac{1}{2}$ oz be enough? **Explain.**

40. **WRITE Math** James and Adam are painting a house. James paints $\frac{2}{5}$ of the house. Adam paints $\frac{3}{4}$ of what is left. **Explain** how to find what fraction of the house is left to paint.

**GO ONLINE Technology** Use *Online Assessment.*

# Enrich • Fraction Patterns

## What Comes Next?

Marcus wrote this list of fractions. If he continues the pattern, what fraction will come next?

$$\frac{5}{6}, \frac{5}{12}, \frac{5}{24}, \frac{5}{48}, \cdots$$

To find the next number in the list, look for a possible rule.

**Example 1** Find the next number in the pattern $\frac{5}{6}, \frac{5}{12}, \frac{5}{24}, \frac{5}{48} \cdots$

$\frac{5}{6} \times \frac{1}{2} = \frac{5}{12}; \frac{5}{12} \times \frac{1}{2} = \frac{5}{24}; \frac{5}{24} \times \frac{1}{2} = \frac{5}{48}$     Compare each fraction with the next.

Multiply by $\frac{1}{2}$.        Find a possible rule.

$\frac{5}{48} \times \frac{1}{2} = \frac{5}{96}$        Find the next number.

So, using the rule, the next fraction in the pattern is $\frac{5}{96}$.

> **Remember**
> If the numbers in a pattern increase, the rule involves most likely addition or multiplication. However, if the rule is multiplication by a fraction less than 1, then the numbers in the pattern will decrease.

Fraction patterns can involve operations other than multiplication.

**Example 2** Find the next number in the pattern $\frac{1}{16}, \frac{3}{16}, \frac{5}{16} \cdots$

$\frac{1}{16} + \frac{2}{16} = \frac{3}{16}; \frac{3}{16} + \frac{2}{16} = \frac{5}{16}$     Compare each fraction with the next.

Add $\frac{2}{16}$.        Find a possible rule.

       Find the next number.

$\frac{5}{16} + \frac{2}{16} = \frac{7}{16}$

So, using the rule, the next number in the pattern is $\frac{7}{16}$.

## Try It

**Find a possible rule. Then find the next number in the pattern.**

1. $1\frac{1}{2}, 3, 4\frac{1}{2}, \cdots$

2. $4, \frac{8}{3}, \frac{16}{9}, \frac{32}{27}, \cdots$

3. $\frac{24}{25}, \frac{21}{25}, \frac{18}{25}, \cdots$

4. $1\frac{1}{3}, 1\frac{7}{9}, 2\frac{10}{27}, \cdots$

5. **Challenge** Michelle wrote the list below:

$$2, 3, 4\frac{1}{2}, 6\frac{3}{4}, 10\frac{1}{8}, \cdots$$

What is a possible rule? What number comes next?

**WRITE Math** A fraction pattern uses a multiplication rule and numbers greater than zero. Is it possible for this pattern to increase and then decrease? **Explain**.

# Achieving the Standards

## Chapters 1 – 3

## Number Sense

1. What is $\frac{10}{13} \times \frac{13}{14}$? (NS 2.1)

   A $\frac{5}{7}$

   B $\frac{23}{27}$

   C $1\frac{1}{140}$

   D 2

2. What is the least common multiple of 15 and 20? (O—n NS 2.4)

   A 5

   B 30

   C 45

   D 60

3. $3\frac{3}{4} - 1\frac{1}{2} =$    (O—n NS 2.0)

   A $2\frac{1}{2}$

   B $2\frac{1}{4}$

   C $1\frac{1}{2}$

   D $1\frac{1}{4}$

4. Which list of numbers is ordered from *least* to *greatest*? (O—n NS 1.1)

   A $\frac{3}{4}, \frac{1}{5}, \frac{2}{3}, \frac{1}{2}$

   B $\frac{1}{2}, \frac{1}{3}, \frac{1}{4}, \frac{1}{5}$

   C $\frac{2}{7}, \frac{2}{5}, \frac{2}{3}, \frac{7}{8}$

   D $\frac{2}{4}, \frac{3}{6}, \frac{4}{8}, \frac{5}{10}$

5. **WRITE Math** ▶ Without multiplying, tell whether the product $\frac{1}{4} \times 5$ is less than or greater than 1. **Explain** your reasoning. (NS 2.1)

## Algebra and Functions

6. What value for *v* makes the following equation true? (Grade 5 AF 1.3)

   $$7 \times 29 = (7 \times 20) + (7 \times v)$$

   A 29        C 9

   B 20        D 7

> **Test Tip** **Get the information you need.**
>
> See item 7. You need information only on Diver A. Information on the other diver is not important.

7. The chart shows the current positions of two scuba divers studying coral formations at a coral reef.

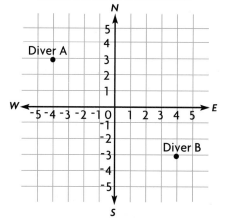

**Scuba Divers at a Coral Reef**

Which ordered pair *best* names the location of Diver A? (Grade 5 O—n AF 1.4)

   A $(3, {}^-4)$        C $(4, {}^-3)$

   B $({}^-3, 4)$        D $({}^-4, 3)$

8. **WRITE Math** ▶ If $y = 6$, what is the value of $4y + 13$? **Explain** how you found your answer. (Grade 5 O—n AF 1.2)

## Measurement and Geometry

**9.** What is the surface area of the box formed by the pattern below? (Grade 5 O━┓ MG 1.2)

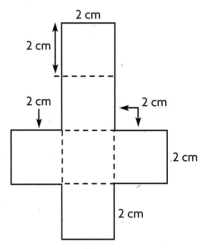

**A** 32 cm²

**B** 24 cm²

**C** 14 cm²

**D** 12 cm²

**10.** This rectangular prism has a length of 14 centimeters, a height of 7 centimeters, and a width of 4 centimeters. What is the volume? (Grade 5 O━┓ MG 1.3)

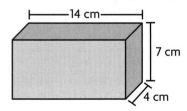

**A** 392 cm³

**B** 98 cm³

**C** 56 cm³

**D** 25 cm³

**11.** ▌WRITE Math ▶ Three angles of a quadrilateral measure 34°, 120°, and 156°. **Explain** how you can find the measure of the fourth angle. (Grade 5 O━┓ MG 2.2)

## Statistics, Data Analysis, and Probability

**12.** Sam's guitar teacher kept a record of his progress on a song that he is memorizing.

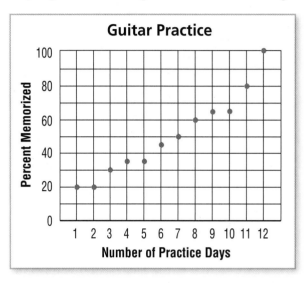

How many days of practice did it take for Sam to memorize half of the song?
(Grade 5 O━┓ SDAP 1.4)

**A** 4 days      **C** 7 days

**B** 6 days      **D** 8 days

**13.** Margot wants to draw a graph that shows the fractional part of each week that she spends on different activities. Which type of graph should she use? (Grade 5 SDAP 1.2)

**A** bar graph

**B** circle graph

**C** line graph

**D** stem-and-leaf plot

**14.** ▌WRITE Math ▶ Ben recorded the number of miles he walked every day for eight days: 2, 3, 4, 2, 3, 6, 3, 5. To the nearest tenth of a mile, what was the mean distance Ben walked each day? **Explain** how you found the answer. (Grade 5 SDAP 1.1)

# 4 Divide Fractions

**The Big Idea** Division of fractions is related to repeated subtraction and can be shown with models.

## CALIFORNIA FAST FACT

California condors soar on wind currents rather than flap their wings, which can measure more than 9 feet from tip to tip.

## Investigate

Suppose you are in charge of feeding three recuperating adult condors at a condor refuge. Each condor is fed 4 times per week. Choose a condor, and explain how you would determine how much food to prepare for each of its meals.

### California Condor Feeding Habits

| Animal ID Number | Week 1 | Week 2 | Week 3 |
|---|---|---|---|
| 21 | $12\frac{1}{3}$ lb | $9\frac{2}{3}$ lb | $11\frac{1}{4}$ lb |
| 89 | $10\frac{1}{6}$ lb | $10\frac{1}{6}$ lb | $11\frac{1}{2}$ lb |
| 103A | $11\frac{1}{2}$ lb | $10\frac{5}{6}$ lb | $12\frac{3}{4}$ lb |

**Technology**
Student pages are available in the Student eBook.

# Show What You Know

Check your understanding of important skills
needed for success in Chapter 4.

▶ **Multiply Fractions**
Find the product. Write it in simplest form.

1. $\frac{1}{2} \times \frac{5}{6}$

2. $\frac{1}{12} \times \frac{1}{6}$

3. $\frac{2}{3} \times \frac{4}{5}$

4. $\frac{5}{7} \times \frac{3}{4}$

5. $\frac{7}{12} \times \frac{1}{3}$

6. $\frac{8}{9} \times \frac{1}{10}$

7. $\frac{1}{8} \times \frac{1}{8}$

8. $\frac{2}{3} \times 2$

9. $9 \times \frac{1}{4}$

10. $\frac{2}{5} \times 5$

11. $\frac{11}{12} \times 3$

12. $44 \times \frac{1}{4}$

13. $\frac{5}{7} \times 5$

14. $\frac{1}{4} \times 8$

15. $12 \times \frac{11}{12}$

▶ **Multiply Mixed Numbers**
Find the product. Write it in simplest form.

16. $\frac{1}{3} \times 1\frac{2}{3}$

17. $2\frac{1}{4} \times \frac{5}{6}$

18. $5\frac{1}{4} \times \frac{1}{12}$

19. $\frac{3}{4} \times 2\frac{3}{10}$

20. $3\frac{1}{7} \times \frac{3}{7}$

21. $1\frac{1}{3} \times 4$

22. $5 \times 2\frac{5}{6}$

23. $1\frac{1}{12} \times 10$

24. $4\frac{3}{4} \times 2$

25. $7 \times 5\frac{1}{10}$

26. $1\frac{1}{2} \times 1\frac{1}{2}$

27. $2\frac{1}{4} \times 3\frac{1}{10}$

28. $4\frac{1}{5} \times 2\frac{3}{5}$

29. $2\frac{1}{10} \times 3\frac{7}{9}$

30. $4\frac{1}{2} \times 10\frac{1}{9}$

31. $\frac{5}{6} \times 2\frac{1}{3}$

32. $1\frac{1}{4} \times \frac{3}{4}$

33. $1\frac{1}{9} \times 9$

34. $7 \times 2\frac{7}{10}$

35. $2\frac{1}{8} \times 3\frac{5}{6}$

# VOCABULARY POWER

**CHAPTER VOCABULARY**

**Associative Property**
divisor
quotient
reciprocals

**WARM-UP WORDS**

**divisor** the number that divides the dividend

**reciprocals** two numbers are reciprocals of each
other if their product equals 1

**Associative Property** the property that states that
whatever way addends are grouped or factors are
grouped does not change the sum or the product

# 1 Division of Fractions

OBJECTIVE: Model division of fractions.

## Investigate

**Materials** ■ fraction circles

Using models will help you understand division of fractions.

Use fraction circles to find $3 \div \frac{1}{3}$, or the number of thirds in 3 wholes.

**A** Trace 3 whole circles on your paper.

**B** Model $3 \div \frac{1}{3}$ by tracing $\frac{1}{3}$-circle pieces on the 3 circles.

**C** 1 whole equals 3 thirds. How many thirds are in 3 wholes?

**D** What is $3 \div \frac{1}{3}$? Record your answer as a number sentence.

**E** Trace another set of 3 whole circles. Use $\frac{1}{4}$-circle pieces to model $3 \div \frac{1}{4}$.

**F** What is $3 \div \frac{1}{4}$? Record your answer as a number sentence.

## Draw Conclusions

1. **Explain** how you found the total number of thirds in 3 wholes.

2. Compare your models and quotients with those of your classmates. What can you conclude? **Explain.**

3. **Analysis** Suppose a whole number is divided by a fraction between 0 and 1. Is the quotient greater than or less than the whole number? **Explain** your answer.

NS 2.2 Explain the meaning of multiplication and division of positive fractions and perform the calculations (e.g., $\frac{5}{8} \div \frac{15}{16} = \frac{5}{8} \times \frac{16}{15} = \frac{2}{3}$). also ◯━┓ NS 2.0, NS 2.1, MR 2.0, MR.2.4, MR 2.5, MR 3.2

# Connect

You can make a model using fraction circles to find the quotient of two fractions.

**Make a model to find $\frac{1}{2} \div \frac{1}{4}$, or the number of fourths in $\frac{1}{2}$.**

**Step 1**

Use a $\frac{1}{2}$-circle piece to model the fraction $\frac{1}{2}$.

**Step 2**

Place as many $\frac{1}{4}$-circle pieces as you can on the $\frac{1}{2}$-circle piece.

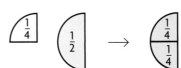

**Step 3**

Find the number of fourths in $\frac{1}{2}$. Two $\frac{1}{4}$-circle pieces can be placed on the $\frac{1}{2}$-circle piece.

$$\frac{1}{2} \div \frac{1}{4} = 2$$

**TALK Math**

Will the quotient $\frac{1}{3} \div \frac{1}{6}$ be greater than or less than $\frac{1}{3}$? **Explain.**

So, $\frac{1}{2} \div \frac{1}{4} = 2$.

# Practice

Write a division number sentence for each model.

1.

2.

3.

☑ 4.

5.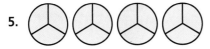

6.

Use fraction circles to find each quotient.

7. $3 \div \frac{1}{6}$   8. $4 \div \frac{1}{2}$   9. $\frac{1}{2} \div \frac{1}{8}$   10. $\frac{5}{6} \div \frac{1}{6}$   11. $\frac{3}{5} \div \frac{1}{10}$   ☑ 12. $\frac{3}{4} \div \frac{1}{8}$

13. Beth ate $\frac{1}{3}$ of a pizza. She wants to divide the rest of the pizza into $\frac{1}{6}$-pizza slices for her family. Use fraction circles to find the number of $\frac{1}{6}$-pizza slices that are left for Beth's family. **Explain** how you solved the problem.

14. **WRITE Math** ▶ Draw a picture or model to show $5 \div \frac{1}{4}$ and its solution. **Explain** how your drawing shows the problem and the solution.

**CD ROM** **Technology**
Use Harcourt Mega Math, Fraction Action, *Fraction Flare Up,* Level P.

## MENTAL MATH
# Divide Fractions

OBJECTIVE: Use mental math to divide fractions.

## Quick Review

Find each product.

1. $14 \times \frac{1}{2}$   2. $6 \times \frac{1}{3}$

3. $25 \times \frac{1}{5}$   4. $28 \times \frac{1}{7}$

5. $8 \times \frac{1}{8}$

## Learn

**PROBLEM** Ricky is pouring free samples of freshly squeezed orange juice at the Riverside Orange Blossom Festival. Each sample is $\frac{1}{2}$ cup. If a pitcher of juice holds 6 cups, how many $\frac{1}{2}$-cup samples can Ricky pour from a pitcher of juice?

Sometimes, you can use mental math to divide with fractions.

### Example 1 Find $6 \div \frac{1}{2}$.

**Step 1**

Write the problem as a number sentence.

$$6 \div \frac{1}{2} = \blacksquare$$

**Step 2**

Write a related multiplication sentence.

$$6 = \blacksquare \times \frac{1}{2}$$

**Step 3**

Use mental math to find the missing factor.

THINK: $6 = 12 \times \frac{1}{2}$, so $\blacksquare = 12$.

**Step 4**

Rewrite the original number sentence with the quotient.

$$6 \div \frac{1}{2} = 12$$

▲ The Riverside Orange Blossom Festival takes place each May in Riverside, California.

So, Ricky can pour twelve $\frac{1}{2}$-cup samples.

• How does knowing that $5 \div \frac{1}{2} = 10$, help you find $7 \div \frac{1}{4}$?

You can use mental math to divide two fractions when the numerators and denominators can be divided evenly.

**ERROR ALERT**

To use the method shown in Example 2, be sure that the divisor's numerator is a factor of the dividend's numerator and that the divisor's denominator is a factor of the dividend's denominator.

### Example 2

**A** Find $\frac{5}{12} \div \frac{1}{4}$.

$$\frac{5}{12} \div \frac{1}{4} = \frac{5 \div 1}{12 \div 4} = \frac{5}{3}, \text{ or } 1\frac{2}{3}$$

So, $\frac{5}{12} \div \frac{1}{4} = \frac{5}{3}$, or $1\frac{2}{3}$.

**B** Find $\frac{9}{16} \div \frac{3}{16}$.

$$\frac{9}{16} \div \frac{3}{16} = \frac{9 \div 3}{16 \div 16} = \frac{3}{1}, \text{ or } 3$$

So, $\frac{9}{16} \div \frac{3}{16} = 3$.

NS 2.1 Solve problems involving addition, subtraction, multiplication, and division of positive fractions and explain why a particular operation was used for a given situation. *also* O—∎ NS 2.0, NS 2.2, MR.2.4, MR 2.5, MR 3.2

1. Use mental math to find the quotient $5 \div \frac{1}{3}$.
   THINK: $5 = \blacksquare \times \frac{1}{3}$, so $5 \div \frac{1}{3} = \blacksquare$.

**Use mental math to find the quotient. Write it in simplest form.**

2. $7 \div \frac{1}{2}$      3. $3 \div \frac{1}{4}$      4. $\frac{2}{3} \div \frac{1}{5}$      ✓5. $4 \div \frac{1}{6}$      ✓6. $\frac{5}{8} \div \frac{3}{4}$

7. **TALK Math** Explain how to use mental math to find the quotient $\frac{8}{9} \div \frac{2}{9}$.

**Independent Practice and Problem Solving**

**Use mental math to find the quotient. Write it in simplest form.**

8. $9 \div \frac{1}{3}$      9. $12 \div \frac{1}{2}$      10. $7 \div \frac{1}{7}$      11. $2 \div \frac{1}{12}$      12. $15 \div \frac{1}{4}$

13. $\frac{3}{4} \div \frac{1}{2}$      14. $\frac{4}{5} \div \frac{2}{5}$      15. $\frac{7}{8} \div \frac{1}{4}$      16. $\frac{10}{11} \div \frac{2}{11}$      17. $\frac{8}{9} \div \frac{2}{3}$

18. $14 \div \frac{1}{4}$      19. $\frac{7}{8} \div \frac{1}{8}$      20. $\frac{5}{6} \div \frac{1}{3}$      21. $20 \div \frac{1}{20}$      22. $\frac{7}{12} \div \frac{1}{4}$

★**Algebra** Find the value of the expression.

23. $12 \div n$ for $n = \frac{1}{8}$      24. $n \div \frac{5}{6}$ for $n = \frac{5}{12}$      25. $\frac{7}{24} \div n$ for $n = \frac{7}{12}$

**Compare. Write $<$, $>$, or $=$.**

26. $3 \div \frac{1}{3} \bullet \frac{7}{8} \div \frac{1}{8}$      27. $\frac{8}{15} \div \frac{1}{3} \bullet \frac{9}{16} \div \frac{3}{4}$      28. $\frac{7}{18} \div \frac{7}{9} \bullet \frac{5}{16} \div \frac{5}{8}$

29. Soon Yee has $\frac{6}{7}$ yd of ribbon to decorate hats. Each hat requires $\frac{2}{7}$ yd of ribbon. How many hats can Soon Yee decorate?

30. **Reasoning** When a number is divided by $\frac{1}{3}$, the quotient is 16 more than the product of the number and $\frac{1}{3}$. What is the number?

31. Alex opens a 1-pt container of orange butter. He spreads $\frac{1}{16}$ of the butter on his bread. Then he divides the rest of the butter into $\frac{3}{4}$-pt containers. How many $\frac{3}{4}$-pt containers is he able to fill?

32. **WRITE Math** What's the Question? Kaitlin buys 2 lb of orange slices. She puts them in bags that hold $\frac{1}{5}$ lb each. The answer is 10.

**Achieving the Standards**

33. What is the greatest common divisor of 32 and 24? (O━┓ NS 2.4, p. 6)

34. If $n = 7$, what is the value of $\frac{n}{8} \div \frac{7}{8}$?
   (Grade 5 O━┓ AF 1.2)

35. One angle in a right triangle measures 30°. What are the measures of the other two angles?
   (Grade 5 O━┓ MG 2.2)

36. **Test Prep** What is $\frac{24}{25} \div \frac{3}{5}$?
   A $1\frac{2}{3}$
   B $1\frac{3}{5}$
   C 5
   D 8

# 3 Reciprocals

OBJECTIVE: Write the reciprocal for a given fraction or mixed number.

## Quick Review

Use mental math to find the quotient.

1. $3 \div \frac{1}{2}$  2. $8 \div \frac{1}{5}$
3. $10 \div \frac{1}{4}$  4. $5 \div \frac{1}{9}$
5. $7 \div \frac{1}{3}$

## Learn

Two numbers whose product is 1 are **reciprocals**.

$$\frac{1}{3} \times 3 = 1 \qquad \frac{4}{5} \times \frac{5}{4} = 1 \qquad 4 \times \frac{1}{4} = 1$$

↑ ↑ reciprocals  ↑ ↑ reciprocals  ↑ ↑ reciprocals

### Vocabulary

reciprocals

### Example 1 Write the reciprocals of $\frac{2}{3}$, $1\frac{4}{5}$, and 7.

| Step 1 | Step 2 | Step 3 |
|---|---|---|
| Write each number as a fraction. | THINK: What other factor will make a product of 1? | Use mental math to find the missing factor. |
| $\frac{2}{3}$ $1\frac{4}{5} = \frac{9}{5}$ $7 = \frac{7}{1}$ | $\frac{2}{3} \times \blacksquare = 1$ $\frac{9}{5} \times \blacksquare = 1$ $\frac{7}{1} \times \blacksquare = 1$ | $\frac{2}{3} \times \frac{3}{2} = 1$ $\frac{9}{5} \times \frac{5}{9} = 1$ $\frac{7}{1} \times \frac{1}{7} = 1$ |

So, $\frac{2}{3}$ and $\frac{3}{2}$, $1\frac{4}{5}$ and $\frac{5}{9}$, and 7 and $\frac{1}{7}$ are reciprocals.

You can use reciprocals and inverse operations to write related number sentences.

$\frac{2}{3} \times \frac{3}{2} = 1 \rightarrow$  $1 \div \frac{2}{3} = \frac{3}{2}$  $1 \div \frac{3}{2} = \frac{2}{3}$  Write related number sentences.

$1\frac{4}{5} \times \frac{5}{9} = 1 \rightarrow$  $1 \div 1\frac{4}{5} = \frac{5}{9}$  $1 \div \frac{5}{9} = 1\frac{4}{5}$  Write related number sentences.

$7 \times \frac{1}{7} = 1 \rightarrow$  $1 \div 7 = \frac{1}{7}$  $1 \div \frac{1}{7} = 7$  Write related number sentences.

### Example 2 Write related division sentences.

**A** $35 \times \frac{1}{7} = 5$    Divide the product by each factor.

$5 \div \frac{1}{7} = 35$    $5 \div 35 = \frac{1}{7}$

**B** $\frac{9}{8} \times \frac{2}{3} = \frac{3}{4}$    Divide the product by each factor.

$\frac{3}{4} \div \frac{2}{3} = \frac{9}{8}$    $\frac{3}{4} \div \frac{9}{8} = \frac{2}{3}$

• For $\frac{3}{4} \div \frac{2}{3} = \frac{3}{4} \times \frac{3}{2}$, what do you notice about the divisor in $\frac{3}{4} \div \frac{2}{3}$ and about the second factor in $\frac{3}{4} \times \frac{3}{2}$?

**NS 2.0** Students calculate and solve problems involving addition, subtraction, multiplication, and division: *also* NS 2.1, NS 2.2, MR 2.2, MR.2.4, MR 2.5, MR 3.0, MR 3.2, MR 3.3

**1.** Write the reciprocal of $3\frac{1}{2}$.  $\text{THINK: } 3\frac{1}{2} = \frac{7}{2}$   $\frac{7}{2} \times \frac{\blacksquare}{\blacksquare} = 1$

**Write the reciprocal of the number.**

**2.** $\frac{1}{2}$   **3.** 17   **4.** $2\frac{5}{8}$   **5.** $\frac{4}{9}$   ✓**6.** $7\frac{1}{3}$

**Write related division sentences.**

**7.** $\frac{4}{5} \times 2 = \frac{8}{5}$   **8.** $\frac{2}{3} \times \frac{5}{3} = \frac{10}{9}$   **9.** $\frac{2}{5} \times 2 = \frac{4}{5}$   **10.** $6 \times \frac{8}{9} = \frac{48}{9}$   ✓**11.** $\frac{2}{9} \times \frac{3}{8} = \frac{1}{12}$

**12.** TALK Math  **Explain** how you can find the reciprocal of any whole number.

## Independent Practice and Problem Solving

**Write the reciprocal of the number.**

**13.** $\frac{5}{8}$   **14.** $1\frac{15}{16}$   **15.** $\frac{7}{6}$   **16.** 30   **17.** $\frac{1}{3}$

**18.** $4\frac{1}{6}$   **19.** 24   **20.** $\frac{5}{9}$   **21.** $2\frac{4}{5}$   **22.** $8\frac{9}{10}$

**Write related division sentences.**

**23.** $\frac{2}{3} \times 8 = \frac{16}{3}$   **24.** $\frac{5}{6} \times \frac{3}{4} = \frac{5}{8}$   **25.** $\frac{1}{3} \times 9 = 3$   **26.** $\frac{8}{9} \times \frac{5}{12} = \frac{10}{27}$   **27.** $\frac{3}{16} \times \frac{8}{9} = \frac{1}{6}$

**28.** $\frac{1}{5} \times 10 = 2$   **29.** $4 \times \frac{11}{12} = \frac{11}{3}$   **30.** $\frac{5}{7} \times \frac{14}{15} = \frac{2}{3}$   **31.** $\frac{16}{3} \times \frac{3}{7} = \frac{16}{7}$   **32.** $40 \times \frac{5}{2} = 100$

**Algebra Find the value of $n$.**

**33.** $\frac{9}{28} \times 3\frac{1}{n} = 1$   **34.** $1 \div \frac{4}{7} = \frac{n}{4}$   **35.** $n \times \frac{1}{6} = 1$   **36.** $\frac{4}{3} \times \frac{3}{n} = 1$   **37.** $1 \div 1\frac{1}{4} = \frac{4}{n}$

**38.** A parade float can travel $\frac{3}{8}$ mi on 1 gal of gas. How many gallons of gas will the float need to travel the 1-mi route?

**39.** WRITE Math ▶ Gus knows that $1 \div \frac{5}{6} = \frac{6}{5}$. **Explain** how he can find the quotients $2 \div \frac{5}{6}$ and $\frac{1}{2} \div \frac{5}{6}$.

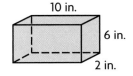

## Achieving the Standards

**40.** If $n = 2$, what is the value of $\frac{21}{2} \times \frac{n}{3}$?
(○━┓ AF 1.2, p. 72)

**41.** The rectangular prism below has a length of 10 in., a height of 6 in., and a width of 2 in. What is the volume? (Grade 5 ○━┓ MG 1.3)

10 in.

6 in.

2 in.

**42.** May's basketball team scored 46, 62, 50, 48, and 44 points in their last five games. What is the best graph to represent this data? Explain.
(Grade 5 ○━┓ SDAP 1.2)

**43.** **Test Prep** What is the reciprocal of $\frac{5}{6}$?

**A** 6

**B** $\frac{6}{5}$

**C** 1

**D** $\frac{1}{6}$

# 4 Use Reciprocals

OBJECTIVE: Divide fractions using reciprocals.

## Learn

**PROBLEM** Winnie needs pieces of string for her craft project. Each piece must be $\frac{1}{3}$ yd long. How many $\frac{1}{3}$-yd pieces of string can she cut from a piece that is $\frac{3}{4}$ yd long?

To divide by a fraction, multiply by the reciprocal.

To find the number of $\frac{1}{3}$-yd pieces, find $\frac{3}{4} \div \frac{1}{3}$.

Think: $1 \div \frac{1}{3} = 1 \times \frac{3}{1}$, so $\frac{3}{4} \div \frac{1}{3} = \frac{3}{4} \times \frac{3}{1}$.

$\frac{3}{4} \div \frac{1}{3} = \frac{3}{4} \times \frac{3}{1}$     Use the reciprocal of the divisor to write a multiplication expression.

$= \frac{9}{4}$, or $2\frac{1}{4}$.     Multiply.

So, Winnie can cut 2 pieces of string. She will have $\frac{1}{4}$ of a piece left.

• **What if** Winnie needed $\frac{1}{8}$-yd piece of string? How many $\frac{1}{8}$-yd pieces of string could she cut?

To see why you can multiply by the reciprocal to find the quotient, use inverse operations.

$\frac{2}{3} \div \frac{4}{5} = \frac{10}{12}$     Start with a division sentence.

$\frac{2}{3} = \frac{10}{12} \times \frac{4}{5}$     Write a related number sentence using inverse operations.

$\frac{2}{3} \times \frac{5}{4} = \left(\frac{10}{12} \times \frac{4}{5}\right) \times \frac{5}{4}$     Multiply both sides of the equation by the reciprocal of $\frac{4}{5}$, $\frac{5}{4}$.

$\frac{2}{3} \times \frac{5}{4} = \frac{10}{12} \times \left(\frac{4}{5} \times \frac{5}{4}\right)$     Use the Associative Property to group the reciprocals.

$\frac{2}{3} \times \frac{5}{4} = \frac{10}{12} \times 1$     Multiply the reciprocals.

$\frac{2}{3} \times \frac{5}{4} = \frac{10}{12}$

So, $\frac{2}{3} \div \frac{4}{5} = \frac{10}{12}$ is the same as $\frac{2}{3} \times \frac{5}{4} = \frac{10}{12}$.

• Write a multiplication expression for $\frac{5}{7} \div \frac{3}{10}$. Then find the product.

**NS 2.1** Solve problems involving addition, subtration, multiplication, and division of positive fractions and explain why a particular operation was used for a given situation, *also* O—n NS 2.0, NS 2.2, O—n NS 2.4, MR 2.2, MR 2.4, MR 2.5, MR 3.0, MR 3.2, MR 3.3

# Divide Whole Numbers and Fractions

You can use reciprocals to divide whole numbers by fractions. Remember, whole numbers can be written as fractions using a denominator of 1.

**Example 2** Toby and his friends are building a backyard fort. They need to cut a 6-ft board into $\frac{1}{4}$-ft pieces. How many $\frac{1}{4}$-ft pieces can they cut?

To find how many pieces they can cut, find $6 \div \frac{1}{4}$.

$6 \div \frac{1}{4} = \frac{6}{1} \div \frac{1}{4}$          Write the whole number as a fraction.

$\qquad = \frac{6}{1} \times \frac{4}{1}$          Use the reciprocal of the divisor, 4, to write a multiplication expression.

$\qquad = \frac{6}{1} \times \frac{4}{1} = \frac{24}{1}$, or 24          Multiply.

So, they can cut 24 pieces that are $\frac{1}{4}$ ft long.

**Math Idea**
To divide by a unit fraction, multiply by the denominator of the unit fraction.

You can also use reciprocals to divide fractions by whole numbers.

**Example 3** Toby has a board that is $\frac{5}{6}$ ft long. He wants to cut the board into 3 equal pieces. How long will each piece be?

To find the length of each piece, find $\frac{5}{6} \div 3$.

$\frac{5}{6} \div 3 = \frac{5}{6} \div \frac{3}{1}$          Write the whole number as a fraction.

$\qquad = \frac{5}{6} \times \frac{1}{3}$          Use the reciprocal of the divisor, 3, to write a multiplication expression.

$\qquad = \frac{5}{6} \times \frac{1}{3} = \frac{5}{18}$          Multiply.

So, each piece will be $\frac{5}{18}$ ft long.

Sometimes, you can simplify the factors before you solve.

**Example 4** Kelly makes wooden bird houses. She needs $\frac{3}{8}$ qt of paint for each bird house. If she has $\frac{3}{4}$ qt of paint, how many bird houses can she paint?

To find how many bird houses she can paint, find $\frac{3}{4} \div \frac{3}{8}$.

$\frac{3}{4} \div \frac{3}{8} = \frac{3}{4} \times \frac{8}{3}$          Use the reciprocal of the divisor to write a multiplication expression.

$\qquad = \frac{\overset{1}{\cancel{3}}}{\underset{1}{\cancel{4}}} \times \frac{\overset{2}{\cancel{8}}}{\underset{1}{\cancel{3}}} = \frac{2}{1}$, or 2          Simplify. Multiply.

So, Kelly can paint 2 bird houses.

Use the reciprocal of the divisor to write a multiplication expression.

1. $\frac{4}{5} \div \frac{1}{4} = \frac{4}{5} \times \frac{\blacksquare}{1}$
2. $\frac{1}{2} \div \frac{3}{8} = \frac{1}{2} \times \frac{\blacksquare}{3}$
3. $4 \div \frac{3}{5} = 4 \times \frac{\blacksquare}{\blacksquare}$
✓4. $6 \div \frac{4}{9} = 6 \times \frac{\blacksquare}{\blacksquare}$

Find the quotient. Write it in simplest form.

5. $\frac{2}{3} \div \frac{5}{12}$
6. $\frac{7}{11} \div 2$
7. $\frac{2}{5} \div \frac{7}{10}$
8. $\frac{11}{12} \div \frac{3}{4}$
✓9. $\frac{5}{6} \div 6$

10. **TALK Math** Explain how to use a reciprocal to find $\frac{5}{6} \div \frac{4}{7}$.

**Independent Practice and Problem Solving**

Use the reciprocal of the divisor to write a multiplication expression.

11. $\frac{2}{9} \div \frac{2}{3}$
12. $\frac{5}{8} \div \frac{1}{6}$
13. $5 \div \frac{3}{4}$
14. $\frac{4}{7} \div \frac{2}{7}$
15. $\frac{3}{4} \div \frac{3}{8}$

16. $\frac{1}{5} \div \frac{1}{3}$
17. $\frac{3}{8} \div 4$
18. $\frac{12}{13} \div \frac{3}{5}$
19. $\frac{7}{8} \div \frac{1}{9}$
20. $\frac{11}{12} \div \frac{2}{3}$

Find the quotient. Write it in simplest form.

21. $\frac{5}{2} \div \frac{5}{6}$
22. $\frac{3}{7} \div \frac{9}{16}$
23. $3 \div \frac{8}{3}$
24. $\frac{2}{3} \div 4$
25. $\frac{1}{2} \div \frac{9}{10}$

26. $\frac{14}{15} \div \frac{2}{7}$
27. $\frac{14}{5} \div 2$
28. $6 \div \frac{5}{6}$
29. $\frac{7}{18} \div \frac{1}{3}$
30. $\frac{4}{5} \div \frac{11}{12}$

**Algebra** Find the value of the expression. Write it in simplest form.

31. $\frac{2}{3} \div n$ for $n = \frac{4}{5}$
32. $\frac{3}{8} \div n$ for $n = \frac{1}{2}$
33. $\frac{9}{10} \div n$ for $n = \frac{3}{5}$

**USE DATA** For 34–37, use the table.

34. Kirsten wants to cut ladder rungs from a 6-ft board. How many ladder rungs can she cut?

35. **Pose a Problem** Look back at Problem 34. Write and solve a new problem by changing the length of the board Kirsten is cutting for ladder rungs.

36. Dan paints a design that has 8 equal parts along the entire length of the windowsill. How long is each part of the design?

37. Dan has a board that is $\frac{15}{16}$ yd. How many "Keep Out" signs can he make if the length of the sign is changed to half the original length?

38. **Reasoning** If $\frac{6}{7} \div \frac{n}{4} = \frac{6}{7} \times \frac{n}{4}$, what is the value of $n$?

39. **WRITE Math** Explain how to divide the fraction $\frac{1}{2}$ by any whole number.

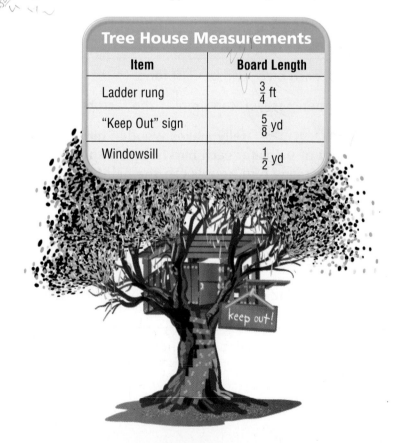

**Tree House Measurements**

| Item | Board Length |
|---|---|
| Ladder rung | $\frac{3}{4}$ ft |
| "Keep Out" sign | $\frac{5}{8}$ yd |
| Windowsill | $\frac{1}{2}$ yd |

**40.** Write $\frac{3}{16}$, $\frac{4}{9}$, and $\frac{2}{5}$ in order from least to greatest.
(O━┓ NS 1.1, p. 18)

**41.** What is $2\frac{2}{5} \times \frac{1}{6}$? (NS 2.2, p. 74)

**42. Test Prep** Which of the following has the greatest quotient?

A $3 \div \frac{3}{4}$

B $7 \div \frac{7}{8}$

C $11 \div \frac{1}{4}$

D $12 \div \frac{1}{2}$

**43.** Give an example of 5 different numbers in which the median equals the mean of the data.
(Grade 5 SDAP 1.1)

**44. Test Prep** Maggy divided $\frac{3}{4}$ pound of flour into 6 bags. Each bag contains the same amount of flour. How many pounds of flour does each bag contain?

A $\frac{3}{16}$ pound

B $\frac{1}{8}$ pound

C $\frac{3}{8}$ pound

D $4\frac{1}{2}$ pounds

## Problem Solving and Reasoning

**MENTAL MATH** You can use mental math to divide two fractions that have the same numerators, but not the same denominators.

**Find $\frac{3}{8} \div \frac{3}{5}$.**

$\frac{3}{8} \div \frac{3}{5} = \frac{3 \div 3}{8 \div 5}$ — Divide the numerators and denominators.

$= \frac{3}{3} \div \frac{8}{5}$ — Rewrite $3 \div 3$ as $\frac{3}{3}$ and $8 \div 5$ as $\frac{8}{5}$.

$= 1 \div \frac{8}{5}$ — Notice that the quotient of the numerators, 1, is divided by the quotient of the denominators, $\frac{8}{5}$.

$= 1 \times \frac{5}{8}$ — Since the reciprocal of $\frac{8}{5}$ is $\frac{5}{8}$, you can write a related number sentence.

$= \frac{5}{8}$ — The answer is the reciprocal of the quotient of the denominators, $\frac{8}{5}$.

So, $\frac{3}{8} \div \frac{3}{5} = \frac{5}{8}$.

**Use mental math to find each quotient.**

**1.** $\frac{4}{7} \div \frac{4}{5}$

**2.** $\frac{2}{3} \div \frac{2}{9}$

**3.** $\frac{3}{7} \div \frac{3}{4}$

**4.** $\frac{11}{12} \div \frac{11}{13}$

**5.** $\frac{3}{10} \div \frac{3}{5}$

**6.** $\frac{7}{8} \div \frac{7}{12}$

## LESSON 5

# Divide Mixed Numbers

**OBJECTIVE:** Divide with fractions and mixed numbers.

## Learn

**PROBLEM** Jamal and his friends looked for gold in the Shasta-Trinity National Forest in Northern California. They searched for $\frac{5}{6}$ hr on Saturday and $2\frac{1}{2}$ hr on Sunday. How many times as long did Jamal and his friends spend searching for gold on Sunday as on Saturday?

To compare, divide the time they spent searching on Sunday by the time they spent searching on Saturday.

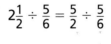

**Example 1  Divide. $2\frac{1}{2} \div \frac{5}{6}$   Estimate. $3 \div 1 = 3$**

**ONE WAY**   Use a model.

Draw 2 wholes and $\frac{1}{2}$ of a whole to model $2\frac{1}{2}$.

Shade as many groups of $\frac{5}{6}$ as you can on the $2\frac{1}{2}$ wholes.

There are 3 groups of $\frac{5}{6}$ in $2\frac{1}{2}$.

$2\frac{1}{2} \div \frac{5}{6} = 3$

Write the answer as a number sentence.

**ANOTHER WAY**   Use a reciprocal.

$2\frac{1}{2} \div \frac{5}{6} = \frac{5}{2} \div \frac{5}{6}$   Write the mixed number as a fraction.

$= \frac{5}{2} \times \frac{6}{5}$   Use the reciprocal of the divisor to write a multiplication expression.

$= \frac{\overset{1}{5}}{2} \times \frac{\overset{3}{6}}{\underset{1}{5}}$   Simplify and multiply.

$= \frac{3}{1}$, or 3

The quotient, 3, is equal to the estimate, so it is reasonable.

So, Jamal and his friends spent 3 times as long searching for gold on Sunday as on Saturday.

You can divide a mixed number by a whole number.

**Example 2  Divide. $6\frac{1}{3} \div 5$**

**ERROR ALERT**

Be sure to multiply by the reciprocal of the **divisor** to divide fractions.

$6\frac{1}{3} \div 5 = \frac{19}{3} \div \frac{5}{1}$   Write the mixed number and the whole number as fractions.

$= \frac{19}{3} \times \frac{1}{5}$   Use the reciprocal of the divisor to write a multiplication expression. Multiply.

$= \frac{19}{15}$, or $1\frac{4}{15}$

So, $6\frac{1}{3} \div 5 = 1\frac{4}{15}$.

NS 2.1 Solve problems involving addition, subtraction, multiplication, and division of positive fractions and explain why a particular operation was used for a given situation. *also* O─┓ NS 2.0, NS 2.2, O─┓ NS 2.4, MR 2.1, MR 2.2, MR.2.4, MR 2.5, MR 3.0, MR 3.2, MR 3.3

**Example 3** Sid and Jill hiked $4\frac{1}{8}$ mi in the morning and $1\frac{7}{8}$ mi in the afternoon. How many times as far did they hike in the morning as in the afternoon?

To compare, divide the distance they hiked in the morning by the distance they hiked in the afternoon.

**Divide.** $4\frac{1}{8} \div 1\frac{7}{8}$     **Estimate.** $4 \div 2 = 2$

$$4\frac{1}{8} \div 1\frac{7}{8} = \frac{33}{8} \div \frac{15}{8}$$ 
Write the mixed numbers as fractions.

$$= \frac{33}{8} \times \frac{8}{15}$$
Use the reciprocal of the divisor to write a multiplication expression.

$$= \frac{\overset{11}{\cancel{33}}}{8} \times \frac{\overset{1}{\cancel{8}}}{\underset{5}{\cancel{15}}} = \frac{11}{5}, \text{ or } 2\frac{1}{5}$$
Simplify and multiply.

Since $2\frac{1}{5}$ is close to the estimate of 2, the answer is reasonable.

So, they hiked $2\frac{1}{5}$ times as far in the morning as in the afternoon.

**Example 4** **Divide.** $\frac{7}{8} \div 1\frac{1}{6}$     **Estimate.** $1 \div 1 = 1$

$$\frac{7}{8} \div 1\frac{1}{6} = \frac{7}{8} \div \frac{7}{6}$$
Write the whole number and the mixed number as fractions.

$$= \frac{7}{8} \times \frac{6}{7}$$
Use the reciprocal of the divisor to write a multiplication problem.

$$= \frac{\overset{1}{\cancel{7}}}{\underset{4}{\cancel{8}}} \times \frac{\overset{3}{\cancel{6}}}{\underset{1}{\cancel{7}}} = \frac{3}{4}$$
Simplify and multiply.

Since $\frac{3}{4}$ is close to the estimate of 1, the answer is reasonable.

So, $\frac{7}{8} \div 1\frac{1}{6} = \frac{3}{4}$.

**Example 5** **Divide.** $6 \div 2\frac{3}{4}$     **Estimate.** $6 \div 3 = 2$

$$6 \div 2\frac{3}{4} = \frac{6}{1} \div \frac{11}{4}$$
Write the whole number and the mixed number as fractions.

$$= \frac{6}{1} \times \frac{4}{11}$$
Use the reciprocal of the divisor to write a multiplication expression. Multiply.

$$= \frac{24}{11}, \text{ or } 2\frac{2}{11}$$

You can also use this key sequence on a calculator.

Since $2\frac{2}{11}$ is close to the estimate of 2, the answer is reasonable.

So, $6 \div 2\frac{3}{4} = 2\frac{2}{11}$.

**Remember**
When rounding fractions, round to 0, $\frac{1}{2}$, or 1. When rounding mixed numbers, round to the nearest whole number.

1. Find $4\frac{1}{3} \div \frac{3}{4}$ in simplest form.  $4\frac{1}{3} \div \frac{3}{4} = \frac{13}{3} \div \frac{3}{4} = \frac{13}{3} \times \frac{\blacksquare}{\blacksquare} = \frac{\blacksquare}{\blacksquare} = \blacksquare\frac{\blacksquare}{\blacksquare}$

**Find the quotient. Write it in simplest form.**

2. $1\frac{2}{7} \div 3$

3. $2\frac{1}{2} \div \frac{1}{4}$

4. $3\frac{1}{3} \div 2\frac{1}{2}$

✓5. $5\frac{2}{3} \div 3$

✓6. $7\frac{1}{2} \div 2\frac{1}{2}$

7. **TALK Math** Explain why a mixed number in a division problem should be written as a fraction.

## Independent Practice and Problem Solving

**Find the quotient. Write it in simplest form.**

8. $2\frac{3}{8} \div 3$

9. $12 \div 1\frac{1}{2}$

10. $5 \div 1\frac{1}{3}$

11. $4\frac{1}{2} \div 3$

12. $\frac{1}{12} \div 3\frac{1}{4}$

13. $\frac{4}{5} \div 1\frac{1}{4}$

14. $3\frac{2}{9} \div \frac{2}{3}$

15. $\frac{7}{12} \div 3\frac{1}{2}$

16. $2\frac{2}{5} \div \frac{9}{10}$

17. $1\frac{5}{9} \div 2\frac{1}{3}$

18. $9\frac{1}{6} \div 3\frac{1}{3}$

19. $2\frac{2}{9} \div 1\frac{3}{7}$

20. $1\frac{7}{8} \div 1\frac{1}{16}$

21. $8\frac{1}{4} \div 2\frac{1}{16}$

22. $15\frac{1}{5} \div 3\frac{1}{10}$

⭐**Algebra** Find the value of each expression.

23. $n \div \frac{1}{2}$ for $n = 4\frac{1}{2}$

24. $1\frac{4}{5} \div n$ for $n = \frac{1}{5}$

25. $1\frac{3}{7} \div n$ for $n = \frac{3}{7}$

26. $n \div 5$ for $n = 1\frac{2}{3}$

27. **≡FAST FACT** At the United States Bullion Depository at Fort Knox, Kentucky, gold is stored in bars about the size of ordinary bricks. Each bar weighs about $27\frac{1}{2}$ lb. If a shipment of gold weighs $687\frac{1}{2}$ lb, how many bars of gold are in the shipment?

28. **Reasoning** A goldsmith has three gold nuggets that weigh $5\frac{1}{3}$ troy oz, $5\frac{1}{10}$ troy oz and $4\frac{4}{5}$ troy oz. She plans to melt one gold nugget to make as many bracelets as possible with the least amount of gold left over. If she needs $\frac{17}{20}$ troy oz of gold to make one bracelet, which of the gold nuggets should she use? **Explain.**

29. Ed poured $\frac{7}{8}$ pt of milk into a $2\frac{1}{2}$ pt bottle. What fraction of the bottle did he fill?

30. When you divide this number by $\frac{2}{3}$, the quotient is $21\frac{1}{2}$. What is the number?

31. A board 10 ft long will be cut into sections that are $1\frac{7}{8}$ ft long. How many sections of that length will there be? Will there be any lumber left over? **Explain.**

32. **WRITE Math** What's the Error? To find $2\frac{1}{2} \div 2$, Deborah wrote $\frac{2}{5} \times \frac{2}{1}$. Explain her error and correct it.

**33.** $5\frac{3}{10} - 3\frac{7}{8}$ (O━▢ NS 1.1, p. 48)

**34.** If $n = 6$, find the value of $\frac{1}{n} \div \frac{2}{3}$.

(Grade 5 O━▢ AF 1.2, p. 96)

**35.** If $x$ represents the number of miles and $y$ represents the number of hours, what is represented by the point shown in the graph.

(Grade 5 O━▢ SDAP 1.4)

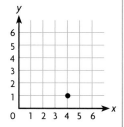

**36. Test Prep** Brett has $3\frac{1}{2}$ cups of rice. How many $\frac{1}{4}$-cup servings can he make?

**A** 6          **C** 12

**B** 7          **D** 14

**37. Test Prep** An O-scale model railroad boxcar is $12\frac{1}{2}$ inches long. The same boxcar in N scale is $3\frac{1}{8}$ inches long. How many times as great is O scale than N scale?

**A** $\frac{3}{10}$          **C** $4\frac{1}{3}$

**B** 4          **D** $16\frac{1}{3}$

## Problem Solving [connects to] Science

Gold is a nonrenewable resource because there is a limited amount on Earth. Gold was probably discovered after weathering broke off pieces of it from deposits in the mountains. People often combine gold with other metals to make alloys, or mixtures of fused metals. The purity of gold is measured in karats. The number of karats indicates the fraction of an alloy that is gold.

| Gold Karats | |
|---|---|
| **Karats (K)** | **Fraction of Pure Gold in Alloy** |
| 10 | $\frac{10}{24}$, or $\frac{5}{12}$ |
| 14 | $\frac{14}{24}$, or $\frac{7}{12}$ |
| 18 | $\frac{18}{24}$, or $\frac{3}{4}$ |
| 24 | $\frac{24}{24}$, pure gold |

**Example** **A goldsmith mixed $1\frac{1}{5}$ troy ounces of pure gold with silver and copper to make 18K gold. How many troy ounces of 18K gold did she make?**

$1\frac{1}{5} \div \frac{3}{4} = \frac{6}{5} \div \frac{3}{4}$     Write the mixed number as a fraction.

$= \frac{6}{5} \times \frac{4}{3}$     Write a multiplication expression.

$= \frac{\overset{2}{\cancel{6}}}{5} \times \frac{4}{\underset{1}{\cancel{3}}} = \frac{8}{5}$, or $1\frac{3}{5}$     Simplify and multiply.

So, she can make $1\frac{3}{5}$ troy ounces of 18K gold.

**Find the number of troy ounces of the alloy that can be made from the given amount of pure gold.**

**1.** 14K gold from $\frac{7}{8}$ troy ounces of pure gold

**2.** 10K gold from $5\frac{1}{3}$ troy ounces of pure gold

**3.** 18K gold from $6\frac{3}{4}$ troy ounces of pure gold

**4.** 14K gold from $7\frac{1}{2}$ troy ounces of pure gold

# Problem Solving Workshop
# Skill: Choose the Operation

**OBJECTIVE:** Solve problems by using the skill *choose the operation*.

## Use the Skill

**PROBLEM** Ricardo makes garden-themed wreaths from old garden hoses. He used $4\frac{1}{8}$-ft, $3\frac{1}{2}$-ft, and $5\frac{3}{8}$-ft lengths of hose to make three wreaths. What is the total length of garden hose he used?

This chart will help you decide which operation or combination of operations you can use to solve the problem.

| Add | Join groups of equal or different sizes |
|---|---|
| Subtract | Take away or compare groups |
| Multiply | Join groups of equal sizes |
| Divide | Separate into groups of equal size or find how many in each group |

The hose lengths are different and you need to find the total length of hose used. So, add the lengths of the hose.

$$4\frac{1}{8} + 3\frac{1}{2} + 5\frac{3}{8} = 4\frac{1}{8} + 3\frac{4}{8} + 5\frac{3}{8}$$    Write equivalent fractions. Add.

$$= 12\frac{8}{8} = 13$$

So, Ricardo used 13 ft of garden hose in all.

## Think and Discuss

**Solve. Name the operation or operations used.**

a. Marcus makes garden planters by stacking tires to form columns. How many tires with a width of $\frac{3}{4}$ ft are needed to make a planter 3 ft high?

b. Lucy makes floral wreaths from wire coat hangers. One stretched-out hanger is $2\frac{2}{3}$ ft long. If she uses one hanger for each wreath and $1\frac{3}{4}$ ft of flower garland for every foot of wire, how many feet of garland does she use for one wreath?

c. Diana makes stamps from potatoes. She stamps a $2\frac{3}{4}$-in. tall design in the middle of a blank card that is $4\frac{5}{8}$ in. tall. How much space on the card is left above the stamp?

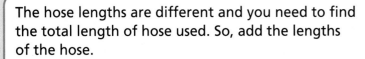

**NS 2.1** Solve problems involving addition, subtraction, multiplication, and division of positive fractions and explain why a particular operation was used for a given situation. *also* O━┓ NS 2.0, O━┓ NS 2.4, MR 1.0, MR 2.0, MR.2.4, MR 2.5, MR 3.0, MR 3.1, MR 3.2, MR 3.3

1. Josh makes picture frames from old CD cases. He glues 3 cases side-by-side to a strip of wood that has a length equal to the total length of the 3 cases. If the length of each CD case is $4\frac{7}{8}$ in., how long is the strip of wood?

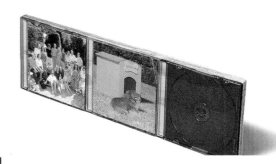

**First,** decide how the numbers in the problem are related. Three cases, with a length of $4\frac{7}{8}$ in. each, will be placed side-by-side on top of a wood strip of the same length.

**Next,** choose the operation and solve.
Addition could be used to find the total length. Multiplication could also be used, since each of the 3 cases has the same length.

$4\frac{7}{8} + 4\frac{7}{8} + 4\frac{7}{8} = \blacksquare$, $3 \times 4\frac{7}{8} = \blacksquare$

2. **What if** Josh made picture frames from 4 CD cases lined up end-to-end? How long would the wooden strip be?

3. Naomi decorates paper towel tubes to make desk organizers. She has cut 5 pieces of tubes. Her first piece is $2\frac{1}{2}$ in. long. If each of the other pieces is $1\frac{1}{2}$ in. longer than the previous piece, how long is the fifth piece?

## Mixed Applications

**USE DATA** For 4–7, use the table.

4. If Margie hikes the Ohio and Erie Canal Towpath in 10 hr, about how far does she hike in 1 hr?

5. Ron hiked all of the California trails and the Buckeye Trail. Tyler hiked the Canal Towpath. Who hiked farther? How much farther?

6. Compare the moderate California trail and the moderate Ohio trail. Which is longer? How much longer?

7. Dina hikes the moderate and difficult trails in Ohio and hikes one-half of the easy trail. How far does she hike?

8. **WRITE Math** Explain how you decide what operation to use when solving a word problem when no operation sign is given.

| Hiking Trails | | | |
|---|---|---|---|
| **State/Park** | **Trail** | **Length (mi)** | **Difficulty** |
| **California: Yosemite National Park** | Bridalveil Fall | $\frac{1}{2}$ | easy |
| | Valley Floor Loop | $6\frac{1}{2}$ | moderate |
| | Vernal Fall | $6\frac{1}{2}$ | difficult |
| **Ohio: Cuyahoga Valley National Park** | Ohio and Erie Canal Towpath | $19\frac{1}{2}$ | easy |
| | Brandywine Gorge | $1\frac{1}{4}$ | moderate |
| | Buckeye Trail (Jaite to Boston) | $5\frac{3}{5}$ | difficult |

9. The Healthy Cuisine Club members had $50.00 to spend on a meal. They spent $13.76 on salad ingredients and $27.82 on the main course. How much money is left?

10. Anna needs 3 bunches of spinach to make a spinach pie that will serve 6 people. How many bunches of spinach does she need to serve 24 people?

# Extra Practice

**Set A** Use mental math to find the quotient. Write it in simplest form. (pp. 92–93)

1. $6 \div \frac{1}{4}$
2. $7 \div \frac{1}{3}$
3. $5 \div \frac{1}{5}$
4. $12 \div \frac{1}{4}$

5. $3 \div \frac{1}{2}$
6. $\frac{4}{5} \div \frac{1}{5}$
7. $\frac{5}{8} \div \frac{1}{4}$
8. $\frac{8}{11} \div \frac{4}{11}$

9. $\frac{5}{6} \div \frac{1}{3}$
10. $\frac{9}{14} \div \frac{3}{7}$
11. $8 \div \frac{1}{2}$
12. $\frac{7}{8} \div \frac{1}{8}$

13. Joseph has a piece of plastic tubing that is $\frac{5}{6}$ ft long. He wants to cut the tubing into four equal pieces. How long will each piece be?

14. Samantha has 8 cups of ice cream to serve to her friends. How many dishes of ice cream can she serve if she puts $\frac{2}{3}$ cup of ice cream in each dish?

**Set B** Write the reciprocal of the number. (pp. 94–95)

1. $\frac{5}{6}$
2. 14
3. $3\frac{3}{5}$
4. $\frac{2}{9}$
5. 9
6. $6\frac{2}{3}$

7. $\frac{1}{4}$
8. $11\frac{1}{12}$
9. $20\frac{1}{2}$
10. 16
11. $3\frac{1}{3}$
12. $\frac{3}{4}$

**Set C** Find the quotient. Write it in simplest form. (pp. 96–99)

1. $\frac{7}{3} \div \frac{2}{3}$
2. $\frac{3}{5} \div \frac{1}{5}$
3. $\frac{7}{10} \div \frac{2}{5}$
4. $\frac{5}{7} \div 15$

5. $\frac{6}{4} \div \frac{3}{8}$
6. $\frac{8}{10} \div 4$
7. $\frac{5}{6} \div 3$
8. $\frac{3}{8} \div \frac{5}{16}$

9. $\frac{11}{12} \div \frac{6}{3}$
10. $\frac{8}{15} \div \frac{2}{5}$
11. $\frac{2}{3} \div \frac{3}{4}$
12. $\frac{3}{5} \div 7$

13. Dion has a piece of wire $\frac{2}{3}$ ft long. He wants to cut the wire into pieces that are $\frac{1}{6}$ ft long. How many pieces will he be able to cut?

14. Marisol makes wooden memory boxes. To paint each memory box, she needs $\frac{1}{10}$ qt of paint. If she has $\frac{2}{5}$ qt of paint, how many memory boxes can she paint?

**Set D** Find the quotient. Write it in simplest form. (pp. 100–103)

1. $1\frac{1}{8} \div 3$
2. $10 \div 2\frac{1}{4}$
3. $6 \div 1\frac{1}{3}$
4. $\frac{1}{10} \div 2\frac{3}{4}$
5. $\frac{2}{3} \div 1\frac{1}{4}$

6. $2\frac{1}{9} \div \frac{1}{3}$
7. $3\frac{2}{5} \div \frac{7}{10}$
8. $1\frac{3}{9} \div 1\frac{1}{3}$
9. $8\frac{1}{4} \div 3\frac{1}{16}$
10. $10\frac{1}{4} \div 4\frac{1}{2}$

11. Brad and Wes are building a tree house. They have to cut a $12\frac{1}{2}$ ft piece of wood into 5 equally-sized pieces. How long is each piece of wood?

12. Sharon has a length of rope that is $10\frac{1}{4}$ ft long. Jill has a length of rope that is $2\frac{1}{2}$ ft long. How many times as long is Sharon's rope compared to Jill's?

**Technology**
Use Harcourt Mega Math, The Number Games, *Up, Up, and Array,* Level J.

# Divide and Find

## On Your Mark!

2 players

## Get Set!

- 8-sided polyhedron labeled 1–8
- 2 different coins
- Divide and Find game sheets, (4 per player)

FINISH

START

## Go!

■ Players choose their coins and place them on START. Each player takes four game sheets.

■ Players take turns tossing the polyhedron and recording the resulting number in one of the empty boxes of Game 1 until all boxes are filled. Fractions greater than 1 are allowed.

■ Each player finds the quotient of his or her numbers. The player with the greater quotient moves his or her coin one space.

■ Play continues using a different game on the game sheets. The first player to reach FINISH wins.

# Chapter 4 Review/Test

## Check Vocabulary and Concepts

**Choose the better term from the box.**

**VOCABULARY**

divisors

reciprocals

quotient

1. Two numbers are __?__ if their product is 1.
   (O— NS 2.0, p. 94)

2. A __?__ is the number, not including the remainder, that results from dividing. (O— NS 2.0, pp. 90–91)

3. Explain how to use mental math to find $5 \div \frac{1}{2}$.

4. Explain how to write the reciprocal of $\frac{2}{3}$.

## Check Skills

**Use mental math to find the quotient. Write it in simplest form.** (NS 2.1, pp. 92–93)

5. $12 \div \frac{1}{3}$

6. $3 \div \frac{1}{6}$

7. $\frac{5}{6} \div \frac{1}{3}$

8. $\frac{9}{14} \div \frac{3}{14}$

9. $5 \div \frac{1}{2}$

**Write the reciprocal of the number.** (O— NS 2.0, pp. 94–95)

10. $\frac{5}{7}$

11. $2\frac{7}{9}$

12. $\frac{9}{5}$

13. $11$

14. $5\frac{2}{3}$

15. $22\frac{1}{2}$

**Use the reciprocal of the divisor to write a multiplication problem.** (NS 2.1, pp. 96–99)

16. $\frac{2}{7} \div \frac{1}{3}$

17. $6 \div \frac{3}{4}$

18. $\frac{4}{5} \div 8$

19. $\frac{2}{3} \div \frac{1}{6}$

20. $\frac{3}{7} \div \frac{5}{8}$

21. $\frac{2}{3} \div \frac{3}{4}$

22. $\frac{5}{6} \div \frac{7}{8}$

23. $\frac{7}{9} \div \frac{14}{15}$

**Find the quotient. Write it in simplest form.** (NS 2.1, pp. 100–103)

24. $2 \div 1\frac{1}{6}$

25. $3\frac{1}{3} \div \frac{1}{6}$

26. $2\frac{1}{4} \div 1\frac{1}{2}$

27. $3\frac{3}{4} \div \frac{2}{3}$

28. $6\frac{1}{2} \div 1\frac{1}{2}$

29. $1\frac{1}{5} \div 1\frac{1}{4}$

30. $5\frac{3}{4} \div 2\frac{1}{8}$

31. $12\frac{1}{3} \div 5\frac{1}{2}$

## Check Problem Solving

**Solve.** (NS 2.1, MR 1.0, pp. 104-105)

32. Erica makes scarecrows that are used by farmers to protect their crops. She starts by stacking bales of hay. If she wants to make a scarecrow that is $5\frac{1}{2}$ ft tall, how many bales of hay with a height of $\frac{5}{6}$ ft each will she need?

33. **WRITE Math** What's the Error? Sergio wanted to find $3\frac{1}{6} \div 3$. He rewrote the problem as show below. Describe his error and write the correct answer.

$$\frac{6}{19} \times \frac{3}{1}$$

**GO ONLINE Technology** Use *Online Assessment.*

# Enrich • Complex Fractions
## Simply Simplifying

A **complex fraction** is a fraction that contains a fraction in its numerator, denominator, or both.

Manuela bought a $\frac{1}{2}$-lb package of peas and a 2-lb package of peas. She wants to divide all the peas into $\frac{3}{4}$-lb containers. How many $\frac{3}{4}$-lb containers will she be able to fill?

**Example** Write the complex fraction $\dfrac{\frac{1}{2}+2}{\frac{3}{4}}$ in simplest form.

$$\frac{\frac{1}{2}+2}{\frac{3}{4}} = \frac{\frac{1}{2}+\frac{4}{2}}{\frac{3}{4}} = \frac{\frac{5}{2}}{\frac{3}{4}}$$

Find the value of the numerator as a simple fraction. Then find the value of the denominator as a simple fraction if needed.

$$= \frac{5}{2} \div \frac{3}{4}$$

Rewrite the problem as the quotient of two fractions.

$$= \frac{5}{2} \times \frac{4}{3}$$

Use the reciprocal of the divisor to write a multiplication expression.

$$= \frac{5}{2} \times \frac{\overset{2}{4}}{3} = \frac{10}{3}, \text{ or } 3\frac{1}{3}$$

Write the answer in simplest form.

**Remember**
The fraction $\frac{a}{b}$ can be written as the division expression $a \div b$.

So, Manuela can fill 3 containers with $\frac{1}{3}$ of a $\frac{3}{4}$-lb container ($\frac{1}{3} \times \frac{3}{4} = \frac{1}{4}$), or $\frac{1}{4}$ lb left over.

## Try It
**Write each complex fraction in simplest form.**

1. $\dfrac{\frac{3}{16}}{\frac{7}{8}}$

2. $\dfrac{1\frac{1}{2}}{\frac{1}{6}+\frac{1}{12}}$

3. $\dfrac{8\frac{1}{2}+\frac{1}{6}}{5-\frac{2}{3}}$

4. $\dfrac{2\frac{7}{10}}{4\frac{4}{5}}$

5. $\dfrac{\frac{7}{24}}{\frac{14}{15}}$

6. **Challenge** Write the complex fraction $\dfrac{2\frac{5}{8}}{2\frac{2}{7} \times \frac{1}{2}}$ in simplest form.

**WRITE Math** Rob is simplifying a complex fraction with mixed numbers in both its numerator and denominator. **Explain** what steps Rob needs to take after he simplifies the numerator and denominator.

## Multiple Choice

1. Marcus saves $\frac{6}{16}$ of his lawn mowing earnings each month. Which of the following is an equivalent fraction for $\frac{6}{16}$? (O━┓ NS 2.4, p. 8)

   A $\frac{1}{4}$

   B $\frac{1}{3}$

   C $\frac{3}{8}$

   D $\frac{8}{3}$

2. A cake is cut into 12 equal slices at a birthday party. Four of the slices are eaten. Which fraction, in simplest form, represents the portion of the cake that is left? (O━┓ NS 2.4, p. 8)

   A $\frac{1}{4}$

   B $\frac{4}{12}$

   C $\frac{2}{3}$

   D $\frac{8}{12}$

3. An art class has 24 students. Last month, $\frac{5}{6}$ of the art class went on a field trip to the art museum. How many students went to the art museum? (NS 2.2, p. 70)

   A 4           C 16

   B 6           D 20

4. What is $\frac{5}{8} \times \frac{2}{5} \times \frac{1}{2}$ written in simplest form? (NS 2.1, p. 72)

   A $\frac{1}{8}$

   B $\frac{10}{80}$

   C $\frac{1}{4}$

   D $\frac{10}{40}$

5. Which list of fractions is ordered from *greatest* to *least*? (O━┓ NS 1.1, p.18)

   A $\frac{3}{5}, \frac{5}{8}, \frac{7}{15}, \frac{1}{4}$

   B $\frac{5}{8}, \frac{3}{5}, \frac{1}{4}, \frac{7}{15}$

   C $\frac{7}{15}, \frac{5}{8}, \frac{3}{5}, \frac{1}{4}$

   D $\frac{5}{8}, \frac{3}{5}, \frac{7}{15}, \frac{1}{4}$

6. $\frac{3}{12} + \frac{1}{8} =$ (O━┓ NS 2.4, p. 38)

   A $\frac{1}{6}$

   B $\frac{1}{5}$

   C $\frac{8}{24}$

   D $\frac{3}{8}$

7. Peter divided $12\frac{1}{4}$ pounds of sand into 6 sandbags. If each sandbag contained the same amount of sand, how many pounds of sand did each sandbag contain? (NS 2.1, p. 100)

   A 2 pounds

   B $2\frac{1}{24}$ pounds

   C $2\frac{1}{12}$ pounds

   D $73\frac{1}{2}$ pounds

8. What is $\frac{5}{6} \div \frac{2}{5}$? (NS 2.1, p. 98)

   A $2\frac{1}{6}$

   B $2\frac{1}{12}$

   C 2

   D $\frac{1}{3}$

**GO ONLINE Technology** Use *Online Assessment.*

9. Which point shows the location of $\frac{4}{3}$ on the number line? (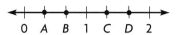 NS 1.1, p. 18)

$$\leftarrow\!\!\!+\!\!-\!\!\bullet\!\!-\!\!\bullet\!\!-\!\!+\!\!-\!\!\bullet\!\!-\!\!\bullet\!\!-\!\!+\!\!\rightarrow$$
0    A    B    1    C    D    2

**A** point A

**B** point B

**C** point C

**D** point D

10. A baker sold loaves of bread weighing $1\frac{2}{3}$ pounds and $1\frac{1}{4}$ pounds. What was the total weight of the bread? (O━┓ NS 2.0, p. 42)

**A** $1\frac{3}{4}$ pounds

**B** $2\frac{3}{4}$ pounds

**C** $2\frac{11}{12}$ pounds

**D** 3 pounds

11. Mike and his friend together have $3\frac{2}{5}$ pounds of marbles. What is $3\frac{2}{5}$ written as a fraction? (O━┓ NS 1.0, p. 12)

**A** $\frac{8}{5}$

**B** $\frac{10}{5}$

**C** $\frac{15}{5}$

**D** $\frac{17}{5}$

12. Jenn and Susie are making a dress. Jenn has $5\frac{2}{3}$ yards of fabric and Susie has $8\frac{1}{4}$ yards of fabric. How much more fabric does Susie have than Jenn? (O━┓ NS 2.0, p. 48)

**A** $2\frac{7}{12}$ yards

**B** 3 yards

**C** $13\frac{3}{12}$ yards

**D** $13\frac{11}{12}$ yards

## Short Response

13. At an archeological site, $\frac{5}{9}$ of the artifacts that were found are tools and the rest were pieces of pottery. What fraction of the artifacts were pieces of pottery? (NS 2.1, p. 38)

14. The Smith family bought three small pizzas. The model shown below shows how much of the pizza was left over. The left over pieces are shaded. How much pizza did the Smith family eat? (NS 2.1, p. 38)

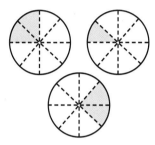

15. If Jorge has three fractions with denominators of 5, 10, and 6, what denominator could Jorge use to add the fractions? (O━┓ NS 2.4, p. 14)

16. Emily and Midge are making 10 bags of popcorn for a party. They have a total of $23\frac{3}{4}$ cups of popcorn. If each bag will hold the same amount of popcorn, how many cups will be in each bag? (NS 2.1, p. 100)

## Extended Response ✏️WRITE Math ▶

17. Russell had 5 hours of free time and spent $\frac{3}{4}$ of it building a table in his woodworking shop. How many hours did he spend building the table? **Explain** how you chose the operation. (O━┓ NS 2.0, p. 70)

18. Maria has an $8\frac{3}{4}$-foot long piece of wooden trim she wants to use to frame some photographs. If she needs $2\frac{5}{8}$ feet of wooden trim to frame each photograph, about how many photographs can she frame? **Explain** how you found your answer. (NS 2.1, p. 102)

# Counting Votes

## THE ELECTORAL COLLEGE VERSUS DIRECT DEMOCRACY

**W**hen citizens vote for President and Vice President of the United States, they are actually choosing people called electors, who will cast ballots for the President and Vice President in the Electoral College. Today the candidate who gets the most votes from citizens of a particular state generally gets all of that state's electoral votes.

In Ancient Greece, people used a direct democracy to govern. This means that all of the people of Greece made and upheld the laws. The only way for a law to be passed was if the majority of the people agreed. This type of governing puts all of the power into the hands of the citizens.

Where the assembly met in Ancient Greece

## FACT·ACTIVITY

**Number of electors in the Electoral College by state as of 2008—total 538.**

**For 1–4, use the map. Write all fractions in simplest form.**

❶ A candidate must receive a majority (more than half) of the electoral votes to become president. How many electoral votes were needed to win the 2008 election? Write this amount as a fraction.

❷ How many electoral votes does California have? Write this amount as a fraction.

❸ Write a fraction addition sentence showing three or more states whose total fraction of votes equals California's.

❹ **Pose a Problem** Write a problem like Problem 2, but use another state.

ALMANAC

**Fact**

As California's population has grown, so has its delegation in the U.S. House of Representatives. After the 1900 census, California had 8 representatives out of a total of 386. After the 2000 census, it had 53 out of 435 representatives!

# How Might You Vote?

Any United States citizen who is 18 years old or older has the right to vote in local, state and national elections. People vote for the leaders of their cities, counties, states, and country. They also vote to decide important local issues such as whether a new school should be built.

A representative has introduced a bill to eliminate the penny. How would you vote on this issue, which would affect everyone in the United States? The chart below offers some arguments in the debate about pennies.

## FACT • ACTIVITY

**Conduct a survey of 30 people. Each person should select *Yes* or *No* and a reason for that choice. You may add other reasons, but there should be an equal number of reasons for each choice.**

- Write a fraction for the part of the total number of people who select each option such as *Yes–Reason A* or *No–Reason B*.
- Write a fraction to represent the part of the total number of people who select *Yes* and the part of the total number of people who select *No*.
- Write a paragraph analyzing your results. Include a statement that orders the fractions from greatest to least.

**Should the United States Stop Making Pennies?**

| Yes | No |
|---|---|
| **A** Vending machines don't take pennies. | **A** Pennies keep prices down. Without the penny, vendors would raise prices to the next highest nickel. |
| **B** Pennies are copper-coated zinc. The price of zinc has increased so much that the penny now costs 1.4 cents to make, according to the United States Mint. | **B** Pennies represent a piece of history and honor President Abraham Lincoln. The Lincoln penny was the first U.S. coin to show a historic figure. Lincoln has been on the penny since 1909, the 100th anniversary of his birth. |
| **C** Pennies are too heavy to carry around. | **C** You can cash in rolls of pennies for dollars. |

# 2 Rational Numbers and Integer Operations

# Math on Location

**①** ▲The topography of Mars has been studied extensively with scientific explorations.

**②** ▲The photographs and data collected from the surface rovers are used to develop and evaluate theories.

**③** ▲Scientists use positive and negative rational numbers to describe altitudes and depths.

# VOCABULARY POWER

## TALK Math

What math do you see in the **Math on Location** photographs? How can you use rational numbers to describe your location?

## READ Math

**REVIEW VOCABULARY** You learned the words below when you learned about rational numbers and integers. How do these words relate to **Math on Location**?

**absolute value** the distance of an integer from zero

**integers** the set of whole numbers and their opposites

**rational number** any number that can be written as $\frac{a}{b}$, where $a$ and $b$ are integers and $b \neq 0$

## WRITE Math

Copy a Venn diagram like the one below. Use what you learn about rational numbers and integers to complete the diagram.

This shows the relationships among rational numbers, integers, whole numbers, and natural numbers.

┌─ **Rational Numbers** ──────────────┐
│ ┌─ **Integers** ───────────────────┐ │
│ │ ┌─ **Whole Numbers** ──────────┐ │ │
│ │ │ ┌─ **Natural Numbers** ───┐ │ │ │
│ │ │ │ the set of counting     │ │ │ │
│ │ │ │ numbers 1, 2, 3, 4      │ │ │ │
│ │ │ └─────────────────────────┘ │ │ │
│ │ └──────────────────────────────┘ │ │
│ └──────────────────────────────────┘ │
└───────────────────────────────────────┘

**Technology**
Multimedia Math Glossary link at
www.harcourtschool.com/hspmath

# 5 Rational Numbers

**The Big Idea** Rational numbers build on an understanding of fractions and their opposites and can be compared and ordered on a number line.

In 2001, Death Valley, California, set a record for hot days—153 consecutive days with high temperatures above 100°F.

## Investigate

The graph at the right shows the average yearly rainfall for seven places in California. Describe some conclusions that you draw from the places listed in this graph.

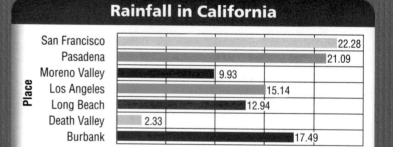

**Rainfall in California**

| Place | Average Yearly Rainfall (inches) |
|---|---|
| San Francisco | 22.28 |
| Pasadena | 21.09 |
| Moreno Valley | 9.93 |
| Los Angeles | 15.14 |
| Long Beach | 12.94 |
| Death Valley | 2.33 |
| Burbank | 17.49 |

**GO ONLINE**

**Technology**
Student pages are available in the Student eBook.

# Show What You Know

Check your understanding of important skills
needed for success in Chapter 5.

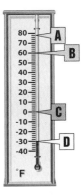

▶ **Read a Thermometer**

Write the temperature shown by each letter on the thermometer.

**1.** A   **2.** B

**3.** C   **4.** D

▶ **Compare and Order Fractions and Mixed Numbers**

Compare. Write <, >, or =.

**5.** $\frac{5}{6}$ ● $\frac{1}{6}$   **6.** $\frac{1}{4}$ ● $\frac{3}{4}$   **7.** $2\frac{2}{5}$ ● $2\frac{3}{5}$   **8.** $\frac{1}{2}$ ● $\frac{1}{3}$

**9.** $4\frac{1}{6}$ ● $4\frac{1}{3}$   **10.** $4\frac{2}{5}$ ● $4\frac{2}{3}$   **11.** $\frac{1}{4}$ ● $\frac{1}{5}$   **12.** $\frac{1}{2}$ ● $\frac{4}{5}$

Order from least to greatest.

**13.** $\frac{1}{3}, \frac{2}{3}, \frac{1}{6}$   **14.** $\frac{2}{5}, \frac{1}{2}, \frac{3}{10}$   **15.** $5\frac{2}{3}, 5\frac{2}{6}, 5\frac{2}{12}$   **16.** $2\frac{3}{4}, 2\frac{1}{8}, 4\frac{1}{12}$

▶ **Practice Division Facts**

Find the quotient.

**17.** $54 \div 9$   **18.** $42 \div 6$   **19.** $24 \div 6$   **20.** $121 \div 11$   **21.** $21 \div 7$

**22.** $84 \div 7$   **23.** $0 \div 7$   **24.** $36 \div 4$   **25.** $32 \div 8$   **26.** $72 \div 12$

**27.** $108 \div 12$   **28.** $56 \div 8$   **29.** $88 \div 8$   **30.** $60 \div 12$   **31.** $49 \div 7$

# VOCABULARY POWER

**CHAPTER VOCABULARY**

absolute value
ratio
rational number
Venn diagram

**WARM-UP WORDS**

**ratio** a comparison of two numbers, $a$ and $b$, that can be
written as a fraction $\frac{a}{b}$

**rational number** any number that can be written as $\frac{a}{b}$,
where $a$ and $b$ are integers and $b \neq 0$

**Venn diagram** a diagram that shows relationships among
sets of things

# 1 Understand Rational Numbers

**OBJECTIVE:** Classify rational numbers and find a rational number between two rational numbers.

## Vocabulary

ratio    rational number

Venn diagram    absolute value

## Learn

A **ratio** is a comparison of two numbers, $a$ and $b$, written as a fraction $\frac{a}{b}$. A **rational number** is any number that can be written as a ratio $\frac{a}{b}$, where $a$ and $b$ are integers and $b$ is not equal to 0.

**Example 1** Write each rational number as a ratio $\frac{a}{b}$.

A. $^-6$    B. $15$    C. $5\frac{1}{4}$    D. $0.86$    E. $^-3\frac{7}{8}$

$^-6 = \frac{^-6}{1}$    $15 = \frac{15}{1}$    $5\frac{1}{4} = \frac{21}{4}$    $0.86 = \frac{86}{100}$    $^-3\frac{7}{8} = \frac{^-31}{8}$

Notice that in E above, $\frac{^-31}{8}$ is a rational number because both $^-31$ and 8 are integers.

• Is $\frac{0}{1}$ a rational number? Is $\frac{1}{0}$ a rational number? **Explain.**

### Remember

Integers include all whole numbers and their opposites. The opposites $^+3$ and $^-3$ are both 3 units from 0.

The **Venn diagram** shows the relationship among the sets of rational numbers, integers, whole numbers, and natural numbers.

**Example 2** Use the Venn diagram to determine the set or sets to which each number belongs.

A. 68    The number 68 belongs in the sets of natural numbers, whole numbers, integers, and rational numbers.

B. $^-9$    The number $^-9$ belongs in the sets of integers and rational numbers, but not in the sets of natural numbers or whole numbers.

C. 7.80    The number 7.80 belongs in the set of rational numbers, but not in the sets of natural numbers, whole numbers, or integers.

D. $\frac{15}{3}$    The number $\frac{15}{3}$ is equal to 5, so it belongs in the sets of natural numbers, whole numbers, integers, and rational numbers.

E. $^-\frac{7}{3}$    The number $^-\frac{7}{3}$ belongs in the set of rational numbers, but not in the sets of natural numbers, whole numbers, or integers.

**Rational Numbers**
Any numbers that can be written as a quotient of two integers $\frac{a}{b}$, where $b \neq 0$

**Integers**
Whole numbers and their opposites

**Whole Numbers**
Zero and natural numbers

**Natural Numbers**
The set of counting numbers 1, 2, 3, 4, 5,.

NS 1.1 Compare and order positive and negative fractions, decimals, and mixed numbers and place them on a number line. *also,* NS 2.0, MR 2.4, MR 2.5, MR 3.2

**Example 3** A bread recipe calls for $1\frac{1}{2}$ tsp of salt. Mary decided the bread was too salty. She baked another loaf using $1\frac{1}{4}$ tsp, but it was not salty enough. If she then uses an amount between $1\frac{1}{4}$ tsp and $1\frac{1}{2}$ tsp, what might it be?

Think of the amounts of salt as rational numbers. You can use a number line to find rational numbers between other rational numbers.

> Use the number line to find an amount between $1\frac{1}{4}$ tsp and $1\frac{1}{2}$ tsp.
>
> $1\frac{1}{4}$     $1\frac{1}{2}$
>
> 1   $1\frac{1}{8}$   $1\frac{2}{8}$   $1\frac{3}{8}$   $1\frac{4}{8}$   $1\frac{5}{8}$   $1\frac{6}{8}$   $1\frac{7}{8}$   2
>
> When the number line is marked in eighths, the mark between $1\frac{1}{4}$ and $1\frac{1}{2}$ represents an amount Mary could use.

So, Mary could use $1\frac{3}{8}$ tsp of salt.

You can use a common denominator to find a rational number between two other rational numbers.

**Example 4** Find a rational number between $^-1\frac{3}{4}$ and $^-1\frac{7}{8}$.

> $^-1\frac{3}{4} = {}^-1\frac{12}{16}$     $^-1\frac{7}{8} = {}^-1\frac{14}{16}$    Use a common denominator to write equivalent fractions
>
> $^-1\frac{13}{16}$ is between $^-1\frac{12}{16}$ and $^-1\frac{14}{16}$    Find a rational number between the two other rational numbers.

**ERROR ALERT**

The farther a negative number is from zero, the less it is.
$$^-1\frac{7}{8} < {}^-1\frac{3}{4}$$

So, $^-1\frac{13}{16}$ is between $^-1\frac{3}{4}$ and $^-1\frac{7}{8}$.

• Explain how to find a rational number between $^-2\frac{1}{3}$ and $^-2\frac{2}{9}$.

You can also find a rational number between two other rational numbers in decimal form.

**Example 5** Find a rational number between 3.5 and 3.6.

> $3.5 = 3.50$    $3.6 = 3.60$    Add a zero to each decimal.
>
> Use a number line marked in hundredths to find a number between 3.50 and 3.60.
>
>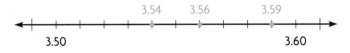
>
> 3.50     3.54    3.56     3.59     3.60

So, 3.54, 3.56, and 3.59 are some of the rational numbers between 3.5 and 3.6.

• Is $^-2.38$ between $^-2.2$ and $^-2.3$? **Explain** your reasoning.

Copy and complete to write the rational number in the form $\frac{a}{b}$.

**1.** $^-12.3$    $^-12.3 = \frac{^-12.3}{1} \times \frac{10}{10} = \frac{\blacksquare}{10}$

**2.** $4.71$    $4.71 = \frac{4.71}{1} \times \frac{100}{100} = \frac{\blacksquare}{100}$

Write the rational number in the form $\frac{a}{b}$.

**3.** $^-6$    **4.** $2\frac{4}{5}$    **5.** $^-0.675$    **6.** $3\frac{5}{6}$    **7.** $^-4\frac{1}{4}$    ✓**8.** $^-5.135$

Use the number line to find a rational number between the two given numbers.

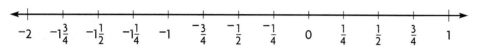

**9.** $^-1\frac{1}{2}$ and $^-1$    **10.** $0$ and $\frac{1}{2}$    **11.** $^-2$ and $^-1\frac{1}{2}$    **12.** $^-\frac{3}{4}$ and $^-\frac{1}{4}$    ✓**13.** $^-\frac{1}{4}$ and $\frac{1}{4}$

**14.** **TALK Math** Explain how a number line can help you decide which of two numbers is greater? Do the signs matter?

Write the rational number in the form $\frac{a}{b}$.

**15.** $3.06$    **16.** $11$    **17.** $^-4\frac{2}{3}$    **18.** $^-0.056$    **19.** $1\frac{5}{8}$    **20.** $^-21$

**21.** $^-72$    **22.** $^-2\frac{4}{5}$    **23.** $53$    **24.** $3\frac{6}{7}$    **25.** $^-3.5$    **26.** $5.86$

Use the number line to find a rational number between the two given numbers.

**27.** $^-1.79$ and $^-1.77$    **28.** $^-1.74$ and $^-1.72$    **29.** $^-1.72$ and $^-1.7$    **30.** $^-1.78$ and $^-1.8$

Find a rational number between the two given rational numbers.

**31.** $\frac{1}{6}$ and $\frac{1}{2}$    **32.** $^-\frac{17}{2}$ and $^-8$    **33.** $2\frac{4}{10}$ and $2.6$    **34.** $^-7.1$ and $^-7.04$    **35.** $4.8$ and $4\frac{7}{8}$

**36.** $^-4\frac{1}{3}$ and $^-\frac{8}{3}$    **37.** $^-87.3$ and $^-87\frac{7}{10}$    **38.** $1\frac{3}{5}$ and $1.5$    **39.** $^-9$ and $^-\frac{29}{3}$    **40.** $^-\frac{15}{7}$ and $^-2\frac{1}{5}$

Tell whether the first rational number is between the second and third rational numbers. Write *yes* or *no*.

**41.** $\frac{3}{4}$; $\frac{5}{8}$ and $\frac{7}{8}$    **42.** $^-0.23$; $^-0.027$ and $^-0.21$    **43.** $^-\frac{5}{6}$; $^-1$ and $^-1\frac{1}{8}$

**44.** $^-4$; $^-\frac{19}{3}$ and $^-\frac{18}{5}$    **45.** $\frac{1}{9}$; $^-\frac{1}{16}$ and $^-\frac{1}{7}$    **46.** $\frac{3}{4}$; $0.54$ and $\frac{13}{20}$

**Solve.**

47. Find a positive number and a negative number between ⁻0.1 and 0.1. Draw a number line and graph the numbers on the number line.

48. **Reasoning** Is it easier to find a rational number between $\frac{3}{8}$ and $\frac{1}{2}$, or between 0.375 and 0.50? **Explain.**

49. Larry's piecrust recipe uses $4\frac{3}{4}$ cups of flour and Judith's recipe uses 5 cups. David wants to use an amount of flour between $4\frac{3}{4}$ cups and 5 cups. What might the amount be?

50. **WRITE Math** **What's the Error?** Jackie says that ⁻3 belongs to three of the four number sets in the Venn diagram on p. 118. Correct Jackie's error.

## Achieving the Standards

51. Muffins are sold for $5.50 per dozen. A club has a weekly order of 120 muffins. What is the total cost of the weekly order? (Grade 5 ⟶ NS 2.1)

52. Graph the ordered pair (1,8) on a coordinate grid. (Grade 5 ⟶ SDAP 1.5)

53. Write an equivalent decimal for 3.5 with two decimal places. (Grade 5 NS 1.0)

54. **Test Prep** Which rational number is between 3.9 and 4.1?

   **A** 3.8    **B** 4    **C** 4.11    **D** 14.2

55. **Test Prep** Which shows $⁻5\frac{2}{3}$ in the form $\frac{a}{b}$?

   **A** $⁻5\frac{17}{3}$    **B** $5\frac{17}{3}$    **C** $\frac{17}{3}$    **D** $\frac{⁻17}{3}$

## MATH POWER — Problem Solving and Reasoning

**NUMBER SENSE** The **absolute value** of a rational number is its distance from 0 on a number line. The symbol for absolute value is | |.

2 units    2 units

Look at 2 and ⁻2. They are both 2 units from 0.

$|2| = 2$ and $|⁻2| = 2$

**Write the absolute value of the rational number.**

**Ⓐ** $|⁻0.4|$

⁻0.4 is 0.4 units from 0.

So, $|⁻0.4| = 0.4$.

**Ⓑ** $\left|\frac{3}{4}\right|$

$\frac{3}{4}$ is $\frac{3}{4}$ units from 0.

So, $\left|\frac{3}{4}\right| = \frac{3}{4}$.

**Ⓒ** $\left|\frac{⁻4}{5}\right|$

$\frac{⁻4}{5}$ is $\frac{4}{5}$ units from 0.

So, $\left|\frac{⁻4}{5}\right| = \frac{4}{5}$.

**Write the absolute value of the rational number.**

1. $\left|\frac{⁻1}{2}\right|$    2. $|⁻4|$    3. $\left|2\frac{1}{4}\right|$    4. $\left|\frac{2}{5}\right|$    5. $|0.2|$    6. $|⁻3.6|$

# Compare and Order Decimals

OBJECTIVE: Compare and order positive and negative decimals.

## Quick Review

Compare. Write <, >, or =.

1. ⁻25 ● ⁻84
2. ⁻11 ● ⁻6
3. 32 ● ⁻39
4. ⁻56 ● ⁻66
5. ⁻15 ● 4

## Learn

On a number line, a number is greater than any number to its left and less than any number to its right. When comparing two negative rational numbers, you can also think about which number is closer to 0. The negative number that is closer to 0 is greater.

### Example 1 Compare ⁻0.47 and ⁻0.83.

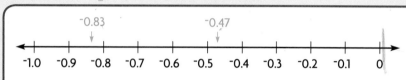

⁻0.83 is between ⁻0.8 and ⁻0.9.

⁻0.47 is between ⁻0.4 and ⁻0.5.

⁻0.83 is to the left of ⁻0.47, so ⁻0.83 is less than ⁻0.47.

So, ⁻0.83 < ⁻0.47 and ⁻0.47 > ⁻0.83.

### More Examples Compare. Use < and >. Think about the positions of the numbers on a number line.

**A** ⁻3.1 ● ⁻3.5
⁻3.1 is to the right of ⁻3.5 on a number line.

**B** ⁻0.08 ● 0.01
0.01 is to the right of ⁻0.08 on a number line.

So, ⁻3.1 > ⁻3.5 and ⁻3.5 < ⁻3.1.   So, 0.01 > ⁻0.08 and ⁻0.08 < 0.01.

**Math Idea**
Grouping rational numbers into positive and negative groups makes it easier to order them.

### Example 2 Order 3.7, ⁻8.35, and 3.74 from least to greatest.

The only negative number is ⁻8.35, so it is the least.
Compare 3.7 and 3.74.

| | | |
|---|---|---|
| 3.7 | 3.74 | Compare the ones digits. They are the same. Compare the tenths digits. They are the same. |
| 3.70 | 3.74 | Write the numbers using the same number of decimal places. |
| 3.70 < 3.74 | 3.74 > 3.70 | Compare the hundredths digits. 4 is greater than 0. |
| ⁻8.35 < 3.7 < 3.74 | | Order the numbers from least to greatest. |

So, in order from least to greatest, the numbers are ⁻8.35, 3.7, and 3.74.

○─┱ NS 1.1 Compare and order positive and negative fractions, decimals, and mixed numbers and place them on a number line. also ○─┱ NS 1.0, MR 2.4, MR 2.5, MR 3.2

Use the number line to compare ⁻5.02 and ⁻4.92. Write < or >.

1. ⁻5.02 ● ⁻4.92

```
        -5.02   -4.92
          ↓       ↓
+----+----+----+----+----+----+
-5.2  -5.1  -5.0  -4.9  -4.8  -4.7
```

Compare. Write < or >.

2. ⁻2.1 ● ⁻1.2        3. ⁻0.87 ● ⁻0.92        ✓4. 0 ● ⁻0.08        ✓5. ⁻0.5 ● 0.3

6. **TALK Math** Explain how to compare ⁻8.3 and ⁻8.15 using a number line and by looking at place values.

## Independent Practice and Problem Solving

Compare. Write < or >.

7. ⁻0.62 ● 0.61        8. 2.8 ● ⁻2.9        9. ⁻0.07 ● ⁻0.06        10. 3.23 ● 3.2

11. ⁻2.34 ● ⁻2.30        12. 8.1 ● ⁻9.6        13. 5.73 ● ⁻5.73        14. ⁻16.26 ● ⁻16.2

Order from least to greatest.

15. 5.82, ⁻0.37, 2.14, ⁻0.05        16. 8.31, 8.42, ⁻0.831, ⁻8.42

17. ⁻0.03, 0.01, 0.2, ⁻0.04, 0.12, ⁻0.34        18. ⁻6.71, 1.06, 10.6, ⁻0.06, 6.10, ⁻6.01

**USE DATA** For 19–24, use the table.

19. Which stock price increased by the greatest amount?

20. Which stock price decreased by the greatest amount?

21. Compare the change in stock prices for stocks PIJ and AOR using < or >.

| Stock | AOR | BPC | ZKL | PIJ |
|-------|-----|-----|-----|-----|
| Change in Price ($) | ⁻0.83 | 1.28 | 0.09 | ⁻1.06 |

22. Write a rational number, expressed as a decimal, which is greater than the number representing the change in the price of stock BPC.

23. Write a rational number, expressed as a decimal, which is less than the number representing the change in the price of stock ACR.

24. **WRITE Math** Graph each change in stock price on a number line. **Explain** how to order the values from greatest to least.

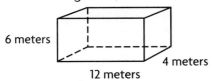

## Achieving the Standards

25. Which unit would you use to measure the volume of this figure? (Grade 5 ●━┓ MG 1.3)

```
6 meters ⌐----------⌐
                    4 meters
         12 meters
```

26. Write 7% as a decimal. (●━┓ NS 1.1, p. 24)

27. Molly needed $3\frac{3}{4}$ cups of flour to make a cake. Write $3\frac{3}{4}$ as a fraction. (●━┓ NS 2.0, p. 12)

28. **Test Prep** Which list of numbers is ordered from greatest to least?

A  ⁻1.05, ⁻0.87, 0.04        C  0.04, ⁻0.87, ⁻1.05

B  ⁻0.87, ⁻1.05, 0.04        D  0.04, ⁻1.05, ⁻0.8

# Compare and Order Fractions and Mixed Numbers

OBJECTIVE: Compare and order positive and negative fractions and mixed numbers.

## Learn

You can compare and order fractions and mixed numbers in several ways.

### Example 1 Compare $^-1\frac{3}{8}$ and $^-1\frac{5}{8}$.

**ONE WAY** Use a number line.

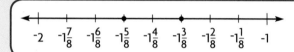

$^-1\frac{3}{8}$ is to the right of $^-1\frac{5}{8}$.

**ANOTHER WAY** When the denominators are the same, compare the numerators.

$^-1\frac{3}{8} = \frac{^-11}{8}$    $^-1\frac{5}{8} = \frac{^-13}{8}$    Write the mixed numbers as fractions.

$^-11 > ^-13$    Since the fractions have the same denominators, compare the numerators.

So, $^-1\frac{3}{8} > ^-1\frac{5}{8}$.

### Example 2 Order $^-\frac{3}{4}$, $1\frac{1}{2}$, and $^-\frac{1}{5}$ from greatest to least.

The only positive fraction is $1\frac{1}{2}$, so it is the greatest. Compare $^-\frac{3}{4}$ and $^-\frac{1}{5}$.

**ONE WAY** Use the LCD.

$^-\frac{3}{4} \bullet ^-\frac{1}{5}$    The LCD of $^-\frac{3}{4}$ and $^-\frac{1}{5}$ is 20.

$^-\frac{3}{4} = \frac{^-15}{20}$    $^-\frac{1}{5} = \frac{^-4}{20}$    Write equivalent fractions by using the LCD.

$^-15 < ^-4$    Compare the numerators.

$^-\frac{3}{4} < ^-\frac{1}{5}$

**ANOTHER WAY** Use cross-multiplication.

$^-\frac{3}{4} \searrow= ^-\frac{1}{5}$    Multiply the numerator of each fraction by the denominator of the other fraction.

$^-3 \times 5$    $^-1 \times 4$

$^-15 < ^-4$    The relationship between the fractions is the same as the relationship between the products.

$^-\frac{3}{4} < ^-\frac{1}{5}$

So, in order from greatest to least, the numbers are $1\frac{1}{2}$, $^-\frac{1}{5}$, $^-\frac{3}{4}$.

- **What if** $\frac{3}{4}$ and $\frac{1}{5}$ were compared? How would the answer change?

NS 1.1 Compare and order positive and negative fractions, decimals, and mixed numbers and place them on a number line. also NS 1.0, NS 2.0, MR 2.4, MR 2.5, MR 3.2

Compare. Write $<$, $>$, or $=$.

1. $\dfrac{^-5}{9}$ ● $\dfrac{^-2}{9}$

A number line from $^-1$ to $0$ marked: $^-\dfrac{8}{9}$ $^-\dfrac{7}{9}$ $^-\dfrac{6}{9}$ $^-\dfrac{5}{9}$ $^-\dfrac{4}{9}$ $^-\dfrac{3}{9}$ $^-\dfrac{2}{9}$ $^-\dfrac{1}{9}$

2. $^-4\dfrac{5}{8}$ ● $^-4\dfrac{7}{8}$

3. $\dfrac{^-1}{6}$ ● $\dfrac{^-2}{12}$

✓4. $\dfrac{^-11}{12}$ ● $\dfrac{^-7}{12}$

✓5. $^-4\dfrac{3}{4}$ ● $^-4\dfrac{9}{12}$

6. **TALK Math** Explain how to use a number line to compare $^-4\dfrac{2}{3}$ and $^-4\dfrac{5}{6}$.

## Independent Practice and Problem Solving

Compare. Write $<$, $>$, or $=$.

7. $\dfrac{^-4}{5}$ ● $\dfrac{4}{5}$

8. $\dfrac{^-3}{8}$ ● $\dfrac{^-1}{8}$

9. $^-6\dfrac{2}{9}$ ● $^-7\dfrac{2}{9}$

10. $^-9\dfrac{4}{11}$ ● $^-9\dfrac{6}{11}$

11. $^-3\dfrac{1}{4}$ ● $^-3\dfrac{1}{3}$

12. $^-1\dfrac{3}{4}$ ● $\dfrac{^-3}{4}$

13. $\dfrac{7}{8}$ ● $\dfrac{^-2}{5}$

14. $^-3\dfrac{2}{3}$ ● $^-3\dfrac{4}{6}$

15. $^-2\dfrac{2}{8}$ ● $2\dfrac{1}{4}$

16. $^-3\dfrac{1}{5}$ ● $^-3\dfrac{7}{8}$

Order from least to greatest.

17. $\dfrac{^-1}{11}$, $^-1$, $\dfrac{^-2}{11}$

18. $\dfrac{5}{8}$, $\dfrac{^-7}{8}$, $\dfrac{^-3}{4}$

19. $\dfrac{^-4}{5}$, $\dfrac{2}{5}$, $\dfrac{^-1}{2}$

20. $^-2\dfrac{1}{6}$, $2\dfrac{1}{3}$, $^-2\dfrac{1}{3}$

21. $\dfrac{^-5}{8}$, $\dfrac{^-4}{5}$, $\dfrac{^-5}{6}$

22. $\dfrac{^-9}{10}$, $\dfrac{3}{5}$, $\dfrac{^-11}{12}$

23. $^-3\dfrac{4}{7}$, $^-3\dfrac{2}{3}$, $3\dfrac{1}{2}$

24. $^-4\dfrac{1}{12}$, $^-4\dfrac{1}{5}$, $^-4\dfrac{1}{6}$

**USE DATA** For 25–26, use the table.

25. **Reasoning** Which month, January or April, had the greater decrease over average? **Explain.**

26. **Pose a Problem** Look back at Problem 25. Write and solve a similar problem using two different months.

27. **WRITE Math** Explain how to use a number line to order $^-1\dfrac{1}{4}$, $^-1\dfrac{1}{3}$, and $\dfrac{^-5}{6}$ from least to greatest.

| 2005 Northern Sierra Precipitation (in.) | | | | | |
|---|---|---|---|---|---|
| **Month** | **Jan** | **Feb** | **Mar** | **Apr** | **May** |
| **Increase or Decrease over Average** | $\dfrac{^-7}{10}$ | $\dfrac{^-18}{5}$ | $\dfrac{12}{5}$ | $\dfrac{^-2}{5}$ | $\dfrac{61}{10}$ |

## Achieving the Standards

28. What is the least common multiple of 4 and 6?
(○━┒ NS 2.4, p. 14)

29. Write $^-6.72$, $^-6.7$, $^-6.27$, and $^-7.72$ in order from least to greatest. (○━┒ NS 1.1, p. 122)

30. How much greater is the mean than the mode of 6, 6, and 9? (Grade 5 SDAP 1.1)

31. **Test Prep** Which list is ordered from least to greatest?

A $\dfrac{^-2}{3}$, $\dfrac{^-5}{6}$, $^-1\dfrac{1}{5}$

B $\dfrac{^-2}{3}$, $^-1\dfrac{1}{5}$, $\dfrac{^-5}{6}$

C $^-1\dfrac{1}{5}$, $\dfrac{^-5}{6}$, $\dfrac{^-2}{3}$

D $\dfrac{^-2}{3}$, $\dfrac{^-5}{6}$, $^-1\dfrac{1}{5}$

# 4 Compare and Order Rational Numbers

OBJECTIVE: Compare and order rational numbers.

## Learn

**PROBLEM** After a storm passes, mountain climbers observe that the temperature has changed from $^-5°$ C to $^-15°$ C. Was the temperature higher before or after the storm?

### Example 1 Compare $^-5$ and $^-15$. Place the numbers on a number line.

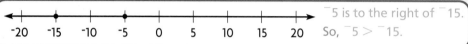

$^-5$ is to the right of $^-15$.
So, $^-5 > ^-15$.

So, the temperature was higher before the storm.

A positive number is always greater than a negative number.

### Example 2 Compare $^-2\frac{1}{5}$ and 2.2. Use < or >.

Think about the positions of the numbers on a number line.

$^-2\frac{1}{5}$ is to the left of 2.2 on a number line.

So, $^-2\frac{1}{5} < 2.2$ and $2.2 > ^-2\frac{1}{5}$.

Rational numbers can be compared easily when they are both expressed as decimals or as fractions with a common denominator.

### Example 3 Compare the numbers. Use < or >.

**A** $\frac{^-2}{5}$ ● $^-0.45$

$\frac{^-2}{5} = \frac{^-40}{100} = ^-0.40$    Write $\frac{^-2}{5}$ as a decimal with the same number of decimal places as $^-0.45$.

$^-0.40 > ^-0.45$    Compare by looking at the place values.

So, $\frac{^-2}{5} > ^-0.45$ and $^-0.45 < \frac{^-2}{5}$.

**B** $^-3\frac{3}{5}$ ● $^-3.75$

$^-3\frac{3}{5} = ^-3\frac{60}{100}$     $^-3.75 = ^-3\frac{75}{100}$    Write both numbers as mixed numbers with denominators of 100.

$^-3\frac{60}{100}$ is to the right of $^-3\frac{75}{100}$.    Think about the positions of the numbers on a number line.

So, $^-3\frac{3}{5} > ^-3.75$ and $^-3.75 < ^-3\frac{3}{5}$.

**NS 1.1** Compare and order positive and negative fractions, decimals, and mixed numbers and place them on a number line. *also* **NS 1.0**, **NS 2.0, MR 2.4, MR 2.5, MR 3.2**

# Order Rational Numbers

Rational numbers can be ordered easily once they are all expressed as decimals or as fractions with a common denominator.

**Example 4** Order $2\frac{3}{5}$, $^-2$, $^-\frac{1}{2}$, 2.4, $^-1.8$, and $\frac{9}{10}$ from least to greatest.

Write each number as a fraction or mixed number.

$$2\frac{3}{5} = 2\frac{3}{5} \qquad ^-2 = \frac{^-2}{1} \qquad ^-\frac{1}{2} = \frac{^-1}{2} \qquad 2.4 = 2\frac{4}{10} \qquad ^-1.8 = ^-1\frac{8}{10} \qquad \frac{9}{10} = \frac{9}{10}$$

Use a common denominator to write equivalent fractions.

$$2\frac{3}{5} = 2\frac{6}{10} \qquad \frac{^-2}{1} = \frac{^-20}{10} \qquad \frac{^-1}{2} = \frac{^-5}{10} \qquad 2\frac{4}{10} = 2\frac{4}{10} \qquad ^-1\frac{8}{10} = ^-1\frac{8}{10} \qquad \frac{9}{10} = \frac{9}{10}$$

Compare the fractions.

$$\frac{^-20}{10} < ^-1\frac{8}{10} < \frac{^-5}{10} < \frac{9}{10} < 2\frac{4}{10} < 2\frac{6}{10}$$

So, $^-2 < ^-1.8 < ^-\frac{1}{2} < \frac{9}{10} < 2.4 < 2\frac{3}{5}$.

So, from least to greatest, the numbers are $^-2$, $^-1.8$, $^-\frac{1}{2}$, $\frac{9}{10}$, 2.4, and $2\frac{3}{5}$.

- What is another way to find the order of $2\frac{3}{5}$, $^-2$, $^-\frac{1}{2}$, 2.4, $^-1.8$, and $\frac{9}{10}$ from least to greatest? Place the numbers on a number line.

**Example 5** If $^-\frac{1}{3}$, $^-4$, and $^-\frac{7}{8}$ were placed on a number line, which number would be closest to $^-1$?

Place the numbers on a number line.

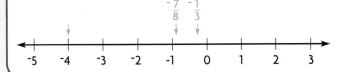

THINK: $\frac{^-3}{3} = ^-1$ and $\frac{^-8}{8} = ^-1$

So, $^-\frac{7}{8}$ would be closest to $^-1$ on a number line.

## Guided Practice

1. Look at the number line below. Which number is greater, $^-0.1$ or $^-\frac{2}{5}$?

Think: $^-\frac{2}{5} = ^-0.4$

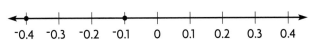

**Compare. Write <, >, or =.**

2. $\frac{-3}{4}$ ● $^-2$

3. $1.25$ ● $^-1$

4. $^-1.5$ ● $^-1\frac{1}{2}$

✓5. $^-2$ ● $\frac{1}{2}$

✓6. $^-0.5$ ● $^-1\frac{1}{2}$

7. **TALK Math** **Explain** how to use a number line to order
$\frac{-1}{2}$, $^-1.5$, and $\frac{-4}{5}$ from least to greatest.

## Independent Practice and Problem Solving

**Compare. Write <, >, or = for each ●.**

8. $^-3$ ● $2$

9. $^-3\frac{1}{8}$ ● $^-3.125$

10. $^-5.5$ ● $^-5$

11. $7.2$ ● $7\frac{1}{10}$

12. $4\frac{1}{4}$ ● $^-4.25$

13. $\frac{-3}{4}$ ● $\frac{-3}{7}$

14. $^-2\frac{1}{5}$ ● $^-2.20$

15. $^-1.5$ ● $^-1.3$

16. $^-1.5$ ● $^-1\frac{7}{8}$

17. $^-8\frac{12}{15}$ ● $^-8\frac{5}{6}$

18. $1.4 + 3.5$ ● $6\frac{3}{4} - 1\frac{1}{2}$

19. $3 \times \frac{5}{8}$ ● $2.4 \div 2$

20. $2.1 + 4\frac{1}{2}$ ● $3\frac{3}{10} + 1.5$

**Order from least to greatest.**

21. $^-7, 0, ^-5, 3$

22. $\frac{-1}{8}, \frac{-1}{4}, 0.75, ^-0.75$

23. $^-4\frac{2}{5}, \frac{2}{5}, ^-4.6, ^-5$

24. $^-2\frac{1}{2}, 2, ^-2, ^-2.1$

25. $\frac{-4}{5}, 0.80, ^-1\frac{3}{10}, ^-1.6, \frac{11}{18}, \frac{7}{9}$

26. $\frac{-5}{8}, \frac{-3}{4}, \frac{-1}{2}, \frac{-7}{8}$

27. $^-3\frac{7}{10}, \frac{2}{5}, 0.96, \frac{11}{15}, ^-3.8, \frac{-26}{8}$

28. Name three numbers in decimal form that can be ordered using this number line. Write the numbers from greatest to least.

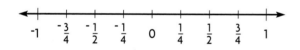

29. **≡FAST FACT** The average cloud temperature on Neptune is $^-200°$ C. Earth has an average surface temperature of $15°$ C. The average cloud temperature on Uranus is $^-193°$ C. Which is the lowest temperature?

30. If $\frac{-2}{5}$, $^-2$, and $\frac{7}{10}$ were placed on a number line, which number would be closest to 0?

31. **WRITE Math** **Explain** how to order a negative fraction, a negative decimal, and a positive integer from greatest to least.

## Achieving the Standards

32. A deep-sea diver is 22 feet below the surface of the water. If 0 represents the surface of the water, what integer represents the location of the diver? (Grade 5, O━▥ NS 1.5)

33. If $y = 8$, what is the value of $6 + y$?
(Grade 5, O━▥ AF 1.2)

34. What is the volume of a rectangular prism with a length of 5 inches, a width of 3 inches, and a height of 8 inches? (Grade 5, O━▥ MS 1.3)

35. **Test Prep** What number is greater than $^-3.2$?

A $^-3.3$

B $^-3\frac{1}{4}$

C $^-3\frac{1}{5}$

D $3\frac{3}{5}$

# Bone Dry

**Reading Skill** Draw Conclusions

◀ The worst drought in the history of California lasted from 1987 to 1992.

The Palmer Drought Severity Index (PDSI) uses temperature and rainfall information to determine dryness. A drought is an extended period of time with less rainfall than is expected. Normal conditions are represented using 0. Negative numbers represent dry conditions and positive numbers represent wet conditions. For example, $^-5.8$ on the index indicates a very dry condition.

The map shows conditions in California in 1992. Which part of the state had conditions rated less than $^-2$, northern or southern California? Are those conditions wet or dry?

Use the map and the index to draw conclusions. Think about the following questions to help you solve the problem.

- What color on the map represents $^-2$?

- What colors on the map represent numbers less than $^-2$?

- What colors are shown in northern California? In southern Calfornia?

The Palmer Drought Severity Index

dry            wet

$^-6$   $^-4$   $^-2$   0   2   4   6

California Drought 1992

## Problem Solving Draw conclusions to solve.

1. Solve the problem above.

2. If you had driven from southern to northern California in 1992, would the conditions have changed from wet to dry or from dry to wet? Would the numbers in the Palmer Drought Severity Index have increased or decreased?

# Problem Solving Workshop
## Strategy: Make a Table

**OBJECTIVE:** Solve problems by using the strategy *make a table*.

## Learn the Strategy

You can make a table to organize information that will help you solve problems.

### A table can show patterns.

Nicky puts 2 pennies in a jar on Monday, 4 pennies on Tuesday, 8 pennies on Wednesday, and 16 pennies on Thursday.

| Day | M | T | W | Th |
|---|---|---|---|---|
| Number of Pennies | 2 | 4 | 8 | 16 |

×2  ×2  ×2

### A table can show schedules.

A 35-min tour of the Science Museum for fourth-grade students starts at 9:30 A.M. Then, fifth-grade students take a 65-min tour. At 1:15 P.M., sixth-grade students go on an hour tour.

| Grade | Start Time | End Time |
|---|---|---|
| 4 | 9:30 A.M. | ? |
| 5 | ? | 11:10 A.M. |
| 6 | 1:15 P.M. | ? |

### A table can show combinations.

Find all possible ways to make 50¢ using only quarters, dimes, and nickels.

Extend the table to show all the possible combinations.

| Quarters | Dimes | Nickels |
|---|---|---|
| 2 | 0 | 0 |
| 1 | 2 | 1 |
| 1 | 1 | 3 |
| 1 | 0 | 5 |
| 0 | 5 | 0 |
| 0 | 4 | 2 |

**TALK Math**

What types of information are organized in tables at your school? How do those tables help you?

NS 1.0 Students compare and order positive and negative fractions, decimals, and mixed numbers. Students solve problems involving fractions, ratios, proportions, and percentages: *also* NS 1.1, MR 1.0, MR 2.0, MR 2.4, MR 2.5, MR 2.7, MR 3.0, MR 3.1, MR 3.2, MR 3.3

# Use the Strategy

**PROBLEM** In a number game, each player chooses two number cards and either a positive or a negative sign card. Players use the numbers and sign to form six possible rational numbers by switching the order of the numbers, inserting a decimal point, or by using the numbers to form fractions. The first player to order his or her numbers from least to greatest wins.

Rachel chooses the numbers 2 and 4 and a negative sign. What is the order of Rachel's numbers from least to greatest?

## Read to Understand

Reading Skill

- **What is the sequence of steps in playing the game?**
- **What information is given?**

## Plan

- **What strategy can you use to solve the problem?**

  You can use *make a table* to help you solve the problem.

## Solve

- **How can you use the strategy to solve the problem?**

  First, make a table to show the 6 possible rational numbers Rachel can make.

| Fraction | | Decimals | | Integers | |
|---|---|---|---|---|---|
| $\frac{^-2}{4}$ | $\frac{^-4}{2}$ | $^-2.4$ | $^-4.2$ | $^-24$ | $^-42$ |

Then, write the fractions and integers as decimals with the same number of decimal places as $^-2.4$ and $^-4.2$ and compare the numbers.

$$^-42.0 < {^-24.0} < {^-4.2} < {^-2.4} < {^-2.0} < {^-0.5}$$

So, Rachel's numbers in order from least to greatest are $^-42$, $^-24$, $^-4.2$, $^-2.4$, $\frac{^-4}{2}$, and $\frac{^-2}{4}$.

## Check

- **How can you check your answer?**

1. Ron is playing the number game with Rachel. He chooses the numbers 6 and 3 and a positive sign. What is the order of Ron's numbers from least to greatest?

   **First,** make a table to show six possible rational numbers Ron can make.

   | Fractions | | Decimals | | Integers | |
   |:---:|:---:|:---:|:---:|:---:|:---:|
   | $\frac{6}{3}$ | $\frac{3}{6}$ | ■ | ■ | ■ | ■ |

   **Then,** write all the numbers as decimals or as fractions with a common denominator.

   **Finally,** compare the numbers and write them in order from least to greatest.

✓ 2. **What if** Ron chooses 6 and 0? Will he still be able to make six rational numbers? **Explain.**

✓ 3. Beth and Mark are playing a number game. Players take turns choosing two number cards and a sign card. Each player uses his or her numbers and sign to form one rational number. The player with the greater number scores 1 point if it is an integer, 2 points if it is a decimal, and 3 points if it is a fraction. What is the score after 5 rounds?

   | Number Game | | | | | |
   |:---:|:---:|:---:|:---:|:---:|:---:|
   | Round | 1 | 2 | 3 | 4 | 5 |
   | Beth | $\frac{6}{5}$ | ⁻12 | ⁻7.8 | ⁻$\frac{5}{2}$ | ⁻4.9 |
   | Mark | ⁻55 | ⁻10 | 11 | ⁻2.4 | ⁻7.4 |

## Problem Solving Strategy Practice

**Use** *make a table* **to solve.**

4. Monica scored 10, 20, or 30 points on each round of a computer game. Her total score after 5 rounds was 90 points. How many different combinations of 10, 20, or 30 points could she have scored? List the combinations.

5. Customers at the local video store get 2 free video game rentals for every 6 video games they rent. Jason got 16 free video game rentals last year. How many video games did he rent?

6. Hector began playing a board game Saturday morning at 10:15. He finished the game 40 min later. Then, Hector played a card game for 70 min. At 1:10 P.M., he finally started his chores. How much time elapsed between the end of Hector's card game and the time he started his chores?

7. The diagram shows the number of squares in each row of a game board that Rosa is designing. If the pattern continues, how many squares will be in Row 8?

   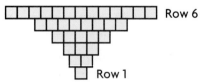

   Row 6
   Row 1

## Mixed Strategy Practice

**Solve.**

8. A square game board is divided into 36 equally-sized squares. Kelly's game piece is in the bottom left square. Game pieces can not be moved diagonally, so she moves her game piece 2 squares up, 3 squares to the right, 3 squares up, 2 squares to the left, 1 square down, and 1 square to the left. What is the fewest number of squares Kelly can move her game piece to return it to the bottom left square?

9. **Open-Ended Problem** Look at Problem 8. Write at least 3 other ways that Kelly could have moved her game piece from the bottom left square to the square where she ended up. Each way should use at least 5 moves of 3 squares or less.

## Problem-Solving STRATEGIES

Use Logical Reasoning

Draw a Diagram or Picture

Make a Model or Act It Out

Make an Organized List

Find a Pattern

Make a Table or Graph

Guess and Check

Work Backward

Solve a Simpler Problem

Write an Equation

**USE DATA** For 10–13, use the bar graph.

10. The number of girls who voted for computer games is $2\frac{1}{2}$ times as great as the number of boys who voted for computer games. How many girls voted for computer games?

11. Ana, Fran, Oscar, and Sam each voted for a different type of game. Ana voted for board games. Oscar did not vote for video games. Fran did not vote for computer games or video games. What type of game did each student vote for?

12. **Pose a Problem** Change the names in Problem 11 to names of your friends or classmates. Then change the clues to describe how you think each person would vote. Have a classmate solve the new problem.

13. The number of students who participated in the survey this year is 14 more than 3.5 times the number of students who participated last year. How many students participated in the survey last year?

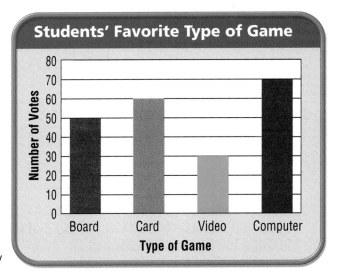

**Students' Favorite Type of Game**

14. **WRITE Math** ▶ **What's the Question?** Each week at a local game café, every 40th customer gets a free drink and every 50th customer gets a free snack. The 200th customer got a free drink and a free snack.

## CHALLENGE YOURSELF

**Ellen, Ray, and Alvin are playing a game with play money. Ellen has 9 dimes, Ray has 5 quarters, and Alvin has 11 nickels.**

15. The amount of money in the game bank is $3.05 less than 6 times the amount that Ellen, Ray, and Alvin have together. How much money is in the game bank?

16. During the next round of the game, Ellen gives Ray 2 dimes, Ray gives Alvin 1 quarter, and Alvin gives Ellen 4 nickels. How much money does each student have now?

# Extra Practice

## Set A Write the rational number in the form $\frac{a}{b}$. (pp. 118–121)

1. 2.6
2. $^-5$
3. $4\frac{3}{8}$
4. $^-0.125$
5. $^-2\frac{1}{6}$
6. 0.15

7. $7\frac{2}{5}$
8. 10
9. $^-2.49$
10. $^-5\frac{2}{3}$
11. 3.75
12. 72

13. Tonya is reading a novel that has 21 chapters. She has read $6\frac{7}{9}$ chapters. Write the amount read by Tonya in the form $\frac{a}{b}$.

14. Alonzo's baked ziti recipe used 4.25 cups of pasta. Write the amount of pasta used in the recipe in the form $\frac{a}{b}$.

## Set B Compare. Write < or >. (pp. 122–123)

1. $^-0.36$ ● $0.32$
2. $4.14$ ● $4.1$
3. $^-0.08$ ● $^-0.02$
4. $5.7$ ● $^-5.9$

5. $7.12$ ● $7.26$
6. $^-0.12$ ● $^-0.13$
7. $^-1.52$ ● $1.52$
8. $12.11$ ● $^-12.12$

Order from least to greatest.

9. $^-3.16, 3.6, ^-3.06, 0.31$

10. $2.04, ^-2.4, ^-0.29, 0.24$

## Set C Compare. Write < or >. (pp. 124–125)

1. $\frac{3}{4}$ ● $\frac{5}{6}$
2. $\frac{12}{13}$ ● $\frac{14}{15}$
3. $\frac{2}{3}$ ● $\frac{3}{5}$
4. $\frac{2}{7}$ ● $\frac{1}{6}$

5. $\frac{6}{7}$ ● $\frac{7}{15}$
6. $\frac{5}{13}$ ● $\frac{3}{4}$
7. $\frac{7}{8}$ ● $\frac{7}{11}$
8. $\frac{15}{16}$ ● $\frac{7}{8}$

Order from least to greatest.

9. $\frac{7}{12}, \frac{1}{12}, \frac{1}{2}$
10. $\frac{^-5}{6}, ^-1, \frac{^-2}{3}$
11. $\frac{^-3}{10}, \frac{^-2}{5}, \frac{^-1}{5}$
12. $3\frac{1}{3}, ^-3\frac{2}{3}, 3\frac{1}{6}$

13 $\frac{1}{4}, \frac{1}{3}, \frac{1}{2}$
14. $\frac{^-1}{4}, \frac{3}{4}, \frac{^-1}{2}$
15. $8\frac{1}{7}, ^-8\frac{1}{5}, 8\frac{5}{7}$
16. $^-2, ^-2\frac{5}{8}, ^-2\frac{1}{4}$

17. Greg, Lem, and Tony painted a fence. Greg painted $\frac{1}{3}$ of the fence. Lem painted $\frac{1}{6}$ of the fence. Tony painted $\frac{1}{2}$ of the fence. Order the men from the one who painted the least amount of fence to the one who painted the greatest amount of fence.

18. Marla wanted to bake a cake for a surprise party. The recipe called for $\frac{2}{3}$ cup sugar, $1\frac{3}{4}$ cups flour, and $1\frac{1}{2}$ cups milk. Order the ingredients from the greatest amount to the least amount.

## Set D Compare. Write <, >, or =. (pp. 126–129)

1. $^-4$ ● $3$
2. $6$ ● $6.5$
3. $2.3$ ● $2$
4. $\frac{4}{5}$ ● $^-2\frac{3}{5}$

5. $^-3\frac{1}{8}$ ● $\frac{5}{8}$
6. $1$ ● $^-1.45$
7. $^-0.6$ ● $\frac{1}{2}$
8. $^-1.10$ ● $^-1\frac{1}{10}$

9. $\frac{1}{3}$ ● $0.36$
10. $\frac{6}{7}$ ● $0.99$
11. $\frac{^-2}{5}$ ● $^-0.30$
12. $^-5.4$ ● $^-5\frac{1}{4}$

Order from least to greatest.

13. $\frac{2}{5}, 0.45, \frac{^-1}{3}, ^-3$

14. $^-1\frac{1}{5}, ^-1.6, \frac{3}{4}, ^-1, \frac{5}{6}$

15. $^-2\frac{4}{5}, ^-2.75, ^-0.25, ^-2.5$

# Is It Rational?

**Players**
2 players

**Materials**
- Rational number cards
- 2 different coins
- Number cube, labeled 1–6

Move back 2 spaces

Lose a turn

Move back 3 spaces

Go again!

Move forward 4 spaces

Lose a turn

Go again!

Move forward 4 spaces

Move back 3 spaces

Lose a turn

FINISH

START

## How to Play

- Place the number cards facedown in a pile.
- Each player selects a coin and places the coin on START. Decide who will go first.
- Player 1 draws one card from the pile and writes the number shown on the card in the form $\frac{a}{b}$.
- Player 2 checks the answer. If it is correct, Player 1 rolls the number cube and moves his or her coin the number of spaces shown.
- If the answer is correct or incorrect, play passes to Player 2.
- The first player to reach FINISH wins.

# Chapter 5 Review/Test

## Check Vocabulary and Concepts

**Choose the best term from the box.**

1. A __?__ is any number that can be written as a ratio $\frac{a}{b}$, where $a$ and $b$ are integers and $b$ is not equal to 0. (O⎯┓ NS 1.0, p. 118)

2. A __?__ is a comparison of two numbers, $a$ and $b$, written as a fraction $\frac{a}{b}$. (O⎯┓ NS 1.0, p. 118)

## Check Skills

**Write the rational number in the form $\frac{a}{b}$.** (O⎯┓ NS 1.2, pp. 118–121)

3. $^-7$          4. 4.3          5. $^-8.54$          6. $2\frac{4}{7}$          7. $^-5\frac{1}{9}$

**Compare. Write $<$ or $>$.** (O⎯┓ NS 1.1, pp. 122–123)

8. 1.5 ● $^-1.5$          9. $^-2.1$ ● 2.2          10. $^-4.31$ ● 4.3          11. 7.2 ● $^-7.24$

12. $^-1.08$ ● $^-1.81$          13. $^-0.48$ ● $^-0.41$          14. $^-1.03$ ● $^-1.0$          15. $^-4.34$ ● $^-4.4$

**Compare. Write $<$, $>$, or $=$.** (O⎯┓ NS 1.1, pp. 124–125, 126–129)

16. $\frac{3}{4}$ ● $\frac{-1}{2}$          17. $^-2\frac{1}{8}$ ● $^-1\frac{5}{8}$          18. $\frac{-1}{4}$ ● $\frac{5}{12}$          19. $^-7\frac{1}{2}$ ● 7.5

20. $^-3$ ● $^-3.3$          21. $^-2\frac{2}{5}$ ● $^-2.45$          22. $^-1\frac{3}{4}$ ● $^-1\frac{4}{5}$          23. $^-8.9$ ● $^-8\frac{8}{10}$

**Order from least to greatest.** (O⎯┓ NS 1.1, pp. 122–123, 124–125, 126–129)

24. $^-0.21$, $^-0.255$, $^-0.2$

25. $\frac{3}{7}$, $\frac{3}{5}$, $\frac{3}{4}$

26. $^-2\frac{7}{8}$, $^-3\frac{1}{4}$, $2\frac{4}{5}$

27. $^-0.45$, 0.83, 0.41, $^-0.87$

28. $\frac{-2}{3}$, 0.62, $^-1\frac{7}{10}$, 1.5, $\frac{10}{15}$, $\frac{6}{7}$

29. $^-3\frac{1}{3}$, 3, $^-3.1$, $3\frac{2}{3}$, $^-3.7$, 3.65

30. $^-0.7$, $\frac{4}{5}$, $1\frac{1}{2}$, $\frac{8}{9}$, $\frac{7}{10}$, $^-3$

31. $^-1\frac{1}{4}$, $\frac{7}{8}$, $\frac{-3}{4}$, $\frac{5}{6}$, $^-2$, $\frac{-2}{5}$

## Check Problem Solving

**Solve.** (O⎯┓ NS 1.0, MR 2.4, pp. 130–133)

32. Lance has only nickels and dimes in his pocket. The total amount of change in his pocket is $0.65. How many different combinations of nickels and dimes could Lance have in his pocket? List the combinations.

33. **WRITE Math** ▶ **What's the Error?** Todd says that decimals are not rational numbers because they do not have a numerator and a denominator. What is wrong with Todd's statement? **Explain.**

# Enrich • Compare Absolute Values

## ⟩ Math Club Challenge ⟨

The Math Club at Fred's school posts problems on the club's website each day for members to solve. Today's problems involve absolute value. Absolute value is the distance of an integer from zero.

### Example 1

Which is greater, $\left|\dfrac{^-3}{5}\right|$ or $|0.7|$?

$\left|\dfrac{^-3}{5}\right| = \dfrac{3}{5}$ $\qquad$ $|0.7| = 0.7$ $\qquad$ Find the absolute value of each number.

$\dfrac{3}{5} = \dfrac{6}{10} = 0.6$ $\qquad$ Write $\dfrac{3}{5}$ as a decimal.

$0.6 < 0.7$ and $0.7 > 0.6$ $\qquad$ Compare the numbers.

So, $|0.7|$ is greater.

### Example 2

Compare $|^-8|$ and $|^-9|$. Which number is less?

$|^-8| = 8$ $\qquad$ $|^-9| = 9$ $\qquad$ Find the absolute value of each number.

$9 > 8$ and $8 < 9$ $\qquad$ Compare the numbers.

So, $|^-8|$ is less.

### Work Out

Compare. Write $<$, $>$, or $=$ for each ●.

1. $\left|\dfrac{^-5}{8}\right|$ ● $|^-0.625|$

2. $|5|$ ● $|5.7|$

3. $\left|^-9\dfrac{3}{4}\right|$ ● $|^-9.75|$

4. $\left|^-6\dfrac{2}{3}\right|$ ● $\left|^-6\dfrac{7}{12}\right|$

5. $\left|1\dfrac{1}{4}\right|$ ● $\left|^-1\dfrac{1}{6}\right|$

6. $|^-3|$ ● $|3|$

7. $\left|\dfrac{^-7}{3}\right|$ ● $\left|\dfrac{^-13}{12}\right|$

8. $|^-2.76|$ ● $|2.78|$

### Cool Down

**WRITE Math** ▶ Explain how to compare $|^-7.9|$ and $\left|^-7\dfrac{4}{5}\right|$.

# Achieving the Standards

 Chapters 1 – 5

## Number Sense

1. Taylor runs 1.5 miles and swims 1.8 miles each day. Which rational number is between 1.5 and 1.8? (O▬ NS 1.1)

   A 2.1

   B 1.9

   C 1.81

   D 1.75

**Test Tip** **Eliminate choices.**

See item 2. First order the choices on a number line. Choose the one closest to 0.

2. Which of the following fractions is closest to 0? (O▬ NS 1.1)

   A $\frac{2}{3}$

   B $\frac{4}{9}$

   C $-\frac{1}{10}$

   D $\frac{-3}{5}$

3. What is the value of $n$ if $\frac{n}{12} = \frac{5}{3}$? (O▬ NS 2.4)

   A 4

   B 12

   C 20

   D 60

4. **WRITE Math** Jan held the record for the 100-meter dash for $\frac{3}{4}$ of the year. Eva held it for $\frac{1}{12}$ of the year, and Amy held it for $\frac{1}{6}$ of the year. **Explain** how to order these fractions from least to greatest. Who held the record for the shortest time, and who held it for the longest time? (O▬ NS 1.1)

## Measurement and Geometry

5. Which of the following *best* describes the figure? (Grade 5 O▬ MG 2.1)

   A acute angle

   B perpendicular lines

   C right angle

   D parallel lines

6. Triangle *PQR* is a right triangle, and the measures of angles *P* and *Q* are equal. What is the measure of angle *P*? (Grade 5 O▬ MG 2.2)

   A 45°         C 25°

   B 35°         D 15°

7. What is the measure of angle *w* in the figure below? (Grade 5 O▬ MG 2.2)

   A 30°

   B 60°

   C 90°

   D 150°

8. **WRITE Math** What's the Error? Zane says that the volume of the rectangular box below is 16 square inches. **Describe** and correct Zane's error. (Grade 5 MG 2.3)

   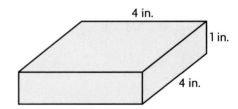

## Algebra and Functions

**9.** If $n = 8$, what is the value of $n + 3$?
(Grade 5 **O—n** AF 1.2)

**A** 3          **C** 11

**B** 5          **D** 24

**10.** What are the coordinates of point $D$?
(Grade 5 **O—n** AF 1.4)

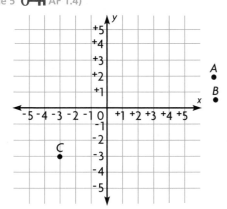

**A** $(^-3,3)$      **C** $(4,3)$

**B** $(3,3)$      **D** $(3,^-3)$

**11.** What value for $n$ makes the following equation true? (Grade 5 AF 1.3)

$$54 \times 6 = (50 \times 6) + (n \times 6)$$

**A** 0          **C** 5

**B** 4          **D** 6

**12.** ◖**WRITE Math**▸ Copy and complete the function table.

$$y = 12 - x$$

| $x$ | 0 | 1 | 2 | 3 | 4 | 5 | 6 |
|-----|---|---|---|---|---|---|---|
| $y$ |   |   |   |   |   |   |   |

**Explain** how you used the table and the equation to find the missing $y$ values.
(Grade 5 **O—n** AF 1.2)

## Statistics, Data Analysis, and Probability

**13.** Mrs. Chang recorded the time it took 5 of her students to complete a test. The times were 22, 26, 29, 32, and 41 minutes. What was the mean time required to complete the test by these students? (Grade 5 SDAP 1.1)

**A** 18 minutes

**B** 29 minutes

**C** 30 minutes

**D** 41 minutes

**14.** Gabriel and Joshua enjoy playing a board game. The differences in their scores for the last 7 games are 42, 77, 66, 102, 12, 39, and 98 points. What was the median difference in their scores for the last 7 games?
(Grade 5 SDAP 1.1)

**A** 12

**B** 66

**C** 77

**D** 102

**15.** ◖**WRITE Math**▸ **Sense or Nonsense** There are 32 students in Mr. Gauss's class and 25 students in Mrs. Taylor's class. Using the circle graphs below, Loretta concluded that Mrs. Taylor's class has more boys than Mr. Gauss's class. Do you agree with Loretta? **Explain.** (Grade 5 SDAP 1.3)

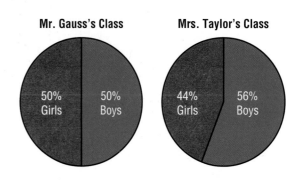

# 6 Add and Subtract Integers

**The Big Idea** The number line can be extended to show negative numbers; operations with integers are based on operations with whole numbers.

## Investigate

Suppose you and your team are hiking along a mountain range and have set up camp for the night at an elevation of 3,135 feet. As navigator, you graph your team's trail for tomorrow's hike as shown below. Describe what you know about tomorrow's hike according to the graph.

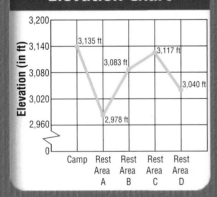

**Elevation Chart**

Elevation (in ft)

3,200
3,140 — 3,135 ft / 3,117 ft
3,083 ft
3,080
3,040 ft
3,020
2,960 — 2,978 ft
0

Camp | Rest Area A | Rest Area B | Rest Area C | Rest Area D

## CALIFORNIA FAST FACT

The Avalanche Gulch route up Mount Shasta, in California, is one of the most popular climbing routes in the United States. Approximately 15,000 climbers each year attempt to reach the summit by that route.

**GO ONLINE**

**Technology**
Student pages are available in the Student eBook.

Check your understanding of important skills
needed for success in Chapter 6.

▶ **Identify Integers on a Number Line**

Copy the number line. Graph the numbers on the number line.

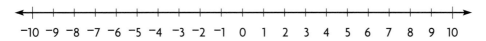

**1.** 5      **2.** 0      **3.** ⁻4      **4.** ⁻1      **5.** 3

**6.** ⁻2      **7.** ⁻5      **8.** 2      **9.** 4      **10.** ⁻3

▶ **Understand Integers**

Write a positive or negative integer to represent the situation.

**11.** 12°F below zero      **12.** 49°F above zero

**13.** 120 ft above sea level      **14.** 15 ft below sea level

**15.** 106 ft above ground level      **16.** a gain of 27 yd

**17.** a bank withdrawal of $440      **18.** a bank deposit of $250

**19.** an increase of 2 cents in the price of gas      **20.** a decrease of 8 cents in the price of gas

**21.** a loss of 5 yd      **22.** 22 ft below ground level

**23.** 21°F above zero      **24.** 13°F below zero

# VOCABULARY POWER

**CHAPTER VOCABULARY**

additive inverse

**WARM-UP WORDS**

**additive inverse** the opposite of a given number

**opposites** two numbers that are an equal distance from zero on the number line

**addends** numbers that are added in an addition problem

# 1 Model Addition

OBJECTIVE: Model addition of integers.

## Investigate

**Materials** ■ two-color counters

You can use counters to find the sum of integers. Use yellow counters to represent positive integers and red counters to represent negative integers.

**A** Use yellow counters to represent 3 and 4.

**B** Combine the yellow counters. The counters represent the sum $3 + 4$.

**C** Use a number sentence to record your sum.

**D** Use red counters to represent ⁻3 and ⁻4.

**E** Combine the red counters. The counters represent the sum ⁻3 + ⁻4.

**F** Use a number sentence to record your sum.

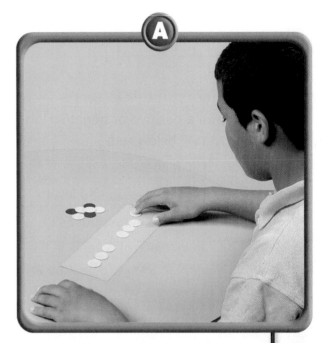

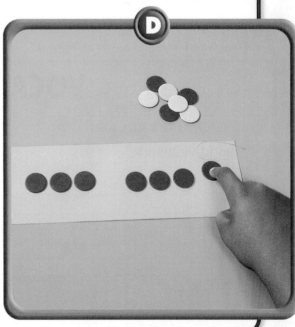

## Draw Conclusions

1. How is adding two negative integers or two positive integers like adding whole numbers? How is it different?

2. Would changing the order of the addends change the sum? Explain.

3. How would you model ⁻2 + ⁻7; how would you model $5 + 6$?

4. **Evaluation** If the signs of the addends are the same, what will be the sign of the sum?

O⊣ **NS 2.3** Solve addition, subtraction, multiplication, and division problems, including those arising in concrete situations, that use positive and negative integers and combinations of these operations. *also*
O⊣ **NS 2.0, MR 2.0, MR 2.4, MR 2.5, MR 3.2**

## Connect

The **additive inverse** of an integer is its opposite. The integers 1 and ⁻1 are additive inverses of each other. When you add an integer and its additive inverse, the sum is always 0.

### Example Find 1 + ⁻1.

Model the sum of 1 and its additive inverse, ⁻1.

 = 0

So, 1 + ⁻1 = 0.

### More Examples

**A** Find ⁻2 + 3.

Model ⁻2 + 3.

Pairs of red and yellow counters equal 0. The remaining counter models the sum.

So, ⁻2 + 3 = 1.

**B** Find 2 + ⁻5.

Model 2 + ⁻5.

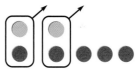

Pairs of yellow and red counters equal 0. The remaining counters model the sum.

So, 2 + ⁻5 = ⁻3.

**TALK Math**

Explain why the sum of 2 and ⁻5 is negative.

## Practice

**Use counters to find the sum of each pair of numbers.**

**1.** 4 + ⁻1 = ▧

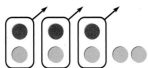

**2.** ⁻5 + 4 = ▧

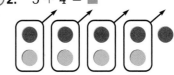

**3.** ⁻3 + 5 = ▧

**4.** 4 + ⁻6 = ▧

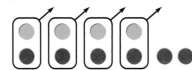

| | | | |
|---|---|---|---|
| **5.** ⁻3 + 6 | **6.** 7 + ⁻7 | **7.** 8 + 2 | **8.** ⁻6 + ⁻3 |
| **9.** ⁻8 + ⁻3 | **10.** 5 + ⁻4 | **11.** 2 + ⁻2 | **12.** ⁻9 + 4 |
| **13.** 8 + ⁻9 | **14.** ⁻4 + 7 | **15.** ⁻3 + 5 | **16.** 2 + ⁻8 |

**17.** **WRITE Math** Explain how to use counters to find the sum ⁻2 + 6.

# Record Addition

OBJECTIVE: Add integers by using number lines and absolute values.

## Quick Review

Use a number line to solve.

1. $7 + 6$     2. $5 + 9$
3. $8 + 4$     4. $14 + 2$
5. $3 + 26$

## Learn

**PROBLEM** On the first play of a football game, the home team gained 7 yd. On the second play, it lost 8 yd. How many yards did the home team gain or lose on the first two plays of the game?

Find $7 + {}^-8$ to solve the problem.

**ONE WAY** Use a model.

**Ⓐ Counters**

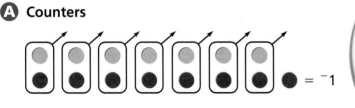

$\bullet = {}^-1$

**Remember**
Pairs of red and yellow counters equal 0.

**Ⓑ Number Line**

Draw a number line.

Start at 0. Move 7 units to the right to show 7.

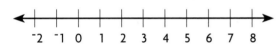

From 7, move 8 units to the left to show $^-8$. This takes you to $^-1$.

So, the sum of the yards in the two plays is $^-1$. This means that the home team lost 1 yd on the first two plays of the game.

- **What if** the team lost 4 yd on the first play and lost 3 yd on the second play of the game? Use a number line to find how many yards the team lost in all.

- When integers are added on a number line, when do the arrows point in the same direction? When do the arrows point in different directions?

NS 2.3 Solve addition, subtraction, multiplication, and division problems, including those arising in concrete situations, that use positive and negative integers and combinations of these operations.
also NS 2.0, MR 2.4, MR 2.5, MR 3.0, MR 3.2, MR 3.3

# Use Absolute Values

> **Adding with the Same Sign**
>
> When adding integers with like signs, add the absolute values of the addends. Use the sign of the addends for the sum.

**ANOTHER WAY**  Use absolute value.

## Example 1 Find ⁻6 + ⁻3.

$$⁻6 + ⁻3$$
$$|⁻6| + |⁻3| = 6 + 3 \qquad \text{Add the absolute values of the integers.}$$
$$= 9$$

Use the sign of the original addends. So, ⁻6 + ⁻3 = ⁻9.

> **Adding with Different Signs**
>
> When adding integers with unlike signs, subtract the lesser absolute value from the greater absolute value. Use the sign of the addend with the greater absolute value for the sum.

## Example 2

**Ⓐ Find ⁻1 + 5.**

$$⁻1 + 5$$
$$|5| − |⁻1| = 5 − 1 \qquad \text{|5| > |⁻1|, so subtract}$$
$$= 4 \qquad \text{|⁻1| from |5|.}$$

Use the sign of the addend with the greater absolute value. Use the positive sign of the 5. The sum is positive.

$$|5| > |⁻1|$$

So, ⁻1 + 5 = 4.

**Ⓑ Find 2 + ⁻8.**

$$2 + ⁻8$$
$$|⁻8| − |2| = 8 − 2 \qquad \text{|⁻8| > |2|, so subtract}$$
$$= 6 \qquad \text{|2| from |⁻8|.}$$

Use the sign of the addend with the greater absolute value. Use the negative sign of the 8. The sum is negative.

$$|⁻8| > |2|$$

So, 2 + ⁻8 = ⁻6.

• How can you check your results in the above problems?

You can use this key sequence on a calculator to find 2 + ⁻8.

2  **+**  **(−)**  8  **Enter =**  $2 + ⁻8 = ⁻6$

---

## Guided Practice

**1.** Use the number line to find ⁻6 + 4.

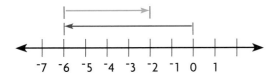

**2.** Use the number line to find 6 + ⁻7.

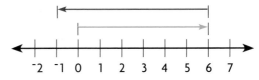

**Write the addition problem modeled on the number line.**

**3.**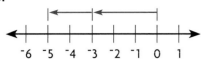

**✓4.**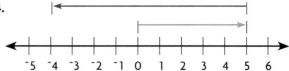

**Find the sum.**

**5.** ⁻4 + 5

**6.** ⁻2 + ⁻6

**7.** 3 + 3

**8.** ⁻7 + 1

**✓9.** ⁻25 + ⁻12

**10.** ⁻9 + ⁻6

**11.** ⁻15 + 3

**12.** 16 + ⁻14

**13.** ⁻23 + ⁻9

**14.** ⁻19 + 24

**15.** TALK Math   **Explain** how you determine the sign of the sum of two integers.

## Independent Practice and Problem Solving

**Write the addition problem modeled on the number line.**

**16.**

**17.**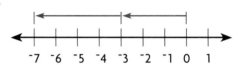

**Find the sum.**

**18.** ⁻2 + ⁻1

**19.** 4 + 2

**20.** ⁻5 + 9

**21.** 3 + ⁻6

**22.** ⁻6 + 4

**23.** 9 + ⁻8

**24.** 0 + ⁻5

**25.** ⁻10 + ⁻16

**26.** ⁻4 + 16

**27.** 15 + ⁻15

**28.** ⁻12 + ⁻7

**29.** ⁻18 + 5

**30.** 17 + 12

**31.** 22 + ⁻19

**32.** ⁻48 + 34

**Use mental math to find the value of the variable.**

**33.** ⁻3 + $x$ = ⁻6

**34.** $n$ + ⁻8 = ⁻10

**35.** 6 + $s$ = 0

**36.** $b$ + 12 = 7

**37.** ⁻4 + $t$ = ⁻14

**38.** $y$ + ⁻3 = 5

**39.** $x$ + 2 = ⁻6

**40.** 38 + $a$ = 1

**41.** A nationally televised football game usually begins at about 6:00 P.M. on the East Coast. Using the number line at the right, what addition number sentence could you write to show the time on the West Coast at the start of the game?

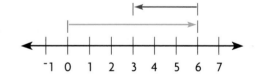

**42.** Write a situation that this addition problem could represent.

$$⁻16 + 9 = ⁻7$$

**43. Reasoning** Is the sum of a positive integer and ⁻7 greater than or less than ⁻7? **Explain.**

**44.** At the start of the game, the Wildcats were penalized 5 yd for delaying the game. Then they were penalized another 5 yd for having too many players on the field. After their first play, they gained 12 yd. How many yards have they gained or lost in all?

**45.** WRITE Math ▸ **What's the Question?** A number line shows a blue arrow beginning at 0 and ending at 5. It also shows a red arrow above the blue arrow beginning at 5 and ending at ⁻3. The answer is ⁻3.

**Technology**
Use Harcourt Mega Math, Fraction
Action, *Number Line Mine*, Level W.

Extra Practice on page 162, Set A

46. Alexandra received the scores 9.820, 9.082, 8.910, 9.258, and 9.750 at her gymnastics competition. Write the scores in order from least to greatest. (O━━ NS 1.1, p. 122)

47. What is the difference $41 - 17$? (Grade 5 NS 1.0)

48. **Test Prep** $^-9 + {}^-3$

   **A** $^-12$

   **B** $^-6$

   **C** $6$

   **D** $12$

49. What is the name of a portion of a line extending in one direction from a single point? (Grade 5 MG 2.0)

50. **Test Prep** The temperature in the morning was $^-3°F$. The temperature rose $8°F$ by noon. What was the temperature at noon?

   **A** $^-11°F$

   **B** $^-5°F$

   **C** $5°F$

   **D** $11°F$

## Problem Solving and Reasoning

**NUMBER SENSE** You can use the Commutative and Associative Properties of Addition to simplify the addition of integers.

### Commutative Property of Addition

$$^-1 + 3 = 3 + {}^-1$$
$$= |3| - |{}^-1|$$
$$= 3 - 1$$
$$= 2$$

Change the order of the addends.

### Associative Property of Addition

$$1 + (3 + {}^-1) = (1 + 3) + {}^-1$$
$$= 4 + {}^-1$$
$$= |4| - |{}^-1|$$
$$= 4 - 1$$
$$= 3$$

Change the grouping of the addends.

You can use both properties together to simplify problems involving the addition of integers.

### Commutative and Associative Properties of Addition

$$17 + (9 + {}^-17) = (17 + {}^-17) + 9$$
$$= 0 + 9$$
$$= 9$$

Change the order and the grouping of the addends.

**Use the Commutative and Associative Properties to help find the sum.**

1. $^-5 + {}^-6 + 5$

2. $(10 + {}^-5) + {}^-2$

3. $^-7 + 2 + {}^-12$

4. $^-6 + (6 + {}^-8)$

5. $^-14 + 19 + {}^-9$

6. $(15 + {}^-3) + 25$

7. $^-23 + ({}^-18 + 23)$

8. $^-19 + 24$

# 3 Model Subtraction

OBJECTIVE: Model subtraction of integers.

## Investigate

**Materials** ■ two-color counters

You can use counters to find the difference of integers.

Ⓐ Find ⁻3 − ⁻1. Use red counters to represent ⁻3.

Ⓑ Take away 1 red counter. The remaining counters represent the difference ⁻3 − ⁻1.

$$^-3 - {^-1} = {^-2}$$

Ⓒ Find 3 − 7. Use yellow counters to represent 3.

Ⓓ Adding a red counter paired with a yellow counter does not change the value of 3. Show another way to model 3 that includes 7 yellow counters.

Ⓔ Use your model to find 3 − 7. Take away 7 yellow counters. The remaining counters represent the difference 3 − 7.

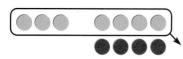

$$3 - 7 = {^-4}$$

## Draw Conclusions

1. Why was it necessary to use pairs of red and yellow counters in Step D?

2. **Synthesis** How could you model the difference ⁻2 − 5?

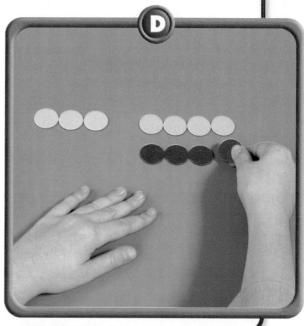

○━┓ NS 2.3 Solve addition, subtraction, multiplication, and division problems, including those arising in concrete situations, that use positive and negative integers and combinations of these operations. *also*
○━┓ NS 2.0, MR 2.0, MR 2.4, MR 2.5, MR 3.2

Addition and subtraction of integers are related.

## Example 1  Find $^-3 - {}^-2$ and $^-3 + 2$.

**A** Model $^-3 - {}^-2$.

$^-3 - {}^-2 = {}^-1$

**B** Model $^-3 + 2$.

$^-3 + 2 = {}^-1$

So, $^-3 - {}^-2 = {}^-1$ and $^-3 + 2 = {}^-1$.

Since both $^-3 - {}^-2$ and $^-3 + 2$ are equal to $^-1$, the expressions are equivalent.

## Example 2  Find $3 - 6$ and $3 + {}^-6$.

**A** Model $3 - 6$.

$3 - 6 = {}^-3$

**B** Model $3 + {}^-6$.

$3 + {}^-6 = {}^-3$

So, $3 - 6 = {}^-3$ and $3 + {}^-6 = {}^-3$.

Since both $3 - 6$ and $3 + {}^-6$ are equal to $^-3$, the expressions are equivalent.

**TALK Math**
Explain how subtracting integers is related to adding integers.

## Practice

**Use counters to find the difference.**

**1.** $4 - {}^-2$

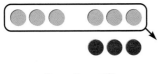

**✓2.** $^-3 - {}^-5$

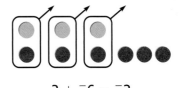

**3.** $5 - 8$  **4.** $^-6 - 6$  **5.** $^-7 - {}^-2$  **6.** $1 - {}^-3$  **✓7.** $^-3 - 1$

**8.** $8 - 9$  **9.** $7 - {}^-6$  **10.** $8 - 3$  **11.** $9 - {}^-4$  **12.** $^-3 - 7$

**Copy and complete the addition problem.**

**13.** $^-3 - {}^-8 = {}^-3 + \blacksquare$  **14.** $^-8 - {}^-2 = {}^-8 + \blacksquare$  **15.** $^-2 - 3 = {}^-2 + \blacksquare$

**16.** $6 - 10 = 6 + \blacksquare$  **17.** $7 - 9 = 7 + \blacksquare$  **18.** $5 - {}^-5 = 5 + \blacksquare$

**19.** **WRITE Math** Explain how to use counters to find the difference $^-3 - {}^-4$.

# 4 Record Subtraction

**OBJECTIVE:** Subtract integers by using a number line or absolute values.

## Learn

**PROBLEM** The temperature in Detroit, Michigan was $^-2°F$ in the morning. It increased to $5°F$ by the afternoon. How much greater was the temperature in the afternoon?

**Find $5 - ^-2$ to solve the problem.**

**ONE WAY** Use a model.

**A Counters**

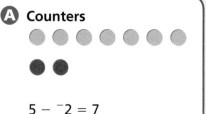

$5 - ^-2 = 7$

**B Number line**

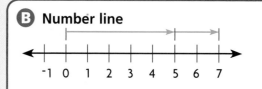

$5 - ^-2 = 7$

Begin at 0. Move to the right 5 units.
To subtract $^-2$, add its opposite.

So, the temperature was $7°F$ greater in the afternoon.

You can find the difference of two integers by adding the opposite of the integer you are subtracting. You can then use the rules for the addition of integers.

**ANOTHER WAY** Use the rules for the addition of integers.

**Example 1** Find $^-5 - ^-2$.

| | |
|---|---|
| $^-5 - ^-2 = ^-5 + 2$ | Write as an addition problem. Use the rules for addition of integers. |
| $^-5 + 2$ | |
| $\|^-5\| - \|^-2\| = 5 - 2$ | Subtract the lesser absolute value from the greater absolute value. |
| $= 3$ | |
| $\|^-5\| > \|2\| \rightarrow ^-5 - ^-2 = ^-3$ | Use the sign of the addend with the greater absolute value. |

So, $^-5 - ^-2 = ^-3$.

You can use this key sequence on a calculator.

(−) 5 − (−) 2 Enter  $^-5 - ^-2 = ^-3$

▲ The Penobscot Building was Detroit's tallest building until 1977.

 NS 2.3 Solve addition, subtraction, multiplication, and division problems, including those arising in concrete situations, that use positive and negative integers and combinations of these operations.
*also* 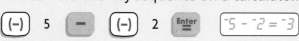 NS 2.0, MR 2.4, MR 2.5, MR 3.2

## Example 2

The low temperature at Camelback ski resort in the Pocono Mountains of Pennsylvania was ⁻7°C. The high temperature was 4°C. What was the range of the temperatures at the resort?

Subtract. $4 - {}^-7$

$4 - {}^-7 = 4 + 7$     Write as an addition problem.
                  Use the rules for addition of integers.
      $= 11$

So, $4 - {}^-7 = 11$, which means the range of temperatures was 11°C.

• **What if** the high temperature was ⁻2°C? What would be the range of temperatures?

## More Examples

**Ⓐ Subtract. 3 − 9**

$3 - 9 = 3 + {}^-9$     Write the subtraction problem as an addition problem. Use the rules for the addition of integers.

$3 + {}^-9$

$|{}^-9| - |3| = 9 - 3$     Subtract the lesser absolute value from the greater absolute value.
       $= 6$

$|{}^-9| > |3| \rightarrow 3 + {}^-9 = {}^-6$     Use the sign of the addend with the greater absolute value.

**Ⓑ Subtract. ⁻2 − 5**

${}^-2 - 5 = {}^-2 + {}^-5$     Write the subtraction problem as an addition problem. Use the rules for the addition of integers.

${}^-2 + {}^-5$

$|{}^-2| + |{}^-5| = 2 + 5$     Add the absolute values of the integers.
       $= 7$

${}^-2 + {}^-5 = {}^-7$     Use the sign of the original addends. The sum is negative.

So, $3 - 9 = {}^-6$.

So, ${}^-2 - 5 = {}^-7$.

• How can you check your answers?

• Explain how to find the difference $0 - 3$.

## Guided Practice

**1.** Use the number line to find $^-5 - {}^-3$.

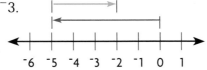

**Rewrite the subtraction problem as an addition problem.**

**2.** $^-2 - {}^-7$      **3.** $^-3 - 8$      **4.** $4 - 19$      **5.** $15 - {}^-11$      ✓ **6.** $23 - {}^-9$

**Find the difference.**

**7.** $^-1 - 4$  **8.** $^-3 - ^-9$  **9.** $18 - ^-6$  **10.** $^-17 - ^-12$  ✓**11.** $13 - 22$

**12.** [ TALK Math ] **Explain** how to use a number line to subtract $^-8 - ^-2$.

## Independent Practice and Problem Solving

**Rewrite the subtraction problem as an addition problem.**

**13.** $^-7 - 4$  **14.** $5 - 7$  **15.** $^-8 - ^-1$  **16.** $5 - 11$  **17.** $9 - ^-5$

**18.** $^-16 - 8$  **19.** $|10| - ^-23$  **20.** $^-24 - |^-37|$  **21.** $|41| - |^-33|$  **22.** $|0| - |^-57|$

**Find the difference.**

**23.** $5 - ^-5$  **24.** $^-6 - 5$  **25.** $^-4 - 16$  **26.** $^-12 - ^-7$  **27.** $2 - 17$

**28.** $0 - ^-36$  **29.** $33 - |^-11|$  **30.** $|^-14| - |^-28|$  **31.** $37 - |^-63|$  **32.** $|^-74| - |^-25|$

**Use mental math to find the value of the variable.**

**33.** $3 - a = 2$  **34.** $n - ^-4 = ^-4$  **35.** $7 - ^-6 = s$  **36.** $b - 7 = ^-15$

**37.** $^-4 - t = ^-13$  **38.** $y - ^-3 = 1$  **39.** $x - 9 = ^-3$  **40.** $1 - x = 5$

**Find each output.**

**41.**

| Rule: Subtract $^-5$. | | |
|---|---|---|
| Input | 7 | $^-1$ | $^-6$ |
| Output | ▓ | ▓ | ▓ |

**42.**

| Rule: Subtract 3. | | |
|---|---|---|
| Input | $^-8$ | $^-3$ | 1 |
| Output | ▓ | ▓ | ▓ |

**43.**

| Rule: Subtract $^-11$. | | |
|---|---|---|
| Input | 0 | 5 | $^-12$ |
| Output | ▓ | ▓ | ▓ |

**USE DATA** For 44–46, use the table.

**44.** How much greater was the low temperature in Tallahassee, FL, than Charlotte, NC?

**45.** Write a subtraction number sentence that could be used to find which city had a temperature 46°F greater than the temperature in Logan, MT.

**46.** What is the difference between the greatest and least temperatures shown in the table?

| Cold Wave of February 1899 | |
|---|---|
| City | Low Temperature (°F) |
| Tallahassee, FL | $^-2$ |
| Washington, DC | $^-15$ |
| Charlotte, NC | $^-5$ |
| Cleveland, OH | $^-16$ |
| Logan, MT | $^-61$ |

**47.** The temperature on Sunday morning was $^-2°F$. The temperature dropped 7° by Monday and then rose 5° by Tuesday. What was the temperature on Tuesday?

**48.** **Reasoning** When Mike subtracted $^-7$ from another integer, the difference was negative. What was the sign of the integer Mike subtracted from?

**49.** [ WRITE Math ] **Sense or Nonsense** Maria says that $^-13 - ^-8 = 21$. Does this make sense? **Explain.**

# Achieving the Standards

**50.** Shara had to walk to school for 12 days. She walked a total of $\frac{3}{4}$ mile each day. How far did Shara walk in all? (O⟊ NS 2.0, p. 70)

**51.** Izzy wants to pass out flyers and stickers for a new skate shop. The flyers come in packages of 10. The stickers come in packages of 15. What is the least number of flyers and stickers Izzy needs to have the same number of each? (O⟊ NS 2.4, p. 14)

**52.** Write, as an ordered pair (x,y), the point located 5 units below the origin and 3 units to the right on a coordinate plane. (Grade 5 O⟊ AF 1.4)

**53. Test Prep** What is ⁻14 − ⁻6?

A ⁻20　　　C 8

B ⁻8　　　D 20

**54. Test Prep** Which shows ⁻23 − 7 written as an addition problem?

A 23 + 7

B 23 + ⁻7

C ⁻23 + ⁻7

D ⁻23 + 7

# Problem Solving connects to Science

Water currents are dynamic forces that shape and sculpt coastlines through weathering, erosion, and deposition. Often, water speed is measured in knots (kt) and its direction is indicated by positive and negative values.

This chart shows approximate water current speeds recorded in San Francisco Bay at the Golden Gate Bridge. Positive values indicate an incoming current. Negative values indicate an outgoing current.

**Use the table to solve.**

1. What was the fastest incoming current and when was it observed?

2. What was the fastest outgoing current and when was it observed?

3. What was the range of current speed from 3 A.M. to 7 A.M.?

4. Describe the current change from 7 A.M. to 2 P.M.?

5. Graph the data shown in this table.

**Water Current Speeds Recorded at Golden Gate Bridge**

| Time | Speed | Time | Speed |
|---|---|---|---|
| 12:00 A.M. | 3 kt | 9:00 A.M. | ⁻2 kt |
| 1:00 A.M. | 2 kt | 10:00 A.M. | ⁻1 kt |
| 2:00 A.M. | 1 kt | 11:00 A.M. | 0 kt |
| 3:00 A.M. | 0 kt | 12:00 P.M. | 1 kt |
| 4:00 A.M. | ⁻1 kt | 1:00 P.M. | 2 kt |
| 5:00 A.M. | ⁻2 kt | 2:00 P.M. | 3 kt |
| 6:00 A.M. | ⁻3 kt | 1:00 P.M. | 2 kt |
| 7:00 A.M. | ⁻4 kt | 2:00 P.M. | 1 kt |
| 8:00 A.M. | ⁻3 kt | 3:00 P.M. | 0 kt |

# Add and Subtract Integers

**OBJECTIVE:** Find the sums and differences of integers.

## Learn

Use what you know about adding and subtracting integers to find the value of expressions with three or more integers.

**PROBLEM** Pat is playing a board game. Her game piece is on START. She moves 3 spaces forward on her first turn, 5 spaces back on her second turn, and 4 spaces forward on her third turn. How many spaces from START is Pat now?

**Example 1** Find the value of $3 - 5 + 4$.

| | |
|---|---|
| $3 - 5 + 4$ | |
| $3 + {}^-5 + 4$ | Write $3 - 5$ as an addition problem. Add. |
| ${}^-2 + 4$ | Add. |
| $2$ | |

So, Pat is 2 spaces in front of START.

• **What if** Pat moved 2 spaces back instead of 3 spaces forward on her first turn? How far is her piece from START at the end of her third turn?

**More Examples** Find the value of the expression.

**A** 
$12 - {}^-5 + 2$
$12 + 5 + 2$
$17 + 2$
$19$

**B** 
${}^-29 + {}^-16 - 9$
${}^-45 - 9$
${}^-45 + {}^-9$
${}^-54$

**C** 
${}^-14 - 53 - {}^-27$
${}^-14 - 53 + 27$
${}^-67 + 27$
${}^-40$

**Remember**
An expression is a mathematical phrase that combines numbers, operation signs, and sometimes variables.

You can use the Commutative Property and the Associative Property to help you find the value of an addition expression more easily using mental math.

**Example 2** Find the value of the expression.

**A** Use the Commutative Property.

$$
\begin{aligned}
{}^-13 + 78 + {}^-7 &= {}^-13 + {}^-7 + 78 \\
&= {}^-20 + 78 \\
&= 58
\end{aligned}
$$

**B** Use the Associative Property.

$$
\begin{aligned}
({}^-94 + 56) + {}^-56 &= {}^-94 + (56 + {}^-56) \\
&= {}^-94 + 0 \\
&= {}^-94
\end{aligned}
$$

• How could you use properties to help you find the value of ${}^-19 + (32 + 19) + {}^-12$?

NS 2.0 Students calculate and solve problems involving addition, subtraction, multiplication, and division: also NS 2.3, MR 1.1, MR 2.4, MR 2.5, MR 3.2

# Integer Patterns

Alvin is playing a computer math game. The game displays the rule for a number pattern and the third number in the pattern. The rule is add 4. The third integer is ⁻3. What are the sixth and first integers in the pattern?

## Example 3

| Step 1 | Step 2 |
|---|---|
| Use the rule to find the three integers that follow the third integer, ⁻3, in the pattern. | Use the inverse operation to find the first two integers in the pattern. |

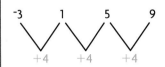

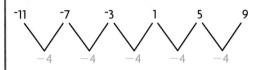

So, the sixth integer is 9 and the first integer is ⁻11.

## Example 4 Find the possible missing integers in the pattern
1, ⁻2, ⁻5, ⁻8, ▪, ▪.

| Step 1 | Step 2 |
|---|---|
| Find a possible rule. | Use your rule to find the missing integers. |

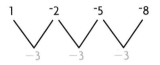

Look for a pattern. Compare each integer to the next.

A possible rule is to subtract 3 to get the next integer.

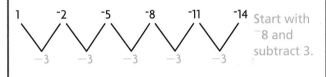

Start with ⁻8 and subtract 3.

So, the next two possible integers are ⁻11 and ⁻14.

## Guided Practice

**Find the value of the expression.**

1.  6 − ⁻2 + 12

    6 + 2 + 12

    8 + 12

    ▪

2.  ⁻2 − ⁻3 + 8

    ⁻2 + 3 + 8

    1 + 8

    ▪

3.  ⁻12 − (17 − 29)

    ⁻12 − ⁻12

    ⁻12 + 12

    ▪

4.  ⁻7 − 3 + 8

5.  13 − ⁻5 − 7

✓6.  22 − (18 + ⁻36)

**Write a possible rule for each pattern. Then find the missing integers.**

7.  2, ⁻1, ⁻4, ⁻7, ▪, ▪

8.  ⁻11, ⁻5, 1, ▪, ▪, 19, 25

✓9.  1, ⁻3, ⁻7, ⁻11, ▪, ▪

10. **TALK Math** Explain how you could use the Associative Property to help find the value of (28 + ⁻47) + ⁻3?

**Find the value of the expression.**

11. $^-2 - (9 + 10)$ 

12. $6 - {}^-5 + 1$ 

13. $^-4 - 3 - {}^-8$

14. $^-14 - 4 + 8$ 

15. $20 + {}^-7 - {}^-6$ 

16. $^-17 - 5 - 7$

17. $^-25 + 4 - {}^-15$ 

18. $^-15 - 28 + {}^-77$ 

19. $^-11 - 87 - ({}^-49 - 5)$

**Write a possible rule for each pattern. Then find the missing integers.**

20. $^-15, {}^-11, {}^-7, {}^-3, \blacksquare, \blacksquare$ 

21. $^-8, {}^-11, {}^-14, {}^-17, \blacksquare, \blacksquare$ 

22. $20, 14, 8, 2, \blacksquare, \blacksquare$

23. $^-14, {}^-9, {}^-4, \blacksquare, 6, 11, \blacksquare$ 

24. $\blacksquare, {}^-35, {}^-25, {}^-15, {}^-5, \blacksquare$ 

25. $\blacksquare, \blacksquare, 8, 15, 22, 29$

26. $\blacksquare, \blacksquare, {}^-22, {}^-26, {}^-30, {}^-34$ 

27. $^-23, {}^-15, {}^-7, \blacksquare, \blacksquare, 17$ 

28. $\blacksquare, {}^-1, {}^-10, {}^-19, {}^-28, \blacksquare$

**Use the Commutative or Associative Property to help you find the sum.**

29. $(^-79 + {}^-14) + {}^-6$ 

30. $^-74 + 56 + 74$ 

31. $(9 + 33) + {}^-3$

32. $82 + ({}^-82 + 83)$ 

33. $^-25 + 365 + {}^-75 + {}^-65$ 

34. $41 + {}^-52 + {}^-8 + {}^-1$

**Compare. Use $<$, $>$ or $=$ for each ●.**

35. $^-3 - (4 - 5)$ ● $^-4 - 4$ 

36. $^-11 + 9 - {}^-7$ ● $11 - {}^-9 + 7$

37. $2 + |{}^-29|$ ● $2 + |29|$ 

38. $|{}^-13| - 13$ ● $8 - |{}^-7|$

**USE DATA For 39–41, use the table.**

39. Number Toss is a game played with a number cube labeled $^-14$, $^-13$, $^-11$, 12, 13, and 15. The table shows the numbers players rolled in one game. The player whose numbers have the greatest sum wins. Who is the winner?

40. **Pose a Problem** Change the numbers tossed by each player in Problem 39. Have a classmate find the new winner.

| Number Toss | | | |
|---|---|---|---|
| **Player** | **Toss 1** | **Toss 2** | **Toss 3** |
| Sam | 12 | $^-14$ | $^-11$ |
| Clyde | $^-11$ | $^-13$ | 13 |
| Pam | 15 | $^-14$ | 12 |
| Rosa | 13 | $^-14$ | 13 |

41. What is the sum of the numbers rolled by all 4 players in Toss 1? How much greater is this than the combined rolls of the 4 players in Toss 2?

42. Ryan and Lee are playing a card game. Red cards are worth $^-1$, and blue cards are worth $^+1$. Each person starts with three of each kind of card. Ryan gives Lee 2 red cards and Lee gives Ryan 1 blue card. How much greater is Ryan's total card value than Lee's?

43. Daya's score in a computer game changed by the same amount each turn. Her score on her first turn was $^-18$. Her scores on her next 3 turns were $^-11$, $^-4$, and 3. What was Daya's score on her sixth turn?

44. Which number does not belong in the pattern below? **Explain** why.

$$9, 3, {}^-3, {}^-9, {}^-15, {}^-18, {}^-21$$

45. **WRITE Math** Kia's teacher made a number pattern with $^-28$, $^-31$, $^-34$, and $^-37$ as the first four integers. Write a possible rule for the pattern. Then find which integer in the pattern is $^-52$.

**46.** What is the greatest common divisor of 96 and 72? (O—π NS 2.4, p. 6)

**47.** What is the total of 8 groups of 4?
(Grade 5 NS 2.0)

**48. Test Prep** What is the value of
⁻4 − ( ⁻2 − ⁻5)?

   **A** 11          **C** ⁻3

   **B** 3           **D** ⁻7

**49.** What is the quotient $\frac{5}{8} \div \frac{1}{2}$ in simplest form?
(O—π NS 2.4, p. 96)

**50. Test Prep** A rule is add ⁻5. What are the next two integers in the pattern?

$$^-15, \; ^-20, \; ^-25, \; ^-30, \; \blacksquare, \; \blacksquare$$

   **A** ⁻40, ⁻5          **C** 35, 40

   **B** ⁻35, ⁻40        **D** 40, 50

## Problem Solving and Reasoning

**VISUAL THINKING** When you add a positive or negative integer, think about how the points "shift" on a number line.

**How does adding 1 shift the points on the number line?**

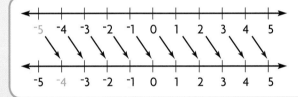

Adding any positive integer, $x$, shifts the points on a number line $x$ units to the right.

⁻5 + 1 = ⁻4

So, adding 1 to each number shifts the points 1 unit to the right.

**How does adding ⁻2 shift the points on the number line?**

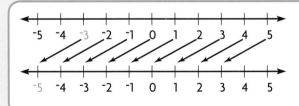

Adding any negative integer, $x$, is the same as subtracting any positive integer, $x$. It shifts the points on a number line $x$ units to the left.

⁻3 + ⁻2 = ⁻5

So, adding ⁻2 to each number shifts the points 2 units to the left.

**Explain how the point on a number line shifts for each expression.
Find the value of each expression.**

  **1.** ⁻3 + ⁻1        **2.** 2 + ⁻5        **3.** ⁻4 + 3        **4.** ⁻5 + ⁻8

  **5.** ⁻4 + 2        **6.** 5 + ⁻7        **7.** 3 + ⁻6        **8.** ⁻2 + 1

# Problem Solving Workshop
## Strategy: Predict and Test

**OBJECTIVE:** Solve problems by using the strategy *predict and test*.

## Learn the Strategy

You can solve some problems by using number sense to predict a possible answer. You should then test your answer and revise your prediction if necessary.

### You can predict and test to find integers with a given sum and difference.

The sum of two negative integers is ⁻7. When the lesser integer is subtracted from the greater integer, the difference is 3. What are the two integers?

| Prediction | | Test | | Result |
|---|---|---|---|---|
| Greater integer | Lesser integer | Sum | Difference | |
| ⁻3 | ⁻4 | ⁻3 + ⁻4 = ⁻7 | ⁻3 − ⁻4 = 1 | The difference is too low; so revise. |
| ⁻1 | ⁻6 | ⁻1 + ⁻6 = ⁻7 | ⁻1 − ⁻6 = 5 | The difference is too high; so revise. |
| ⁻2 | ⁻5 | ⁻2 + ⁻5 = ⁻7 | ⁻2 − ⁻5 = 3 | Correct. |

### You can predict and test to solve some geometry problems.

The perimeter of a rectangle is 40 m. The length is 3 times as great as the width. What are the length and the width of the rectangle?

| Prediction | | Test | Result |
|---|---|---|---|
| Width | Length | Perimeter $P = 2(l + w)$ | |
| 10 | 3 × 10 = 30 | $P = 2(30 + 10)$ $= 2(40) = 80$ | The perimeter is too high, so revise. |
| 4 | 3 × 4 = 12 | $P = 2(12 + 4)$ $= 2(16) = 32$ | The perimeter is too low, so revise. |
| 5 | 3 × 5 = 15 | $P = 2(15 + 5)$ $= 2(20) = 40$ | Correct. |

**TALK Math**

Explain how you revised your predictions to solve each problem.

O━┓ NS 2.0 Students calculate and solve problems involving addition, subtraction, multiplication, and division: *also* O━┓ NS 2.3, MR 1.0, MR 2.0, MR 2.4, MR 2.5, MR 2.7, MR 3.0, MR 3.1, MR 3.2, MR 3.3

# Use the Strategy

**PROBLEM** Copy the diagram to arrange the integers ⁻10, ⁻8, ⁻7, ⁻6, ⁻5, and ⁻4 in the square so the sum of the integers in each row and each column is ⁻19. Use each integer only once.

|  |  |  |
|---|---|---|
| ⁻12 |  | ⁻2 |
|  |  |  |
| ⁻3 |  |  |

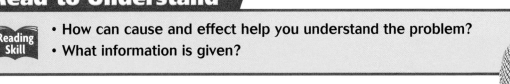

## Read to Understand

**Reading Skill**

• How can cause and effect help you understand the problem?
• What information is given?

## Plan

• **What strategy can you use to solve the problem?**
You can use *predict and test* to solve the problem.

## Solve

• **How can you use the strategy to solve the problem?**
Find the values that can be found by calculation. Then, predict the other values and their placement in the square.
Since ⁻12 + ⁻2 = ⁻14, use ⁻5 for the first row. ⁻14 + ⁻5 = ⁻19
Since ⁻12 + ⁻3 = ⁻15, use ⁻4 for the first column. ⁻15 + ⁻4 = ⁻19

**Prediction**

| ⁻12 | ⁻5 | ⁻2 |
|---|---|---|
| ⁻4 | ⁻7 | ⁻8 |
| ⁻3 | ⁻6 | ⁻10 |

| Prediction | | Test | Result |
|---|---|---|---|
| **Integers** | | **Sum** | |
| ⁻8 | ⁻10 | ⁻4 + ⁻8 + ⁻10 = ⁻22 | too low, so revise |
| ⁻7 | ⁻8 | ⁻4 + ⁻7 + ⁻8 = ⁻19 | correct |

← Second row

Use ⁻7 and ⁻8 for the second row and the remaining numbers, ⁻6 and ⁻10, for the third row. Now, test the sums of columns 2 and 3.

**Revision**

| ⁻12 | ⁻5 | ⁻2 |
|---|---|---|
| ⁻4 | ⁻8 | ⁻7 |
| ⁻3 | ⁻6 | ⁻10 |

| Prediction | | Test | Result |
|---|---|---|---|
| **Integers** | | **Sum of Columns 2 and 3** | |
| ⁻7 | ⁻6 | ⁻5 + ⁻7 + ⁻6 = ⁻18 | too high, so revise |
| ⁻8 | ⁻10 | ⁻2 + ⁻8 + ⁻10 = ⁻20 | too low, so revise |

Exchange ⁻7 and ⁻8 in the second row. Test the sums.
⁻5 + ⁻8 + ⁻6 = ⁻19          ⁻2 + ⁻7 + ⁻10 = ⁻19
Both columns now have a sum of ⁻19.

## Check

• **What other strategy could you use?**

## Guided Problem Solving

1. Copy the diagram to arrange the integers ⁻6, ⁻7, ⁻8, ⁻10, ⁻11, and ⁻12 in the circles so the sum of the integers on each side of the triangle is ⁻10. Use each integer only once.

   **First,** predict and test integers for one side of the triangle.

   **Then,** if the sum of the integers is ⁻10, predict and test integers for another side of the triangle. If your prediction is incorrect, adjust your prediction and then test it.

   **Finally,** continue until you have placed all the integers in the circles and the sum of the integers on each side of the triangle is ⁻10.

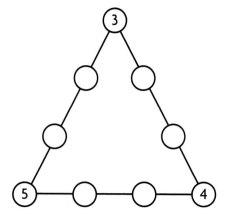

✓2. **What if** the integers to be arranged were ⁻6, ⁻2, ⁻1, 0, 2, and 7 and the sum of the integers on each side of the triangle was 8? If you could only use each integer only once, what would be the arrangement of the integers?

✓3. The perimeter of a triangle is 39 in. The length of the second side is one more than the length of the first side. The length of the third side is two more than the length of the first side. What is the length of each side?

## Problem Solving Strategy Practice

**Predict and test to solve.**

4. Arrange the digits 1 through 9 in a 3-by-3 grid to form one 3-digit number in each of the rows. Make the number in the second row 2 times as great as than the number in the first row, and make the number in the third row 3 times as great as the number in the first row.

5. The Mighty Mathematicians competed in 25 math competitions. They won 9 more competitions than they lost. Two competitions ended in a tie. How many competitions did they win?

6. The perimeter of a rectangle is 32 units. If the width is $\frac{1}{3}$ that of the length, what are the length and width of the rectangle?

7. The sum of two 4-digit numbers is 5,555. The same 4 digits are used in each number without any digits repeating. Find two such numbers.

8. Harry has $37.72 in his toy bank. The amount of bills is the same as the amount of coins. What are possible bills and coins in Harry's toy bank?

Mighty Mathematicians
First Place

9. **WRITE Math** ▸ In Problem 7, how did your first prediction help you to make your second prediction?

## Mixed Strategy Practice

**Solve.**

10. Copy the diagram to arrange the integers ⁻1 through ⁻19 in the circles so the sum of the numbers on each line is ⁻30.

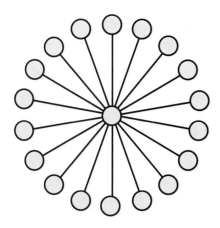

**Problem-Solving STRATEGIES**

Use Logical Reasoning
Draw a Diagram or Picture
Make a Model or Act It Out
Make an Organized List
Find a Pattern
Make a Table or Graph
Predict and Test
Work Backward
Solve a Simpler Problem
Write an Equation

11. If Jack gives one of his pencils to Kim, they will each have the same number of pencils. But if Kim gives Jack one of her pencils, Jack will have twice as many pencils as Kim. How many pencils does each student have?

12. Liz, Keith, Olivia, and Alvin are standing in line. Alvin is ahead of Olivia, but he is not first. Liz is behind Alvin. Olivia is last. In what order are the students?

**USE DATA** For 13–16, use the number cards.

13. How many different two-digit numbers can you make with the cards?

14. **Pose a Problem** Make a pattern with the cards. Write a problem to go along with your pattern.

15. **Open-Ended Problem** Choose four cards. Arrange the numbers on the cards to write an equation.

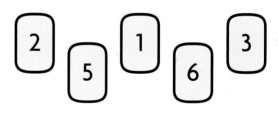

16. If you add 3 to the number on one of the cards, subtract 5 from the sum, and end up with ⁻1, what number was on the card you started with?

**CHALLENGE YOURSELF**

A magic square is a square array of numbers consisting of integers arranged such that the sum of the numbers in any horizontal, vertical, or main diagonal line is always the same number.

17. Draw a 3-by-3 square. Arrange any or all of the numbers 1 through 5 so that the sum is 9. Some numbers will repeat.

18. Look at the figure at the right. Copy and complete the 4-by-4 magic square using each of the numbers 1 through 16 only once.

| 16 |    |    | 13 |
|----|----|----|----|
|    | 10 |    |    |
|    |    | 7  |    |
|    | 15 |    | 1  |

# Extra Practice

1. ⁻1 + 8
2. 9 + ⁻7
3. 6 + ⁻4
4. ⁻8 + ⁻2
5. ⁻3 + 7

6. ⁻5 + ⁻8
7. ⁻2 + 2
8. ⁻4 + 5
9. 6 + ⁻6
10. 1 + ⁻9

11. ⁻9 + ⁻3
12. ⁻4 + 4
13. ⁻7 + ⁻12
14. ⁻10 + 10
15. 5 + ⁻13

16. ⁻15 + ⁻6
17. 3 + ⁻11
18. ⁻14 + 3
19. ⁻21 + 6
20. ⁻9 + ⁻14

21. On the first play of a football game, the home team lost 2 yd. If the team gained 8 yd on the second play, how many yards did the team gain or lose on the first two plays?

22. The temperature in the early part of the afternoon was ⁻6°F. The temperature rose 5°F by late afternoon. What was the temperature in the late afternoon?

**Set B** Find the difference. (pp. 150–153)

1. ⁻3 − 5
2. 5 − ⁻12
3. ⁻6 − ⁻8
4. ⁻12 − 3
5. 7 − ⁻7

6. 0 − ⁻9
7. ⁻25 − ⁻8
8. 15 − ⁻12
9. ⁻9 − 17
10. 14 − ⁻6

11. 0 − ⁻14
12. ⁻4 − ⁻12
13. ⁻15 − 7
14. ⁻8 − ⁻9
15. 23 − ⁻7

16. 13 − 31
17. ⁻6 − ⁻11
18. 17 − ⁻6
19. ⁻15 − ⁻8
20. ⁻4 − 6

21. Jen scuba dives 32 m below sea level. She then rises 18 m to look at a school of fish. How many meters below sea level is the school of fish?

22. The temperature in Jack's town was ⁻7°F in the morning. It rose to 12°F by the afternoon. How much greater was the temperature in the afternoon?

**Set C** Find the value of the expression. (pp. 154–157)

1. ⁻56 + 8 − 16
2. ⁻36 − 89 + 36
3. 12 + 48 + ⁻9

4. 6 − ⁻31 − ⁻11
5. ⁻15 + 22 − ⁻49
6. ⁻76 + ⁻19 + ⁻3

7. 5 − ⁻17 + ⁻16
8. ⁻21 + 13 − 31
9. ⁻4 − (⁻67 + ⁻3)

10. ⁻35 + 65 − ⁻18 + ⁻27
11. 87 − ⁻34 − (⁻12 − ⁻1)
12. ⁻28 + ⁻65 + 148 + ⁻57

13. The temperature Monday evening was ⁻8°F. The temperature dropped 6°F by Tuesday morning and then rose 15°F during the day Tuesday. What was the temperature by Tuesday evening?

14. Sophia gets on an elevator on the 18th floor, travels down 3 floors and then up 7 floors. She gets off the elevator to attend a meeting. Later she gets on the elevator and travels down 16 floors. What floor is she on now?

**CD ROM** **Technology**
Use Harcourt Mega Math, Fraction Action, *Number Line Mine*, Level W.

# Integer Express

## Get Ready!
2 players

## Get Set!
- Integer cards
- Operation cards
- 2 different coins
- Number cube, labeled 1–6

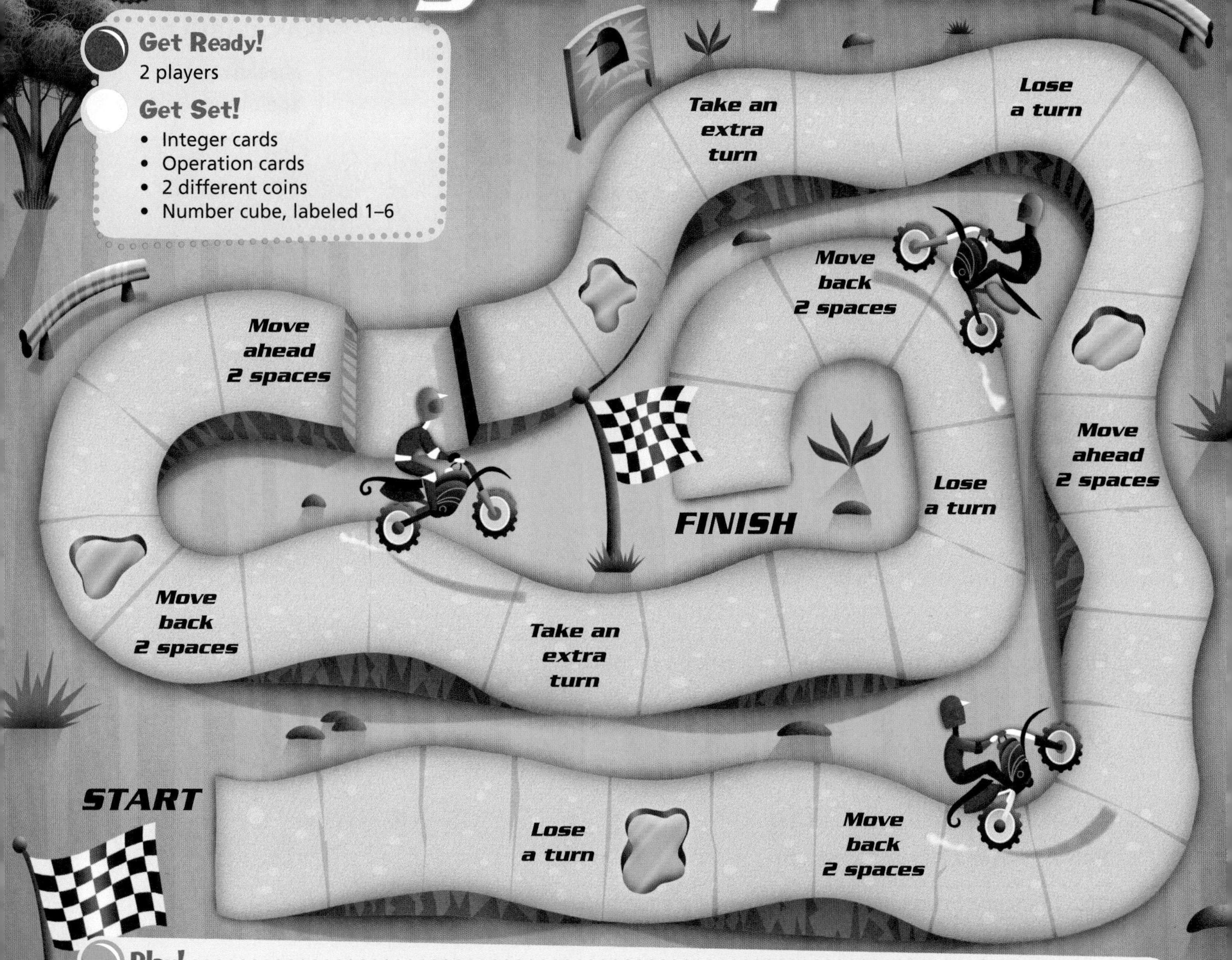

**Take an extra turn**

**Lose a turn**

**Move back 2 spaces**

**Move ahead 2 spaces**

**Move ahead 2 spaces**

**Lose a turn**

**FINISH**

**Move back 2 spaces**

**Take an extra turn**

**START**

**Lose a turn**

**Move back 2 spaces**

## Play!

- Shuffle the integer cards and operation cards separately and place each set facedown in a pile.

- Each player selects a coin and places it on START. Decide which player will go first.

- Player 1 draws two integer cards and one operation card from the piles.

- The player uses the cards to write an expression, such as ⁻1 + ⁻3, and then finds its value.

- Player 2 checks the answer. If it is correct, Player 1 tosses the number cube and moves his or her coin the number of spaces shown.

- If the answer is correct or incorrect, play passes to Player 2.

- The first player to reach FINISH wins.

# Chapter 6 Review/Test

## Check Vocabulary and Concepts

1. The __?__ of an integer is its opposite. Choose the better term from the box. (O⊓ NS 2.3, p. 143)

2. Explain how you would model ⁻5 + 3 to find the sum.
   (O⊓ NS 2.3, pp. 142–143)

3. Explain how subtracting integers is related to adding integers.
   (O⊓ NS 2.3, pp. 148–149)

## Check Skills

**Find the sum.** (O⊓ NS 2.3, pp. 144–147)

| | | | | |
|---|---|---|---|---|
| 4. ⁻8 + ⁻9 | 5. ⁻3 + 12 | 6. 4 + ⁻7 | 7. 4 + 8 | 8. 5 + ⁻1 |
| 9. 6 + ⁻8 | 10. ⁻5 + ⁻7 | 11. ⁻3 + 11 | 12. 0 + ⁻7 | 13. ⁻9 + 3 |

**Find the difference.** (O⊓ NS 2.3, pp. 150–153)

| | | | | |
|---|---|---|---|---|
| 14. 3 − 5 | 15. ⁻3 − 11 | 16. ⁻9 − ⁻5 | 17. 4 − ⁻7 | 18. ⁻8 − ⁻15 |
| 19. ⁻9 − ⁻10 | 20. 0 − ⁻15 | 21. ⁻13 − 12 | 22. ⁻8 − ⁻16 | 23. 7 − ⁻7 |

**Find the value of the expression.** (O⊓ NS 2.3, pp. 154–157)

24. (⁻15 + 7) − ⁻18

25. (25 + ⁻9) − ⁻5

26. (⁻19 − 9) + 12

27. (⁻2 + 9) + 15

28. (⁻4 − 8) − ⁻3

29. (21 − ⁻6) + 2

## Check Problem Solving

**Solve.** (O⊓ NS 2.0, MR 2.0, pp. 158–161)

30. The sum of two integers is ⁻3. The difference between the greater integer and the lesser integer is 11. What are the two integers?

31. The Basketball All–Stars competed in 28 games during the season. They won 8 more games than they lost. How many games did they win?

32. Copy the diagram at the right. Arrange the digits 1–9 in the magic square so that the sum of each row and each column is 15.

33. **WRITE Math** Michael has $15.15 in his pocket. The number of coins is the same as the number of bills. **Explain** how using predict and test can help you to find the bills and coins in Michael's pocket.

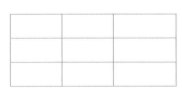

# Enrich • Input-Output Tables
## Integers RULE!

You can use a rule to complete an input-output table. What are the missing input and output values for this table?

| Rule: Add ⁻3. ||
|---|---|
| Input | Output |
| ⁻6 | ▓ |
| ⁻4 | ⁻7 |
| ▓ | ⁻1 |

←— THINK: ⁻6 + ⁻3 = ▓
⁻6 + ⁻3 = ⁻9

←— THINK: ▓ + ⁻3 = ⁻1
2 + ⁻3 = ⁻1

So, the missing output value is ⁻9. The missing input value is 2.

You can use input and output values to find a rule for an input-output table.

### Example Find a possible rule for the input-output table.

| Rule: ? ||
|---|---|
| Input | Output |
| 3 | ⁻2 |
| 1 | ⁻4 |
| ⁻4 | ⁻9 |

THINK: What rule changes 3 to ⁻2?
←——— 3 − 5 = ⁻2
←——— 1 − 5 = ⁻4
←——— ⁻4 − 5 = ⁻9

So, a possible rule for the table is *subtract 5*.

### More Examples

**A**

| Rule: Subtract ⁻4. ||
|---|---|
| Input | Output |
| ⁻8 | ▓ |
| ⁻2 | 2 |
| ▓ | 10 |

THINK: Subtract ⁻4 is the same as *add 4*.
⁻8 + 4 = ⁻4

6 + 4 = 10

So, the missing values are ⁻4 and 6.

**B**

| Rule: ? ||
|---|---|
| Input | Output |
| ⁻5 | 1 |
| ⁻2 | 4 |
| ⁻8 | ⁻2 |

THINK: What rule changes ⁻5 to 1?
⁻5 + 6 = 1
⁻2 + 6 = 4
⁻8 + 6 = ⁻2

So, a possible rule is *add 6*.

### Try It

Find the missing values or a possible rule.

**1.**

| Rule: Subtract 7. ||
|---|---|
| Input | Output |
| 1 | ▓ |
| ▓ | ⁻5 |
| 5 | ▓ |

**2.**

| Rule: Add 8. ||
|---|---|
| Input | Output |
| ▓ | ⁻7 |
| ▓ | ⁻4 |
| ⁻7 | ▓ |

**3.**

| Rule: ? ||
|---|---|
| Input | Output |
| ⁻13 | ⁻11 |
| ⁻10 | ⁻8 |
| ⁻8 | ⁻6 |

**WRITE Math** ▶ Explain how you found the rule for Exercise 3.

# Achieving the Standards

## Chapters 1 – 6

## Number Sense

**1.** What is the sum of 8 and ‾4?
(O━┓ NS 2.3)

  **A** 12       **C** ‾4

  **B** 4        **D** ‾32

**Test Tip** **Look for important words.**

See item 1. The important word is sum.
Remember that this tells you to add.

**2.** $\frac{4}{5} \div \frac{3}{10} =$    (NS 2.1)

  **A** $\frac{8}{3}$       **C** $\frac{7}{15}$

  **B** $\frac{1}{2}$       **D** $\frac{1}{5}$

**3.** Which list of numbers is ordered from *least* to *greatest*? (O━┓ NS 1.1)

  **A** 1.1, 1.001, 0.9, 1.01

  **B** 0.9, 1.001, 1.01, 1.1

  **C** 1.001, 1.01, 1.1, 0.9

  **D** 0.9, 1.1, 1.01, 1.001

**4.** What is the the least common multiple of 9 and 12? (O━┓ NS 2.4)

  **A** 3       **C** 27

  **B** 21      **D** 36

**5.** **WRITE Math** ▸ **What's the Error?** Julie correctly answered $\frac{7}{8}$ of the items on a math exam and David correctly answered $\frac{13}{16}$ of the items. David told his friends that he scored higher on the exam than Julie. Explain why David is wrong. (O━┓ NS 1.1)

## Measurement and Geometry

**6.** In the figure below, *WXYZ* is a parallelogram.

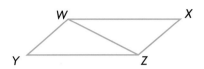

If the area of the parallelogram is 18 square inches, what is the area of triangle *WYZ*? (Grade 5 O━┓ MG 1.1)

  **A** 2 square inches

  **B** 6 square inches

  **C** 9 square inches

  **D** 18 square inches

**7.** What is the approximate measure of this angle in degrees? (Grade 5 O━┓ MG 2.1)

  **A** 15°

  **B** 45°

  **C** 110°

  **D** 135°

**8.** **WRITE Math** ▸ Based on the drawing below, Marcus claimed the measure of angle *A* was 115°. Is Marcus's claim valid? **Explain.** (Grade 5 O━┓ MG 2.2)

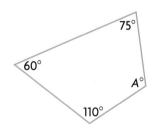

## Algebra and Functions

9. If $x = 12$, what is the value of $x - 7$?
   (Grade 5 AF 1.2)

   **A** 19  **B** 12  **C** 5  **D** $^-7$

10. The map below shows the locations of the houses of 4 different students.

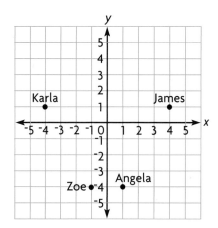

   Which student's house is located at the point $(1, ^-4)$? (Grade 5 AF 1.4)

   **A** Karla  **C** Zoe

   **B** James  **D** Angela

11. What value for $z$ makes the following equation true? (Grade 5 AF 1.3)

   $$2 \times 10 = (z \times 5) + (2 \times 5)$$

   **A** 2  **B** 5  **C** 10  **D** 20

12. **WRITE Math** **Explain** how to find an equation that could have been used to make this function table. Find an equation.
   (Grade 5 AF 1.5)

   | $x$ | $^-3$ | $^-1$ | 2 | 4 |
   |---|---|---|---|---|
   | $y$ | 0 | 2 | 5 | 7 |

## Statistics, Data Analysis, and Probability

13. There are has 5 children in Melinda's family, including herself. The ages of the children are 7, 3, 1, 4, and 10. What is the median of these ages? (Grade 5 SDAP 1.1)

   **A** 1  **C** 5

   **B** 4  **D** 10

14. Jack spent 10 hours reading a book. He kept a record of his progress based on the time he had spent reading.

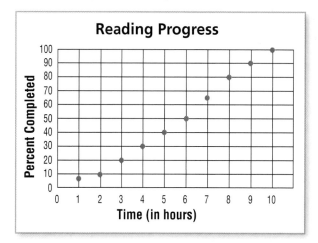

   Approximately how many hours did it take for Jack to read 40% of the book?
   (Grade 5 SDAP 1.4)

   **A** 4 hours  **C** 6 hours

   **B** 5 hours  **D** 7 hours

15. **WRITE Math** Suppose a data set contains: 0, 1, 1, 2, 2, 3, 4, and 20. Later, it was realized that a mistake was made when collecting the data. The item 20 in the data set should have been 4. **Explain** what effect, if any, this change has on the mean of the data.

   (Grade 5 SDAP 1.1)

# 7 Multiply and Divide Integers

**The Big Idea** The number line can be extended to show negative numbers; operations with integers are based on operations with whole numbers.

## CALIFORNIA FAST FACT

The USS *Topeka* is a submarine that can travel more than 25 knots (28.8 mi per hr) when submerged. The USS *Topeka's* home port is Naval Base Point Loma, in San Diego.

## Investigate

Suppose you are tracking a submarine and have recorded its distance below the surface in the graph at the right. Your captain has asked for a report on the submarine's progress. Interpret your findings.

### Submarine Tracking

| Distance Below Surface (in ft) | 25 | 27 | 29 | 31 | 32 | 34 | 35 | 41 | 47 | 53 | 58 | 104 | 150 |
|---|---|---|---|---|---|---|---|---|---|---|---|---|---|
| Time (in sec) | 0 | 30 | 60 | 90 | 120 | 150 | 180 | 210 | 240 | 270 | 300 | 330 | 360 |

**GO ONLINE Technology**
Student pages are available in the Student eBook.

Check your understanding of important skills
needed for success in Chapter 7.

▶ **Use Parentheses**

**Find the value of the expression.**

**1.** $2 \times (4 + 3) \times 6$     **2.** $1 + (2 + 5) + 7$     **3.** $7 - (2 - 1) - 5$

**4.** $5 \times (1 + 6) \times 3$     **5.** $14 - (2 \times 5) + 2$     **6.** $(6 - 4) \times (5 - 3)$

**7.** $10 - 6 + (2 \times 5)$     **8.** $(5 + 2) \times 3 - 9$     **9.** $5 \times (1 + 8) \times 3$

**10.** $6 - (7 - 5) - 1$     **11.** $25 - (3 \times 7) + 4$     **12.** $18 - 12 + (4 \times 8)$

▶ **Practice Multiplication Facts**

**Multiply.**

**13.** $5 \times 6$     **14.** $7 \times 9$     **15.** $8 \times 4$     **16.** $11 \times 8$

**17.** $12 \times 3$     **18.** $11 \times 12$     **19.** $12 \times 12$     **20.** $8 \times 8$

**21.** $9 \times 9$     **22.** $2 \times 8$     **23.** $7 \times 6$     **24.** $4 \times 5$

▶ **Practice Division Facts**

**Divide.**

**25.** $12 \div 4$     **26.** $21 \div 3$     **27.** $8 \overline{)32}$     **28.** $5 \overline{)40}$

**29.** $7 \overline{)49}$     **30.** $6 \overline{)36}$     **31.** $16 \div 8$     **32.** $30 \div 6$

**33.** $24 \div 4$     **34.** $96 \div 8$     **35.** $11 \overline{)121}$     **36.** $10 \overline{)90}$

# VOCABULARY POWER

**CHAPTER VOCABULARY**

Commutative Property of
  Multiplication
product
Property of Zero

**WARM-UP WORDS**

**product** the answer in a multiplication problem

**Property of Zero** the property that states that the product
of any number and zero is zero

**Commutative Property of Multiplication** the property
that states that if the order of factors is changed, the
product stays the same

# 1 Model Multiplication

OBJECTIVE: Model multiplication of integers.

## Quick Review

Add.

1. $3 + 3 + 3 + 3$
2. $2 + 2 + 2 + 2 + 2$
3. $5 + 5 + 5 + 5 + 5 + 5$
4. $6 + 6 + 6$
5. $4 + 4 + 4 + 4$

## Investigate

**Materials** ■ two-color counters

You can use counters to find the product of integers. Remember, a yellow counter represents $^+1$ and a red counter represents $^-1$.

**A** Use yellow counters to model the product $2 \times 4$.

  ← 2 groups of $^+4$

$2 \times 4 = 8$

**B** Use red counters to model the product $2 \times {}^-4$.

●●●●   ●●●●   ← 2 groups of $^-4$

$2 \times {}^-4 = {}^-8$

**C** Use red counters to model the product $^-2 \times 4$. Using the Commutative Property, you can write $^-2 \times 4$ as $4 \times {}^-2$.

●● ●● ●● ●●   ← 4 groups of $^-2$

$^-2 \times 4 = 4 \times {}^-2 = {}^-8$

## Draw Conclusions

1. How would you model the product $3 \times 5$?

2. How would you model the product $3 \times {}^-4$?

3. **Synthesis** What do you notice about the sign of the product of two positive integers? What do you notice about the sign of a positive integer and a negative integer?

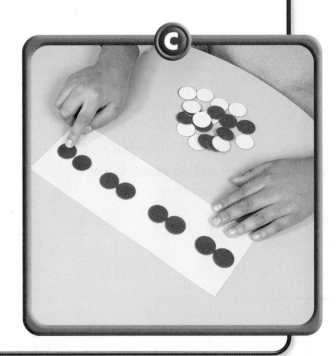

🐻 **O━┓ NS 2.3** Solve addition, subtraction, multiplication, and division problems, including those arising in concrete situations, that use positive and negative integers and combinations of these operations. *also* **O━┓ NS 2.0, MR 2.0, MR 2.4, MR 2.5, MR 3.2**

# Connect

You can also use a number line to multiply integers.

---

**Ⓐ Find the product 4 × 3.**

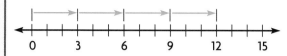

Start at 0.
Add 3 four times.

The number line shows that

$4 \times 3 = 3 + 3 + 3 + 3 = 12$.

So, $4 \times 3 = 12$.

---

**Ⓑ Find the product 5 × ⁻2.**

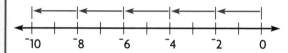

Start at 0.
Add ⁻2 five times.

The number line shows that

$5 \times {}^-2 = {}^-2 + {}^-2 + {}^-2 + {}^-2 + {}^-2 = {}^-10$.

So, $5 \times {}^-2 = {}^-10$.

**TALK Math**

**Explain** how using a number line to multiply two positive integers is like using a number line to multiply a positive and a negative integer.

---

# Practice

**Use counters to find the product.**

**1.** $2 \times {}^-5$    **2.** $2 \times 3$    **3.** $3 \times {}^-6$    **4.** ${}^-3 \times 5$    ☑**5.** ${}^-6 \times 2$

**Use the number line to find the product.**

**6.**

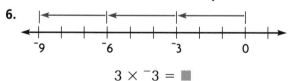

$3 \times {}^-3 = \blacksquare$

☑**7.**

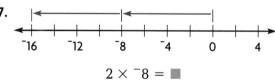

$2 \times {}^-8 = \blacksquare$

**Find the product.**

**8.** ${}^-4 \times 6$    **9.** $7 \times {}^-1$    **10.** $3 \times 9$    **11.** ${}^-5 \times 3$    **12.** $4 \times {}^-5$

**13.** $6 \times {}^-5$    **14.** ${}^-2 \times 7$    **15.** $3 \times 8$    **16.** $4 \times {}^-4$    **17.** $5 \times {}^-1$

**Solve.**

**18.** Sam uses 4 groups of 4 red counters to model a multiplication expression. What is the value of the expression?

**19.** Rick uses counters to model $5 \times 5$. Describe the model. What is the product $5 \times 5$?

**20.** **WRITE Math** **Explain** how to use a number line to find $6 \times {}^-3$.

---

**Technology**
Use Harcourt Mega Math, Fraction
Action, *Number Line Mine,* Level X.

# Record Multiplication

OBJECTIVE: Find the product of integers.

## Learn

**PROBLEM** Many shipwrecks are located off the coast of California. The *Newbern* is about 20 ft below sea level or at ⁻20. The *Yukon* is about 5 times as deep as the *Newbern*. At what depth is the *Yukon*?

**Example 1** Use a number line to find $5 \times {}^-20$.

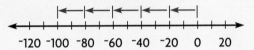

⁻120 ⁻100 ⁻80 ⁻60 ⁻40 ⁻20 0 20

The number line shows that $5 \times {}^-20 = {}^-100$. So, the Yukon lies 100 ft below sea level or at ⁻100.

• **What if** another shipwreck is 2 times as deep as the *Yukon*? How could you use the number line to find the depth of this shipwreck?

You can use patterns to find rules for multiplying integers.

▲ The *Yukon* was sunk completely intact off Mission Bay, near San Diego, on July 14, 2000.

### Example 2 Complete the pattern.

| | | |
|---|---|---|
| $5 \times 3 = 15$ | Study the pattern. As the second factor | $5 \times 3 = 15$ |
| $5 \times 2 = 10$ | decreases by 1, the product decreases by 5. | $5 \times 2 = 10$ |
| $5 \times 1 = 5$ | Use this rule to complete the pattern. | $5 \times 1 = 5$ |
| $5 \times 0 = 0$ | | $5 \times 0 = 0$ |
| $5 \times {}^-1 = \blacksquare$ | | $5 \times {}^-1 = {}^-5$ |
| $5 \times {}^-2 = \blacksquare$ | | $5 \times {}^-2 = {}^-10$ |
| $5 \times {}^-3 = \blacksquare$ | | $5 \times {}^-3 = {}^-15$ |

So, the missing products are ⁻5, ⁻10, and ⁻15.

### Example 3 Complete the pattern.

| | | |
|---|---|---|
| $^-5 \times 3 = {}^-15$ | Study the pattern. As the second factor | $^-5 \times 3 = {}^-15$ |
| $^-5 \times 2 = {}^-10$ | decreases by 1, the product increases by 5. | $^-5 \times 2 = {}^-10$ |
| $^-5 \times 1 = {}^-5$ | Use this rule to complete the pattern. | $^-5 \times 1 = {}^-5$ |
| $^-5 \times 0 = 0$ | | $^-5 \times 0 = 0$ |
| $^-5 \times {}^-1 = \blacksquare$ | | $^-5 \times {}^-1 = 5$ |
| $^-5 \times {}^-2 = \blacksquare$ | | $^-5 \times {}^-2 = 10$ |
| $^-5 \times {}^-3 = \blacksquare$ | | $^-5 \times {}^-3 = 15$ |

So, the missing products are 5, 10, and 15.

NS 2.3 Solve addition, subtraction, multiplication, and division problems, including those arising in concrete situations, that use positive and negative integers and combinations of these operations. *also* NS 2.0, AF 1.3, MR 2.4, MR 2.5, MR 3.2

# Rules for Integer Products

Examples 2 and 3 lead to the rules below.

> The product of two integers with like signs is positive.
> $$5 \times 6 = 30 \qquad {}^-4 \times {}^-3 = 12$$
> The product of two integers with unlike signs is negative.
> $$2 \times {}^-3 = {}^-6 \qquad {}^-7 \times 4 = {}^-28$$

The Zero Property of Multiplication holds for integers. So, the product of any integer and 0 is 0.

### Example 4 Find ⁻3 × ⁻9.

| | |
|---|---|
| $${}^-3 \times {}^-9 = \blacksquare$$ $${}^-3 \times {}^-9 = 27$$ | Multiply as with whole numbers. The sign of the product is positive because the integers have like signs. |

So, $${}^-3 \times {}^-9 = 27$$.

### Example 5

A scuba diver is 4 m below the surface of the water. An underwater vehicle is 6 times as deep as the scuba diver. At what depth is the underwater vehicle?

| | |
|---|---|
| Find $6 \times {}^-4$. $$6 \times {}^-4 = \blacksquare$$ $$6 \times {}^-4 = {}^-24$$ | Multiply as with whole numbers. The sign of the product is negative because the integers have unlike signs. |

So, the underwater vehicle is 24 m below sea level.

You can use mental math to find missing factors.

### Example 6 Use mental math to find the value of *y*.

| | |
|---|---|
| $${}^-7 \times y = {}^-84$$ | The product is negative. The product of two integers with unlike signs is negative. |

Since the first factor is negative, the second factor must be positive. So, the value of *y* is 12.

## Guided Practice

**1.** Use the number line to find $4 \times {}^-2$.

**2.** Use the number line to find $3 \times {}^-12$.

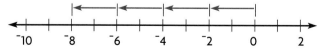

**Tell whether the sign of the product is positive or negative.**

**3.** ${}^-3 \times {}^-6$  **4.** ${}^-5 \times 4$  **5.** $8 \times 18$  **6.** $13 \times {}^-9$  ✓**7.** ${}^-17 \times {}^-4$

**Find the product.**

**8.** $9 \times 0$

**9.** $6 \times {}^-13$

**10.** ${}^-5 \times 9$

**11.** ${}^-7 \times {}^-83$

**✓12.** ${}^-2 \times 57$

**13.** **TALK Math** Explain how to determine the sign of a product when you multiply two integers.

## Independent Practice and Problem Solving

**Tell whether the sign of the product is positive or negative.**

**14.** ${}^-8 \times {}^-24$

**15.** $5 \times {}^-2$

**16.** ${}^-7 \times 4$

**17.** $5 \times 11$

**18.** ${}^-68 \times 12$

**19.** $9 \times {}^-54$

**20.** ${}^-4 \times {}^-7$

**21.** $75 \times {}^-3$

**22.** ${}^-8 \times 6$

**23.** ${}^-2 \times {}^-9$

**Find the product.**

**24.** ${}^-8 \times 12$

**25.** $0 \times {}^-5$

**26.** $42 \times {}^-6$

**27.** ${}^-4 \times {}^-10$

**28.** ${}^-1 \times 11$

**29.** ${}^-3 \times 7$

**30.** $84 \times {}^-6$

**31.** ${}^-37 \times {}^-3$

**32.** $4 \times {}^-95$

**33.** $66 \times {}^-7$

**34.** ${}^-12 \times 4$

**35.** $20 \times {}^-5$

**36.** ${}^-15 \times {}^-3$

**37.** $88 \times {}^-8$

**38.** ${}^-4 \times {}^-12$

**Use mental math to find the value of the variable.**

**39.** $4 \times z = 12$

**40.** ${}^-5 \times n = {}^-35$

**41.** $8 \times s = {}^-40$

**42.** $12 \times b = 48$

**43.** ${}^-6 \times t = {}^-30$

**44.** ${}^-7 \times y = 56$

**45.** $2 \times z = {}^-20$

**46.** ${}^-3 \times a = 0$

**47.** ${}^-5 \times s = {}^-40$

**48.** $5 \times r = {}^-60$

**49.** ${}^-9 \times p = 27$

**50.** ${}^-4 \times t = 36$

**51.** An underwater robot is 30 ft below the surface of the water. A shipwreck is 5 times as deep as the robot. How many feet deeper is the shipwreck than the robot?

**52.** **Pose a Problem** Look back at Problem 51. Write and solve a similar problem.

**53.** Horace used the table below right to find a pattern and write a rule for finding the sign of the product of three or more negative integers.

    **a.** What is the sign of the product of 3, 5, or 7 negative integers? of 4, 6, or 8 negative integers?

    **b.** What does this tell you about the product of an even number of negative integers? What does this tell you about the product of an odd number of negative integers?

**54.** **Reasoning** The product of four integers is negative. How many of the integers are negative?

**55.** **WRITE Math** What's the Question? The answer is the product ${}^-36$.

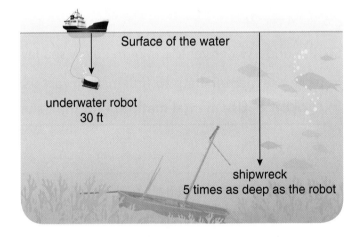

Surface of the water

underwater robot
30 ft

shipwreck
5 times as deep as the robot

| |
|---|
| ${}^-2 \times {}^-2 \times {}^-2 = {}^-8$ |
| ${}^-2 \times {}^-2 \times {}^-2 \times {}^-2 = 16$ |
| ${}^-2 \times {}^-2 \times {}^-2 \times {}^-2 \times {}^-2 = {}^-32$ |
| ${}^-2 \times {}^-2 \times {}^-2 \times {}^-2 \times {}^-2 \times {}^-2 = 64$ |
| ${}^-2 \times {}^-2 \times {}^-2 \times {}^-2 \times {}^-2 \times {}^-2 \times {}^-2 = {}^-128$ |
| ${}^-2 \times {}^-2 \times {}^-2 \times {}^-2 \times {}^-2 \times {}^-2 \times {}^-2 \times {}^-2 = 256$ |

**56.** A baker uses $2\frac{3}{4}$ cups of raisins to make one batch of raisin cookies. How many cups of raisins does the baker use to make 5 batches of cookies? (O⎯⊓ NS 2.0, p. 76)

**57.** Sam had a rope that was 7.65 meters long. He cut off 2.80 meters. What is the length of the rope now? (Grade 5 O⎯⊓ NS 2.1)

**58. Test Prep** What is ⁻6 × ⁻11?

A ⁻66        C 17

B ⁻17        D 66

**59.** A snack bar sold 387 hot dogs in 3 days. If the snack bar sold the same number each day, how many hot dogs did it sell in one day? (Grade 5 NS 1.0)

**60. Test Prep** Janet is snorkeling 2 feet below the surface or at ⁻2. A starfish is 3 times as deep as Janet. What number best describes the position of the starfish?

A ⁻6        C 1

B ⁻5        D 6

 **Problem Solving and Reasoning**

**ALGEBRA** You can use the Commutative and Associative Properties of multiplication to help simplify the products of integers.

### Commutative Property

$$3 \times {}^-12 \times {}^-2 = 3 \times {}^-2 \times {}^-12 \qquad \text{Change the order of the factors.}$$
$$= {}^-6 \times {}^-12$$
$$= 72$$

### Associative Property

$$25 \times ({}^-4 \times 8) = (25 \times {}^-4) \times 8 \qquad \text{Change the grouping of the factors.}$$
$$= {}^-100 \times 8$$
$$= {}^-800$$

### Commutative and Associative Properties

$${}^-20 \times ({}^-45 \times {}^-5) = {}^-20 \times ({}^-5 \times {}^-45) \qquad \text{Change the order of the factors.}$$
$$= ({}^-20 \times {}^-5) \times {}^-45 \qquad \text{Change the grouping of the factors.}$$
$$= 100 \times {}^-45$$
$$= {}^-4,500$$

**Use a property to help simplify the expression.**

**1.** ⁻2 × (5 × ⁻36)        **2.** ⁻50 × ⁻13 × 2        **3.** (⁻12 × ⁻4) × ⁻2        **4.** 5 × ⁻78 × ⁻2

## Quick Review

Divide.

1. $81 \div 9$
2. $32 \div 4$
3. $560 \div 8$
4. $200 \div 10$
5. $420 \div 70$

## Learn

Multiplication and division are inverse operations. To solve a division problem, think about the related multiplication problem.

$63 \div 7 = \blacksquare$     **Think:** What number multiplied by 7 equals 63?

$7 \times 9 = 63$, so $63 \div 7 = 9$.

You can use related multiplication problems to determine the sign of the quotient when dividing integers.

Look at the sign of the quotient of two positive integers and the sign of the quotient of two negative integers.

$5 \times 8 = 40$, so $40 \div 5 = 8$.
$^-5 \times 8 = {}^-40$, so $^-40 \div {}^-5 = 8$.

Look at the sign of the quotient of a positive integer and a negative integer.

$^-5 \times {}^-8 = 40$, so $40 \div {}^-5 = {}^-8$.
$5 \times {}^-8 = {}^-40$, so $^-40 \div 5 = {}^-8$.

The rules below apply when dividing integers.

> The quotient of two integers with like signs is positive.
>
> The quotient of two integers with unlike signs is negative.

### Example 1 Find the quotient.

**A** $^-219 \div {}^-3$
$^-219 \div {}^-3 = 73$

Divide as with whole numbers. The quotient is positive because the integers have like signs.

**B** $^-154 \div 11$
$^-154 \div 11 = {}^-14$

Divide as with whole numbers. The quotient is negative because the integers have unlike signs.

• Is the quotient $108 \div {}^-9$ positive or negative? Is the quotient $^-108 \div {}^-9$ positive or negative? **Explain.**

• How do the rules for the sign of the quotient of two integers compare with the rules for the sign of the product of two integers?

**NS 2.3** Solve addition, subtraction, multiplication, and division problems, including those arising in concrete situations, that use positive and negative integers and combinations of these operations. *also*
**NS 2.0, SDAP 1.1, MR 2.4, MR 2.5, MR 3.2, MR 3.3**

## Example 2

The table shows the monthly profit and loss for Cindy's snow shoveling business. What is the average monthly profit or loss?

| Monthly Profit and Loss | | | | | | |
|---|---|---|---|---|---|---|
| Month | Nov | Dec | Jan | Feb | Mar | Apr |
| Profit or Loss | ⁻$12 | ⁻$10 | ⁻$5 | $7 | ⁻$9 | $5 |

> **READ Math**
> You should read ⁻4 as "negative 4" and not as "minus 4."

$$^-12 + {}^-10 + {}^-5 + 7 + {}^-9 + 5 = {}^-24 \qquad \text{Find the sum.}$$

$$^-24 \div 6 = {}^-4 \qquad \text{Divide by the number of months.}$$

So, since the quotient is negative, there is an average monthly loss of $4.

- **What if** Cindy's snow shoveling business had a profit of $20 in December instead of a loss of $10? What would be the average monthly profit or loss?

## Example 3

Cindy recorded the hourly temperature during a snowstorm. What was the average temperature from 4:00 A.M. to 7:00 A.M.?

| Hourly Temperature | | | |
|---|---|---|---|
| Time (A.M.) | 4:00 | 5:00 | 6:00 | 7:00 |
| Temperature (°F) | ⁻9 | ⁻6 | ⁻2 | 1 |

$$^-9 + {}^-6 + {}^-2 + 1 = {}^-16 \qquad \text{Find the sum.}$$

$$^-16 \div 4 = {}^-4 \qquad \text{Divide by the number of temperatures.}$$

So, the average temperature was ⁻4°F.

- How can you use multiplication to check the answer to Example 3?
- **What if** the sum of the temperatures was 0°F? What would the average temperature be? **Explain.**

## Guided Practice

**Use the multiplication problem to help you solve each division problem.**

1. ⁻3 × ⁻6 = 18,
   so 18 ÷ ⁻3 = ■.

2. ⁻10 × 4 = ⁻40,
   so ⁻40 ÷ ⁻10 = ■.

3. 8 × ⁻5 = ⁻40,
   so ⁻40 ÷ 8 = ■.

4. ⁻2 × 0 = 0,
   so 0 ÷ ⁻2 = ■.

**Find the quotient.**

5. 32 ÷ 4

6. ⁻90 ÷ ⁻10

7. ⁻72 ÷ 8

8. 49 ÷ ⁻7

9. ⁻36 ÷ ⁻3

10. 36 ÷ ⁻6

11. 144 ÷ 4

12. ⁻225 ÷ ⁻5

✓13. ⁻328 ÷ 8

✓14. ⁻190 ÷ ⁻2

15. **TALK Math** **Explain** how to find the sign of a quotient when you divide integers.

**Find the product or quotient.**

| | | | | |
|---|---|---|---|---|
| **16.** $^-63 \div ^-7$ | **17.** $88 \div ^-8$ | **18.** $^-30 \div 3$ | **19.** $64 \div 8$ | **20.** $92 \div ^-4$ |
| **21.** $^-75 \div ^-5$ | **22.** $64 \div 8$ | **23.** $20 \div ^-4$ | **24.** $96 \div ^-3$ | **25.** $0 \div ^-3$ |
| **26.** $^-252 \div 12$ | **27.** $^-12 \times ^-5$ | **28.** $420 \div ^-15$ | **29.** $6 \times 40$ | **30.** $644 \div ^-14$ |
| **31.** $144 \div ^-3$ | **32.** $^-35 \times ^-1$ | **33.** $^-300 \div 6$ | **34.** $^-75 \times 3$ | **35.** $^-819 \div ^-13$ |
| **36.** $585 \div ^-13$ | **37.** $^-60 \times 90$ | **38.** $24 \times ^-12$ | **39.** $300 \div ^-50$ | **40.** $^-980 \div ^-14$ |

**Compare. Write $<$, $>$, or $=$.**

**41.** $48 \div ^-2 \bullet 8 \times 3$     **42.** $^-54 \div ^-2 \bullet 81 \div 3$     **43.** $21 \times 8 \bullet 14 \times ^-12$    **44.** $^-28 \div ^-14 \bullet 84 \div ^-42$

**Use mental math to find the value of the variable.**

| | | | |
|---|---|---|---|
| **45.** $x \div 4 = 7$ | **46.** $^-18 \div n = ^-9$ | **47.** $s \div ^-5 = ^-12$ | **48.** $^-48 \div b = 4$ |
| **49.** $^-40 \div t = ^-8$ | **50.** $y \div ^-9 = 6$ | **51.** $c \div 3 = ^-13$ | **52.** $^-60 \div a = 10$ |
| **53.** $^-10 \div a = 1$ | **54.** $^-45 \div t = ^-5$ | **55.** $y \div ^-4 = 0$ | **56.** $c \div 3 = ^-15$ |

**USE DATA** For 57–58, use the table.

**57.** What is the average temperature in Barrow, Alaska, for November through April?

**58.** The average temperature in Barrow for January is twice as far below zero as the average temperature in McKinley Park, Alaska, for February. What is the average temperature in McKinley Park for February?

**Average Temperature (2005–2006) Barrow, Alaska**

| Month | Nov | Dec | Jan | Feb | Mar | Apr |
|---|---|---|---|---|---|---|
| Temperature (°F) | $^-1$ | $^-4$ | $^-12$ | $^-9$ | $^-18$ | $^-4$ |

**59.** **≡FAST FACT** The record low January temperature in California, $^-45°$ F, was set in 1937 in Boca, CA. That is three times as far below zero as the record low May temperature set in 1964, in White Mountain, CA. What is the record low May temperature in White Mountain?

**60.** Mia had a loss of \$50 for the first month of operating a ski-rental business. She had no profit or loss for the next 3 months. Then, she had a profit of \$120 for the fifth month. What is Mia's average monthly profit or loss for the 5 months?

**61.** **Pose a Problem** Look back at Problem 60. Write and solve a new problem by changing the profit and loss for each month.

**62.** **Reasoning** The dividend, divisor, and quotient of a division problem all have the same sign. Is that sign positive or negative?

**63.** The counters below represent a multiplication problem. Write the multiplication problem and two related division problems.

**64.** **Reasoning** The quotient $^-5 \div 2$ can be written as $^-2$ r $^-1$. What is the quotient $^-10 \div 7$?

**65.** Which is the greatest quotient? **Explain.**
$36 \div ^-12$     $^-36 \div ^-12$     $^-36 \div 12$

**66.** **WRITE Math** ▸ Explain how you can use $^-24 \times 5 = ^-120$ to find $^-120 \div ^-24$.

**67.** What is the volume of this rectangular prism?

(Grade 5 ⊙━┓ MG 1.3)

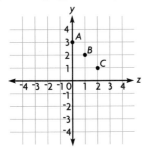

2 centimeters
4 centimeters
12 centimeters

**68.** What ordered pair best names the location of Point *C*? (Grade 5 ⊙━┓ SDAP 1.5)

**69.** What is the product of ⁻14 and 6?

(⊙━┓ NS 2.3, p. 172)

**70. Test Prep** What is the quotient of ⁻48 and ⁻2?

| | |
|---|---|
| **A** ⁻42 | **C** 24 |
| **B** ⁻24 | **D** 42 |

**71. Test Prep** The average monthly low temperature in a city for four months was 3°F, 2°F, 4°F, and ⁻5°F. What was the average monthly low temperature for the four-month period?

| | |
|---|---|
| **A** ⁻4°F | **C** 1°F |
| **B** ⁻1°F | **D** 4°F |

---

## Problem Solving connects to Science

Earth is composed of many different layers. The outer layer is the lithosphere. It includes the crust and the upper mantle. The base of the crust is about 40 km below Earth's surface. The base of the upper mantle is about 400 km below Earth's surface. How many times as far below Earth's surface is the base of the upper mantle as compared with the base of the crust?

$$^-400 \div ^-40 = 10$$

So, the base of the upper mantle is 10 times as far below Earth's surface as the base of the crust.

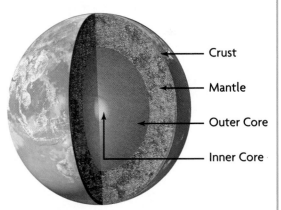

Crust

Mantle

Outer Core

Inner Core

**Solve.**

**1.** There are two types of crust, continental and oceanic. The base of the continental crust is about 40 km below Earth's surface. That is about five times as far below Earth's surface as the base of the oceanic crust. About how far below Earth's surface is the base of the oceanic crust?

**2.** Earth's inner core is about 6,400 km below Earth's surface. The base of the crust is about 40 km below Earth's surface. About how many times as far below Earth's surface is the inner core as compared with the base of the crust?

# 4 Multiply and Divide Integers

OBJECTIVE: Find the product and quotient of integers.

## Quick Review

Find the product or quotient.

1. $^-5 \times 6$
2. $^-21 \div 3$
3. $8 \times ^-7$
4. $^-40 \div ^-8$
5. $^-9 \times ^-6$

## Learn

You can use the rules for multiplying and dividing integers to find missing signs for integers in multiplication and division sentences.

### HANDS ON Activity

**A** Find all possible signs for the factors that make each multiplication sentence true.

$■7 \times ■4 = ^-28$          $■5 \times ■8 = 40$

$^-7 \times ^+4 = ^-28$          $^-5 \times ^-8 = 40$

$^+7 \times ^-4 = ^-28$          $^+5 \times ^+8 = 40$

• What do you know about the signs of two integers whose product is negative?

**B** Find all possible signs for the dividend and divisor that make each division sentence true.

$■36 \div ■4 = 9$          $■10 \div ■2 = ^-5$

$^+36 \div ^+4 = 9$          $^-10 \div ^+2 = ^-5$

$^-36 \div ^-4 = 9$          $^+10 \div ^-2 = ^-5$

• What do you know about the signs of two integers whose quotient is positive?

**C** Find all possible signs to make the number sentence true.

$■3 \times ■3 = ^-9$          $■45 \div ■9 = 5$

$■6 \times ■5 = 30$          $■64 \div ■8 = ^-8$

$■8 \times ■7 = ^-56$          $■12 \div ■12 = 1$

### Math Idea

Perform all operations inside parentheses first, using the rules for finding products and quotients of integers.

## Example 1

**Find the value of each expression.**

**A** $^-4 \times (^-81 \div 9)$

$^-4 \times (^-81 \div 9)$   Divide.

$^-4 \times ^-9$   Multiply.

$36$

So, $^-4 \times (^-81 \div 9) = 36$.

**B** $64 \div (^-4 \times ^-8)$

$64 \div (^-4 \times ^-8)$   Multiply.

$64 \div 32$   Divide.

$2$

So, $64 \div (^-4 \times ^-8) = 2$.

NS 2.3 Solve addition, subtraction, multiplication, and division problems, including those arising in concrete situations, that use positive and negative integers and combinations of these operations. *also* NS 2.0, MR 2.4, MR 2.5, MR 3.2

**Find all possible signs that make the number sentences true.**

1. ☐3 × ⁺6 = 18
⁻3 × ☐6 = 18

2. ⁻30 ÷ ☐10 = ⁻3
☐30 ÷ ☐10 = ⁻3

3. ☐91 ÷ ☐13 = ⁻7
☐91 ÷ ☐13 = ⁻7

✓4. ☐6 × ☐8 = 48
☐6 × ☐8 = 48

**Find the value of the expression.**

5. ⁻3 × (⁻63 ÷ 7)

6. (⁻4 × ⁻6) ÷ 2

7. ⁻81 ÷ (⁻3 × ⁻3)

✓8. 8 × (16 ÷ ⁻8)

9. **TALK Math** Explain how you decide the possible signs for the factors of a product.

## Independent Practice and Problem Solving

**Find the value of the expression.**

10. ⁻3 × (⁻56 ÷ 8)

11. ⁻18 ÷ ⁻3 × 9

12. ⁻3 × (⁻24 ÷ ⁻6)

13. 72 ÷ ⁻9 × 4

14. 7 × (⁻55 ÷ 5)

15. ⁻18 ÷ (2 × 9)

16. 4 × (⁻49 ÷ 7)

17. ⁻54 ÷ ⁻9 × 6

18. 2 × (⁻35 ÷ 7)

19. ⁻42 ÷ (⁻1 × ⁻6)

20. ⁻25 × (4 ÷ ⁻2)

21. ⁻72 ÷ 6 × ⁻4

22. 12 × (⁻48 ÷ 3)

23. ⁻196 ÷ (49 × ⁻2)

24. 25 × (⁻65 ÷ 5)

25. ⁻225 ÷ ⁻15 × 6

**Use mental math to find the value of the variable.**

26. 2 × z = ⁻20

27. y ÷ ⁻9 = 6

28. ⁻3 × a = 0

29. ⁻60 ÷ b = 10

30. 8 × c = 32

31. d ÷ ⁻7 = 8

32. 42 ÷ r = 7

33. 13 × p = 0

34. **Reasoning** Neil writes a number sentence using each of the following integers only once: ⁻6, ⁻3, 24, and 48. What is a number sentence he could have written?

35. The challenge problem on a math test is to solve the equation 2 × (⁻25 ÷ y) = ⁻10. What is the value of y?

36. Beth uses two multiplication sentences to check the solution to ⁻18 ÷ ☐ = 9. What are the multiplication sentences?

37. **WRITE Math** Explain how to use the rules for dividing integers to find missing signs for the dividend and quotient in ☐56 ÷ ☐7 = 8.

## Achieving the Standards

38. Marta divided $1\frac{1}{2}$ pounds of fruit salad into 4 equal servings. What fraction of a pound is in each serving? (NS 2.1, p. 100)

39. What is the difference between the median and mode of the data set below?
(Grade 5 SDAP 1.1)

12, 10, 9, 10, 14

40. What is ⁻17 − 8? (O━┓ NS 2.3, p. 154)

41. **Test Prep** What is the value of ⁻60 ÷ (⁻5 × 2)?

A ⁻24

B ⁻6

C 6

D 24

Extra Practice on page 188, Set C

OBJECTIVE: Add, subtract, multiply, and divide integers.

## Quick Review

Solve.

1. $^-5 \times 6$    2. $3 - 5$
3. $8 + {}^-7$    4. $^-40 \div {}^-8$
5. $^-9 - {}^-6$

## Learn

**PROBLEM** The stock price of Fab Jeans Industries stock was on the decline. It fell $5 in January and $8 in February. By the end of March, the price had declined an additional $14. Evan wanted to find how much the price of the stock changed for the three months using the expression $^-5 - 8 + {}^-14$.

You can use the rules for integers to find the value of expressions involving combinations of operations with integers.

### Example 1  Find the value of $^-5 - 8 + {}^-14$.

$^-5 - 8 + {}^-14$
$^-5 + {}^-8 + {}^-14$    Write $^-5 - 8$ as an addition expression. Add.
$^-13 + {}^-14$    Add.
$^-27$

So, the price of Fab Jeans Industries stock dropped $27.

### Example 2  Find the value of $^-24 \div ({}^-6 - 2)$.

$^-24 \div ({}^-6 - 2)$    Perform operations in parentheses. Write as an addition expression.
$^-24 \div ({}^-6 + {}^-2)$    Add.
$^-24 \div {}^-8$    Divide.
$3$

**ERROR ALERT**

When you write a subtraction expression as an addition expression, be sure to add the opposite of the number you are subtracting.

### Example 3  Use mental math to find a possible value for *y* to make $(y - {}^-5) \div 2$ equal to a positive integer.

$(y - {}^-5) \div 2$    Write as an addition expression.
$(y + 5) \div 2$    **Think:** To get a positive integer, the dividend, $(y + 5)$, must be greater than or equal to 2. It must also be divisible by 2.
$({}^-3 + 5) \div 2$    Use mental math. Try $y = {}^-3$. Then add.
$2 \div 2$    Divide.
$1$

So, $^-3$ is a possible value for *y*.

- Replace *y* with $^-5$, $^-1$, 1, and 3. Then find the value of each expression. Look for a pattern. What does this tell you about the values of *y* that will make the expression equal to a positive integer?

**NS 2.3** Solve addition, subtraction, multiplication, and division problems, including those arising in concrete situations, that use positive and negative integers and combinations of these operations.
*also* **NS 2.0, AF 1.3, MR 2.4, MR 2.5, MR 3.2**

# Integer Patterns

A number pattern can repeat the operations of addition, subtraction, multiplication, division, or a combination of these operations.

**Example 4** **Find a possible rule. Then find the next two numbers in the pattern. 1, $^-$2, $^-$5, $^-$8, ■, ■**

| Step 1 | Step 2 |
|---|---|
| **Find a possible rule.** | **Use the rule.** |
| Try subtract 3 because $1 - 3 = {}^-2$. | 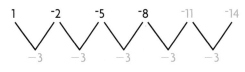 |
| $^-2 - 3 = {}^-2 + ({}^-3) = {}^-5$ | |
| $^-5 - 3 = {}^-5 + ({}^-3) = {}^-8$ | |
| A possible rule is to subtract 3. | $^-8 - 3 = {}^-8 + {}^-3 = {}^-11$    $^-11 - 3 = {}^-11 + {}^-3 = {}^-14$ |

So, $^-11$ and $^-14$ are the next two numbers in the pattern.

You can also use a rule to find missing numbers in a pattern.

**Example 5** **Find a possible rule. Then find the missing numbers in the pattern. 4, 8, 3, 6, 1, ■, ■, $^-$6, $^-$11**

| Step 1 | Step 2 |
|---|---|
| **Find a possible rule.** | **Use the rule.** |
| Look at the pattern. The numbers increase and decrease, so try two operations. | $1 \times 2 = 2$        $2 - 5 = 2 + {}^-5 = {}^-3$ |
| | Check the last numbers in the pattern. |
| Try multiply by 2, and then subtract 5, because $4 \times 2 = 8$ and $8 - 5 = 3$ $3 \times 2 = 6$ and $6 - 5 = 1$ | $^-3 \times 2 = {}^-6$    $^-6 - 5 = {}^-6 + {}^-5 = {}^-11$ |
| A possible rule is to multiply by 2, and then subtract 5. | |

So, the missing numbers in the pattern are 2 and $^-3$.

## Guided Practice

**Find the value of the expression.**

1. $(2 - {}^-7) + 10$

   $(2 + 7) + 10$

   $9 + 10 = $ ■

2. $({}^-12 - 3) \div {}^-5$

   $({}^-12 + {}^-3) \div {}^-5$

   $^-15 \div {}^-5 = $ ■

✓3. $^-11 \times (3 - 6)$

   $^-11 \times (3 + {}^-6)$

   $^-11 \times {}^-3 = $ ■

**Write a possible rule for each pattern. Then find the missing numbers.**

4. $^-7, {}^-11, {}^-15, {}^-19,$ ■, ■

✓5. $1, {}^-3, 9, {}^-27,$ ■, ■, $729, {}^-2{,}187$

6. **TALK Math** Explain how to find a possible rule for a pattern.

## Independent Practice and Problem Solving

**Find the value of the expression.**

**7.** $(^-9 - 6) \div {}^-5$  **8.** $(2 - {}^-3) \times 4$  **9.** $^-12 + (^-9 - {}^-5)$  **10.** $^-4 \times 6 + 14$

**11.** $(^-10 - {}^-10) \div 2$  **12.** $(6 - {}^-7) \times {}^-8$  **13.** $^-1 + 8 - {}^-6$  **14.** $8 + (^-10 \times 4)$

**15.** $(^-18 - 2) \div {}^-4$  **16.** $^-7 + 13 - {}^-4$  **17.** $25 \div (6 - 7)$  **18.** $11 \times (48 \div {}^-8)$

**Write a possible rule for each pattern. Then find the missing numbers.**

**19.** $^-5, {}^-7, {}^-9, {}^-11, \blacksquare, \blacksquare$

**20.** $14, 5, {}^-4, {}^-13, \blacksquare, \blacksquare, {}^-40$

**21.** $^-2, 6, {}^-18, 54, \blacksquare, 486, \blacksquare$

**22.** $6, {}^-6, 6, {}^-6, \blacksquare, \blacksquare, 6$

**23.** $^-11, {}^-6, {}^-1, 4, \blacksquare, 14, \blacksquare$

**24.** $^-1, {}^-4, {}^-16, {}^-64, \blacksquare, \blacksquare, {}^-4{,}096$

**Compare. Write >, <, or =.**

**25.** $(5 - {}^-7) \times 8 \ \blacksquare\ (6 + {}^-3) \times 9$

**26.** $^-24 \div (1 - {}^-5) \ \blacksquare\ {}^-24 \div 4$

**27.** $(7 - {}^-4) + |{}^-5| \ \blacksquare\ (9 + {}^-5) \times 4$

**28.** $(^-1 \times 7) \div {}^-7 \ \blacksquare\ (7 \div {}^-1) \times {}^-1$

**29.** New Orleans, Louisiana, has an elevation of 8 ft below sea level. Ohio's highest elevation is Campbell Hill. The elevation of Campbell Hill is 1,565 ft higher than a point twice as far below sea level as is New Orleans. What is the elevation of Campbell Hill?

**30.** The temperature dropped 5°F on Monday, another 8°F on Tuesday, and then dropped 12°F more on Wednesday. By how much did the temperature change over the three days?

**31. Reasoning** Write two different rules that can be used to find the next number in the pattern. Then find the next number.

$^-29, {}^-18, {}^-7, 4, \blacksquare$

**32. Pose a Problem** Look back at Problem 30. Write a similar problem by changing the daily temperature changes and the number of days.

**33.** During one week, Built-Up Industries' stock increased $2 for 3 days, and decreased $3 for 2 days. By how much did the stock's value change at the end of the week?

**34.** **WRITE Math** Explain how to find the next two integers in the following pattern. Then find the integers.

$100{,}000, {}^-10{,}000, 1{,}000, {}^-100, \blacksquare, \blacksquare$

## Achieving the Standards

**35.** After 6 weeks, Steve's Sandwich Shop has lost $96. What is the average loss each week?
(NS 2.3, p. 176)

**36.** Use a straightedge to draw two parallel lines.
(Grade 5 MG 2.1)

**37.** In Pete's class, 15 out of 25 students have traveled outside of their state. What percent of the class is that? (NS 1.0, p. 24)

**38. Test Prep** What is the value of $(^-7 - {}^-11) \times {}^-5$?

**A** $^-90$

**B** $^-20$

**C** $20$

**D** $90$

**184**    **Extra Practice** on page 188, Set D

# Pose a Problem

There are different ways to pose problems. One way is to change the conditions in a problem you are given. For example, you can change the numbers in a problem or exchange known and unknown information. You can also make a problem more open-ended.

Solve the problem. Then use all three methods to change it.

**Problem** Tammy rides the museum elevator up 6 floors from the ground floor to the art exhibit. Then she rides down 8 floors to the parking garage. How many floors below ground level is the parking gargage. Answer: 2 floors

## Change the Numbers

Tammy rides the museum elevator up 3 floors from the ground floor to the art exhibit. Then she rides down 4 floors to the parking garage. How many floors below the ground floor is the parking garage?
Answer: 1 floor

## Exchange the Known and Unknown Information

Tammy rides the museum elevator from the ground floor up to the art exhibit. Then she rides down 8 floors to the parking garage. The parking garage is 3 floors below the ground floor. How many floors up did Tammy ride to the art exhibit?
Answer: 5 floors

## Make the Problem More Open-Ended

Tammy rides the museum elevator up 4 floors from the ground floor. Then she rides down to a floor below the ground floor. If there are 4 floors below the ground floor, how many floors down might she have ridden the elevator?
Answer: 5, 6, 7, or 8 floors

### Tips

- Changing the numbers can make the problem easier or more difficult. You don't have to change the situation.
- Exchanging the known and unknown information requires you to rewrite some of the information given in the original situation.
- Making a problem more open-ended requires you to change the conditions of the problem so that more than one correct answer is possible.

**Problem Solving** Use all three methods to change the problem. Then solve.

Jason is delivering packages to a museum. He enters an elevator 2 floors below the ground floor. He rides up 6 floors to the first delivery, down 3 floors to the second delivery, and up 1 floor to the last delivery. On which floor is Jason's last delivery?
Answer: the second floor

# Problem Solving Workshop
## Skill: Multistep Problems
OBJECTIVE: Solve problems by using the skill solve multistep problems.

## Use the Skill

**PROBLEM** A shortage of rain caused the water level of a California reservoir to change by a 3 ft drop in May, a 5 ft drop in June, and a 10 ft drop in July. What was the average monthly change in the water level?

This problem involves more than one step. To solve a multistep problem, break it into single steps.

### Step 1

First, find the *total amount of change* in the water level of the reservoir.

$^-3 + {}^-5 + {}^-10 = {}^-18$    Add to find the total amount of change in the water level.

### Step 2

Then, find the *average monthly change* in the water level.

$^-18 \div 3 = {}^-6$    Divide the total amount of change by the number of months.

So, the average monthly change in the water level was a drop of 6 ft.

## Think and Discuss
**Solve by breaking down each problem into single steps.**

**a.** The table at the right shows the monthly profit or loss of Gloria's Produce Market for 6 months. What was the average monthly profit or loss?

**b.** The temperature was 5°F at 3:00 P.M., $^-2$°F at 7:00 P.M., and $^-6$°F at 11:00 P.M. Was the temperature decrease greater between 3:00 P.M. and 7:00 P.M. or between 7:00 P.M. and 11:00 P.M.?

| Gloria's Produce Market | | | | | | |
|---|---|---|---|---|---|---|
| **Month** | Jan | Feb | Mar | Apr | May | Jun |
| **Profit or Loss** | $^-$$15 | $^-$$22 | $^-$$30 | $^-$$8 | $9 | $12 |

**c.** A vegetable garden has 6 spinach plants in each of 3 rows, 4 squash plants in each of 2 rows, and 5 turnip plants in each of 6 rows. How many plants are in the vegetable garden?

**d.** Nick earns $30 per hr as a gardener. Sandy earns $42 per hr as a landscape designer. How much more does Sandy earn when Nick and Sandy each work a 40-hr work week?

NS 2.3 Solve addition, subtraction, multiplication, and division problems, including these arising in concrete situations, that use positive and negative integers and combinations of these operations. *also* NS 2.0, MR 1.0, MR 1.3, MR 2.0, MR 2.4, MR 2.5, MR 3.0, MR 3.1, MR 3.2, MR 3.3

1. Mike recorded the low temperature each day for a week for science class. What was the average low temperature?

   **First,** decide what steps are needed to find the average low temperature.

   **Then,** decide what operation you will use in each step.

   **Finally,** solve the problem.

2. **What if** the low temperature on Saturday was ⁻1°F? How would the average low temperature change?

3. The table below shows Maria's profits and losses during a three-day weekend. What was the average daily profit or loss for Maria's lemonade stand?

| Low Temperatures | |
| --- | --- |
| Day | Temperature (°F) |
| Sun | ⁻3 |
| Mon | ⁻4 |
| Tues | ⁻5 |
| Wed | ⁻1 |
| Thu | ⁻6 |
| Fri | ⁻1 |
| Sat | ⁻8 |

| Maria's Lemonade Stand | | | |
| --- | --- | --- | --- |
| Day | Fri | Sat | Sun |
| Profit of Loss | ⁻$4 | $14 | ⁻$1 |

## Mixed Applications

4. A vegetable garden has an area of 108 ft². Radishes grow in $\frac{1}{4}$ of the garden. Tomatoes grow in the rest of the garden. How many more square feet of the garden are used to grow tomatoes than to grow radishes?

5. Rachel has enough garden space to plant 100 seeds. She has 25 cucumber seeds, 41 zucchini seeds, and 53 beet seeds. Does Rachel have enough garden space to plant all the seeds? Do you need to find an estimate or an exact number? Solve.

6. Salima bought 6 packets of cucumber seeds and 3 packets of zucchini seeds. Is there enough information to find how many seeds Salima bought in all? **Explain.**

7. Write a product that is greater than the quotient of ⁻56 and 4, and less than the quotient of 54 and 9.

**USE DATA** For 8–10, use the seed packets.

8. Heidi is planting a vegetable garden 7 ft long and 4 ft wide. She buys 3 packets of carrot seeds and 2 packets of artichoke seeds. She pays the clerk with a $20 bill. How much change should Heidi get back?

9. Students want to plant 115 artichoke seeds in the school garden. How many packets of artichoke seeds should they buy?

10. **WRITE Math** ▸ **What's the Error?** The sales clerk said that the cost of 4 packets of carrot seeds is $11.25. **Describe** his error and find the correct amount.

11. **Reasoning** Copy and complete the puzzle at the right. Each row, column, and diagonal has the same sum. Use any numbers from ⁻3 to 5 for the missing numbers. (Hɪɴᴛ: What is the sum of the top row?)

| ⁻2 | 3 | 2 |
| --- | --- | --- |
| 5 | ▪ | ▪ |
| ▪ | ▪ | 4 |

# Extra Practice

## Set A  Find the product. (pp. 172–175)

1. $^-3 \times 0$
2. $2 \times {^-7}$
3. $^-3 \times {^-6}$
4. $2 \times {^-5}$
5. $^-11 \times {^-4}$

6. $^-9 \times {^-8}$
7. $3 \times {^-12}$
8. $10 \times {^-8}$
9. $^-5 \times {^-11}$
10. $6 \times {^-1}$

11. $4 \times {^-6}$
12. $^-7 \times {^-7}$
13. $^-12 \times {^-4}$
14. $9 \times {^-10}$
15. $^-12 \times {^-1}$

16. Marcus is snorkeling 3 ft below the surface, or at $^-3$. A parrotfish is 2 times as deep as Marcus. What number best descries the position of the parrotfish?

17. A scuba diver is 20 ft below the surface of the water. A nurse shark is 3 times as deep as the diver. How many feet deeper is the nurse shark than the diver?

## Set B  Find the quotient. (pp. 176–179)

1. $21 \div 7$
2. $15 \div {^-3}$
3. $12 \div {^-1}$
4. $^-48 \div {^-4}$
5. $^-36 \div 6$

6. $42 \div {^-7}$
7. $^-20 \div {^-2}$
8. $^-56 \div {^-8}$
9. $75 \div {^-5}$
10. $^-128 \div {^-8}$

11. $121 \div {^-11}$
12. $^-49 \div {^-7}$
13. $225 \div {^-15}$
14. $^-169 \div {^-13}$
15. $220 \div {^-10}$

## Set C  Find the value of the expression. (pp. 180–181)

1. $2 \times (^-54 \div 9)$
2. $^-3 \times (^-35 \div 7)$
3. $^-45 \div (3 \times 5)$
4. $^-16 \div (^-2 \times 8)$

5. $^-60 \div (5 \times 4)$
6. $10 \times (36 \div {^-6})$
7. $7 \times (^-48 \div {^-12})$
8. $^-120 \div (5 \times 6)$

9. $^-4 \times (^-32 \div 8)$
10. $^-36 \div (3 \times 2)$
11. $12 \times (^-48 \div 6)$
12. $^-150 \div (^-3 \times {^-2})$

13. Melissa orders 6 large pizzas. Each pizza has 8 slices. If the pizzas are split evenly among 12 people, how many slices will each person get?

14. George earned a total of $240 last week after working 8 hours a day for 5 days. How much did George earn for each hour of work?

## Set D  Find the value of the expression. (pp. 182–185)

1. $(^-6 + 10) \div 4$
2. $(^-6 + 8) - {^-9}$
3. $(42 \div {^-7}) \times {^-4}$
4. $(^-9 - {^-12}) \div 3$

5. $(^-20 - 2) \div {^-11}$
6. $(40 \div {^-8}) \times {^-5}$
7. $(^-10 - 5) \div {^-5}$
8. $(^-6 \times 4) + 10$

9. $(^-7 + {^-5}) \times {^-12}$
10. $(^-15 + {^-3}) \times {^-4}$
11. $(^-8 \times 7) + 18$
12. $(^-30 - {^-9}) \div {^-7}$

13. On his math test, Charlie answered 21 of 25 problems correctly. Suppose each correct answer was worth 4 points and each incorrect answer was worth $^-1$ point. Write and find the value of an expression to show the number of points Charlie earned.

14. A shop owner buys T-shirts for $5 each and sells them for $12 each. On a certain day, the shop owner sells 11 T-shirts. Write and find the value of an expression to show the amount of money the shop owner made on the sale of the T-shirts.

**CD ROM  Technology**
Use Harcourt Mega Math, Fraction Action, *Number Line Mine*, Level X.

# integer spin

**On Your Mark!**
2 players

**Get Set!**
• Integer cards
• Operation cards
• 2 different coins
• Spinner, labeled 1–4

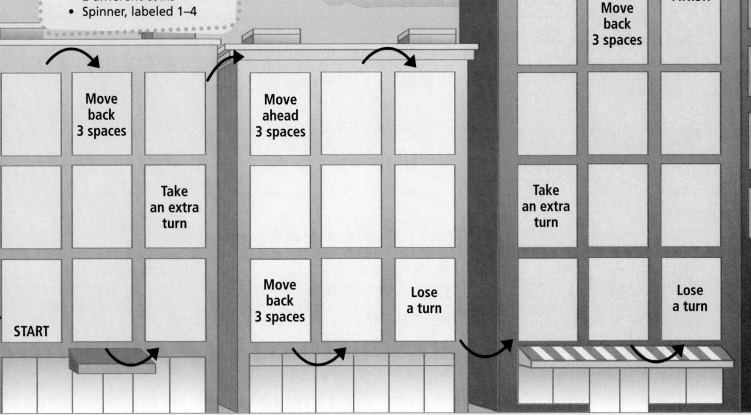

START

Move back 3 spaces

Take an extra turn

Move ahead 3 spaces

Move back 3 spaces

Lose a turn

Move back 3 spaces

FINISH

Take an extra turn

Lose a turn

**Go!**

■ Shuffle the integer cards and operation cards separately and place each set facedown in a pile.

■ Each player selects a coin and places it on START. Decide who will go first.

■ Player 1 draws two integer cards and one operation card from the piles.

■ Player 1 uses the cards to write an expression, such as ⁻1 × ⁻3, and then find its value.

■ Player 2 checks the answer. If it is correct, Player 1 spins the pointer to find the number of spaces to advance.

■ If the answer is correct or incorrect, play passes to Player 2.

■ The first player to reach FINISH wins.

  # Chapter 7 Review/Test

## Check Concepts

1. Explain how to model the product $^-4 \times {}^-2$. (O—ㄲ NS 2.3, pp. 170–171)

2. What do you know about the signs of two integers that have a negative product? (O—ㄲ NS 2.3, pp. 170–171)

## Check Skills

**Find the product.** (O—ㄲ NS 2.3, pp. 172–175)

| | | | | |
|---|---|---|---|---|
| **3.** $8 \times {}^-2$ | **4.** $^-3 \times 3$ | **5.** $9 \times {}^-4$ | **6.** $0 \times {}^-1$ | **7.** $^-1 \times {}^-12$ |
| **8.** $^-11 \times {}^-8$ | **9.** $12 \times {}^-5$ | **10** $^-8 \times {}^-9$ | **11.** $^-6 \times 3$ | **12.** $^-4 \times 0$ |

**Find the quotient.** (O—ㄲ NS 2.3, pp. 176–179)

| | | | | |
|---|---|---|---|---|
| **13.** $36 \div {}^-3$ | **14.** $^-33 \div {}^-11$ | **15.** $24 \div {}^-2$ | **16.** $^-18 \div 3$ | **17.** $30 \div {}^-6$ |
| **18.** $^-15 \div {}^-1$ | **19.** $^-56 \div {}^-7$ | **20.** $40 \div {}^-2$ | **21.** $160 \div {}^-4$ | **22.** $99 \div {}^-11$ |

**Find the value of the expression.** (O—ㄲ NS 2.3, pp. 180–181, 182–185)

| | | |
|---|---|---|
| **23.** $^-32 \div ({}^-2 \times {}^-4)$ | **24.** $6 \times (51 \div 3)$ | **25.** $(4 - {}^-8) \times 9$ |
| **26.** $(12 + 24) \div {}^-6$ | **27.** $({}^-16 - 2) \div {}^-3$ | **28.** $({}^-45 \div {}^-9) \times 2$ |
| **29.** $({}^-1 + 3) - {}^-9$ | **30.** $({}^-7 \times 5) + 19$ | **31.** $^-16 \times ({}^-10 \div 2)$ |
| **32.** $({}^-121 \div 11) + 19$ | **33.** $({}^-144 - 6) \div 10$ | **34.** $^-48 \div (31 - 15)$ |
| **35.** $^-81 - (54 \div 6)$ | **36.** $^-63 + ({}^-21 \times 4)$ | **37.** $({}^-56 \div {}^-7) - 18$ |

## Check Problem Solving

**Solve.** (O—ㄲ NS 2.0, MR 2.0, pp. 186-187)

38. The price of gasoline changes frequently. During four days last week, the price of a gallon of gas had the following changes (in cents): $^-2$, 4, 7, and $^-1$. What is the average change in gas price for those four days?

39. Suppose that a large pizza has 12 slices, a medium pizza has 8 slices, and a small pizza has 6 slices. If James orders 3 large pizzas, 4 medium pizzas, and 2 small pizzas, how many slices of pizza will James receive?

40. **⟦WRITE Math⟧** Explain how to find the next two numbers in the pattern: 128, $^-64$, 32, $^-16$, ■, ■.

**GO ONLINE Technology** Use *Online Assessment.*

# Enrich • Integer Puzzles
## Integer Mystery

Mystery squares are a way to have fun while you practice multiplying integers. Each row, column, and diagonal of a mystery square must have the same product.

**Use the clues to complete the mystery square.**

Each square contains either 1 or ⁻1. The number of 1's is one more than the number of ⁻1's. The product of each row, column, and diagonal is 1. What are the missing values?

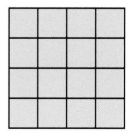

|   |   |   |
|---|---|---|
|   |   |   |
|   | 1 | 1 |
| ⁻1 |  | ⁻1 |

According to the clues, five squares contain 1 and four squares contain ⁻1. The product of each row, column, and diagonal must equal 1, so each row, column, or diagonal must have either only 1's or exactly two ⁻1's.

| ⁻1 | 1 | ⁻1 |
|---|---|---|
| 1 | 1 | 1 |
| ⁻1 | 1 | ⁻1 |

## Solve the Mystery

**Copy the mystery square. Then use the clues to complete.**

**1.** Each square contains either 1 or ⁻1. The number of 1's is one less than the number of ⁻1's. The product of each row, column, and diagonal is ⁻1.

| 1 |   |   |
|---|---|---|
|   | ⁻1 |   |
|   |   | 1 |

**2.** Each square contains either 1 or ⁻1. The number of 1's is the same as the number of ⁻1's. The product of each row, column, and diagonal is 1.

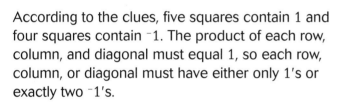

|   |   |   | ⁻1 |
|---|---|---|---|
|   |   |   |   |
|   |   |   |   |
|   |   |   |   |

**3.** Each square contains either 0 or ⁻1. There are three times as many ⁻1's as 0's. The product of each row, column, and diagonal is 0.

|   |   |   |   |
|---|---|---|---|
|   |   |   |   |
|   |   |   |   |
|   |   |   |   |

## Try It

**WRITE Math** Is it possible to complete a 3 × 3 mystery square with twice as many ⁻1's as 1's if the product of each row, column, and diagonal is ⁻1? **Explain.**

## Unit Review/Test
### Chapters 5–7

## Multiple Choice

1. Which of the following rational numbers is between ⁻1.36 and ⁻0.92? (O—ᴛ NS 1.1, p. 118)

   A $\frac{99}{100}$

   B $-\frac{1}{2}$

   C $-\frac{99}{100}$

   D $^-1\frac{2}{3}$

2. Which list of numbers is ordered from *least* to *greatest*? (O—ᴛ NS 1.1, p. 122)

   A ⁻2.06, ⁻2.16, ⁻2.26, ⁻2.36

   B ⁻0.41, ⁻0.30, ⁻0.29, ⁻0.01

   C ⁻1.01, 1.02, ⁻1.03, 1.04

   D 2.15, 3.17, 2.45, 3.21

3. Which list of numbers is ordered from *least* to *greatest*? (O—ᴛ NS 1.1, p. 124)

   A $\frac{1}{2}, \frac{2}{3}, \frac{1}{4}, \frac{2}{5}$

   B $^-1\frac{1}{2}, ^-1\frac{2}{3}, ^-1\frac{3}{4}, ^-1\frac{4}{5}$

   C $^-1\frac{1}{2}, ^-1\frac{1}{4}, ^-1\frac{1}{5}, ^-1\frac{1}{6}$

   D $\frac{3}{4}, ^-2\frac{6}{7}, ^-1\frac{7}{9}, \frac{8}{11}$

4. What is 7 + ⁻3? (O—ᴛ NS 2.3, p. 144)

   A ⁻10

   B ⁻7

   C 4

   D 10

5. Jim runs $2\frac{3}{4}$ miles each day and Lori runs $2\frac{1}{8}$ miles each day. If Carl runs an amount that is between the distances Jim and Lori run, which of the following could be Carl's distance? (O—ᴛ NS 1.1, p. 118)

   A $2\frac{1}{16}$ miles

   B $2\frac{19}{32}$ miles

   C $2\frac{25}{32}$ miles

   D $2\frac{7}{8}$ miles

6. 8 − ⁻14 = (O—ᴛ NS 2.3, p. 150)

   A ⁻22

   B ⁻6

   C 6

   D 22

7. The stock market was down 10 points at the start of the day. By the end of the day, it had fallen 3 more points. What was the total change in the stock market for the day? (O—ᴛ NS 2.3, p. 150)

   A ⁻13

   B ⁻7

   C 7

   D 13

8. ⁻2 + (5 − ⁻7) = (O—ᴛ NS 2.3, p. 154)

   A ⁻10

   B ⁻4

   C 5

   D 10

**GO Technology** Use *Online Assessment.*

**9.** If the rule is to add 7 to get the next term, what are the missing integers in this pattern? (O—n NS 2.3, p. 154)

$$■, \ ^-12, \ ^-5, \ ■, \ 9, \ 16$$

**A** $^-19, \ ^-2$

**B** $^-17, \ 0$

**C** $^-19, \ 0$

**D** $^-19, \ 2$

**10.** What is the product of 11 and $^-5$? (O—n NS 2.3, p. 172)

**A** $^-55$

**B** $^-16$

**C** 16

**D** 55

**11.** What is $^-6 \times \ ^-8$? (O—n NS 2.3, p. 172)

**A** $^-48$

**B** $^-14$

**C** 24

**D** 48

**12.** Jessica wants to divide 18 marbles evenly among herself and 5 of her friends. How many marbles does each person get? (O—n NS 2.3, p. 176)

**A** $^-6$          **C** 12

**B** 3          **D** 24

**13.** What is the quotient of $^-56$ and $^-8$? (O—n NS 2.3, p. 176)

**A** 48          **C** $^-7$

**B** 7          **D** $^-48$

**14.** $^-90 \div (^-6 \times \ ^-5) =$          (O—n NS 2.3, p. 180)

**A** $^-30$          **C** 3

**B** $^-3$          **D** 30

## Short Response

**15.** Mrs. Jenkins had $25 in her checking account. Then she wrote 3 checks for $7 each. How much does Mrs. Jenkins have left in her account? (O—n NS 2.3, p. 182)

**16.** Maria wrote the expression $(^-12 - 8) \div \ ^-4$ on her paper. Find the value of the expression. (O—n NS 2.3, p. 182)

**17.** Order the rational numbers from *least* to *greatest*: $1\frac{2}{3}, \ ^-0.75, \ 1.8, \ ^-\frac{3}{8}$. (O—n NS 1.1, p. 126)

**18.** Tessa and Karen are playing a game. They each start with $100 in play money. During the game, Tessa gives Karen $28, and then Karen gives Tessa $39. At the end of the game, how much more money does Tessa have than Karen? (O—n NS 2.3, p. 154)

**19.** Sara runs a jewelry store. She sold 5 pieces a day for 6 days, 3 pieces a day for 2 days, and 8 pieces a day for 4 days. Find the total number of pieces that Sara sold during the 12 days. (O—n NS 2.3, p. 186)

## Extended Response ⟨ WRITE Math ⟩

**20.** **Explain** how to use the rules for dividing integers to find the possible signs for the dividend and divisor in $■72 \div \ ■8 = 9$. (O—n NS 2.3, p. 176)

**21.** Jason wakes up at 6:30 A.M. He spends 25 minutes getting ready for the day and then 15 minutes eating breakfast. School starts at 8:10 A.M. **Explain** how to find how much time Jason has between finishing breakfast and when school starts. (O—n NS 1.1, p. 130)

# Highs and Lows in California

## HOW LOW (AND HIGH) CAN YOU GO?

California's landscape spans from high mountain peaks to low valleys. Mount Whitney (14,494 feet high), in Inyo County, is the highest peak in California. Badwater Basin in Death Valley, at 282 feet below sea level, is the lowest point in California. It just happens to be the lowest point in the United States and in the Western Hemisphere, too. Badwater Basin is also located in Inyo County.

**Mount Whitney**

## FACT·ACTIVITY

Suppose you are the host for a travel program on television. Use the table and other sources to prepare a report on the highest and lowest points in California.

❶ Find the difference between the lowest and highest elevations in California.

❷ Compare and order the elevations in California from least to greatest.

❸ Find the difference in feet between the elevations of Thunder Mountain and the Salton Sea.

❹ **Pose a Problem** Write a problem like Problem 3 using two different elevations from the table.

| Elevations in California | |
|---|---|
| Name | Elevation (feet) |
| Mt. Whitney | 14,494 |
| Mt. Davidson | 925 |
| Salton Sea | ⁻228 |
| Thunder Mountain | 13,517 |
| Los Angeles (highest point) | 5,074 |
| Snow Mountain | 7,056 |
| San Francisco (highest point) | 934 |
| Death Valley | ⁻282 |
| Sonora Peak | 11,459 |

# THE DEEPEST DEPTHS

T he average height of the surface of the world's oceans is called sea level. The elevations of places on Earth are often compared to this level. Elevations above sea level are expressed using positive numbers. Heights below sea level are expressed using negative numbers. Of course, most places below sea level are underwater, but there are some on dry land.

In July, marathon runners run from Badwater Basin in Death Valley to the base of Mount Whitney. The race begins 282 feet below sea level and ends 8,360 feet above sea level. The marathon winner in 2000 ran the distance in 25 hours, 9 minutes, and 5 seconds!

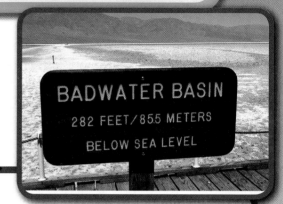

## FACT·ACTIVITY

**Use the tables and graph to answer the questions.**

1. List the following in order from least to greatest elevation: Furnace Creek, Badwater Basin, Landing Strip, and Stovepipe Wells.

2. What is the difference in elevation between Furnace Creek and Badwater Basin?

3. Hikers at Death Valley National Park walk to the Landing Strip from Stovepipe Wells and back. What is the total change in elevation they experience during their walk?

4. **WRITE Math** Most commercial jets fly at a height of 35,000 ft. Many military submarines can travel 800 ft below sea level. How do these figures compare with the highest and lowest places in California? Explain how they compare with each other.

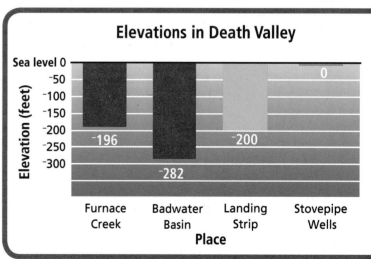

**Elevations in Death Valley**

Elevation (feet) vs Place

- Furnace Creek: −196
- Badwater Basin: −282
- Landing Strip: −200
- Stovepipe Wells: 0

# Math on Location

▲ Data gathered from samples of plants grown in greenhouses are used in making agriculture decisions.

▲ Tomatoes picked from the fields are sorted and graded before they are packaged and shipped to stores.

▲ As more stores sell organically-grown produce, more farms will use this system of growing purer foods.

# VOCABULARY POWER

## TALK Math

How are statistics used in the **Math on Location**? How can farmers use statistics to determine if their methods are improving their crops?

## READ Math

**REVIEW VOCABULARY** You learned the words below when you learned about statistics. How do these words relate to **Math on Location**?

**population** the entire group of objects or individuals considered for a survey

**random sample** a sample in which each subject in the population has an equal chance of being selected

## WRITE Math

Copy and complete a tree map like the one below. Use what you know about statistics to fill in the map.

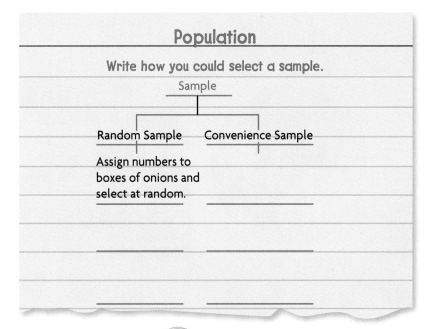

**Population**

Write how you could select a sample.

Sample

Random Sample    Convenience Sample

Assign numbers to boxes of onions and select at random.

**Technology**
Multimedia Math Glossary link at
www.harcourtschool.com/hspmath

# 8 Data and Sampling

## The Big Idea
Data can be collected in various formats and analyzed.

## Investigate
A researcher asked people walking past Grauman's Chinese Theatre, "Do you agree that action movies are the best, or do you prefer some other type better?" What observations can you make about the survey and its results as shown in this graph?

**Best Type of Movie**

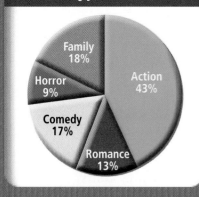

- Family 18%
- Action 43%
- Horror 9%
- Comedy 17%
- Romance 13%

**CALIFORNIA FAST FACT**

Grauman's Chinese Theatre, located in Hollywood, is a world-famous movie theater built in 1927.

**GO ONLINE**

**Technology**
Student pages are available in the Student eBook.

# Show What You Know

**Check your understanding of important skills needed for success in Chapter 8.**

▶ **Read and Interpret a Table**

For 1–5, use the table at the right.

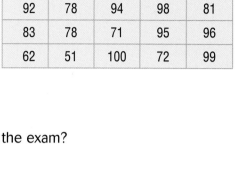

| Scores on the English Exam | | | | |
|---|---|---|---|---|
| 98 | 89 | 76 | 83 | 36 |
| 78 | 90 | 100 | 96 | 70 |
| 92 | 78 | 94 | 98 | 81 |
| 83 | 78 | 71 | 95 | 96 |
| 62 | 51 | 100 | 72 | 99 |

1. How many grades were given for this exam?

2. If an A is a grade of 90 or above, how many students earned an A on this exam?

3. If a perfect score is a 100, how many perfect scores were earned on this exam?

4. If a passing score is 70 or better, how many students passed the exam?

5. A failing score is below 70. How many students failed the exam?

▶ **Read a Venn Diagram**

For 6–10, use the Venn diagram at the right.

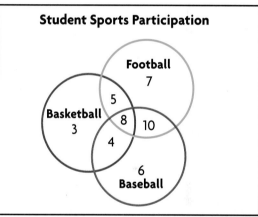

**Student Sports Participation**

6. How many students play all three sports?

7. How many students play only baseball?

8. How many students either play only baseball or play only football?

9. How many students do not play basketball?

10. How many students play basketball and baseball but not football?

# VOCABULARY POWER

**CHAPTER VOCABULARY**

biased question
biased sample
convenience sample
population
random sample
sample
survey
unbiased question
unbiased sample

**WARM-UP WORDS**

**survey** a method of gathering information about a population

**population** the entire group of objects or individuals considered for a survey

**sample** a representative part of a population

# 1 Samples and Populations

**OBJECTIVE:** Identify when it makes sense to use a sample, and compare data from samples with data from the population.

## Quick Review

Complete.

1. 85 out of 100 = __?__ %
2. 12 out of 48 = __?__ %
3. 45 out of 90 = __?__ %
4. 20 out of 200 = __?__ %
5. 36 out of 180 = __?__ %

## Vocabulary

survey     population     sample

## Learn

A **survey** is a method of gathering information about a population. The **population** is the entire group of objects or individuals considered for a survey. When a population in a survey is large, you can survey a representative part of the group, called a **sample**.

**Example 1** Patty wants to find out which day of the week students in her homeroom do most of their shopping. Describe the population. Should Patty survey the population or use a sample?

> The population is students in her homeroom. The population is small.

So, Patty should survey the entire population.

• If the population in Patty's survey were all 1,500 students in her school, would she survey the population or use a sample? Explain.

## Example 2

Liam wants to find out the number of students in his middle school who prefer rock music more than all other types of music. He surveys two samples and then the entire population of the school. How do the results from the two samples compare with the results from the population?

| Middle School Students' Favorite Music | | | |
|---|---|---|---|
| Survey | Number Choosing Rock Music | Number of Students Surveyed | Percent Choosing Rock Music |
| Sample A | 28 | 80 | 35% |
| Sample B | 37 | 100 | 37% |
| Population | 288 | 800 | 36% |

The results of the two samples are about the same as the results of the population.

So, both samples are good representations of the population.

## Guided Practice

1. A soccer coach wants to find out what brand of soccer equipment students on the soccer team buy most often. If there are 15 players on the team, should the coach survey a sample or the population?

SDAP 2.0 Students use data samples of a population and describe the characteristics and limitations of the samples. *also* SDAP 2.1, MR 2.4, MR 2.5, MR 3.0, MR 3.2, MR 3.3

**Tell whether you would survey the population or use a sample.**

2. Rachel wants to know whether students in her computer class buy new or used computers.

3. Celinda wants to know whether more people in San Francisco drive or take a bus to work.

4. The owner of an electronics store wants to find out which brand of portable music players is most popular among middle school students.

5. **TALK Math** Explain why a sample is often used instead of a population when conducting a survey.

## Independent Practice and Problem Solving

**Tell whether you would survey the population or use a sample.**

6. Ben wants to find out whether the 23 teachers at Roosevelt Elementary School bring their lunch or buy food from the cafeteria.

7. The owners of a baseball stadium want to find out what food baseball fans would most like to buy when they attend games.

**USE DATA** For 8–10, use the circle graphs at the right.

8. The results shown are from a survey asking students, "Do you prefer shopping online, at the mall, or in a catalog?" How do the results from the sample compare with the results from the population?

9. Which type of shopping showed the greatest difference between the sample and the population?

10. **ALGEBRA** The results of this survey show that 40 students prefer shopping at the mall. Of the students surveyed, 21 preferred only indoor malls, and $n$ students prefered outdoor malls. What is the value of $n$?

11. **WRITE Math** Write a question you would like to ask in a survey. Define the population you would use.

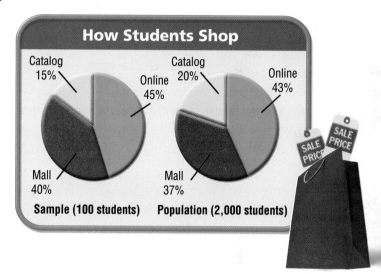

**How Students Shop**

Catalog 15%
Online 45%
Mall 40%
**Sample (100 students)**

Catalog 20%
Online 43%
Mall 37%
**Population (2,000 students)**

## Achieving the Standards

12. Nick bought $1\frac{3}{4}$ pounds of potato salad and $2\frac{5}{8}$ pounds of fruit salad for a picnic. How many pounds of salad did Nick buy in all?
(O⟋ NS 2.0, p.42)

13. Subtract $^-9 - {}^-4$. (O⟋ NS 2.0, p. 154)

14. Stephen conducts a survey in which he asks a question of every fourth student who walks into school. Do you think his survey represents the population of the school? **Explain.**
(Grade 4 SDAP 1.1)

15. **Test Prep** Choose the topic you could survey by using a population.

   A favorite song of teenagers in a large city

   B most popular song of students nationwide

   C best beach among all surfers in California

   D favorite poem of students in a poetry club

**Extra Practice** on page 216, Set A

# Sampling Methods

**OBJECTIVE:** Identify different types of samples and determine whether a sample is representative of the population.

## Quick Review

Sylvia wants to know the most popular magazine read by students in San Diego. Should she survey the population or use a sample?

## Vocabulary

**convenience sample**

**random sample**

## Learn

There are many types of sampling methods. The table shows three different methods.

| Sampling Method | Definition | Example |
|---|---|---|
| Convenience Sample | The most available individuals or objects in the population are selected to obtain results quickly. | Choose a specific location, such as the library or cafeteria, and survey students as they walk in. |
| Random Sample | Every individual or object in the population has an equal chance of being selected. This produces the sample that is most representative of the population. | Assign a number to each student in the school, and then randomly select numbers using a computer. |
| Responses to a Survey | Individuals participate in mail, Internet, or phone surveys. | E-mail a questionnaire to students at home. |

Convenience samples and responses in mail, phone, and e-mail surveys are less likely to be representative of the population because every member of the population may not have an equal chance of being selected.

**Example** Ron wants to find out whether students in his school prefer using landline phones or cell phones. He is choosing a sample for his survey by writing each student's name on an index card and picking cards without looking. What sampling method is Ron using?

> Every student in his school has an equal chance of being chosen for the survey.

So, Ron is using a random sample.

### Math Idea

It is important to choose a sample that accurately represents the population. For example, if the population of Ron's middle school is sixth, seventh, and eighth graders, then all grades should be used in his samples.

### More Examples Identify which sampling method is being used.

**A** Luis wants to know how often students in his community buy phone cards. He asks students in his apartment building.

Luis is using a convenience sample.

**B** Beth wants to know what students in her community think of television commercials. She calls selected students in the community.

Beth is using responses to a survey.

- **Explain** why the samples in Luis's and Beth's surveys may not be representative of the population.

**SDAP 2.2** Identify different ways of selecting a sample (e.g., convenience sampling, responses to a survey, random sampling) and which method makes a sample more represenative of a population. *Also* SDAP 2.0, SDAP 2.1, **SDAP 2.4**, MR 2.4, MR 2.5, MR 3.2

## Activity

**Materials** ▪ recording sheet

Conduct a survey.

**A** Choose one of the following survey topics.

- Favorite movie

- Number of hours spent online each day

- Favorite electronic game

**B** Decide what population you want to survey. Do you want to include students in all grades at your school or just sixth-grade students?

**C** Write a question for your survey. The question should be clear and simple, include words that have the same meaning to everyone, and have only one response, or answer, per person.

**D** Survey a random sample of at least 30 students from the population, and record the data on a recording sheet.

| Student | Response |
|---------|----------|
| 1 | |
| 2 | |
| 3 | |

**E** Organize the data in a frequency table, and draw a graph to display the data.

**F** Use your graph to draw conclusions about the survey topic and population.

**G** Compare the results of your survey with the results of a classmate who chose the same topic.

## Guided Practice

1. Anita wants to know if sixth-grade students would prefer to use e-mail or text messaging. She surveys 50 students. If every sixth-grade student has an equal chance of being selected for the survey, what sampling method is Anita using?

**Identify which sampling method is being used. Write** *convenience,* *random,* **or** *responses to a survey.*

2. A greeting-card company wants to know how many greeting cards teenagers in California send each year. The company conducts an online survey of California students who visit their website.

✓3. A large company wants to find out whether current employees are planning to attend their company picnic. The company surveys a randomly generated list of employees.

**Identify which sampling method is being used. Write** *convenience,* *random,* **or** *responses to a survey.*

4. Juan wants to know the favorite radio station of teenagers in his community. He asks students in his math class.

✓5. Ana wants to find out if students at her school own camera phones. She surveys a randomly generated list of students enrolled at the school.

6. **TALK Math** **Explain** how you know whether a sample is representative of a population.

## Independent Practice and Problem Solving

**Identify which sampling method is being used. Write** *convenience,* *random,* **or** *responses to a survey.*

7. An Internet service provider wants to find out how many minutes of music teenagers download each month. The provider asks teenagers at the local deli.

8. A newspaper reporter wants to know what topics students in the community like to read about in the newspaper. She calls students in the community for their opinions.

9. Sam wants to know how much money students in sixth grade are willing to pay for a portable digital music player. He surveys 40 randomly chosen sixth-graders.

10. Sue wants to know if students at her school enjoy reality television shows. She asks students as they are getting off a school bus.

11. A long-distance phone company employee wants to know how customers rate the quality of their phone service. He surveys customers whose names are on a randomly generated list.

12. A cable company wants to know which television channels customers like best. The company asks customers to complete a mail-in survey.

**USE DATA For 13–15, use the tables at the right.**

13. David asked Reed Middle School students to indicate their favorite subject. He first surveyed two samples. Then he surveyed the population of 450 students. How do the results from the two samples compare with the results from the population?

| Sample | Students Choosing Science | Percent of Sample |
|--------|--------------------------|-------------------|
| 10 | 3 | 30% |
| 50 | 26 | 52% |

14. **Reasoning** If the population is 1,000 students, about how many students would choose science? **Explain** your reasoning.

| Population | Students Choosing Science | Percent of Population |
|-----------|--------------------------|----------------------|
| 450 | 225 | 50% |

15. **WRITE Math** The larger sample used in the survey is representative of the population. The population includes all students at a middle school. **Describe** how the sample may have been chosen.

16. Sarah had $2\frac{5}{8}$ yards of ribbon. She used $\frac{2}{3}$ of the ribbon to wrap a package. How many yards of ribbon did Sarah use? (p. 38, NS 2.1)

17. John is ordering pizza for his friends. Each slice is $\frac{1}{8}$ of the pizza. If John wants to order a total of 24 slices, how many pizzas will John need? (p. 70, O━┱ NS 2.0)

18. You want to conduct a survey of other sixth-grade students to find out how many think your science fair project is excellent. Write the question you would ask in your survey. Does your question suggest or lead to the response you want? Explain.

(Grade 4, SDAP 1.1)

19. **Test Prep** Jenny wants to find out how much allowance students in sixth grade receive. She conducts the survey in a way that gives every person an equal chance of being selected. Which sampling method is Jenny using?

A convenience     C responses to a survey

B random     D another method

20. **Test Prep** Mike wants to know the most popular website of students at his school. He asks students as they walk into the cafeteria. Which sampling method is Mike using?

A convenience     C responses to a survey

B random     D another method

## Problem Solving connects to Science

An individual ecosystem can contain many types of organisms. Ecosystems that are in areas with plentiful rainfall and warm temperatures will support many kinds of life.

Scientists use a method called "mark, release, recapture" for estimating population size of animals in an ecosystem. To use this method, scientists capture a few members of a population, mark them with tags, and release them back into the ecosystem. Later, a new sample from the population is captured. If tagged individuals are found in the new sample it is possible to estimate the size of the population by counting the number of recaptured individuals in the new sample.

> Suppose 50 individuals of a certain kind of fish in a pond are captured, tagged, and released. Later, in a sample of 20 such fish, 2 have tags. Then an estimate for the population is $50 \times \frac{20}{2} = 500$.

1. In Lana's butterfly study, she marked 100 individuals during her first visit to the habitat area. On her second visit to the area, she recaptured 10 marked butterflies in a sample of 100. Based on this sample, what is an estimate of the entire butterfly population?

2. An ecologist marks and releases 250 squirrels on her first research visit at a local park. When she returns, she captures another 100 squirrels, of which 40 are tagged. Based on the results, what is an estimate of the whole squirrel population in the park?

3. What are some things that could make a mark, release, recapture study inaccurate?

# Bias in Surveys

**OBJECTIVE:** Determine whether a sample or a question in a survey is biased.

## Quick Review

Bob wants to find out the most popular song of students in grade 6. He surveys students randomly chosen from a list of all students in his school in grade 6. What method of sampling is Bob using?

_____

## Vocabulary

**unbiased sample**   **biased sample**

**biased question**   **unbiased question**

## Learn

When all individuals in the population have an equal chance of being selected, the sample is an **unbiased sample**. If certain groups from the population are not represented appropriately in the sample, then the sample is a **biased sample**.

**PROBLEM** Joshua wants to know if students at a middle school are interested in performing in a school play. He surveys an unbiased sample of students from the school. Does he use a sample of 70 randomly selected boys or 70 randomly selected students?

### Example 1

> The sample of 70 randomly selected boys is biased because it excludes girls from the population.
>
> The sample of 70 randomly selected students is unbiased because all students have an equal chance of being selected.

So, Joshua uses the sample of 70 randomly selected students.

A **biased question** suggests or leads to a specific response or excludes a certain group. When a specific response is not suggested and no groups are excluded, it is an **unbiased question**.

### Example 2 Is the question "Did you like the play that has received excellent reviews?", biased or unbiased?

The question suggests that we should say that we liked the play. So, the question is biased.

• How could you ask the question so it is unbiased?

## Guided Practice

**Tell whether the sample is biased or unbiased. Explain.**

The art museum is conducting a survey to find out what type of exhibits students in the community enjoy.

1. 75 randomly selected students from local art clubs. (This sample excludes people who are not in art clubs.)

✓2. 75 randomly selected students from all of the community.

**○—┱ SDAP 2.3** Analyze data displays and explain why the way in which the question was asked might have influenced the results obtained and why the way in which the results were displayed might have influenced the conclusions reached. *also* **○—┱ SDAP 2.4, MR 2.4, MR 2.5, MR 3.2**

**Tell whether the question is biased or unbiased.**

3. What type of art exhibit would you like to see at the art museum?

4. Poems are better than short stories, don't you agree?

5. Do you agree with most students that modern art exhibits are wonderful?

✓ 6. What is your favorite animal to see at the zoo?

7. (TALK Math) **Explain** how you know whether a question is biased.

## Independent Practice and Problem Solving

**Tell whether the sample is biased or unbiased.**

A dance studio wants to find out the favorite dance of students at a high school.

8. 90 randomly selected tenth-grade students from the high school

9. 90 randomly selected students at the high school football game

10. 90 randomly selected students from the high school

11. 90 randomly selected girls from the high school

**Tell whether the question is biased or unbiased.**

12. Is ballroom dancing your favorite dance style?

13. What is your favorite dance style?

14. Do you agree with most students that square dancing is fun?

15. Do you think, as I do, that break dancing is the best style of dance?

**Tell whether the question is biased or unbiased. If it is biased, rewrite it to make it unbiased.**

16. Do you like the beautiful parrot more than the cockatiel?

17. Which is your favorite professional sports team?

18. (WRITE Math) **What's the Question?** The answer is that the sample is unbiased.

## Achieving the Standards

19. Order from least to greatest. (O—¬ NS 1.1, p.124)

$$\frac{5}{8}, \frac{1}{2}, \frac{3}{4}$$

20. Rita hiked $6\frac{5}{12}$ miles on Saturday and 6.375 miles on Sunday. On which day did she hike the greater distance? (O—¬ NS 1.0, p. 126)

21. Find the mean of the set of data.

(Grade 5, SDAP 1.1)

15, 8, 11, 9, 6, 8, 13

22. **Test Prep** Which question is unbiased?

A Do you prefer rock music, as do most students?

B Is the very popular country western music your favorite type of music?

C What is your favorite type of music?

D Do you agree with a popular rap star that rap music is awesome?

# 4 Claims Based on Data

OBJECTIVE: Identify and evaluate the validity of claims based on data.

**Quick Review**

Tell whether the question is biased or unbiased.

Do you agree with most students that ice hockey is exciting?

## Learn

**PROBLEM** Baseball fans claim that Ted is the best pitcher in his division because he pitched a no-hitter in game 8. Is their claim valid?

**Example 1** Use the data in the table.

| Opposing Team Hits in Division A | | | | | | | | |
|---|---|---|---|---|---|---|---|---|
| Pitcher | Game 1 | Game 2 | Game 3 | Game 4 | Game 5 | Game 6 | Game 7 | Game 8 |
| Inez | 4 | 3 | 2 | 3 | 3 | 2 | 1 | 1 |
| Pedro | 5 | 5 | 3 | 5 | 4 | 3 | 2 | 3 |
| Hannah | 4 | 5 | 6 | 4 | 4 | 1 | 2 | 3 |
| Ted | 10 | 9 | 7 | 6 | 5 | 4 | 3 | 0 |
| Cathy | 4 | 4 | 4 | 5 | 4 | 3 | 2 | 4 |
| Bill | 6 | 7 | 6 | 4 | 3 | 3 | 2 | 6 |

A claim is not valid unless it is supported by the given data.

The baseball fans use the data for game 8 to justify their claim. However, game 8 is only a small part of all the data in the table. If they analyze all the data, the fans will find that in each of the other games, Ted allowed the opposing team more hits than any other pitcher in his division.

So, the baseball fans' claim is not valid.

Valid claims are made by analyzing all of the relevant data. Below is a chart of the claims that can be made from the data above.

| Analyze the Data | Claim |
|---|---|
| • In games 1–8, Inez allowed fewer hits to the opposing team than most of the other pitchers. | • Overall, Inez is the best pitcher in the division. |
| • Pedro and Cathy allowed nearly the same number of hits in each game. Both allowed 30 hits total. | • Cathy and Pedro are equally good pitchers. |
| • Ted's game 8 was the only no-hitter pitched in the division. | • Ted pitched the best game in the division. |

• What claim could you make about Ted's pitching from game 1 through game 8? Justify your answer.

SDAP 2.5 Identify claims based on statistical data and, in simple cases, evaluate the validity of the claims. *also* MR 2.4, MR 2.5, MR 3.1, MR 3.2

# Biased Samples and Questions

## Example 2 Biased or unbiased samples

Rhonda wants to find out the favorite sport of students at her school. She surveys the cheerleaders, and they all vote for football. So, Rhonda claims that football is the favorite sport of students at her school. Is Rhonda's claim valid?

> A claim is not valid if the sample used in the survey is biased. The sample Rhonda used in the survey is biased because it excludes students who are not cheerleaders.

So, Rhonda's claim is not valid.

- What unbiased sample could Rhonda survey to make a valid claim?

- What if Rhonda wanted to know the favorite sport of the cheerleaders at her school? Would her claim be valid? Explain.

## Example 3 Biased or unbiased questions

Patrick wants to know which of four events in his school's track-and-field program is most popular to watch. The choices are the high jump, the pole vault, the long jump, the triple jump. He decides to survey all his classmates. After looking at the results, Patrick claims that the most popular event is the pole vault. Is his claim valid?

**ERROR ALERT**

Even if the survey data supports the claim, the claim is valid only if both the sample and the questions are unbiased.

**Patrick's Survey Question**

At a track meet, do you prefer to watch the high jump, the extremely exciting pole vault, the long jump, or the triple jump?

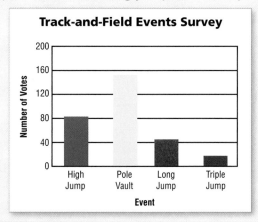

> A claim is not valid if the question asked in the survey is biased. The data seem to support Patrick's claim, but his question suggests responses in favor of the pole vault. The question is biased.

So, Patrick's claim is not valid.

- What unbiased question could Patrick ask to make a valid claim?

1. Ana's friend claims that Ana is the best player on the basketball team because she scored more points in the first game than any other player. Look at how well Ana did in the remaining games compared to her teammates. Does the data support the claim? Justify your answer.

**Points Scored in Basketball**

| Game | Jane | Cindy | Ana | Gloria | Liz |
|------|------|-------|-----|--------|-----|
| 1 | 6 | 6 | 12 | 4 | 8 |
| 2 | 4 | 8 | 6 | 2 | 14 |
| 3 | 10 | 11 | 6 | 2 | 9 |
| 4 | 8 | 14 | 14 | 8 | 16 |

**Determine whether the claim is valid. Explain your answer.**

2. Jeff surveys 80 randomly selected students from his school. He asks the following question: "Wouldn't a pep rally before soccer games be great?" They all respond *yes*. So, Jeff claims that students at his school want to have a pep rally before soccer games.

3. Barb asks a group of her friends whether they prefer ice-skating or cross-country skiing. Most say they prefer cross-country skiing. So, Barb claims that most students at her school prefer cross-country skiing to ice-skating.

4. **TALK Math** Explain how you determine whether a claim is valid.

## Independent Practice and Problem Solving

**For 5–7, use the table. Determine if the claim is valid. Explain.**

5. Trevor claims he is a better runner than Pete because he finished before Pete in the 400-m run.

6. Pete claims he is a better runner than Marco.

7. **Pose a Problem** Write a new claim that could be made. Explain why the claim is valid or not valid.

8. **≡FAST FACT** The L.A. Lakers won three NBA championships between 1999 and 2002. Bruce surveyed a group of students at his school. He asked, "Are the champion L.A. Lakers your favorite team?" Based on the results, Bruce claims that the favorite basketball team of most students is the Lakers. Is Bruce's claim valid? Explain.

**Track Meet Results**

| | 100-m Dash | 110-m Dash | 400-m Run | 800-m Run |
|---|---|---|---|---|
| **Pete** | 1st place | 2nd place | 3rd place | 1st place |
| **Ryan** | 2nd place | 1st place | 1st place | 2nd place |
| **Marco** | 4th place | 4th place | 4th place | 4th place |
| **Trevor** | 3rd place | 3rd place | 2nd place | 3rd place |

**USE DATA For 9–11, use the line graph. Determine if the claim is valid. Explain.**

9. Timothy claims that a total of about 300 more students played sports in year 4 than played in year 1.

10. **Reasoning** Andrea claims that with the trend in participation in summer sports, about 550 students will participate in year 5.

11. **WRITE Math** What's the Error? Mavis claims winter sports are more popular than summer sports. She says her claim is valid because each year, participation increases more for winter sports than summer sports.

**Extra Practice** on page 216, Set D

12. Paula wants to find who her school's favorite baseball player is. She is standing outside the cafeteria and needs results quickly. She surveys students as they leave the cafeteria. What sampling method is Paula using? ( 0—┓ SDAP 2.2, p. 202)

13. What is the measure of angle *b* in the figure? (Grade 5 0—┓ MG 2.2)

70°
70°
*b*

14. Order the data from least to greatest, and find the median value. (Grade 5 SDAP 1.1)

   17, 22, 16, 19, 16, 21, 10

15. **Test Prep** Debby claims that Mr. Jackson is the best coach at the school. She asks all the sixth-grade girls from her school who is their favorite coach. Tell whether Debby's claim is valid or not valid. **Explain.**

16. **Test Prep** Use the table to decide which claim is valid.

| Goals Scored in Soccer Games | | | | | |
|---|---|---|---|---|---|
| Game | Frank | Gary | Devon | Ellis | Hector |
| 1 | 1 | 0 | 3 | 2 | 2 |
| 2 | 1 | 2 | 3 | 2 | 1 |
| 3 | 1 | 1 | 2 | 0 | 0 |
| 4 | 1 | 0 | 2 | 1 | 0 |

A Hector is a better goal scorer than Gary.

B Frank is a better goal scorer than Ellis.

C Devon is the best goal scorer.

D Gary is the best goal scorer.

# Problem Solving connects to Science

Populations of organisms can be categorized by the functions they serve in an ecosystem. When a species becomes endangered and cannot provide its function completely, the balance of life in an ecosystem can be affected. To help monitor the species within an ecosystem, studies are conducted.

Evan is observing the wildlife in a nature preserve by his house. He records the species he sees while walking through the wild. Based on his results, he claims that the gray fox may be endangered in his region. Name some reasons that his claim may be or may not be valid.

His claim may not be valid. Possible reason: It is possible the gray foxes heard Evan approaching and ran away before he could see them.

| Wildlife Observations | | |
|---|---|---|
| | Species | Number |
| | Gray fox | 0 |
| | Cooper's hawk | 2 |
| | Desert cottontail | 6 |
| | California ground squirrel | 21 |

**Solve.**

1. During his observations, Evan hears a coyote howl in the distance, but he never sees it in the wild. He claims the coyote must not be endangered in his region, even though he did not see any. Name some reasons his claim may or may not be valid.

2. **Reasoning** Use the table. The Cooper's hawk is a natural predator of the California ground squirrel. Based on the number of ground squirrels present, make a claim about the Cooper's hawk. Justify your claim.

# Problem Solving Workshop
## Strategy: Use Logical Reasoning

OBJECTIVE: Solve problems by *using logical reasoning.*

## Learn the Strategy

Logical reasoning helps you solve challenging problems. Use logical reasoning to organize information in lists, tables, and diagrams.

### Use logical reasoning by making an organized list to help you eliminate choices.

Survey question: Is your commute to work 20, 30, 35, 45, 65, or 90 minutes?

Survey results: Most commuters say not as much as 1 hr, not as little as $\frac{1}{2}$ hr, and not 35 minutes.

### Use logical reasoning by making a table to record information and eliminate choices.

Survey question: What is your daily cost for riding a bus, sharing a van, or driving alone in a car?

Survey results: Most commuters say that sharing a van costs twice as much as riding a bus and that daily commuting costs are either $6.00, $4.00, or $2.00.

| Daily Commuting Costs | | | |
|---|---|---|---|
| | $2.00 | $4.00 | $6.00 |
| Van | no | yes | no |
| Car | no | no | yes |
| Bus | yes | no | no |

### Use logical reasoning by making a Venn diagram to show relationships among groups.

Survey question: Do you sit in traffic going to work, going home, or both?

Survey results: A total of 50 people responded. Fifteen people sit in traffic going to work, and 40 sit in traffic going home. Five people sit in traffic both going to work and going home.

**TALK Math**
How does each example organize the information?

**SDAP 2.0** Students use data samples of a population and describe the characteristics and limitations of the samples: *also* MR 1.0, MR 1.1, MR 2.0, MR 2.4, MR 2.5, MR 3.0, MR 3.1, MR 3.2, MR 3.3

# Use the Strategy

Read to
Understand
Plan
Solve
Check

**PROBLEM** Ben conducted a survey about the methods of transportation used by a group of commuters in southern California. The results show that 25 people commute by Metro Rail, 35 by bicycle, and 40 by car. Six people use both Metro Rail and bicycle, 10 use both bicycle and car, and 9 use both Metro Rail and car. Four people use all three methods of transportation. How many people were in the survey?

## Read to Understand

**Reading Skill**
- Use graphic aids to organize information from the problem.
- What information is given?

## Plan

- **What strategy can you use to solve the problem?**
  You can use logical reasoning to solve the problem.

## Solve

- **How can you use the strategy to solve the problem?**
  Draw a Venn diagram that has three overlapping circles, and add the information from the problem. Label each circle with a form of transportation used.

  Four people use Metro Rail, bicycle, and car.

  Since 6 people commute by both Metro Rail and bicycle, subtract $6 - 4 = 2$. So, 2 people use only Metro Rail and bicycle.

  Since 9 people commute by both Metro Rail and car, subtract $9 - 4 = 5$. So, 5 people use only Metro Rail and car.

  25 people commute by Metro Rail. Since $4 + 2 + 5 = 11$ and $25 - 11 = 14$, 14 people use only Metro Rail.

  Use the same process to complete the other parts of the diagram. Then add all the numbers in the diagram.

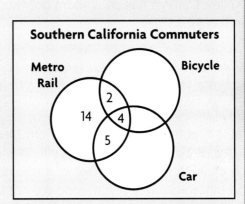

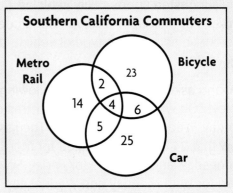

$$14 + 2 + 23 + 5 + 4 + 6 + 25 = 79$$

So, 79 people were in the survey.

## Check

- **How can you check your answer?**

Commuters in San Diego were asked in a survey what types of roads they travel on to go to work. The results of the survey show that 90 commuters use freeways, 75 use expressways, and 85 use the interstate. Fifteen commuters use both freeways and expressways. Twenty-one use both expressways and the interstate. Eleven use both freeways and the interstate. Nine commuters use all three types of roads.

1. How many commuters were in the survey?

   **First,** draw a Venn diagram.

   **Next,** complete all parts of the diagram.

   **Last,** add the numbers in the diagram.

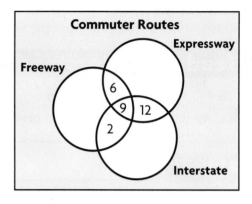

Commuter Routes

✓2. **What if** the number of commuters who in Exercise 1 took all three types of roads changed? Which portions of the Venn diagram would change?

✓3. Carolyn, Tim, Kelley, and Quinton emptied their banks. They found $7.50, $4.35, $5.00, and $10.00, but not necessarily in that order. Tim has twice as much money as Kelley. Carolyn has an amount between Kelley and Tim. Who has $4.35?

## Problem Solving Strategy Practice

**Use logical reasoning to solve.**

4. A radio broadcaster asked Patty, Ron, Joe, and Sue to help her decide what types of vehicles to include in a survey. Each chose one of the following: minivans, pick-up trucks, sport-utility vehicles, or cars. Joe did not suggest minivans. Patty suggested sports-utility vehicles. Ron did not suggest minivans or pick-up trucks. All four students chose a different vehicle. Which type of vehicle did each of them suggest?

5. Santiago asked commuters the following question in a survey: "On which day is rush hour traffic the worst— Monday, Wednesday, or Friday?" The results of the survey show that 24 commuters voted for Monday, 19 voted for Wednesday, and 30 voted for Friday. Seven commuters voted for both Monday and Wednesday. Nine voted for Wednesday and Friday. Ten voted for Monday and Friday. Three commuters voted for all 3 days. How many commuters were in the survey?

6. **WRITE Math** Explain how to determine whether a Venn diagram would help you solve a complicated problem.

## Mixed Strategy Practice

**USE DATA** For 7–11, use the train survey.

**7.** Karen commutes to and from San Francisco 20 days each month. She chooses the train pass that is least expensive for her commute. Which pass does Karen choose? How much does she save in one month by using that pass instead of the next least expensive pass?

**8.** Larry chooses the ten-ride train pass. When he buys the pass, he hands the clerk 3 bills, and she gives him $5.25 in change. What 3 bills does Larry hand the clerk?

**9.** Olivia, Frank, Armando, and Elaine each choose a different train pass in the survey. Olivia did not choose the ten-ride pass. Frank did not choose the ten-ride pass or the monthly pass. Armando chose the one-way pass. Which pass did Olivia, Frank, Armando, and Elaine each choose?

**10. Pose a Problem** Look back at problem 9. Change the known and unknown information to write a new problem.

**11. Open-Ended Problem** Lenora buys several different train passes for her family. Last week, she spent a total of $147.25 for several passes. What is one possible combination of passes Lenora purchased? What information about the costs could lead you to a second possible combination?

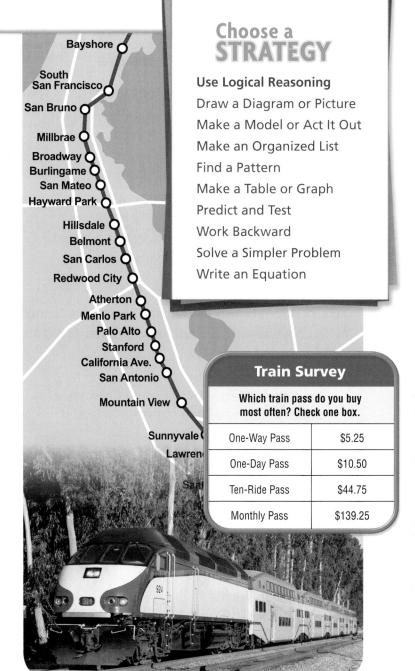

### Choose a STRATEGY

Use Logical Reasoning

Draw a Diagram or Picture

Make a Model or Act It Out

Make an Organized List

Find a Pattern

Make a Table or Graph

Predict and Test

Work Backward

Solve a Simpler Problem

Write an Equation

**Train Survey**

| Which train pass do you buy most often? Check one box. | |
| --- | --- |
| One-Way Pass | $5.25 |
| One-Day Pass | $10.50 |
| Ten-Ride Pass | $44.75 |
| Monthly Pass | $139.25 |

## CHALLENGE YOURSELF

Students who live far from Samuel's school take the bus to school every day. Those who live closer either ride to school in a car, walk, or bike, depending on the weather.

**12.** One week, half of Samuel's class took the bus to school every day. In that week, more students walked or biked to school every day than rode in a car. Two students rode in cars only some days that week. If there are 24 students in Samuel's class, how many could there be who walked or biked to school every day?

**13.** A group of 60 students in Samuel's grade ride the bus to school. Another group of students is five-sixths the size of the first group. Those students ride in a car or walk to school. Of those students, one-fifth alternate between riding and walking. If 19 students always walk, how many more always ride than walk?

 **Extra Practice**

**Set A** Tell whether you would survey the population or use a sample. (pp. 200–201)

1. Thomas wants to know whether students in his class prefer to draw with crayons or with magic markers.

2. Janice wants to know the amount of time it takes people in her state to drive to work each morning.

3. Saralee wants to know whether people in Anaheim prefer scary or romantic movies.

4. Raul wants to know if the employees at his job would rather work 4 or 5 days a week.

5. Judy wants to know if her soccer teammates enjoy practicing on weekends.

6. Marcus wants to know if boyscouts across the country prefer camping in fall or spring.

**Set B** Identify which sampling method is being used.
Write *convenience, random,* or *responses to a survey.* (pp. 202–205)

1. The mayor wants to find out how many of the city's residents would be willing to help fund a new library for the community. He sends out surveys to a randomly-selected list of registered voters.

2. A butcher at a local supermarket wants to know the preferred cut of beef of his customers. He surveys the first 25 customers that appear at his counter. He asks them to name their preferred cut of beef.

3. Joe wants to find out the number of students at his school who enjoy playing chess. He surveys 100 students randomly chosen from the list of all students at his school.

4. A principal wants to know how many elementary students in her school district play video games. She sends a survey to all the elementary students in her school district.

**Set C** Tell whether the question is biased or unbiased. (pp. 206–207)

1. What is your preferred method of travel?

2. I love to fly in an airplane. Do you?

3. Chocolate desserts are the best, don't you agree?

4. Do you agree with most people that flat-screen TVs are the best?

5. Do you like the smooth sound of jazz?

6. What is your favorite restaurant?

**Set D** Determine if the claim is valid. Explain your answer. (pp. 208–211)

1. Rodney wants to determine the favorite hobby of people in his town. He surveys 100 members of his community as they leave the city pool. They all say that their favorite hobby is swimming. Rodney claims that the favorite hobby of the people in his town is swimming.

2. Lisa randomly surveys 50 of her schoolmates as they enter the school one morning. She asks, "Do you prefer country or rock music?" Most of her schoolmates say that they prefer rock music. Lisa claims that most students at her school prefer rock music to country music.

# BIASED OR UNBIASED

### Players
2 teams of 2 players each

### Materials
• Different coins
• Game cards

## How to Play

■ Shuffle the question cards, and place them facedown in a pile.

■ The teams take turns playing offense and defense. The defense is the team reading the question, and the offense is the team responding.

■ Toss a coin to determine which team will play offense first.

■ The defense reads a question aloud to the offense and then asks, "Biased or unbiased?"

■ If the answer is *biased*, the offense must restate the question so that it is unbiased.

■ Teams check each other's answers. If its answer is correct, the offense scores a point. If the answer is incorrect, the defense scores the point.

■ The teams then switch roles, and the new defense reads a survey question. The new offense has to say whether the question is biased or unbiased.

■ Play continues until all the questions have been read. The team with the higher point total wins!

 **Chapter 8 Review/Test**

## Check Vocabulary and Concepts

**Choose the best term from the box.**

1. The entire group of objects or individuals considered for a survey is called the __?__ . (SDAP 2.0, p. 200)

2. A __?__ is a sampling method where every individual or object in the population has an equal chance of being selected. (O—n SDAP 2.2, p. 202)

3. A __?__ is a method of gathering information about a population. (SDAP 2.0, p. 200)

> **VOCABULARY**
>
> biased sample
>
> survey
>
> unbiased sample
>
> population
>
> random sample

## Check Skills

**Tell whether you would survey the population or use a sample.** (SDAP 2.0, pp. 200–201)

4. An education agency wants to determine what math textbook sixth-graders prefer.

5. A baseball coach wants to know whether his players like hot dogs or hamburgers.

**Identify which sampling method is being used. Write** *convenience,* *random,* **or** *responses to a survey.* (O—n SDAP 2.2, pp. 202–205)

6. Mary wants to know the favorite teacher of students in her school. She leaves survey forms in the cafeteria for students to fill out and return to her.

7. Kostas wonders what foods are most popular among students in his grade. He asks ten of his friends from science class for their opinion.

**Tell whether the sample is biased or unbiased.** (O—n SDAP 2.3, pp. 206–207)

8. A researcher wants to determine how long, on average, the members of a community spend exercising each week. He spends one day at a men's gymnasium asking the members about their exercise habits.

**Determine if the claim is valid. Explain your answer.** (O—n SDAP 2.5, pp. 208–211)

9. Stacy surveys 100 randomly selected students from her school. She asks, "Wouldn't having no tests on Fridays be great?" They all respond yes. So Stacy claims that students at her school do not want to take tests on Friday.

## Check Problem Solving

**Solve.** (SDAP 2.0 MR 1.1, MR 2.4, pp. 212-215)

10. **WRITE Math**  When Dana asked 130 students about the sports they enjoyed, 40 said they enjoyed baseball, 35 said table tennis, 55 said swimming, 10 said both baseball and table tennis, 17 said baseball and swimming, and 5 said all three. What could you use to best display this data. Explain.

**GO ONLINE Technology** Use *Online Assessment.*

# Enrich • Stratified Sample
# Try a Sample

For a sample to be useful, it must fairly represent the population you are studying. Several sampling methods can be used to gather data about a population. If you are conducting a survey and want to make sure that particular characteristics of a population, such as particular ages or grade levels, are fairly represented, you can use a stratified sample. In **stratified sampling**, the population is separated into smaller populations, each with a characteristic you want represented in your survey. These smaller populations are called **strata**. The samples for the survey are chosen randomly from each stratum and are based on the sizes of the strata.

## Sample It

Megan wants to know the favorite national park of students attending public schools in Middletown Unified School District in California. She plans to use a stratified sample to make sure students of all school levels are fairly represented. Which strata should she use? Which school level will have the largest sample?

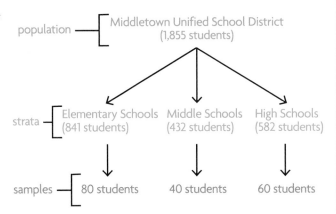

Since she wants all school levels to be fairly represented, Megan separates her population into strata by school level. She bases the number of students in each sample on the sizes of the strata. The stratum with the greatest number of people should have the greatest sample size.

So, the strata are school levels, and elementary schools will have the largest sample.

## Try It
**Solve.**

1. Jordan wants to know what transportation students aged 9–12 take to school. He wants to use stratified sampling to make sure all ages are represented. What strata should Jordan use?

2. Sophia is conducting a survey of favorite types of pets. She wants to make sure students in each grade level at her middle school are represented. Her strata are Grade 6 (125 students), Grade 7 (104 students), and Grade 8 (151 students). Which sample should be the largest? Which should be the smallest?

**WRITE Math** Explain how you would use stratified sampling to determine the favorite sport of students in your school.

# Achieving the Standards
 Chapters 1 – 8

## Number Sense

**1.** What value of *k* makes the following equation true? (O━┓ NS 2.4)

$$\frac{5}{8} = \frac{k}{24}$$

**A** $k = 5$

**B** $k = 8$

**C** $k = 15$

**D** $k = 21$

**2.** Which of the following decimals is closest to 0? (O━┓ NS 1.1)

**A** 0.3

**B** 0.1

**C** 0.02

**D** 0.003

**3.** Which list of numbers is ordered from *least* to *greatest*? (O━┓ NS 1.1)

**A** 0.02, 0.003, 0.0004, 0.00005

**B** $\frac{1}{2}, \frac{1}{3}, \frac{1}{5}, \frac{1}{7}$

**C** 0.02, 0.03, 1, 1.02

**D** 0.01, 1, 0.02, 2

**4.** Mary got 45 out of 100 questions correct on her science test. What percent of the questions did she get wrong? (O━┓ NS 1.1)

**A** 45%          **C** 100%

**B** 55%          **D** 145%

**5.** **WRITE Math** ▶ Four-fifths of a tour group said they had never been on a jungle cruise before. Is that more than, less than, or equal to 60%? **Explain.** (O━┓ NS 1.1)

## Statistics, Data Analysis, and Probability

 **Test Tip** Look for important words.

See item 6. Note that the problem states that every 15th person thereafter will be selected. These words are key to answering the problem.

**6.** Joey is researching overall student satisfaction with cafeteria food at his school. He uses an alphabetical list of all students in his school. He randomly selects a starting point in the list, and then chooses every 15th person thereafter. Which sampling method is Joey using? (O━┓ SDAP 2.2)

**A** convenience sample

**B** random sample

**C** responses to a survey

**D** cluster sample

**7.** Use the table to decide which claim is valid. (O━┓ SDAP 2.5)

| Exam Scores | | | | |
|---|---|---|---|---|
| Exam | Krista | Barry | Lisa | Mark |
| 1 | 99 | 98 | 96 | 92 |
| 2 | 87 | 98 | 83 | 94 |
| 3 | 90 | 95 | 97 | 93 |

**A** Krista has a higher average than Barry.

**B** Barry has the highest exam average.

**C** Mark has the lowest exam average.

**D** Lisa has a higher average than Krista.

**8.** **WRITE Math** ▶ **Explain** how you would find each student's average exam score in Problem 7. (SDAP 1.1)

## Algebra and Functions

**9.** At 1:00, 12 customers were in a store. At 1:20, 5 of the customers left and 3 more entered. At 1:40, $x$ additional customers entered the store. Which expression represents how many customers were in the store at 1:40? (Grade 5 AF 1.2)

**A** $x + 3 - 12 - 5$

**B** $12 + 5 + 3 - x$

**C** $12 - 5 + 3 + x$

**D** $x - 3 - 12 - 5$

**10.** What value of $m$ makes the following equation true? (Grade 5 AF 1.3)

$$5 \times (6 + 2) = (5 \times m) + (5 \times 2)$$

**A** 10      **C** 5

**B** 6      **D** 2

**11.** Look at the table below.

| x | y |
|---|---|
| 1 | 4 |
| 2 | 6 |
| 3 | |

Which of the following is the value of $y$ when $x = 3$? (Grade 5 AF 1.5)

**A** 5

**B** 6

**C** 7

**D** 8

**12.** **WRITE Math** ▶ **Explain** where you would find the point (1,4) on the coordinate plane. (Grade 5 AF 1.4)

## Measurement and Geometry

**13.** The measure of angle $A$ is twice the measure of angle $C$. What is the measure of angle $A$? (Grade 5 MG 2.2)

**A** 30°

**B** 60°

**C** 75°

**D** 90°

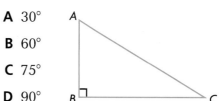

**14.** What is the surface area of the box formed by the pattern below? (Grade 5 MG 1.2)

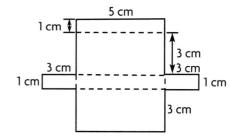

**A** 15 square centimeters

**B** 23 square centimeters

**C** 37 square centimeters

**D** 46 square centimeters

**15.** What is the approximate measure of the angle in the figure below? (Grade 5 MG 2.1)

**A** 5°      **C** 120°

**B** 45°      **D** 180°

**16.** **WRITE Math** ▶ **Explain** how you would find the measure of angle $z$ in the figure below. (Grade 5 MG 2.2)

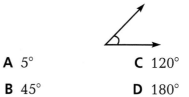

# 9 Analyze Data

**The Big Idea** Data can be collected in various formats and analyzed.

Dale "Daily" Webster has a legendary streak of consecutive days surfed—10,407. For more than 28 years, Mr. Webster has surfed each day, regardless of the weather.

| Wave Height | | | |
|---|---|---|---|
| Time | Height (in ft) | Time | Height (in ft) |
| 12:00 A.M | 3.97 | 12:00 P.M | 4.20 |
| 1:00 A.M. | 4.10 | 1:00 P.M. | 4.00 |
| 2:00 A.M. | 3.97 | 2:00 P.M. | 3.84 |
| 3:00 A.M | 4.13 | 3:00 P.M. | 3.74 |
| 4:00 A.M. | 4.13 | 4:00 P.M. | 4.00 |
| 5:00 A.M | 4.30 | 5:00 P.M. | 4.10 |
| 6:00 A.M. | 4.53 | 6:00 P.M. | 3.38 |
| 7:00 A.M. | 4.53 | 7:00 P.M. | 3.05 |
| 8:00 A.M. | 4.46 | 8:00 P.M. | 2.92 |
| 9:00 A.M. | 4.23 | 9:00 P.M. | 3.22 |
| 10:00 A.M. | 4.46 | 10:00 P.M | 3.28 |
| 11:00 A.M. | 4.07 | 11:00 P.M | 3.61 |

## Investigate

The table at the left displays some of the wave height data reported in the *Los Angeles Times* for July 20, 2006. What observations can you make about the data?

**Technology**
Student pages are available in the Student eBook.

Check your understanding of important skills
needed for success in Chapter 9.

▶ **Compare Whole Numbers to 100,000**

Compare the numbers. Write <, >, or = for each ●.

**1.** 4 ● 10

**2.** 19 ● 180

**3.** 1,700 ● 18

**4.** 99,246 ● 78,123

**5.** 71,456 ● 71,456

**6.** 19,561 ● 19,516

**7.** 999 ● 4,580

**8.** 10,000 ● 1,000

**9.** 100,000 ● 100,000

▶ **Mean**

Find the mean for each set of data.

**10.** 2, 2, 3, 4, 5, 6, 8, 10

**11.** 21, 25, 26, 27, 28, 30, 32, 32, 40

**12.** 15, 8, 17, 21, 56, 9, 32, 45, 41, 14, 17

**13.** 210, 210, 210, 221, 215, 212, 210, 210

**14.** 4,256; 1,900; 5,716; 2,213; 1,785; 3,999; 3,000

**15.** 999; 991;1,043; 1,025; 989; 994; 1,000; 1,003

▶ **Median and Mode**

Find the median and mode for each set of data.

**16.** 1, 1, 1, 1, 2, 2, 2, 3, 4

**17.** 6, 1, 4, 6, 7, 4, 3, 1, 5, 7, 8

**18.** 16, 14, 13, 21, 32, 18, 25, 27

**19.** 145, 137, 142, 147, 138, 137, 141

**20.** 58, 81, 59, 77, 81, 90, 61, 59, 66

**21.** 875; 1,120; 1,075; 992; 1,176; 1,075

# VOCABULARY POWER

**CHAPTER VOCABULARY**

outlier

**WARM-UP WORDS**

**outlier** a value that is very small or very large compared to the majority of the values in a data set

**mean** the sum of a group of numbers divided by the number of addends

**median** the middle value in a group numbers arranged in order

# Mean, Median, Mode, and Range

OBJECTIVE: Find the mean, median, mode, and range of a set of data.

## Quick Review

Order the numbers from least to greatest.

1. 96, 85, 89, 91, 89

2. 1.2, 0.6, 2.1, 0.1, 1.1

3. $\frac{2}{3}, \frac{5}{9}, \frac{5}{18}, \frac{1}{3}, \frac{1}{2}$

4. 7, 6.8, 7.2, 6.3, 6, 7.6

5. 403, 340, 440, 304, 430

## Learn

The mean and median are measures of central tendency. The mode is the number that occurs most often in a data set. The range indicates the amount of spread in the data. The mean, median, mode, and range can help describe a set of data.

**PROBLEM** The table shows the ages of the first eight Presidents of the United States when they were inaugurated. What are the mean, median, mode, and range of the data?

### Ages of Presidents at Inauguration

| President | Age |
|-----------|-----|
| Washington | 57 |
| J. Adams | 61 |
| Jefferson | 57 |
| Madison | 57 |
| Monroe | 58 |
| J. Q. Adams | 57 |
| Jackson | 61 |
| Van Buren | 54 |

### Example 1 Find the mean, median, mode, and range.

The mean is the number found by dividing the sum of a set of numbers by the number of addends.

$(57 + 61 + 57 + 57 + 58 + 57 + 61 + 54) \div 8 = 462 \div 8 = 57.75$

Mean: 57.75

The median is the middle number or the average of the two middle numbers in an ordered data set.

54    57    57    57    57    58    61    61

Median: $(57 + 57) \div 2 = 57$

The mode is the number that occurs most often in a data set. There can be more than one mode or no mode at all.

57    61    57    57    58    57    61    54

Mode: 57

The range is the difference between the greatest and least numbers in a data set.

54    57    57    57    57    58    61    61

Range: $61 - 54 = 7$

**ERROR ALERT**

Be sure to include each instance of repeated data when finding the mean or median of a data set.

So, the mean of the presidential ages at inauguration is 57.75 years, the median is 57 years, the mode is 57 years, and the range of ages is 7 years.

• For which measure of central tendency do you need to write data in ascending or descending order? Explain.

SDAP 1.1 Compute the range, mean, median, and mode of a data set. *also* SDAP 1.0, MR 2.4, MR 2.5, MR 3.0, MR 3.2, MR 3.3.

1. The local theater is holding auditions for a play about the Civil War. Order the ages of those who auditioned.

   Find the mean, median, mode, and range of the ages.

| Ages of People Who Auditioned on Tuesday | |
|---|---|
| 15 | 56 |
| 18 | 35 |
| 27 | 22 |
| 42 | 18 |

**Find the mean, median, mode, and range.**

✓ 2. 80, 74, 82, 74, 86, 75, 74, 74, 75, 80, 82, 86

✓ 3. $\frac{1}{2}, \frac{3}{4}, \frac{1}{4}, \frac{3}{4}, \frac{1}{4}$

4. [ TALK Math ] **Explain** why not all data sets have a mode. Give an example of a set of at least five data values with no mode.

## Independent Practice and Problem Solving

**Find the mean, median, mode, and range.**

5. 140, 183, 85, 93, 97, 101, 85

6. 450, 325, 500, 450, 325, 50, 450, 450

7. 32.5, 41.9, 30.5, 32.6, 37.3, 39.8, 40.6, 41.2

8. $\frac{5}{6}, \frac{1}{4}, \frac{5}{12}, \frac{1}{4}, \frac{1}{2}, \frac{3}{4}$

**Algebra** For 9–11, use the given mean to find the value of $n$ in each data set.

9. 9, 6, 12, 3, $n$; mean: 9

10. 8.4, 3.2, 6.8, $n$; mean: 4.8

11. 36, 42, 18, $n$; mean: 36

12. Half the people standing in line with Ellen at a voting booth are older than she is. Half are younger. Give a possible data set of the ages of all the people in line. Use at least five ages.

13. **Reasoning** The mean voter turnout in five recent elections was 52%. The mode was 55%. What might the voter turnout have been in the five different elections?

**USE DATA** For 14–15, use the line graph.

14. Find the range of voter turnout for presidential elections from 1984 to 2004.

15. [ WRITE Math ] ▶ **What's the Error?** Kent says the mean voter turnout for presidential elections from 1984 to 2004 was 54% because $(53 + 55) \div 2 = 54$.

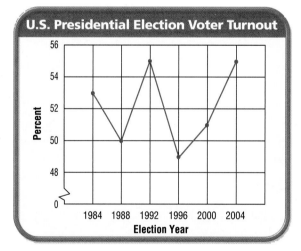

## Achieving the Standards

16. Nancy earns $5 for each car she washes. If she washes 16 cars, how much money will she earn? (○━┓ NS 2.0, p. 172)

17. Pedro wants to know the favorite sport of students in his school. He asks students as they walk into the library. What sampling method is Pedro using? (○━┓ SDAP 2.2, p. 202)

18. Find the mean voter turnout rounded to the nearest tenth for presidential elections from 1984 to 2004. What years in the graph were below the mean voter turnout? (Grade 5 SDAP 1.1)

19. **Test Prep** What is the range of the data set?

   9.6, 8.4, 6, 9, 7.8, 6

   **A** 3.6    **B** 6    **C** 7.8    **D** 8.1

# 2 Outliers

**OBJECTIVE:** Describe how outliers affect the mean, median, and mode.

## Quick Review

The monthly snowfalls for ski season were 9, 16, 13, 20, 16, 22, and 16 inches. Find the mean, median, and mode of the snowfall data.

---

## Vocabulary

**outlier**

## Learn

A value that is very small or very large compared to the majority of the values in a data set is called an **outlier**.

**PROBLEM** Hannah is researching the number of animals that students in her class have at their homes. Her results are shown on the line plot. Find the mean, median, and mode of the data with the outliers included and excluded. Then, compare the values and explain how the outliers affect the mean, median, and mode.

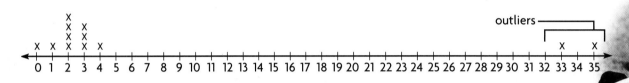

### Example 1

**Step 1**

Find the mean, median, and mode with the outliers included.

**Mean:** 90 ÷ 12 = 7.5

**Median:** 0, 1, 2, 2, 2, 2, 3, 3, 3, 4, 33, 35; (2 + 3) ÷ 2 = 2.5     **Mode:** 2

With the outliers included, the mean is 7.5, the median is 2.5, and the mode is 2.

> **Math Idea**
> You can quickly find the mode in a line plot by finding the tallest stack on the number line.

**Step 2**

Find the mean, median, and mode with the outliers excluded. The outliers are 33 and 35, so exclude 33 and 35 from the data set.

**Mean:** 22 ÷ 10 = 2.2

**Median:** 0, 1, 2, 2, 2, 2, 3, 3, 3, 4; (2 + 2) ÷ 2 = 2          **Mode:** 2

With the outliers excluded, the mean is 2.2, the median is 2, and the mode is 2.

**Step 3**

Compare the mean, median, and mode with the outliers included to the mean, median, and mode with the outliers excluded.

mean: 7.5 > 2.2   median: 2.5 > 2   mode: 2 = 2

So, when the outliers are excluded the mean and median decrease. Since 2 still occurs four times, the mode remains the same.

SDAP 1.3 Understand how the inclusion of exclusion of outliers affects these computatons.
*also* SDAP 1.0, SDAP 1.1, SDAP 1.2, MR 2.4, MR 2.5, MR 3.2

## Example 2

Jim wants to move to California. The table shows the population, in thousands, of each of the counties he is considering. Find the mean, median, and mode of the data with the outlier included and excluded. Then compare the values and explain how the outlier affects the mean, median, and mode.

| County Population (in thousands) | |
|---|---|
| 250 | 185 |
| 18 | 242 |
| 317 | 255 |
| 214 | 247 |

**Step 1**

Order the data from least to greatest and identify the outlier.

18, 185, 214, 242, 247, 250, 255, 317; outlier: 18

**Step 2**

Find the mean, median, and mode with the outlier included.

**Mean:** 1,728 ÷ 8 = 216

**Median:** 18, 185, 214, 242, 247, 250, 255, 317; (242 + 247) ÷ 2 = 244.5

**Mode:** no mode

With the outlier included, the mean is 216, the median is 244.5, and the data does not contain a mode.

**Step 3**

Find the mean, median, and mode with the outlier excluded. The outlier is 18, so exclude 18 from the data set.

**Mean:** 1,710 ÷ 7 ≈ 244.3

**Median:** 185, 214, 242, 247, 250, 255, 317; 247          **Mode:** no mode

With the outliers excluded, the mean is about 244.3, the median is 247, and the data does not contain a mode.

**Step 4**

Compare the mean, median, and mode with the outliers included to the mean, median, and mode with the outliers excluded.

mean: 216 < 244.3     median: 244.5 = 247     mode: no mode

So, when the outliers are excluded, the mean and median increase. However, there is no mode in the data set.

## Guided Practice

1. The line plot shows the numbers of kilometers sixteen different people hiked. The outliers are 0.9 and 1. Find the mean, median, and mode of the data with the outliers included and excluded.

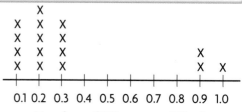

**Number of Kilometers Hiked**

**Find the mean, median, and mode with the outliers included and excluded. Explain how the outliers affect the mean, median, and mode.**

**2.** 55, 52, 55, 50, 17, 47

**3.** 36, 42, 52, 42, 38, 40, 52, 42, 34, 42, 218

**✓4.** 24, 34, 56, 25, 58, 26, 32, 27

**✓ 5.** 0.1, 0.9, 1.3, 1.2, 0.9, 0.1, 1.1

**6.** **TALK Math** Explain when it is possible for a data set to have a mean that is less with the outliers included than with the outliers excluded. Give an example.

## Independent Practice and Problem Solving

**Find the mean, median, and mode with the outliers included and excluded. Explain how the outliers affect the mean, median, and mode.**

**7.** 81, 72, 79, 12, 86, 79, 80, 11

**8.** 5, 21, 4.6, 5.3, 5, 4.8, 5.3, 5, 5.2

**9.** 125, 158, 135, 166, 31, 166, 31,

**10.** $1\frac{1}{2}$, $1\frac{2}{5}$, 3, $26\frac{2}{5}$, $1\frac{1}{2}$, $2\frac{3}{5}$

**11.**

```
                              X
                              X      X
          X                   X   X X
          X                   X X X X
  +-+-+-+-+-+-+-+-+-+-+-+-+-+-+-+-+-+-+-+->
    6 7 8 9 10 11 12 13 14 15 16 17 18 19 20 21 22 23 24 25
```
**Number of Kites Flown Each Day**

**12.**

| Number of Miles Biked | | | | | |
|---|---|---|---|---|---|
| 2.5 | 2.2 | 0.2 | 2.5 | 3.0 | 2.4 |
| 3.0 | 2.5 | 2.2 | 3.0 | 0.4 | 2.5 |

**USE DATA** For 13–14, use the table.

**13.** What is the difference between the mean growth with and without the outlier included?

**14.** During July, each plant grows half of what it grew in June. Find the mean, median and mode, with the outlier included and excluded, of the total plant growth in June and July for all plants.

**15.** Pose a Problem Write and answer a new question for problem 13 by coming up with a different set of data.

**16.** **WRITE Math** What's the Question? The answer is the mean of the data set decreases.

| Plant Growth for June | |
|---|---|
| **Plant** | **Growth (cm)** |
| A | 8 |
| B | 10 |
| C | 32 |
| D | 12 |

## Achieving the Standards

**17.** Daryl wants to know what subject students in his school like best. He uses a randomly generated list of students for a sample. Is his sample representative of the population? Explain. (○━┓ SDAP 2.2, p. 200)

**18.** Find the sum of $\frac{1}{4}$, $\frac{5}{12}$, and $\frac{1}{2}$. (○━┓ NS 2.0, p. 38)

**19.** Find the mean of the following data set.
(SDAP 1.1, p. 224)

100, 97, 100, 98, 103, 100, 95

**20.** **Test Prep** How does the outlier affect the mean, median, and mode?

1.5, 0.75, 1.5, 3.75, 0.5, 1.5, 1

**A** The mean, median, and mode increase.

**B** The mean and mode increase.

**C** The mean and median increase.

**D** The mean and median decrease.

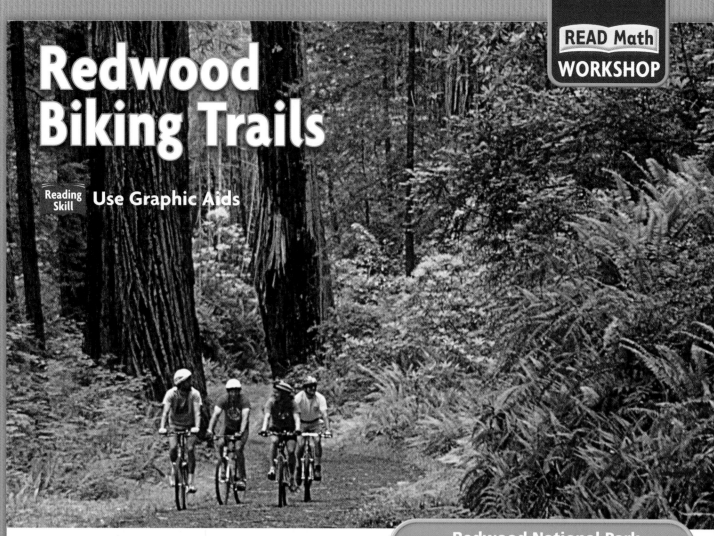

# Redwood Biking Trails

**Reading Skill** Use Graphic Aids

▲ Bikers in Redwood National Park

Biking and hiking are forms of exercise enjoyed by people of all ages. Bike trails across the country weave through a variety of scenic environments that enhance the biking experience. The trails at Redwood National Park lead bikers through prairies, old-growth redwood forests, and along beaches. The table at the right shows the length of some randomly chosen trails at the park.

| Redwood National Park | |
|---|---|
| **Trails** | **Approx. Length (mi)** |
| Lost Man Creek Trail | 11 |
| Coastal Trail | 6 |
| Little Bald Hill Trail | 8 |
| Ossagan Trail Loop | 19 |
| Davison Road | 8 |
| Davison Trail | 8 |

**Problem Solving** Read the graphic aid. Use the information to solve the problems.

1. What is the mean length of the trails with and without the outlier included?

2. Is the mode useful to describe the data? Why or why not?

3. **Reasoning** The median length of three trails that Rick biked on is 11 miles. Which two trails must Rick have biked on?

4. **Explain** how to find the range of the trail lengths. What is the range?

# LESSON 3

# Choose the Most Useful Measure

OBJECTIVE: Decide if the mean, median, or mode best describes a set of data.

### Quick Review

Identify the outliers.

1. 98, 102, 98, 280,103,100
2. 23.8, 24.1, 23.5, 23.8, 0.8, 23.8
3. 710, 689, 698, 121, 710, 699
4. 6.25, 6.09, 6.11, 6.09, 61
5. 555, 560, 52, 554, 545

## Learn

**PROBLEM** Death Valley, California, has the warmest climate in the United States. The table shows the high temperature in Death Valley on 7 summer days. Which measure is most useful to describe the temperatures: the mean, the median, or the mode?

| Summer High Temperatures in Death Valley | | | | | | | |
|---|---|---|---|---|---|---|---|
| Day | 1 | 2 | 3 | 4 | 5 | 6 | 7 |
| Temperature (°F) | 104 | 110 | 106 | 104 | 112 | 105 | 108 |

### Example 1

Mean: 749 ÷ 7 = 107

Median: 104   104   105   106   108   110   112; 106

Mode: 104

The mean, 107°F, and the median, 106°F, are close to most of the data. The mode, 104°F, is close to the low end of the data, so the mode is not as useful.

So, either the mean or the median is most useful to describe the data.

• Suppose the high temperature for 5 of the 7 days were 106°F. Would the mode be more useful than the other measures to describe the data? Explain.

Outliers affect the usefulness of measures of central tendency.

### Example 2

Which measure is most useful to describe the following data: the mean, the median, or the mode?

9.8   9.1   9.9   9.2   0.4   9.9   8.4

Mean: 56.7 ÷ 7 = 8.1

Median: 0.4   8.4   9.1   9.2   9.8   9.9   9.9; 9.2

Mode: 9.9

The outlier, 0.4, makes the mean, 8.1, less than most of the data. So the mean is not as useful. The mode, 9.9, is at the high end of the data, so the mode is not as useful. The median, 9.2, is closest to most of the data.

So, the median is most useful to describe the data.

▲ The highest temperature ever officially observed in the United States was 134°F, in Death Valley, California, on July 10, 1913.

SDAP 1.4 Know why a specific measure of central tendency (mean, median, mode) provides the most useful information in a given context. *also* SDAP 1.0, SDAP 1.1, SDAP 1.3, MR 2.4, MR 2.5, MR 3.2

## Guided Practice

1. The weather forecast in the table on the right shows the chance of rain in Los Angeles for the next 7 days. The mean chance is 40%, the median is 60%, and the mode is 60%. The median and mode are close to most of the data. Which measure is most useful to describe the data?

| Weekly Forecast for Los Angeles | | | | | | | |
|---|---|---|---|---|---|---|---|
| **Day** | Mon | Tue | Wed | Thu | Fri | Sat | Sun |
| **Chance of Rain** | 0% | 0% | 30% | 60% | 70% | 60% | 60% |

**Find the mean, median, and mode. Tell which measure is most useful to describe the data. Explain.**

2. 17, 12, 14, 14, 13, 11    ✓3. 0.6, 0.8, 0.2, 7.1, 0.2    ✓4. 97, 85, 97, 90, 92, 87, 80, 94, 88

5. **TALK Math** **Explain** how to determine if the mean, median, or mode is the most useful to describe a set of data.

## Independent Practice and Problem Solving

**Find the mean, median, and mode. Tell which measure is most useful to describe the data. Explain.**

6. 13, 9, 5, 8, 10, 5, 12, 5, 14

7. 9.1, 8.2, 9.5, 8.2, 9, 9.3, 9.5, 9.2

8. 350, 324, 320, 475, 346, 321

9. 71.6, 70.8, 71.6, 71.8, 71.6

**USE DATA** For 10–11, use the map.

10. Find the mean, median, and mode of the temperatures. Tell which measure is most useful to describe the data. **Explain.**

11. **≡FAST FACT** The lowest temperature ever recorded in California was in 1937, in Boca, when the temperature dropped to ⁻42.8°C. Including this temperature with the temperatures from the map, tell if the mean, median, or mode is most useful to describe the data.

12. **WRITE Math** **Explain** how an outlier that is greater than all of the data will affect the mean.

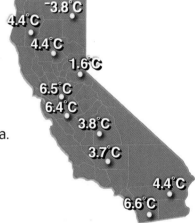

## Achieving the Standards

13. Draw $\overleftrightarrow{AB}$ and $\overleftrightarrow{XY}$ as parallel lines.
   (Grade 5 ○━┓ MG 2.1)

14. The annual rainfall in a city was $73\frac{4}{5}$ in. last year and $73\frac{2}{3}$ in. this year. In which year was the rainfall greater? (○━┓ NS 1.1, p. 18)

15. Find the mean of the following data set.
   (SDAP 1.1, p. 224)

   6.9, 7.4, 6.9, 5.2, 8.7, 6.9

16. **Test Prep** Find the mean, median, and mode of the data. Which measure is most useful to describe the data?

   0.6, 0.9, 0.5, 0.6, 8.0, 0.6, 0.7

   **A** The mean and the median are most useful.

   **B** The median and the mode are most useful.

   **C** The mean and the mode are most useful.

   **D** The mean, median, and mode are most useful.

**Extra Practice** on page 236, Set C

# Additional Data

OBJECTIVE: Show how additional data affect the mean, median, and mode.

**Quick Review**

The wingspans of 6 paper airplanes are 6 in., 6.5 in., 8 in., 6.5 in., 7.5 in., and 7.5 in. What are the mean, median, and mode of the wingspans?

## Learn

**PROBLEM** Beth is entering five paper airplanes in a competition. The table shows the maximum distance flown by each plane. Find the mean, median, and mode of the distances.

### Example 1

**Mean:** $1{,}659 \div 5 = 331.8$

**Median:** 319   319   331   342   348; 331

**Mode:** 348   319   342   319   331; 319

So, the mean is 331.8 in., the median is 331 in., and the mode is 319 in.

| Beth's Paper Airplanes | |
| --- | --- |
| Name | Maximum Distance Flown (in.) |
| Streamer | 348 |
| Spike | 319 |
| Panther | 342 |
| Dart | 319 |
| Whiz | 331 |

### Example 2

Beth enters another airplane in the competition. It has flown a maximum distance of 345 in. How does this additional data affect the mean, median, and mode?

**Mean:** $2{,}004 \div 6 = 334$

**Median:** 319   319   331   342   345   348; $(331 + 342) \div 2 = 336.5$

**Mode:** 319

So, the additional distance increases the mean and the median. The mode remains the same.

- **What if** Beth enters a seventh paper airplane in the competition? Describe the plane's maximum distance that would decrease the mean of all of Beth's entries and change the median to 331.

**Remember**
When finding the mean, increase the divisor when you add data to the data set.

## Guided Practice

1. The table shows the flight times of five direct flights from Sacramento to San Francisco. The mean time is 45 min, and the median and mode are both 44 min.

   Suppose a sixth flight lasting 42 min is added to the list. Find the new mean, median, and mode. How does the new flight time affect the original mean, median, and mode?

   new mean: $(45 + 50 + 44 + 42 + 44 + 42) \div 6 =$ ■

| Flights Times to San Francisco (min) | |
| --- | --- |
| Flight 1 | 45 |
| Flight 2 | 50 |
| Flight 3 | 44 |
| Flight 4 | 42 |
| Flight 5 | 44 |

SDAP 1.2 Understand how additional data added to data sets may affect these computations of measure of central tendency. *also* SDAP 1.0, SDAP 1.1, MR 2.4, MR 2.5, MR 3.1, MR 3.2

**Find the mean, median, and mode. Then describe how the additional data affects the mean, median, and mode.**

2. 284, 296, 275, 288, 296

   additional data: 275

✓3. 8.2, 6.6, 8.6, 6.8, 8.2, 6.6, 8.2

   additional data: 6.8

✓4. $\frac{3}{4}, \frac{5}{12}, \frac{1}{2}, \frac{5}{6}$

   additional data: $\frac{5}{6}$

5. **TALK Math** **Explain** how the mean, median, and mode of a data set change when a value greater than all of the other values is added to the data set. Give an example.

## Independent Practice and Problem Solving

**Find the mean, median, and mode. Then describe how the additional data affects the mean, median, and mode.**

6. 36, 30, 48, 50, 32 additional data: 32

7. 800, 925, 915, 790, 800 additional data: 925, 949

8. 60.2, 71.5, 60.2, 70.4, 63.5, 70.4, 60.2

   additional data: 57.1, 63.4

9. $\frac{3}{8}, \frac{1}{4}, \frac{5}{8}, \frac{1}{2}, \frac{1}{4}$ additional data: $\frac{1}{2}$

**USE DATA For 10–11, use the bar graph.**

10. **Reasoning** One of the paper airplanes in the competition was disqualified. The median time in the air of the remaining planes is 8 sec. Which of the paper airplanes could have been disqualified?

11. **FAST FACT** The world indoor record for a paper airplane's time in the air is 27.6 sec. If the world record had been set by a sixth plane in this competition, by how many seconds would that sixth plane have increased the mean for these planes?

12. **WRITE Math** **Sense or Nonsense?** Lou says adding a value that is less than every other value in the data set is guaranteed to decrease the mean, median, and mode. Does this make sense? **Explain.**

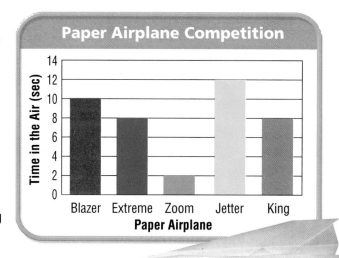

Paper Airplane Competition

## Achieving the Standards

13. Jonathon has $24\frac{1}{5}$ cups of flour. If he uses $2\frac{1}{5}$ cups of flour to make a batch of his famous cookies, how many batches of cookies can Jonathon make? (**O—n** NS 2.0, p. 100)

14. If $n = 2$, what is the value of $8 \times n - 3$.
    (Grade 5 **O—n** AF 1.2)

15. Find the median of the following data set.
    (SDAP 1.1, p. 224)

    6.04, 5.76, 6.24, 5.04

16. **Test Prep** What is the mean when 74 is added to the following data set?

    68, 74, 74, 66, 76

    **A** 72    **B** 71.6    **C** 74    **D** 74.5

Extra Practice on page 236, Set D

# Problem Solving Workshop
## Skill: Too Much or Too Little Information

OBJECTIVE: Solve problems by using the skill *too much or too little information.*

## Use the Skill

**PROBLEM** Nick uses an online puzzle generator to create word search puzzles. He spent 2 hours making 10 puzzles. What is the mean number of words in Nick's puzzles?

### Nick's Word Search Puzzles

| Puzzle | 1 | 2 | 3 | 4 | 5 | 6 | 7 | 8 | 9 | 10 |
|---|---|---|---|---|---|---|---|---|---|---|
| Number of Words | 20 | 15 | 18 | 15 | 22 | 20 | 18 | 17 | 15 | 30 |

If a problem has too much information, decide which information you need for solving the problem.

- **You want to find** the mean number of words in Nick's puzzles.

- **You need to know** the number of puzzles Nick made and the total number of words in the puzzles.

- **You don't need to know** that Nick spent 2 hours making the puzzles.

$$20 + 15 + 18 + 15 + 22 + 20 + 18 + 17 + 15 + 30 = 190$$

$$190 \div 10 = 19$$

So, the mean number of words in Nick's puzzles is 19.

## Think and Discuss

**Tell if each problem has *too much*, *too little*, or *the right amount* of information. Then solve the problem, if possible, or describe the information you would need to solve it.**

**a.** Some word puzzles are made by reordering the letters of a word or phrase. What is the median number of letters in the following puzzles?

| | | | | |
|---|---|---|---|---|
| rgite | feiragf | tnpelhea | lgrloia | noli |

**b.** Hayley won $\frac{5}{8}$ of the crossword puzzle competitions she entered last year. How many competitions did she win in all?

**c.** Harold started a jigsaw puzzle collection 4 years ago. He now has 15 puzzles in his collection. The puzzles have these numbers of pieces: 1,000; 2,000; 1,500; 2,000; 50; 1,000; 50; 1,000; 500; 3,000; 5,000; 1,000; 2,000; 1,500; and 5,000. What is the mode of the numbers of pieces in Harold's jigsaw puzzles?

SDAP 1.0 Students compute and analyze statistical measures for data sets: *also* SDAP 1.1, MR 1.0, MR 1.1, MR 2.0, MR 2.4, MR 2.5, MR 3.0, MR 3.1, MR 3.2, MR 3.3

Tell if each problem has *too much, too little,* or *the right amount* of information. Then solve the problem, if possible, or describe the information you would need to solve it.

1. Six of the most popular three-dimensional puzzles are marked down for a special sale. The sale prices are $39.99, $25.50, $22.99, and $25.50. What is the median sale price of the 6 puzzles?

   **First,** decide what you need to find and what you need to know.

   **Then,** determine if the problem has *too much, too little,* or *the right amount* of information.

   **Finally,** solve the problem or describe the information you need to solve it.

2. **What if** the puzzle prices in Exercise 1 were for the 4 most popular puzzles? What would be the median sale price of the 4 most popular puzzles?

3. Julian jogged 2 km, 6 km, 8 km, 6 km, 4 km, 3 km, and 6 km in the past week. He also walked 3 km and 2 km on the past 2 days. Find the mean of the distances he jogged.

## Mixed Applications

4. The first published crossword puzzle appeared in a Sunday newspaper on December 21, 1913. The longest word in that puzzle had 7 letters. What is the range of the number of letters in the words in the crossword puzzle?

5. Rachel started a crossword puzzle by writing 7 words. She erased 2 of the words, wrote 5 more words, erased 3 of those words, and then finished the puzzle by writing 8 more words. How many words are in the crossword puzzle?

6. Donna is buying 4 crossword puzzle books for $2.75 each, 2 word search puzzle books for $3.15 each, and 1 math puzzle book for $3.75. How much do the books cost in all?

7. The greatest common factor of the number of letters in the puzzle below and in another puzzle is 8. The least common multiple is 24. How many letters are in the other puzzle?

**For 8–9, use the table at the right.**

8. How much greater is the median number of entries in the Puzzle Design Competition with the outliers excluded than with the outliers included?

9. **WRITE Math** Explain which measure is most useful for describing the following data about favorite puzzles: the mean, the median, or the mode. Explain your thinking.

   Favorite puzzle: mixed letters, crossword, jigsaw, crossword, word search, jigsaw

```
GROTHTEE
```

| **Puzzle Design Competition** | | | | | | | |
|---|---|---|---|---|---|---|---|
| Year | 1 | 2 | 3 | 4 | 5 | 6 | 7 |
| Number of Entries | 35 | 9 | 42 | 36 | 40 | 8 | 42 |

# Extra Practice

## Set A Find the mean, median, mode, and range. (pp. 224-225)

1. 12, 25, 14, 31, 27, 18, 9, 13

2. 101, 105, 96, 96, 113, 108, 104, 106, 98

3. $\frac{1}{3}, \frac{2}{3}, \frac{2}{3}, \frac{1}{4}, \frac{3}{4}, \frac{1}{2}$

4. $\frac{1}{4}, 1, \frac{2}{3}, 2, \frac{5}{6}, 1, \frac{1}{4}$

5. 2.5, 4.1, 3.7, 3.2, 3.7, 3.9, 3.7

6. 4, 6, 4, 8, 9, 6, 8, 7, 3, 2

## Set B Find the mean, median, and mode with the outliers included and excluded. Explain how the outliers affect the mean, median, and mode. (pp. 226-229)

1. 12, 4, 12, 4, 6, 7, 10, 9, 35

2. 120, 52, 125, 121, 126, 128, 126

3. 0.9, 1.2, 0.8, 55, 0.7, 1.4

4. 47, 49, 318, 45, 44, 45, 312, 45, 40

5. The table at the right shows the number of students who have been absent for each day of the week.

| Absences | | | | | |
|---|---|---|---|---|---|
| **Day** | Mon | Tues | Wed | Thurs | Fri |
| **Number of Absences** | 55 | 49 | 12 | 47 | 57 |

## Set C Find the mean, median, and mode. Tell which measure is most useful to describe the data. Explain. (pp. 230-231)

1. 10, 12, 15, 16, 16, 17, 20, 10

2. 0.01, 0.05, 0.03, 0.01, 0.08, 0.09, 0.1

3. 51, 25, 51, 56, 52, 55, 51, 58, 60

4. 0, 1, 2, 2, 3, 5, 5, 5, 6, 6, 7, 8, 9

5. 125, 153, 308, 156, 147, 145, 156

6. $\frac{3}{8}, \frac{1}{5}, \frac{1}{4}, 2, \frac{7}{8}, \frac{1}{5}, 1, \frac{1}{10}$

## Set D Find the mean, median, and mode. Then describe how the additional data affects the mean, median, and mode. (pp. 232-233)

1. 3, 8, 4, 4, 5, 7, 4
   additional data: 8

2. 16, 18, 11, 21, 19, 15, 20, 14
   addtitional data: 19

3. Trent recorded the weights of 5 newborn babies. Their weights, in ounces, were 120, 117, 97, 109, and 128. He later was able to add more data: a sixth baby, weighing 80 oz.

4. Julie surveys the costs of a haircut and styling at 5 local salons. Their fees are $25, $45, $30, $55, and $60. Two weeks after she finishes her survey, the salon that was charging $25 raises its price to $80.

5. The table at the right shows the grades of 20 students on a recent exam. Another student missed the exam due to an illness. The teacher allows him to make up the grade. When he takes the exam, his score is 91.

| Exam Scores | | | | |
|---|---|---|---|---|
| 32 | 51 | 58 | 67 | 70 |
| 71 | 78 | 82 | 82 | 83 |
| 84 | 85 | 87 | 89 | 91 |
| 92 | 94 | 97 | 99 | 100 |

# Mean, Median, & Mode March

## One!
2 players

## Two!
- Number cards (1–50)
- 2 number cubes, each labeled 1–6
- 2 different-colored counters

**START**

**FINISH**

## Three! Four!

- Shuffle the number cards, and place them facedown in a pile.

- Each player selects a counter and places it on START. Decide who will go first.

- The first player tosses the number cubes.

- The player draws the same number of cards as the sum of the numbers tossed.

- The player then tosses one number cube.

- If a 1 or a 2 is tossed, the player calculates the mean of the values on the number cards.

- If a 3 or a 4 is tossed, the player calculates the median.

- If a 5 or a 6 is tossed, the player calculates the mode.

- The other player checks the first player's answer. If it is correct, the first player moves his or her counter one space on the gameboard and play passes to the opposing player.

- If the answer is incorrect, play passes to the opposing player.

- When all cards have been used, reshuffle them and place them facedown to be used again.

- The first player to reach FINISH wins.

# Chapter 9 Review/Test

## Check Vocabulary and Concepts

Choose the best term from the box.

1. A data value that is very small or very large compared to the majority of values in a data set is a(n) ___?___. (SDAP 1.3, p. 226)

2. Explain the steps you would take to find the median of the following data set: 143, 127, 205, 315, and 180. (SDAP 1.1, pp. 224–225)

## Check Skills

**Find the mean, median, mode, and range.** (SDAP 1.1, pp. 224–225)

3. 5, 7, 12, 15, 10, 5

4. 1, 2, 3, 3, 3, 4, 5

5. 15, 15, 14, 19, 11, 15, 14, 17

**Find the mean, median, and mode with and without the outliers. Explain how the outliers affect the mean, median, and mode.** (SDAP 1.3, pp. 226–229)

6. 25, 22, 25, 20, 42, 28

7. 85, 82, 86, 82, 16, 88, 93

8. 205, 203, 213, 201, 44, 208

**Find the mean, median, and mode. Which measure or measures are most useful to describe the data? Explain.** (SDAP 1.3, pp. 230–231)

9. 3.5, 4.8, 2.1, 10.7, 1.9

10. 27, 31, 48, 52, 18, 52

11. 10, 115, 119, 117, 110, 107, 115

**Find the mean, median, and mode. Then describe the effect the additional data has on the mean, median, and mode.** (SDAP 1.2, pp. 232–233)

12. 1, 2, 3, 4, 5, 6, 7
additional data: 4

13. 17, 12, 17, 10
additional data: 111

14. 101, 103, 101, 103, 102
additional data: 10

15. 0.2, 0.8, 1.2, 1.6
additional data: 0.2

16. $\frac{2}{3}, \frac{1}{2}, \frac{1}{2}, \frac{1}{6}$
additional data: $\frac{1}{4}$

17. 5, 7, 12, 10, 10, 40
additional data: 40

## Check Problem Solving

**Solve.** (SDAP 1.0 MR 1.1, pp. 234–235)

18. Kyla completed 2 mi, 3 mi, 1 mi, and 4 mi jogging this week. He also rode his bike 2 mi and 5 mi the last two days. What is the mean number of miles he jogged?

19. Tommy spent $2.87, $3.02, and $2.99 per gallon on gas this month. It takes 15 gal to fill up his car. What is the mean and median cost per gallon on gas?

20. **WRITE Math** **What's the Error?** Eight pairs of shoes are shown in a catalog. Some of the prices listed for the shoes are $79.99, $64.99, $101.99, $80.00 and, $99.50. Beth makes the claim that the median price for a pair of shoes from this catalog is $80.00.

**GO Technology** Use *Online Assessment*.

# Enrich • Mean, Median, Mode, and Range
## Math Mysteries

Use clues and your knowledge of mean, median, mode, and range to solve math mysteries. Be prepared to share how you solved the mysteries!

### Investigate

Clues:

• There are three numbers in a set.
• The mean is 5.
• The mode is 6.

What is the set of numbers?

| **Step 1** | Use the mean and the number of addends to find the sum of the numbers in the set. |

$5 \times 3 = 15$

The sum of the numbers in the set is 15.

| **Step 2** | Use the mode to help you find three numbers with a sum of 15. |

$6 + 6 + \blacksquare = 15$
$6 + 6 + 3 = 15$

**Math Idea**
To find the mean of a data set, you divide. So, to find the sum of the numbers in a set when you know the mean, you multiply.

So, the numbers in the set are 6, 6, and 3.

### Solve the Mysteries

**Use the clues to find each set of numbers.**

1. • There are three numbers in a set.
   • The range is 23.
   • The median is 26.
   • One number in the set is 40.

2. • There are four numbers in a set.
   • The mode is 10.
   • The median is 7.
   • The range is 8.

3. • There are four numbers in a set.
   • The mean is 12.
   • The range is 11.
   • The mode is 7.
   • One number in the set is 16.

4. • There are four numbers in a set.
   • The median is 22.
   • The range is 40.
   • One number in the set is 57.
   • The mode is 22.

### Think About It

**WRITE Math** Explain how you solved Mystery 2.

# Achieving the Standards
## Chapters 1–9

## Number Sense

**1.** $4 \times {}^-8 =$  (O━┓ NS 2.3)

    **A** $^-32$

    **C** $12$

    **B** $^-4$

    **D** $32$

**Test Tip** Eliminate choices.

See item 1. Remember that when you multiply two numbers with different signs, the result is negative.

**2.** What is the greatest common multiple of 4, 12, and 20? (O━┓ NS 2.4)

    **A** $4$         **C** $32$

    **B** $28$       **D** $60$

**3.** $10 \times \frac{3}{5} =$  (O━┓ NS 2.0)

    **A** $1\frac{3}{5}$      **C** $6$

    **B** $\frac{13}{5}$      **D** $15$

**4.** Which list of numbers is ordered from greatest to least? (O━┓ NS 1.1)

    **A** 0.4, 0.004, 0.04, 4

    **B** 4, 0.004, 0.4, 0.04

    **C** 4, 0.4, 0.04, 0.004

    **D** 0.004, 0.04, 0.4, 4

**5.** **WRITE Math** **What's the Error?** Jessie constructed the number line below. (O━┓ NS 1.1)

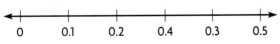

## Statistics, Data Analysis, and Probability

**6.** George took 5 math exams during a semester of school. His scores were 88, 67, 75, 89, and 92. Which shows George's median exam score? (SDAP 1.1)

    **A** 88         **C** 75

    **B** 82.2      **D** 25

**7.** Which statement is valid about the points scored by these players? (O━┓ SDAP 2.5)

| Points Scored | | | | | |
|---|---|---|---|---|---|
| Game | Tom | Mary | Rick | Alice | Paul |
| 1 | 1 | 2 | 1 | 0 | 3 |
| 2 | 0 | 2 | 2 | 1 | 3 |

    **A** Alice is a better player than Tom.

    **B** Tom is a better player than Mary.

    **C** Paul is the best player.

    **D** Rick is the best player.

**8.** Maria is interested in determining the mean amount that people spend when buying a new car. She goes to a local car lot for a day and obtains the amount spent by each customer who purchases a new car. Which sampling method did Maria use to obtain this information? (O━┓ SDAP 2.2)

    **A** convenience sampling

    **B** random sampling

    **C** systematic sampling

    **D** stratified sampling

**9.** **WRITE Math** After Brad weighed all 12 kittens at the veterinary clinic to determine their median weight, the lightest kitten lost two pounds. **Explain** how this will affect the median weight. (SDAP 1.2)

## Algebra and Functions

**10.** Miguel went to the grocery store. He started with $100. If he spent x number of dollars, which expression represents how much money he had when he left the store? (Grade 5 AF 1.2)

**A** $x + 100$

**B** $x - 100$

**C** $100 - x$

**D** $100 + x$

**11.** Rochelle bought 5 tickets to a baseball game, each priced at $21. To find the total cost, she added the product $5 \times 20$ to the product $5 \times 1$, for a total of $105. Which property did Rochelle use? (Grade 5 AF 1.3)

**A** Commutative Property

**B** Associative Property

**C** Identity Property

**D** Distributive Property

**12.** What value of $p$ makes the following equation true? (Grade 5 AF 1.3)

$$17 \times 3 = (10 \times 3) + (p \times 3)$$

**A** 3        **C** 10

**B** 7        **D** 17

**13.** **WRITE Math** ▸ The steps Roger took to evaluate the expression $n - 7$ when $n = 12$ are shown below. Explain what Roger should have done differently in order to evaluate the expression. (Grade 5 AF 1.2)

$$n - 7$$
$$n - 7 = 12 + 7$$
$$12 + 7 = 19$$

## Measurement and Geometry

**14.** What is the measure of the angle shown below? (Grade 5 MG 2.1)

**A** 180°

**B** 120°

**C** 90°

**D** 45°

**15.** The angle measures of a triangle are 90°, 45°, and $x$. What is the measure of the unknown angle? (Grade 5 MG 2.2)

**A** 15°

**B** 45°

**C** 90°

**D** 135°

**16.** The rectangle shown below has length 5 centimeters and width 4 centimeters. What is the area of the rectangle? (Grade 5 MG 1.4)

**A** 1 square centimeter

**B** 9 square centimeters

**C** 12 square centimeters

**D** 20 square centimeters

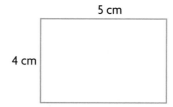

5 cm

4 cm

**17.** **WRITE Math** ▸ What's the Question? Suppose you are shown a picture of a cube with an edge that measures 8 centimeters. The answer is 512. (Grade 5 MG 1.3)

# 10

# Graph Data

**The Big Idea** Data can be analyzed and displayed in various graphical formats.

## Investigate

The graph at the right shows the seating capacities of some famous baseball stadiums. Make a new graph using different intervals.

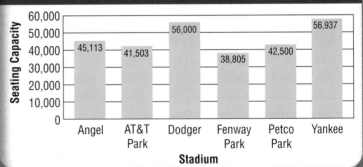

**Baseball Stadium Seating Capacity**

| Stadium | Seating Capacity |
|---|---|
| Angel | 45,113 |
| AT&T Park | 41,503 |
| Dodger | 56,000 |
| Fenway Park | 38,805 |
| Petco Park | 42,500 |
| Yankee | 56,937 |

**GO ONLINE**

**Technology**
Student pages are available in the Student eBook.

Check your understanding of important skills
needed for success in Chapter 10.

## ▶ Read Circle Graphs

**For 1–4, use the circle graph at the right.**

1. Which part of exercise takes up the most time?

2. Which part of exercise takes up the least time?

3. What percent of time exercising is spent on strength training?

4. If a person spends 5 minutes warming up, how much time do they spend cooling down?

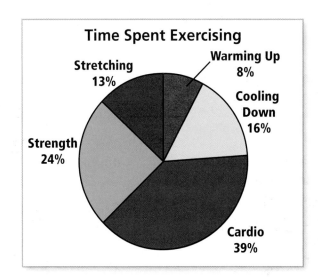

**Time Spent Exercising**

## ▶ Read Bar Graphs

**For 5–8, use the bar graph at the right.**

5. Which subject is preferred by the most people?

6. Which subject is preferred the least?

7. How many students list science as their favorite subject?

8. How many more students prefer English than math?

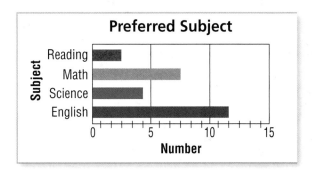

**Preferred Subject**

# VOCABULARY POWER

**CHAPTER VOCABULARY**

circle graph
double-bar graph
double-line graph

**WARM-UP WORDS**

**double-bar graph** a graph that helps to compare two sets of data

**double-line graph** a graph that helps to compare two sets of data that change over time

**circle graph** a graph that lets you compare parts to the whole and to other parts

# 1 Bar Graphs

OBJECTIVE: Analyze and display data in bar graphs.

## Learn

**PROBLEM** Many schools sponsor activities focused on the arts. The table shows the percents of elementary schools that offer extracurricular arts programs in two different regions of the country. Which region has a greater percent of schools offering field trips to art museums?

A bar graph is a useful way to display and analyze data that is grouped in categories. A **double-bar graph** helps to compare two sets of data.

### Example 1 Use the data in the table to make a double-bar graph.

| Elementary Schools with Arts Programs | | | |
|---|---|---|---|
| Region | Field trips to performances | Field trips to art museums | Visiting artists |
| Southeast | 82% | 38% | 37% |
| West | 75% | 69% | 34% |

**Step 1**

Determine an appropriate scale. Numbers vary from 34% to 82%. So, use a scale from 0 to 100%.

**Step 2**

Use the data to determine the length of the bars. Make the bars of equal width.

**Step 3**

Use different colors to represent the different sets of data.

In comparing the field trips to art museums, the West region has the taller bar.

So, the West region offers a greater percent of trips to art museums.

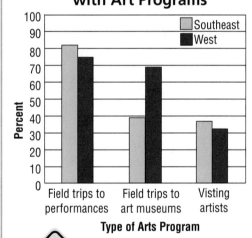

**Elementary Schools with Art Programs**

*Type of Arts Program*

**ERROR ALERT**

Be sure to
• include a title.
• label the scales.
• provide a key.

## Guided Practice

1. Suppose you added the data at the right to the graph above. Would the bars be longer than some of the bars shown? If so, which bars?

| Region | After-school arts program |
|---|---|
| Southeast | 42% |
| West | 55% |

**SDAP 2.3** Analyze data displays and explain why the way in which the question was asked might have influenced the results obtained and why the way in which the results were displayed might have influenced the conclusions reached. *also* MR 1.1, MR 2.4, MR 2.5, MR 3.1, MR 3.2

**For 2–5, use the table.**

2. Make a double-bar graph using the data in the table.

3. Compare the matching bars for men and women. Which shows the greatest difference?

4. What type of entertainment should Mr. and Mrs. Jones choose so that they would most likely enjoy it equally?

5. **TALK Math** **Explain** the steps you should follow when making a bar graph. In your explanation, refer to the graph you made in Exercise 2.

**Favorite Types of Entertainment**

|  | Men | Women |
|---|---|---|
| Movies | 19% | 40% |
| Television | 46% | 31% |
| Live Shows | 35% | 29% |

## Independent Practice and Problem Solving

**For 6–8, use the table.**

6. Use the data in the table to make a double-bar graph.

7. Which type of financial support has declined from ten years ago to this season?

8. Compare the total financial support from ten years ago with the total for this season. Which type of support shows the greatest difference?

**Financial Support for Symphony (in millions of dollars)**

|  | Income from Concerts | Private Contributions | Government Grants |
|---|---|---|---|
| Ten years ago | 470 | 350 | 60 |
| This season | 520 | 570 | 50 |

**For 9–11, use the bar graph.**

9. Which two types of films, when combined, are about as popular as action films?

10. Each percent represents the number of people out of 100 who chose each type of movie. If the graph shows the results for 400 people, how many people favored each type of film?

11. **WRITE Math** **What's the Error?** Stephanie claims that if 5,000 people took the survey, then 65 people chose science fiction. Find her error and correct it.

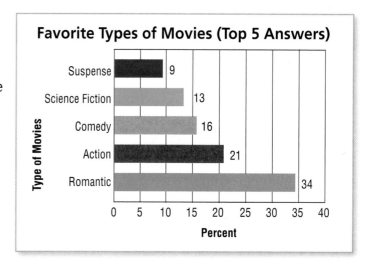

Favorite Types of Movies (Top 5 Answers)

## Achieving the Standards

12. If $x$ is a number that satisfies $2x + 3 = 11$, can $x$ be equal to 4? (Grade 5 ⊶ AF 1.2)

13. Find the range of the following list of numbers: 24, 35, 16, 52, 37, 13, and 49. (SDAP 1.1, p. 224)

14. Which type of graph shows changes in data over a period of time? (Grade 5 SDAP 1.2)

15. **Test Prep** Look at the bar graph for Exercises 9–11. Which type of movie is about half as popular as romantic movies?

   **A** suspense       **C** science fiction

   **B** comedy         **D** action

## Quick Review

The data below was collected about people's favorite sports. What scale could be used to graph this data?

Baseball – 38     Football – 22
Tennis – 15       Soccer – 57

## Vocabulary

**double-line graph**

## Learn

**PROBLEM** Over 80% of consumers buy music CDs from stores. The table shows the type of stores where people have bought music. Analyze the data. How have people's CD-buying habits changed during the time shown?

A **double-line graph** helps to compare two sets of data that change over time.

## Example   Use the data in the table to make a double-line graph.

| Music CDs Sold | | | | |
|---|---|---|---|---|
| Store Type | 2000 | 2001 | 2002 | 2003 |
| Music Store | 54% | 43% | 37% | 33% |
| Department Store | 41% | 42% | 51% | 53% |

**Step 1**

Determine an appropriate scale. Numbers vary from 33% to 54%. So, use a scale from 0% to 60%.

**Step 2**

Mark a point in one color for each year's percent sold at music stores, and connect the points.

**Step 3**

Mark a point in another color for each year's percent sold at department stores. Connect the points.

The red line shows that the trend from one year to the next in percent purchased at music stores has gone down, while the blue line shows the percent purchased at department stores has gone up.

So, people are buying a lesser percent of CDs at music stores than at department stores.

• Look at the double-line graph above. What conclusion could you make about music CD sales in 2001? Explain.

**Remember**

The jagged line on the scale shows a break in the scale. Some numbers are left out.

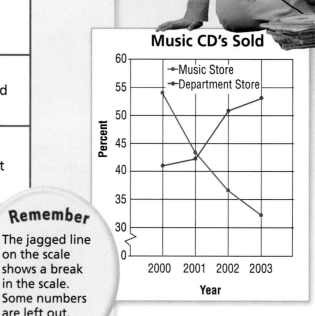

Music CD's Sold

## Guided Practice

1. Suppose you added the data at the right to the graph above. Would the trends for each type of store remain the same?

| Department | 2004 |
|---|---|
| Music Store | 32% |
| Department Store | 54% |

**SDAP 2.3** Analyze data displays and explain why the way in which the question was asked might have influenced the results obtained and why the way in which the results were displayed might have influenced the conclusions reached. *also* MR 1.1, MR 2.4, MR 2.5, MR 3.2

**For 2–5, use the table.**

2. Use the data in the table at the right to make a double-line graph.

3. Between which years did the percent of hip-hop music sales increase the most?

4. Find the difference in percent of sales between the two types of music for each year. Order the differences from least to greatest.

5. **TALK Math** Explain how you can use the double-line graph in Exercise 2 to make predictions about the future percents of sales of the two types of music.

| Percent of Music by Type Sold | | |
|---|---|---|
| Type of music | Hip-Hop | Rhythm and Blues |
| 1995 | 7% | 11% |
| 1998 | 8% | 13% |
| 2001 | 11% | 11% |
| 2004 | 12% | 11% |

## Independent Practice and Problem Solving

**For 6–7, use the table.**

6. Use the data in the table to make a double-line graph.

7. **Reasoning** Describe the trend of listening time from age 8 to age 18. **Explain** your reasoning.

| Minutes Per Day Listening to Audio Media | | | |
|---|---|---|---|
| Listening Device | 8-10 year-olds | 11-14 year-olds | 15-18 year-olds |
| Radio | 29 | 57 | 75 |
| CD/Tapes/MP3s | 30 | 45 | 69 |

**For 8–10, use the line graph.**

8. Which two years show the same percent of music sales for jazz music?

9. Find the difference in the percent of jazz music sales between each pair of years. Between which two years was the greatest increase?

10. **WRITE Math** Melissa says that the trend for purchases of jazz music have been declining in recent years. Do you agree or disagree?

## Achieving the Standards

**Explain.**

11. Order the fractions below from least to greatest. (**O—πι** NS 1.1, p.18)

$$\frac{2}{5}, \frac{3}{10}, \frac{1}{2}$$

12. Find the area of a rectangle when the length is 5 cm and the width is 6 cm. (Grade 5 MG 1.0)

13. Write $\frac{90}{360}$ as a percent. (**O—πι** NS 1.1, p.24)

14. **Test Prep** Use the line graph about jazz music above. Between which two years is there the greatest decrease in sales of jazz music?

A 1999-2000     C 2001-2002

B 2000-2001     D 2002-2003

# 3 Circle Graphs

OBJECTIVE: Analyze data in circle graphs.

## Quick Review

**Write each as a fraction in simplest form.**

1. 6 out of 10
2. 12 out of 32
3. 45 out of 135
4. 78 out of 99
5. 125 out of 500

## Quick Review

**Write each as a fraction in simplest form.**

1. 6 out of 10
2. 12 out of 32
3. 45 out of 135
4. 78 out of 99
5. 125 out of 500

## Vocabulary

circle graph

## Learn

**PROBLEM** Almost everyone has a favorite color. Many people also have colors they favor the least. How does the percent of people who choose purple as their least favorite color compare with the percent of people who choose yellow? The circle graph below, which shows the results of a survey, can help you answer that question.

A **circle graph** helps you compare parts of the data with the whole and with other parts.

**Example 1** Use the circle graph at the right.

> Find the parts that represent purple and yellow. Compare the percents of people choosing purple and yellow as their least favorite color.
>
> Purple was chosen by 26% of the people, and yellow was chosen by 13%.
>
> $26 \div 13 = 2$

So, twice as many people chose purple as their least favorite color as chose yellow.

**Example 2** Use the circle graph at the right.

Of all girls surveyed, what fraction chose blue?

> Find the part that represents the number of girls who chose blue as their favorite color.
>
> 105 girls chose blue as their favorite color.
>
> Find the total number of girls who participated in the survey by adding the number of girls who chose each color.
>
> $105 + 18 + 9 + 60 + 69 + 27 + 12 = 300$
>
> Write as a fraction in simplest form. $\frac{105}{300} = \frac{7}{20}$

So, $\frac{7}{20}$ of all girls surveyed chose blue as their favorite color.

• What percent of girls chose blue as their favorite color?

**Least Favorite Color**

Red 4%
Blue 2%
Yellow 13%
Purple 26%
Green 13%
Gray 12%
Orange 30%

**Favorite Color of Girls**

18  9
60
105
69
12  27

**Math Idea**
You can also display the data in the circle graph above by using percents. Convert each fraction to a decimal and then to a percent.

## Guided Practice

1. In Example 1, 4% of the people surveyed chose red as their least favorite color and 12% chose gray. How does the percent who chose gray compare with the percent who chose red?

 **SDAP 2.3** Analyze data displays and explain why the way in which the question was asked might have influenced the results obtained and why the way in which the results were displayed might have influenced the conclusions reached. *also* **MR 1.1, MR 2.4, MR 2.5, MR 3.2**

**For 2–4, use the circle graph at the right.**

**Boy's Least Favorite Color**

✓ 2. Write a fraction in simplest form to represent the number of boys who chose purple or gray as their least favorite color.

3. What percent of boys chose yellow as their least favorite color?

✓ 4. How does the number of boys who chose gray as their least favorite color compare with the number who chose green?

5. **TALK Math** **Explain** why you would use a circle graph to compare the results of a survey.

## Independent Practice and Problem Solving

**For 6–9, use the circle graph at the right.**

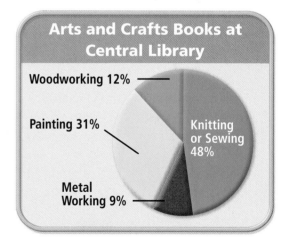

**Cost of Painting Supplies**

Drop Cloth, $5
Blue Paint, $18
Brush/Roller, $10
White Paint, $15
Paint Thinner, $12

6. Write a fraction in simplest form that represents the cost of the paint thinner compared to the total cost of the painting supplies.

7. Which three items combine to make up $\frac{3}{4}$ of the total cost?

8. What conclusion could you make about the cost of paint? Is your conclusion valid? **Explain.**

9. How does the cost of a drop cloth compare with the cost of white paint and a brush/roller combined?

**For 10–12, use the circle graph at the right.**

**Arts and Crafts Books at Central Library**

Woodworking 12%
Painting 31%
Metal Working 9%
Knitting or Sewing 48%

10. What two types of books make up $\frac{2}{5}$ of the books in the arts and crafts section? **Explain.**

11. **Reasoning** Clay counted 120 knitting or sewing books in the central library. Based on the data given, how many woodworking books does the library have? **Explain.**

12. **WRITE Math** **What's the Question?** The answer is that when combined, they are almost double the percent of painting books.

## Achieving the Standards

13. Barbara purchased three items that cost $3.75, $9.15, and $4.35. What is the mean of her purchases? (SDAP 1.1, p. 224)

14. Find $\frac{2}{5} + \frac{1}{2}$. (NS 2.1, p.42)

15. Would asking "Would you like the delicious Greek salad or the tomato salad?" affect the results of a survey? **Explain.** (O─┐SDAP 2.4, p. 206)

16. **Test Prep** A circle graph shows the results of 320 people surveyed. What fraction of the graph would represent the 100 people who answered yes?

   A. $\frac{4}{15}$   B. $\frac{3}{10}$   C. $\frac{5}{16}$   D. $\frac{3}{8}$

**Extra Practice** on page 260, Set C

# LESSON 4

# Misleading Graphs

**OBJECTIVE:** Analyze data displays and determine how results and conclusions may have been influenced.

## Learn

**PROBLEM** Josh and David both conducted random surveys all over California about favorite California major league baseball teams. Which of their graphs is likely to be misleading?

Sometimes, the way data is displayed can be misleading. Misleading displays of data can be a result of biased survey questions.

### Example 1 Biased Question

David asked, "Which of these five major league baseball teams is your favorite: the Los Angeles Angels, the Oakland Athletics, the San Diego Padres, the San Francisco Giants, or the Los Angeles Dodgers?"

Josh asked, "Which major league baseball team is your favorite: the spectacular Los Angeles Angels, the Oakland Athletics, the San Diego Padres, the San Francisco Giants, or the Los Angeles Dodgers?"

**Favorite Baseball Team**

**Favorite Baseball Team**

Josh's question is biased since it singles out one team as better than the others. This leads people to choose the Los Angeles Angels as their favorite. So, Josh's graph is likely to be misleading.

When graphs are misleading, they can lead to conclusions that are not valid. There are several factors that can make a graph misleading.

### Example 2 Broken Scale

Raya concluded that the average attendance at the San Francisco Giants' stadium is about three times the average attendance at the Oakland Athletics' stadium. Why is Raya's conclusion not valid?

The bar for the Giants' stadium appears to be about three times the length of the Athletics' bar. The attendance numbers show that this is misleading since the Giants' attendance is 38,000 and the Athletics' attendance is 26,000 people. The graph is misleading because the scale is broken between 0 and 25.

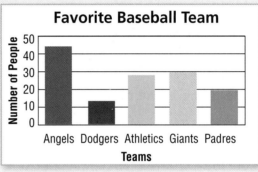

So, Raya's conclusion is not valid because the graph has a broken scale.

 **SDAP 2.3** Analyze data displays and explain why the way in which the question was asked might have influenced the results obtained and why the way in which the results were displayed might have influenced the conclusions reached. *also* **SDAP 2.4, MR 1.1, MR 2.4, MR 2.5, MR 3.1, MR 3.2**

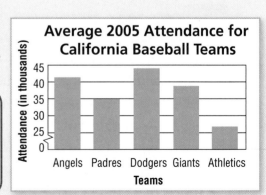

## Example 3 Different Intervals

Both graphs show attendance data for the first four games of a baseball season. Martin concluded that Giants games had greater attendance than Dodgers games. Why is Martin's conclusion not valid?

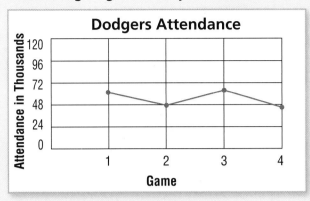

**Dodgers Attendance**

**Giants Attendance**

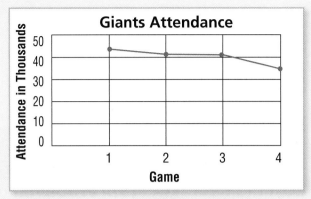

> Different intervals on the scales make the graphs misleading. The graph for the Dodgers has intervals of 24 but the Giants graph has intervals of 10 over the same space. To compare graphs, you need to use the same scale and interval.

So, Martin's conclusion is not valid because the intervals and the scales on the two graphs are different.

## Example 4 Unequal Intervals

Jasmine looked at the graph at the right and concluded that the Padres recorded about twice as many stolen bases as the Giants. Why is Jasmine's conclusion not valid?

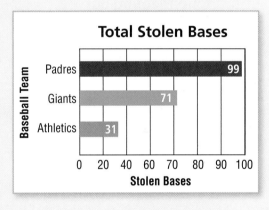

**Total Stolen Bases**

> The lengths of the bars make it appear as if the Padres recorded almost twice as many stolen bases as the Giants. The actual numbers show this is not true since the Padres recorded 99 stolen bases and the Giants recorded 71 stolen bases. The graph is misleading because the scale changes from intervals of 20 to intervals of 10. To compare data, you need equal scale intervals on the graph.

So, Jasmine's conclusion is not valid because the scale does not have equal intervals.

## Guided Practice

1. Jessica looked at the graph of total runs scored at home. She concluded that the Red Sox and Yankees scored almost twice as many runs as the Athletics.

   Look at the graph's scale. Why is Jessica's conclusion not valid?
   Hint: look at the scale and the intervals.

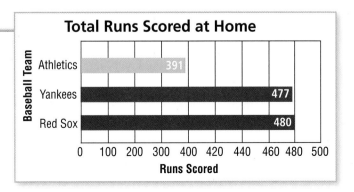

**Total Runs Scored at Home**

**For 2-3, use the graph at the right.**

2. The Wildcats' shortstop concluded that his team recorded about four times as many hits as the Hawks. Why is his conclusion not valid?

3. Is the graph misleading? If so, explain why and tell how you could fix it.

4. **TALK Math** Explain why this question can cause bias in the data and a misleading graph. "Which sport is your favorite sport to watch: exciting football, baseball, or basketball?" Rewrite the question so it is not biased.

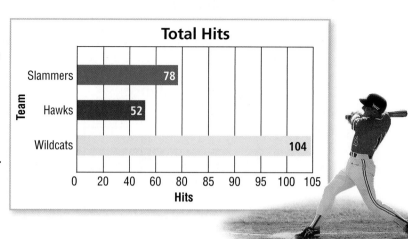

## Independent Practice and Problem Solving

**Use the graph below each problem. Determine if the claim is valid. Then tell whether the graph is misleading. If so, explain why and tell how you could fix it.**

5. Joseph concluded that Friday is the preferred day for the club meeting.

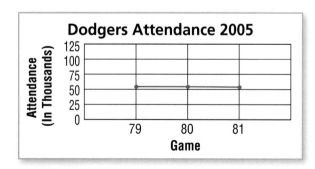

6. Hannah concluded that the Dodgers scored about one-third as many runs as the Giants scored at home.

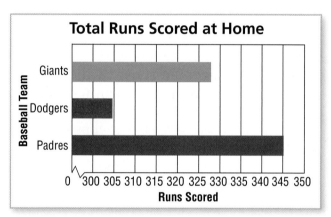

7. George came up with the following conclusion: more people attended the last three Dodgers games in 2005 than in 2006.

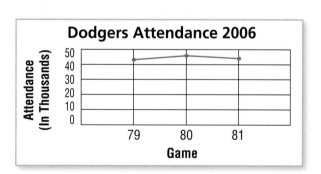

8. **WRITE Math** What's the Error? Bill made a bar graph of the number of home-runs hit last season. The vertical axis began at 0 with intervals of 20 up to 40. From 40, he used intervals of 5. How would Bill's graph be misleading? How would you correct his graph?

9. Claudia has 14 erasers and 35 pencils. She wants to combine equal numbers of erasers with equal numbers of pencils to form sets. What is the greatest number of sets that she can make if she uses all the pencils and erasers? (○━┓ NS2.4, p.7)

10. Order from least to greatest. 12.45, 12.36, 12.33 (○━┓ NS1.4, p. 122)

11. **Test Prep** Nick is recording the results of his research in a line graph. He begins by labeling his x-axis from 0 to 30 with intervals of 10. He then notices he has more data and uses intervals of 5 from 30 to 50. Will Nick's graph be misleading? **Explain.**

12. **Test Prep** Why is the graph misleading?

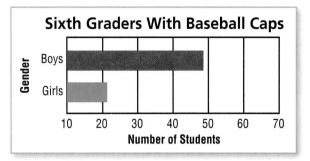

**Sixth Graders With Baseball Caps**

A The axes are labeled wrong.

B A break in the scale exaggerates the difference.

C The scale does not have even intervals.

D The scale does not begin at 0.

## Problem Solving and Reasoning

**REASONING** A stacked bar graph like the one at the right can show more than one category in each bar. The data in one category is added to data in the previous category. Can you tell from the graph how much time each girl spent in softball batting practice?

The graph shows the percent of total practice time each girl spent training in three different ways. Each colored section represents a percent of that girl's total practice time, and that total is always 100%. However, it does not give the total number of minutes or hours represented by that 100%, and that can differ from girl to girl. This can be misleading for someone who does not read the graph carefully.

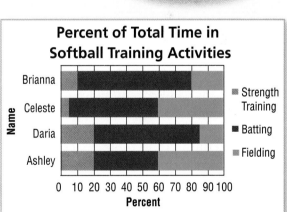

**Percent of Total Time in Softball Training Activities**

■ Strength Training

■ Batting

■ Fielding

So, you cannot tell how much time each girl spent on batting practice from this stacked bar graph.

**Use the bar graph for 1–4. Write *true, false,* or *cannot be determined.***

1. Daria and Ashley spent the same amount of time in strength training.

2. Brianna spent about twice as long in batting practice as in fielding practice.

3. All four girls practiced for the same amount of time.

4. What other type of graph would be appropriate for showing the percent of time Celeste spent on each type of training? Explain.

# 5 Find Unknown Values

**OBJECTIVE:** Estimate unknown values from a graph and solve for the values by using logic, arithmetic, and algebra.

## Learn

**PROBLEM** Brittany is training for a triathlon, which is a swimming, biking, and running race. The following table shows how long it takes Brittany to swim different distances.

How many yards can Brittany swim in 3.5 min?

| Brittany's Swimming Rate | | | | | |
|---|---|---|---|---|---|
| Time (min) | 1 | 2 | 3 | 4 | 5 |
| Distance (yd) | 40 | 80 | 120 | 160 | 200 |

You can use a line graph to display the data and find the unknown data.

### Example 1 Use a line graph.

> Make a line graph for the given data. Locate the point on the line for 3.5 min on the horizontal scale. The vertical scale for that point shows 140 yd.

So, Brittany can swim 140 yd in 3.5 min.

- How would you use the line graph to predict how many yards Brittany can swim in 6 min?

### Example 2 Use logical reasoning and arithmetic.

How many yards can Brittany swim in 8 min if she continues to swim at a constant rate?

> Look at the data in the table. Since the rate is constant, you can logically find how far she swims in 8 min by using what you already know about the times she has recorded. You know how far she swims in 5 min, how far she swims in 3 min, and that 5 + 3 = 8.
>
> 200 + 120 = 320   Add the yards she swims in 5 min to the yards she swims in 3 min.

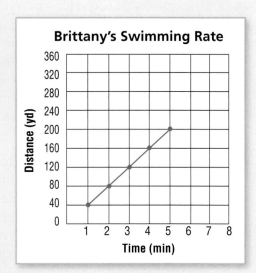

**Brittany's Swimming Rate**

So, Brittany can swim 320 yd in 8 min.

- Use logical reasoning and arithmetic to find out how many yards she can swim in 10 min. Explain.

O—π AF 2.0 Students analyze and use tables, graphs, and rules to solve problems involving rates and proportions.
*also* AF 2.3, MR 1.1, MR 2.3, MR 2.4, MR 2.5, MR 3.0, MR 3.2, MR 3.3

# Example 3

If Brittany continues to swim at a constant rate, how many minutes will it take her to swim 240 yd?

> Look at the data in the table on the previous page. As Brittany's time increases by 1 min, the distance increases 40 yd.
>
> $240 \div 40 = 6$   Divide the total distance by 40.

Because each 40-yd distance takes 1 minute to swim and because $240 \div 40 = 6$, it takes Brittany 6 min to swim 240 yd.

- If Brittany swims at the same rate, how many seconds will it take her to swim 320 yd?

**ERROR ALERT**

Be sure the units are the same. Since the rate is per minute, the time must be minutes as well.

## Guided Practice

**For 1–3, use the graph.**

1. The graph at the right shows the speed Brittany can run. Look between 1 hr and 2 hr on the horizontal axis of the graph. How far will Brittany run in $1\frac{1}{2}$ hr?

✓ 2. Brittany can run 15 mi in 3 hr. At the same rate, how many miles can she run in twice the time?

3. What if Brittany can run at a rate of 5 miles per hour? Use the formula $d = rt$ to find how much time it will take her to run 40 mi.

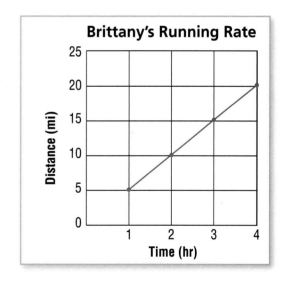

**Brittany's Running Rate**

**For 4–8, use the table.**

4. Make a line graph to display Marco's swimming speed.

5. At this rate, how far does Marco swim in $1\frac{1}{2}$ min?

✓ 6. Marco has been swimming at the same rate for 8 min. How many yards has Marco gone?

7. If Marco swam at the same rate to the buoy 600 yd from the start, how long did it take?

8. **TALK Math** **Explain** how you can use a line graph of the data in the table to determine how far Marco can swim in $3\frac{1}{2}$ min.

| Marco's Swimming Rate | | | |
|---|---|---|---|
| Time (min) | 1 | 2 | 3 | 4 |
| Distance(yd) | 50 | 100 | 150 | 200 |

## Independent Practice (and Problem Solving)

**For 9–11, use the table.**

9. Make a line graph using the data in the table. How long does it take Janine to walk 5 mi?

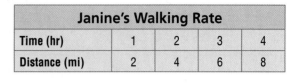

| Janine's Walking Rate | | | | |
|---|---|---|---|---|
| Time (hr) | 1 | 2 | 3 | 4 |
| Distance (mi) | 2 | 4 | 6 | 8 |

10. If Janine continues walking at the same rate for 6 hr, how far will she go?

11. Find how many miles Janine goes if she walks at the same rate for 90 min.

12. ≡**FAST FACT** In the 2002 International Association of Athletics Federations Grand Prix, Tim Montgomery ran at an average rate of 23 mi per hr, breaking the previous world record. If he could keep up this incredible pace for 30 min, how far would he run?

**For 13–15, use the graph.**

13. Mike bicycles 1 mi in 4 min, or 15 mi per hr. If he continues this rate, how far will Mike travel in 7 hr?

14. Mike has been biking for 1 hr 15 min. Is it more likely that Mike has traveled more than or less than 20 mi?

15. **Pose a Problem** Look back at Problem 13. Write a similar question by changing the amount of time Mike bikes.

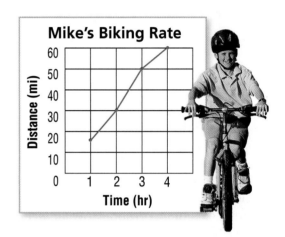

**For 16–18, use the table.**

16. The table shows how Katie's average swim times changed with practice. Make a line graph. Use the graph to estimate what Katie's average swim time could be after $2\frac{1}{2}$ months of practice.

17. Find what Katie's time could be in month 7.

| Katie's Average Swim Time for 200 yd | | | | | |
|---|---|---|---|---|---|
| Month | 1 | 2 | 3 | 4 | 5 |
| Time (min) | 6 | 5.7 | 5.4 | 5.1 | 4.8 |

18. **WRITE Math** **Explain** how you can use logical reasoning to find your answer for Exercise 17.

## Achieving the Standards

19. Find the LCM of the set of numbers.
(O—ⁿ NS 2.0, p.14) 6, 9, 18

20. Find the range, mean, median, and mode of the following numbers: 83, 105, 84, 92, 86, and 84.
(O—ⁿ SDAP 1.1, p. 224)

21. Identify the property being used.
$6 \times (x + 7) = (6 \times x) + (6 \times 7)$ (Grade 5, AF 1.3, )

22. **Test Prep** In approximately how many hours can Nick ride 100 mi?

| Nick's Biking Speed | | | | |
|---|---|---|---|---|
| Time (hours) | 1 | 2 | 3 | 4 |
| Distance (miles) | 19 | 38 | 57 | 76 |

**A** 2 hr    **C** 6 hr

**B** 5 hr    **D** 8 hr

# Write Questions

Students in Mr. James's class learned that a population pyramid is a special kind of histogram. It is a graph that shows the distribution of population by age and gender. Age intervals are written on the vertical scale, and the bars appear to the left and right of that scale. The bars compare the population in millions of males and females in different age intervals. The population pyramid is like a double-bar graph because it displays data about two groups. Students wrote the following questions and answers about the 2000 population pyramid:

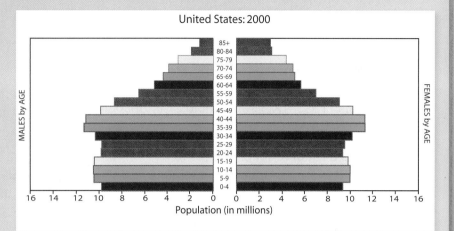

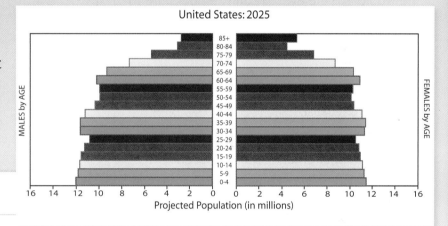

- About how many males 20–24 years old were there in 2000?

  Look at the red bar to the left. There were about 10 million males.

- Were there more males or more females who were 75–79?

  Compare the left and right yellow bars. There were more females.

- About how many more males than females were there who were 10–14 years old?

  Estimate the numbers for the left and right green bars. There were about 1 million more males.

**Problem Solving** Use the data in the population pyramids to write questions. Answer your questions.

1. Write a question about people 5–9 years old in 2000.

2. Write a comparison question about people 60–64 years old in 2000.

3. Write a subtraction question and an addition question about the 2025 graph.

4. Write two questions that compare data on the 2000 and 2025 graphs.

# Problem Solving Workshop
## Skill: Use a Graph

**OBJECTIVE:** Solve problems by using the skill *use a graph*.

## Use the Skill

**PROBLEM** Rachel lives in Sacramento, CA, where the average January temperature is 46°F and the average July temperature is 75°F. She will be moving and must choose one of five cities: El Paso, TX; Grand Rapids, MI; Anaheim, CA; San Francisco, CA; or Columbus, OH.

Rachel made a list of requirements. She would like the average January temperature to be within 15°F of Sacramento's average January temperature.

She would like the average July temperature to be at least 70°F. Finally, she would like to live near the Pacific ocean. Which city should Rachel choose?

Identify the details by using the graph. Then make a checklist.

Anaheim is the only city that fits all three of Rachel's requirements. So, Rachel should move to Anaheim, CA.

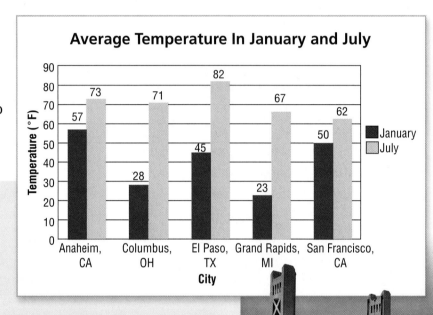

**Average Temperature In January and July**

| Requirements | El Paso, TX | Grand Rapids, MI | Anaheim, CA | San Francisco, CA | Columbus, OH |
|---|---|---|---|---|---|
| Within 15°F of January Temperature | ✔ | | ✔ | ✔ | |
| Average July Temperature at Least 70°F | ✔ | | ✔ | | ✔ |
| Near the Pacific Ocean | | | ✔ | ✔ | |

## Think and Discuss
**Find information in the graph to answer each question.**

a. Which city has the least range of average temperatures between January and July? What is the range?

b. Find the range of the average temperatures for each of the five cities, and order the ranges from least to greatest.

c. Find the difference in average temperature between Columbus and Grand Rapids in January. Which two cities have the same difference in July? What is that difference?

d. Why is a double-bar graph an appropriate graph to display this data?

○━┱ **SDAP 2.3** Analyze data displays and explain why the way in which the question was asked might have influenced the results obtained and why the way in which the results were displayed might have influenced the conclusions reached. *also* ○━┱ **MR 1.0, MR 1.1, MR 2.0, MR 2.4, MR 2.5, MR 3.0, MR 3.1, MR 3.2, MR 3.3**

**For 1–3, use the graph.**

1. Chris is moving from Stockton, CA. Stockton has an average January temperature of 46°F and an average July temperature of 77°F. Which city in the graph should he choose if he prefers an average July temperature warmer than Stockton's and an average January temperature about equal to Stockton's?

   **First,** make a chart of cities and of Chris's requirements.

   | City | July Temp. | Jan. Temp. |
   |---|---|---|
   | Houghton Lake, MI | | |
   | Miami, FL | | |
   | Springfield, IL | | |
   | Williamsport, PA | | |
   | Redding, CA | | |

   **Then,** check off the requirements each city fulfills.

   **Finally,** identify the city that fulfills all of Chris's requirements.

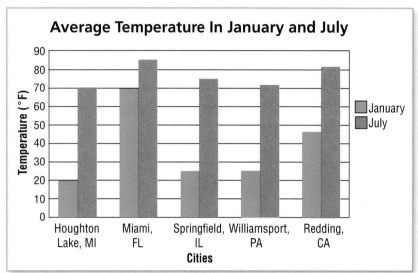

2. **What if** Chris also considered Birmingham, AL, where the January temperature is 43°F and the July temperature is 80°F. Would that change the city he chose? Why or why not?

3. Daniel's grandparents live in the city with the least range of temperatures between January and July. In which city do they live?

## Mixed Applications

**Use the circle graph for 4–8.**

4. Which three types of music combined have the popularity of hip-hop music? Give the percent for each.

5. How many times as many students prefer hip-hop music to other music?

6. Suppose 10 students stated they prefer other music. How many students would you expect to choose hip-hop? **Explain.**

7. Write a fraction in simplest form that is equivalent to the percent of sixth-graders who chose country as their favorite music.

8. **WRITE Math** ▶ Explain why a circle graph is used to display the favorite music of sixth-graders.

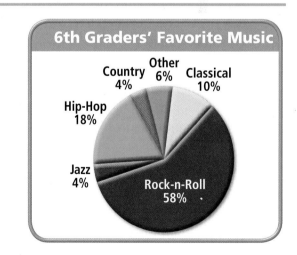

 **Extra Practice**

## Set A Use the table at the right. (pp. 244–245)

1. Use the data in the table to make a double-bar graph.

2. On which day was there the greatest difference between the number of bottles of water and sports drink sold?

| Concession Stand Sales | | | |
|---|---|---|---|
| | Friday | Saturday | Sunday |
| **Bottled Water** | 19 | 25 | 21 |
| **Sports Drink** | 13 | 26 | 14 |

## Set B Use the table at the right. (pp. 246–247)

1. Use the data in the table to make a double-line graph.

2. Between which years did science increase the most as the favorite subject?

| Favorite Subject (in Percent) | | | |
|---|---|---|---|
| | 2000 | 2002 | 2004 |
| **Math** | 23 | 18 | 10 |
| **Science** | 9 | 11 | 29 |

## Set C Use the circle graph at the right. (pp. 248–249)

1. Which item makes up the largest percent of the student's expenditures?

2. Which items combine to make up just over one quarter of the student's expenditures?

3. What 3 items combined make up half of the students expenditures?

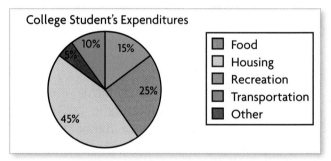

## Set D Use the graph at the right. (pp. 250–253)

1. Bryan concluded that night was the preferred time to watch a movie. Is his conclusion valid?

2. The survey asked, "I love to watch movies at night. When do you prefer to watch movies?" Is the graph misleading? If the graph is misleading, explain why?

## Set E Use the graph at the right. (pp. 254–257)

1. The graph shows the number of rooms that Tommy can paint in a given amount of time. How many rooms can Tommy paint in 2 hours?

2. If Tommy paints for 8 hours, how many rooms could he paint?

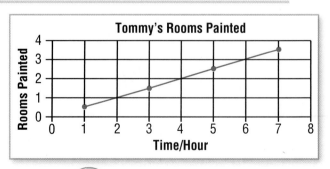

 **Technology**
Use Harcourt Mega Math, The Number Games
ROM *ArachnaGraph*, Levels B and C.

# GRAPHS GALORE!

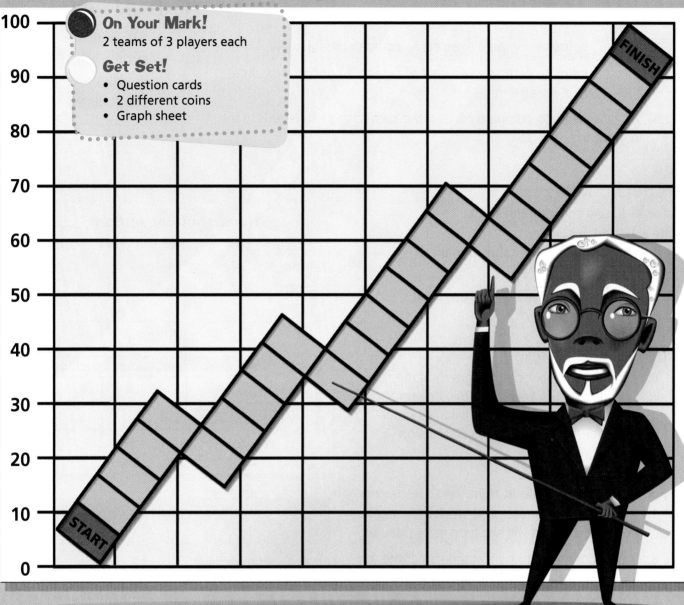

**On Your Mark!**
2 teams of 3 players each

**Get Set!**
- Question cards
- 2 different coins
- Graph sheet

START

FINISH

**Go!**

- Shuffle the question cards, and place them facedown in a pile.

- Players toss a coin to determine which team will be Team 1 and which will be Team 2.

- Each team selects a coin and places it on START.

- Team 1 draws a question card from the pile and answers the question looking at the graph sheet.

- Team 2 checks the answer. If it is correct, Team 1 moves its coin the number of spaces shown on the card and play passes to Team 2.

- If the answer is incorrect, play passes to the other team.

- The first team to reach FINISH wins.

# Chapter 10 Review/Test

## Check Vocabulary and Concepts

Choose the best term from the box.

1. A __?__ helps to compare two sets of countable data. (O━ SDAP 2.3, p. 244)

2. A __?__ helps to compare two sets of data that change over time. (O━ SDAP 2.3, p. 246)

3. A __?__ helps to compare parts of the data to the whole and to the other parts. (O━ SDAP 2.3, p. 248)

> **VOCABULARY**
>
> bar graph
> circle graph
> double-bar graph
> double-line graph

## Check Skills

**For 4–5, use the table at right.**
(O━ SDAP 2.3, pp. 246–247)

4. Use the data in the table to make a double-line graph.

5. Between which years were the most males born?

### Number of Babies Born

|        | 2002 | 2003 | 2004 | 2005 |
|--------|------|------|------|------|
| Male   | 47   | 39   | 61   | 58   |
| Female | 53   | 46   | 42   | 39   |

**Use the graph at right.** (O━ SDAP 2.3, pp. 250–253)

6. When Mario looked at the graph of the total sales for James, Mark, and Bill, he concluded that James sold more than twice as much as either Mark or Bill. Is his conclusion valid? Explain.

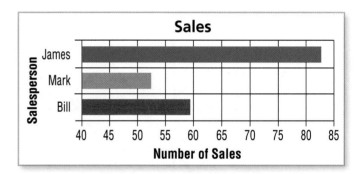

**For 7–9, use the table at right.** (AF 2.0, pp. 254–257)

7. If Pam types at a rate of 52 words per minute, how many words will she type in $2\frac{1}{2}$ minutes?

8. If Pam continues to type at the same rate for 10 minutes, how many words will she type?

9. If Pam has typed 312 words, how long has she been typing?

### Pam's Typing Speed

| Time (minutes) | 1  | 2   | 3   | 4   |
|----------------|----|-----|-----|-----|
| Male           | 52 | 104 | 156 | 208 |

## Check Problem Solving

**Solve.** (O━ SDAP 2.3, MR 1.1, pp. 258–259)

10. **WRITE Math** Look at the graph of the number of artifacts found by Jesse. Explain why a line graph is an appropriate graph to display the trend of this data.

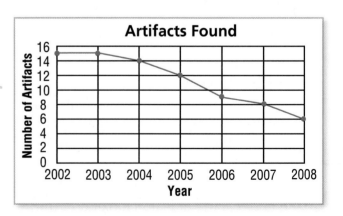

**GO Technology** Use *Online Assessment*.

# Enrich • Graph Relationships
# PEDAL POWER

Stephanie goes for a ride on her bike. The graph below tells a story about her ride. It shows the relationship between her speed and the time.

- Stephanie's speed increases gradually.

- Then she rides at a constant speed.

- She slows down when going up a hill.

- She pedals at a slow constant speed and then increases her speed again going downhill.

- She reaches a faster speed than before and maintains it until she slows to an abrupt stop.

**Stephanie's Bike Ride**

Speed

Time

## Example

You ride your bike to a park, play tennis, and then ride home. Draw a graph showing time and the distance traveled on your bike.

**Your Bike Ride**

Distance

Time

Your graph will show an increase in distance until you stop at the park.
The time you spend at the park shows no change in the distance.
As you ride home, the distance increases again until you reach your destination.

## Try It

**Describe the story that is told by each graph.**

1.
**Home Run Ball**

Height Above the Ground

Feet from Home Plate

2.
**Kayla Jumping on a Trampoline**

Height (in feet) Above the Ground

Time

**Draw a graph that tells the story.**

3. Draw a graph showing time and speed as you walk to the bus stop, wait for the bus, and then ride the bus as it stops two times on the way to school.

4. Draw a graph showing time and volume of water in a bathtub. You fill a tub, soak, add more hot water, soak some more, and then empty the tub.

**WRITE Math** Explain how the graph in Problem 1 would change if an outfielder caught the ball.

# Unit Review/Test
## Chapters 8–10

## Multiple Choice

1. Lisa stands outside a local supermarket and asks the customers who are exiting, "What is your favorite brand of ice cream?" Which sampling method is Lisa using? (O—n SDAP 2.2, p. 202)

   **A** cluster

   **B** convenience

   **C** random

   **D** responses to a survey

2. Thomas wants to know the percentage of pet owners in his community who adopted their pet from the animal shelter. He gets a list of pet owners based on the city's registration records. The owners included in his sample are obtained by assigning a number to each owner on the list and then randomly selecting numbers. Which sampling method is Thomas using? (O—n SDAP 2.2, p. 202)

   **A** systematic        **C** random

   **B** convenience       **D** responses to a survey

3. Which of the following questions is not biased? (O—n SDAP 2.3, p. 206)

   **A** Do you prefer the new song, or do you prefer the all-time favorite song?

   **B** I just love Italian food. What is your favorite type of food?

   **C** Cruise ships go to many different destinations. So far, the Caribbean is the most preferred stop. Where would you like your ship to stop?

   **D** Out of all the sports, which do you enjoy the most?

4. The table shows the annual profits for four companies.

   | 2008 Profits | |
   | --- | --- |
   | Company | Profit |
   | I | $254,000 |
   | II | $375,000 |
   | III | $300,000 |
   | IV | $299,000 |

   Which statement is valid about the annual profits of these four companies? (O—n SDAP 2.5, p. 208)

   **A** Companies III and IV made the same profit.

   **B** Company II made $75,000 more profit than company III.

   **C** No company made less than $275,000 profit.

   **D** No company made more than a profit of $350,000.

5. Bailey worked for 4 days. Her mean amount earned for the 4 days was $26. She earned $29, $25, and $26 on the first three days she worked. How much did she earn on the fourth day? (SDAP 1.1, p. 224)

   **A** $24.00        **C** $26.67

   **B** $26.00        **D** $80.00

6. What is the median of the following data set? (SDAP 1.1, p. 224)

   14, 12, 15, 15, 16, 16, 10, 16

   **A** 6            **C** 15

   **B** 14.25        **D** 16

**GO ONLINE Technology** Use *Online Assessment.*

**7.** Find the mean, median, and mode. Which measures are most useful to describe the data? (SDAP 1.3, p. 230)

$$7, 12, 2, 10, 12, 8, 12, 158$$

**A** mean and median

**B** median and mode

**C** mean and mode

**D** mean, median, and mode

**8.** The table below shows the weights for one baby's checkups.

| Jace's Weight (in Ounces) | | | | | | |
|---|---|---|---|---|---|---|
| Birth | 1 Month | 2 Months | 4 Months | 6 Months | 9 Months | 12 Months |
| 120 | 163 | 184 | 218 | 260 | 288 | 352 |

Which of the following graphs is the best way to show these weights? (O—┑ SDAP 2.3, p. 246)

**A** circle graph      **C** line graph

**B** bar graph        **D** histogram

**9.** The following graph shows the number of students enrolled in math classes.

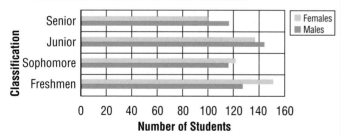

Which of the following statements is true? (O—┑ SDAP 2.3, p. 244)

**A** There are more junior females than males enrolled in math classes.

**B** There are more juniors enrolled in math classes than sophomores.

**C** There are over 140 male freshmen enrolled in math classes.

**D** Twice the number of juniors are enrolled in math classes than seniors.

## Short Response

**10.** Lisa wants to know whether the 78,000 people that live in her town like cold weather. Should she survey the population or use a sample? (O—┑ SDAP 2.2, p. 200)

**11.** Which type of graph is the best way to display and analyze two sets of countable data? (SDAP 2.0, p. 244)

**12.** The table below shows the attendance for the first 4 baseball games of the season. Assume the trend continues. Use logical reasoning to estimate the attendance for game 8. (AF 2.0, p. 254)

| | Game 1 | Game 2 | Game 3 | Game 4 |
|---|---|---|---|---|
| Attendance | 30 | 90 | 150 | 210 |

## Extended Response 〔WRITE Math〕

**13.** 〔WRITE Math〕 **What's the Question?** An announcer at a baseball game asks fans to choose a song to be played during the next break in the game: "Should it be 'The Sidewalks of New York,' 'America the Beautiful,' or that beloved classic, 'Take Me Out to the Ball Game'?" The answer is: the fans are being signaled to choose "Take Me Out to the Ball Game." What is the question? **Explain.** (O—┑ SDAP 2.3, p. 206)

**14.** The table below shows data collected on the number of days that randomly-selected people spent vacationing last year. Find the mean, median, and mode with the outliers included and excluded. **Explain** how the outliers affect the mean, median, and mode. (SDAP 1.3, p. 226)

| 3 | 18 | 14 | 13 | 12 |
|---|---|---|---|---|
| 14 | 1 | 18 | 21 | 14 |

# Population Trends

## CALIFORNIA IS NUMBER 1!

**E**very 10 years, the U.S. Census Bureau takes a census of the population. A census counts the number of people who live in the country and where they live. A census also indicates the backgrounds of the populations throughout the country. The census taken in 1970 showed California as the most populous state for the first time. This is an honor that California still holds.

FACT·ACTIVITY

**Use the table to answer the questions.**

❶ Round each population to the nearest million and then use the information in the table to make a line graph.

❷ How would you describe the change in California's population since 1900?

❸ Does the graph show any decreases in population? If so, when?

❹ In which 10-year period since 1900 did the population grow most?

❺ In which 10-year periods were the population growths about 4,000,000?

❻ **WRITE Math** ▸ Make a reasonable prediction about the population of California in 2030. **Explain** your reasoning.

### California's Populations

| Year | Population | Year | Population |
|------|-----------|------|-----------|
| 1900 | 1,485,053 | 1960 | 15,717,204 |
| 1910 | 2,377,549 | 1970 | 19,953,134 |
| 1920 | 3,426,861 | 1980 | 23,667,902 |
| 1930 | 5,677,251 | 1990 | 29,760,021 |
| 1940 | 6,907,387 | 2000 | 33,871,648 |
| 1950 | 10,586,223 | | |

# PREDICTING THE FUTURE

**C**ensus data tell us about changes in the number of people living in a certain place. With this information the government can see how the population is changing and predict what population changes may happen in the future. There can be many factors that affect an area's population.

**FACT·ACTIVITY**

**Gold**

**Suppose you work for the United States Census Bureau and have been asked to research population trends.**

① Based on the population density map, what conclusion can you make about how the population of the California is distributed?

② Choose 5 counties, 5 cities, or 5 towns in California to research. Make sure one is where you live.

▶ Research the population of each location in the past two censuses, 1990 and 2000.

▶ Now, show the information in a double-bar graph.

▶ What trends does your graph show? How could your graph be useful to someone moving to California?

▶ Compare your graph with a classmate's. Describe any similarities or differences.

**People per sq. mi**

- 400 or more
- 200 to 399
- 100 to 199
- 25 to 99
- Less than 25

# 4 Algebra: Expressions and Equations

# Math on Location

▲ A wind analyst uses equations to decide which sites are best to build wind turbines.

▲ Once the best site for a wind turbine is established, construction begins.

▲ The wind turns the blades at about 14 revolutions per minute. Each wind turbine produces enough energy for 750 homes.

# VOCABULARY POWER

## TALK Math

What math do you see in the **Math on Location** photographs? How can you determine how many homes can be powered by the turbines?

## READ Math

**REVIEW VOCABULARY** You learned the words below when you learned about expressions and equations. How do these words relate to **Math on Location**?

**algebraic expression** an expression that includes at least one variable

**equation** an algebraic or numerical statement that shows that two quantities are equal

**numerical expression** a mathematical phrase that uses only numbers and operation symbols.

## WRITE Math

Copy and complete a Venn diagram like the one below. Then use what you know about equations and expressions to describe the differences and similarities between them.

### Equations vs. Expressions

Write 5 examples of each.

| Equations | Expressions |
|-----------|-------------|
| $15 = 2x + 5$ | $2x + 5$ |
| $4 = 3 + 1$ | $3 \times 9$ |
| $7x = 21$ | $18y$ |

**GO ONLINE**

**Technology**
Multimedia Math Glossary link at
www.harcourtschool.com/hspmath

# 11 Expressions

**The Big Idea** Properties and the concepts of algebra are used to evaluate expressions.

CALIFORNIA
FAST
FACT

In 2005, Pebble Beach Golf Links was ranked the number one public golf course in America. The course features 18 holes, with a combined length of 6,737 yd and a par of 72.

## Investigate

You are a caddy trying to determine the distance a player's golf ball traveled. Choose three of the holes from the table at the right. Write and evaluate an algebraic expression to find the total distance the player's golf ball traveled on each of the holes you chose.

### Caddy's Yardage Book

| Hole | 1st Shot (yd) | 2nd Shot (yd) | 3rd Shot (yd) | 4th Shot (yd) | 5th Shot (yd) |
|------|---------------|---------------|---------------|---------------|---------------|
| 1 | 216 | 135 | 80 | 3 | none |
| 2 | 275 | 231 | 52 | 9 | 1 |
| 3 | 172 | 6 | 2 | none | none |
| 4 | 266 | 182 | 101 | 8 | 2.5 |
| 5 | 282 | 104 | 47 | 5 | none |

GO
ONLINE

**Technology**
Student pages are available in the Student eBook.

Check your understanding of important skills
needed for success in Chapter 11.

▶ **Exponents**

**Find the value.**

1. $3^3$
2. $5^2$
3. $4^3$
4. $10^2$

5. $2^4$
6. $4^4$
7. $3^1$
8. $5^3$

9. $7^2$
10. $6^3$
11. $3^4$
12. $2^6$

▶ **Use Parentheses**

**Evaluate the expression.**

13. $(3 + 6) \times 6$
14. $3 \times (5 + 7) + 3$
15. $8 - (9 - 3) - 3$

16. $4 \times (3 + 7)$
17. $4 \times (8 - 5)$
18. $(2 + 6) \times (2 + 9)$

19. $(2 + 6) \times 3$
20. $(16 \div 8) + (72 \div 9)$
21. $34 + (12 - 5) + 12$

▶ **Evaluate Expressions**

**Evaluate the expression for the given value of the variable.**

22. $x + 4$ for $x = 2$
23. $\frac{z}{3}$ for $z = 24$
24. $g - 6$ for $g = 9$

25. $6a$ for $a = 2$
26. $r + 12$ for $r = 8$
27. $\frac{c}{2}$ for $c = 100$

28. $100k$ for $k = 3$
29. $\frac{k}{3}$ for $k = 66$
30. $7p$ for $p = 3$

# VOCABULARY POWER

**CHAPTER VOCABULARY**

algebraic expression
Algebraic Operating System
like terms
numerical expression
order of operations
terms

**WARM-UP WORDS**

**numerical expression** a mathematical phrase that uses numbers and operation symbols

**order of operations** the process for evaluating expressions: first perform the operations in parentheses, clear the exponents, perform all multiplication and division, and then perform all addition and subtraction

**Algebraic Operating System** a way for calculators to follow the order of operations when evaluating expressions

# Properties and Expressions

OBJECTIVE: Use the Commutative, Associative, and Distributive Properties to evaluate expressions.

## Quick Review

Mark bought 12 books at $5 each. Marge bought 5 books at $12 each. Did they spend the same amount? Explain.

## Vocabulary

**numerical expression**

**evaluate**

## Learn

**PROBLEM** Christopher stacks 12 boxes of baseballs on shelves at the local sporting goods store. Each box holds 32 baseballs. How many baseballs does Christopher put on the shelves?

A **numerical expression** is a mathematical phrase that includes only numbers and operating symbols. Some examples of numerical expressions appear in the table below.

| Examples of Numerical Expressions | | | | |
|---|---|---|---|---|
| $6 + 8$ | $5 \times 7$ | $15 - 4$ | $36 \div 9$ | $3 + 16 \div 2$ |

To represent the total number of baseballs Christopher puts on the shelves, you can use a numerical expression.

total number of baseballs on the shelf
↓
$12 \times 32$

To simplify this numerical expression, you can use the Distributive Property. The Distributive Property can help you evaluate some expressions mentally.

To **evaluate** an expression, find the value of the expression.

### Example 1  Evaluate $12 \times 32$.

Multiply 12 boxes by 32 baseballs per box.

$12 \times 32 = 12 \times (30 + 2)$ — Rewrite the expression by using the Distributive Property.

$\quad\quad = (12 \times 30) + (12 \times 2)$ — Multiply 12 by each number.

$\quad\quad = 360 + 24$ — Add.

$\quad\quad = 384$

So, Christopher put 384 baseballs on the shelves.

• Evaluate $7 \times 78$ using the Distributive Property.

Other examples of the Distributive Property are shown in the table below.

| Distributive Property | |
|---|---|
| $8 \times (3 + 5) = (8 \times 3) + (8 \times 5)$ | $9 \times 47 = 9 \times (40 + 7) = (9 \times 40) + (9 \times 7)$ |

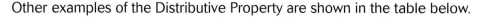
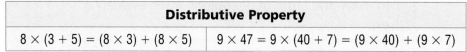

AF 1.3 Apply algebraic order of operations and the commutative, associative, and distributive properties to evaluate expressions; and justify each step in the process. *also* O—n NS 2.0, MR 1.3, MR 2.0, MR 2.4, MR 2.5, MR 3.2

# Commutative and Associative Properties

The Commutative and Associative Properties can also help you evaluate expressions mentally. Both the Commutative and Associative Properties hold for addition and multiplication. Examples of both properties appear in the tables below.

| Commutative Property | |
|---|---|
| **Addition** | **Multiplication** |
| $6 + 5 = 5 + 6$ | $8 \times 6 = 6 \times 8$ |

| Associative Property | |
|---|---|
| **Addition** | **Multiplication** |
| $(4 + 7) + 9 = 4 + (7 + 9)$ | $(3 \times 5) \times 2 = 3 \times (5 \times 2)$ |

Use the Commutative and Associative Properties to add and multiply mentally.

## Example 2 Use the Commutative Property.

**Ⓐ Add. 14 + 9 + 6**

$14 + 9 + 6 = 14 + 6 + 9$    Rewrite using the Commutative Property.

$= 20 + 9$    Add.

$= 29$

So, $14 + 9 + 6 = 29$.

**Ⓑ Multiply. 4 × 7 × 5**

$4 \times 7 \times 5 = 4 \times 5 \times 7$    Rewrite using the Commutative Property.

$= 20 \times 7$    Multiply.

$= 140$

So, $4 \times 7 \times 5 = 140$.

## Example 3 Use the Associative Property.

**Ⓐ Add. (23 + 18) + 2**

$(23 + 18) + 2 = 23 + (18 + 2)$    Rewrite using the Associative Property. Add the numbers in the parentheses first.

$= 23 + 20$    Add.

$= 43$

**Ⓑ Multiply. (7 × 6) × 5**

$(7 \times 6) \times 5 = 7 \times (6 \times 5)$    Rewrite using the Associative Property. Multiply the numbers in parentheses first.

$= 7 \times 30$    Multiply.

$= 210$

• What if 5 was negative? How would the answer change?

**1.** Evaluate $7 \times 48$ mentally using the Distributive Property.

$7 \times 48 = 7 \times (40 + 8)$    Rewrite using the Distributive Property.

$\quad\quad = (7 \times 40) + (7 \times 8)$    Inside the parentheses, multiply 7 by each number.

$\quad\quad = 280 + 56$    Add.

$\quad\quad = \blacksquare$

**Evaluate the expression. Tell what property you used.**

**2.** $5 \times 27$

**3.** $2 \times 9 \times 15$

**4.** $25 \times 46$

**5.** $22 + (8 + 4)$

**6.** $23 + 16 + 17$

**7.** $^-9 \times 19$

**8.** $8 + 14 + 12$

**9.** $6 \times 7 \times 5$

**10.** $(17 + 11) + 9$

**11.** $(12 \times 6) \times 25$

✓**12.** $12 \times 41$

✓**13.** $^-5 \times (8 \times 9)$

**14.** **TALK Math** **Explain** how the Associative Property can help you find the sum $80 + (20 + 75)$ mentally.

**Evaluate the expression. Tell what property or properties you used.**

**15.** $6 \times 47$

**16.** $17 + 15 + 33$

**17.** $9 \times 13$

**18.** $(9 \times 12) \times 5$

**19.** $6 \times 23$

**20.** $^-5 \times 7 \times 2$

**21.** $12 + 19 + 18$

**22.** $^-7 \times 12 \times 10$

**23.** $(22 + 53) + 37$

**24.** $11 \times 21$

**25.** $20 \times (5 \times 15)$

**26.** $11 + (19 + 27)$

**27.** $54 \times 12$

**28.** $36 + 48 + 22$

**29.** $10 \times 9 \times 5$

**30.** $31 + (9 + 16)$

**31.** $14 + 9 + 6 + (11 + 30)$

**32.** $23 + 5 + 17 + (5 + 11) + 9$

**Write _true_ or _false_ for each statement. Explain your answer.**

**33.** $(6 \times 12) \times 25 = 6 \times (12 \times 25)$ **34.** $17 + 45 + 23 = 17 + 23 + 45$ **35.** $(3 \times 6) + 18 = 3 \times (6 + 18)$

**36.** Larry bought 14 packages of juice. Each package had 8 juice boxes in it. How many juice boxes did he buy?

**37.** Juanita bought 8 concert tickets that cost $47 each. She wanted to spend less than $380. Did she achieve her goal? **Explain.**

**38.** Juan bought 8 tickets to a basketball game, each costing $17. To find the total cost, he added the product $8 \times 10$ to the product $8 \times 7$ for a total of $136. Which property did he use?

**39.** Jimmy said, "$(20 - 10) - 5 = 20 - (10 - 5)$, so the Associative Property works for subtraction." Do you agree with Jimmy's statement? **Explain.**

**40.** **Pose a Problem** Look back at Problem 36. Write and solve a similar problem by changing the number of juice boxes in each package.

**41. Reasoning** Why does the Commutative Property not apply to subtraction or division? **Explain.**

**42.**  **WRITE Math** ▸ **Explain** how the Commutative Property can help you find the product $25 \times 55 \times 4$ mentally.

## Achieving the Standards

**43.** Joseph surveyed 80 people. If $x$ people chose blue as their favorite color and 57 people chose a different color, what is the value of $x$, and how many people chose blue?

(O━ AF 1.1, p. 304)

**44. Test Prep** Which of the following shows the Distributive Property?

 **A** $9 \times (7 + 4) = (9 \times 7) + (9 \times 4)$

 **B** $9 + 7 + 4 = 4 + 7 + 9$

 **C** $(9 + 7) + 4 = 9 + (7 + 4)$

 **D** $9 \times 7 \times 4 = 7 \times 4 \times 9$

**45.** Rachel had the following scores on her last 5 math tests: 87, 92, $x$, 94, 100. Her mean score for the 5 tests was 92. What is the value of $x$?

(SDAP 1.1, p. 224)

**46.** Find the value of $3^5$. (Grade 5, NS 1.3)

**47. Test Prep** Which of the following statements is true?

 **A** $5 \times (6 + 7) = (5 + 6) + (5 + 7)$

 **B** $14 \times 6 \times 5 = (14 + 6) \times (14 + 5)$

 **C** $12 + 6 + 8 = 12 + 8 + 6$

 **D** $15 + 9 \times 8 = 15 \times 8 + 9$

**MATH POWER** ## Problem Solving and Reasoning

**REASONING** You can use the Distributive Property to help you multiply a number with any number of digits.

### Example Multiply.

$12 \times 8,752$

$12 \times 8,752 = 12 \times (8,000 + 700 + 50 + 2)$     Rewrite the expression by using the Distributive Property.

$= (12 \times 8,000) + (12 \times 700) + (12 \times 50) + (12 \times 2)$    Multiply.

$= 96,000 + 8,400 + 600 + 24$

$= 96,000 + (8,400 + 600) + 24$     Regroup.

$= 96,000 + 9,000 + 24$     Add.

$= 105,024$

So, $12 \times 8,752 = 105,024$.

**Use the Distributive Property to help you evaluate the expression.**

**1.** $9 \times 1,268$       **2.** $15 \times 8,451$       **3.** $4 \times 6,897$

**4.** $11 \times 4,372$      **5.** $5 \times 12,056$      **6.** $25 \times 4,208$

# Order of Operations with Exponents

**OBJECTIVE:** Use the order of operations to find the value of expressions.

## Quick Review

**Evaluate.**

1. $4^2$
2. $3^4$
3. $2^5$
4. $(^-5)^2$
5. $(^-4)^3$

## Vocabulary

order of operations

Algebraic Operating System (AOS)

## Learn

Many tasks that people do every day must follow a certain order of steps. For instance if you make scrambled eggs, you crack the eggs, mix them up, cook them in a pan, and then remove them from the pan. You can't very well change the order of the steps and still get scrambled eggs.

In mathematics, when you evaluate expressions that have more than one operation, you must follow rules called the **order of operations**.

| Order of Operations |
|---|
| **1.** Perform all operations inside parentheses or brackets. If there is a set of parentheses or brackets inside another set, work in the inner set first. |
| **2.** Evaluate numbers that have exponents. |
| **3.** Multiply and divide from left to right. |
| **4.** Add and subtract from left to right. |

### Example 1 Evaluate $5 \times 9 + 3^2$.

| | |
|---|---|
| $5 \times 9 + 3^2$ | Clear exponents. |
| $5 \times 9 + 9$ | Multiply. |
| $45 + 9$ | Add. |
| $54$ | |

- Evaluate the expression $14 + 2^2 \times 9$.

### Example 2 Evaluate $(4^3 + 7) - (5 - 8)^3$.

| | |
|---|---|
| $(4^3 + 7) - (5 - 8)^3$ | Operate inside parentheses. |
| $(64 + 7) - (^-3)^3$ | Operate inside parentheses. |
| $71 - (^-3)^3$ | Clear exponents. |
| $71 - (^-27)$ | Rewrite as an addition problem. |
| $71 + 27$ | Add. |
| $98$ | |

**Remember**
To evaluate numbers that have exponents, use repeated multiplication.
$2^3 = 2 \times 2 \times 2$
$3^4 = 3 \times 3 \times 3 \times 3$

- Evaluate the expression $(^-5 + 6)^2 - (3^4 + 4)$.

**AF1.3** Apply algebraic order of operations and the commutative, associative, and distributive properties to evaluate expressions; and justify each step in the process. *also* O—n NS 2.0, O—n NS 2.3, AF 1.4, MR 2.4, MR 2.5, MR 3.1, MR 3.2

**Example 3** Evaluate $11 \times [5 \times 7^2 - 3^2 - 12 \times (20 + 5.4 + 2)]$.

| | |
|---|---|
| $11 \times [5 \times 7^2 - 3^2 - 12 \times (20 + 5.4 + 2)]$ | Operate inside the inner parentheses. |
| $11 \times [5 \times 7^2 - 3^2 - 12 \times 27.4]$ | Operate inside the brackets. |
| $11 \times [5 \times 49 - 9 - 12 \times 27.4]$ | Multiply. |
| $11 \times [245 - 9 - 328.8]$ | Subtract. |
| $11 \times {}^-92.8$ | Multiply. |
| ${}^-1{,}020.8$ | |

You can use a calculator to evaluate expressions. Most calculators use an **algebraic operating system (AOS)**, which automatically follows the order of operations.

## Activity

**Materials** ■ calculator

**Step 1**

Use your calculator to evaluate $3 + 5 \times 2^3 - 6$. Then follow the order of operations and use pencil and paper to evaluate $3 + 5 \times 2^3 - 6$.

**Step 2**

Exchange papers with another student. Check each other's work.

**Step 3**

How does the calculator value for $3 + 5 \times 2^3 - 6$ compare with the value you got by using paper and pencil? Check to see if your calculator uses an AOS.

**Step 4**

If your calculator does not use an AOS, follow the order of operations.

**Using order of operations**
$3 + 5 \times 2^3 - 6$

 2  3  5  3  6  `2^3X5+3-6=37`

**Using memory keys**
$3^2 + 7 \times 4 - 9$

 3  2    7  4  9

  `M 7X4-9+9=28`

**Complete each step to evaluate the expression.**

**1.** $4^3 - 3 \times 8$       Clear exponents.
     $64 - 3 \times 8$      Multiply.
     $64 - 24$      Subtract.
     ▩

**2.** $(5 - 11)^2 \div 9$      Operate inside parentheses.
     $(^-6)^2 \div 9$      Clear exponents.
     $36 \div 9$      Divide.
     ▩

**Evaluate the expression.**

**3.** $2 \times (5 - 3) + 8$

**4.** $5 \times (2.5 + 7) - 8$

**✔5.** $4^2 - 6 \times 3$

**6.** $8 \times (6 - 2)^2 + 15$

**7.** $(4 - 1)^4 \times (6 + 5)$

**8.** $(5^2 - 21)^2 \times 6 + 18$

**9.** $24 \div (^-8 - 4) - 4^3$

**10.** $5 \times [(6 + 3.2) \times 7 - 2^5 \div 8]$

**✔11.** $8 \times [(3 - 6 + 9)^2 + 4.8 \div 16]$

**12.** **TALK Math** Explain in order, the steps you would use to evaluate the expression $[3 - (13 - 10)^2] \times 15$.

## Independent Practice and Problem Solving

**Evaluate the expression.**

**13.** $(^-6)^2 + 20 \div 4$

**14.** $12 \times (5.9 + 18) - 6$

**15.** $4.6 \times (9 - 4)^3 + 102$

**16.** $(9 - 2)^2 - 3 \times (14 - 20)$

**17.** $(2^6 - 60)^2 + 45 \div 5$

**18.** $100 \div (2 - 12)^2 + 1^9$

**19.** $72 + (36 \div 3^2)^2 - 154$

**20.** $6 \times [(15.1 + 8) \times (6 - 3^4) \div 25]$

**21.** $3 \times [(6 - 5 + 9)^2 - 72] \div 12$

**Tell whether the statement is *true* or *false*. Explain.**

**22.** $(18 \div 2) \div 3 = 18 \div (2 \div 3)$

**23.** $(5 + 16) \times 3 = 5 + 16 \times 3$

**24.** $6 \times 4^2 + 10 = (6 \times 4)^2 + 10$

**25.** $6 \times 5 \times 4 + 10 = (6 \times 5) \times 4 + 10$

**26.** A restaurant has 16 tables for 2 and 14 tables for 4, but 9 chairs are missing. Write and evaluate a numerical expression that tells the number of chairs.

**27.** Brooke bought 3 tickets that cost $3.45 each, 2 tickets that cost $1.75 each, and one ticket that cost $4.99. How much did she spend on all the tickets she bought?

**28.** Tickets for a fundraiser cost $15 for adults and $7.50 for children. A total of 175 adult tickets were sold. The remaining tickets were sold to children. The room can seat 596 people, but 100 tickets were not sold. How much money was earned from ticket sales?

**29.** The Terrace Movie Theater holds 418 people. From Monday to Thursday, 2,145 people visited the theater. On Friday, Saturday, and Sunday, each of its 5 shows per day was sold out. How many people attended the theater during the entire week?

**30.** The temperature at noon was 76°F. The temperature increased 2°F each hour until 4:00 P.M. and then dropped 3°F each hour after that. What was the temperature at 9:00 P.M.?

**31.** **Pose a Problem** Look back at Problem 26. Write and solve a similar problem by changing the number of tables of each type.

**32.** **WRITE Math** What's the Error? Joel wrote $17 - 5 \times 2 = 24$. Find his error and give the correct answer.

**33.** **WRITE Math** Explain how you would use the order of operations to evaluate the expression $6 \times 100 \div 3 + 4^2 - (4 - 2)$.

**Technology**
Use Harcourt Mega Math, Ice Station Exploration, *Arctic Algebra*, Level X.

**Extra Practice** on page 292, Set B

**34.** Maria has to unpack 34 boxes of compact discs. Each box contains 12 discs. Show how she can use the Distributive Property to help her find the total number of discs. (AF 1.3, p. 272)

**35.** Margaret is making gift bags for a party. Each bag contains 4 stickers, 3 postcards, 1 magic marker, and 10 pieces of candy. Margaret decides to take out 5 pieces of candy from each bag. How many items are left in each gift bag? (AF 1.3, p. 272)

**36.** A music store lost an average of $1,766 during each of its first 3 months in business. How much will the store need to make in profit for each of the next 2 months to make up for the losses? (NS 2.1, p. 180)

**37. Test Prep** Which shows the correct value of the expression $20 \div (5 - 3) + 6^2$?

  **A** 37      **B** 46      **C** 49      **D** 256

**38. Test Prep** Jim took the steps below to evaluate the expression $2 \times 9 - 15 \div 3$.

$$2 \times 9 = 18$$
$$18 - 15 = 3$$
$$3 \div 3 = 1$$

What should Jim have done differently in order to evaluate the expression?

  **A** divided $(18 - 15)$ by $(18 \times 15)$

  **B** divided $(18 - 15)$ by $(18 - 15)$

  **C** subtracted $(15 \div 3)$ from 18

  **D** subtracted 15 from $(18 \div 3)$

 **Problem Solving and Reasoning**

**REASONING** You can use reasoning to determine where to place parentheses to get a certain value for an expression.

**Example** Place parentheses in the expression so that the expression is equal to 10.

| | |
|---|---|
| $4 \times 5 - 3 + 18 \div 2 + 7$ | **THINK:** Multiplication and division come before addition and subtraction. Try placing parentheses around numbers that are being added or subtracted. |
| $4 \times (5 - 3) + 18 \div (2 + 7)$ | Try parentheses around $5 - 3$ and $2 + 7$. |
| $4 \times 2 + 18 \div 9$ | |
| $8 + 2$ | |
| $10$ | The expression now equals 10. |

**Place parentheses in the expression so the expression is equal to the given value.**

  **1.** $2 + 3 - 5 \times 12 - 6;\ ^-25$                        **2.** $36 \div 4 + 5 + 72 \div 9 - 6 \times 3;\ 76$

# Write Algebraic Expressions

OBJECTIVE: Write an algebraic expression for a given situation.

## Learn

**PROBLEM** Irene's cell phone plan allows 200 text messages each month for a flat rate of $4.99, with $0.10 charged for each text message beyond 200. Write an algebraic expression for the amount Irene will have to pay for text messages each month.

An **algebraic expression** is an expression that includes at least one variable.

## Quick Review

Write a numerical expression.

1. seven plus five
2. eighteen minus sixteen
3. forty-two times six
4. twenty-four divided by 6
5. six less than the product of seven and eight

## Vocabulary

algebraic expression

### Example 1 Write an algebraic expression.

Write a word expression to represent the monthly charge for text messages. Use $m$ to represent the number of text messages over the limit.

| $4.99 for the month | plus | $0.10 for each of the $m$ text messages over 200 |
|:---:|:---:|:---:|
| ↓ | ↓ | ↓ |
| 4.99 | + | $0.10 \times m$ |

So, $4.99 + 0.10m$ represents the monthly cost of Irene's text messages.

Sometimes, you need two or more variables to write an algebraic expression.

### Example 2 Write an algebraic expression using two variables.
A cell phone company charges $0.03 per minute for local calls and $0.12 per minute for long-distance calls. Write an algebraic expression that gives the total cost where $a$ represents minutes of local calls and $b$ represents minutes of long-distance calls.

| word expression: | algebraic expression |
|---|---|
| $0.03 per minute for local calls | $0.03a$ |
| $0.12 per minute for long distance-calls | $0.12b$ |

So, an algebraic expression that represents the total cost is $0.03a + 0.12b$.

### Example 3 Write an algebraic expression for each word expression.

| thirty more than the product four and some number, $x$ | $4x + 30$ |
|---|---|
| four times the quantity of $x + 30$ | $4(x + 30)$ |
| some number, $w$, divided by 5 times another number, $t$ | $\frac{w}{5t}$ |

**Remember**
Multiplication using a variable can be represented in several different ways.
$8 \times m$ $8 \cdot m$
$8(m)$ $8m$

AF 1.2 Write and evaluate an algebraic expression for a given situation, using up to three variables. *also* AF 1.0, MR 2.4, MR 2.5, MR 3.2

**Example 4 Write an algebraic expression using three variables.**

A cell phone company is offering a special deal. For the first month, you pay half the basic monthly service fee plus the charges for text messages and the charges for phone calls. Write an algebraic expression for the total cost.

> Choose your variables. Let $b$ represent the basic monthly service fee, $t$ represent the cost of text messages, and $p$ represent the cost of phone calls.
>
> Write numbers and symbols for the parts of the word expression.
>
> one-half basic monthly service: $\frac{1}{2}b$
>
> cost of text messages: $t$
>
> cost of phone calls: $p$

So, the total cost can be represented by $\frac{1}{2}b + t + p$.

• Write an algebraic expression for the total monthly cost if the basic monthly service fee is doubled instead of halved.

You can use algebraic properties to write equivalent algebraic expressions.

**Example 5 Use the properties.**

Use the Commutative, Associative, or Distributive Property to write an equivalent algebraic expression.

| Property | Expression | Equivalent Expression |
|---|---|---|
| Commutative | $3x + 5y$ | $5y + 3x$ |
| Associative | $(3x + 5y) + 8z$ | $3x + (5y + 8z)$ |
| Distributive | $3(2a + 5b)$ | $6a + 15b$ |

• Show how the Distributive Property allows you to write $3(2a + 5b) = 6a + 15b$.

## Guided Practice

1. Use a multiplication symbol to write an algebraic expression for $x$ multiplied by 7.

2. Use an addition symbol to write an algebraic expression for $m$ increased by 14.

**Write an algebraic expression for the word expression.**

3. $g$ divided by 2.39

4. 2 less than 4 multiplied by $d$

✓5. 17 more than $x$

✓6. one-half of some number plus the number squared

7. **TALK Math** **Explain** how to write an algebraic expression for the following: If you buy 3 shirts, at $s$ dollars each, then you get $5 off the total price.

**Write an algebraic expression for the word expression.**

**8.** some number increased by 32

**9.** $3\frac{1}{2}$ decreased by some number

**10.** the product of a number and 36

**11.** length times width times height

**12.** some number decreased by 45

**13.** 24 less than two thirds of some number

**14.** the square of some number which is then divided by 8

**15.** some number increased by 5, then increased by the same number cubed

**Use the indicated property to write an equivalent algebraic expression.**

**16.** Commutative Property
$2x + 4y$

**17.** Associative Property
$a + (2b + 3c)$

**18.** Distributive Property
$5(3n + 2m)$

**Write a word expression for each algebraic expression.**

**19.** $n - 14$

**20.** $36 \div 2n$

**21.** $n + \frac{2}{5} + n^2$

**22.** $3(n + 1) \div 4$

**Solve.**

**23.** A cell phone company charges $0.01 for each extra kilobyte of data usage and $0.05 for each extra text message. Write an algebraic expression that gives the total extra cost where $k$ represents the number of extra kilobytes and $t$ represents the number of extra text messages.

**24.** On their first month's bill, new customers pay one-fourth the basic service fee, one-half the text messaging fee, and an additional $10 off the entire bill. Write an algebraic expression for the total cost for the first month, if $s$ represents the total bill without the discounts.

**25. Pose a Problem** Look back at Problem 24. Write a similar problem in which new customers get a smaller discount on the cost of data usage and text messages. Choose your own discount percentage.

**26.**  Hazel purchases a new cell phone for $99, and signs up for a plan that will cost $29.99 per month. **Explain** how to write an expression for the total cost of the phone and the monthly plan for a certain number of months.

## Achieving the Standards

**27.** What is the median of the following prices: $35, $23, $40, $28, and $37? (SDAP 1.1, p. 224)

**28.** Oscar said the measures of the angles of a triangle he drew were 50°, 85°, and 65°. Could that be correct? Explain. (Grade 5 ○━┓ MG 2.2)

**29.** Evaluate the expression $3^3 \div (17 - 8)$.
(AF 1.3, p. 276)

**30. Test Prep** A camp site costs $15, plus an additional charge of $2.50 for each camper, $c$. Which algebraic expression represents the total cost?

**A** $15 + c$

**C** $15c$

**B** $15 + 2.50 + c$

**D** $15 + 2.50c$

# Write a Problem

Math is a language of digits, symbols, and words. You use algebra to translate the words to numbers and symbols. You need to understand key words and phrases, know what each variable represents, and how to follow the order of operations to evaluate expressions.

Mr. Becker asked his students to write a question that can be represented by $7.5y + 6$.

Read the steps that Jenny followed to write her problem.

| Key Words and Phrases | Operation |
| --- | --- |
| added to, combined, increased by, more than, sum of, together, total of | addition (+) |
| decreased by, difference between/of, fewer than, less, less than, minus, how many more than, how many fewer than, are left | subtraction (−) |
| product of, multiplied by, times | multiplication (×) |
| per, out of, percent (divide by 100), quotient of, ratio of, shared by, split among, divided among | division (÷) |

**Step 1**  The problem could be about buying items that cost $7.50 each and then buying another item that costs $6.00

**Step 2**  Think of a situation.

**Step 3**  Write a problem based on the situation. "Jenny, her little brother, and some friends are going to the movies. The tickets cost $7.50 each for Jenny and her friends and cost $6.00 for her little brother. Write an expression for the total cost of going to the movies."

**Problem Solving** Write a problem for each expression.

**1.** $12(x + 4y)$

**2.** $12x + 4y$

**3.** $x(29.5 - 5) + 12.5$

**4.** $\dfrac{x + y}{3}$

# Evaluate Algebraic Expressions

**OBJECTIVE:** Evaluate algebraic expressions.

## Learn

To evaluate algebraic expressions, you replace the variables with values and then follow the order of operations.

**Example 1** Evaluate $4m - 18 \div 3$ for $m = 7$.

| | |
|---|---|
| $4m - 18 \div 3$ | |
| $4 \times 7 - 18 \div 3$ | Replace $m$ with 7. Multiply. |
| $28 - 18 \div 3$ | Divide. |
| $28 - 6$ | Subtract. |
| $22$ | |

So, for $m = 7$, the expression $4m - 18 \div 3 = 22$.

- Will evaluating the algebraic expression $4m - 18 \div 3$ for some value of $m$ give the same result as evaluating $(4m - 18) \div 3$? Explain.

You can evaluate an algebraic expression for different values of the variable.

**Example 2** Evaluate $x^2 + 11$ for $x = 7, 4, {}^-3$ and ${}^-5$.

| | |
|---|---|
| $x = 7$ | |
| $x^2 + 11$ | |
| $7^2 + 11$ | Replace $x$ with 7. Clear the exponent. |
| $49 + 11$ | Add. |
| $60$ | |

So, for $x = 7$, $x^2 + 11 = 60$.

| | |
|---|---|
| $x = 4$ | |
| $x^2 + 11$ | |
| $4^2 + 11$ | Replace $x$ with 4. Clear the exponent. |
| $16 + 11$ | Add. |
| $27$ | |

So, for $x = 4$, $x^2 + 11 = 27$.

**ERROR ALERT**

When squaring a number, be sure to multiply the number by itself and not multiply it by 2.

| | |
|---|---|
| $x = {}^-3$ | |
| $x^2 + 11$ | |
| $({}^-3)^2 + 11$ | Replace $x$ with ${}^-3$. Clear the exponent. |
| $9 + 11$ | Add. |
| $20$ | |

So, for $x = {}^-3$, $x^2 + 11 = 20$.

| | |
|---|---|
| $x = {}^-5$ | |
| $x^2 + 11$ | |
| $({}^-5)^2 + 11$ | Replace $x$ with ${}^-5$. Clear the exponent. |
| $25 + 11$ | Add. |
| $36$ | |

So, for $x = {}^-5$, $x^2 + 11 = 36$.

AF 1.2 Write and evaluate an algebraic expression for a given situation, using up to three variables. *also* NS 2.3, AF 1.0, AF 1.3, MR 2.2, MR 2.4, MR 2.5, MR 3.1, MR 3.2

The parts of an expression that are separated by an addition or subtraction sign are called **terms**. Before you evaluate some algebraic expressions, you can simplify them by combining like terms. **Like terms** have the same variable, raised to the same power.

| Algebraic Expression | Like Terms |
|---|---|
| $3x + 10x + 9$ | $3x$ and $10x$ |
| $15y - 8 - 12y$ | $15y$ and $12y$ |
| $8z^2 + 17 + 4z + 12z^2$ | $8z^2$ and $12z^2$ |

To make an algebraic expression simpler, combine like terms by adding or subtracting them.

| Algebraic Expression | Simplified |
|---|---|
| $3x + 10x + 9$ | $13x + 9$ |
| $15y - 8 - 12y$ | $3y - 8$ |
| $8z^2 + 17 + 4z + 12z^2$ | $20z^2 + 4z + 17$ |

If possible, simplify an expression before you evaluate it. Combine like terms, and then evaluate the expression for the given value of the variable.

## Example 3 Evaluate $6y + 12 + 3y$ for $y = 10$.

$$
\begin{aligned}
6y + 12 + 3y &= 6y + 3y + 12 \quad &&\text{Use the Commutative Property.} \\
&&&\text{Combine like terms.} \\
&= 9y + 12 \\
&= 9 \times 10 + 12 \quad &&\text{Replace } y \text{ with 10 and multiply.} \\
&= 90 + 12 \quad &&\text{Add.} \\
&= 102
\end{aligned}
$$

So, for $y = 10$, $6y + 12 + 3y = 102$.

**PROBLEM** A rectangular lot is being made into a skateboard park. The length, $l$, is 45 yd, and the width, $w$, is 30 yd. To find the perimeter, the algebraic expression $l + w + l + w$, where $l$ is the length and $w$ is the width is being used. What is the perimeter of the lot?

## Example 4 Combine like terms and evaluate.

$$
\begin{aligned}
l + w + l + w &= l + l + w + w \quad &&\text{Use the Commutative Property.} \\
&&&\text{Combine like terms.} \\
&= 2l + 2w \\
&= 2 \times 45 + 2 \times 30 \quad &&\text{Replace } l \text{ with 45 and } w \text{ with 30 and multiply.} \\
&= 90 + 60 \quad &&\text{Add.} \\
&= 150
\end{aligned}
$$

So, the perimeter of the lot is 150 yd.

Guided Prac

1. Evaluate 2
   multiply

Evaluate

3. 10

Sin
   v

$y + 4$ for $y = 3$. Replace $y$ with 3, 3 by 2, and then add 4.

**2.** Evaluate $4g + 21g - 21$ for $g = 2$. Combine like terms, then replace $g$ with 2, multiply, and then subtract 21.

the expression for $x = 3, 2, 1,$ and 0.

$+ 5x$

**4.** $4x - 29$

**5.** $17 + 4x + x^2$

✓**6.** $0.5x + x^3$

**plify the expression. Then evaluate the expression for the given value of the variable.**

**7.** $9a + 15a - 6$ for $a = 3$

**8.** $4x - 12 + 5x$ for $x = 6$

✓**9.** $4c + c + 2c$ for $c = 2$

**10.** [ **TALK Math** ] **Explain** how to evaluate the expression $3y - 15 + 8y$ for $y = 12$.

## Independent Practice (and Problem Solving)

**Evaluate the expression for $a = 3, 0, ^-1,$ and $^-3$.**

**11.** $4a$

**12.** $^-6a$

**13.** $8 - \frac{1}{2}a$

**14.** $7 + 2a$

**15.** $(a + 6)^2 - 15$

**16.** $(a + 1)^3 + 2$

**17.** $a^2 + 3a - 5$

**18.** $a^2 + a + 2$

**Simplify the expression. Then evaluate the expression for the given value of the variable.**

**19.** $3x + 8x - 11$ for $x = 2$

**20.** $33n - 15 + 7n$ for $n = 1$

**21.** $6d + 6d - 6d$ for $d = 6$

**22.** $5k + 2k + 17$ for $k = ^-2$

**23.** $24y + 6 - 19y$ for $y = ^-3$

**24.** $14b + 12b - 7b$ for $b = ^-4$

**25.** The tread area of a skateboard wheel can be estimated by using the expression $6.28rw$, where $r$ is the radius and $w$ is the width of the wheel. What is the tread area of a wheel with a radius of 25 mm and a width of 15 mm?

**26.** The skate park charges $5 admission and a $2 rental fee. To find the total cost for 3 people, the cashier used the expression $a + r + a + r + a + r$ where $a$ is the admission cost and $r$ is the rental cost. What was the total cost for 3 people?

**USE DATA For 27–29, use the cost chart.**

The cost chart shows how much a company charges for skateboard wheels. Each pack of 8 wheels costs $50. Shipping costs $7 for any order.

**27.** Copy and complete the cost chart.

**28.** **Reasoning** Suppose your skateboard club has a budget of $200 to spend on new wheels this year. How many packs of wheels can you order?

**29.** The company sold 12 packs of wheels on one order last week. How much did the company charge for the wheels, including shipping?

| Cost Chart for Skateboard Wheels | | |
|---|---|---|
| Number of Packs | $50 \times n + 7$ | Cost |
| 1 | $50 \times 1 + 7$ | $57 |
| 2 | $50 \times 2 + 7$ | |
| 3 | | |
| 4 | | |
| 5 | | |

**Technology**

Use Harcourt Mega Math, Ice Station Exploration, *Arctic Algebra*, Levels F, G, H, and I.

( **Extra Practice** ) on page 292, Set D

**30.** Another company sells packs of wheel bearings for $50 each. It charges $1.50 to ship each pack. Write an algebraic expression to represent the cost of $p$ packs, including shipping. Make a cost chart for up to five packs.

**31.** [WRITE Math] ▸ **What's the Error?** Bob evaluated $3m - 3 \div 3$ this way for $m = 8$:

$$3 \times 8 = 24$$
$$24 - 3 = 21$$
$$21 \div 3 = 7$$

Describe Bob's error. What is the correct value?

## Mixed Review and Test Prep

**32.** What is the volume of a box that measures 12 inches by 12 inches by 18 inches?

(Grade 5 ◯━┓ MG 1.3)

**33.** A reporter conducting a survey asks 35 people in her office their political opinions. What sort of sample is she using?

(◯━┓ SDAP 2.2, p. 202)

**34.** Find the value of $2x^2$ for $x = 5$. (AF 1.2, p. 284)

**35.** **Test Prep** Evaluate $2a + c^2$ for $a = 3$ and $c = 6$.

**A** 11    **B** 12    **C** 42    **D** 144

**36.** **Test Prep** A roller skating rink charges a $7.50-per-person entry fee plus a $2.00-per-person rental fee for skates. Write and evaluate an algebraic expression for the total cost for a family of 4 to go skating.

## MATH POWER ⟩ Problem Solving and Reasoning

**NUMBER SENSE** You can use the Distributive Property and mental math to evaluate algebraic expressions.

**Evaluate** $lw$ **for** $l = 5$ **and** $w = 68$.

| $lw$ | |
|---|---|
| $5 \times 68$ | Replace $l$ with 5 and $w$ with 68. |
| $5(60 + 8)$ | Think of 68 as $60 + 8$. |
| $5 \times 60 + 5 \times 8$ | Use the Distributive Property and mental math. |
| $300 + 40$ | |
| $340$ | |

So, for $l = 5$ and $w = 68$, $lw = 340$.

**Evaluate** $bh$ **for** $b = 3$ **and** $h = 4.7$.

| $bh$ | |
|---|---|
| $3 \times 4.7$ | Replace $b$ with 3 and $h$ with 4.7. |
| $3(4 + 0.7)$ | Think of 4.7 as $4 + 0.7$. |
| $3 \times 4 + 3 \times 0.7$ | Use the Distributive Property and mental math. |
| $12 + 2.1$ | |
| $14.1$ | |

So, for $b = 3$ and $h = 4.7$, $bh = 14.1$.

**Use the Distributive Property and mental math to evaluate each expression.**

**1.** $xy$ for $x = 4$ and $y = 79$    **2.** $rs$ for $r = 5$ and $s = 37$    **3.** $ma$ for $m = 3$ and $a = 9.8$

**4.** The cost for the band to ride a bus is $12 per student. Write an algebraic expression to represent the cost of $s$ students riding the bus. If there are 65 students in the band, how much does it cost to ride the bus?

LESSON **5**

# Use Three Variables

OBJECTIVE: Evaluate algebraic expressions with three variables.

**Quick Review**

Evaluate the algebraic expression for $x = 12$.

1. $7x + 15$
2. $3(x + 7)$
3. $14 + 4x - 2x$
4. $\dfrac{5x + 6}{3}$
5. $8(4x^2 - 3x + 15)$

## Learn

**PROBLEM** Gary saves all of his loose change. He gives all of his pennies to his younger sister. Then he puts all of his nickels, dimes, and quarters into a bank. Write an algebraic expression that will show the total amount that he has saved from all the loose change in his bank.

Algebraic expressions may contain more than two variables.

**Example 1** Write an algebraic expression for Gary's savings using three variables.

**Step 1**

Choose variables. Let $n$ = number of nickels, $d$ = number of dimes, and $q$ = number of quarters.

**Step 2**

Write an expression.

| value of nickels | | value of dimes | | value of quarters |
|---|---|---|---|---|
| ↓ | | ↓ | | ↓ |
| $0.05n$ | + | $0.10d$ | + | $0.25q$ |

So, the total amount that Gary has saved can be shown using the algebraic expression $0.05n + 0.10d + 0.25q$.

• If Gary has 53 nickels, 31 dimes, and 27 quarters, how much money does he have in his bank?

**Example 2** Combine like terms to simplify an expression. Evaluate the following for $x = 2$, $y = 3$, and $z = 15$.

| | |
|---|---|
| $8x + 14 - 3y + 14x + 8y - 4z - 5$ | |
| $8x + 14 - 3y + 14x + 8y - 4z - 5$ | Combine all the $x$ terms. |
| $22x + 14 - 3y + 8y - 4z - 5$ | Combine all the $y$ terms. |
| $22x + 14 + 5y - 4z - 5$ | Combine all terms with no variables. |
| $22x + 5y - 4z + 9$ | |
| $22 \times 2 + 5 \times 3 - 4 \times 15 + 9$ | Replace $x$ with 2, $y$ with 3, and $z$ with 15. |
| $44 + 15 - 60 + 9$ | Evaluate. |
| $8$ | |

So, the expression is equal to 8.

**Math Idea**
Terms that have the same variable and exponent, such as $4x^2$ and $9x^2$, are like terms. Two terms with the same variable but different exponents, such as $3x^2$ and $5x^3$, are not like terms.

**AF 1.2** Write and evaluate an algebraic expression for a given situation, using up to three variables. *also* **NS 2.0, NS 2.3, AF 1.0, AF 1.3, MR 2.2, MR 2.4, MR 2.5, MR 3.1, MR 3.2**

Simplify the expression if possible. Evaluate the expression for
$a = 3$, $b = 6$, and $c = {}^-2$.

**1.** $3a - 4b + 2c + 7$
$3 \times 3 - 4 \times 6 + 2 \times {}^-2 + 7$
$9 - 24 - 4 + 7$
▪

**2.** $6a - 8b + 6 - 9c + 3b - 4a + 12$
$2a - 8b + 6 - 9c + 3b + 12$
$2a - 5b + 6 - 9c + 12$
$2a - 5b - 9c + 18$
$2 \times 3 - 5 \times 6 - 9 \times {}^-2 + 18$
$6 - 30 + 18 + 18$
▪

Simplify the expression if possible. Evaluate the expression for
$x = 9$, $y = 5$, and $z = 15$.

**3.** $8x + 9y - 5z$

**✓4.** $12x + 5z - 14 + 7z - 6y + 12x$

**✓5.** $9x - 9y + 9z + 14y$

**6.** **TALK Math** **Explain** how to evaluate the expression $3p + 4q - 5r + 2p$
for $p = 5$, $q = 3$, and $r = 1$.

Simplify the expression if possible. Evaluate the expression for
$x = 6$, $y = 12$, and $z = 7$.

**7.** $2x + 5y - 10z$

**8.** $5x - 8y + 3y + 5z$

**9.** $4z + 2y + 2z - 8y + 3x$

**10.** $3x + 6y - 9z$

**11.** $8x + 12z - 6y + 7z - 3z + 12x$

**12.** $11x - 4y + 8z + 2y$

**13.** $20z - 4x + 11z - 6y$

**14.** $12z + 8x + 5y - 3z - z$

**15.** $2y^2 + 6x^2 + 19x + 12z$

**16.** Morgan has 10 one-dollar bills, 17 five-dollar bills, and 2 ten-dollar
bills. Write and evaluate an algebraic expression to find the total
amount of money she has.

**17.** Mary has 13 nickels, 7 dimes, and 14 quarters. Write and evaluate an
algebraic expression to find the total number of money she has.

**18.** **WRITE Math** ▸ **What's the Question?** The answer is $3x + y + z = 12$.

### Achieving the Standards

**19.** What is the prime factorization of 36?
(Grade 5 O━━┓ NS1.4)

**20.** There are 9 red and 5 blue marbles in a bag.
What is the probability that a blue marble will
be drawn from the bag? (Grade 4 SDAP 2.0)

**21.** Write as an algebraic expression: a number is
increased by seven times the number.
(p. 280, AF 1.2)

**22.** **Test Prep** Which is the value of the expression
$8a + 7b + 3c^2$ for $a = 4$, $b = 3$, and $c = 9$?

**A** 8      **B** 34      **C** 79      **D** 296

# Problem Solving Workshop
## Skill: Sequence and Prioritize Information

**OBJECTIVE:** Solve problems by using the problem solving skill *sequence and prioritize* information.

## Use the Skill

**PROBLEM** At the start of the month, Jon has 24 copies of Ultradog comic books and 31 copies of Aquacat comic books in his store. He orders and receives 2 boxes of each. Each box holds 48 copies. In one month, he sells 87 copies of Ultradog comic books and 95 copies of Aquacat comic books. How many comic books in all does he have at the end of the month?

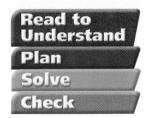

Sometimes a complex problem describes a sequence of events. It is often helpful to follow that sequence when solving the problem. You may also need to prioritize parts of the problem, or decide which parts are especially important.

| Sequence | Event | Ultradog | Aquacat |
|----------|-------|----------|---------|
| 1st | John starts with certain numbers. | 24 | 31 |
| 2nd | He orders 2 boxes. Priority: Find $2 \times 48$ for each comic book. | $2 \times 48$ | $2 \times 48$ |
| 3rd | He adds comic books from the boxes. | $24 + 2 \times 48$ | $31 + 2 \times 48$ |
| 4th | He sells some. | $24 + 2 \times 48 - 87$ | $31 + 2 \times 48 - 95$ |
| 5th | He has a total at the end of the month. | $(24 + 2 \times 48 - 87) + (31 + 2 \times 48 - 95)$ | |

$(24 + 2 \times 48 - 87) + (31 + 2 \times 48 - 95) = 33 + 32 = 65$

So, Jon has a total of 65 comic books.

## Think and Discuss
**Use the information below to solve the problems.**

Greg is in charge of ordering food and supplies for the Snack Hut. At the start of the month, he has 129 hot dogs. During the month, the Snack Hut sells 327 hot dogs. Also during the month, Greg orders and receives 4 cases of hot dogs. Each case holds 75 hot dogs.

**a.** Sequence and prioritize the steps for finding the total number of hot dogs, if any, that were left.

**b.** Did Greg order enough hot dogs? Explain.

**c.** Could Greg have ordered one less case of hot dogs and still have had enough? Explain.

AF 1.3 Apply algebraic order of operations and the commutative, associative, and distributive properties to evaluate expressions; and justify each step in the process. *also* O━┓ NS 2.0, AF 1.4, MR 1.0, MR 1.1, MR 2.0, MR 2.4, MR 2.5, MR 3.0, MR 3.2 , MR 3.3

1. Jen starts the year with 24 copies of Ultradog, 26 copies of Aquacat, and 38 copies of Green Shield comic books. Every month, she orders 2 boxes each of Ultradog and Aquacat, and 1 box of Green Shield comic books. There are 48 copies in each box. How many comic books does she have at the end of March?

| Monthly Comic Sales | | | |
|---|---|---|---|
| Month | Ultradog | Aquacat | Green Shield |
| Jan | 82 | 98 | 44 |
| Feb | 93 | 89 | 52 |
| Mar | 102 | 90 | 47 |

**First,** find out how many copies of each comic book she bought over the three months.

**Then,** add the number of each comic book bought to the number she started with at the beginning of the year.

**Finally,** subtract the sales for the three months from the total of the numbers she started with and bought.

2. **What if** there were 52 copies in each box ordered? How many copies of Green Shield would she have at the end of March?

3. Which comic book has the highest average monthly sales? What is that average to the nearest whole number?

## Mixed Applications

**USE DATA** For 4–6, use the table.

4. Find the number of copies of Aquacat comic books that were sold in June.

5. Find the number of copies of Cool Kid comic books that were sold during June. Explain the sequence of steps you followed.

| Comic | Sales Comparison for June |
|---|---|
| Ultradog | 33 more copies than Green Shield sales |
| Aquacat | 11 more copies than Ultradog sales |
| Green Shield | 54 copies sold |
| Cool Kid | 43 copies less than Aquacat sales |

6. **Reasoning** List the number of copies for each comic book sold in June in order from least to greatest.

7. Forty-two sixth graders subscribe to the magazine Sixth Grade World. The magazine sells for $2.95. Estimate the total amount of money that was spent on the magazine over 5 months.

8. Jen's store receives 3 boxes of Red Runner comic books at the beginning of June. Each box holds 48 copies. At the end of the month, she has 34 copies left. How many copies were sold in June? Is there enough or too little information to solve this problem?

9. **FAST FACT** In 2005, comic book sales amounted to about $450 million. Suppose the average cost of a comic book in 2005 was $1.80. Was the number of comic books sold in 2005 more or less than 275,000,000?

10. Allen has twice as many comic books as Josie. Josie has three more comic books than Sarah. Sarah has 12 comic books. How many comic books does Allen have?

11. **Pose a Problem** Look back at Problem 10. Write and solve a similar problem by changing the number of comic books Sarah has.

12. **WRITE Math** **Explain** how sequencing and prioritizing information help you to solve some problems.

 **Extra Practice**

**Set A** Write *true* or *false* for each statement. Explain your answer. (pp. 272–275)

1. $16 + 35 + 24 = 16 + 24 + 35$

2. $12 + 24 \times 28 = 12 \times 28 + 24$

3. $(7 \times 4) + 12 = 7 \times (4 + 12)$

4. $6 \times (3 + 7) = (6 \times 3) + (6 \times 7)$

5. $(4 \times 9) \times 34 = 4 \times (9 \times 34)$

6. $11 + 35 + 29 = 11 + 29 + 35$

**Set B** Evaluate the expression. (pp. 276–279)

1. $6^2 + 12 \div 3$

2. $11 \times (9 + 14) - 3$

3. $121 \div (14 - 3)^2 + 2^3$

4. $3 \times (5 - 3)^4 + 21$

5. $3^3 \times [(5 - 3^2) \div 2 + 9]$

6. $4 \times [(1 - 3 + 5)^2 + 6]$

7. The school cafeteria has 12 tables for 4 and 14 tables for 8, but 5 chairs are missing. Write and evaluate a numerical expression that gives the number of chairs available for the students.

**Set C** Write an algebraic expression for the word expression. (pp. 280–283)

1. a number increased by 12

2. the product of a number and 15

3. 17 less than one half of a number

4. the square of some number which is then divided by 6

5. New internet customers pay one-third the basic monthly service charge for the first month of service. Write an algebraic expression that represents the first month's cost.

6. Customers pay half the cost of a new phone plus one-fourth the basic monthly service fee for the first month. Write an algebraic expression that represents the cost of a new phone and first month's service.

**Set D** Evaluate the expression for $x = 3, 2, 1,$ and $0$. (pp. 284–287)

1. $2 \times (x + 15)$

2. $239 - x^3$

3. $\frac{3x}{3} + 2$

4. $6x + x^2$

5. $x^2 + 3x + 5$

6. $5x - 21$

7. $13x^2 - 2x$

8. $1.5x + 2$

9. $11x$

10. $(x - 1)^2$

**Set E** Simplify the expression if possible. Evaluate the expression for $a = 6, b = 4,$ and $c = 3$. (pp. 288–289)

1. $a - 5c + 4b$

2. $12b + 3c + a$

3. $5a + 8b + 6c - 3a$

4. $11c + 5a - 1 + 4b$

5. $a^2 + 2b - c + 2a$

6. $10c - 9a + 2b^2 - 2c + a$

7. $2a + 3b + 4c - a - 2b$

8. $a^2 + b^2 + c^2 + 2a^2$

9. $10c + 3b - 14c - 8a + 18c$

**CD ROM Technology**
Use Harcourt Mega Math, Ice Station
Exploration, *Arctic Algebra*, Levels F, G, H and I.

# expression exploration

### Players

2 players

### Materials

- Number cube labeled 1–6
- 3-section spinner labeled 1–3
- Timer or watch
- 2 different coins
- 30 expression cards

**START**

**FINISH**

## How to Play

- Shuffle the expression cards and place them facedown in a pile.
- Each player selects a coin and places it on START. Decide who will go first.
- The first player draws an expression card from the pile and rolls the number cube.
- The player then evaluates the expression on the expression card by replacing the variable with the number on the number cube. The other player checks the answer.

- If the answer is correct, the player spins the pointer, advances the number of spaces shown, and draws another card.
- If the answer is incorrect, or after a player gets 3 correct answers in a row, play passes to the other player.
- Play continues until a player lands on or beyond FINISH. The first player reaching or passing FINISH is the winner.

# Chapter 11 Review/Test

## Check Vocabulary and Concepts

**Choose the best term from the box.**

1. A mathematical phrase that includes only numbers and operating symbols is called a(n) __?__. (AF 1.3, p. 272)

2. When you evaluate expressions that have more than one operation, you follow rules called the __?__. (AF 1.3, p. 276)

3. An expression that includes at least one variable is a(n) __?__.
(AF 1.2, p. 280)

> **VOCABULARY**
> algebraic expression
> like terms
> numerical expression
> order of operations

## Check Skills

**Write true or false for each statement. Explain your answer.** (AF 1.3, pp. 272–275)

4. $(16 + 4) + 2 = 16 + (4 + 2)$

5. $5 \times 3 + 12 = 5 \times 12 + 3$

6. $(16 \times \frac{1}{2}) \times \frac{1}{4} = 16 \times (\frac{1}{2} \times \frac{1}{4})$

7. $2 + (6 \times 7) = (2 + 6) \times 7$

**Evaluate the expression.** (AF 1.3, pp. 276–279)

8. $5^2 - 60 \div 3$

9. $9 \times (5 - 3) + 16$

10. $(5 - 3)^2 - 2 \times 12$

11. $(2^6 - 50) \times 2 + 35 \div 5$

12. $4^3 \times [(4 + 3^2) \div 4 - 5]$

13. $4 \times [(2 - 6 + 14)^2 + 20] \div 20$

**Write an algebraic expression for the word expression.** (AF 1.2, pp. 280–283)

14. 34 less than $\frac{1}{4}$ of $y$

15. a number decreased by 26

16. the product of a number and 12

17. $h$ times $j$ times $k$

**Evaluate the expression for $x = 3, 2, 1$, and $0$.** (AF 1.2, pp. 284–287)

18. $45 + 2x$

19. $2 \times (x + 0.5) - 3x$

20. $x^2 + 2x - 4$

**Simplify the expression if possible. Evaluate the expression for $x = 5, y = 8$, and $z = 4$.** (AF 1.2, pp. 288–289)

21. $10z + 4x + 6y - 2z$

22. $3y^2 + 2x^2 + 13z$

23. $7x + 11z - 4y + 6z - 2z + 10x$

## Check Problem Solving

**Solve.** (AF 1,3, MR 2.0, pp. 290-291)

24. Karen's trip will last 4 days and 3 nights. Transportation costs $75 round trip, and the hotel costs $100 per night. If she has a budget of $675, how much will she have left to spend each day if she spends the same amount each day?

25. **WRITE Math** ▶ Mr. Sanchez had 12 boxes that held 5 skateboards each. He sold all but 7 of them. How many skateboards did he sell?
**Explain** the steps you followed to solve the problem.

**GO Technology** Use *Online Assessment.*

# Enrich • Writing Expressions to Find Sums
## Expressions and Consecutive Integers

Given any integer $n$, you can generate a list of consecutive integers using the expressions $n$, $n + 1$, $n + 2$, $n + 3$, and so on. For example, if $n$ is equal to 17, then the expressions will produce the integers 17, 18, 19, 20, and so on.

| $n$ | 17 |
|---|---|
| $n + 1$ | $17 + 1 = 18$ |
| $n + 2$ | $17 + 2 = 19$ |
| $n + 3$ | $17 + 3 = 20$ |

In the same way, you can produce a list of consecutive odd or even integers using the expressions $n$, $n + 2$, $n + 4$, $n + 6$, and so on. If $n$ is odd, then the list will contain odd integers. If $n$ is even, then the list will contain even integers. For example, if $n$ is equal to 34, then the expressions will produce the integers 34, 36, 38, 40, and so on.

| $n$ | 34 |
|---|---|
| $n + 2$ | $34 + 2 = 36$ |
| $n + 4$ | $34 + 4 = 38$ |
| $n + 6$ | $34 + 6 = 40$ |

## Example

Find 3 consecutive even integers whose sum is equal to 24.

Let $n$ = the first integer, $n + 2$ = the second integer, and $n + 4$ = the third integer.

$n + (n + 2) + (n + 4)$ — Write an expression that represents the sum of 3 consecutive even integers.

$n + n + 2 + n + 4$ — Remove the parentheses.

$3n + 6$ — Simplify by combining like terms.

Use predict and test to choose values for $n$ so that $3n + 6 = 24$.

Next, evaluate $n$, $n + 2$, and $n + 4$ for $n = 6$ to find the consecutive even integers whose sum is 24.

$n = 6$      $n + 2 = 6 + 2 = 8$      $n + 4 = 6 + 4 = 10$

Check: $6 + 8 + 10 = 24$

| $n$ | $3n + 6$ | Result |
|---|---|---|
| 4 | $3(4) + 6 = 18$ | Too low |
| 8 | $3(8) + 8 = 32$ | Too high |
| 6 | $3(6) + 6 = 24$ | Correct |

So, three consecutive even integers whose sum is 24 are 6, 8, and 10.

## Try It

**Find the given integers for the given sum.**

1. 3 consecutive integers whose sum is 12

2. 3 consecutive integers whose sum is 15

3. 3 consecutive odd integers whose sum is 27

4. 3 consecutive even integers whose sum is 48

5. 4 consecutive odd integers whose sum is 16

6. 4 consecutive even integers whose sum is 28

**WRITE Math** ▸ **Explain** how using subtraction expressions to find consecutive integers would give different integers than using addition expressions.

# Achieving the Standards

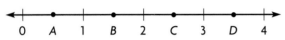 Chapters 1 – 11

## Number Sense

1. Which point shows the location of $\frac{7}{2}$ on the number line? (O━ NS 1.1)

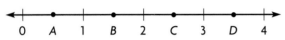

   **A** point $A$

   **B** point $B$

   **C** point $C$

   **D** point $D$

2. What is the greatest common divisor of 20, 16, and 8? (O━ NS 2.4)

   **A** 2

   **B** 4

   **C** 8

   **D** 16

3. What is the sum $\frac{3}{8} + \frac{1}{2}$? (NS 2.1)

   **A** $\frac{3}{16}$

   **B** $\frac{2}{5}$

   **C** $\frac{4}{10}$

   **D** $\frac{7}{8}$

4. What is the product of $\frac{1}{5}$ and $\frac{3}{5}$? (NS 2.1)

   **A** $\frac{3}{25}$

   **B** $\frac{1}{3}$

   **C** $\frac{3}{5}$

   **D** $\frac{4}{5}$

5. **WRITE Math** ▶ Describe how to write $\frac{4}{6}$ in simplest form. (O━ NS 2.4)

## Algebra and Functions

6. Which of the following statements is true? (AF 1.3)

   **A** $16 \times 7 \times 4 = (16 + 7) \times (16 + 4)$

   **B** $10 + 8 \times 7 = 10 \times 7 + 8$

   **C** $5 \times (6 + 7) = (5 + 6) + (5 + 7)$

   **D** $11 + 7 + 8 = 11 + 8 + 7$

7. If $c = 5$, what is the value of $7 \times c - 4$? (AF 1.2)

   **A** 31        **C** 11

   **B** 28        **D** 7

8. Which expression represents the product of $x$ and 34? (AF 1.2)

   **A** $34 - x$        **C** $34 + x$

   **B** $34x$           **D** $34 \div x$

9. Which equation could have been used to make the function table? (Grade 5 O━ AF 1.5)

   | $x$ | $y$ |
   |---|---|
   | $^{-}10$ | $^{-}4$ |
   | $^{-}3$ | 3 |
   | 5 | 11 |
   | 12 | 18 |

   **A** $y = \frac{x}{3}$

   **B** $y = 3x$

   **C** $y = x - 6$

   **D** $y = x + 6$

10. **WRITE Math** ▶ **Explain** how to find the value of $6y - 11$ for $y = 4$. (AF 1.2)

## Measurement and Geometry

**Test Tip**  Decide on a plan.

See item 11. You can calculate the surface area of the large rectangle in the center first, and then add the surface areas of the smaller rectangles.

**11.** What is the surface area of the box formed by the pattern below? (Grade 5 O—┑ MG 1.2)

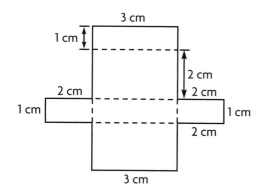

**A** 22 square centimeters

**B** 20 square centimeters

**C** 17 square centimeters

**D** 11 square centimeters

**12.** What is the measure of angle $c$ in the figure below? (Grade 5 O—┑ MG 2.2)

**A** 125°

**B** 115°

**C** 105°

**D** 65°

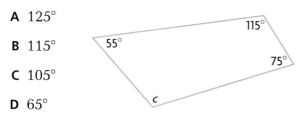

**13.** **WRITE Math** What's the Error? Aki says that the volume of a cube is 20 square centimeters. Describe his error. (Grade 5 O—┑ MG 1.3)

## Statistics, Data Analysis, and Probability

**14.** Keisha found the mean and median of this list of numbers. (SDAP 1.2)

$$3, 4, 8$$

If the number 3 were added to the list, then

**A** the mean and median would increase.

**B** the mean and median would decrease.

**C** the mean and median would stay the same.

**D** the median would stay the same and the mean would decrease.

**15.** How many more house sparrows than blue jays were spotted? (Grade 5 SDAP 1.0)

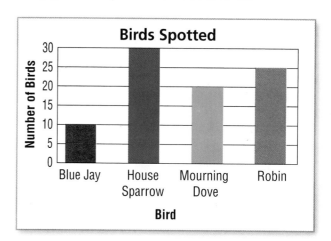

**A** 3          **C** 20

**B** 15          **D** 35

**16.** What is the mode of this list of numbers? (SDAP 1.1)

$$8, 4, 2, 8, 6, 5, 9$$

**A** 8          **C** 4

**B** 6          **D** 2

**17.** **WRITE Math** Explain how data added to a data set could affect the mean of the original data set. (SDAP 1.2)

# 12 Addition Equations

**The Big Idea** Properties and the concepts of algebra are used to solve addition equations.

## Investigate

Suppose you are an event coordinator at a Special Olympics competition. You have just received the status report. Choose two of the events below and show how you could use addition equations to find the number of athletes that have not yet competed.

| Event | Athletes Who Have Competed Already | Total Number of Athletes Competing |
|---|---|---|
| 100-m dash | 45 | 87 |
| High jump | 6 | 32 |
| Hurdles | 18 | 51 |
| Long jump | 98 | 107 |

Event Status Report: 2:30 P.M.

**CALIFORNIA FAST FACT**

**Special Olympics Southern California serves more than 11,000 children and adults, ranging in age from 8 to 80. Athletes receive at least eight weeks of training before a competition.**

**GO ONLINE**
**Technology**
Student pages are available in the Student eBook.

# Show What You Know

Check your understanding of important skills
needed for success in Chapter 12.

▶ **Write Expressions**

**Write an algebraic expression for the word expression.**

**1.** the total, $t$, increased by 25

**2.** the sum of $k$ and 4.5

**3.** 9 more than $\frac{2}{3}m$

**4.** the sum of $15s$ and 2.4

**5.** the sum of $5g$ and 3.5

**6.** the sum of $\frac{1}{2}j$ and $\frac{1}{3}k$

**7.** 1.5 more than $\frac{2}{3}p$

**8.** 8 more than $2a$

**9.** 34 more than a number, $n$

**10.** the number of students, $s$, increased by 5

**11.** 17 increased by a number, $p$

**12.** the number $x$, added to 12

**13.** 15 more than a number, $y$

**14.** 234 added to a number $m$

▶ **Subtract Whole Numbers, Decimals, and Fractions**

**Subtract.**

**15.** $2.3 - 1.1$

**16.** $\frac{2}{3} - \frac{1}{2}$

**17.** $1,225 - 925$

**18.** $12.45 - 10.23$

**19.** $20\frac{1}{2} - 10\frac{1}{4}$

**20.** $1\frac{4}{5} - \frac{1}{10}$

**21.** $10\frac{5}{6} - 8$

**22.** $10.2 - 8.3$

**23.** $234.4 - 102.3$

**24.** $18.75 - 2.6$

**25.** $2\frac{3}{4} - 1\frac{1}{3}$

**26.** $\frac{9}{10} - \frac{2}{3}$

**27.** $\frac{7}{8} - \frac{3}{4}$

**28.** $9.5 - 7.9$

**29.** $12\frac{1}{2} - 5\frac{3}{8}$

# VOCABULARY POWER

**CHAPTER VOCABULARY**

equation
Subtraction Property of Equality

**WARM-UP WORDS**

**equation** a statement that shows that two quantities are
equal

**Subtraction Property of Equality** the property that
states that if you subtract a number from both sides of an
equation, the two sides remain equal

**variable** a letter or symbol that stands for one or more
numbers

# 1 Words and Equations

OBJECTIVE: Write linear equations that model problem situations.

## Learn

**PROBLEM** It costs $59.60 to fill up the soccer team's van with gas. If gas costs $2.98 per gallon, how many gallons does it take to fill up the gas tank?

You can write an equation to help find the number of gallons. An **equation** is a statement that shows that two quantities are equal. These are examples of equations:

$$8 + 12 = 20 \qquad 15 \times 3 = 45 \qquad a - 3 = 14 \qquad d \div 3 = 7$$

### Example 1 Write an equation.

Use numbers, variables, and operations to translate words into equations.

**Step 1**

**Choose a variable.** Let $g$ represent the number of gallons of gas in the tank.

**Step 2**

Know the operation. Divide the total cost by the cost per gallon to find the number of gallons.

**Step 3**

Write an equation. Translate the words into an equation.

| gallons of gas in van's gas tank | equals | cost to fill up gas tank | divided by | price per gallon |
|:---:|:---:|:---:|:---:|:---:|
| ↓ | ↓ | ↓ | ↓ | ↓ |
| $g$ | = | 59.60 | ÷ | 2.98 |

So, an equation is $g = 59.60 \div 2.98$.

### Example 2 Write an equation for a word sentence.

Write an equation for the following word sentence:

The original amount in Jim's savings account plus the $219.00 he deposited totals $876.54.

Choose a variable. Let $a$ represent the original amount in Jim's savings account.

| original amount | plus | $219.00 deposited | totals | $876.54 |
|:---:|:---:|:---:|:---:|:---:|
| ↓ | ↓ | ↓ | ↓ | ↓ |
| $a$ | + | 219 | = | 876.54 |

So, an equation is $a + 219 = 876.54$.

AF 1.1 Write and solve one-step linear equations in one variable. *also* **AF 1.0, MR 2.4, MR 2.5, MR 3.1, MR 3.2**

**Choose the correct equation for the word sentence.**

**1.** 25 is 13 more than a number.

$$25 = n + 13$$
$$13 = n + 25$$

**2.** 10 times the number of balloons is 120.

$$10 + n = 120$$
$$10 \times n = 120$$

**Write an equation for the word sentence.**

✓ **3.** 6 fewer than a number is $12\frac{2}{3}$.

✓ **4.** The quotient of 20.7 and a number is 9.

**5.** ⌈TALK Math⌋ **Explain** how to translate a word sentence into an equation.

## Independent Practice and Problem Solving

**Write an equation for the word sentence.**

**6.** Two-thirds of a number is 18.

**7.** 56 fewer than $g$ is 40.

**8.** 18.5 is 75 more than twice a number.

**9.** 3.67 less than a number equals 46.33.

**10.** 8 times a number is 62.

**11.** The quotient of a number and 3 is 16.

**Write a word sentence for each equation.**

**12.** $x - 21 = 6$    **13.** $25 = \frac{1}{3}n$    **14.** $15g = 135$    **15.** $w \div 3\frac{1}{3} = \frac{5}{6}$    **16.** $g - 9 = 10$

**USE DATA** For 17–18, use the chart.

**17.** Write an equation you could use to find how many miles a hybrid SUV can travel in the city on 20 gal of gas.

**18.** A sedan traveled 504 mi on the highway on a full tank of gas. Write an equation to find the number of gallons the tank holds.

**19.** ⌈WRITE Math⌉ **What's the Error?** Tony is planning a 560-mi trip. He travels 313 mi the first day. He says that the equation $m - 313 = 560$ will help find the number of miles he has left on his trip. Describe his error.

### Fuel-Efficiency (mi per gal)

| Automobile | mi per gal city | mi per gal highway |
|---|---|---|
| Mini van | 19 | 26 |
| SUV | 22 | 26 |
| Hybrid SUV | 36 | 31 |
| Van | 14 | 17 |
| Sedan | 20 | 28 |

Fuel efficiency is measured in miles per gallon.

## Achieving the Standards

**20.** Which is greater, $\frac{2}{3}$ or $\frac{5}{7}$? (O➤ NS 1.1, p. 18)

**21.** Find the sum. $^-6 + {}^-7$ (O➤ NS 2.3, p. 144)

**22.** Write this word expression as an algebraic expression: a number increased by 6.

(AF 1.0, p. 280)

**23.** **Test Prep** Which represents the word sentence "12 less than a number, $n$, is 17"?

**A** $12n = 17$

**B** $\frac{n}{12} = 17$

**C** $n + 12 = 17$

**D** $n - 12 = 17$

# 2 Model Addition Equations

OBJECTIVE: Model solving one-step linear addition equations.

## Investigate

**Materials** ■ algebra tiles

You can use algebra tiles to model and solve addition equations.

**A** Model $x + 2 = 5$. Use a green rectangle to represent the variable. Use a yellow square to represent 1.

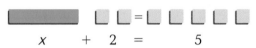

$$x \quad + \quad 2 \quad = \quad 5$$

**B** Solve $x + 2 = 5$. To solve the equation, you must get the variable alone on one side. To do this, take away 2 ones from each side.

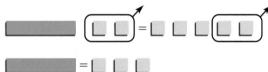

• What is the solution of the equation $x + 2 = 5$?

**C** Model $x + 2 = {}^-5$. Use a red tile to represent $^-1$.

$$x \quad + \quad 2 \quad = \quad {}^-5$$

**D** Solve $x + 2 = {}^-5$. A red tile and a yellow tile together form a zero pair and represent 0. To solve the equation, you must get the variable alone on one side. Use 2 red squares to make 2 zero pairs on the left side, and place 2 red squares on the right side.

• What is the solution of the equation $x + 2 = {}^-5$?

**E** Model and solve $x + 3 = {}^-6$.

## Draw Conclusions

1. What operation did you model in part B? in part D?

2. **Synthesis** What would you do to model and solve the equation $x + 9 = 12$?

○━┓ AF 1.1 Write and solve one-step linear equations in one variable. *also* AF 1.0, MR 2.4, MR 2.5, MR 3.2

## Connect

You can solve addition equations by drawing a model.

Let a rectangle represent the variable. Let an unfilled square represent 1 and a shaded square represent ⁻1.

**Solve $x + 3 = 7$.**

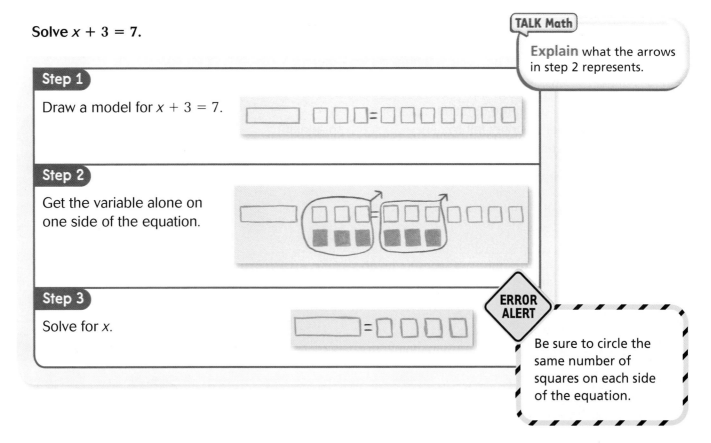

> **TALK Math**
>
> **Explain** what the arrows in step 2 represents.

**Step 1**

Draw a model for $x + 3 = 7$.

**Step 2**

Get the variable alone on one side of the equation.

**Step 3**

Solve for $x$.

> **ERROR ALERT**
>
> Be sure to circle the same number of squares on each side of the equation.

## Practice

**Copy the model and use it to solve the equation.**

1. $x + 3 = 4$

2. $5 = x + 2$

3. $x + 2 = {}^{-}7$

**Solve each equation by using algebra tiles or by drawing a picture.**

4. $x + 1 = 6$

5. $8 = x + 2$

6. $x + 6 = 6$

✓7. $x + 9 = 11$

8. $x + 1 = {}^{-}5$

9. ${}^{-}7 = x + 4$

10. $x + 3 = {}^{-}2$

✓11. $x + 3 = {}^{-}1$

12. $x + 2 = 4$

13. $6 = x + 4$

14. ${}^{-}8 = x + 3$

15. ${}^{-}4 = x + 3$

16. $7 = x + 6$

17. ${}^{-}3 = x + 6$

18. $x + 4 = 5$

19. $x + 3 = 7$

20. **WRITE Math** Explain how modeling with algebra tiles or pictures helps you solve addition equations.

# Solve Addition Equations

OBJECTIVE: Solve one-step linear addition equations.

## Quick Review

1. $14 - 6$
2. $4\frac{2}{3} - 1\frac{5}{6}$
3. $7.75 - 5.25$
4. $59 - 23.8$
5. $61.2 - 18.5$

## Vocabulary

**Subtraction Property of Equality**

## Learn

**PROBLEM** The world record for a dance marathon is 52 hr. If you have been dancing for 24 hr, how much longer do you have to dance to match the world record?

Solve the problem by using the addition equation $h + 24 = 52$, where $h$ is the number of hours left to dance. To solve an addition equation, use the inverse operation, subtraction.

| Subtraction Property of Equality | |
|---|---|
| If you subtract the same number from both sides of an equation, the two sides remain equal. | $7 = 7$ <br> $7 - 3 = 7 - 3$ <br> $4 = 4$ |

### Example 1  Solve and check. $h + 24 = 52$

| | |
|---|---|
| $h + 24 = 52$ | Write the equation. |
| $h + 24 - 24 = 52 - 24$ | Use the Subtraction Property of Equality. |
| $h + 0 = 28$ | Use the Identity Property. |
| $h = 28$ | |
| | |
| $h + 24 = 52$ | Check your solution. |
| $28 + 24 \stackrel{?}{=} 52$ | Replace $h$ with 28. |
| $52 = 52 \checkmark$ | The solution checks. |

So, you have to dance 28 hr longer.

• Solve $n + 13 = 37$.

Sometimes the variable will be on the right side of the equation.

### Example 2  Solve and check. $10 = 1.5 + x$

| | |
|---|---|
| $10 = 1.5 + x$ | Write the equation. |
| $10 = x + 1.5$ | Use the Commutative Property. |
| $10 - 1.5 = x + 1.5 - 1.5$ | Use the Subtraction Property of Equality. |
| $8.5 = x + 0$ | Use the Identity Property. |
| $8.5 = x$ | |
| | |
| $10 = 1.5 + x$ | Check your solution. |
| $10 \stackrel{?}{=} 1.5 + 8.5$ | Replace $x$ with 8.5. |
| $10 = 10 \checkmark$ | The solution checks. |

So, $x = 8.5$.

### Math Idea

When solving addition equations, subtract the number that is on the same side of the equation as the variable from both sides of the equation.

AF 1.1 Write and solve one-step linear equations in one variable. *also* NS 2.0, NS 2.1, AF 1.0, MR 2.4, MR 2.5, MR 3.2

Solve and check.

**1.** $x + 8 = 15$
$x + 8 - 8 = 15 - 8$
$x = \blacksquare$

**2.** $g + 23 = 20$
$g + 23 - 23 = 20 - 23$
$g = \blacksquare$

**3.** $a + 16 = {}^-25$
$a + 16 - \blacksquare = {}^-25 - \blacksquare$
$a = \blacksquare$

**4.** $42 = s + 20$
$42 - \blacksquare = s + 20 - \blacksquare$
$\blacksquare = s$

**5.** $b + 7 = 15$

**✓6.** $y + 6.7 = 9.8$

**7.** $8\frac{2}{5} = d + 2\frac{2}{5}$

**✓8.** ${}^-25 = k + 2$

**9.** **TALK Math** Explain how you get a variable alone on one side of an addition equation.

## Independent Practice and Problem Solving

Solve and check.

**10.** $n + 9 = 25$

**11.** $y + 11 = 26$

**12.** $16\frac{1}{2} = x + 4$

**13.** $4\frac{3}{4} + v = 12\frac{1}{2}$

**14.** $z + 6.8 = 15$

**15.** $18.7 + k = 32.2$

**16.** $p + 13 = {}^-42$

**17.** ${}^-12 = r + 12$

**18. Reasoning** Which of the numerical values 1, 2, and 3 is the solution of the equation $x + 5 = 7$?

**19.** What value of $k$ makes the equation $k + 5 = 9$ true?

**USE DATA** For 20–22, use the table at the right. Write an equation and solve.

**20.** Suppose you jump on a pogo stick 1,600 times in a row. How many more jumps would it take to match the world record?

**21.** Suppose you want to match the world record for eating ice cream. If you eat 100 g in the first 10 sec, and 98 g in the next 10 sec, how many more grams do you need to eat?

**22.** **WRITE Math** What's the Question? A friend tells you, "I made 3 sets of five hundred jumps each." The answer is 399 more jumps.

| World Records | | |
|---|---|---|
| **Name** | **Record** | **Amount** |
| Diego Siu | most ice cream eaten in 30 sec | 264g (9.3 oz) |
| Ashrita Furman | most pogo stick jumps | 1,899 jumps |
| Susan Williams | biggest bubble-gum bubble | 58.4 cm wide (23 in.) |

**23. ≡FAST FACT** • The record for the hottest temperature of 136° F was in El Azizia, Libya. This is 23° F greater than the record temperature in Canada. Write and solve an equation to find the record temperature in Canada.

## Achieving the Standards

**24.** Find the volume of a cube that measures 3 feet by 3 feet by 3 feet. (Grade 5 0—ᴨ MG 1.3)

**25.** How does the outlier 36 affect the mean when added to the data 3, 5, 7, 4, 6, and 2?
(SDAP 1.3, p. 226)

**26.** Write $7b$ as a word sentence. (AF 1.0, p. 280)

**27. Test Prep** Fran is buying an $88 bicycle in two payments. The first payment is $42. Which equation can be used to find the amount of the second payment, $x$?

**A** $42 = x - 88$     **C** $x + 88 = 42$

**B** $x - 88 = 42$     **D** $88 = 42 + x$

**Extra Practice** on page 310, Set B

# Problem Solving Workshop
## Strategy: Write an Equation

OBJECTIVE: Solve problems by using the strategy *write an equation*.

## Learn the Strategy

You can solve problems by using the strategy *write an equation* and carefully translating a word sentence into an equation.

### An equation can help you find a total.

Eric collects baseball cards as a hobby. On Monday, he went to a baseball card show and bought 37 baseball cards. On Tuesday, he went to a store and bought 29 baseball cards. How many cards did he buy all together?

Let *b* represent the total number of cards. Add to find the total number of cards.

$$\underset{\downarrow}{\text{total number of cards}} = \underset{\downarrow}{\text{number on Monday}} + \underset{\downarrow}{\text{number on Tuesday}}$$
$$b = 37 + 29$$

### An equation can help you find an addend.

Julie has a collection of music CDs. On Friday, she bought 13 CDs and then had a total of 123 CDs in her collection. How many CDs did she have in her collection on Thursday?

Let *n* represent the number of CDs in Julie's collection on Thursday. Add the 13 CDs she bought, and set the addition equal to the total of 123 CDs in her collection on Friday.

$$\underset{\downarrow}{\text{CDs on Thursday}} + \underset{\downarrow}{\text{CDs bought on Friday}} = \underset{\downarrow}{\text{total CDs in collection}}$$
$$n + 13 = 123$$

**TALK Math**

What would the next step be to solve the equation in the second problem above?

306

AF 1.1 Write and solve one-step linear equations in one variable. *also* AF 1.0, MR 1.0, MR 2.0, MR 2.4, MR 2.5, MR 3.0, MR 3.1, MR 3.2, MR 3.3

# Use the Strategy

**PROBLEM** Jerry and Kayla are playing a guessing game. Jerry has formed a number pattern by choosing two numbers and then adding them together to get the next number in the pattern. The beginning of his pattern is shown below.

9, 12, 21, 33, 54, . . .

9 + 12 ——→
12 + 21 ——→
21 + 33 ——→

Jerry starts with 9 and 12.
Next he adds 9 and 12 to get 21, then adds
12 and 21 to get 33, and 21 and 33 to get 54.

Jerry tells Kayla that two numbers next to each other in the pattern are 228 and 369. Kayla has to find the number that comes before 228. How can she find the number?

## Read to Understand

Reading Skill

- **Summarize what you are asked to find.**
- **What information is given?**

## Plan

- **What strategy can you use to solve the problem?**

  Write an equation to find the number that comes before 228.

## Solve

- **How can you use the strategy to solve the problem?**

  Choose a variable to represent the number before 228. Then write an equation to show the relationship between the variable and what you know.

  number before 228   plus   228   equals   369
  ↓                          ↓     ↓        ↓
  $a$                   +    228   =        369          Let $a$ represent the number before 228.

  $a + 228 = 369$                                         Write an equation.

  $a + 228 - 228 = 369 - 228$                             Use the Subtraction Property of Equality.

  $a + 0 = 141$                                           Use the Identity Property.

  $a = 141$

So, 141 comes before 228 in the pattern.

## Check

- **How can you check your answer?**
- **What other ways could you solve the problem?**

1. Pearl forms a number pattern by starting with 7 and 11. She adds 7 and 11 to get the next number, 18. Then she adds 11 and 18 to get the next number, 29. She continues the pattern:

   7, 11, 18, 29, 47, . . .

   In the pattern, the number 843 comes after 521. Find the number that comes before 521.

   **First,** choose a variable to represent the number before 521.

   Let $n$ represent the number before 521.

   **Then,** write an equation.

   $n + 521 = 843$

   **Finally,** solve the equation to find the number that comes before 521.

✓ 2. **What if** you need to find the seventh number in the pattern in Exercise 1? The sixth number is 76, and the eighth number is 199? Write and solve an equation to find the seventh number.

✓ 3. Fran is buying a $144 necklace in two payments. The first payment is $57. How much is her second payment?

## Problem Solving Strategy Practice

**Write an equation and solve.**

4. Lucas forms the number pattern on the right using the same pattern as in Exercise 1. He extends the pattern. Find the number that comes before 403.

   10, 13, 23, 36, 59, —, —, —, 403, 652, . . .

5. Eliana spent $5.75 on a sandwich and a drink. The drink cost $1.25. Find the cost of the sandwich.

6. Yura is 5 years older than his sister Marina. Marina is 11 years old. How old is Yura?

**USE DATA** For 7–9, use the temperature chart. Write an equation and solve.

7. In January, the average monthly high temperature in Los Angeles is 27°F higher than the average monthly high in Lake Tahoe. What is January's average monthly high temperature in Lake Tahoe?

8. In February, the average monthly low temperature in Los Angeles is 33°F higher than the average monthly low in Lake Tahoe. What is February's average monthly low temperature in Lake Tahoe?

| Average Monthly Temperatures Los Angeles, CA | | | |
|---|---|---|---|
| **Month** | **Jan** | **Feb** | **Mar** | **Apr** |
| **High (°F)** | 68° | 70° | 70° | 73° |
| **Low (°F)** | 48° | 50° | 52° | 54° |

9. **WRITE Math** **Explain** how you used the strategy *write an equation* to solve Exercise 6.

## Mixed Strategy Practice

### Problem-Solving STRATEGIES

Draw a Diagram

Make a Model or Act It Out

Make an Organized List

Find a Pattern

Make a Table or Graph

Predict and Test

Work Backward

Solve a Simpler Problem

Write an Equation

Use Logical Reasoning

**10. Reasoning** Salim owns 13 CDs. His brother, Lou, has 7 more CDs than he does. Their older sister, Bella, has more CDs than either of the boys. Together, the three siblings have 58 CDs. How many CDs does Bella have?

**11.** Caroline centered a table holding her CD player against a wall that was 13 ft wide. The table was $3\frac{1}{2}$ ft wide. How far was the left end of the table from the left end of the wall?

**USE DATA For 12–15, use the table.**

**12. Reasoning** A band wants to donate some of its royalties to charity. It could donate either $1 for every CD sold or all of its royalties for the first 12,000 CDs sold. How many CDs would the band need to sell for it to donate the same amount either way?

**13.** Advertising Company A can provide advertising for one third the cost shown in the table. Advertising Company B offers $1.50 less than the cost shown in the table. Which company can advertise for less? How much less?

**14. Pose a Problem** Write a problem using at least three of the data items in the table.

**15. Open Ended** Suppose you are in charge of advertising a CD that is expected to sell 800,000 copies. Find how much money you can spend. Decide the percents you will spend on ads using TV, radio, newspapers, magazines, and the Internet. Find the amount you will spend on each.

### Where The Money From A Single CD Sale Goes

| Expense | Amount |
|---|---|
| Artist Royalties | $1.60 |
| Manufacturing/Distribution | $1.70 |
| Label Overhead | $2.91 |
| Label Profit | $1.70 |
| Advertising | $2.40 |
| Musicians' Unions | $0.17 |
| Publishing Royalties | $0.82 |
| Retail Overhead | $3.88 |
| Retail Profit | $0.82 |

## CHALLENGE YOURSELF

A local store sells single CDs for half their original prices and CD box sets for three-fourths their original prices.

**16.** Malerie bought a discounted CD for $7.68 and two discounted box sets for $38.85 each. How much in all did she save off the regular prices?

**17.** In one week, the store sold 872 single CDs that originally cost $12.98 each, and it sold 64 box sets that originally cost $59.96 each. How much money did the store take in during this week?

# Extra Practice

## Set A  Write an equation for the word sentence. (pp. 300–301)

1. 4.34 less than a number equals 67.43.

2. Three quarters of a number is 12.

3. One half of a number is 34.4.

4. $k$ fewer than 48 is 36.

5. 145 is 45 more than four times a number.

6. 20.3 is 18 more than twice a number.

7. $\frac{1}{2}$ less than a number is $4\frac{3}{4}$.

8. $x$ more than 35 is 56.

9. Mark recorded 8 inches of rainfall for the past month. Suppose he records that amount for the next 4 months. Write an equation that could be used to find the total amount of rainfall during the next 4 months.

10. A concert sold out with 1,440 people attending its first performance. Suppose the concert is only half-full during the second performance. Write an equation that could be used to find the number of people attending the concert during the second performance.

### Write a word sentence for each equation. (pp. 300–301)

11. $a \times 2\frac{1}{2} = 5$

12. $y - 54 = 72$

13. $z \div \frac{1}{2} = 4$

14. $76 - p = 23$

15. $12c - 4 = 100$

16. $30 = \frac{1}{5}n$

17. $w - 32 = 3$

18. $3n = 10$

19. $20x = 140$

20. $d \div 3 = 9$

21. $x - 2 = 2\frac{1}{2}$

22. $24y + 7 = 2$

23. $7t = 150.5$

24. $a + \frac{3}{4} = 5\frac{1}{4}$

25. $2w - 3 = 11$

## Set B  Solve and check. (pp. 304–305)

1. $x + 3\frac{5}{6} = 10$

2. $45 = 11 + n$

3. $3 = 4 + s$

4. $12 + h = {}^-2$

5. $23 = 5 + v$

6. $r + 5\frac{1}{2} = 8$

7. $21.5 = d + 11.3$

8. $4\frac{1}{12} + q = 8$

9. $31.7 = q + 7.4$

10. $5\frac{7}{12} + k = 13$

11. $5\frac{5}{8} + p = 13$

12. $v + 11\frac{3}{4} = 23\frac{1}{2}$

13. $b + 12 = 44$

14. ${}^-19 = m - 6$

15. $4\frac{1}{3} = 3\frac{2}{3} + p$

16. ${}^-15 + r = {}^-22$

17. Roberto is buying a leather briefcase for $75. If he has given the cashier $28, how much more does he still have to pay for the briefcase? Write and solve an equation to find the amount he still has to pay.

18. Mr. Powell spent 12 hr at the gym this week, which is $4\frac{1}{2}$ hr longer than last week. Write and solve an equation to find the number of hours Mr. Powell spent at the gym last week.

19. For a science experiment, Minnie and Jennifer recorded the temperatures every Saturday for a month. On the first Saturday, the temperature was 3°C. This is 11° greater than the temperature on the second Saturday. Write and solve an equation to find the temperature on the second Saturday.

**Technology**
Use Harcourt Mega Math, Ice Station Exploration, *Arctic Algebra*, Levels *S*, and *Y*.

# Can You Solve It?

Finish

Start

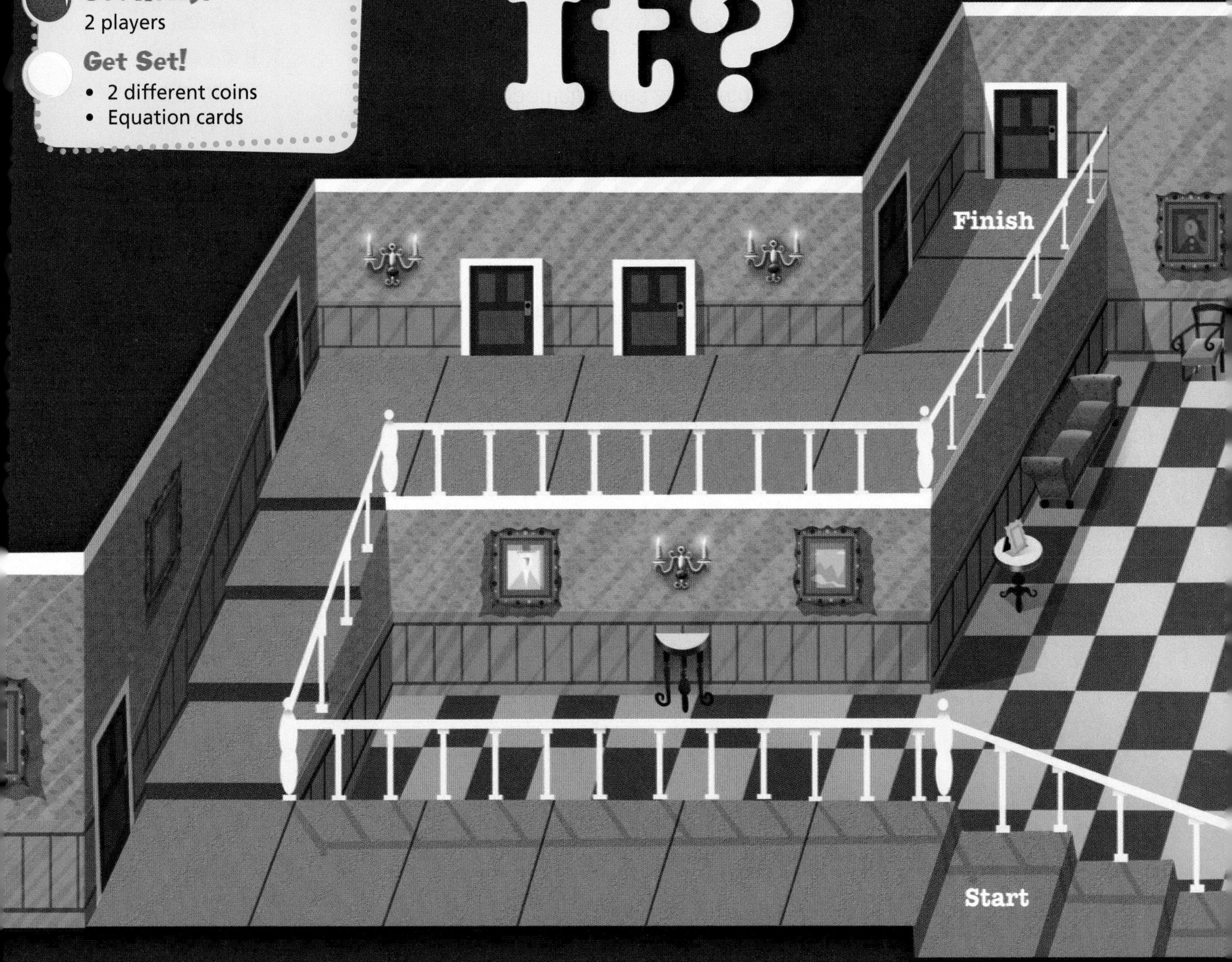

## Play!

- Shuffle the equation cards and place them facedown in a pile.

- Each player selects a coin and places the coin on START. Decide who will go first.

- The first player selects an equation card from the pile and solves the equation. The other player checks the answer.

- If the solution is correct, the player advances the number of spaces shown on the card. Play then passes to the other player.

- If the solution is incorrect, play passes to the other player.

- Play continues until a player's coin moves onto or beyond FINISH. The first player reaching or passing FINISH is the winner.

#  Chapter 12 Review/Test

## Check Vocabulary and Concepts

Choose the best term from the box.

1. An ___?___ is a statement that shows that two quantities are equal and includes an equals sign. (O—⊓ AF 1.1, p. 300)

2. The ___?___ states that if you subtract the same number from both sides of an equation, the two sides remain equal. (O—⊓ AF 1.1, p. 304)

## Check Skills

Write an equation for the word sentence. (O—⊓ AF 1.1, pp. 300-301)

3. 34.9 is 14 more than three times a number.

4. One half of a number is 16.

5. 4.45 subtracted from a number equals 12.89.

6. $k$ fewer than 89 is 40.

Write a word sentence for each equation. (O—⊓ AF 1.1, pp. 300-301)

7. $3h = 6$

8. $12 - x = 8$

9. $16k = 80$

10. $n - 45 = 672$

11. $n \div 4\frac{1}{4} = 1$

12. $12 = 2k + 70$

13. $5g - 12 = 96$

14. $a + 2\frac{1}{8} = 3$

Solve and check. (O—⊓ AF 1.1, pp. 304-305)

15. $14 = 6 + x$

16. $x + 2 = 5$

17. $x + 1 = {}^-3$

18. $^-5 = x + 3$

19. $x + 8 = 12$

20. $^-6 = x + 4$

21. $10 = x + 5$

22. $x + 7 = 7$

23. $72 = 12 + k$

24. $10.2 = x + 2$

25. $5\frac{1}{5} + v = 10$

26. $5 + n = {}^-12$

27. $x + 5\frac{1}{12} = 20$

28. $3.2 = s + 1.1$

29. $16 = w + 5$

30. $41.6 = r + 9.2$

## Check Problem Solving

Solve. (O—⊓ AF 1.1, MR 2.0, MR 2.4, pp. 306-309)

31. Christie formed the number pattern 3, 8, 11, 19, 30, ___, ___, 128, 207 by adding the two previous numbers to get the next number. Find the number that comes right before 128 in the pattern.

32. John and Sam collected a total of 105 baseball cards. John collected 41 baseball cards. How many baseball cards did Sam collect?

33. **WRITE Math** ▶ **Explain** how you could use the strategy *write an equation* to solve Problem 32.

# Enrich • Absolute Value Equations

## THINK POSITIVE!

Recall that since ⁻3 and and 3 are both 3 units from 0 on a number line, the absolute value of ⁻3 is 3 and the absolute value of 3 is 3. This suggests that an equation like $|x| = 2$ will have two solutions. The solutions will be the numbers whose distance from 0 on the number line is 2.

## Two Sides to Every Story

> **A** Solve $|x| = 2$.
>
> **Think:** Find numbers whose absolute value is 2.
>
> $|2| = 2$ and $|⁻2| = 2$

So, $x = ⁻2$ and $x = 2$.

> **B** Solve $|x| + 3 = 8$.
>
> | **Step 1** | **Step 2** |
> |---|---|
> | Begin by solving as you would an addition equation. Get $\lvert x \rvert$ by itself on one side of the equation.<br><br>$\lvert x \rvert + 3 = 8$<br>$\lvert x \rvert + 3 - 3 = 8 - 3$<br>$\lvert x \rvert = 5$ | Find numbers whose absolute value is 5.<br><br>$\lvert 5 \rvert = 5$ and $\lvert ⁻5 \rvert = 5$ |

So, $x = ⁻5$ and $x = 5$.

## Here We Go

**Solve for x.**

1. $|x| = 18$
2. $|x| = 92$
3. $|x| + 4 = 16$
4. $|x| + 17 = 32$
5. $15 + |x| = 16$

6. $41 + |x| = 75$
7. $2.3 + |x| = 7.7$
8. $19.7 + |x| = 29.6$
9. $|x| + 3\frac{1}{4} = 5\frac{1}{2}$
10. $|x| + 12\frac{3}{5} = 15\frac{2}{3}$

## Tell It Like It Is

**WRITE Math** ▸ **Explain** why there are two solutions for some absolute value equations.

## Number Sense

**1.** Which list of numbers is ordered from *greatest* to *least*? (○━┓ NS 1.1)

**A** $\frac{3}{8}, \frac{3}{7}, \frac{3}{11}, \frac{3}{5}$

**B** $\frac{3}{7}, \frac{3}{5}, \frac{3}{11}, \frac{3}{8}$

**C** $\frac{3}{11}, \frac{3}{8}, \frac{3}{7}, \frac{3}{5}$

**D** $\frac{3}{5}, \frac{3}{7}, \frac{3}{8}, \frac{3}{11}$

**2.** Which point shows the location of $\frac{1}{2}$ on the number line? (○━┓ NS 1.1)

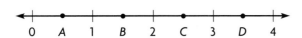

**A** point *A*

**B** point *B*

**C** point *C*

**D** point *D*

**3.** $16 \div {}^-4 =$     (○━┓ NS 2.3)

**A** 12

**B** 4

**C** $\frac{-1}{4}$

**D** $^-4$

**4.** What is the greatest common divisor of 24, 32, and 64? (○━┓ NS 2.4)

**A** 12        **C** 6

**B** 8         **D** 4

**5.** ▐ WRITE Math ▶ **Explain** how to find the product of $\frac{1}{2}$ and $\frac{5}{6}$. (NS 2.1)

## Algebra and Functions

**6.** The Desmond family went on vacation. They started with $1,500. If they spent $175 each day, which expression represents how much money they had left after *n* days? (AF 1.2)

**A** 1,325*n*       **C** 175*n*

**B** $1,500 - 175n$    **D** $1,500 + 175n$

**7.** Mr. Judson had some change in his pocket. After his wife gave him $0.55, Mr. Judson had $5.25 altogether. Which equation can he use to find the original amount of money, *d*, he had in his pocket? (○━┓ AF 1.1)

**A** $d + 0.55 = 5.25$

**B** $5.25 = d - 0.55$

**C** $d = 5.25 \times 0.55$

**D** $d + 5.25 = 0.55$

**8.** The table below shows how many medals the United States won at the 2006 Winter Olympics.

| Medal Count | | | | |
|---|---|---|---|---|
| Country | Gold | Silver | Bronze | Total |
| United States | 9 | *s* | 7 | 25 |

Which equation could be used to find the number of silver medals won by the United States? (○━┓ AF 1.1)

**A** $s + 17 = 25$     **C** $s + 7 = 25$

**B** $s + 9 = 25$      **D** $s + 16 = 25$

**9.** ▐ WRITE Math ▶ **Explain** how to solve the equation $g + 1\frac{1}{3} = 3$ and how to check your answer. (○━┓ AF 1.1)

## Measurement and Geometry

10. In the figure below, *ABCD* is a parallelogram.

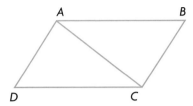

   If the area of triangle *ABC* is 18 square inches, what is the area of *ABCD*? (Grade 5 O—¬ MG 1.1)

   A  9 square inches

   B  18 square inches

   C  27 square inches

   D  36 square inches

 **Test Tip** **Get the information you need.**

See item 11. Triangles are classified by sides and angles. What do you know about the sum of this triangle's angles?

11. Triangle *MNO* is a right triangle. Angle *N* measures 60°. What is the measure of angle *O*? (Grade 5 O—¬ MG 2.2)

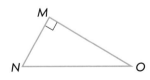

   A  15°            C  60°

   B  30°            D  90°

12. **WRITE Math** **What's the Error?** Darren says that a right triangle can have an obtuse angle. Is he correct? **Explain** your reasoning.
    (Grade 5 O—¬ MG 2.2)

## Statistics, Data Analysis, and Probability

13. Tyrell scored the following point totals in 5 dart games.

   $$85, 92, 110, 123, 145$$

   What is the median of the data?
   (SDAP 1.1)

   A  66            C  110

   B  85            D  111

14. The table shows the annual profit for five companies.

| Annual Profits | |
|---|---|
| **Company** | **Profit** |
| I | $150,000 |
| II | $120,000 |
| III | $100,000 |
| IV | $175,000 |
| V | $150,000 |

   Which statement is valid about the annual profits of these five companies?
   (O—¬ SDAP 2.5)

   A  Companies I and IV made the same profit.

   B  No company made less than $125,000 profit.

   C  No company made more than $150,000 profit.

   D  Company IV made $25,000 more profit than Company I.

15. **WRITE Math** **Explain** how to calculate the mean of a set of data. (SDAP 1.1)

# 13 Subtraction Equations

**The Big Idea** Properties and the concepts of algebra are used to solve subtraction equations.

The Bixby Creek Bridge, commonly referred to as Bixby Bridge, is 260 ft above the water and more than 700 ft long. The bridge is 18 mi south of Carmel.

## Investigate

Suppose you are a construction worker repaving bridges. For each bridge, you know the length of the main span and the length of the side spans. Choose two of the bridges at the right, and show how you can use a subtraction equation to find the total length of the bridge.

### California Bridge Lengths

| Names | Side Spans (in feet) | Main Span (in feet) |
|---|---|---|
| Golden Gate Bridge | 2,250 | 4,200 |
| West Bay Bridge | 0 | 2,310 |
| Vincent Thomas Bridge | 1,012 | 1,500 |

**Technology**
Student pages are available in the Student eBook.

# Show What You Know

Check your understanding of important skills
needed for success in Chapter 13.

▶ **Add Whole Numbers, Decimals, and Fractions**

**Add.**

1. $4.5 + 3.1$

2. $\frac{3}{4} + \frac{1}{2}$

3. $1{,}034 + 923$

4. $13\frac{1}{4} + 3\frac{1}{6}$

5. $1\frac{4}{5} + \frac{1}{15}$

6. $10\frac{5}{6} + 2$

7. $123.4 + 10.23$

8. $10.23 + 3.89$

9. $20 + 12.34$

▶ **Mental Math and Equations**

**Solve each equation by using mental math.**

10. $c + 6 = 9$

11. $2 = v - 9$

12. $q + 6 = 67$

13. $b - 2 = 7$

14. $r - 3 = 21$

15. $12 = p - 8$

16. $x - 6 = 11$

17. $9 = t + 4$

18. $25 = 10 + w$

▶ **Write Expressions**

**Write an algebraic expression for the word expression.**

19. the total, $t$, reduced by 12

20. $k$ decreased by 5

21. 4.53 less than a number, $x$

22. the difference of 23 and $h$

23. 78 fewer than $s$

24. $b$ reduced by 234

25. a number, $n$, decreased by 175

26. 27 decreased by a number $y$

# VOCABULARY POWER

**CHAPTER VOCABULARY**

**Addition Property of Equality**

**WARM-UP WORDS**

**Addition Property of Equality** the property that states
that if you add the same number to both sides of an
equation, the sides remain equal

**equation** a statement that shows that two quantities
are equal

**Identity Property of Addition** the property that states
that the sum of zero and any number is that number

# 1 Model Subtraction Equations

**OBJECTIVE:** Model solving one-step linear subtraction equations.

**Quick Review**

Add.

1. $24 + 8$
2. $6 + 9$
3. $73 + 25.5$
4. $43 + {}^-7$
5. $10 + {}^-60$

## Investigate

**Materials** ■ algebra tiles

You can use algebra tiles to model and solve subtraction equations.

**Ⓐ** Model and solve $x - 3 = 5$. Use a green rectangle to represent the variable. Use a yellow square to represent 1 and a red square to represent $^-1$.

$$x \quad - \quad 3 \quad = \quad 5$$

**Ⓑ** To solve the equation, you must get the variable alone on one side. Use 3 yellow squares to make 3 zero pairs on the left side, and place 3 more yellow squares on the right side.

- What is the solution of the equation $x - 3 = 5$?

**Ⓒ** Model and solve $x - 4 = 10$.

## Draw Conclusions

1. What is the solution of $x - 4 = 10$?

2. What operation did you model in part B?

3. **Synthesis** Explain how you would model and solve the equation $x - 2 = 8$.

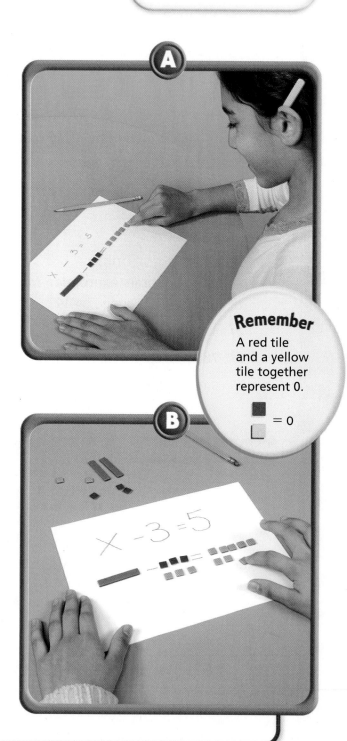

**Remember**

A red tile and a yellow tile together represent 0.

■ □ = 0

0—⊓ **AF 1.1** Write and solve one-step linear equations in one variable. *also* **AF 1.0, MR 2.0, MR 2.4, MR 2.5, MR 3.2**

## Connect

You can solve subtraction equations by drawing a model.

Let a rectangle represent the variable. Let an unfilled square represent 1 and a shaded square represent $^-1$.

Solve $x - 3 = 7$.

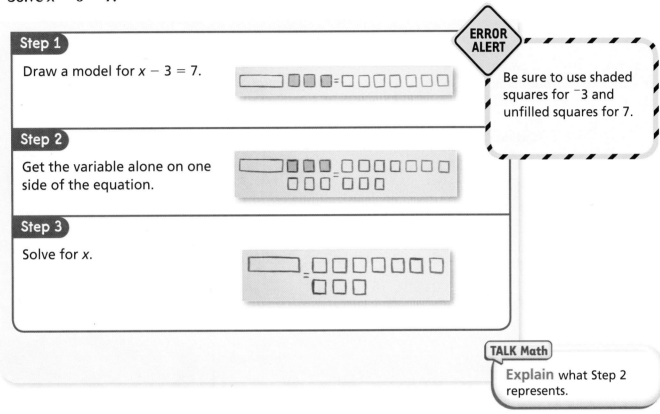

**Step 1**

Draw a model for $x - 3 = 7$.

**ERROR ALERT**

Be sure to use shaded squares for $^-3$ and unfilled squares for 7.

**Step 2**

Get the variable alone on one side of the equation.

**Step 3**

Solve for $x$.

**TALK Math**

**Explain** what Step 2 represents.

## Practice

**Copy the model and use it to solve the equation.**

**1.** $x - 3 = 6$

**2.** $5 = x - 2$

**3.** $x - 2 = 3$

**Solve each equation by using algebra tiles or by drawing a picture.**

**4.** $x - 7 = 6$
**5.** $x - 3 = 1$
**6.** $x - 6 = 6$
**✓7.** $x - 1 = 5$

**8.** $x - 9 = 11$
**9.** $7 = x - 4$
**10.** $x - 5 = 2$
**✓11.** $8 = x - 2$

**12.** $x - 2 = 4$
**13.** $x - 3 = 1$
**14.** $x - 1 = 6$
**15.** $x - 4 = {}^-2$

**16.** $x - 5 = {}^-1$
**17.** $x - 2 = {}^-7$
**18.** $x - 4 = 3$
**19.** $x - 5 = {}^-5$

**20.** **WRITE Math** **Explain** how modeling with algebra tiles or pictures helps you solve subtraction equations.

# Solve Subtraction Equations

OBJECTIVE: Solve one-step linear subtraction equations.

## Quick Review

Solve.
1. $x + 14 = 86$
2. $5\frac{2}{3} = p + 3\frac{5}{6}$
3. $9.75 = y + 4.25$
4. $14.7 = 12.8 + w$
5. $a + 45.6 = 65.4$

## Vocabulary

Addition Property of Equality

## Learn

**PROBLEM** A cable station manager at KIDS-TV hired 12 students and had to turn away 36 students. How many students wanted to work at KIDS-TV? Solve the problem by using the subtraction equation $s - 36 = 12$, where $s$ is the total number of students who applied. To solve a subtraction equation, use the inverse operation, addition.

**Addition Property of Equality**

If you add the same number to both sides of an equation, the two sides remain equal.

$$7 = 7$$
$$7 + 2 = 7 + 2$$
$$9 = 9$$

### Example 1 Solve and check. $s - 36 = 12$

| | |
|---|---|
| $s - 36 = 12$ | Write the equation. |
| $s - 36 + 36 = 12 + 36$ | Use the Addition Property of Equality. |
| $s + 0 = 48$ | Use the Identity Property. |
| $s = 48$ | |
| $s - 36 = 12$ | Check your solution. |
| $48 - 36 \stackrel{?}{=} 12$ | Replace $s$ with 48. |
| $12 = 12$ ✓ | The solution checks. |

So, 48 students wanted to work at KIDS-TV.

• Solve $x - 9 = {}^-23$.

Sometimes the variable will be on the right side of the equation.

### Example 2 Solve and check. $6.5 = d - 15.5$

| | |
|---|---|
| $6.5 = d - 15.5$ | Write the equation. |
| $6.5 + 15.5 = d - 15.5 + 15.5$ | Use the Addition Property of Equality. |
| $22 = d + 0$ | Use the Identity Property. |
| $22 = d$ | |
| $6.5 = d - 15.5$ | Check your solution. |
| $6.5 \stackrel{?}{=} 22 - 15.5$ | Replace $d$ with 22. |
| $6.5 = 6.5$ ✓ | The solution checks. |

So, $d = 22$.

AF 1.1 Write and solve one-step linear equations in one variable. *also* NS 2.0, NS 2.1, AF 1.0, MR 2.4, MR 2.5, MR 3.2

Solve and check.

**1.** $x - 7 = 15$
$x - 7 + 7 = 15 + 7$
$x = \blacksquare$

**2.** $a - 32 = {}^-49$
$a - 32 + 32 = {}^-49 + 32$
$a = \blacksquare$

**3.** $78 = w - 39$
$78 + \blacksquare = w - 39 + \blacksquare$
$w = \blacksquare$

**4.** $9.8 = d - 7.2$
$9.8 + \blacksquare = d - 7.2 + \blacksquare$
$d = \blacksquare$

**✓5.** $y - 4.9 = 9.1$

**6.** $10 = p - 6\frac{5}{8}$

**7.** $^-52.2 = s - 14.8$

**✓8.** $w - 2\frac{3}{5} = 4\frac{2}{5}$

**9.** **TALK Math** Explain how to use the Addition Property of Equality to solve $x - 15 = {}^-6$.

Solve and check.

**10.** $n - 26 = 11$

**11.** $22 = x - 9$

**12.** $z - \frac{3}{5} = \frac{5}{6}$

**13.** $a - 9\frac{2}{3} = 15\frac{1}{3}$

**14.** $y - 3.7 = 13.8$

**15.** $2.5 = k - 9.9$

**16.** $p - 22 = {}^-30$

**17.** $^-6 = m - 12$

**18.** **Reasoning** Which of the numerical values 19, 20, and 21, is the solution of the equation $x - 12 = 7$?

**19.** What value of $y$ makes the equation $y - 6 = {}^-10$ true?

**USE DATA** For 20–21, use the bar graph. Write an equation and solve it.

**20.** The amount of water used for showering is 7.5 gal less than the amount used for washing clothes. How many gallons are used for washing clothes?

**21.** The amount of water that the average person drinks each week, minus $\frac{1}{5}$ of the water used washing dishes daily, is equal to $\frac{1}{2}$ gal. How much water does the average person drink in a week?

**22.** **WRITE Math** What's the Error? Rolando says that the solution of the equation $x - 3 = 12$ is $x = 9$. Find his error and then solve the equation.

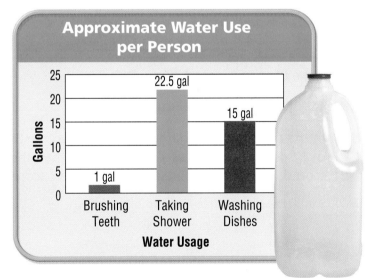

Approximate Water Use per Person

Gallons — Brushing Teeth 1 gal, Taking Shower 22.5 gal, Washing Dishes 15 gal
Water Usage

**23.** Sherri's store logo says "best fruit," because everyone in her family agrees that her fruit is the best. Is Sherri's claim valid?
(O–¬ SDAP 2.5, p. 208)

**24.** Order the numbers from least to greatest.
3, $^-2$, 2, $^-3$, $^-1$, 0 (O–¬ NS 1.0, p. 126)

**25.** Write an equation for the word sentence "15 less than $x$ is 36." (O–¬ AF 1.1, p. 300)

**26.** **Test Prep** Which is the solution of $y - 12 = 16$?

**A** $y = {}^-28$

**C** $y = 4$

**B** $y = {}^-4$

**D** $y = 28$

# Addition and Subtraction Equations

OBJECTIVE: Solve one-step linear addition and subtraction equations.

## Learn

**PROBLEM** The Bears scored 59 points in a playoff basketball game. This was 14 points fewer than their opponents, the Panthers, scored. How many points did the Panthers score?

### Example 1 Subtraction Equation

You can solve this problem by writing and solving an equation.

| Panthers' score | minus | 14 points | equals | Bears' score. |
|---|---|---|---|---|
| ↓ | ↓ | ↓ | ↓ | ↓ |
| $p$ | $-$ | $14$ | $=$ | $59$ |

| | |
|---|---|
| $p - 14 = 59$ | Write the equation. |
| $p - 14 + 14 = 59 + 14$ | Use the Addition Property of Equality. |
| $p + 0 = 73$ | Use the Identity Property. |
| $p = 73$ | |
| $p - 14 = 59$ | Check your solution. |
| $73 - 14 \overset{?}{=} 59$ | Replace $p$ with 73. |
| $59 = 59 \checkmark$ | The solution checks. |

**Math Idea**
When using the Addition or Subtraction Property of Equality, remember to add or subtract the same number from each side of an equation so that the two sides remain equal.

So, the Panthers scored 73 points.

### Example 2 Addition Equation

In the championship game, the Eagles won with a score of 67 points, which was 13 points more than the Panthers scored. How many points did the Panthers score?

| Panthers' score | plus | 13 points | equals | Eagles' score. |
|---|---|---|---|---|
| ↓ | ↓ | ↓ | ↓ | ↓ |
| $p$ | $+$ | $13$ | $=$ | $67$ |

| | |
|---|---|
| $p + 13 = 67$ | Write the equation. |
| $p + 13 - 13 = 67 - 13$ | Use the Subtraction Property of Equality. |
| $p + 0 = 54$ | Use the Identity Property. |
| $p = 54$ | |
| $p + 13 = 67$ | Check your solution. |
| $54 + 13 \overset{?}{=} 67$ | Replace $p$ with 54. |
| $67 = 67 \checkmark$ | The solution checks. |

So, the Panthers scored 54 points.

AF 1.1 Write and solve one-step linear equations in one variable. *also* NS 2.0, NS 2.1, NS 2.3, AF 1.0, MR 2.4, MR 2.5, MR 3.2

1. At a track meet, there was a 24-point difference between first place and second place. First place went to the Chavez Middle School track team. The second-place team earned 96 points. How many points did the Chavez team earn?

| Chavez score | minus | 24 | equals | 2nd place score |
|:---:|:---:|:---:|:---:|:---:|
| ↓ | ↓ | ↓ | ↓ | ↓ |
| $c$ | $-$ | 24 | $=$ | 96 |

$$c - 24 = 96$$
$$c - 24 + 24 = 96 + 24$$
$$c + 0 = \blacksquare$$

**Solve and check.**

✅ **2.** $q - 36 = 19$     **3.** $d - 7.25 = 10.75$     **4.** $v + 4\frac{3}{5} = 5\frac{1}{10}$     ✅ **5.** $a + 15 = {}^{-}3$

**6.** **TALK Math** **Explain** how to decide whether to use an addition equation or a subtraction equation to solve a word problem.

## Independent Practice and Problem Solving

**Solve and check.**

**7.** $n + 15 = 36$     **8.** $y - 12 = 17$     **9.** $x + 4.7 = 16.5$     **10.** $q + 8 = {}^{-}25$

**11.** $6 + n = 36$     **12.** ${}^{-}6 = r - 13$     **13.** $z - \frac{2}{3} = \frac{3}{4}$     **14.** $x - 3\frac{3}{8} = 9\frac{5}{12}$

**USE DATA** For 15–17, use the table. Write an equation and solve.

**15.** The Bulls lost to the Knights by 15 points. What was the final score for the Bulls?

**16.** The Tigers beat the Cubs by 7 points. What was the final score for the Cubs?

**17.** **Pose a Problem** Look back at Problem 15. Write and solve a similar problem about the scores of the Hawks and the Cougars.

**Football Scores**

| Knights 31 | Bulls ▨ |
|:---|:---|
| Tigers 24 | Cubs ▨ |
| Hawks 42 | Cougars ▨ |

**18.** **≡FAST FACT** The length of a football field is 120 yd. The width of a football field is $66\frac{2}{3}$ yd less than the length. Is the width of a football field greater than 60 yd?

**19.** **WRITE Math** **What's the Question?** Lisa and Rodney went to a football game. Lisa spent $8.50 at the concession stand. Rodney spent $3.75 more than Lisa. The answer is $12.25.

## Achieving the Standards

**20.** Evaluate $12 - 3^2 \times (8 - 24)$. (AF 1.3, p. 276)

**21.** Two angles of a triangle measure $37°$ and $59°$. What is the measure of the third angle of the triangle? (Grade 5 ⊶ MG 2.2)

**22.** Evaluate $9n$ for $n = 7.5$. (AF 1.2, p. 284)

**23.** Sarah collects money for the track team. She keeps the money in a box. After she put $2.25 in the box, Sarah had a total of $19.75. Which is the original amount of money in the box?

  **A** $2.25           **C** $19.75

  **B** $17.50         **D** $22.00

**Extra Practice** on page 326, Set B

**CD ROM** **Technology** Use Harcourt Mega Math, Ice Station Exploration, *Arctic Algebra,* Levels S, Y, Z. **Chapter 13** 323

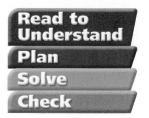

## LESSON 4

# Problem Solving Workshop
# Strategy: Compare Strategies

**OBJECTIVE:** Use the strategies *predict and test* and *write an equation* to solve problems.

## Use the Strategy

**PROBLEM** A school club is building a 450-square-foot house out of bales of straw. Several farmers donated $3\frac{1}{4}$ tons of straw bales. The club must get an additional $1\frac{1}{8}$ tons. How many tons of straw bales does the club need in all to build the house?

### Read to Understand

Reading Skill

• **What you are asked to find?**

• **Identify the details that are given.**

• **Is there information you will not use? If so, what?**

### Plan

• **What strategy can you use to solve the problem?**

Use *predict and test* or *write an equation*.

### Solve

• **How can you use each strategy to solve the problem?**

**Predict and Test**

Predict a total number of tons.

| Predict | Test | |
|---------|------|---|
| $4\frac{1}{4}$ tons | $4\frac{1}{4} - 1\frac{1}{8} = 3\frac{1}{8}$ | too low, so revise |
| $4\frac{1}{2}$ tons | $4\frac{1}{2} - 1\frac{1}{8} = 3\frac{3}{8}$ | too high, so revise |
| $4\frac{3}{8}$ tons | $4\frac{3}{8} - 1\frac{1}{8} = 3\frac{1}{4}$ | correct |

**Write an Equation**

Write and solve an equation for the situation.

Total tons − tons donated = tons still needed.

$$\downarrow \qquad\qquad \downarrow \qquad\qquad \downarrow$$
$$x \quad - \quad 3\frac{1}{4} \quad = \quad 1\frac{1}{8}$$

$$x - 3\frac{1}{4} = 1\frac{1}{8}$$
$$x - 3\frac{1}{4} + 3\frac{1}{4} = 1\frac{1}{8} + 3\frac{1}{4}$$
$$x = 4\frac{3}{8}$$

So, the club needs $4\frac{3}{8}$ tons of straw bales in all.

### Check

• **How do you know the answer is correct?**

**324**

○━┓ **AF 1.1** Write and solve one-step linear equations in one variable. *also* **MR 1.0, MR 1.1, MR 2.0, MR 2.4, MR 2.5, MR 2.7, MR 3.0, MR 3.1, MR 3.2, MR 3.3**

### Problem-Solving STRATEGIES

Draw a Diagram
Make a Model or Act It Out
Make an Organized List
Find a Pattern
Make a Table or Graph
Predict and Test
Work Backward
Solve a Simpler Problem
Write an Equation
Use Logical Reasoning

1. The members of the club are waiting for the final layer of stucco on their straw bale house to dry. The total number of hours they need to wait is 5.5 hr less than the 18.75 hr it took to install the windows and doors. How many hours must they wait for the final layer of stucco to dry?

   **First,** write the equation $n + 5.5 = 18.75$.

   **Then,** solve the equation.

   **Finally,** check your solution.

2. **What if** it took 14.75 hr for the stucco to dry? How long did it take to install the windows and doors?

3. So far, the club members have used 6 gal of paint on the interior of the house. $3\frac{1}{2}$ gal of that paint was donated. How much paint did the members have to buy?

## Mixed Strategy Practice

4. Several volunteers are sorting through a pile of used floor tiles. Out of the 560 tiles, 105 are damaged. How many of the floor tiles are not damaged?

5. On the walls of the kitchen, a repeating pattern of 4 colored rectangular tiles is going to be installed. The colors are blue, green, red, and yellow. In how many ways can one set of these four different color tiles be arranged in one row?

6. The homeowners paid $40,000 for 25 acres surrounding the home. They want to buy 15 acres more at the same price per acre. How much will the 15 acres cost in all?

**USE DATA** For 7–8, use the cost chart.

7. Another building requires 200 bales of straw, and each bale weighs 50 lb. What is the least possible amount that could be charged for 200 bales of straw?

8. The club has to buy $1\frac{1}{8}$ tons of straw. There are 40 bales in each ton. What is the most that the club might pay for the straw? (1 ton = 2,000 lb)

9. **Reasoning** Melani, Trevor, and Lee all worked on the straw bale house. Melani worked 15 hr more than Trevor, who worked twice as many hours as Lee. If Lee worked 20 hr, how many hours did Melanie work?

10. **WRITE Math** **Explain** how using the problem solving strategies *predict and test* and *write an equation* are helpful when solving problem 4.

| Straw Bale Costs | | |
|---|---|---|
| store | per bale | per ton |
| A | $2.25 | $80 |
| B | $2.75 | $120 |
| C | $4.15 | $160 |

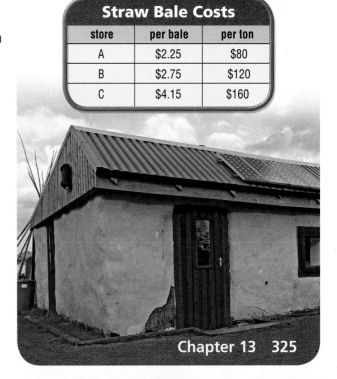

# Extra Practice

**Set A** Solve and check. (pp. 320–321)

1. $n - 13 = 10$
2. $s - 7\frac{1}{3} = 14\frac{2}{3}$
3. $27 = a - 52$
4. $4.5 = y - 2.5$
5. $k - 1\frac{1}{2} = 5$
6. $x - 26 = 2$
7. $14.3 = b - 2.4$
8. $8 = k - 17$
9. $m - 9\frac{1}{6} = 12\frac{5}{6}$
10. $a - 5 = 7$
11. $10 = q - 7\frac{1}{5}$
12. $7.5 = y - 21.7$
13. $91 = x - 2$
14. $2\frac{5}{8} = x - 1\frac{1}{8}$
15. $15.2 = n - 21.2$
16. $7\frac{1}{2} = a - \frac{1}{2}$
17. $k - 21.3 = 10.5$
18. $x - 9 = 19$
19. $36 = n - 32$
20. $21\frac{1}{8} = a - 14$
21. $^-27 = x - 12$

22. There are 14 seventh-grade students participating in the school musical. This is 8 less than the number of sixth-graders. Write and solve an equation to find the number of sixth-graders in the musical.

23. At a junior robotics competition, first place went to the team from Einstein Junior High. The second place team finished 10 points behind, earning 125 points. Write and solve an equation to find how many points the team from Einstein Junior High earned?

**Set B** Solve and check. (pp. 322-323)

1. $s - 11 = 22$
2. $12 + n = 21$
3. $5\frac{1}{4} = x - 7\frac{3}{4}$
4. $x - 2\frac{1}{5} = 9\frac{3}{5}$
5. $a + 6 = {}^-12$
6. $9 + q = {}^-31$
7. $k - 4\frac{1}{4} = 2$
8. $5 = m - 4.2$
9. $16 + n = 35$
10. $a - 7 = {}^-16$
11. $a + 12\frac{4}{5} = 102$
12. $38 = n - 42$
13. $3.9 = 2.1 + k$
14. $x - 2 = {}^-4$
15. $y + 5 = {}^-15$
16. $v - 3\frac{1}{3} = 16\frac{2}{3}$
17. $6\frac{4}{5} = k - 1\frac{1}{5}$
18. $7 + a = 96$
19. $z - 1\frac{1}{16} = 9\frac{1}{8}$
20. $4.5 + x = 9.2$
21. $\frac{1}{2} + y = \frac{5}{6}$

22. Mrs. Sanchez keeps the money she collects for the local nature center in a large envelope. After she put $15.25 in the envelope, Mrs. Sanchez had a total of $34.75. Write and solve an equation to find the amount of money originally in the envelope.

23. Sam is 4 years older than Keisha, who is 2 years younger than Jim. Jim is 12 years old. Write and solve an equation to find Keisha's age. Then write and solve another equation to find Sam's age.

**Technology**
CD ROM
Use Harcourt Mega Math, Ice Station Exploration, *Arctic Algebra*, Levels S, Y, and Z.

# Mystery Equation

**On Your Mark!**
2 players

**Get Set!**
- Mystery Equation game cards
- Watch or timer

$$b - \boxed{\phantom{XX}} = \boxed{\phantom{XXX}}$$

**Go!**

- Shuffle the game cards, and place them facedown in a pile.

- Toss a coin to determine who will be Player 1.

- Player 2 draws two game cards from the pile and places them in the empty spaces in the equation.

- Player 1 has one minute to solve the equation. Player 2 keeps time.

- Player 2 checks the answer. If the answer is correct, Player 1 gets one point. If the answer is incorrect, no points are awarded.

- The cards on the board are returned to the pile, which is reshuffled, and play passes to Player 2.

- Play continues until a player wins by earning 5 points.

Chapter 13 Review/Test

## Check Vocabulary and Concepts

**Choose the best term from the box.**

1. The __?__ states that if you add the same number to both sides of an equation, the two sides remain equal. (⊙━┓ AF 1.1, p. 320)

2. Explain how you can use algebra tiles to solve the subtraction equation $x - 4 = 5$. (⊙━┓ AF 1.1, pp. 318–319)

## Check Skills

**Solve and check.** (⊙━┓ AF 1.1, pp. 320–321)

3. $x - 9 = 2$
4. $a - 7 = 15$
5. $k - 7\frac{2}{3} = 10\frac{1}{3}$
6. $7.6 = d - 5.2$

7. $36 = q - 1\frac{3}{4}$
8. $s - 1\frac{3}{4} = 7\frac{1}{4}$
9. $72.2 = y - 21.2$
10. $t - 3.2 = 8.2$

11. $w - 9\frac{3}{5} = 4\frac{1}{5}$
12. $b - 4 = 6\frac{3}{8}$
13. $10 = k - 5.3$
14. $6.5 = y - 2.2$

**Solve and check.** (⊙━┓ AF 1.1, pp. 322–323)

15. $s - 13 = 24$
16. $x + 5 = {}^-21.5$
17. $15 + k = 30$
18. $x - 2\frac{1}{5} = 7\frac{2}{5}$

19. $9 + s = {}^-20$
20. $w - 12 = {}^-8$
21. $d + 2\frac{1}{2} = 6$
22. $w - 8 = {}^-12$

23. $a + 12 = 38$
24. $x + 2\frac{3}{5} = 4\frac{1}{10}$
25. $m - 2.25 = 19.75$
26. $12.5 + s = 21.2$

27. $b - 6 = {}^-6$
28. $7 + m = 14.15$
29. $p - 4 = 12$
30. ${}^-5 + r = 6$

## Check Problem Solving

**Solve.** (⊙━┓ AF 1.1, MR 2.0, MR 2.4, pp. 324–325)

31. Fourteen members of the student choir were not able to travel to the concert. The remaining 26 members gave a successful concert. How many members are there in the student choir?

32. Mr. Jones is in the waiting room at a doctor's office. He has already been waiting $1\frac{1}{2}$ hr. A nurse says he will need to wait another $\frac{3}{4}$ hr. How many hours must Mr. Jones wait to see the doctor?

33. **⟨WRITE Math⟩** **Explain** how using the strategies *predict and test* and *write an equation* could help you solve Problem 31.

**GO ONLINE. Technology** Use *Online Assessment.*

# Enrich • Equations
# Cryptography Revealed

Cryptography is a system of secret writing. For centuries, people have devised ways to send coded secret messages. You can take a basic code and secure it with an equation to send coded messages of your own. The charts below show two separate codes connected by an equation.

| | | | | | Values for $y$ | | | | | | | |
|---|---|---|---|---|---|---|---|---|---|---|---|---|
| A | B | C | D | E | F | G | H | I | J | K | L | M |
| 4 | 10 | 18 | 23 | -2 | 7 | 20 | 22 | 0 | 12 | 21 | 6 | 8 |
| N | O | P | Q | R | S | T | U | V | W | X | Y | Z |
| 16 | 2 | 14 | 19 | -1 | 11 | 15 | 3 | 9 | 17 | 1 | 13 | 5 |

| | | | | | Decoded Letters for $x$ | | | | | | | |
|---|---|---|---|---|---|---|---|---|---|---|---|---|
| A | B | C | D | E | F | G | H | I | J | K | L | M |
| 1 | 2 | 3 | 4 | 5 | 6 | 7 | 8 | 9 | 10 | 11 | 12 | 13 |
| N | O | P | Q | R | S | T | U | V | W | X | Y | Z |
| 14 | 15 | 16 | 17 | 18 | 19 | 20 | 21 | 22 | 23 | 24 | 25 | 26 |

To make the code difficult to crack, you need to have a secret key.

## Crack the Code

You have received a secret message: GLS WJXEH. The decoding equation is $x - 3 = y$. To decode the message, follow the steps below.

| Step 1 | Step 2 |
|---|---|
| $x - 3 = y$   Replace $y$ with $G$, the first | Look at the *Decoded-Letters-for-x* chart. |
| $x - 3 = G$   letter in the secret message. | Since $x = 23$, the corresponding letter is $W$. |
| $x - 3 = 20$   Replace $G$ with 20, its value | |
| $x = 23$   in the *Values-for-y* chart.   Solve for $x$. | So, the first letter in the secret message is $W$. |

Repeat Steps 1 and 2 for the rest of the letters in the secret message. So, the secret message is WIN TODAY.

## Use the Key

**Decode the message. Use the decoding equation $x - 3 = y$.**

1. LU HJC IES
2. TOEX WZLN
3. WZESM HJCT
4. WOEIZOT
5. ROVLOQO LS
6. HJCT XTOEBN
7. GJTM ZETX
8. UJT WZOB

## Make Your Own

WRITE Math ▶ **Explain** how to decode a secret message using an equation. Write your own coded message, and then show the key.

# Achieving the Standards
 **Chapters 1 – 13**

## Number Sense

**1.** Which fraction is closest to 0? (○━┓ NS 1.1)

  **A** $\dfrac{^-7}{12}$

  **B** $\dfrac{^-1}{3}$

  **C** $\dfrac{1}{4}$

  **D** $\dfrac{5}{6}$

**2.** Which point shows the location of $\dfrac{5}{2}$ on the number line? (○━┓ NS 1.1)

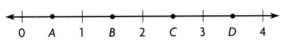

  **A** point $A$

  **B** point $B$

  **C** point $C$

  **D** point $D$

**3.** Which list of numbers is ordered from *greatest* to *least*? (○━┓ NS 1.1)

  **A** $\dfrac{1}{2}$, $2\dfrac{1}{2}$, 0.45, 0.045

  **B** $2\dfrac{1}{2}$, $\dfrac{1}{2}$, 0.045, 0.45

  **C** 0.045, 0.45, $\dfrac{1}{2}$, $2\dfrac{1}{2}$

  **D** $2\dfrac{1}{2}$, $\dfrac{1}{2}$, 0.45, 0.045

**4.** $2\dfrac{1}{2} \times \dfrac{4}{5} =$      (NS 2.1)

  **A** $\dfrac{2}{5}$

  **B** 2

  **C** $2\dfrac{1}{5}$

  **D** $3\dfrac{1}{5}$

**5.** **▐WRITE Math** ▶ **Explain** how to find the sum of $\dfrac{1}{2}$ and $\dfrac{5}{6}$. (NS 2.1)

## Algebra and Functions

**6.** Jamal had some change on his desk. After Mark gave him $0.35, Jamal had $2.15 in all. Write and solve an equation to find the amount of money, $m$, he had on his desk? (○━┓ AF 1.1)

  **A** $m = {^-}1.80$

  **B** $m = 0.75$

  **C** $m = 1.80$

  **D** $m = 6.14$

**7.** The table shows how many quarts of ice cream the Corner Ice Cream Store ordered last month.

| Corner Ice Cream Store | | | |
|---|---|---|---|
| Vanilla | Chocolate | Strawberry | Total |
| 8 | 14 | $s$ | 32 |

Which equation can you use to find the number of quarts of strawberry ice cream ordered by the store last month? (○━┓ AF 1.1)

  **A** $s + 8 = 32$

  **B** $s + 14 = 32$

  **C** $s + 22 = 32$

  **D** $s + 24 = 32$

**8.** What value of $d$ makes the following equation true? (○━┓ AF 1.1)

$$24 = d - 11\dfrac{1}{3}$$

  **A** $d = 12\dfrac{2}{3}$      **C** $d = 35\dfrac{1}{3}$

  **B** $d = 13$         **D** $d = 37\dfrac{1}{3}$

**9.** **▐WRITE Math** ▶ **Explain** how to solve the equation $a + 9\dfrac{2}{3} = 15\dfrac{1}{4}$. (○━┓ AF 1.1)

## Measurement and Geometry

**10.** What is the volume of the rectangular prism?

(Grade 5 ⊙🔑 MG 1.3)

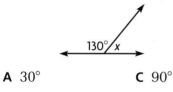

6 inches
4 inches
19 inches

**A** 29 cubic inches  **C** 190 cubic inches

**B** 72 cubic inches  **D** 456 cubic inches

**11.** What is the measure of angle *x* in the figure below? (Grade 5 ⊙🔑 MG 2.1)

130°/*x*

**A** 30°  **C** 90°

**B** 50°  **D** 120°

---

**Test Tip** **Understand the problem.**

See item 12. You are given the measures of three angles of a quadrilateral. What do you know about the sum of the angle measures of a quadrilateral?

---

**12.** What is the measure of angle *a* in the figure?

(Grade 5 ⊙🔑 MG 2.2)

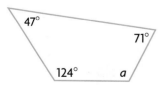

47°
71°
124°  *a*

**A** 56°  **C** 118°

**B** 109°  **D** 242°

**13.** **WRITE Math** Susan knows the perimeter and width of a rectangular door. **Explain** how she can find the height of the door.

(Grade 5 MG 1.4)

## Statistics, Data Analysis, and Probability

**14.** There are 5 sixth-grade classes at Kim's school.

| Number of 6th Graders Per Class | | | | | |
|---|---|---|---|---|---|
| **Class** | 1 | 2 | 3 | 4 | 5 |
| **Number** | 15 | 17 | 18 | 15 | 16 |

What is the median of the data set?

(SDAP 1.1)

**A** 15  **C** 17

**B** 16  **D** 18

**15.** A professional golfer recorded the scores below during a four-day tournament.

68, 70, 73, 69

What is the mean of the data set? (SDAP 1.1)

**A** 73  **C** 70

**B** 71  **D** 68

**16.** Which point represents (4,3) on the graph below? (Grade 5 ⊙🔑 SDAP 1.4)

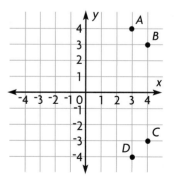

**A** point *A*  **C** point *C*

**B** point *B*  **D** point *D*

**17.** **WRITE Math** **Explain** how to locate the point represented by (2,5) on a graph.

(Grade 5 ⊙🔑 SDAP 1.4)

**The Big Idea** Properties and the concepts of algebra are used to solve multiplication and division equations.

## Investigate

You work for the San Francisco cable car system. Suppose each cable car can carry 58 people. Choose two or three stops. Explain how you can write a multiplication equation and solve it to find the number of cable cars needed to transport all of the passengers waiting at those stops.

| Passengers Waiting to Ride the Powell-Hyde Cable Car Line | |
|---|---|
| **Stop Name** | **Waiting Passengers** |
| Hyde and Beach Terminal | 450 |
| Hyde Street | 90 |
| Jackson Street | 100 |
| California Street | 115 |
| Market Street | 275 |

**CALIFORNIA FAST FACT**

On August 2, 1873, Andrew Hallidie became the first person to ride the San Francisco cable car system. Mr. Hallidie happened also to be the inventor of the cable car.

**GO ONLINE**

**Technology**
Student pages are available in the Student eBook.

Check your understanding of important skills
needed for success in Chapter 14.

▶ **Evaluate Expressions**

Evaluate the expression for the given value of the variable.

**1.** $5d$ for $d = 12$

**2.** $\frac{w}{9}$ for $w = 45$

**3.** $6c$ for $c = 12$

**4.** $4 \times a$ for $a = 4$

**5.** $x \div 10$ for $x = 100$

**6.** $z \div 18$ for $z = 54$

**7.** $c \div 5$ for $c = 75$

**8.** $8j$ for $j = 7$

**9.** $54 \div p$ for $p = 6$

▶ **Words to Equations**

Write an equation for the word expression.

**10.** $b$ divided by 7 is 4

**11.** the product of 6 and $h$ is 48

**12.** 100 is 20 times $p$

**13.** 14 is $c$ divided by 45

▶ **The Coordinate Plane**

Write the ordered pair for the given point.

**14.** point $A$

**15.** point $B$

**16.** point $C$

**17.** point $D$

**18.** point $E$

**19.** point $F$

**20.** point $G$

**21.** point $H$

**22.** point $I$

**23.** point $J$

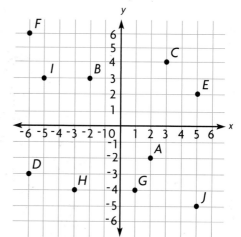

# VOCABULARY POWER

**CHAPTER VOCABULARY**

Division Property of Equality
function
linear equation
Multiplication Property
   of Equality

**WARM-UP WORDS**

**Division Property of Equality** the property that states
that if you divide both sides of an equation by the same
nonzero number, the sides remain equal

**Multiplication Property of Equality** the property that
states that if you multiply both sides of an equation by the
same number, the sides remain equal

**function** a relationship between two quantities in which
one quantity depends uniquely on the other

# 1 Model Multiplication Equations

OBJECTIVE: Use models to solve multiplication equations.

## Investigate

**Materials** ■ algebra tiles

You can use algebra tiles to model and solve multiplication equations.

**A** Model $3c = 15$. Use a green rectangle to represent the variable. Use a yellow square to represent 1.

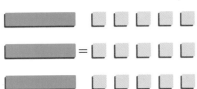

$$3c \quad = \quad 15$$

**B** Solve $3c = 15$. Since $c$ is multiplied by 3, you need to divide each side of the model into 3 equal groups.

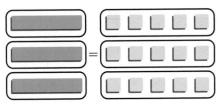

**C** Look at one group on each side. Observe what is in this pair of equal groups. What equation does this pair model?

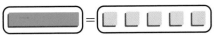

• What is the solution of the equation $3c = 15$?

**D** Model and solve $4c = 12$.

## Draw Conclusions

1. What operation did you model in part B? How is this operation related to multiplication?

2. **Synthesis** How do you think you would solve an algebraic equation like $\frac{x}{4} = 12$?

O—π **AF 1.1** Write and solve one-step linear equations in one variable. *also* O—π **NS 2.0, AF 1.0, MR 2.4, MR 2.5, MR 3.2**

## Connect

You can solve multiplication equations by drawing a model.

Draw a rectangle to represent the variable. Draw a square to represent 1.

**Solve $2y = 6$.**

**Step 1**

Draw a model for $2y = 6$.

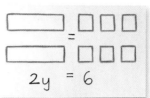

$2y = 6$

**Step 2**

Divide each side of the model into equal groups.

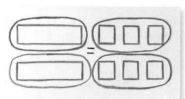

**Step 3**

Look at one group on each side.
This pair of groups represents the solution.

**TALK Math**

**Explain** how you would model and solve $4x = 24$.

## Practice

**Model each equation using algebra tiles and solve.**

**1.** $4x = 16$

**2.** $3y = 12$

**3.** $2c = 6$

**Solve each equation by using algebra tiles or by drawing a picture.**

**4.** $2a = 6$  **5.** $8y = 24$  **6.** $6b = 12$  **7.** $4x = 8$

**8.** $5a = 35$  **9.** $10 = 2b$  ✓**10.** $3x = 9$  ✓**11.** $15 = 5y$

**12.** $3k = 9$  **13.** $4b = 4$  **14.** $5c = 10$  **15.** $2m = 18$

**16.** **WRITE Math** **Explain** how modeling a multiplication equation with algebra tiles or by drawing a model can help you solve it.

# Solve Multiplication Equations

OBJECTIVE: Solve one-step linear multiplication equations.

## Learn

**PROBLEM** Jake, Melissa, Larry, Beth, and Sal are buying tickets to see a new movie. All tickets are the same price. If the tickets cost $45 altogether, how much does one ticket cost?

| number of people | times | price of one ticket | equals | total cost |
|:---:|:---:|:---:|:---:|:---:|
| ↓ | | ↓ | | ↓ |
| 5 | × | $n$ | = | 45 |

Multiplication and division are inverse operations. To solve a multiplication equation, you use the inverse operation, division, to get the variable alone on one side of the equation.

| **Division Property of Equality** | $12 = 12$ |
|---|---|
| When you divide both sides of an equation by the same nonzero number, the two sides remain equal. | $\dfrac{12}{2} = \dfrac{12}{2}$ <br> $6 = 6$ |

### Example 1  Solve and check. $5n = 45$

| | |
|---|---|
| $5n = 45$ | Write the equation. |
| $\dfrac{5n}{5} = \dfrac{45}{5}$ | Use the Division Property of Equality. |
| $1 \times n = 9$ | $5 \div 5 = 1; 45 \div 5 = 9$ |
| $n = 9$ | Use the Identity Property. |
| | |
| $5n = 45$ | Check your solution. |
| $5 \times 9 \stackrel{?}{=} 45$ | Replace $n$ with 9. |
| $45 = 45✔$ | The solution checks. |

So, the cost of one movie ticket is $9.

### Example 2  Solve and check. $2y = 3.2$

| | |
|---|---|
| $2y = 3.2$ | Write the equation. |
| $\dfrac{2y}{2} = \dfrac{3.2}{2}$ | Use the Division Property of Equality. |
| $1 \times y = 1.6$ | $2 \div 2 = 1; 3.2 \div 2 = 1.6$ |
| $y = 1.6$ | Use the Identity Property. |
| | |
| $2y = 3.2$ | Check your solution. |
| $2 \times 1.6 \stackrel{?}{=} 3.2$ | Replace $y$ with 1.6. |
| $3.2 = 3.2✔$ | The solution checks. |

So, $y = 1.6$.

**Remember**

Division can be written using the symbol ÷ or as a fraction. For example, 24 divided by 6 can be written as $24 \div 6$ or as $\frac{24}{6}$.

 AF 1.1 Write and solve one-step linear equations in one variable. *also* O━┓ NS 2.0, NS 2.1, O━┓ NS 2.3, AF 1.0, MR 2.4, MR 2.5, MR 3.2

# Equations with Fractions and Integers

Equations can involve negative integers and fractions.

## Example 3 Solve and check. $^-3a = ^-24$

| | |
|---|---|
| $^-3a = ^-24$ | Write the equation. |
| $\dfrac{^-3a}{^-3} = \dfrac{^-24}{^-3}$ | Use the Division Property of Equality. |
| $1 \times a = 8$ | $^-3 \div ^-3 = 1;\ ^-24 \div ^-3 = 8$ |
| $a = 8$ | Use the Identity Property. |
| $^-3a = ^-24$ | Check your solution. |
| $^-3 \times 8 \overset{?}{=} ^-24$ | Replace $a$ with 8. |
| $^-24 = ^-24$ ✔ | The solution checks. |

So, $a = 8$.

- Is solving an equation with negative integers different than solving an equation with whole numbers? Explain.

## Example 4 Solve and check $\dfrac{2}{3} = 4z$

| | |
|---|---|
| $\dfrac{2}{3} = 4z$ | Write the equation. |
| $\dfrac{\frac{2}{3}}{4} = \dfrac{4z}{4}$ | Use the Division Property of Equality. |
| $\dfrac{2}{3} \div 4 = 1 \times z$ | $4 \div 4 = 1$ |
| $\dfrac{2}{3} \times \dfrac{1}{4} = z$ | Multiply by the reciprocal. Use the Identity Property. |
| $\dfrac{1}{6} = z$ | |
| $\dfrac{2}{3} = 4z$ | Check your solution. |
| $\dfrac{2}{3} \overset{?}{=} 4 \times \dfrac{1}{6}$ | Replace $z$ with $\dfrac{1}{6}$. |
| $\dfrac{2}{3} = \dfrac{2}{3}$ ✔ | The solution checks. |

**Math Idea**
The Division Property of Equality is used to solve multiplication equations because division is the inverse operation of multiplication.

So, $z = \dfrac{1}{6}$.

- Solve and check. $\dfrac{3}{4}k = 12$

## Guided Practice

Solve and check.

**1.** $3x = 21$

$\dfrac{3x}{3} = \dfrac{21}{3}$

$x = \blacksquare$

**2.** $^-32 = 4y$

$\dfrac{^-32}{4} = \dfrac{4y}{4}$

$y = \blacksquare$

**3.** $\dfrac{1}{2}z = 12$

$\dfrac{\frac{1}{2}z}{\frac{1}{2}} = \dfrac{12}{\frac{1}{2}}$

$z = \blacksquare$

**4.** $5.6 = 7a$

$\dfrac{5.6}{7} = \dfrac{7a}{7}$

$a = \blacksquare$

**5.** $2.8b = 19.6$

$\dfrac{2.8b}{2.8} = \dfrac{19.6}{2.8}$

$b = \blacksquare$

**Solve and check.**

**6.** $7x = 63$    **⊘7.** $12y = 60$    **8.** $^-54 = 9z$    **9.** $1.4c = 70$    **⊘10.** $\frac{2}{5}a = 7$

**11.** (**TALK Math**) **Explain** how the Division Property of Equality is used to solve multiplication equations.

## Independent Practice and Problem Solving

**Solve and check.**

**12.** $36 = 4x$    **13.** $8y = 32$    **14.** $32 = 4g$    **15.** $38 = 2.5a$    **16.** $3z = 72$

**17.** $4.25 = 3.4f$    **18.** $12c = 56$    **19.** $^-3b = ^-39$    **20.** $128 = ^-8x$    **21.** $6g = ^-72$

**22.** $7x = \frac{1}{3}$    **23.** $\frac{2}{5}k = \frac{3}{5}$    **24.** $1.2y = 6.84$    **25.** $18 = 7.5h$    **26.** $2\frac{4}{9} = \frac{5}{6}z$

**27.** What value of $y$ makes $3y = ^-72$ true?

**28.** What value of $x$ makes $4x = 25$ true?

**29. Reasoning** Which of the numerical values 2, 4, and 6, is the solution of the euation $3x = 12$?

**30. Reasoning** Which of the numerical values $^-8$, $^-10$, and $^-12$ is the solution of the equation $5x = ^-40$?

**USE DATA For 31–32, use the table. Write an equation and solve.**

**31.** Adult and child tickets are sold at the movie theater. If the total amount of money made in ticket sales for Super Action was $2,176, what was the average cost per ticket?

**32.** The total amount of money made in ticket sales for all the movies was $8,083.25. What was the average cost per ticket?

**33.** Beth and her friends buy several buckets of popcorn when they go to see The Amazing Ring. If each bucket costs $5.75 and the total cost of the popcorn is $34.50, how many buckets do they buy?

| Movie Title | Tickets Sold |
|---|---|
| Three Friends | 128 |
| Super Action | 272 |
| The Big Game | 98 |
| Star Journey | 347 |
| The Amazing Ring | 198 |

**34. Pose a Problem** Look back at Problem 31. Write a similar problem by exchanging known and unknown information.

**35.** (**WRITE Math**) **What's the Error?** Michael solves the equation $8x = 2$ and gets the solution $x = 16$. **Explain** Michael's error and give the correct solution.

## Achieving the Standards

**36.** Miriam is conducting a survey at her school about students' favorite hobbies. She surveys the students in her math class since she needs the results quickly. What type of sampling method did Miriam use? (○━ SDAP 2.2, p. 202)

**37.** What value of $z$ makes $z - 12 = ^-3$ true?
(○━ AF 1.1, p. 320)

**38.** Evaluate $\frac{14}{y}$ for $y = 7$. (AF 1.2, p. 284)

**39. TEST PREP** Richard earned $399 for 42 hours of work. How much is he paid per hour?

A  $0.11            C  $357

B  $9.50            D  $16,758

# Theater Seating–Sections

**Reading Skill** Use Generalizations

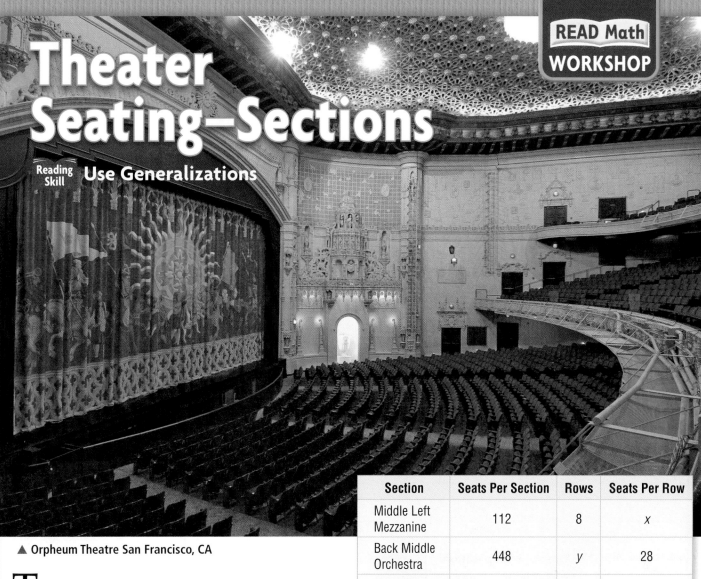

▲ Orpheum Theatre San Francisco, CA

| Section | Seats Per Section | Rows | Seats Per Row |
|---|---|---|---|
| Middle Left Mezzanine | 112 | 8 | $x$ |
| Back Middle Orchestra | 448 | $y$ | 28 |
| Right Loge | 42 | 3 | 14 |

$T$he Orpheum Theatre in San Francisco boasts many historical and decorative features. Since being built in 1926, the theatre has featured vaudeville shows, silent films, movies, musicals, and many other forms of entertainment. The interior of the theatre includes a lobby decorated like a twelfth century Spanish palace, an enormous tapestry covering the stage, and sculptures of lions around the ceiling. It is easy to see why the Orpheum is considered a historical landmark by the city!

When setting ticket prices at events, one thing to consider is how many seats are in various sections. Look at the data for the Right Loge section of the theater. The number of seats equals the number of rows times the number of seats per row, or $(42 = 3 \times 14)$.

If every row in a section has the same number of seats, you can make the generalization below.

total seats = number of rows $\times$ seats per row

**Problem Solving** Use generalizations to solve.

1. Write and solve equations to find the values for $x$ and $y$ in the table.

2. Tickets for the back middle orchestra section cost $50 each. If the theater makes $20,450 from ticket sales in this section, how many tickets were sold?

**LESSON**

# 3 Solve Division Equations

OBJECTIVE: Solve one-step linear division equations.

## Quick Review

Evaluate for $x = 48$.

1. $\frac{x}{2}$        2. $\frac{x}{6}$

3. $\frac{x}{16}$       4. $\frac{x}{24}$

5. $\frac{x}{10}$

## Vocabulary

**Multiplication Property of Equality**

## Learn

**PROBLEM** Megan buys a box filled with trading cards. She divides the cards into 4 equal piles and gives a pile to each of her friends. If each pile contains 12 cards, how many total cards were in the box when she bought it?

To solve division equations, use the inverse operation, multiplication.

| **Multiplication Property of Equality** | $8 = 8$ |
|---|---|
| When you multiply both sides of an equation by the same number, the two sides remain equal. | $3 \times 8 = 3 \times 8$ $24 = 24$ |

### Example 1 Find the total number of cards in the box.
Write an equaiton.

total cards in box ÷ number of piles = 12
$\downarrow$          $\downarrow$          $\downarrow$
$c$         ÷         $4$         =         $12$

| | | | |
|---|---|---|---|
| $\frac{c}{4} = 12$ | Write the equation. | $\frac{c}{4} = 12$ | Check your solution. |
| $4 \times \frac{c}{4} = 4 \times 12$ | Use the Multiplication Property of Equality. | $\frac{48}{4} \stackrel{?}{=} 12$ | Replace $c$ with 48. |
| $\frac{4}{1} \times \frac{c}{4} = 48$ | | $12 = 12 ✔$ | The solution checks. |
| $\frac{4c}{4} = 48$ | | | |
| $c = 48$ | $4 \div 4 = 1$ and $1 \times c = c$. | | |

So, there were 48 cards in the box when Megan bought it.

### Example 2 Solve and check. $3.5 = \frac{k}{6}$

| | | | |
|---|---|---|---|
| $3.5 = \frac{k}{6}$ | Write the equation. | $3.5 = \frac{k}{6}$ | Check your solution. |
| $6 \times 3.5 = 6 \times \frac{k}{6}$ | Use the Multiplication Property of Equality. | $3.5 \stackrel{?}{=} \frac{21}{6}$ | Replace $k$ with 21. |
| $21 = \frac{6}{1} \times \frac{k}{6}$ | | $3.5 = 3.5 ✔$ | The solution checks. |
| $21 = \frac{6k}{6}$ | | | |
| $21 = k$ | $6 \div 6 = 1$ and $1 \times k = k$. | | |

So, $k = 21$.

**340**

AF 1.1 Write and solve one-step linear equations in one variable. *also* NS 2.0, NS 2.1, NS 2.3, AF 1.0, MR 2.4, MR 2.5, MR 3.2

**Solve and check.**

1. $\frac{y}{5} = 12$ 

$\frac{y}{5} = 12$
$5 \times \frac{y}{5} = 5 \times 12$
$y = 5 \times 12$
$y = \blacksquare$

2. $\frac{z}{4} = 2.7$

$\frac{z}{4} = 2.7$
$4 \times \frac{z}{4} = 4 \times 2.7$
$z = 4 \times 2.7$
$z = \blacksquare$

3. $\frac{x}{8} = 2$

4. $\frac{a}{4} = {}^-15$

5. $\frac{m}{20} = \frac{9}{30}$

✓6. $\frac{p}{2} = 27$

✓7. $2.6 = \frac{r}{9}$

8. **TALK Math** **Explain** why the Multiplication Property of Equality is used to solve division equations.

## Independent Practice and Problem Solving

**Solve and check.**

9. $\frac{x}{10} = 12$

10. $\frac{y}{7} = 8$

11. $\frac{m}{4} = 2.5$

12. $\frac{n}{3} = 13$

13. $6 = \frac{z}{9}$

14. $14 = \frac{b}{4}$

15. $\frac{j}{3} = 4.9$

16. $2.8 = \frac{p}{9}$

17. $-\frac{s}{4} = {}^-3$

18. $14 = \frac{r}{13}$

19. $4.25 = \frac{w}{20}$

20. $\frac{d}{12} = {}^-6$

21. $\frac{h}{6} = \frac{1}{2}$

22. $\frac{4}{15} = \frac{g}{30}$

23. $\frac{a}{9} = \frac{7}{12}$

24. What number $x$ makes $\frac{x}{3} = 15$ true?

25. What number $y$ makes $\frac{y}{12} = \frac{1}{4}$ true?

26. **Reasoning** Which of the numerical values 27, 29, and 31, is the solution of the equation $\frac{x}{3} = 9$?

27. **Reasoning** Which of the numerical values ${}^-31$, ${}^-33$, and ${}^-35$, is the solution of the equation $\frac{a}{5} = {}^-7$?

28. Mary has a game that comes with playing tokens. She divides all the tokens between herself and 3 friends. If each player has 15 tokens, how many tokens are in the game?

29. Wanda is selling her trading card collection in batches of 4. By the time she finishes selling 12 batches, she only has 2 cards remaining. How many cards were in Wanda's collection?

30. **Reasoning** In the equation $\frac{48}{x} = 12$, the variable is in the denominator. Explain how you would solve the equation.

31. **WRITE Math** **What's the Question?** Mario has a coin collection that he displays in 8 display cases. There are 12 coins in each display case. The answer is 96 coins.

## Achieving the Standards

32. A rectangular solid has a length of 3 feet, a width of 4 feet, and a height of 5 feet. What is the volume? (Grade 5 O—⊓ MG 1.3)

33. Marissa buys $\frac{1}{5}$ of a roll of fabric from a roll that is 10 yards long. How much fabric does she buy? (O—⊓ NS 2.0, p. 70)

34. Solve $5y = 75$. (O—⊓ AF 1.1, p. 336)

35. **Test Prep** What number $x$ makes $\frac{x}{4} = 20$ true?

    **A** $x = 5$

    **B** $x = 6$

    **C** $x = 80$

    **D** $x = 100$

# Practice Solving Equations

OBJECTIVE: Practice solving all four types of one-step linear equations.

## Learn

**PROBLEM** Mark charges the same amount for each lawn he mows. Last week, he made $180 for mowing 12 lawns. How much does Mark charge for mowing a lawn?

### Example 1

First choose which type of equation you will use to solve the problem. You know that the total amount of money Mark earned, $180, is the number of lawns he mowed times the dollar amount he charges per lawn. You can use a multiplication equation.

| number of lawns | times | amount per lawn | equals | total |
|:---:|:---:|:---:|:---:|:---:|
| ↓ | ↓ | ↓ | ↓ | ↓ |
| 12 | × | $c$ | = | 180 |

| | | | |
|---|---|---|---|
| $12c = 180$ | Write the equation. | $12c = 180$ | Check your solution. |
| $\frac{12c}{12} = \frac{180}{12}$ | Use the Division Property of Equality. | $12 \times 15 = 180$ | Replace $c$ with 15. |
| $c = 15$ | | $180 = 180$✔ | The solution checks. |

**ERROR ALERT**

When solving one-step equations, be sure you are using the correct Property of Equality.

So, Mark charges $15 for each lawn he mows.

• What division equation could you write to solve this problem?

### Example 2

Louis deposited $152 into his bank account. His balance is now $437. How much was the balance before the deposit?

Since Louis deposited $152, he added it to his balance. Therefore, his balance before the deposit plus $152 gives him a new balance of $437. You can use an addition equation.

**Remember**
To deposit means to "add" to a previous balance.

| balance before deposit | plus | deposit | equals | new balance |
|:---:|:---:|:---:|:---:|:---:|
| ↓ | ↓ | ↓ | ↓ | ↓ |
| $b$ | + | 152 | = | 437 |

| | | | |
|---|---|---|---|
| $b + 152 = 437$ | Write the equation. | $b + 152 = 437$ | Check your solution. |
| $b + 152 - 152 = 437 - 152$ | Use the Subtraction Property of Equality. | $285 + 152 = 437$ | Replace $b$ with 285. |
| $b = 285$ | | $437 = 437$✔ | The solution checks. |

So, Louis's balance before the deposit was $285.

• What subtraction equation could you write to solve this problem?

○━┓ AF 1.1 Write and solve one-step linear equations in one variable. *also* ○━┓ NS 2.0, NS 2.1, ○━┓ NS 2.3, AF 1.0, MR 2.4, MR 2.5, MR 3.2

1. Richard had 71 stickers. After giving a number of stickers away, he now has 54 left. Write and solve an equation to find the number of stickers he gave away.

   $n + 54 = 71$
   $n + 54 - 54 = 71 - 54$
   $n = \blacksquare$

**Solve and check.**

2. $x + 89 = 104$     3. $12y = 90$     4. $64 = \frac{z}{8}$     ✓5. $r - 46 = 53$     ✓6. $3a = 9.6$

7. **TALK Math** Explain how you decide what kind of equation to use to solve problems.

## Independent Practice and Problem Solving

**Solve and check.**

8. $9x = 153$     9. $35 = y + 19$     10. $m - 87 = 54$     11. $12 = \frac{s}{15}$     12. $\frac{h}{5} = 55.5$

13. $p + 7.8 = 15.2$     14. $8n = {}^{-}144$     15. $k + \frac{4}{5} = 3\frac{9}{10}$     16. $^{-}53 = t - 61$     17. $\frac{w}{3} = \frac{8}{9}$

**Write an equation and solve.**

18. Helen makes $18 for every lawn she rakes. If she was paid $108 last week, how many lawns did she rake?

19. After Jessica made a $72 withdrawal, her balance was $417. What was her balance before she made the withdrawal?

20. Kendall opens an 18-lb bag of fertilizer. After she spread some fertilizer on the garden, the bag weighed $10\frac{5}{6}$ lb. How many pounds of fertilizer did she use?

21. Forrest has 3 chores to complete for his parents. He divides his time evenly among all 3 so that each chore takes him 20 min. How long does Forrest spend doing all his chores?

22. Marc and April combine their money to buy a rose bush. Marc contributes $10.20. April adds her money to Marc's. Together they buy a rose bush for $16.55 and get $0.15 in change. How much money did April contribute?

23. **WRITE Math** What's the Question? Melanie walks her dog 4 times around the block in 35 minutes. The answer is $8\frac{3}{4}$ min.

## Achieving the Standards

24. Evaluate $2z - 34$ for $z = 3.5$. (AF 1.2, p. 284)

25. Find the value of $(^{-}15 - 5) \div 4$.
    (O━┓ NS 2.3, p. 182)

26. How does the outlier 32 affect the mean when added to the data set 2, 5, 6, 6, 9?
    (SDAP 1.3, p. 226)

27. **Test Prep** Chris mowed 57 lawns during the month of August. He makes $19 per lawn. How much did he make during the month of August?

    **A** $3          **C** $1,003

    **B** $76         **D** $1,083

# 5 Number Patterns and Functions

OBJECTIVE: Write an equation to represent a function.

## Quick Review

**Evaluate each expression.**

1. $4b + 5$, for $b = 6$
2. $3 \times (4 + c)$, for $c = 3.5$
3. $120 \div n$, for $n = 15$
4. $14 - x$, for $x = 24$
5. $60w \div 5$, for $w = \frac{2}{3}$

## Vocabulary

function

## Learn

**SCIENCE PROBLEM** The drama club is making costumes for the school musical. The fabric the students want costs $5.50 per yard. They need 37 yd of fabric. If there is $209 in the costume budget, does the drama club have enough money to buy all the fabric it needs?

### Example 1 Write an equation to represent a function.

A **function** is a relationship between two quantities in which one quantity depends uniquely on the other. For every input, there is exactly one output. Look for a pattern in the input/output table.

The pattern is that as the number of yards of fabric increases by 1, the cost increases by $5.50. The drama club can use the rule for this pattern to write an equation. Then they can determine if they have enough money to buy the fabric they need.

| Input | Output |
|-------|--------|
| Yards of Fabrics | Cost |
| 1 | $5.50 |
| 2 | $11.00 |
| 3 | $16.50 |
| 4 | $22.00 |
| 5 | $27.50 |

| | |
|---|---|
| **Rule:** $5.5n$ | $n$ = number of yards of fabric |
| $5.5n = c$ | Write an equation. Let $c$ = total cost of fabric. |
| $5.5n = 209$ | Replace $c$ with 209. |
| $\dfrac{5.5n}{5.5} = \dfrac{209}{5.5}$ | Solve the equation. |
| $n = 38$ | |

So, the drama club has enough money to buy 38 yd of fabric.

### Example 2 Write an equation to represent a two-step function.

At a local skating rink, you pay $1.75 to rent skates, plus $3.00 for each hour you skate. Use the input/output table to find a pattern.

| Input | hour, $h$ | 1 | 2 | 3 | 4 |
|-------|-----------|---|---|---|---|
| **Rule** | $3h + 1.75$ | $3 \times 1 + 1.75$ | $3 \times 2 + 1.75$ | $3 \times 3 + 1.75$ | $3 \times 4 + 1.75$ |
| **Output** | total cost, $c$ | $4.75 | $7.75 | $10.75 | $13.75 |

Each output term increases by 3. Let $h$ = hours and $c$ = total cost.

Rule: $3h + 1.75 = c$

The pattern is to multiply the number of hours you skate by 3, and then add 1.75.

So, an equation is $c = 3h + 1.75$.

• Does a change in $h$ result in a change in $c$? Explain.

AF 1.0 Students write verbal expressions and sentences as algebraic expressions and equations; they evaluate expressions, solve simple linear equations, and graph and interpret their results. *also* O━┓ NS 2.0, O━┓ NS 2.3, O━┓ AF 1.1, MR 1.1, MR 2.4, MR 2.5, MR 3.2

# Finding Missing Terms

### Example 3 Write an equation to represent the function. Use the equation to find the missing term.

| x | 1 | 2 | 3 | 4 | 5 |
|---|---|---|---|---|---|
| y | 1 | 8 | 27 | 64 | ■ |

**Think:** Each $y$-value is greater than or equal to the corresponding $x$-value. Since the pattern is increasing, the rule could use either multiplication or addition.

Pattern: Each $x$-value is cubed to find the $y$-value.

Rule: $x^3$

Equation: $y = x^3$     Use the rule to write an equation.

$y = 5^3$     Let $x = 5$

$y = 125$     Solve for $y$.

So, an equation is $y = x^3$, and the missing term is 125.

• Does this equation describe a function? Explain.

### Example 4 Write an equation to represent the two-step function. Use the equation to find the missing term.

| x | 1 | 2 | 3 | 4 | 5 |
|---|---|---|---|---|---|
| y | 2.65 | 4.65 | 6.65 | ■ | 10.65 |

**Think:** Compare $x$ and $y$. The $y$-value is 0.65 more than twice the $x$-value.

Pattern: Multiply each $x$-value by 2. Then add 0.65.

Rule: $2x + 0.65$

Equation: $y = 2x + 0.65$     Use the rule to write an equation.

$y = 2 \times 4 + 0.65$     Let $x = 4$

$y = 8.65$     Solve for $y$.

So, an equation is $y = 2x + 0.65$, and the missing term is 8.65.

## Guided Practice

**Write an equation to represent the function.**

1. Compare $d$ and $r$ in the table at the right. The variable $r$ is always 7 less than $d$.

| d | 20 | 19 | 18 | 17 | 16 |
|---|---|---|---|---|---|
| r | 13 | 12 | 11 | 10 | 9 |

2.

| w | 30 | 35 | 40 | 45 | 50 |
|---|---|---|---|---|---|
| t | 6 | 7 | 8 | 9 | 10 |

3.

| x | 5 | 4 | 3 | 2 | 1 |
|---|---|---|---|---|---|
| y | 11 | 9 | 7 | 5 | 3 |

4. **TALK Math** Explain how to write an equation to describe a function shown by an input/output table.

**Write an equation to represent the function.**

**5.**

| a | 5 | 7 | 9 | 11 | 13 |
|---|---|---|---|----|----|
| b | 8.5 | 10.5 | 12.5 | 14.5 | 16.5 |

**6.**

| c | 65 | 50 | 35 | 20 | 5 |
|---|----|----|----|----|---|
| d | 50 | 35 | 20 | 5 | ⁻10 |

**7.**

| p | 1 | 2 | 3 | 4 | 5 |
|---|---|---|---|---|---|
| w | 3 | 6 | 9 | 12 | 15 |

**8.**

| m | 10 | 11 | 12 | 13 | 14 |
|---|----|----|----|----|----|
| t | 31 | 34 | 37 | 40 | 43 |

**Write an equation to represent the function. Then use the equation to find the missing term.**

**9.**

| r | 10 | 12 | 14 | 16 | 18 |
|---|----|----|----|----|----|
| d | 5 | 6 | 7 | ■ | 9 |

**10.**

| x | 20 | 25 | 30 | 35 | 40 |
|---|----|----|----|----|----|
| y | 5 | ■ | 15 | 20 | 25 |

**11.**

| k | 3 | 6 | 9 | 12 | 15 |
|---|---|---|---|----|----|
| g | 8 | 14 | ■ | 26 | 32 |

**12.**

| m | 180 | 160 | 140 | 120 | 100 |
|---|-----|-----|-----|-----|-----|
| h | 167 | 147 | ■ | 107 | 87 |

**USE DATA** For 13–15, use the chart.

**13.** Describe in words what the pattern shows for the first 5 costumes. Then write an equation to describe the function. Let c equal the number of costumes and y equal the amount of fabric.

**14.** How many costumes can be made from 36 yd of fabric?

| Number of Costumes | Amount of Fabric (in yards) |
|--------------------|----------------------------|
| 1 | 3.5 |
| 2 | 7.0 |
| 3 | 10.5 |
| 4 | 14.0 |
| 5 | 17.5 |

**15.** How much do 5 costumes cost, if fabric is $5.50 per yard? Write an equation to describe the function. Let c equal the number of costumes and t equal the cost.

**16.** ≡**FAST FACT** During the Middle Ages, a typical child's outfit used 3.5 yd of fabric. Today, a typical child's outfit uses 1.75 yd of fabric. Write an equation that compares the different amounts of fabric used.

**17.** Laura wants to make necklaces for the costumes. The beads she wants cost $3.50 per bag. She needs 22 bags of beads. If she has $75 to spend, will she have enough money to buy all the beads she needs?

**18.** ⬛**WRITE Math** Reasoning Look at Exercise 15. Suppose that each costume needs a zipper that costs $0.75. Write an equation to describe the new function. **Explain** how a change in one quantity affects a change in the other.

**Technology**
**CD ROM** Use Harcourt Mega Math, The Number Games, *Tiny's Think Tank,* Level K and V.

**19.** Are lines $AB$ and $CD$ perpendicular or parallel?

(🔑 Grade 5 MG 2.1)

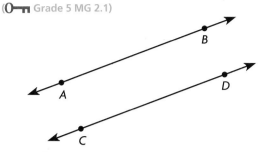

**20.** Dave took the steps below to evaluate the expression $3^2 - 2 \times 3$. (AF 1.3, p. 276)

$$3^2 = 9$$
$$9 - 2 = 7$$
$$7 \times 3 = 21$$

Describe his error.

**21.** Write an equation for the word expression.

(AF 1.0, p. 300)

8 more than a number is 24.

**22. Test Prep** Which equation could represent the function in the table?

| x | ⁻2 | ⁻1 | 0 | 1 | 2 |
|---|---|---|---|---|---|
| y | ⁻10 | ⁻5 | 0 | 5 | 10 |

**A** $y = x - 5$

**B** $y = 5x$

**C** $x = y + 5$

**D** $x = 5y$

**23. Test Prep** A cell-phone company charges a $33.00 monthly rate and $0.02 per call. Which equation represents the total cost, $t$, if $n$ equals the number of calls?

**A** $t = 33 + 0.02$

**B** $n = 0.02 + 33$

**C** $t = 0.02 + 33n$

**D** $t = 0.02n + 33$

## MATH POWER — Problem Solving and Reasoning

**NUMBER SENSE** The binary, or base-two, number system uses only the digits 0 and 1. In the decimal system, each place value is ten times the place value to the right. In the binary system, each place value is twice the place value to the right. You can use powers of 2 to find the decimal equivalent of a binary number.

**Find the decimal equivalent of $10101_{two}$.**

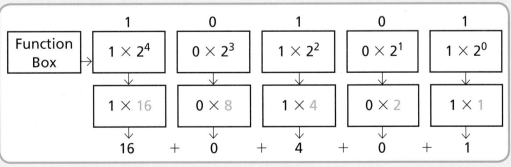

So, $10101_{two} = 21$

**Find the decimal equivalent for each binary number.**

**1.** $1100_{two}$

**2.** $1111_{two}$

**3.** $10110_{two}$

**4.** $11101_{two}$

# 6 Graph Functions

OBJECTIVE: Graph functions.

## Learn

**PROBLEM** A local store buys old computers. The store reuses parts that are still good to make a working computer, which they then sell. The table at the right shows how much money the store earns selling the computers. Write ordered pairs and use them to graph the data. Use the graph to help write an equation for the function.

| Reused Computers Sales | |
|---|---|
| Computers Sold | Money Earned |
| 1 | $200 |
| 2 | $400 |
| 3 | $600 |
| 4 | $800 |
| 5 | $1000 |

### Example 1

**A** **Write the ordered pairs and then graph them.**

(1,200)  (2,400)  (3,600)  (4,800)  (5,1,000)

The ordered pairs represent a function. Graph the ordered pairs to show the function on a graph.

**B** **Use the graph to help write an equation for the function.**

As the number of computers sold increases by 1, the amount of money earned increases by $200.

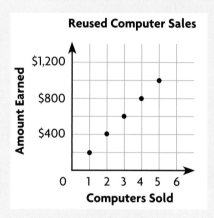

Reused Computer Sales

So, an equation for the function could be $A = 200c$, where $A$ is the amount earned and $c$ is the number of computers sold.

### Example 2 Use ordered pairs to graph data from a function table.

**A** **Graph the data on a coordinate plane.**

Write the data in the table as ordered pairs.

$({}^-5, {}^-3)$, $({}^-3.5, {}^-1.5)$, $({}^-2,0)$, $(0,2)$, $(1.5,3.5)$

Plot the points on a coordinate plane.

**B** **Write an equation relating $y$ to $x$. Use the equation to find the missing value of $y$.**

The $y$-value is always 2 more than the $x$-value.

Equation: $y = x + 2$        $y = 2.5 + 2 = 4.5$

| x | y |
|---|---|
| $^-5$ | $^-3$ |
| $^-3.5$ | $^-1.5$ |
| $^-2$ | 0 |
| 0 | 2 |
| 1.5 | 3.5 |
| 2.5 | ■ |

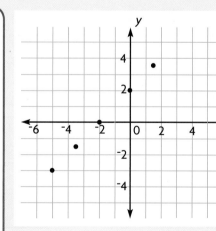

So the missing value is $y = 4.5$.

**AF 1.0** Students write verbal expressions and sentences as algebraic expressions and equations; they evaluate algebraic expressions, solve simple linear equations, and graph and interpret their results. *also* ○━┓ NS 2.3, ○━┓ AF 1.1, MR 1.1, MR 2.4, MR 2.5

1. The local sporting goods store sells baseballs. The data in the chart at the right shows a record of some of the sales. Graph the data and use the graph to help write an equation for the function. First write ordered pairs: (1,3.5), (2,7), (3,10.5), (4,14), (5,17.5), (6,21). Next, plot the points. Use the graph to help write an equation for the function.

| Baseballs Sold | Amount |
|---|---|
| 1 | $3.50 |
| 2 | $7.00 |
| 3 | $10.50 |
| 4 | $14.00 |
| 5 | $17.50 |
| 6 | $21.00 |

**Graph the data on a coordinate plane. Write an equation relating y to x. Use the equation to find the missing value of y.**

2.

| x | ⁻5 | ⁻2.5 | 0 | 4 | 10 |
|---|---|---|---|---|---|
| y | ⁻20 | ⁻10 | ■ | 16 | 40 |

3.

| x | ⁻4 | ⁻1 | 0 | 2 | 5 |
|---|---|---|---|---|---|
| y | ■ | ⁻2 | 1 | 7 | 16 |

4. **TALK Math** Explain how you can use the graph of a function to find a missing y-value.

## Independent Practice and Problem Solving

**Graph the data on a coordinate plane. Write an equation relating y to x. Use the equation to find the missing value of y.**

5.

| x | ⁻6 | ⁻3 | 0 | 2 | 9 |
|---|---|---|---|---|---|
| y | ⁻3 | ■ | 0 | 1 | 4.5 |

6.

| x | ⁻4 | ⁻2 | 0 | 1 | 3 |
|---|---|---|---|---|---|
| y | ■ | ⁻20 | 0 | 10 | 30 |

7.

| x | 7 | 6 | 5 | 4 | 3 |
|---|---|---|---|---|---|
| y | 21 | ■ | 15 | 12 | 9 |

8.

| x | 16 | 18 | 20 | 22 | 24 |
|---|---|---|---|---|---|
| y | 4 | 4.5 | 5 | 5.5 | ■ |

9. **Reasoning** A table relating distance traveled by a car, d, and time, t, is shown below.

| d (mi) | 55 | 110 | 165 | 220 |
|---|---|---|---|---|
| t (hr) | 1 | 2 | 3 | 4 |

Will distance always increase over time? Use a graph to support your answer.

10. **WRITE Math** **Sense or Nonsense** Sue earns three credits per win, w, on a computer game. Use ordered pairs to show the number of credits earned, c, for 7, 8, 9, and 10 wins. Graph the data. Sue says the equation c = w + 3 relates c to w. Does Sue's statement make sense? **Explain.**

## Achieving the Standards

11. For a school survey, Janine surveyed 4 girls from each of her classes. What kind of sample did she use? (O—Π SDAP 2.2, p. 202)

12. Find the sum $5\frac{1}{4} + 3\frac{2}{3}$ (NS 2.1, p. 42)

13. If x + 1.5 is evaluated for x = 2, is the result less than or greater than 3? (AF 1.2, p. 284)

14. **Test Prep** Which equation could be used to represent the function in the table?

| x | ⁻2 | ⁻1 | 0 | 1 | 2 |
|---|---|---|---|---|---|
| y | 3 | 4 | 5 | 6 | 7 |

A $x = y + 5$     C $y = x + 5$

B $x = y - 5$     D $y = x - 5$

# Graph Linear Equations

**OBJECTIVE:** Graph and interpret linear equations.

## Quick Review

Find *y* for *x* = 3.

**1.** $y = {}^-x$      **2.** $y = x + 6$

**3.** $y = x - 7$      **4.** $y = 4x$

**5.** $y = x^2 + 1$

## Vocabulary

**linear equation**

## Learn

**PROBLEM** Patricio is exchanging euros, the currency in Spain, and U.S. dollars. On one day, the exchange rate is 1 euro equals about 1.29 U.S. dollars. An equation relating euros, *y*, to U.S. dollars, *x*, is $y = 1.29x$. Graph this equation.

### Example 1 Graph the equation.

Use the equation to find values for *x* and *y* to form ordered pairs. Replace values for *x* and find the corresponding values for *y*.

| | |
|---|---|
| $y = 1.29(1) = 1.29$ | Replace *x* with 1, 2, and 3 in the equation. |
| $y = 1.29(2) = 2.58$ | Find the corresponding values for *y*. |
| $y = 1.29(3) = 3.87$ | Record your findings in a table. |

Make a table and write ordered pairs.

| U.S. Dollars (*x*) | 1 | 2 | 3 |
|---|---|---|---|
| Euros (*y*) | 1.29 | 2.58 | 3.87 |

(1,1.29) (2,2.58) (3,3.87)

Plot the ordered pairs. Since this is a linear equation, draw a line through the points. The line represents all possible solutions to the equation.

The graph of some functions form a straight line. Equations that are straight lines when graphed are called **linear equations**.

### Example 2 Graph the linear equation $y = x + 4$.

Find values for *x* and *y* so you can form ordered pairs. Replace values for *x* and find the corresponding values for *y*.

| | |
|---|---|
| $y = {}^-2 + 4 = 2$ | Replace *x* with $^-2$, 0, and 2 in the equation. |
| $y = 0 + 4 = 4$ | Find the corresponding values for *y*. |
| $y = 2 + 4 = 6$ | Record your findings in a table. |

Make a table and write ordered pairs.

| *x* | $^-2$ | 0 | 2 |
|---|---|---|---|
| *y* | 2 | 4 | 6 |

($^-$2,2), (0,4), (2,6)

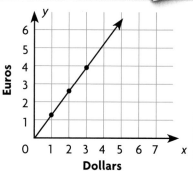

Plot the ordered pairs. Since this a linear equation, draw a line through the points. The line represents all possible solutions to the equation.

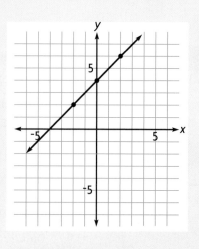

**AF 1.0** Students write verbal expressions and sentences as algebraic expressions and equations; they evaluate algebraic expressions, solve simple linear equations, and graph and interpret their results. *also* MR 2.3, MR 2.4, MR 2.5, MR 3.2

**Example 3** Which table corresponds to the graph on the coordinate plane?

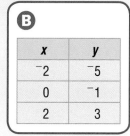

**A**

| x | y |
|---|---|
| ⁻2 | ⁻6 |
| 0 | 0 |
| 2 | 6 |

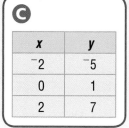

**B**

| x | y |
|---|---|
| ⁻2 | ⁻5 |
| 0 | ⁻1 |
| 2 | 3 |

**C**

| x | y |
|---|---|
| ⁻2 | ⁻5 |
| 0 | 1 |
| 2 | 7 |

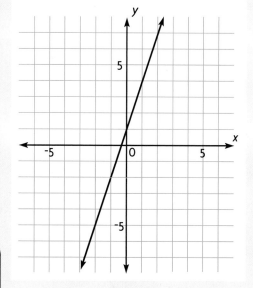

Check the ordered pairs from each table to see if they are on the line. If at least one of the ordered pairs is not on the line, then the table does not correspond to the graph. If all of the ordered pairs are on the line, then the table does correspond to the graph.

> **TABLE A:** Check (⁻2, ⁻6). (⁻2, ⁻6) is not on the line, so table A does not correspond to the graph.
>
> **TABLE B:** Check (⁻2, ⁻5). (⁻2, ⁻5) is on the line. Check (0, ⁻1). (0, ⁻1) is not on the line, so table B does not correspond to the graph.
>
> **TABLE C:** Check (⁻2, ⁻5). (⁻2, ⁻5) is on the line. Check (0,1). (0,1) is on the line. Check (2,7). (2,7) is on the line.

So, table C corresponds to the graph.

- Why are there arrows on the ends of the line?

# Guided Practice

1. Graph the equation $y = 2x + 5$ on a coordinate plane. Find values for x and y so you can form ordered pairs. Replace x with different values and find the corresponding values for y. Write ordered pairs, plot them, and draw a line through the points.

| x | ⁻3 | 0 | 2 |
|---|---|---|---|
| y | ⁻1 | 5 | 9 |

**Tell which table corresponds to the graph on the coordinate plane.**

2. **A**

| x | y |
|---|---|
| ⁻1 | 3 |
| 0 | 4 |
| 1 | 5 |

**B**

| x | y |
|---|---|
| ⁻2 | ⁻4 |
| 0 | 0 |
| 3 | 6 |

**C**

| x | y |
|---|---|
| ⁻1 | ⁻4 |
| 0 | ⁻3 |
| 2 | ⁻1 |

**Graph the equation on a coordinate plane.**

3. $y = x - 2$

4. $y = x + 6$

✓5. $y = 2x + 1$

✓6. $y = 3x - 2$

7. **TALK Math** Explain how you use the data in a table to identify the graph of a linear equation.

## Independent Practice and Problem Solving

**Tell which table corresponds to the graph on the coordinate plane.**

**8.** A

| x | ⁻2 | 0 | 2 |
|---|---|---|---|
| y | ⁻7 | ⁻3 | 1 |

B

| x | ⁻1 | 0 | 1 |
|---|---|---|---|
| y | ⁻3 | ⁻2 | ⁻1 |

C

| x | ⁻1 | 0 | 2 |
|---|---|---|---|
| y | ⁻1 | 1 | 5 |

**9.** Q

| x | ⁻3 | 0 | 2 |
|---|---|---|---|
| y | 6 | 0 | ⁻4 |

R

| x | ⁻2 | ⁻1 | 1 |
|---|---|---|---|
| y | 3 | 1 | ⁻3 |

S

| x | ⁻2 | 0 | 5 |
|---|---|---|---|
| y | 7 | 5 | 0 |

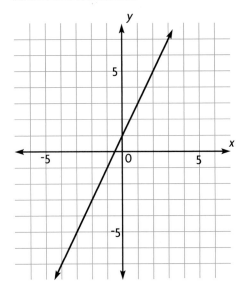

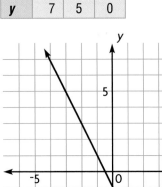

**Graph the equation on a coordinate plane.**

**10.** $y = 2x$

**11.** $y = x - 5$

**12.** $y = x + 2$

**13.** $y = 3x$

**14.** $y = {}^-3x$

**15.** $y = 2x + 1$

**16.** $y = 3x - 2$

**17.** $y = {}^-4x + 5$

**18.** Graph the equation $y = 5x$ for values of $x$ from ⁻3 to 3.

**19.** Graph the equation $y = 2x - 2$ for values of $x$ from ⁻3 to 3.

**20.** On the day Amanda travels to Canada, the currency exchange rate is 1 U.S. dollar equals about 1.12 Canadian dollars. An equation relating U.S. dollars, $x$, to Canadian dollars, $y$, is $y = 1.12x$. Graph this equation. About how many Canadian dollars can Amanda get for 6 U.S. dollars?

**21.** While in Canada, Amanda goes hiking. She hikes at an average rate of 4 mi per hr. An equation relating the distance she travels, $y$, to the time in hours she hikes, $x$, is $y = 4x$. Graph this equation. About how far will Amanda hike in $2\frac{3}{4}$ hr?

**22.** **WRITE Math** ▸ Look back at Problems 20 and 21. **Explain** how the graph helped you answer the questions.

**352** Extra Practice on page 358, Set F

**23.** What is the greatest common factor of 50 and 45? (🔑 NS 2.4, p. 6)

**24.** The price of a quart of milk at 5 different stores was $1.35, $1.50, $1.60, $1.25, and $1.20. What is the mean price? (SDAP 1.1, p. 224)

**25.** Evaluate $(50 - 14) \div 3^2$.

(AF 1.3, p. 276)

**26. Test Prep** In order to graph the linear equation $y = x + 7$, Caroline replaced $x$ with $^-2$, 0, and 2 and found the corresponding values for $y$. Which shows the ordered pairs Caroline used?

(🔑 NS 2.0)

**A** $(^-2, ^-9)$, $(0, ^-7)$, $(2, ^-5)$

**B** $(^-2, ^-14)$, $(0, 0)$, $(2, 14)$

**C** $(^-2, 5)$, $(0, 7)$, $(2, 9)$

**D** $(5, ^-2)$, $(7, 0)$, $(2, 9)$

**27. Test Prep** The graph of $y = 2x$ is shown below.

(🔑 NS 2.0)

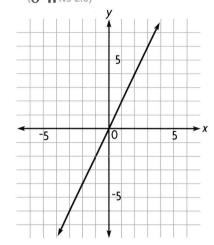

Which ordered pair is a solution of $y = 2x$?

**A** $(1, 1)$    **C** $(3, 5)$

**B** $(0, 2)$    **D** $(2, 4)$

---

## MATH POWER — Problem Solving and Reasoning

**TECHNOLOGY** You can use a graphing calculator to graph and analyze linear equations.

Use a graphing calculator to graph $y = 4x$.

**Step 1**

Press . Press **CLEAR**, ,   **ENTER** .

**Step 2**

Press **GRAPH** to show the graph.

Use a graphing calculator to graph each equation. Then sketch the graph on paper.

**1.** $y = 3x$

**2.** $y = ^-0.7x$

**3.** $y = 5.2x$

**4.** $y = x - 5$

**5.** $y = ^-x + 1.2$

**6.** $y = ^-0.67x$

# Problem Solving Workshop
## Strategy: Work Backward

**OBJECTIVE:** Solve problems using the strategy *work backward*.

## Learn the Strategy

Working backward can help you solve problems that involve
a seqence of events.

### Work backward to find a position or location.

At the amusement park, a train drops Abdul off
at an unknown level in the Fun House. He gets
out and climbs up 3 flights of stairs. Then he
climbs down 5 flights of stairs, climbs up
2 flights, and then climbs down 7 flights to
the 2nd level. On what level did the train drop
Abdul off?

Start on the last level and work backward to
find the level where Abdul got off the train.

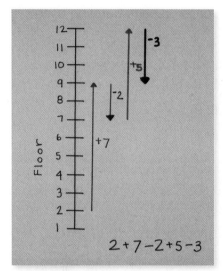

$2 + 7 - 2 + 5 - 3$

### Work backward to find an original amount.

Joe and his brother Tim go shopping. They use half their money to buy
a video game. They spend half the money they have left on pizza. Then
they spend half the remaining money to rent a video. After this, they
have $4.50 remaining. How much money did they have at the start?

Start with the amount of money Joe and Tim had remaining and work
backward to find the money they had at the start.

$4.50: twice the amount before the video →$9.00

$9.00: twice the amount before the pizza →$18.00

$18.00: twice the amount before the video game →$36.00

**TALK Math**

Describe what happens to
the operations when you
work backward.

**AF 1.0** Students write verbal expressions and sentences as algebraic expressions and equations; they
evaluate algebraic expressions, solve simple linear equations, and graph and interpret their results. *also*,
**MR 1.0, MR 1.1, MR 2.0, MR 2.4, MR 2.5, MR 2.7, MR 3.0, MR 3.1, MR 3.2, MR 3.3**

# Use the Strategy

**PROBLEM** A bike team left at 7:00 A.M. for a 60-mi tour. In the first hour, they had to stop and fill up 6 water bottles. The team traveled only 8 mi per hr that first hour. For the rest of the ride, they averaged 13 mi per hr. How long did it take the team to ride 60 mi?

## Read to Understand

Reading Skill

- What is the sequence of events?
- Is there information you will not use? If so, what?

## Plan

- What strategy can you use to solve the problem?

  You can *work backward* to help you solve the problem.

## Solve

- How can you use the strategy to solve the problem?

  The number of additional hours can be found this way:

  | number of additional hours | × | average miles per additional hour | + | number of miles ridden in first hour | = | total miles |
  |---|---|---|---|---|---|---|
  |  | × | 13 | + | 8 | = | 60 |

  You can work backward by reversing the operations and the order.

  | total miles | − | number of miles ridden in first hour | ÷ | average miles per additional hour | = | number of additional hours |
  |---|---|---|---|---|---|---|
  | (60 | − | 8) | ÷ | 13 | = | 4 |

  first hour + additional hours = total time

  1 hr + 4 hr = 5 hr

So, the team took 5 hr to ride 60 mi.

## Check

- How do you know the answer is correct?

1. The coach bought $130.80 worth of supplies for the team to use during a 40-mi bike ride. She bought 4 cases of water, energy bars for $36, and oranges for $15. How much did each case of water cost?

   **First,** write a number sentence.

   ▬ × 4 + 36 + 15 = 130.80

   **Then,** work backward by reversing the operations and the order.

   (130.80 − 15 − 36) ÷ 4 = ▬

   **Finally,** find the cost of one case of water.

✓2. **What if** the coach had spent $115 for the supplies in Problem 1? How much would each case of water have cost?

✓3. To repair a bike a bike shop charges $10.95 for the first hour and $6.95 for each additional hour. Lee paid $31.80 to have her bike fixed. How many hours did the shop mechanic spend on her bike?

**Problem Solving Strategy Practice**

**Use the strategy *work backward* to solve.**

4. A local bike store, E-Z-Spokes, is sponsoring some cyclists to race in France. The store is paying airfare, which is $325 per cyclist, plus $600 to ship all the bikes. The total cost is $2,225. How many cyclists is E-Z-Spokes sponsoring?

5. Felix made his own racing bike. He bought a bike frame, two tires, and one set of new brakes from E-Z-Spokes. The tires cost $45 each, and the brakes cost $79. If his total bill at E-Z-Spokes was $649, how much did he pay for the bike frame?

6. Amanda is passing out fliers to promote the grand opening of a bike shop. She gave out 20 fliers the first hour and 45 in the second hour. During the third hour, she handed out twice as many as she had in the previous two hours. She has 100 fliers left to hand out. How many fliers did Amanda start with?

7. A catering company is providing food for a two-day cycling race. It will cost the company $52.50 per day for each employee that will work at the event and $10 for each cyclist's meals. They spent $1,660 on meals for the event. How many cyclists competed?

8. One company pays bike messengers $3.00 for each delivery. After 5:00 P.M., it pays $15 for each delivery. Suppose a bike messenger worked from 9:00 A.M. to 5:00 P.M. and then made 2 deliveries after 5:00 P.M. If she earned $150, how many deliveries per hour did she average from 9:00 A.M. to 5:00 P.M.?

## Mixed Strategy Practice

9. The security guard for a sporting goods store is making her rounds. First, she walks down 1 flight to the men's bikes section, on the 1st floor. From there, she walks up several flights to clothing. Then, she walks down 2 flights to women's bikes, which is 1 floor above where she started. On which floor is clothing?

**USE DATA** For 10-14, use the table.

10. Karl weighs 150 lb, and Lonnie weighs 200 lb. Karl ran four 6-minute miles at 10 mi per hr. Lonnie jumped rope for half an hour. Who burned more energy?

11. Noel jogged for 1 hr and 27 min, and then bicycled at 12 mi per hr for 33 min. Noel weighs 150 lb. About how many calories did he burn?

12. **Pose a Problem** Look back at Problem 11. Write a similar problem by changing the weight and the types of activity.

13. **Open-Ended** Leah weighs 150 lb. She can exercise each day for 60 min. She wants to do 2 different activities in each 60-min session and burn between 400 and 600 calories. Suggest two possible 60-min workouts she could do.

14. **WRITE Math ▸** Bert burned 500 calories in half an hour. **Explain** how to find Bert's weight and the activity.

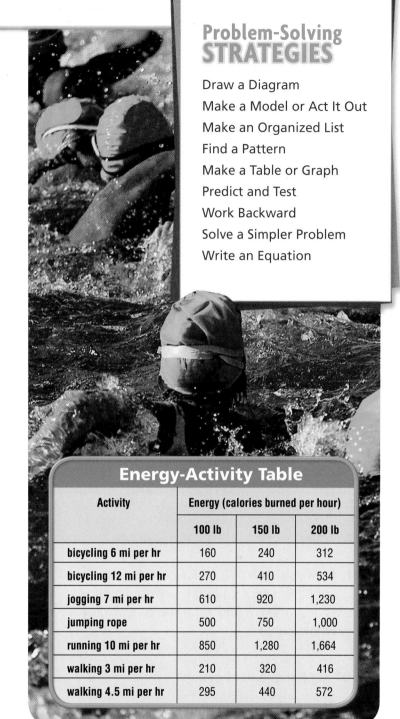

**Problem-Solving STRATEGIES**

Draw a Diagram
Make a Model or Act It Out
Make an Organized List
Find a Pattern
Make a Table or Graph
Predict and Test
Work Backward
Solve a Simpler Problem
Write an Equation

### Energy-Activity Table

| Activity | Energy (calories burned per hour) | | |
|---|---|---|---|
| | 100 lb | 150 lb | 200 lb |
| bicycling 6 mi per hr | 160 | 240 | 312 |
| bicycling 12 mi per hr | 270 | 410 | 534 |
| jogging 7 mi per hr | 610 | 920 | 1,230 |
| jumping rope | 500 | 750 | 1,000 |
| running 10 mi per hr | 850 | 1,280 | 1,664 |
| walking 3 mi per hr | 210 | 320 | 416 |
| walking 4.5 mi per hr | 295 | 440 | 572 |

**CHALLENGE YOURSELF**

In a triathlon, athletes perform in three different sports in a single race. The race begins with swimming, which is followed by bicycling and finally running.

15. Jacob finished the running portion of the triathlon in 12 min 20 sec, which was half the time that it took him to complete the bike portion. He completed the swim in one-eighth the time that it took him to complete the bike portion. What was Jacob's total time?

16. Amanda averaged 13.2 mi per hr for the last 2 mi of the bike portion. That was 0.3 mi per hr slower than she averaged in the first mile. If Amanda's average speed overall for the 6-mi bike portion was 13.35 mi per hr, what was her average speed for miles 2, 3, and 4?

# Extra Practice

## Set A Solve and check. (pp. 336–339)

**1.** $24 = 3x$      **2.** $6y = 36$      **3.** $36 = 1.5b$      **4.** $72 = 8k$

**5.** $\frac{1}{4} = 2r$      **6.** $105 = {}^{-}15x$      **7.** ${}^{-}9v = {}^{-}108$      **8.** $16 = 6.4h$

**9.** $4b = 52$      **10.** $4x = \frac{8}{11}$      **11.** $10x = {}^{-}350$      **12.** $8m = 9.6$

**13.** $1.5 = 3y$      **14.** $42 = 7n$      **15.** $2t = \frac{1}{2}$      **16.** $3x = 24$

**17.** ${}^{-}8y = 36$      **18.** $1{,}200 = 15z$      **19.** $\frac{2}{3} = \frac{3}{4}k$      **20.** $5x = 125$

**21.** Enrique made a total of $625 during the summer painting fences. He painted 25 fences. Write and solve an equation to find how much he was paid per fence.

**22.** Nine shipping containers hold a total of 36 oil paintings. Write and solve an equation to find the number of oil paintings in each container.

## Set B Solve and check. (pp. 340–341)

**1.** $\frac{x}{8} = 6$      **2.** $\frac{k}{3} = 2.5$      **3.** $8 = \frac{a}{6}$      **4.** $12 = \frac{c}{7}$

**5.** $\frac{x}{2} = 3.9$      **6.** $1.8 = \frac{q}{9}$      **7.** $\frac{u}{3} = {}^{-}4$      **8.** $2.25 = \frac{d}{10}$

**9.** $\frac{v}{8} = \frac{1}{2}$      **10.** $\frac{1}{15} = \frac{g}{45}$      **11.** $\frac{k}{5} = \frac{16}{20}$      **12.** ${}^{-}7 = \frac{b}{4}$

**13.** $\frac{m}{2} = 12$      **14.** $1.75 = \frac{h}{5}$      **15.** $\frac{y}{6} = {}^{-}48$      **16.** $\frac{p}{7} = 9$

**17.** $1.5 = \frac{m}{3}$      **18.** $1{,}523 = \frac{a}{24}$      **19.** $\frac{b}{12} = {}^{-}9$      **20.** ${}^{-}5 = \frac{c}{3}$

**21.** Samantha pays $8.95 for each figurine in a set of 8 collector figurines. Write and solve an equation to find what she pays for the whole set of figurines.

**22.** Robert is selling his comic book collection. He separated his comic books into stacks of 8 and ended up with 21 stacks. Write and solve an equation to find the number of comic books he had in his collection.

## Set C Solve and check. (pp. 342–343)

**1.** $8t = 136$      **2.** $29 = x + 17$      **3.** $p - 77 = 34$      **4.** $9 = \frac{s}{13}$

**5.** $\frac{x}{3} = 11.1$      **6.** $l + 5.7 = 14.6$      **7.** $9v = {}^{-}162$      **8.** $n + \frac{2}{3} = 2\frac{5}{6}$

**9.** ${}^{-}21 = u - 48$      **10.** $\frac{w}{4} = \frac{9}{12}$      **11.** $x + 7.9 = 16.5$      **12.** $2\frac{3}{4} = \frac{1}{4}x$

**13.** Alana bought a 5-lb bag of potatoes to make mashed potatoes for dinner. When she was done, the bag weighed $3\frac{1}{4}$ lb. Write and solve an equation to find how many pounds of potatoes Alana used.

**14.** Miguel spent $225 last week on collectible bobble-head dolls. He paid $15 for each bobble-head. Write and solve an equation to find how many bobble-head dolls he bought.

**Technology**
Use Harcourt Mega Math, Ice Station Exploration, *Arctic Algebra*, Levels S, T, Y, X, AA, and BB.

## Set D  Write an equation to represent the function. Then use the equation to find the missing term. (pp. 344–347)

**1.**

| r | 8 | 18 | 28 | 38 | 48 |
|---|---|----|----|----|----|
| s | 16 | 36 |  | 76 | 96 |

**2.**

| v | 16 | 26 | 36 | 46 | 56 |
|---|----|----|----|----|----|
| t | 8 | ■ | 18 | 23 | 28 |

**3.**

| c | 2 | 6 | 10 | 14 | 18 |
|---|---|---|----|----|----|
| d | 0 | 4 | 8 | ■ | 16 |

**4.**

| a | 100 | 80 | 60 | 40 | 20 |
|---|-----|----|----|----|----|
| c | 25 | 20 | ■ | 10 | 5 |

**5.**

| x | 6 | 7 | 8 | 9 | 10 |
|---|---|---|---|---|----|
| y | 3 | 4 | 5 | ■ | 7 |

**6.**

| m | 1 | 2 | 3 | 4 | 5 |
|---|---|---|---|----|----|
| n | 3 | 6 | ■ | 12 | 15 |

## Set E  Graph the data on a coordinate plane. Write an equation relating y to x. Use the equation to find the missing value of y. (pp. 348–349)

**1.**

| x | ⁻6 | ⁻3 | 0 | 9 | 12 |
|---|----|----|---|---|----|
| y | ⁻2 | ⁻1 | 0 | ■ | 4 |

**2.**

| x | ⁻4 | ⁻2 | 0 | 1 | 3 |
|---|----|----|---|---|---|
| y | ⁻24 | ⁻12 | 0 | 6 | ■ |

**3.**

| x | 12 | 14 | 16 | 18 | 20 |
|---|----|----|----|----|----|
| y | 6 | ■ | 8 | 9 | 10 |

**4.**

| x | 8 | 7 | 6 | 5 | 4 |
|---|---|----|----|----|----|
| y | ■ | 28 | 24 | 20 | 16 |

## Set F  Which table represents the graph on the coordinate plane? (pp. 350–353)

**1.**

A

| x | y |
|----|----|
| ⁻1 | ⁻3 |
| 0 | 0 |
| 1 | 3 |

B

| x | y |
|----|----|
| ⁻2 | ⁻4 |
| 0 | 0 |
| 2 | 4 |

C

| x | y |
|----|----|
| ⁻2 | ⁻3 |
| 0 | 1 |
| 2 | 4 |

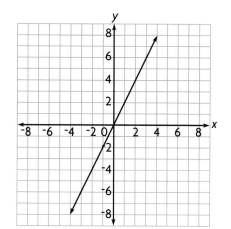

**Graph the equation on a coordinate plane.** (pp. 350–353)

**2.** $y = 3x$

**3.** $y = 5x - 1$

**4.** $y = {}^{-}3x - 4$

**5.** $y = {}^{-}4x + 2$

**6.** $y = {}^{-}2x$

**7.** $y = 3x + 1$

**8.** $y = x + 4$

**9.** $y = x$

# Chapter 14 Review/Test

## Check Vocabulary and Concepts

Choose the best term from the box.

1. The __?__ states that when you divide both sides of an equation by the same nonzero number, the two sides remain equal. (O─┓ AF 1.1, p. 336)

2. A __?__ is a relationship between two quantities in which one quantity depends uniquely on the other. (O─┓ NS 2.0, p. 344)

## Check Skills

Solve and check. (O─┓ AF 1.1, pp. 336–339, 340–341, 342–343)

3. $4z = 64$

4. $\frac{j}{4} = 42.5$

5. $1.6 = \frac{b}{7}$

6. $q + 2.2 = 19.8$

7. $t - \frac{2}{3} = 4\frac{4}{9}$

8. $10 = \frac{s}{15}$

9. $^-2n = \frac{7}{11}$

10. $2.2x = 33$

11. $\frac{n}{2} = \frac{11}{22}$

12. $13 = 6.5v$

Write an equation to represent the function. Then use the equation to find the missing term. (O─┓ AF 1.1, pp. 344–347)

13.

| r | 1 | 2 | 3 | 4 | 5 |
|---|---|---|---|---|---|
| s | 2 | 4 | 6 | 8 | ■ |

14.

| m | 10 | 8 | 6 | 4 | 2 |
|---|----|---|---|---|---|
| n | 5 | 4 | 3 | ■ | 1 |

Graph the data on a coordinate plane. Write an equation relating y to x. Use the equation to find the missing value of y. (AF 1.0, pp. 348–349)

15.

| x | 2 | 3 | 4 | 5 | 6 |
|---|---|---|---|---|---|
| y | 5 | 6 | ■ | 8 | 9 |

16.

| x | $^-10$ | $^-6$ | $^-2$ | 0 | 2 |
|---|-----|-----|-----|---|---|
| y | ■ | 12 | 4 | 0 | $^-4$ |

Graph the equation on a coordinate plane.

(AF 1.0, pp. 350–353)

17. $y = 3x$

18. $y = 4x + 3$

19. $y = 2x - 1$

20. $y = ^-5x + 1$

21. $y = x - 1$

## Check Problem Solving

Solve. (AF 1.0, MR 1.0, MR 2.5, pp. 354–357)

22. Mitchell spent $146 for 4 saw blades and a wrench. The wrench cost $28. How much was each saw blade?

23. Juan paid $12.75 for the first hour of tutoring and $9.95 for each additional hour. He spent $42.60 on tutoring. How many hours did Juan spend on tutoring?

24. If you divide this number by 4, add 8, and multiply by 3, the result is 42. What is the number?

25. **WRITE Math** Suppose Mitchell spent $128 for all the tools in Problem 22. **Explain** how this affects the cost of each saw blade.

**GO ONLINE Technology** Use *Online Assessment.*

# Enrich • Systems of Equations
# What's the Point?

A **system of equations** is a set of two or more equations. To solve a system of equations, you can graph the equations on a coordinate plane and find the intersection point. That point is the solution of the system.

**Gear Up!** Solve the system of equations $y = 2x + 1$ and $y = 3x - 1$.

**Step 1** Graph each equation on the same coordinate plane.

Make an input-output table for each equation. Choose values for $x$, and solve for $y$.

$y = 2x + 1$

| x | 0 | 1 | 2 | 3 |
|---|---|---|---|---|
| y | 1 | 3 | 5 | 7 |

$y = 3x - 1$

| x | 0 | 1 | 2 | 3 |
|---|---|---|---|---|
| y | ⁻1 | 2 | 5 | 8 |

Use the tables to write ordered pairs.

(0,1), (1,3), (2,5), (3,7)          (0,⁻1), (1,2), (2,5), (3,8)

Graph the ordered pairs for each equation on the coordinate plane and draw a line through the points.

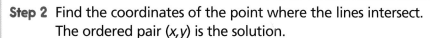

**Step 2** Find the coordinates of the point where the lines intersect. The ordered pair $(x,y)$ is the solution.

$x$-coordinate = 2          $y$-coordinate = 5          (2,5)

**Step 3** Check the solution, (2,5).

Substitute the values into the equation $y = 2x + 1$.

$$y = 2x + 1$$
$$5 = (2 \times 2) + 1$$
$$5 = 5$$

Substitute the values into the equation $y = 3x - 1$.

$$y = 3x - 1$$
$$5 = (3 \times 2) - 1$$
$$5 = 5$$

So, the solution of the system of equations is (2,5).

## Try It

**Solve each system of equations.**

**1.** $y = {}^-2x + 1$
   $y = 2x - 3$

**2.** $y = 3x + 5$
   $y = {}^-3x - 1$

**3.** $y = x - 2$
   $y = 2x - 1$

**4.** $y = 0.5x + 1$
   $y = 4x - 6$

**5.** $y = {}^-2x - 2$
   $y = x + 4$

**6.** $y = {}^-x + 3$
   $y = 3x - 3$

**WRITE Math** ► Ronald solves a system of equations and writes an ordered pair $(x,y)$ as the solution. **Explain** how he could check that his solution is correct.

# Unit Review/Test
## Chapters 11–14

## Multiple Choice

1. Evaluate $3b + 3b^2 + b$ for $b = 3$. (AF 1.2, p. 284)

   **A** 39

   **B** 48

   **C** 84

   **D** 87

2. A local skating rink charges $3 for each skater. Which expression represents the total cost in dollars for $n$ skaters? (AF 1.2, p. 280)

   **A** $\frac{n}{3}$

   **B** $3 + n$

   **C** $3n$

   **D** $n - 3$

3. Armando wanted to find out how much money he began the day with before going shopping. He wrote the equation $m - 15 = 49$. What value of $m$ makes Armando's equation true? (O━┓ AF 1.1, p. 320)

   **A** $^-64$

   **B** $^-34$

   **C** 34

   **D** 64

4. Steve is paying for a $102 digital music player in two payments. The first payment is $45. Which equation can he use to find the amount of the second payment?
   (O━┓ AF 1.1, p. 304)

   **A** $102 = 45 + p$

   **B** $p - 102 = 45$

   **C** $p - 45 = 102 - 45$

   **D** $45 = p + 102$

5. Mario had some change in his pocket. After his friends gave him $1.25, Mario had a total of $3.55 in his pocket. Which equation can he use to find the original amount of money, $p$, he had in his pocket?
   (O━┓ AF 1.1, p. 300)

   **A** $3.55 = p - 1.25$

   **B** $p = 1.25 \times 3.55$

   **C** $p + 1.25 = 3.55$

   **D** $p + 3.55 = 1.25$

6. What value of $h$ makes the following equation true? (O━┓ AF 1.1, p. 320)

   $$\frac{h}{6} = 7$$

   **A** 42

   **B** 3

   **C** $1\frac{1}{6}$

   **D** 1

7. Each of 8 boxes holds the same number of yearbooks. If there are 128 yearbooks, which equation can be used to find the number of yearbooks in each box? (O━┓ AF 1.1, p. 336)

   **A** $8 + b = 128$

   **B** $\frac{b}{8} = 128$

   **C** $128b = 8$

   **D** $128 = 8b$

8. Use the Commutative Property to help evaluate $6 + 23 + 14$. (AF 1.3, p. 272)

   **A** 29

   **B** 37

   **C** 43

   **D** 53

**GO ONLINE Technology** Use *Online Assessment.*

9. Which equation could represent the function in the table? (O—ᴨ AF 1.1, p. 344)

| x | 10 | 12 | 14 | 16 | 18 |
|---|----|----|----|----|----|
| y | 32 | 38 | 44 | 50 | 56 |

**A** $y = 3x$

**B** $y = 3x + 2$

**C** $x = 3y$

**D** $x = 3y + 2$

10. What value of $x$ makes the following equation true? (O—ᴨ AF 1.1, p. 320)

$$x - 13 = 12$$

**A** 25      **C** $^{-}1$

**B** 1      **D** $^{-}5$

11. Kirsten is paid $295 for cutting yards in her neighborhood. She works for 25 hours. How much is she paid per hour? (O—ᴨ AF 1.1, p. 336)

**A** $0.11      **C** $11.08

**B** $1.18      **D** $11.80

12. The table below shows the relationship between the number of ceramic pots, $x$, in a box, and the weight of the box, $y$, in pounds. Which equation represents the function in the table? (O—ᴨ AF 1.1, p. 344)

| x | 3 | 5 | 7 | 9 |
|---|---|----|----|----|
| y | 7 | 11 | 15 | 19 |

**A** $y = x + 4$      **C** $y = 2x$

**B** $y = x + 10$      **D** $y = 2x + 1$

13. Which expression represents 21.6 times a number $b$? (AF 1.2, p. 280)

**A** $\frac{6}{21.6}$

**B** $21.6b$

**C** $21.6 - b$

**D** $21.6 + b$

## Short Response

14. Samuel's age is 4 years greater than the sum of Moishe's age, $m$, and twice Abigail's age, $a$. Write an expression that shows how to find Samuel's age. (AF 1.2, p. 280)

15. Eileen makes $24 for every scarf that she sews. If she was paid $408 last week, how many scarves did she make? (O—ᴨ AF 1.1, p. 342)

16. Write an equation that represents the word sentence "two fifths of a number, $n$, is 24." (O—ᴨ AF 1.1, p. 300)

17. The table below shows the number of tickets sold at a local amusement park.

| Amusement Park Tickets | |
|---|---|
| **Ride** | **Tickets Sold** |
| Super Coaster | 1,934 |
| Danger Alley | 876 |
| Teacup Spin | 543 |

If the total amount of money made in ticket sales for Super Coaster was $3,384.50, how much did each ticket cost? (O—ᴨ AF 1.1, p. 336)

## Extended Response   WRITE Math ▶

18. Jorge says that the expression $60h$ can be used to find the number of minutes in $h$ hours. Is he correct? **Explain** why or why not. (AF 1.2, p. 280)

19. At a beach, 48 people are snorkeling. That is three times the number of people scuba diving. If $s$ represents the number of scuba divers, what equation can you write to find the number of people scuba diving? **Explain** how to determine the solution to the equation. (O—ᴨ AF 1.1, p. 342)

# The Sound of Speed

## Breaking the "Sound Barrier"

At sea level, on a dry day, sound travels about 760 mi per hr. For a long time, many people did not believe that a plane could fly that fast. In 1946, pilots at Edwards Air Force Base in California began testing experimental planes that were faster than ever before. The next year, a test pilot named Chuck Yeager flew an X-1 plane faster than the speed of sound and "broke the sound barrier." Scientists use a ratio called a Mach number to compare the speed of an airplane to the speed of sound. For example, an airplane traveling at Mach 3 is traveling at 3 times the speed of sound. The fastest known speed for a winged aircraft flown by a pilot is Mach 6.7. This record was set in 1967, again by a test pilot from Edwards Air Force Base.

Chuck Yeager and the X-1 research aircraft at Edwards Air Force Base in California.

### FACT·ACTIVITY

**Use the table to help answer the questions.**

| Mach Number | 1 | 2 | 3 | 4 | 5 | 6 |
|---|---|---|---|---|---|---|
| Speed | 760 | ▨ | ▨ | ▨ | ▨ | ▨ |

1 The first Mach number, Mach 1, is approximately 760 mi per hr. Copy and complete the table showing the first six Mach numbers. Then make a graph of the data.

2 **WRITE Math** Explain what the shape and direction of the line in your graph tells you about the relationship between Mach number and speed?

3 The Concorde jet had a cruising speed of 1,350 mi per hr. Find the point for that speed on the graph. What was the approximate Mach number of the Concorde jet?

4 An F-15 military jet has a top speed of Mach 2.5. Find the point for that speed on the line graph. What is the approximate speed of an F-15 in miles per hour?

5 The distance between California's northern border with Oregon and its southern border with Mexico is about 770 miles. How long would it take to fly that distance at Mach 2?

The X-43A is an unmanned experimental aircraft that flew at Mach 7 for 10 seconds. The aircraft, stationed at Dryden Flight Research Center in California, broke the world record as the plane flew over the Pacific Ocean west of California.

# SONIC BOOM!

**A** sonic boom is sound made by an object traveling faster than the speed of sound. The boom is caused by the compression of sound waves in front of the object. If a plane causes a sonic boom, the people on the ground can hear it, but the pilot cannot.

**X-43A Hyper-X hypersonic aircraft**

# FACT·ACTIVITY

**1** The sound barrier has been broken by vehicles other than aircrafts. The first land vehicle to break the sound barrier was driven by Andy Green, a British fighter pilot, at Black Rock Desert in Nevada. On October 15, 1997, Green reached a world-record land speed of 763.035 mi per hr. At what Mach number was Green traveling?

**2** Mach numbers can also be used to describe objects traveling slower than the speed of sound. For example, an object traveling 570 mi per hr is traveling at Mach 0.75.

This equation can be used to calculate the Mach number for any speed in miles per hour: $y = \frac{x}{760}$ when $y$ is the Mach number and $x$ is the speed in miles per hour.

▶ Do some research to identify three fast animals, three fast humans, and three fast vehicles.

▶ Find their speeds in miles per hour, and convert their speeds into Mach numbers. How many times as fast would each have to travel in order to break the sound barrier?

▶ Calculate your own top speed and convert it to a Mach number. How many times as fast would you have to travel to break the sound barrier?

▶ Decide how to best display all the data you have collected. Present your findings to the class.

**3** **WRITE Math** ▶ **Explain** how you could use logical reasoning to find the equivalent speed in mi per hr of Mach 0.25.

# UNIT
# 5 Geometry: Two-Dimensional Figures

## Math on Location

**1**

▲ Landscape architects create beautiful spaces near buildings, using sculptures, water, and plants.

**2**

▲ Parallel lines and congruent angles form views of pleasing and restful patterns.

**3**

▲ Being surrounded by beautiful space forms an amazing contrast to tall buildings in a city.

# VOCABULARY POWER

**TALK Math**

What math is shown in the **Math on Location** photographs? How are parallel and perpendicular lines used in landscape architecture?

**READ Math**

**REVIEW VOCABULARY**  You learned the words below when you learned about two-dimensional figures. How do these words relate to **Math on Location**?

**congruent** having the same size and shape

**parallel lines** lines in a plane that are always the same distance apart

**perpendicular lines** two lines that intersect to form right, or 90°, angles

**WRITE Math**

Copy and complete a double bubble map like the one below. Use what you know about two-dimensional figures to compare and contrast the properties of squares and rhombi.

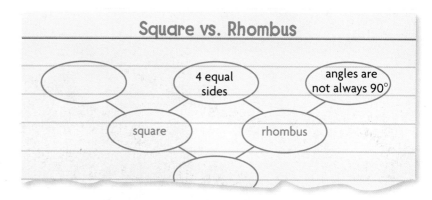

Square vs. Rhombus

4 equal sides

angles are not always 90°

square        rhombus

**Technology**
Multimedia Math Glossary link at
**www.harcourtschool.com/hspmath**

# 15 Angle Relationships

**The Big Idea** Angles and their relationships can be identified, described, and classified.

## Investigate

Make a list of the different types of angles that you see in the bridge, including acute, obtuse, and right angles. Then look for pairs of angles that have special relationships. Give any examples of vertical angles, adjacent angles, complementary angles, and supplementary angles that you can find.

### Types of Angles

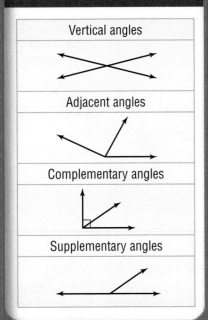

Vertical angles

Adjacent angles

Complementary angles

Supplementary angles

## CALIFORNIA FAST FACT

The San Francisco-Oakland Bay Bridge is one of the longest high-level steel bridges in the world. From one approach to the other, the bridge is 8.4 miles long.

**GO ONLINE**

**Technology**
Student pages are available in the Student eBook.

Check your understanding of important skills
needed for success in Chapter 15.

▶ **Name Angles**

Name the angle formed by the blue rays.

1.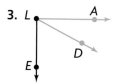

2.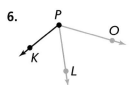

3. 

4.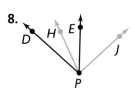

5. 

6. 

7. 

8. 

▶ **Use a Protractor to Measure Angles**

For 9–14, use the figure at the right. Copy the figure.
Then use a protractor to measure each angle.

9. ∠ABD      10. ∠DBF

11. ∠FBA      12. ∠EBC

13. ∠CBD      14. ∠FBC

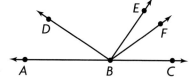

# VOCABULARY POWER

**CHAPTER VOCABULARY**

adjacent angles
complementary angles
congruent
supplementary angles
vertical angles

**WARM-UP WORDS**

**vertical angles** a pair of opposite congruent angles
formed where two lines intersect

**congruent** having the same size and shape

**adjacent angles** side-by-side pairs of angles that have a
common vertex and a common ray

# 1 Types of Angles

**OBJECTIVE:** Classify angles and identify vertical and adjacent angles.

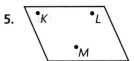
## Quick Review

**Name each figure.**

1. $\overleftrightarrow{O \quad R}$
2. • $C$
3. $D \quad E$ →
4. $A \quad\quad B$
5. [parallelogram with points $K$, $L$, $M$]

## Vocabulary

**vertical angles**

**congruent**      **adjacent angles**

## Learn

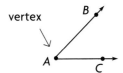

Two rays with a common endpoint form an angle. The endpoint is called the vertex of the angle.

vertex → [angle diagram with vertex $A$, rays to $B$ and $C$]

You can name the angle with the three points shown or with the vertex.

$$\angle BAC, \angle CAB, \text{ or } \angle A$$

The angle is measured in degrees. One degree is $\frac{1}{360}$ of a circle. An angle is classified by the number of degrees in it.

**PROBLEM** A stone has the best chance of skipping across water when it is tossed at an angle of 20° to the water. What type of angle is an angle that measures 20°?

You can classify angles by their measures.

| | |
|---|---|
| An acute angle measures less than 90°. | [acute angle diagram] |
| A right angle measures 90°. | [right angle diagram] |
| An obtuse angle measures more than 90° but less than 180°. | [obtuse angle diagram] |
| A straight angle measures 180°. | [straight angle diagram] |

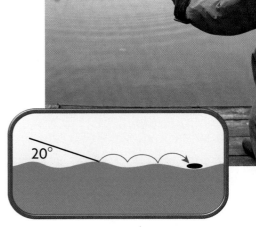

20°

Since 20° < 90°, an angle that measures 20° is an acute angle.

You can use the measure of one or more angles to find the measure of another angle.

### Example 1  What is m∠JKM?

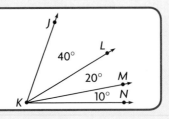

m∠JKM = m∠JKL + m∠LKM

m∠JKL = 40°   m∠LKM = 20°

m∠JKM = 40° + 20°

[angle diagram with vertex $K$, rays to $J$, $L$, $M$, $N$ showing 40°, 20°, 10°]

**READ Math**

Read m∠JKM as the measure of angle JKM.

So, m∠JKM is 60°.

• Why are the angles above not named by using only the letter of the vertex?

• What is the measure of ∠JKN? Explain how you found the answer.

**MG 2.1** Identify angles as vertical, adjacent, complementary, or supplementary and provide descriptions of these terms. *also* **MR 2.0, MR 2.2, MR 2.4, MR 2.5, MR 3.0, MR 3.2**

# Special Angle Names

Certain angle pairs have special names.

**Vertical angles** are pairs of angles formed opposite each other when two lines intersect. Vertical angles have the same measure. Angles with the same measure are said to be **congruent**. Use the symbol ≅ to show that two angles are congruent.

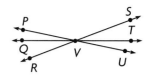

∠PVS and ∠RVU are vertical angles. They each measure 150°, so ∠PVS ≅ ∠RVU.

**Adjacent angles** are side-by-side pairs of angles that have a common vertex and a common ray.

Both pairs of angles, ∠QVR and ∠QVS and ∠QVR and ∠RVU, are adjacent angles.

**Math Idea**

An angle can be a part of a vertical angle pair and part of an adjacent angle pair. ∠RVU and ∠PVS are vertical angles. ∠RVU and ∠QVR are adjacent angles.

**Example 2** Look at the figure above. Is ∠PVQ adjacent to ∠RVU?

> ∠PVQ and ∠RVU have a common vertex, V, but they do not have a common ray. So, ∠PVQ is not adjacent to ∠RVU.

**Example 3** Look at the figure above. Find an angle vertical to the given angle. Then find two angles adjacent to the given angle.

**Ⓐ** ∠SVT

Vertical angle: ∠QVR

Adjacent angles: ∠PVS, ∠TVU

**Ⓑ** ∠PVQ

Vertical angle: ∠TVU

Adjacent angles: ∠QVR, ∠PVS

• Can you name other angles adjacent to ∠SVT? ∠PVQ?

**Example 4** Tell if the pair of angles is *vertical*, *adjacent*, or *neither*.

**Ⓐ** ∠1 and ∠2

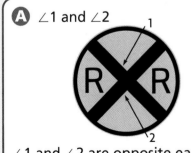

∠1 and ∠2 are opposite each other and are formed by two intersecting lines.

So, ∠1 and ∠2 are vertical angles.

**Ⓑ** ∠A and ∠B

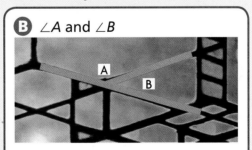

∠A and ∠B are side-by-side and have a common vertex and a common ray.

So, ∠A and ∠B are adjacent angles.

## Guided Practice

1. ∠AEB is opposite ∠DEC and these angles are formed with two intersecting lines. Name the angle vertical to ∠DEC.

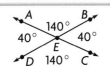

**For 2-4, use the figure at the right. Find an angle vertical to the given angle. Then find two angles adjacent to the given angle.**

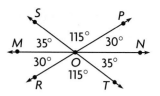

**2.** ∠MOS　　　　**3.** ∠PON　　　　**4.** ∠TOR

**5.** **TALK Math** Explain how you know if a pair of angles is vertical or adjacent.

---

## Independent Practice and Problem Solving

**For 6-9, use the figure at the right. Find an angle vertical to the given angle. Then find two angles adjacent to the given angle.**

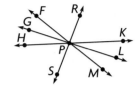

**6.** ∠FPR　　　　　　　**7.** ∠KPL

**8.** ∠RPK　　　　　　　**9.** ∠MPL

**For 10-15, use the figure at the right. Tell if the pair of angles is *vertical, adjacent,* or *neither*.**

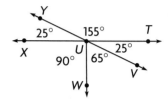

**10.** ∠TUV and ∠YUT　　　　**11.** ∠XUY and ∠WUV

**12.** ∠XUY and ∠TUV　　　　**13.** ∠XUV and ∠YUX

**14.** ∠YUW and ∠WUV　　　　**15.** ∠YUT and ∠XUV

**16.** ★**Algebra** Use the figure at the right. Clea wants to find m∠ABE. If ∠ABC and ∠DBE measure 15° and ∠CBD measures 20°, what is the measure of ∠ABE? What is the difference between the measure of ∠ABE and the measure of ∠CBE? **Explain.**

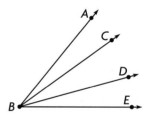

**17.** **Reasoning** Rod says the letter X forms two pairs of congruent angles. Kelly says the letter X forms two pairs of vertical angles. Who is correct? **Explain.**

**18.** **WRITE Math** **What's the Error?** Paul says that all vertical angles are acute. Describe Paul's error. Justify your answer with examples.

---

## Achieving the Standards

**19.** What value of *k* makes the following equation true? $k \times 4 = 48$ (○━┓ AF 1.1, p. 336)

**20.** Use mental math to solve. ■ + 135 = 190
(Grade 5 NS 1.0)

**21.** Patty wants to know where sixth-grade students want to go on their next field trip. She surveys 50 students randomly chosen from a list of all sixth-grade students. What sampling method is she using? (○━┓ SDAP 2.2, p. 202)

**22.** **Test Prep** Which is a true statement?

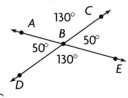

**A** ∠CBE is vertical to ∠ABC.

**B** ∠ABD is adjacent to ∠CBE.

**C** ∠DBE is vertical to ∠ABD.

**D** ∠DBE is adjacent to ∠ABD.

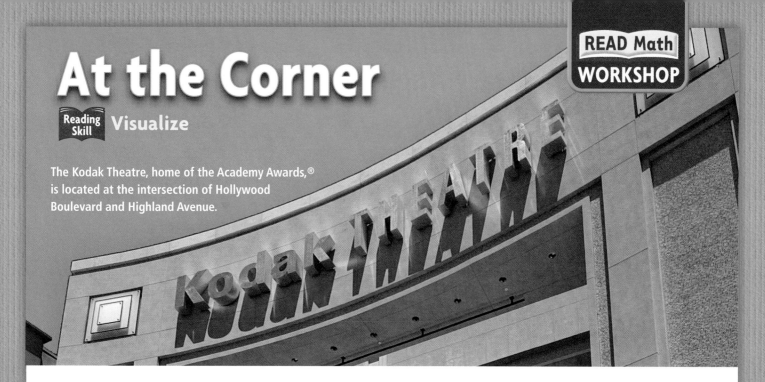

# At the Corner

**Reading Skill** Visualize

The Kodak Theatre, home of the Academy Awards,® is located at the intersection of Hollywood Boulevard and Highland Avenue.

$H$ollywood Boulevard provides many shopping and entertainment choices. At the intersection of Hollywood and Highland, the Kodak Theatre attracts thousands of visitors each year.

The table shows approximate angle measures of intersections formed by some Hollywood roads. You can visualize information given in a problem to help you understand the situation. When you visualize, you picture something in your mind.

### Approximate Angles of Intersection

| Roads | Measure |
|---|---|
| Hollywood and Highland | 90° |
| Wilshire and Santa Monica | 45° |
| Wilshire and N. La Ciennega | 150° |

**Example** Classify all of the angles formed by the intersection of Hollywood Blvd. and Highland Ave. in front of the Kodak Theatre.

**Step 1**

Picture what the intersection of the two streets might look like from an airplane or on a map. Simplify the picture in your mind so it looks like intersecting lines.

Highland
90°
90° Hollywood

**Step 2**

Use what you know about the types of angles formed by intersecting lines to help you.

**Problem Solving** Visualize to understand the problem.

1. Solve the problem above.

2. Classify all of the angles formed by the intersection of Wilshire and Santa Monica.

# Complementary Angles

**OBJECTIVE:** Identify complementary angles.

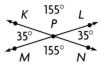
## Learn

### Activity

**Materials** ■ protractor ■ tracing paper ■ scissors

• Trace ∠BOC and ∠AOD on tracing paper.

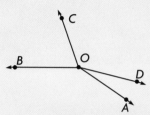 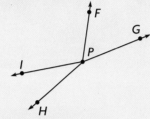

• Use a protractor to measure both angles.

• Cut out the angles and lay $\overrightarrow{OC}$ over $\overrightarrow{OD}$.

• Find m∠BOA.

• Repeat for ∠FPG and ∠IPH, lay $\overrightarrow{PF}$ over $\overrightarrow{PI}$.

Then find m∠HPG.

• What do you notice about ∠BOA and ∠HPG?

**ERROR ALERT**

It is important to read the appropriate scale on a protractor. Read the scale that starts with 0° at $\overrightarrow{YZ}$. ∠XYZ is an acute angle. The m∠XYZ = 75°.

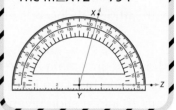

Two angles whose measures have a sum of 90° are called **complementary angles**. They can be adjacent or nonadjacent.

**Example** The Auburn-Foresthill Bridge is the second-highest bridge in California. Are the angles formed by the cross beams of the bridge complementary angles?

$$45° + 45° = 90°$$

Yes, the angles are complementary angles.

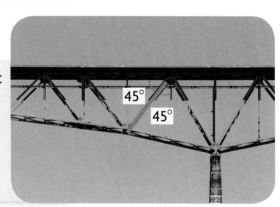

## Guided Practice

**1.** Are ∠SWV and ∠TWU complementary angles?

∠SWV measures 35°. ∠TWU measures 55°.

35° + 55° = ■°

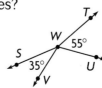

**MG 2.1** Identify angles as vertical, adjacent, complementary, or supplementary and provide descriptions of these terms. *also* **MR 2.0, MR 2.2, MR 2.4, MR 2.5, MR 3.0, MR 3.2**

For 2–5, use the figure at the right. Tell if the pair of angles is *adjacent, complementary, both of these,* or *none of these.*

2. ∠JPO and ∠KPJ

3. ∠NPO and ∠LPK

✓4. ∠LPK and ∠MPN

✓5. ∠NPO and ∠MPN

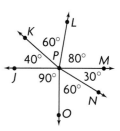

6. **TALK Math** Explain how you know if two angles are complementary.

## Independent Practice and Problem Solving

For 7–12, use the figure at the right. Tell if the pair of angles is *adjacent, complementary, both of these,* or *none of these.*

7. ∠FGE and ∠CGD

8. ∠AGF and ∠BGC

9. ∠AGB and ∠BGC

10. ∠DGE and ∠BGC

11. ∠AGF and ∠FGE

12. ∠BGC and ∠CGD

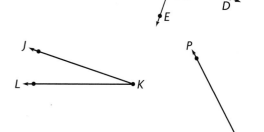

13. Estimate the measures of ∠JKL and ∠PQR at the right. Then measure the angles with a protractor, and tell if they are complementary angles. Were your estimates reasonable? Explain.

14. **Reasoning** The difference between the measures of two complementary angles is 18°. What is the measure of each angle?

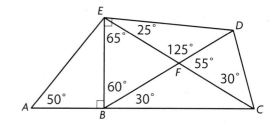

For 15–16, use the figure at the right.

15. **Algebra** The measure of ∠EFD is $2\frac{1}{2}$ times the measure of one of the other angles. Which angle is it? What is its measure?

16. **WRITE Math** What's the Question? The answer is ∠BEF and ∠DEF.

## Achieving the Standards

17. The temperature in the evening was 8°F. It dropped 15°F overnight. What was the temperature the next morning?

   (○━ NS 2.3, p. 150)

18. Solve using mental math. 95 + ▧ = 180

   (Grade 5 NS 1.0)

19. What is the measure of ∠PQR?

   (Grade 5 ○━ MG 2.1)

20. **Test Prep** Which pair of angles is complementary?

   A ∠BGE and ∠AGB

   B ∠AGF and ∠FGD

   C ∠EGD and ∠AGF

   D ∠AGF and ∠BGE

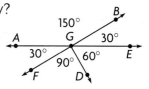

# Supplementary Angles

**OBJECTIVE:** Identify supplementary angles.

## Learn

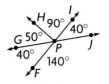
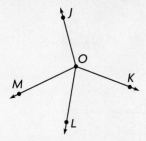

### Activity

**Materials** ▪ protractor ▪ tracing paper ▪ scissors

*   Trace ∠*JOM* and ∠*LOK* on tracing paper.

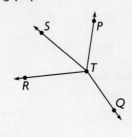

*   Use a protractor to measure both angles.
*   Cut out the two angles and lay one ray over another.
*   Measure the new angle.
*   Repeat for ∠*RTS* and ∠*PTQ*.
*   What do you notice about the new angles?

Two angles whose measures have a sum of 180° are **supplementary angles**. The angles may be adjacent or nonadjacent.

**Example** The stained glass window shown at the right was designed by Arthur Stern and is known as *Frozen Music*. Look at the labeled angles. Are they supplementary?

$$135° + 45° = 180°$$

So, the two angles are supplementary.

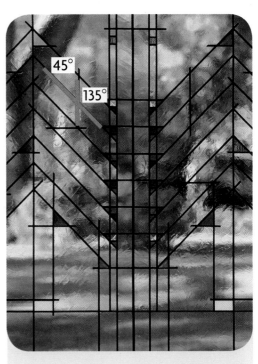

▲ Arthur Stern is considered an expert on Frank Lloyd Wright and the Prairie School.

## Guided Practice

1.  Are ∠*AED* and ∠*BEC* supplementary angles?

    ∠*AED* measures 115°.

    ∠*BEC* measures 65°.

    $$115° + 65° = \blacksquare°$$

**MG 2.1** Identify angles as vertical, adjacent, complementary, or supplementary and provide descriptions of these terms. *also* **MR 2.0, MR 2.2, MR 2.4, MR 2.5, MR 3.0, MR 3.2**

**For 2–5, use the figure at the right. Tell if the pair of angles is** *complementary,* *supplementary,* **or** *neither.*

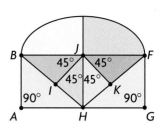

**2.** ∠IJB and ∠HJK

**3.** ∠IJH and ∠HJK

✓ **4.** ∠BAH and ∠FGH

✓ **5.** ∠HGF and ∠IJH

**6.** TALK Math Explain how you know if two angles are supplementary.

## Independent Practice and Problem Solving

**For 7–12, use the figure at the right. Tell if the pair of angles is** *complementary,* *supplementary,* **or** *neither.*

**7.** ∠AOB and ∠BOC

**8.** ∠DOC and ∠AOB

**9.** ∠DOE and ∠AOB

**10.** ∠BOC and ∠DOC

**11.** ∠DOC and ∠DOE

**12.** ∠AOE and ∠COE

**Complete. Write** *always, sometimes,* **or** *never.*

**13.** Two acute angles are __?__ complementary.

**14.** Two obtuse angles are __?__ supplementary.

**15.** Two obtuse angles are __?__ complementary.

**16.** Two right angles are __?__ supplementary.

**17.** ≡**FAST FACT** From 1885 to 1923, Frank Lloyd Wright designed more than 4,500 decorative glass windows. The figure at the right shows angles from Arthur Stern's *Frozen Music.* Find an angle that is complementary to ∠2 and supplementary to the angle formed by angles 5 and 6.

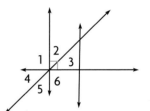

**18. Reasoning** Angle *PQR* is formed by two adjacent supplementary angles. One of the angles is ∠*PQS*. What is the name of the other angle?

**19.** WRITE Math ▸ Explain how to draw a pair of supplementary angles without using a protractor.

## Achieving the Standards

**20.** How does the outlier affect the mean, median, and mode of the following data set? 2.5, 12.2, 2.8, 4.6, 2.5 (SDAP 1.3, p. 226)

**21.** Solve by using mental math. (Grade 5 NS 1.0)
20 + 38 + __?__ = 180

**22.** What is $4 \times 3^2 - (17 - 8)$? (AF 1.4, p. 276)

**23. Test Prep** What is the measure of angle 1 in the figure?

**A** 35°

**B** 45°

**C** 65°

**D** 85°

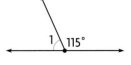

Extra Practice on page 384, Set C

# LESSON 4

# Unknown Angle Measures

**OBJECTIVE:** Use angle relationships to find unknown angle measures.

**Quick Review**

Name two pairs of supplementary angles in the figure.

## Learn

You can use the properties of vertical and adjacent angles to find unknown angle measures.

**Example 1** Find m∠LNM.

∠JNK and ∠LNM are vertical angles.
∠JNK ≅ ∠LNM.

Since m∠JNK is 145°, the m∠LNM is 145°.

**Example 2** The measure of ∠YZW is 65°. Find m∠WZX.

∠YZX and ∠WZX are adjacent angles.

m∠YZX + m∠WZX = m∠YZW

40° + ■ = 65°    The sum of the measures is 65°.

65° − 40° = 25°    Subtract to find the unknown measure.

So, m∠WZX is 25°.

You can also use the properties of complementary and supplementary angles to find the measures of unknown angles.

**Example 3** Ski jumpers lean forward to help them extend the distance of their jumps. What is the angle between this ski jumper and the front of his skis?

In the photo, ∠DCE and ∠BCD are supplementary angles.

m∠DCE + m∠BCD = 180°

160° + ■ = 180°    The sum of the measures is 180°.

180° − 160° = 20°    Subtract to find the unknown measure.

So, the ski jumper is at a 20° angle to the front of his skis.

• **What if** the ski jumper were at a 145° angle to the back of his skis? At what angle would he be to the front of his skis?

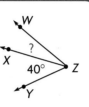

**378**

MG 2.2 Use the properties of complementary and supplementary angles and the sum of the angles of a triangle to solve problems involving an unknown angle. *also* MG 2.1, MR 2.2, MR 2.4, MR 2.5, MR 3.0, MR 3.2, MR 3.3

## Example 4 Find m∠IGH.

∠FGI and ∠IGH are complementary angles.

m∠FGI + m∠IGH = 90°

30° + ■ = 90°    The sum of the measures is 90°.

90° − 30° = 60°    Subtract to find the unknown measure.

So, the m∠IGH is 60°.

## Example 5 In the figure, $\overleftrightarrow{PQ}$ intersects $\overleftrightarrow{MN}$ at O, m∠NOP = 55°, and ∠MOQ ≅ ∠MOR. What is m∠POR?

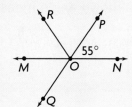

| Unknown Angle Measure | Angle Relationship |
|---|---|
| m∠MOQ is 55°. | ∠MOQ and ∠NOP are vertical angles.<br>m∠MOQ = m∠NOP |
| m∠MOR is 55°. | ∠MOQ ≅ ∠MOR, so m∠MOQ = m∠MOR. |
| m∠POR is 70°. | ∠MON is a straight angle, so ∠MON is 180°.<br>m∠MON = m∠MOR + m∠POR + m∠NOP<br>   180° = 55° + m∠POR + 55°<br>   180° = 110° + m∠POR<br>    70° = m∠POR |

When an object bounces off a surface, it always rebounds at the angle at which it hit. In the figure, ∠PSR and ∠VST have the same measure.

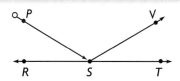

## Example 6

A hockey puck hits $\overline{BD}$, the straight wall of an ice rink, at an angle of 25°. $\overline{FC}$ is drawn so that ∠BCF and ∠DCF are right angles. Find the measures of ∠1 and ∠3.

The puck rebounds at the angle at which it hit, so the measure of ∠3 is 25°.

∠BCA and ∠1 are complementary angles.

25° + ■ = 90°

90° − 25° = 65°, so m∠1 is 65°.

• What is m∠2?

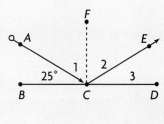

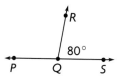

## Guided Practice

1. Find m∠PQR.

   m∠PQS is 180°. ∠RQS and ∠PQR are supplementary angles.

   80° + ∠PQR = 180°    m∠PQR is ■°.

**Find the unknown angle measure. Explain your answer.**

2.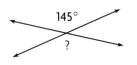
145°
?

3.
?
147°

✓4.
?
39°

✓5.
?  48°

6. **TALK Math** Explain how to find the measure of an angle that is complementary to another angle with a known measure.

## Independent Practice and Problem Solving

**Find the unknown angle measure. Explain your answer.**

7. 72°
?

8. ?  35°

9. ?  65°

10. 90°
?

11. ?  116°

12. ?  84°

13. ?  23°

14. ?  56°

**For 15–18, use the figure at the right. Find the unknown angle measure. Explain your answer.**

15. ∠LMQ

16. ∠QMN

17. ∠NMR

18. ∠RMP

L
30°  M  Q
P
N
R

**For 19–22, use the figure at the right.**

19. Which pair(s) of vertical angles include ∠2?

20. Which angles are not adjacent to ∠6?

21. If m∠8 is 41°, what are the measures of ∠5, ∠6, ∠7?

22. If m∠3 is 139°, what are the measures of ∠1, ∠2, and ∠4? What do you notice about the sum of the measures of ∠1, ∠2, ∠3, and ∠4?

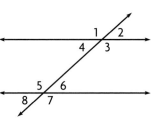
1  2
4  3
5  6
8  7

**For 23–24, use the figure at the right.**

23. If m∠2 is 38.25°, what is m∠1?

24. **Algebra** What if m∠2 is the same as $\frac{2}{3} \times (36 + (3 \times 3))$? What are m∠1 and m∠2?

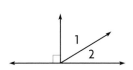
1
2

25. **Reasoning** John says that two complementary angles that are congruent both measure 45°. Is John's statement *always true*, *sometimes true*, or *never true*? Explain.

26. Angles A and B are complementary angles. If the measure of ∠B is 75°, what is the measure of the angle that is supplementary to angle A?

27. **Pose a Problem** Change Problem 26 so that the angle that is supplementary to ∠A measures less than 100°. Solve the new problem.

28. **WRITE Math** What's the Question? The answer is 165°.

**Extra Practice** on page 384, Set D

**CD ROM** **Technology** Use Harcourt Mega Math, Ice Station Exploration, *Polar Planes*, Level B.

**29.** What is the range of the following data set?
(SDAP 1.1, p. 224)

72, 63, 81, 68, 88, 72, 69

**30.** What is the missing number? (Grade 5 NS 1.0)

12 + 9 + ___ = 180

**31. Test Prep** Which of the following is the unknown angle measure?

**A** 41°　　**C** 139°

**B** 131°　　**D** 229°

**32.** What is the volume of this figure?
(Grade 5 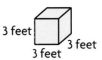 MG 1.3)

3 feet, 3 feet, 3 feet

**33. Test Prep** Which of the following is the unknown angle measure?

**A** 30°　　**C** 70°

**B** 50°　　**D** 160°

20°, ?

 **Problem Solving and Reasoning**

**LOGICAL REASONING** Inductive and deductive reasoning are ways to use information to draw conclusions.

You use inductive reasoning when you look for patterns in specific examples to draw conclusions. You use deductive reasoning when you use known facts to draw conclusions.

**Example** **Use inductive and deductive reasoning to support the following statement.**

Two complementary adjacent angles form a right angle.

**Ⓐ Inductive Reasoning**

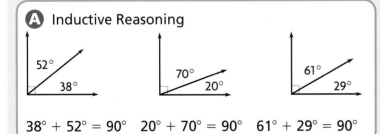

52°, 38°　　70°, 20°　　61°, 29°

38° + 52° = 90°　20° + 70° = 90°　61° + 29° = 90°

**Ⓑ Deductive Reasoning**

- A right angle measures 90°.
- The sum of two complementary angles is 90°.
- Adjacent angles have a common ray and common vertex.

So, the statement is true.

**Identify the type of reasoning used. Explain your answer.**

**1.** Two supplementary adjacent angles form a straight angle.

- A straight angle measures 180°.
- The sum of two supplementary angles is 180°.
- Adjacent angles have a common ray and a common vertex.

**2.** Vertical angles have the same measure.

105°, 105°

135°, 45°, 45°, 135°

# Problem Solving Workshop
## Strategy: Draw a Diagram

OBJECTIVE: Solve problems by using the strategy draw a diagram.

## Use the Strategy

**PROBLEM** Angle 1 measures 30°. Angles 1 and 4 are vertical angles. Angles 1 and 2 are adjacent, complementary angles. Angle 3 is adjacent to angle 2 and angle 4. The sum of the measures of angles 2, 3, and 4 is 180°. What are the measures of angles 2, 3, and 4?

### Read to Understand

Reading Skill

• **How can context clues help you understand the problem?**
• **What information is given?**

### Plan

• **What strategy can you use to solve the problem?**

You can draw a diagram to solve the problem.

### Solve

• **How can you use the strategy to solve the problem?**

Draw a diagram that shows the relationships between the angles.

Angles 1 and 4 are vertical angles. Vertical angles are formed opposite each other when two lines intersect. They have the same measure. Draw ∠1 and ∠4. Label m∠1 and m∠4 as 30°.

Angles 1 and 2 are adjacent complementary angles. Adjacent complementary angles have a common ray and a total measure of 90°. Draw ∠2 adjacent to ∠1 to form a right angle. 90° − 30° = 60°, so m∠2 is 60°. Label m∠2 as 60°.

Angle 3 is adjacent to angles 2 and 4. Mark ∠3 on the diagram adjacent to ∠2 and ∠4. The sum of the measures of angles 2, 3, and 4 is 180°.

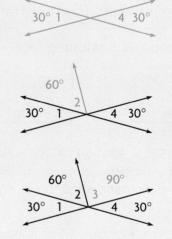

30° + 60° = 90° and 180° − 90° = 90°, so m∠3 is 90°. Label m∠3 as 90°.

So, m∠2 is 60°, m∠3 is 90°, and m∠4 is 30°.

### Check

• **How can you check your answer?**

MG 2.2 Use the properties of complementary and supplementary angles and the sum of the angles of a triangle to solve problems involving an unknown angle. *also* MG 2.1, MR 1.0, MR 2.0, MR 2.4, MR 2.5, MR 2.7, MR 3.0, MR 3.1, MR 3.2, MR 3.3

### Problem-Solving
### STRATEGIES

Use Logical Reasoning

Draw a Diagram or Picture

Make a Model or Act It Out

Make an Organized List

Find a Pattern

Make a Table or Graph

Predict and Test

Work Backward

Solve a Simpler Problem

Write an Equation

1. Angle 1 is a right angle. Angles 1 and 3 are vertical. What are the measures of angles 2, 3, and 4?

   **First**, draw ∠1 and label its measure.

   **Next**, use angle relationships to draw and find the measure of angle 3.

   **Finally**, use angle relationships to draw and find the measures of angles 2 and 4.

2. **What if**, in Problem 1, angles 2 and 4 are supplementary angles rather than vertical angles? Would the measures of angles 2 and 4 be the same? Explain.

3. A game board is made up of 25 squares in 5 equal rows. The colors of the squares alternate between red and blue going across and down. The square in the top left corner is blue. How many squares on the game board are blue? How many are red?

## Mixed Strategy Practice

**Solve.**

4. Farber Middle School is hosting a board game marathon. Twenty-one students are playing only chess, and 36 students are playing only checkers. A total of 75 students are playing chess, checkers, or both games. How many students are playing both games?

**USE DATA For 5–8, use the table.**

5. Myra's combined score for creativity and graphics is half of Brian's combined score in the same categories. Brian scored 8 more points for creativity than graphics. What are Brian's scores for creativity and graphics?

6. **Pose a Problem** Look at Problem 5. Change the difference between Brian's scores for creativity and graphics. Solve the new problem.

7. Pam's total score for the competition is 4 more than 2 times Myra's total score. What is Pam's total score?

8. **WRITE Math** ▸ **Explain** how you used a strategy to solve Problem 7.

| Game Design Competition | |
|---|---|
| **Category** | **Myra's Points** |
| Creativity | 9 |
| Graphics | 4 |
| Fairness of Rules | 10 |
| Entertainment Value | 6 |

# Extra Practice

## Set A
For 1–6, use the figure at the right. Tell if the pair of angles is *vertical*, *adjacent*, or *neither*. (pp. 370–373)

1. ∠AGF and ∠CGD
2. ∠BGC and ∠DGE
3. ∠DGE and ∠EGF
4. ∠BGC and ∠EGF
5. ∠FGA and ∠AGB
6. ∠CGD and ∠EGF

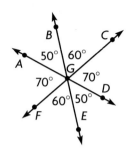

## Set B
For 1–6, use the figure at the right. Tell if the pair of angles is *vertical*, *adjacent*, *complementary*, or *none of these*. (pp. 374–375)

1. ∠DGE and ∠EGF
2. ∠AGF and ∠CGD
3. ∠CGD and ∠AGB
4. ∠AGF and ∠BGC
5. ∠AGF and ∠DGE
6. ∠CGD and ∠EGF

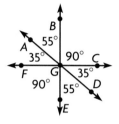

## Set C
For 1–6, use the figure at the right. Tell if the pair of angles is *complementary*, *supplementary*, or *neither*. (pp. 376–377)

1. ∠AED and ∠BEC
2. ∠CED and ∠BEC
3. ∠AED and ∠CED
4. ∠CED and ∠AEB
5. ∠AED and ∠AEB
6. ∠AEB and ∠BEC

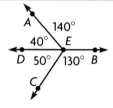

## Set D
For 1–3, use the figure at the right.
Find the unknown angle measure. Explain your answer. (pp. 378–381)

1. ∠AFB
2. ∠BFC
3. ∠CFD
4. ∠AFC
5. ∠DFB
6. ∠EFB

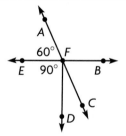

7. Angles A and B are complementary angles. If the measure of angle B is 35°, what is the measure of an angle that is supplementary to angle A?

8. Angles C and D are supplementary angles. If the measure of angle D is 121°, what is the measure of an angle that is complementary to angle C?

 **Technology**
Use Harcourt Mega Math, Ice Station Exploration, *Polar Planes*, Level B.

# WHAT'S THE ANGLE?

FINISH

## Get Ready
2 players

## Get Set
- 2 different coins
- Protractor
- Ruler
- Number cube labeled 1–6

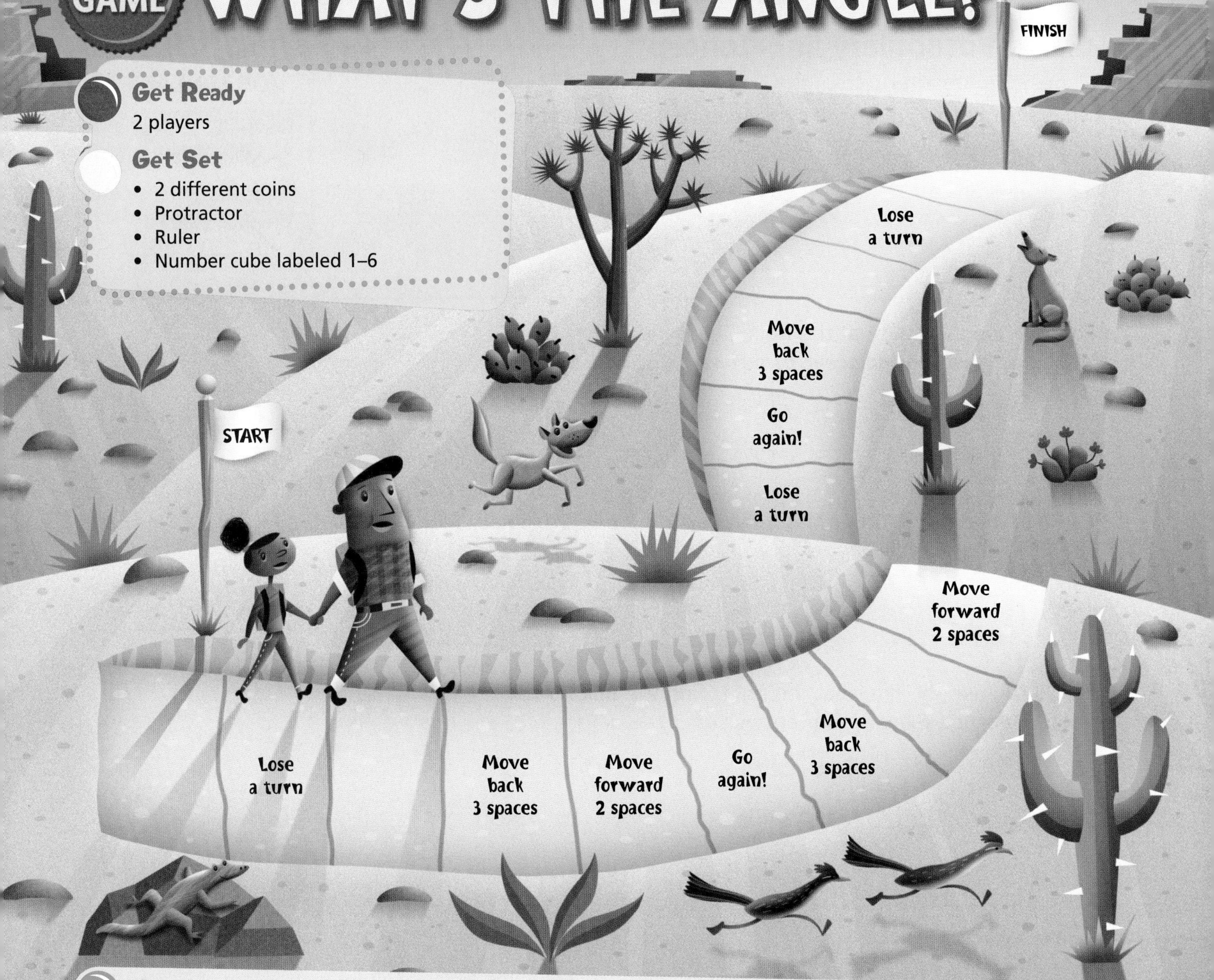

START

Lose a turn

Move back 3 spaces

Go again!

Lose a turn

Move forward 2 spaces

Lose a turn

Move back 3 spaces

Move forward 2 spaces

Go again!

Move back 3 spaces

## Play

- Each player selects a coin and places it on START. Decide which player will go first.
- Player 2 draws two rays to form an acute angle.
- Player 1 measures the angle with a protractor and records the angle measure.
- Player 1 tosses a coin to determine an angle relationship.

- If the player tosses heads he or she draws a nonadjacent complementary angle and records the angle measure. If tails, the player draws a nonadjacent supplementary angle and records the angle measure.
- Player 2 checks the angle measure. If the answer is correct, Player 1 rolls the number cube and moves his or her coin that many spaces. If the answer is incorrect, Player 1 does not move. Play passes to the other player.
- The first player to reach FINISH wins.

# Chapter 15 Review/Test

## Check Vocabulary and Concepts

Choose the best term from the box.

VOCABULARY

adjacent
complementary
vertical
supplementary

1. Pairs of angles that have a common vertex and a common ray are ___ angles. (MG 2.1 p. 370)

2. Two angles whose measures have a sum of 90° are called ___ angles. (MG 2.1, p. 374)

## Check Skills

**For 3-8, use the figure at the right. Tell if the pair of angles is *vertical, adjacent,* or *neither*.** (MG 2.1, pp. 370–373)

3. ∠EFA and ∠AFB     4. ∠DFE and ∠BFC     5. ∠CFD and ∠AFB

6. ∠CFD and ∠BFC     7. ∠CFD and ∠AFE     8. ∠DFA and ∠BFC

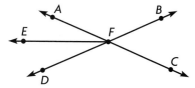

**For 9-14, use the figure at the right. Tell if the pair of angles is *complementary, supplementary,* or *neither*.** (MG 2.1, pp. 374–375, 376–377)

9. ∠AFE and ∠EFD     10. ∠CFD and ∠DFE     11. ∠AFB and ∠CFD

12. ∠BFC and ∠AFE     13. ∠EFD and ∠AFB     14. ∠AFE and ∠AFB

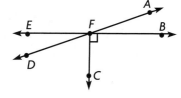

**For 15-20, use the figure at the right. Find the unknown angle measure. Explain your answer.** (MG 2.2, pp. 378–381)

15. ∠AGB     16. ∠BGC     17. ∠CGD

18. ∠DGE     19. ∠AGE     20. ∠AGD

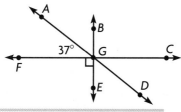

## Check Problem Solving

**Solve.** (MG 2.2, pp. 382–383)

21. Angles A and B are adjacent complementary angles. Angles A and C are adjacent supplementary angles. If angle A is 45°, what are the measures of angles B and C?

22. Lines $\overleftrightarrow{AB}$ and $\overleftrightarrow{CD}$ intersect at point E. ∠AED and ∠DEB are adjacent supplementary angles. What is the sum of ∠AEC and ∠CEB?

23. Maple Street and Oak Street intersect to form right angles. Pine Street forms a 28° angle with Maple Street. What angle does this form with Oak Street?

24. Serena lifts one page of her open math textbook to make a 55° angle with the left side of the book. What angle does it make with the right side of the textbook?

25. **WRITE Math** ▶ Ryan says that two supplementary angles that are congruent both measure 90°. Is his statement always true, sometimes true, or never true? **Explain.**

# Enrich • Use Properties of Angles
# Transversals

A line that intersects two or more lines is called a **transversal**.

Angles formed inside the two lines are called **interior angles**, and angles formed outside the two lines are called **exterior angles**. Angles 3, 4, 5, and 6 are interior angles. Angles 1, 2, 7, and 8 are exterior angles.

**Corresponding angles** are angles that appear in the same position in relation to a transversal and the lines it intersects. Corresponding angles are congruent when the lines the transversal intersects are parallel. In figure 1, ∠1 and ∠5, ∠3 and ∠7, ∠2 and ∠6, and ∠4 and ∠8 are pairs of corresponding angles.

Interior angles on opposite sides of the transversal are called **alternate interior angles**. Alternate interior angles are congruent when the lines the transversal intersects are parallel. In figure 1, angles 3 and 6 and angles 4 and 5 are pairs of alternate interior angles.

Exterior angles on opposite sides of the transversal are called **alternate exterior angles**. Alternate exterior angles are congruent when the lines the transversal intersects are parallel. In figure 1, angles 1 and 8 and angles 2 and 7 are pairs of alternate exterior angles.

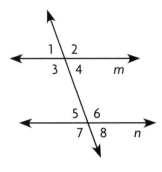

**Figure 1**

**Example** Look at Figure 2. Lines *m* and *n* are parallel. If $m\angle 3 = 65°$, find $m\angle 5$.

∠3 and ∠7 are corresponding angles, so $m\angle 7 = 65°$.

∠5 and ∠7 are supplementary angles, so $m\angle 5 = 180° − 65° = 115°$.

So, $m\angle 5 = 115°$.

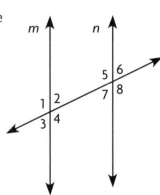

## Try It

For 1–6, use Figure 3. Lines *m* and *n* are parallel. Write *corresponding*, *alternate interior*, or *alternate exterior* for each.

**Figure 2**

1. ∠3 and ∠7

2. ∠2 and ∠6

3. ∠8 and ∠1

4. ∠5 and ∠4

5. ∠7 and ∠2

6. ∠8 and ∠4

 **Explain** how you could use the properties of angles to find the measure of ∠7 in Figure 3 if the measure of ∠2 is 79°.

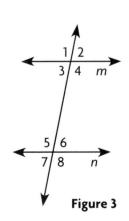

**Figure 3**

## Number Sense

**1.** What is the greatest common divisor of 42 and 18? (O—n NS 2.4)

  **A** 3

  **B** 6

  **C** 72

  **D** 126

**2.** What is the least common multiple of 4, 6, and 10? (O—n NS 2.4)

  **A** 2

  **B** 30

  **C** 60

  **D** 120

**3.** What is the product of $1\frac{1}{3}$ and $\frac{1}{2}$? (NS 2.2)

  **A** $\frac{1}{3}$

  **B** $\frac{2}{3}$

  **C** $1\frac{1}{6}$

  **D** $2\frac{2}{3}$

**4.** What is $1\frac{2}{7} \div \frac{3}{5}$? (NS 2.1)

  **A** $2\frac{6}{7}$

  **B** $2\frac{1}{4}$

  **C** $2\frac{1}{7}$

  **D** $\frac{27}{35}$

**5.** **WRITE Math** ▷ Sunni wrote 4.05, 4.5, 4.055, and 4.505 on her paper. **Explain** how to order the decimals from *greatest* to *least*. (O—n NS 1.1)

## Algebra and Functions

**6.** The table shows how much a company charges for pencils. Each pack of 4 pencils costs $2. Shipping costs $5 for any order. Which completes the cost chart below? (AF 1.2)

| Packs | 2x + 5 | Cost (in dollars) |
|---|---|---|
| 1 | $(2 \times 1) + 5$ | 7 |
| 2 | $(2 \times 2) + 5$ | 9 |
| 3 | $(2 \times 3) + 5$ | 11 |
| 4 | $(2 \times 4) + 5$ | ■ |

  **A** 12          **C** 14

  **B** 13          **D** 15

 **Test Tip** **Understand the problem.**

See item 7. The equation says that one half of a number, $x$, is 13. The value for $x$, then, must be twice the value of 13.

**7.** What value for $x$ makes the following equation true? (O—n AF 1.1)

$$0.5x = 13$$

  **A** 65          **C** 13

  **B** 26          **D** 12.5

**8.** What value for $n$ makes the following equation true? (O—n AF 1.1)

$$\frac{120}{n} = 10$$

  **A** 1,200          **C** 12

  **B** 100          **D** 10

**9.** **WRITE Math** ▷ If Gina can take 23 seconds off her best time for running a mile, she will be 10 seconds short of breaking the school record of 6 minutes 53 seconds. **Explain** how you can write an equation to find Gina's best time. (O—n AF 1.1)

## Measurement and Geometry

**10.** Armando drew a triangle with angle measures 90°, 45°, and $x$. What is the measure of the unknown angle? (Grade 5 O—n MG 2.2)

  **A** 45°      **C** 90°

  **B** 60°      **D** 180°

**11.** If two angles are adjacent angles, what do they have in common? (MG 2.1)

  **A** only a vertex

  **B** a vertex and a ray

  **C** two vertices

  **D** two rays

**12.** If two angles are vertical angles, what do they have in common? (MG 2.1)

  **A** only a vertex

  **B** a vertex and a ray

  **C** two vertices

  **D** two rays

**13.** If $m\angle A$ is 42° and $m\angle B$ is 138°, what word describes the two angles? (MG 2.1)

  **A** vertical      **C** supplementary

  **B** complementary  **D** congruent

**14.** **WRITE Math** Angles $A$ and $B$ are vertical angles. Angles $B$ and $C$ are complementary angles. Angles $C$ and $D$ are supplementary angles and Angles $D$ and $E$ are vertical angles. **Explain** how you can find $m\angle E$, if $m\angle A$ is 66°. (O—n MG 2.2)

## Statistics, Data Analysis, and Probability

**15.** Jacob wants to know the most popular sport of students at his school. He asks students as they walk into the library. Which sampling method is Jacob using? (O—n SDAP 2.2)

  **A** convenience    **C** survey responses

  **B** random        **D** another method

| Weekday Attendance | | | | |
|---|---|---|---|---|
| **Mon** | **Tue** | **Wed** | **Thu** | **Fri** |
| 14 | 21 | 13 | 22 | 20 |

**16.** What is the median of the attendance listed in the table above? (SDAP 1.1)

  **A** 18

  **B** 20

  **C** 20.5

  **D** 21

**17.** Marla claims that tennis is the favorite sport at her school. Which survey shows that Marla's claim is valid? (O—n SDAP 2.5)

  **A** Marla asks 4 of her best friends what their favorite sport is.

  **B** Marla asks 40 randomly selected students if tennis is their favorite sport.

  **C** Marla asks all sixth-graders at her school what their favorite sport is.

  **D** Marla asks 40 randomly selected students what their favorite sport is.

**18.** **WRITE Math** Explain why the question "Is hockey your favorite sport to watch?" causes bias in the data and a misleading graph. (O—n SDAP 2.3)

# 16 Plane Figures

**The Big Idea** Two-dimensional figures can be classified according to their geometric properties.

 **CALIFORNIA FAST FACT**

The Wells Fargo Center in Los Angeles is home to a three-story, glass-enclosed atrium that links the Wells Fargo Tower and the KPMG Tower, two trapezoidal office towers.

## Investigate

Look at the photo above. Draw an example of the types of quadrilaterals you see. Classify the figures in as many ways as you can.

### Types of Quadrilaterals

| Parallelogram | Rectangle | Rhombus |
|---|---|---|
| | | |
| Square | Trapezoid | General |
| | | |

 **GO ONLINE**

**Technology**
Student pages are available in the Student eBook.

# Show What You Know

Check your understanding of important skills
needed for success in Chapter 16.

▶ **Classify Angles**

Classify each angle as acute, obtuse, right, or straight.

**1.**

**2.**

**3.**

**4.**

**5.**

**6.**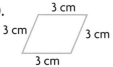

**7.**

**8.**

▶ **Identify Quadrilaterals**

Give the most exact name for the figure. Write parallelogram,
rectangle, rhombus, square, or trapezoid.

**9.**
3 cm
3 cm      3 cm
3 cm

**10.**
2 m
2 m      2 m
2 m

**11.**

**12.**
4 in.
2 in.

**13.**
6 cm
2 cm
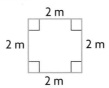

**14.**
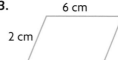

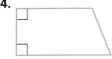

# VOCABULARY POWER

**CHAPTER VOCABULARY**

acute triangle
conjecture
diagonal
equilateral triangle
isosceles triangle
obtuse triangle
right triangle
scalene triangle

**WARM-UP WORDS**

**acute triangle** a triangle with all angles less than 90°

**right triangle** a triangle with one right angle

**obtuse triangle** a triangle with one angle greater than 90°

# Triangles

**OBJECTIVE:** Use the properties of a triangle to classify triangles and find unknown angle measures.

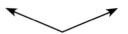
## Learn

A triangle can be classified by the angles it contains. An **acute triangle** contains only acute angles. A **right triangle** contains one right angle. An **obtuse triangle** contains one obtuse angle.

## Vocabulary

acute triangle    isosceles triangle

right triangle    scalene triangle

obtuse triangle   diagonal

equilateral triangle

### Classify by Angles

Acute Triangle

Right Triangle

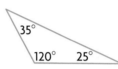

Obtuse Triangle

A triangle can also be classified by the lengths of its sides. Sides with the same length are congruent. An **equilateral triangle** has three congruent sides. An **isosceles triangle** has exactly two congruent sides. A **scalene triangle** has no congruent sides.

### Classify by Sides

Equilateral Triangle

Isosceles Triangle

Scalene Triangle

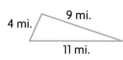

**Example 1** Christina made a sketch of one of the triangles shown on the building at the right. Classify the triangle by its sides.

The triangle has exactly two sides that are congruent.

So, △*ABC* is an isosceles triangle.

**Example 2** Classify the triangle by its sides and angles.

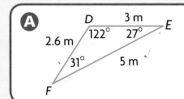

The triangle has no congruent sides and one obtuse angle.

The triangle has 2 congruent sides and one right angle.

So, △*DEF* is a scalene obtuse triangle.    So, △*GHJ* is an isosceles right triangle.

**MG 2.2** Use the properties of complementary and supplementary angles and the sum of the angles of a triangle to solve problems involving an unknown angle. *also* MG 2.0, MR 2.4, MR 2.5, MR 3.2

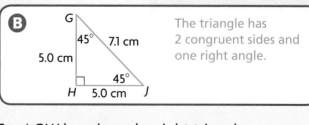

# Triangle Angle Measures

You can use what you know about rectangles to find the sum of the measures of the angles of a right triangle.

Each angle of a rectangle measures 90°. So, the sum of the angles of a rectangle is 4 × 90°, or 360°. If a diagonal is drawn, two congruent right triangles are formed. A **diagonal** is a line segment that connects two non-adjacent vertices of a polygon. Since the two triangles are congruent, the sum of the angles in each of these right triangles is 360° ÷ 2, or 180°.

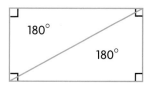

For triangles other than right triangles, look at △ABC. A line segment drawn from vertex C perpendicular to $\overline{AB}$ forms right triangles ADC and BDC as shown. A vertex is the point of intersection of two sides of a polygon.

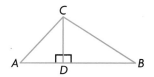

The sum of the angle measures in both right triangles is 180°, so the total measure of all the angles in both triangles combined is 360°. If the sum of the two right angle measures is subtracted, 180° remains. The 180° comes from the measures of ∠CAB, ∠ABC, and ∠BCA, the three angles of △ABC. So, the sum of the angle measures of △ABC must be 180°.

So, the sum of the measures of the angles of a triangle is 180°.

**Remember**

Two lines are perpendicular if they intersect to form right angles.

## Example 3 Find the measure of ∠B. Then classify △ABC by its angles.

$$x + 41 + 26 = 180$$     The sum of the angle measures in a triangle is 180°. Add.

$$x + 67 = 180$$

$$x + 67 - 67 = 180 - 67$$     Use the Subtraction Property of Equality.

$$x + 0 = 113$$     Use the Identity Property.

$$x = 113$$

So, the measure of ∠B is 113°. Since △ABC has one obtuse angle, △ABC is an obtuse triangle.

## Guided Practice

1. Find the measure of the unknown angle. Then classify the triangle by its angles.

$$x + 40 + 110 = 180$$
$$x + 150 = 180$$
$$x + 150 - 150 = 180 - 150$$
$$x + 0 = 30$$
$$x = \blacksquare$$
So, △ABC is a(n) ▊ triangle.

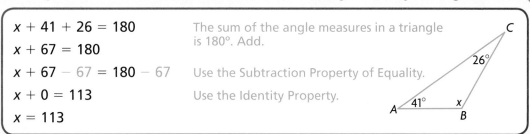

**Classify each triangle by its angles and the lengths of its sides.**

2.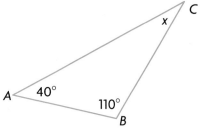

3.

4.

✓5.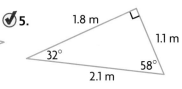

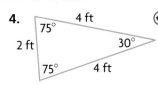

★**Algebra** Find the measure of ∠B and classify △ ABC by its angles.

6.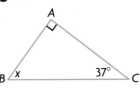

7.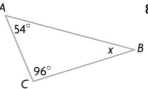

8.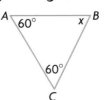

✓9.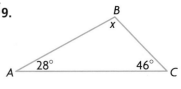

10. **TALK Math** Explain why a triangle cannot have two obtuse angles.

## Independent Practice and Problem Solving

**Classify each triangle by its angles and the lengths of its sides.**

11.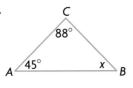

12.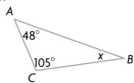

13.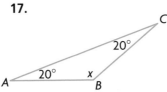

14.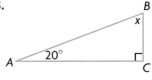

★**Algebra** Find the measure of ∠B and classify △ ABC by its angles.

15.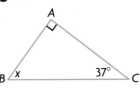

16.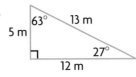

17.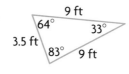

18.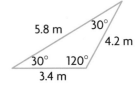

**Classify each triangle by the given side lengths and angle measures.**

19. sides: 15 m, 18 m, 20 m
angles: 46°, 60°, 74°

20. sides: 4.5 cm, 4.9 cm, 5.6 cm
angles: 50°, 58°, 72°

21. sides: 8 mi, 8 mi, 8 mi
angles: 60°, 60°, 60°

22. Triangle *PQR* is a right triangle with angle *Q* measuring 90°. Are angles *P* and *R* complementary or supplementary?

23. Triangle *XYZ* is a right triangle. If one of the acute angles measures 46°, what is the measure of the other acute angle? **Explain.**

24. If you extend a side of a triangle, you form an exterior angle. ∠*CJL* is an exterior angle of △*GCJ*. Find the measure of ∠*CJL*. **Explain.**

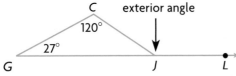

25. Look at the figure below. Name all of the triangles. Then classify each triangle by its angles and the lengths of its sides.

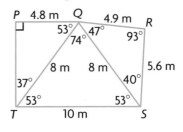

26. **Reasoning** In △*ABC*, the measure of ∠*A* is twice the combined measure of ∠*B* and ∠*C*. The measure of ∠*B* is twice the measure of ∠*C*. What are the measures of the angles of △*ABC*? **Explain** how you know.

27. **Pose a Problem** Look back at Problem 26. Write a similar problem by changing the relationships among the angle measures of the triangle. Then solve.

Extra Practice on page 410, Set A

**Technology**
Use Harcourt Mega Math, Ice Station
Exploration, *Polar Planes*, Levels E and F.

**For 28–29, use the figure at the right.**

28. Find all unknown angle measures. Name all triangles and classify them by angles.

29. **WRITE Math** ▶ What's the Question? The answer is ∠MBA and ∠DBA.

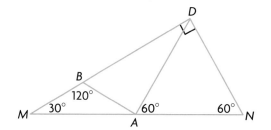

 **Achieving the Standards**

30. Jay's rectangular garden is 30 feet long. If the perimeter is 90 feet, what is the width of the garden? (Grade 5 MG 1.4)

31. Cal has 332 trading cards. This is twice as many as Margo has. How many cards does Margo have? (O-π AF 1.1, p. 336)

32. Solve for *n*. (O-π AF 1.1, p. 304)

$$189 + n = 360$$

33. **Test Prep** Triangle *FGH* is an acute triangle. Which shows possible angle measures for triangle *FGH*?

   **A** 90°, 35°, 55°     **C** 40°, 65°, 75°

   **B** 30°, 115°, 35°   **D** 20°, 140°, 20°

34. **Test Prep** An isosceles obtuse triangle has angles that measure 112°, 34°, and *x*°. What is the value of *x*?

   **A** 180    **B** 112    **C** 68    **D** 34

 **Problem Solving and Reasoning**

**REASONING** An exterior angle is formed by one side of a triangle and the extension of another side. The measure of an exterior angle of a triangle is equal to the sum of the measures of its two nonadjacent interior angles.

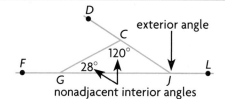

In the figure, ∠CJL is an exterior angle of △CGJ. The angles *JCG* and *CGJ* are nonadjacent interior angles to ∠CJL. Find m∠CJL.

| | |
|---|---|
| m∠CJL = m∠JCG + m∠CGJ | Angles *JCG* and *CGJ* are the nonadjacent interior angles to ∠CJL. |
| m∠CJL = 120° + 28° | Add. |
| m∠CJL = 148° | |

So, the measure of ∠CJL is 148°.

**For each triangle, find the unknown angle.**

1.
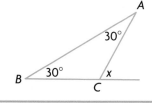

2.
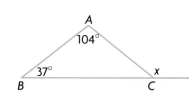

3.
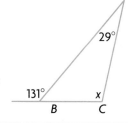

# LESSON 2

# Make Conjectures

OBJECTIVE: Make conjectures using the properties of triangles.

## Learn

**PROBLEM** Nathan builds a birdhouse with a triangular roof. He wants the roof to form an isosceles triangle in the front with 5.2 cm sides and a base of 9 cm. Nathan made one of the base angles 30°. What should be the measure of the other base angle?

A **conjecture** in mathematics is a statement, based on observations, that has been proposed to be true. A conjecture is believed to be true but has not yet been proven true or false. To prove that a conjecture is not true, you need to find one false example.

Nathan made a conjecture about isosceles triangles: "If a triangle is isosceles, then the two angles opposite the two congruent sides are also congruent." The following activity will test Nathan's conjecture.

### Quick Review

For each set of angle measures, classify the triangle as acute, obtuse, or right.

1. 79°, 81°, 20°
2. 120°, 30°, 30°
3. 174°, 1°, 5°
4. 90°, 45°, 45°
5. 30°, 60°, 90°

### Vocabulary

conjecture

## HANDS ON Activity

**Materials** ■ ruler ■ protractor

• Trace △ABC. Measure ∠B and ∠C with a protractor.

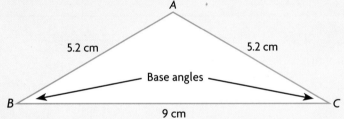

• Compare the measures of ∠B and ∠C. Then compare the lengths of $\overline{AB}$ and $\overline{AC}$.

Since $\overline{AB} \cong \overline{AC}$, △ABC is an isosceles triangle. Since ∠B ≅ ∠C, the conjecture is true for this example.

So, the other base angle of Nathan's birdhouse should be 30°.

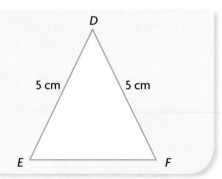

**Example 1** Test Nathan's conjecture about isosceles triangles.

Conjecture: If △DEF is an isosceles triangle, then ∠E ≅ ∠F.

Measure ∠E and ∠F with a protractor. Then compare the measures. Triangle DEF is an isosceles triangle with congruent sides $\overline{DE}$ and $\overline{DF}$.

∠E and ∠F have equal measures. So, the conjecture is true for this example.

**MG 2.0** Students identify and describe the properties of two-dimensional figures. *also* **MR 1.2, MR 2.4, MR 2.5, MR 3.2**

1.  Measure angles *A*, *B*, and *C*. Then compare the measures to prove the conjecture true or false.

   Conjecture: The angles opposite congruent sides of a triangle are congruent.

**Write *always*, *sometimes*, or *never* for each conjecture.**

✓ 2. A scalene triangle is a right triangle.

✓ 3. An acute triangle has one right angle.

4. **TALK Math** **Explain** how you can prove the following conjecture to be false: "A triangle has two obtuse angles."

## Independent Practice and Problem Solving

**Write *always*, *sometimes*, or *never* for each conjecture.**

5. The sum of two even numbers is an even number.

6. The product of two odd numbers is an odd number.

7. A right triangle is an equilateral triangle.

8. An obtuse triangle has only one acute angle.

**For 9–12, give an example that proves the conjecture to be false.**

9. A right triangle has three different angle measures.

10. All polygons with 3 or more sides are triangles.

11. All prime numbers are odd.

12. An isosceles triangle is an acute triangle.

13. Draw a triangle with three angle measures of 60°. Make a conjecture about the side lengths of this triangle.

14. **Reasoning** Draw and connect three points using a straightedge. Will connecting any three points always form a triangle? **Explain.**

15. **Pose a Problem** Look back at Problem 11. Make a conjecture about integers and show if it is true or false.

16. **WRITE Math** **Explain** the difference between a conjecture and a false statement.

## Achieving the Standards

17. Are the two smaller angles in a right triangle acute, obtuse, or right angles? (MG 2.3, p. 392)

18. Jorge needs 0.25 pound of apricots for a trail mix recipe. If apricots are sold in packages weighing 1.50 pounds, how many batches of trail mix can he make from 1 package of apricots? (Grade 5 ○━┓ NS 2.2)

19. Name the type of lines that never intersect and are the same distance apart at every point. (Grade 5 ○━┓ MG 2.1)

20. **Test Prep** Which of the following completes this statement: "An obtuse triangle can __?__ be an isosceles triangle?"

   **A** always

   **B** usually

   **C** sometimes

   **D** never

# Draw Triangles

**OBJECTIVE:** Use the properties of triangles to draw different types of triangles.

## Learn

You can use the properties of triangles to draw them on dot paper.

### Activity

**Materials** ■ square dot paper ■ isometric dot paper

• Use properties to draw an isosceles right triangle.

Square dot paper can be used to help you draw figures with right angles.

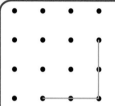

**Think:** The triangle must have two congruent sides that form a right angle. From the same dot, draw two congruent line segments perpendicular to each other. Make sure they both have the same length of 2 units.

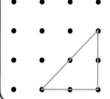

The triangle also must have two congruent angles. Connect the endpoints to form the third side.

**Math Idea**
Isometric dot paper is used to draw an equilateral triangle since different rows of dots form a 60° angle with each other.

• Use properties to draw an equilateral triangle.

Isometric dot paper can be used to help you draw figures with congruent sides and no right angles.

**Think:** The triangle must have three congruent sides. From the same dot, draw two congruent line segments as shown. Make sure they both have the same length of 4 units. Connect their endpoints to form the third side of 4 units.

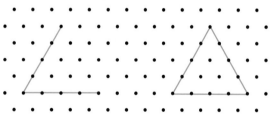

• Is it possible to draw a right triangle with an obtuse angle? Explain.

**MG 2.3** Draw quadrilaterals and triangles from given information about them (e.g., a quadrilateral having equal sides but no right angles, a right isosceles triangle). *also* **MG 1.0, MG 2.0, MR 2.4, MR 2.5, MR 3.2**

1. Copy and complete the drawing at the right to draw an isosceles obtuse triangle with two sides that are 3 units in length.

**Draw the triangle. Use square dot paper or isometric dot paper.**

2. an isosceles right triangle

3. an equilateral triangle

4. a scalene right triangle

✓5. an isosceles obtuse triangle

6. an isosceles obtuse triangle with sides that each have a length of 4 units

✓7. a scalene right triangle with one side that has a length of 3 units

8. **TALK Math** **Explain** the difference between square dot paper and isometric dot paper.

**Draw the triangle. Use square dot paper or isometric dot paper.**

9. a scalene right triangle with one side that has a length of 6 units

10. an equilateral triangle with sides that each have a length of 8 units

11. an isosceles right triangle with 2 sides that each have a length of 7 units

12. an equilateral triangle with sides that each have a length of 4 units

13. Mary drew equilateral triangle *ABC*. Then she drew a line segment to connect vertex *A* to the middle of line segment *BC*. What type of triangles did she form?

14. Draw an isosceles right triangle *ABC*. Let $\angle A$ be a right angle. Find the measures of the other two angles.

15. **Reasoning** An exterior angle of an isosceles triangle measures 126°. Find two possible measures for the angles of the triangle.

exterior angle
126°

16. **WRITE Math** **Explain** why you would use square dot paper rather than isometric dot paper to draw a scalene right triangle.

17. The temperature at sunset was 4°F. By midnight, the temperature had fallen 8°F. What was the temperature at midnight?
(O━┓ NS 2.3, p. 154)

18. What are the range, mean, median, and mode of the data set 8, 12, 9, 10, 16, 12, 19, 10, 12?
(SDAP 1.1, p. 224)

19. A triangle has angles that measure 56°, 49°, and *x*°. What is the value of *x*? (O━┓ MG 2.2, p. 392)

20. **Test Prep** For which of the following would you use isometric dot paper to draw the figure?

   **A** scalene right triangle

   **B** isosceles right triangle

   **C** equilateral triangle

   **D** right angle

**Extra Practice** on page 410, Set C

# 4 Quadrilaterals

OBJECTIVE: Identify, classify, and compare quadrilaterals.

## Quick Review

Find the measure of the unknown angle.

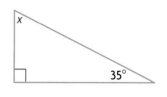

## Learn

Five types of quadrilaterals are especially important: parallelogram, rectangle, rhombus, square, and trapezoid. Their names and properties are listed below. Note: The same marking on two sides or more of a figure indicates that those sides are congruent.

| Quadrilateral | Figure | Properties |
|---|---|---|
| parallelogram | | opposite sides are parallel and congruent |
| rectangle | | parallelogram with four right angles |
| rhombus | | parallelogram with four congruent sides |
| square | | rectangle with four congruent sides |
| trapezoid | | quadrilateral with exactly two parallel sides |
| general | | 4 sides and 4 angles |

Notice that some quadrilaterals have common properties. You can use a diagram to organize quadrilaterals by their properties. For example, the diagram shows that a rectangle has the same properties as a parallelogram.

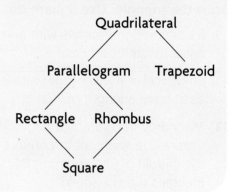

The figure at the right has four sides, so it is a quadrilateral. A more exact name for the figure, however, is a *rectangle*, because the name *rectangle* describes the figure's properties more completely than the name *quadrilateral* does.

Quadrilateral: 4 sides, 4 angles
Rectangle: parallelogram with 4 right angles

## Example 1 Give the most exact name for the figure.

**A**

The figure is a rectangle with 4 congruent sides and a rhombus with 4 right angles, so the most exact name is a square.

**B**

The figure is a quadrilateral with opposites sides that are parallel and congruent. The figure is a parallelogram.

**C**

The figure is a parallelogram with four congruent sides but no right angles. The figure is a rhombus.

• If a given figure is a rhombus, then it also is what other figures?

MG 2.0 Students identify and describe the properties of two-dimensional figures: *also* AF 1.0, MG 1.0, MR 2.4, MR 2.5, MR 3.2

## Activity

**Materials** ■ square dot paper ■ ruler

Jeremy makes a statement that the two diagonals of a square are congruent.

You can test whether Jeremy's statement is true by drawing a square, connecting the opposite vertices to draw the diagonals, and measuring the lengths of the diagonals.

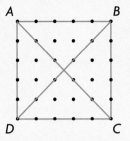

- Draw a square. Label the vertices $A$, $B$, $C$, and $D$.
- Connect the opposite vertices to draw diagonals $\overline{AC}$ and $\overline{BD}$.
- Measure the length of each diagonal. Compare the lengths.

Each diagonal has the same length. So, $\overline{AC} \cong \overline{BD}$.

So, based on your observations, the statement that the diagonals of a square are congruent is true.

As with triangles, the sum of the four interior angles of any quadrilateral is also always the same measure. The sum of the four interior angles of any quadrilateral is 360°.

**Example 2** Find the unknown measure in the quadrilateral.

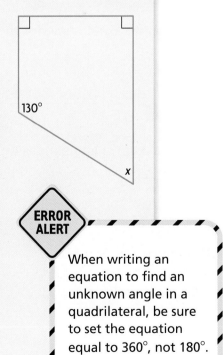

The trapezoid has two right angles, a 130° angle, and an unknown angle measure.

To find the measure of the unknown angle, write and solve an equation.

$x + 130 + 90 + 90 = 360$      The sum of the angles in a quadrilateral is 360°. Add.

$x + 310 = 360$

$x + 310 - 310 = 360 - 310$      Use the Subtraction Property of Equality.

$x + 0 = 50$      Use the Identity Property.

$x = 50$

So, the unknown angle measure is 50°.

**ERROR ALERT**

When writing an equation to find an unknown angle in a quadrilateral, be sure to set the equation equal to 360°, not 180°.

- What if the known angle measures of the quadrilateral above were 113°, 90°, and 90°? How would the unknown angle measure change?

## Guided Practice

**1.** Find the unknown angle measure.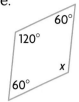

$x + 120° + 60° + 60° = 360°$

$x + 240° = 360°$

$x + 240° - 240° = 360° - 240°$

$x + 0° = \blacksquare$

$x = \blacksquare$

**2.** Find the unknown angle measure.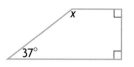

$x + 37° + 90° + 90° = 360°$

$x + 217° = 360°$

$x + 217° - 217° = 360° - 217°$

$x + 0° = \blacksquare$

$x = \blacksquare$

**Give the most exact name for the figure.**

**3.**

**4.**

☑**5.**

**Find the unknown angle measure.**

**6.**

**7.**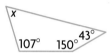

☑**8.**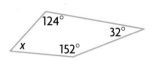

**9.** [TALK Math] **Explain** why a square is a rectangle, a parallelogram, and a rhombus.

## Independent Practice and Problem Solving

**Give the most exact name for the figure.**

**10.**

**11.**

**12.**

**Find the unknown angle measure.**

**13.**

**14.**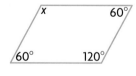

**15.**

**16.**

**17.**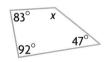

**18.**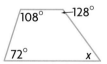

**Complete the statement.**

**19.** A rectangle is always a ___?___.

**20.** A trapezoid is always a ___?___.

**21.** A parallelogram is always a ___?___.

**22.** A rhombus is sometimes a ___?___.

Extra Practice on page 410, Set D

**23.** **≡FAST FACT** Some artists use simple geometric shapes such as quadrilaterals to make their works of art. How many quadrilaterals can you find in this shape?

**24.** Find the measures of angles *a, b, c, d, e,* and *f.*

54°
b
d e 42°
56°
c
a 100° f

**25.** **Reasoning** Draw a rhombus that does not have right angles. Then draw the diagonals of the rhombus. Are the diagonals of the rhombus congruent? What type of rhombus has congruent diagonals? **Explain.**

**26.** **WRITE Math** **What's the Error?** Jackie says that a rhombus can have 4 obtuse angles. Describe her error.

## Achieving the Standards

**27.** How many eggs does Joan have if she has $\frac{1}{2}$ dozen? (O⊸ NS 2.0, p. 70)

**28.** Which of the numerical values, 2, 4, or 6, is the solution to the equation $x + 4 = 8$?
(O⊸ AF 1.1, p. 304)

**29.** How many total angles do 3 hexagons have?
(Grade 5 MG 2.0)

**30.** **Test Prep** Which quadrilateral has congruent sides, but not right angles?

**A** square      **C** rhombus

**B** trapezoid      **D** parallelogram

**31.** **Test Prep** A quadrilateral has angles that measure 75°, 143°, 95°, and *x*°. What is the value of *x*?

**A** 47    **B** 57    **C** 74    **D** 313

## Problem Solving connects to Art

**Architecture** I.M. Pei, or Ieoh Ming Pei, is considered a master of architecture. Architecture is the art and science of designing and constructing buildings. Pei uses abstract forms to make structures of stone, concrete, glass, and steel. He is one of the twentieth century's most successful architects.

Pei worked with his son, Chien Chung Pei, to complete the Louvre Pyramid at the entrance of the world famous museum in Paris, France, in 1989.

**Solve.**

**1.** If I.M. Pei's design used glass cut into quadrilaterals with angle measures of 115°, 65°, 115°, and *x*°, what would be the value of *x*?

**2.** Give the most exact name for all of the quadrilaterals that you can see in the Louvre Pyramid.

# Draw Quadrilaterals

**OBJECTIVE:** Use the properties of quadrilaterals to draw different types of quadrilaterals.

## Quick Review

Marcus drew a four-sided figure that has two pairs of congruent sides and four right angles. What type of quadrilateral did he draw?

## Learn

**PROBLEM** Julia draws a diagram of her parents' kitchen. The diagram is a quadrilateral with two pairs of parallel sides. The sides are all congruent and meet at right angles. What kind of quadrilateral is the shape of the kitchen floor?

### Activity

**Materials** ■ square dot paper ■ isometric dot paper

• Use properties to draw the quadrilateral.

Recall the properties of the quadrilateral.

| Step 1 | Step 2 | Step 3 |
|---|---|---|
| Draw two congruent line segments perpendicular to each other. | Use the endpoint of one of the line segments to draw a congruent perpendicular line segment. | Connect the endpoints of the line segments. |
|  |  |  |

Notice that the drawing shows that the kitchen floor has two pairs of parallel sides, four congruent sides, and four right angles. So, the kitchen floor is in the shape of a square.

• Use properties to draw a parallelogram.

Draw a quadrilateral with no right angles that has opposite sides congruent and parallel. Name the quadrilateral.

| Step 1 | Step 2 |
|---|---|
| Draw two congruent parallel line segments shifted right or left as shown. | Connect the endpoints of the line segments as shown below. |
| 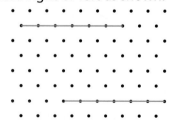 | 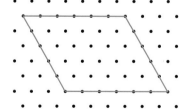 |

The quadrilateral is a parallelogram.

MG 2.3 Draw quadrilaterals and triangles from given information about them (e.g., a quadrilateral having equal sides but no right angles, a right isosceles triangle). *also* MG 1.0, MG 2.0, MR 2.4, MR 2.5, MR 3.2

1. Copy and complete to draw a quadrilateral with four congruent sides.

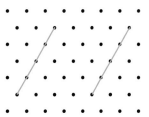

**Draw the figure. Use square dot paper or isometric dot paper.**

2. a square    3. a parallelogram    4. a rectangle    ✔5. a rhombus

6. a quadrilateral with congruent sides but no right angles    ✔7. a quadrilateral with two sides of length 6 units and two sides of length 8 units

8. (**TALK Math**) **Explain** which quadrilaterals would be easier to draw using square dot paper and which would be easier to draw using isometric dot paper.

## Independent Practice and Problem Solving

**Draw the figure. Use square dot paper or isometric dot paper.**

9. a quadrilateral with exactly one pair of parallel sides    10. a quadrilateral with all sides of length 5 units

11. a trapezoid with two congruent sides    12. a parallelogram with congruent sides

**Draw each quadrilateral as described. If it is not possible to draw, explain why.**

13. a rectangle that is also a square    14. a parallelogram that is not a rectangle

15. a square that is not a rhombus    16. a rhombus that is also a trapezoid

17. (**WRITE Math**) ▶ Describe how to draw a trapezoid on isometric dot paper.

##  Achieving the Standards

18. Evaluate the expression. (AF 1.3, p. 276)

$$(3^3 + 9) - (4 - 7)^2$$

19. Amanda drew one polygon with four sides and another with four angles. What types of polygons did Amanda draw? (Grade 5 MG 2.0)

20. What is $3\frac{1}{4} \times 8$? (NS 2.0, p. 76)

21. **Test Prep** Which of the following figures would you draw on isometric dot paper?

   **A** rhombus    **C** rectangle

   **B** circle    **D** right angle

# Problem Solving Workshop
## Strategy: Find a Pattern

**OBJECTIVE:** Solve problems by using the strategy *find a pattern*.

## Learn the Strategy

Finding patterns in problems can help you identify values or other kinds of information that are not given in the problem. There are different types of patterns in different types of problems.

### Number patterns can increase, decrease, repeat, or stop.

Kelly opens a new savings account and deposits $32 into the account each week. What will be her balance after 5 weeks?

| Week | 1 | 2 | 3 | 4 | 5 |
|---------|------|------|------|------|------|
| Balance | $32 | $64 | $96 | $128 | $160 |

### Geometric patterns can be related to size, shape, position, color, or number of figures.

Leslie is using stencils to paint a border on her wall. If she continues her pattern, what geometric figure could she paint next?

### Some visual patterns can be described using numbers.

Vera is drawing plane geometric shapes. She draws an equilateral triangle followed by a square. Her third shape is a regular pentagon, and her fourth shape is a regular hexagon. If the pattern continues, what could be the eighth shape?

**TALK Math**

How can finding a pattern help you solve each problem?

**MG 1.0** Students deepen their understanding of the measurement of plane and solid shapes and use this understanding to solve problems. *also* **MG 2.0, MR 1.0, MR 1.1, MR 1.3, MR 2.0, MR 2.4, MR 2.5, MR 2.7, MR 3.0, MR 3.1, MR 3.2, MR 3.3**

# Use the Strategy

**PROBLEM** Jason is building a garden area in the shape of a regular octagon. All sides are congruent and all angles are congruent in a regular polygon. So, a regular octagon has 8 congruent sides and 8 congruent angles. What is the measure of each angle of the regular octagon?

## Read to Understand

**Reading Skill**
• What information is given?
• How can you organize the information to help you solve the problem?

## Plan

• What strategy can you use to solve the problem?
  You can look for a pattern in the sums of the measures of the angles of polygons with fewer sides than an octagon.

## Solve

**Reading Skill**
• How can you use the strategy and graphic aids to solve the problem?
  You can write a rule for the pattern.

Draw polygons. Divide each into triangles.

$1 \times 180° = 180°$

$2 \times 180° = 360°$

$3 \times 180° = 540°$

$4 \times 180° = 720°$

| Polygon | Sides | Triangles | Sum of Angle Measures |
|---|---|---|---|
| Triangle | 3 | 1 | $1 \times 180° = 180°$ |
| Quadrilateral | 4 | 2 | $2 \times 180° = 360°$ |
| Pentagon | 5 | 3 | $3 \times 180° = 540°$ |
| Hexagon | 6 | 4 | $4 \times 180° = 720°$ |

**Remember**
The sum of the angles of a triangle is 180°.

The number of triangles is always 2 fewer than the number of sides. Let $n$ represent the number of sides of a polygon. You can use $(n - 2) \times 180°$ to find the sum of the interior angles of an octagon by replacing $n$ with 8.

$$(8 - 2) \times 180° = 6 \times 180°, \text{ or } 1{,}080°$$

So, an octagon can be divided into $8 - 2 = 6$ triangles. The sum of the interior angles of an octagon is $1{,}080°$. To find the measure of each angle in a regular octagon, divide the sum by 8.

$$1{,}080° \div 8 = 135°$$

So, each angle of a regular octagon measures $135°$.

## Check

• How can you check your answer?

1. The figures to the right show how many diagonals can be drawn in a quadrilateral, pentagon, hexagon, and heptagon. How many diagonals can be drawn in an octagon?

 4 sides, 2 diagonals
 5 sides, 5 diagonals
 6 sides, 9 diagonals
 7 sides, 14 diagonals

**First,** organize the information using a table.

**Then,** find a rule for the pattern in the table to show how many diagonals can be drawn in a polygon with *n* sides.

**Finally,** use the rule to find the number of diagonals in an octagon.

| Polygon | Quadrilateral | Pentagon | Hexagon | Heptagon |
|---|---|---|---|---|
| Number of sides | 4 | 5 | 6 | 7 |
| Diagonals Drawn from a Vertex | 1 | 2 | 3 | 4 |
| Total Number of Diagonals | 2 ($4 \times 1 \div 2 = 2$) | 5 ($5 \times 2 \div 2 = 5$) | 9 ($6 \times 3 \div 2 = 9$) | 14 ($7 \times 4 \div 2 = 14$) |

2. **What if** you were asked to find the number of diagonals that can be drawn in a polygon with 14 sides? How many diagonals can be drawn?

3. Irena draws a regular octagon with a perimeter of 48 cm and a regular heptagon with a perimeter of 35 cm. She then draws a regular hexagon with a perimeter of 24 cm and a regular pentagon with a perimeter of 15 cm. What is a rule for this pattern? If Irena continues this pattern, what will be the length of each side of her equilateral triangle?

**Problem Solving Strategy Practice**

**Find a pattern to solve.**

4. Lewis drew 40 triangles in the first row of a 4-row design he made in art class. He drew 30 rectangles in the second row and 24 pentagons in the third row. If his pattern continued, what shape did he draw in the fourth row, and how many did he draw? What is a possible rule for the pattern?

5. Edward stacks square boxes to create larger squares. If he stacks boxes to create a square with 8 units per side, how many total boxes will he use, and what will be the perimeter of the larger square?

Units = 1  Units = 4  Units = 9  Units = 16
Perimeter = 4  Perimeter = 8  Perimeter = 12  Perimeter = 16

6. **WRITE Math** Describe two ways to find the area of Triangle 5 if the pattern in the table continues.

| | Triangle 1 | Triangle 2 | Triangle 3 | Triangle 4 |
|---|---|---|---|---|
| Height (in.) | 2 | 4 | 6 | 8 |
| Area (in.²) | 6 | 12 | 18 | 24 |

## Mixed Strategy Practice

**USE DATA For 7–11, use the diagram and the table.**

7. Kendra is making a large tile triangle for an art class using light and dark green tiles in the shape of isosceles triangles. She arranges the tiles as shown in the diagram. How many tiles will she need to make a triangle with 6 rows?

8. How many light green tiles will there be in the seventh row? How many dark green tiles will there be?

9. If Kendra wants the base of the large triangle to measure exactly 80 cm, how many rows will she need?

10. Kendra has $48 to spend on purchasing tiles. What are the side and base lengths of the largest triangle she can make?

11. **Pose a Problem** Write and solve a new problem about Kendra's triangle using different costs for the light green tiles and dark green tiles.

12. Lucy draws a pentagon. The figure has three interior right angles. The two remaining interior angles have equal measures. What are the measures of the five interior angles?

13. **Open-Ended Problem** Terry is making a pattern of polygons using toothpicks for the sides. He uses exactly two toothpicks for each side of each polygon. What combination of regular hexagons, pentagons, and octagons can Terry make if he wants to use exactly 150 toothpicks? Is it possible for him to make only octagons? **Explain.**

## Problem-Solving
## STRATEGIES

Draw a Diagram

Make a Model

Make an Organized List

Find a Pattern

Make a Table or Graph

Predict and Test

Work Backward

Solve a Simpler Problem

Write an Equation

Use Logical Reasoning

| Light and Dark Green Tiles | |
|---|---|
| **Base Length (1 tile)** | 8 cm |
| **Side Length (1 tile)** | 5 cm |
| **Cost per tile** | $0.75 |

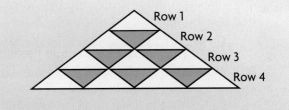

## CHALLENGE YOURSELF

**Anna bought a box of 100 tiles that contained the shapes shown below.**

14. One-half of the tiles in Anna's box contain at least one right angle. Three-fifths of those tiles are rectangles and one-half of the rectangles do not have sides that are all equal. How many of the tiles in the box are rectangles but not squares?

15. The quadrilaterals in the Anna's box have a total of 304 sides. One-half of these tiles are rectangles, and there are 10 more parallelograms with no right angles than there are trapezoids. How many of the tiles in the box are trapezoids?

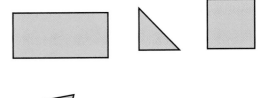

# Extra Practice

**Set A** Classify each triangle by its angles and the lengths of its sides. (pp. 392–395)

1.
3.5 cm  60°  2.5 cm
45°  75°
3 cm

2.
4.6 m  100°  4.6 m
45°  45°
8 m

3.
4 ft  5 ft
30°
60°
3 ft

4.
45°  8.5 cm
6.0 cm
45°
6.0 cm

5. A triangle has sides that measure 8 feet, 8 feet, and 8 feet. Classify the triangle by the lengths of its sides.

6. A triangle has angles that measure 32°, 32°, and 116°. Classify the triangle by its angles.

**Set B** Write *always*, *sometimes*, or *never* for each conjecture. (pp. 396–397)

1. An equilateral triangle has congruent sides.

2. An obtuse triangle has one right angle.

3. A right triangle has two acute angles.

4. A scalene triangle is an acute triangle.

**Set C** Draw the triangle. Use square dot paper or isometric dot paper. (pp. 398–399)

1. an isosceles right triangle with two sides that are 4 units

2. an isosceles acute triangle with two sides that are 3 units

3. One angle in an isosceles triangle measures 92°. What are the other two angle measures?

4. One angle in an equilateral triangle measures 60°. What are the other two angle measures?

**Set D** Complete the statement. (pp. 400–403)

1. A square is always a __?__ .

2. A rectangle is sometimes a __?__.

3. A trapezoid is never a __?__ .

4. A rhombus is always a __?__.

**Set E** Draw the figure. Use square dot paper or isometric dot paper. (pp. 404–405)

1. a rhombus with all sides of length 3 units

2. a rectangle that measures 2 units by 4 units

3. a trapezoid with two right angles

4. an quadrilateral with no congruent sides

5. Kenza drew a parallelogram with four congruent sides and no right angles. What type of figure did Kenza draw?

6. Maria drew a quadrilateral with four congruent sides and four right angles. What type of figure did Maria draw?

 **Technology**
Use Harcourt Mega Math, Ice Station Exploration, *Polar Planes*, Level G.

# It All Adds Up!

## On Your Mark!
2 players

## Get Set!
- Game cards
- 2 different coins

## Go!

- Shuffle the game cards, and place them facedown in a pile.
- Each player chooses a coin and places it behind START. Decide who will go first.
- Player 1 take draws a card from the pile.
- Player 1 finds the unknown angle measure in the figure on the card.

- Player 2 checks the answer. If it is correct, Player 1 moves his or her coin one space on the gameboard and play passes to the other player.
- If the answer is incorrect the player does not move. Play passes to the other player.
- The first player to reach FINISH wins.

**Chapter 16   411**

# Chapter 16 Review/Test

## Check Vocabulary and Concepts

**Choose the best term from the box.**

1. A triangle with no congruent sides is called a(n) __?__. (O━┓ MG 2.2, p. 392)

2. A(n) __?__ has three congruent sides. (O━┓ MG 2.2, p. 392)

3. A(n) __?__ in mathematics is a statement, based on observations, that has been proposed to be true. (MG 2.0, p. 396)

## Check Skills

**Classify each triangle by its angles and the lengths of its sides.** (O━┓ MG 2.2, pp. 392–395)

4.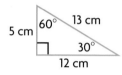

5.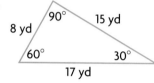

6.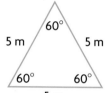

7.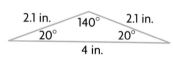

**Write *always*, *sometimes*, or *never* for each conjecture.** (MG 2.0, pp. 396–397)

8. A scalene triangle has three acute angles.

9. A right triangle is a scalene triangle.

10. An equilateral triangle has one right angle.

11. An acute triangle has three acute angles.

**Draw the figure. Use square dot paper or isometric dot paper.** (MG 2.3, pp. 398–399, 404–405)

12. an isosceles obtuse triangle

13. a quadrilateral with exactly one pair of parallel sides

14. a quadrilateral with equal sides but no right angles

**Find the unknown angle measure.** (MG 2.0, O━┓ MG 2.2, pp. 392–395, 400–403)

15.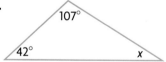

16.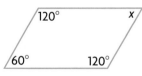

17.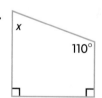

## Check Problem Solving

**Solve.** (MG 1.0, pp. 406–409)

18. Mark draws a triangle, square, and pentagon. If his pattern continues, what shape should Mark draw sixth?

19. Elaine stacks square boxes. If she stacks boxes to create a square with 4 units on each side, how many boxes will she use?

20. **⬛ WRITE Math ▸** Paul drew a hexagon with an area of 30 square meters, a pentagon with an area of 20 square meters, and a rectangle with an area of 12 square meters. If Paul continues the pattern, what will be the area of his triangle? **Explain.**

**GO ONLINE Technology** Use *Online Assessment.*

# Enrich • Draw Shapes Using Ordered Pairs

## Shapes on a Coordinate Plane

Keisha is drawing rhombus *ABCD* on a coordinate plane. She has drawn three points on the coordinate plane: *A* (4,7), *B* (1,5), and *C* (4,3). Where should she place point *D*?

Complete the activity to find the coordinates of point *D*.

### Activity

**Materials**  grid paper, ruler

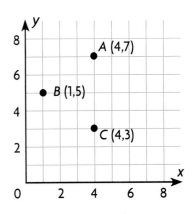

**A** In order to find the location of point *D*, you need to know the properties of a rhombus. A rhombus has opposite sides parallel and four congruent sides.

**B** Point *D* has the same relationship to point *C* as point *A* has to point *B*. Compare point *A* (4,7) with point *B* (1,5). Point *A* is three units to the right and two units up from point *B*.

**C** To locate point *D*, count three units to the right and two units up from point *C* (4,3). Point *D* is located at (7,5).

**D** Use a ruler to connect points *A*, *B*, *C*, and *D* to form rhombus *ABCD*.

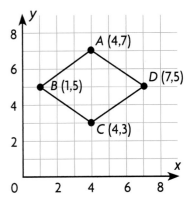

**E** To make sure that the four sides of rhombus *ABCD* are congruent, measure the lengths of the sides with a ruler.

So, Keisha should place point *D* to form rhombus *ABCD* at (7,5).

## Try It

**Find the unknown point to complete the given shape.**

**1.** rectangle

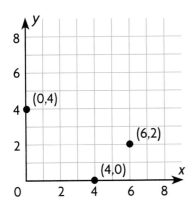

**2.** parallelogram

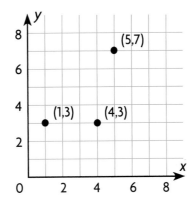

**3.** trapezoid with 2 right angles

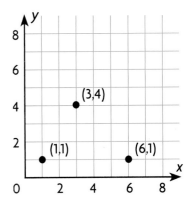

**WRITE Math** Explain how you found the unknown point in Problem 2.

# Achieving the Standards

## Chapters 1 – 16

## Number Sense

**1.** What is $\frac{14}{8}$ in simplest form? (NS 1.0)

**A** $1\frac{3}{4}$

**B** $1\frac{6}{8}$

**C** $1\frac{6}{7}$

**D** $2\frac{1}{4}$

**2.** What is the *best* estimate for $3\frac{1}{7} + 4\frac{8}{9} + 2\frac{3}{5}$?
(NS 2.1)

**A** 12

**B** $10\frac{1}{2}$

**C** $9\frac{1}{2}$

**D** 9

**3.** Which list of numbers is ordered from *least*
to *greatest*? (NS 1.0)

**A** $\frac{3}{7}, \frac{3}{8}, \frac{4}{9}, \frac{2}{5}$

**B** $\frac{4}{9}, \frac{3}{8}, \frac{2}{5}, \frac{3}{7}$

**C** $\frac{2}{5}, \frac{3}{7}, \frac{4}{9}, \frac{3}{8}$

**D** $\frac{3}{8}, \frac{2}{5}, \frac{3}{7}, \frac{4}{9}$

**4.** Which list of numbers is ordered from
*greatest* to *least*? (NS 1.0)

**A** $\frac{1}{5}, 0.05, 0.5, 5\frac{1}{5}$

**B** $0.05, \frac{1}{5}, 0.5, 0.5, 5\frac{1}{5}$

**C** $5\frac{1}{5}, 0.5, \frac{1}{5}, 0.05$

**D** $5\frac{1}{5}, 0.5, 0.05, \frac{1}{5}$

**5.** **WRITE Math** **Explain** how to rename
5 before you can find $5 - 2\frac{1}{4}$. Give the
difference in simplest form. (O–π NS 2.0)

## Algebra and Functions

**6.** $(^-7 + 3) \div ^-2 =$
(AF 1.4)

**A** $^-5$

**B** 2

**C** 5

**D** 8

**7.** What value for *x* makes the following
equation true? (O–π AF 1.1)

$$x + 13 = ^-17$$

**A** $^-30$      **C** 4

**B** $^-4$      **D** 30

**8.** The table lists costs for skating and skate
rental at the Harney Skate Center. Which
expression gives the total cost, in dollars,
for *x* hours of skating? (AF 1.2)

| Harney Skate Center | |
|---|---|
| Skating: | $7.50 per hour |
| Skate rental: | $5 |

**A** $7.5x + 5$      **C** $5x + 7.5$

**B** $7.5x - 5$      **D** $5x - 7.5$

**9.** What value for *s* makes the following
equation true? (O–π AF 1.1)

$$\frac{s}{3} = 15$$

**A** 3      **C** 30

**B** 5      **D** 45

**10.** **WRITE Math** **Explain** how to find
the value of *p* in the equation $\frac{p}{7} = 13.5$.
(O–π AF 1.1)

## Measurement and Geometry

**11.** Which is always a true statement about two angles that are complementary?

(MG 2.1)

  **A** Their measures add up to 90°.

  **B** Their measures add up to 180°.

  **C** They are the same size.

  **D** Their measures add up to 360°.

**12.** Which of the following is not a quadrilateral with two pairs of parallel sides?

(MG 2.0)

  **A** a parallelogram

  **B** a trapezoid

  **C** a rhombus

  **D** a rectangle

### Test Tip   Look for important words.

See item 13. The scenario asks you about an isosceles triangle. What do you know about isosceles triangles that could help you find the missing angle measures?

**13.** **WRITE Math** Pablo drew an isosceles triangle on grid paper. He measured one of the angles and found that its angle measure was 70°. What are two possibilities for the other angles in his isosceles triangle? **Explain** your reasoning.  (MG 2.2)

## Statistics, Data Analysis, and Probability

**14.** Abigail has been tracking the temperature of the pool over the last 4 weeks. Which of the following types of graphs is the *best* way for her to display her data? (SDAP 2.3)

  **A** a bar graph      **C** a circle graph

  **B** a line graph      **D** a mean

**15.** The table shows the test scores for 5 students on a spelling test. What is the range of the scores on the spelling test?

(SDAP 1.1)

| Spelling Test Scores | | | | |
|---|---|---|---|---|
| **Tom** | **Dina** | **Lindsey** | **Kalo** | **Devon** |
| 53 | 42 | 75 | 98 | 62 |

  **A** 98          **C** 56

  **B** 62          **D** 42

**16.** Nate added up all the items in a data set and then divided by the number of items in the set. Which of the following measures did Nate find? (SDAP 1.1)

  **A** mean          **C** mode

  **B** median       **D** range

**17.** **WRITE Math** A small village contains 10 residents. Nine of the residents are poor and the tenth is a millionaire. Would the mean give a good representation of the average income? If not, which measure of central tendency should be used? **Explain.** (SDAP 1.3)

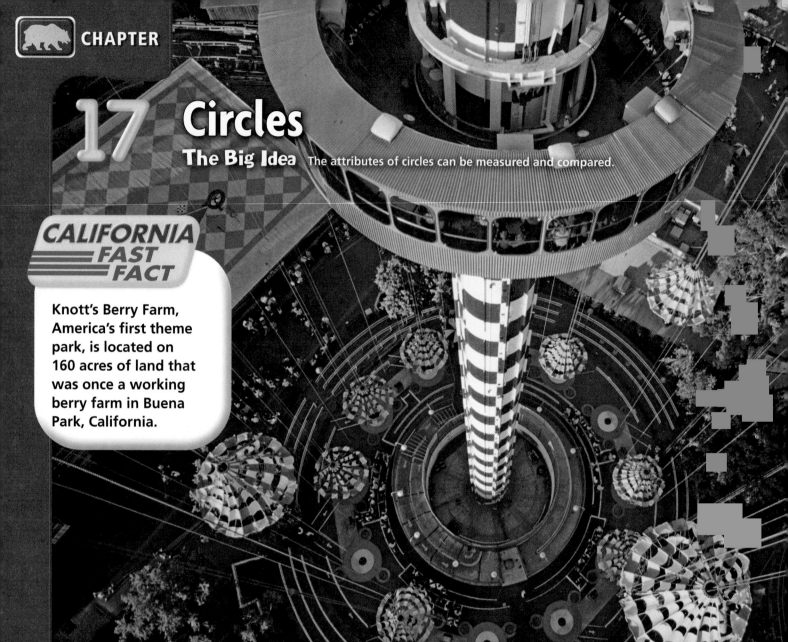

# 17 Circles

**The Big Idea** The attributes of circles can be measured and compared.

## CALIFORNIA FAST FACT

Knott's Berry Farm, America's first theme park, is located on 160 acres of land that was once a working berry farm in Buena Park, California.

## Investigate

The bar graph shows the approximate diameters of five Ferris wheels. Choose three of the wheels and find the circumference of each and the corresponding area.

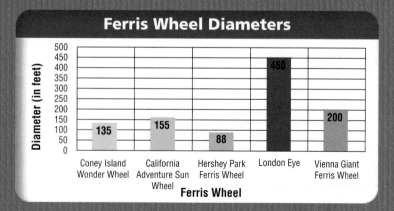

**Ferris Wheel Diameters**

Diameter (in feet)

| Ferris Wheel | Diameter |
|---|---|
| Coney Island Wonder Wheel | 135 |
| California Adventure Sun Wheel | 155 |
| Hershey Park Ferris Wheel | 88 |
| London Eye | 450 |
| Vienna Giant Ferris Wheel | 200 |

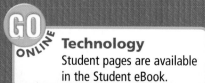

**GO ONLINE**

**Technology**
Student pages are available in the Student eBook.

# Show What You Know

Check your understanding of important skills
needed for success in Chapter 17.

▶ **Multiply Whole Numbers and Decimals**

Find the product.

1. $5 \times 1.2$
2. $2.4 \times 12$
3. $36 \times 0.5$
4. $3.14 \times 8$

5. $2.25 \times 40$
6. $100 \times 0.18$
7. $9 \times 5.12$
8. $420 \times 0.24$

9. $220 \times 9.05$
10. $18 \times 3.14$
11. $92 \times 8.1$
12. $10 \times 7.42$

▶ **Multiply Fractions by Whole Numbers**

Find the product.

13. $20 \times \frac{3}{5}$
14. $9 \times \frac{5}{18}$
15. $\frac{22}{7} \times 28$
16. $\frac{16}{25} \times 5$

17. $\frac{8}{3} \times 18$
18. $49 \times \frac{22}{7}$
19. $55 \times \frac{3}{10}$
20. $\frac{5}{21} \times 63$

21. $\frac{22}{7} \times 77$
22. $40 \times \frac{5}{16}$
23. $75 \times \frac{24}{25}$
24. $40 \times \frac{5}{32}$

▶ **Exponents**

Evaluate.

25. $9^2$
26. $1.3^2$
27. $25^2$
28. $3.1^2$

29. $7.5^2$
30. $100^2$
31. $2.7^2$
32. $18^2$

33. $0.8^2$
34. $22.4^2$
35. $11^2$
36. $90^2$

# VOCABULARY POWER

**CHAPTER VOCABULARY**

area
circumference
pi
radius
semicircle
unit circle

**WARM-UP WORDS**

**area** the number of square units to cover a given surface

**radius** a line segment with one end point at the center of a circle and the other end point on the circle

**unit circle** a circle that has a radius of 1

# 1 Area of Circles

**OBJECTIVE:** Discover pi and a formula for the area of circles.

## Investigate

**Materials** ■ unit circle graph paper ■ calculator

The **area** of a figure is the number of square units needed to cover it. Be sure to label area by using square units. The **radius** of a circle is a line segment with one endpoint at the center of the circle and the other endpoint on the circle. A **unit circle** has a radius of 1. You can use grid paper to estimate the area of a circle.

**A** The circle on the graph paper is a unit circle. Divide the unit circle into four equal parts, making four quarter circles. Shade one of the quarter circles.

**B** Count the shaded full squares and the shaded almost full squares inside the shaded quarter circle. Do not count the squares that are shaded less than half full. Record your result.

**C** The area of each square is $\frac{1}{10} \times \frac{1}{10} = \frac{1}{100}$ units$^2$, or 0.01 units$^2$. To estimate the area of the quarter circle, multiply your result from Part B by 0.01. Record your result.

**D** Then, to estimate the area of the entire unit circle, multiply your result in Part C by 4. Record your result.

## Draw Conclusions

1. Why did you need to multiply the area of the quarter circle by 4?

2. **Analysis** What is the area of your circle? Compare your result to the results of four other students. How do your results compare?

The number **pi,** or $\pi$, can be defined as the area of a unit circle. Pi is not a rational number, but it is approximately equal to 3.14, or $\frac{22}{7}$.

○━┓ **MG 1.1** Understand the concept of a constant such as $\pi$; know the formulas for the circumference and area of a circle. *also* ○━┓ **NS 2.0, NS 2.1, AF 3.0, AF 3.1, AF 3.2, MG 1.0, MG 1.2, MR 1.1, MR 1.2, MR 2.0, MR 2.4, MR 2.5, MR 3.2**

You can use the area of a unit circle and area relationships to discover a formula for the area of a circle. Look at the squares below.

**Square A**

Side Length: 1
Area: $1^2$, or 1 unit$^2$

**Square B**
Side Length: 2, or double that of square A.
Area: $2^2$, or 4 units$^2$

**Square C**

Side Length: 3, or triple that of square A.
Area: $3^2$, or 9 units$^2$

Doubling the side length of square A multiplies the area by $2^2$, or 4.
Tripling the side length of square A multiplies the area by $3^2$, or 9.

Look at the circles below. Circle A is a unit circle, which has an area of $\pi$ units$^2$.

**Circle A**

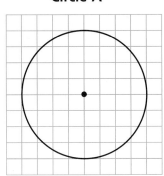

**Circle B**

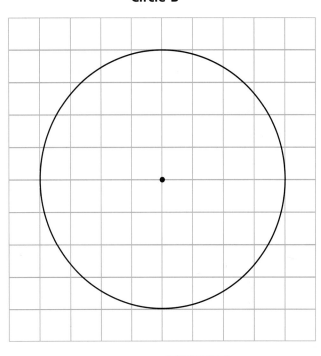

The sides of the squares on the grid of circle B have been magnified to twice the length of the sides of the squares on the grid of circle A. So, the radius of circle B is twice the radius of circle A. As a result, the area of circle B has $2^2$ times, or 4 times, the area of circle A. That's because the area of each magnified square in circle B is $2^2$ times, or 4 times, the area of each square in circle A. Since the area of circle A is $\pi$ units$^2$, then the area of circle B is $\pi \times 2^2$ units$^2$.

**TALK Math**

Why is the area of a square inside circle B four times the area of a square inside circle A?

If you magnify circle A by $r$, then the area of each magnified square will be $r^2$ as much. So the area of any circle magnified by $r$ would be $\pi \times r^2$, or $\pi r^2$. This gives the formula $A = \pi r^2$ for the area of a circle.

**Practice**

**Find the area of a circle with a radius of 4 cm. Use 3.14 for $\pi$.**

1. $A = \pi r^2$
   $A \approx 3.14 \times 4^2 \approx 3.14 \times 16$
   $A \approx$ ▮

2. **WRITE Math** Explain how the area of a circle is related to the radius of the circle squared.

**ALGEBRA**
# Area of Circles

OBJECTIVE: Find the area of circles.

## Vocabulary

diameter

semicircle

## Learn

The irrigation system on Mr. Martin's farm consists of 10 rotating sprinklers, each of which waters a circular area that has a radius of 9.3 m. What is the area of the plot watered by each sprinkler?

The **diameter** of a circle is a line segment that passes through the center and has its endpoints on the circle. If you know the radius or diameter of a circle, you can find the area by using the formula $A = \pi r^2$.

**Example 1** Find the area of the plot to the nearest whole number. Use 3.14 for $\pi$.

| | |
|---|---|
| $A = \pi r^2$ | Write the formula. |
| $A \approx 3.14 \times (9.3)^2$ | Replace $\pi$ with 3.14 and $r$ with 9.3. |
| $A \approx 3.14 \times 86.49$ | Multiply. |
| $A \approx 271.5786$ | |

9.3 m

▲ Large farms use sprinklers that have a greater radius.

So, the area of the plot watered by each sprinkler is about 272 m².

You can also find the area by using a calculator.

 $\boxed{271.7163486}$

The result from the calculator is slightly different since it uses more digits as an approximation to $\pi$.

A **semicircle** is one-half of a circle. Because of that, you can use the formula $A = \frac{1}{2} \pi r^2$ to find its area.

**Example 2** Find the area of the semicircle. Use $\frac{22}{7}$ for $\pi$.

Divide the diameter by 2 to find the length of the radius.

$28 \div 2 = 14$, or 14 in.

| | |
|---|---|
| $A = \frac{1}{2}\pi r^2$ | Write the formula. |
| $A \approx \frac{1}{2} \times \frac{22}{7} \times (14)^2$ | Replace $\pi$ with $\frac{22}{7}$ and $r$ with 14. |
| $A \approx \frac{1}{2} \times \frac{22}{7} \times 196$ | |
| $A \approx \frac{1}{\overset{1}{2}} \times \frac{\overset{11}{22}}{\overset{1}{7}} \times \frac{\overset{28}{196}}{1}$ | Simplify and multiply. |
| $A \approx 308$ | |

28 in.

**Math Idea**
Use $\frac{22}{7}$ for $\pi$ when it can be simplified using the square of the radius.

So, the area of the semicircle is about 308 in.²

MG 1.2 Know common estimates of $\pi$ (3.14; $\frac{22}{7}$) and use these values to estimate and calculate the circumference and area of circles; compare with actual measurements. *also* O—ᴨ NS 2.0, NS 2.1, AF 3.1, AF 3.2, MG 1.0, O—ᴨ MG 1.1, MR 2.4, MR 2.5, MR 3.2

Find the area to the nearest whole number. Use 3.14 or $\frac{22}{7}$ for $\pi$.

**1.**    3 in.

$A = \pi r^2$
$A \approx 3.14 \times (3)^2$
$A \approx \blacksquare$

**2.**    16 cm

$A = \pi r^2$
$A \approx 3.14 \times 8^2$
$A \approx \blacksquare$

**3.**    7 yd

**4.**    10 cm

✔**5.**    10 in.

✔**6.**    12.2 m

**7.** [TALK Math] **Explain** how to find the area of a circle if you know the diameter.

**Independent Practice and Problem Solving**

Find the area to the nearest whole number. Use 3.14 or $\frac{22}{7}$ for $\pi$.

**8.**    15 m

**9.** 21 ft

**10.**    40 mm

**11.** 8.6 yd

**12.**    semicircle   16 cm

**13.** $\frac{1}{4}$ circle   2 cm

**14.**    $\frac{1}{3}$ circle   6 in.

**15.**     $\frac{2}{3}$ circle   8 ft

**16.** A normal sprinkler on Mr. Martin's farm waters a circular plot with a radius of 9.3 m. However, the last sprinkler receives only enough water pressure to water a circular plot with a radius of 8.5 m. How much smaller is the area watered by this sprinkler than that of a normal sprinkler?

**17. Reasoning** Mrs. Brown also uses rotating sprinklers to water her farm. If a sprinkler that can water a circular plot with a diameter of 15 m is placed in the center of a square plot of land that measures 15 m on a side, how much of the plot will not be watered?

**18.** Use a compass to draw a circle on grid paper and estimate its area. Then calculate the area using a formula. Compare your results.

**19.** [WRITE Math] ▸ **What's the Error?** Mike said the area of a circle with a radius of 6 cm was about 18.84 cm². Describe his error and find the correct area. Use 3.14 for $\pi$.

**Achieving the Standards**

**20.** What is $\frac{3}{10}$ mile plus $\frac{3}{8}$ mile? (NS 2.1, p. 38)

**21.** A teacher recorded the following quiz scores for 7 students: 82, 63, 75, 91, 75, 62, and 75. What is the mode of the data? (SDAP 1.1, p. 224)

**22.** Write $\frac{10}{12}$ in simplest form. (O⎯ʀ NS 2.4, p. 8)

**23. Test Prep** Which equation could be used to find the area in square inches of a circle with a radius of 5 inches?

**A** $A = 5 \times \pi$       **C** $A = 10 \times \pi$

**B** $A = \pi \times 5^2$       **D** $A = \pi \times 10^2$

# 3 Estimate Circumference

**OBJECTIVE:** Investigate the relationship between the diameter and circumference of circles and estimate the circumference of circles.

## Quick Review

**Calculate.**

1. $37.2 \div 12$
2. $43.2 \div 13.5$
3. $7.5 \div 3$
4. $14.7 \div 3$
5. $5.2 \div 2$

## Vocabulary

circumference

## Investigate

**Materials** ■ compass ■ ruler ■ string ■ calculator

**Circumference** is the distance around a circle. You can use string and a ruler to estimate the circumference of a circle.

**A** Use a compass to draw a circle. Mark the center of the circle. Use a ruler to draw a diameter of the circle. Remember that the diameter passes through the center of the circle.

**B** Measure the diameter of the circle to the nearest tenth of a centimeter. Record your measurement.

**C** Lay the string around the circle. Mark the string where it meets itself.

**D** Use the ruler to measure the string from its end to the mark you made. Measure to the nearest tenth of a centimeter. Record your measurement.

**E** Use a calculator to divide the circumference of your circle by the diameter. Record your result.

**F** Display your results on the chalkboard with those of other students in the class by making a table like the one below.

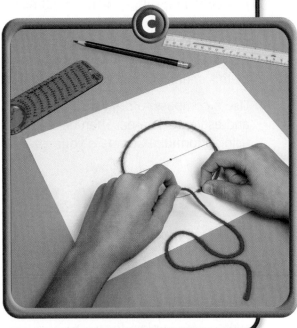

| Student Name | Circumference (*C*) | Diameter (*d*) | *C* ÷ *d* |
|---|---|---|---|
| | | | |
| | | | |
| | | | |

## Draw Conclusions

1. About how many times as long as the diameter is the circumference of your circle?

2. **Synthesis** About how many times as long as the diameter is the circumference of the circles drawn by other students? What approximate value is $\frac{C}{d}$ for any circle?

🐻 ●━┓ MG 1.1 Understand the concept of a constant such as $\pi$; know the formulas for the circumference and area of a circle. *also* AF 3.0, MG 1.0, MR 1.2, MR 2.0, MR 2.4, MR 2.5, MR 2.6, MR 3.2

# Connect

You can use the relationship between the diameter and the circumference of a circle to estimate the circumference of a circle when you know its diameter.

| Step 1 | Step 2 | Step 3 |
|---|---|---|
| Find the diameter of the circle.  The diameter is 10 in. | Multiply the diameter of the circle by 3. 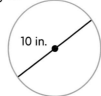 $3 \times 10 = 30$ | Estimate the circumference of the circle. 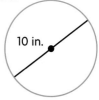 So, the circumference is approximately 30 in. |

It is important to understand that since the circumference of a circle is a little more than 3 times its diameter, multiplying by 3 is an estimate.

So, as the length of the diameter increases, the estimate becomes less accurate.

**TALK Math**

**Describe** the relationship between the diameter and the circumference of a circle.

# Practice

Use a compass and a ruler to draw a circle with the given radius.
Estimate the circumference of the circle by using a string and ruler.

1. radius = 4 cm
2. radius = 10 cm
3. radius = 8 cm
4. radius = 5 cm
5. radius = 6.2 cm
✓6. radius = 7.3 cm

Estimate the circumference of the circle.

7. 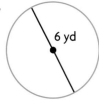 6 yd

8. 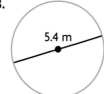 5.4 m

9. 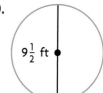 $9\frac{1}{2}$ ft

10. 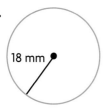 18 mm

11.  25 in.

✓12.  $\frac{1}{2}$ in.

13. **WRITE Math** **Explain** how you could estimate the circumference of a circle using only a ruler.

ALGEBRA
# Find Circumference

OBJECTIVE: Find the circumference of circles.

## Learn

The View is a circular revolving restaurant that overlooks Times Square in New York City. It is 47 stories high, providing views in every direction. The restaurant has a diameter of 112 ft. To the nearest foot, about how far does a person seated at the edge of the restaurant travel in one revolution?

In the previous lesson, you found that the value of the circumference divided by the diameter is a little more than 3 for any circle. For any circle, the circumference divided by the diameter is about 3.14, or exactly equal to $\pi$. This relationship can be written as $\frac{C}{d} = \pi$, where $C$ is the circumference of the circle and $d$ is the diameter of the circle.

Since $\frac{C}{d} = \pi$, you can get the formula $C = \pi d$ by multiplying both sides of the equation by $d$. Since the diameter of a circle is twice the length of the radius, or $d = 2r$, you can also write $C = \pi \times 2r$, or $C = 2\pi r$.

So, you can find the circumference of any circle by using the formula $C = \pi d$ or $C = 2\pi r$.

**Remember**
You can use 3.14 or $\frac{22}{7}$ for $\pi$. These are common estimates of $\pi$.

### Example 1 Find the circumference to the nearest foot. Use 3.14 for $\pi$.

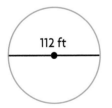

112 ft

Use the formula $C = \pi d$.

| | |
|---|---|
| $C = \pi d$ | Write the formula. |
| $C \approx 3.14 \times 112$ | Replace $\pi$ with 3.14 and $d$ with 112. Multiply. |
| $C \approx 351.68$ | |
| $C \approx 352$ | Round to the nearest foot. |

So, a person seated at the edge of the restaurant travels about 352 ft in one revolution.

- **What if** a person were seated 5 ft from the edge of the restaurant? About how far would that person travel in one revolution?
  HINT: The diameter decreases by $2 \times 5 = 10$, or 10 ft.

MG 1.2 Know common estimates of $\pi$ (3.14; $\frac{22}{7}$) and use these values to estimate and calculate the circumference and area of circles; compare with actual measurements. *also* AF 3.1, AF 3.2, MG 1.0, MG 1.1, MR 2.2, MR 2.4, MR 2.5, MR 3.2

# Use the Radius

When the radius of a circle is given, use $C = 2\pi r$ to find circumference.

**Example 2** Jeanette has a circular tablecloth with a radius of $3\frac{1}{2}$ ft. She wants to trim the tablecloth with fringe. How many feet of fringe will she need? Use $\frac{22}{7}$ for $\pi$.

| | |
|---|---|
| $C = 2\pi r$ | Write the formula. |
| $C \approx 2 \times \frac{22}{7} \times 3\frac{1}{2}$ | Replace $\pi$ with $\frac{22}{7}$ and $r$ with $3\frac{1}{2}$. |
| $C \approx \frac{2}{1} \times \overset{11}{\underset{1}{\frac{22}{7}}} \times \overset{1}{\underset{2}{\frac{7}{2}}}$ | Write 2 and $3\frac{1}{2}$ as fractions. Simplify. Multiply. |
| $C \approx \frac{22}{1}$, or 22 | |

So, she will need about 22 ft of fringe.

**ERROR ALERT**

Be sure you are using the correct circumference formula, depending on whether you know the diameter or the radius.

You can find the diameter or radius of a circle when the circumference is known.

**Example 3** The circumference of a basketball hoop is 141.3 cm. What is the diameter of the hoop? Use 3.14 for $\pi$.

| | |
|---|---|
| $C = \pi d$ | Write the formula. |
| $141.3 \approx 3.14d$ | Replace C with 141.3 and $\pi$ with 3.14. |
| $\dfrac{141.3}{3.14} \approx \dfrac{3.14d}{3.14}$ | Solve. |
| $45 \approx d$ | |

So, the diameter of the basketball hoop is about 45 cm.

**Example 4** Find the circumference of a circle with diameter 6.45 m. Round to the nearest tenth.

You can use this key sequence on a calculator.

| $\pi$ | $\times$ | 6 | $\cdot$ | 4 | 5 | $=$ | 20.26327262 |

$C \approx 20.26327262$

$C \approx 20.3$     Round to the nearest tenth.

So, the circumference is about 20.3 m.

## Guided Practice

Find the circumference to the nearest whole number. Use 3.14 for $\pi$.

**1.**  8 cm

$C = \pi d$
$C \approx 3.14 \times 8$
$C \approx \blacksquare$

**2.**  3 ft

$C = 2\pi r$
$C \approx 2 \times 3.14 \times 3$
$C \approx \blacksquare$

**Find the circumference to the nearest whole number.**
**Use 3.14 or $\frac{22}{7}$ for $\pi$.**

3.
7 m

✓4.
$17\frac{1}{2}$ yd

5.
2.8 cm

✓6.
$5\frac{1}{2}$ in.

7. **[ TALK Math ]** **Explain** how you can find the circumference of a circle if you know its radius.

## Independent Practice and Problem Solving

**Find the circumference to the nearest whole number.**
**Use 3.14 or $\frac{22}{7}$ for $\pi$.**

8.
20 in.

9.
$10\frac{1}{2}$ ft

10.
6.7 mm

11.
4.5 km

12.
6.4 m

13.
$14\frac{1}{4}$ yd

14.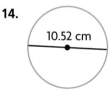
10.52 cm

15.
$62\frac{1}{2}$ in.

16. diameter = 23 yd

17. radius = 40 mm

18. radius = 1.8 m

19. diameter = $4\frac{5}{11}$ mi

**Find the diameter to the nearest whole number. Use 3.14 or $\frac{22}{7}$ for $\pi$.**

20. circumference = 39.25 m

21. circumference = $13\frac{2}{7}$ yd

22. circumference = 19.625 km

23. **≡FAST FACT** George W. G. Ferris built the first Ferris wheel in 1892. This wheel was 250 ft in diameter. About how far would a person sitting in one of the cars travel in 3 revolutions?

24. **Reasoning** How many segments, $x$, will fit on the circumference of the circle? **Explain.**

25. Draw a circle with radius 5 cm. Use string to estimate its circumference. Then calculate the circumference. Compare your results.

26. **[ WRITE Math ]** **What's the Error?** Lin said the circumference of a circle with an 11 ft radius was about 35 ft. Find and correct her error.

## Achieving the Standards

27. Kirk is three years older than Brian. If $n$ represents Brian's age, what expression can be used to represent Kirk's age? (AF 1.0, p. 280)

28. Tyler had test scores of 89, 92, 80, 99, 85, and 83 on his last 6 math tests. Is Tyler's mean test score greater than 90? (SDAP 1.1, p. 224)

29. **Test Prep** A band is being placed around a circular hat with a diameter of 8 inches. Which measure is closest to the length of the band that will go around the hat?

   **A** 10 inches   **C** 25 inches

   **B** 15 inches   **D** 50 inches

# Write to Describe an Error

Finding and describing an error in another student's work or in your own work helps you avoid making errors on similar types of problems.

Will and Devon's class is assigned this problem to solve.

Bev's dog Riley has a leash that is 9 ft long. When Riley is outside, his leash is attached to a stake in the ground. To the nearest tenth of a foot, what is the length of the longest circular path that Riley can run when leashed to the stake?

This is Will's solution:

$C = \pi d$
$C \approx 3.14 \times 9$
$C \approx 28.26$

So, the longest circular path is about 28.3 ft.

Devon identified and described Will's error and showed her solution to the problem.

Will did not understand that the length of the leash represented the radius of the circle, not the diameter. So, he should have used the formula $C = 2\pi r$.

$$C = 2 \times 3.14 \times 9$$
$$C = 56.52$$

So, the longest circular path is about 56.5 ft.

**Problem Solving** Find and describe the error that led to the given incorrect solution. Then find the correct answer.

1. The circumference of the center circle on a basketball court is 11.492 m. To the nearest tenth of a meter, what is the radius of the circle? Claire's incorrect solution is 3.7 m.

2. Snowball's leash is attached to the back of a house. If the length of the longest semi-circular path that Snowball can run is 22.61 ft, how long is Snowball's leash? Jimmy's incorrect solution is 3.6 ft.

# LESSON 5

## Problem Solving Workshop
## Strategy: Compare Strategies

OBJECTIVE: Solve problems using the strategies *draw a diagram* and *make a table*.

**Read to Understand**
**Plan**
**Solve**
**Check**

**PROBLEM** George is planning to build a large circular garden with a circular pond within the garden. The garden will have a radius of 10 yd. The pond will have a radius of 5 yd. How many square yards of area does George need to cover with topsoil? Use 3.14 for $\pi$.

## Read to Understand

Reading Skill

• Identify the details of the problem.
• What information will you use?

## Plan

• What strategies can you use to solve the problem?

You can draw a diagram or make a table.

## Solve

• How can you use the strategies to solve the problem?

**Draw a Diagram**

The garden is circular with a radius of 10 yd. The pond is also circular with a radius of 5 yd. Use this information to draw a diagram.

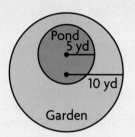

Pond 5 yd
10 yd
Garden

The region shaded in green is the area that requires topsoil. Subtract the area of the small circle from the area of the large circle to find the area of the region shaded in green.

$$Area = \pi \times 10^2 - \pi \times 5^2$$
$$\approx 3.14 \times 100 - 3.14 \times 25$$
$$\approx 314 - 78.5$$
$$\approx 235.5$$

**Make a Table**

Make a table showing the measurements for each circle. Use the measurements to calculate the area of each circle. Then find the difference between the areas.

|  | $r$ | $r^2$ | $\pi r^2$ | Area |
|---|---|---|---|---|
| **Large Circle** | 10 | 100 | 3.14 × 100 | ≈ 314 yd² |
| **Small Circle** | 5 | 25 | 3.14 × 25 | ≈ 78.5 yd² |
| **Difference** |  |  |  | ≈ 235.5 yd² |

So, George will need to cover about 235.5 yd² with topsoil.

## Check

• How can you estimate to check your answer?

MG 1.2 Know common estimates of $\pi$ (3.14; $\frac{22}{7}$) and use these values to estimate and calculate the circumference and area of circles; compare with actual measurements. *also* ⊶ NS 2.0, AF 3.1, AF 3.2, ⊶ MG 1.1, MR 1.0, MR 2.0, MR 2.2, MR 2.4, MR 2.5, MR 2.7, MR 3.0, MR 3.1, MR 3.2, MR 3.3

Use Logical Reasoning

Draw a Diagram or Picture

Make a Model

Make an Organized List

Find a Pattern

Make a Table or Graph

Guess and Check

Work Backward

Solve a Simpler Problem

Write an Equation

1. The Smiths are planning to have a circular patio built in their new backyard. The rest of the yard will be planted with grass seed. The yard is circular with a diameter of 40 ft. If the patio will have a radius of 9 ft, what is the area of the part of the yard that will need to be seeded?

   **First,** draw and label a diagram.

   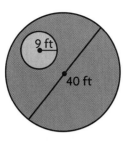

   **Next,** find the area of each shape.

   **Finally,** subtract the area of the small circle from the area of the large circle.

2. **What if** the Smiths decide they want a larger patio with a radius of 12 ft? What is the area of the part of the yard that will need to be seeded?

3. Mr. Hernandez is adding on to a deck in his backyard. The plans for the deck are shown on the right. The section he is adding on is shaded in blue. The area of the original deck is 145 ft$^2$. What is the total area of the deck? Use $3.14$ for $\pi$.

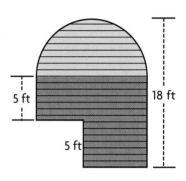

## Mixed Strategy Practice

4. A fundraiser is being held at school. Manny sells adult tickets for $3.50 and student tickets for $2.50. Manny sells 10 more adult tickets than student tickets. He collects $155 in ticket sales. If a total of 50 people attend the fundraiser, how many student tickets did Manny sell?

5. Alexander is making an herb garden. He plans to surround his rectangular garden with a border of edging. Each piece of edging is 1 ft in length. If he has 24 pieces of edging, what are the dimensions, in feet, of the different rectangular gardens he can make?

6. The Washingtons are having a party in their backyard. One of the games they have planned is darts. The dart board is shown at right. If you can throw 3 darts to score points and each dart lands within the target area, how many different total scores are possible?

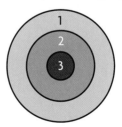

7. **Reasoning** Yi's flower garden is circular with a diameter of 8 yd. In the center there is a square with an area of 4 yd$^2$. Yi needs to find the area of his garden so he can buy fertilizer. Find the area of the garden to the nearest square yard.

8. The Davidsons want to buy a circular tarp to cover the circular pool in their backyard. If the circumference of their pool is 38 yd, what is the area of the smallest tarp they can buy? Give your answer to the nearest square yard.

9. **WRITE Math** ▶ **What's the Error?** Look back at Problem 7. Yi calculated the area of the garden to be about 197 yd. **Describe** his error.

# Extra Practice

**Set A** Find the area to the nearest whole number. Use 3.14 or $\frac{22}{7}$ for $\pi$. (pp. 420–421)

**1.**
12 m

**2.**
9.8 m

**3.**
35 in.

**4.**
266 mm

**5.**
19.4 yd

**6.**
12 mi

**7.**
19 cm

**8.**
26.2 m

**9.** radius = 3.4 cm    **10.** radius = 15 km    **11.** diameter = 196 ft    **12.** diameter = 17.5 in.

**13.** What is the area of a circular tabletop with a radius of 40 in.?

**14.** A circular parachute has a diameter of 15 ft. What is the area of the parachute?

**Find the area of the partial circle to the nearest whole number.**
Use 3.14 or $\frac{22}{7}$ for $\pi$. (pp. 420–421)

**15.**
144 cm

semicircle

**16.**
9 in.

$\frac{3}{4}$ circle

**17.**
4 mm

$\frac{1}{4}$ circle

**18.**
11.8 yd

$\frac{2}{3}$ circle

**Set B** Find the circumference to the nearest whole number. Use 3.14 or $\frac{22}{7}$ for $\pi$. (pp. 424–427)

**1.**
34 yd

**2.**
0.56 km

**3.**
215 mm

**4.**
2.3 ft

**5.**
14.7 m

**6.**
159 ft

**7.**
3 cm

**8.**
9.6 m

**9.** radius = 9.7 in.    **10.** diameter = 8.25 ft    **11.** radius = 25 cm    **12.** diameter = 2.3 m

**Find the diameter of the circle. Use 3.14 or $\frac{22}{7}$ for $\pi$. Round to the nearest whole number.**

**13.** circumference = 67.51 m    **14.** circumference = 44 ft    **15.** circumference = 392.5 cm

**16.** One of the coins in Larissa's coin collection has a circumference of 60 millimeters. What is the diameter of the coin?

**17.** Jon paints a 4-in. yellow line along the diameter of a hockey puck. What is the circumference of the hockey puck?

# Going in Circles

**Circle Up**
2 teams of 2 players each

**Round Everything Up**
- Game cards
- 2 different coins

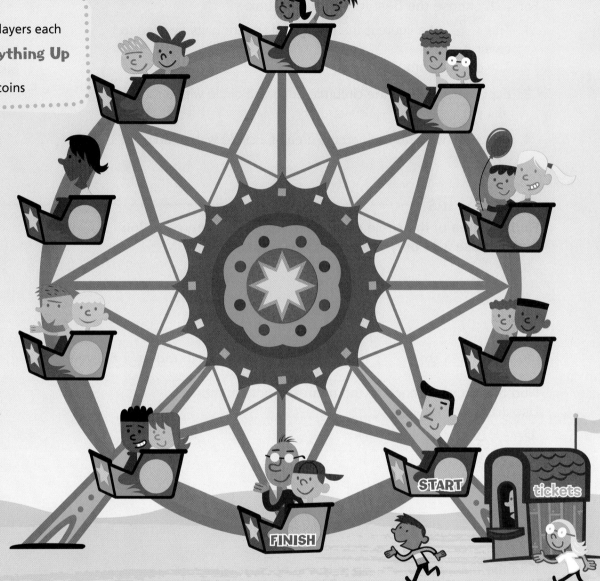

START

FINISH

tickets

## Around you Go

- Each team selects a different coin and places it on START.
- Shuffle the game cards, and place them facedown in a pile. Decide who will go first.
- Team 1 draws a game card from the pile.
- Teammates work together to find the radius, circumference, diameter, or area of the circle. (Use 3.14 for π. Round your answer to the nearest whole number.)

- Team 2 checks the answer. If the answer is correct, Team 1 moves its coin one space counterclockwise and play passes to Team 2.
- If the answer is incorrect, the team does not move. Play passes to the other team.
- The first team to reach FINISH wins.

**Chapter 17 Review/Test**

## Check Vocabulary and Concepts

For 1–2, choose the best term from the box.

**VOCABULARY**

area

circumference

radius

1. The ___?___ of a figure is the number of square units needed to cover it. (MG 1.0, p. 418)

2. The distance around a circle is called the ___?___. (O━┓ MG 1.1, p. 422)

3. Explain how to find the circumference of a circle with a radius of 4 cm. (O━┓ MG 1.1, pp. 424–427)

4. Describe how you can find the area of a circle with a radius of 10 in. (O━┓ MG 1.1, pp. 420–421)

## Check Skills

Find the area of the circle or partial circle to the nearest whole number. Use 3.14 or $\frac{22}{7}$ for $\pi$. (MG 1.2, pp. 420–421)

5.

8 km

6.

3.6 in.

7.

14 cm

8.

22 ft
$\frac{2}{3}$ circle

9. radius = 5 km

10. diameter = 12 ft

11. radius = 6.5 yd

12. diameter = 17.2 m

Find the circumference to the nearest whole number.
Use 3.14 or $\frac{22}{7}$ for $\pi$. (MG 1.2, pp. 424–427)

13.

5.5 yd

14.

22 km

15.

8.44 cm

16.

19 in.

17. radius = 5.9 m

18. diameter = 15 ft

19. diameter = 17.5 cm

20. radius = 2.75 mi

Find the diameter of the circle to the nearest whole number. Use 3.14 for $\pi$. (MG 1.2, pp. 424–427)

21. circumference = 67.75 ft

22. circumference = 1,592 mm

## Check Problem Solving

Solve. (MG 1.2, MR 1.0, MR 2.0, pp. 428–429)

23. Marco had a plate with a diameter of 20 cm. If he paints a sun in the center of the plate with a radius of 5 cm, what is the area of the part of the plate not covered by the sun?

24. Ken made a circular placemat with a design within the mat. The mat has a radius of 12 in. If the design has a radius of 4 in, what is the circumference of the design?

25. **WRITE Math** Explain how to find the diameter of a circle when the circumference is given.

**GO ONLINE Technology** Use *Online Assessment.*

# Enrich • Central Angles and Area of Sectors
## Part of the Circle

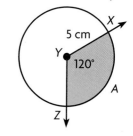

Christie knows how to find the area of a circle. She wants to know how she can find the area of a *part* of a circle, such as the part shaded in pink, sector *XYZA*, in the figure shown at right.

An **arc** is part of a circle. A **sector** is a region enclosed by two radii and the arc joining their endpoints. A **central angle** has its vertex at the center of a circle. An arc has the same measure as the central angle that forms it.

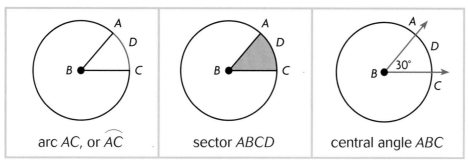

| arc *AC*, or $\overarc{AC}$ | sector *ABCD* | central angle *ABC* |

You can find the area of a sector of a circle by using the measure of the central angle and the radius.

## Circle Up! Find the area of sector *XYZA* to the nearest whole number.

Since an arc has the same measure as the central angle that forms it, $\overarc{XZ}$ measures 120°. The total angle measure of a circle is 360°. So, the area of the sector is $\frac{120°}{360°}$ or $\frac{1}{3}$ of the area of the circle. To find the area of sector *XYZA*, multiply the area of the entire circle by $\frac{120°}{360°}$ or $\frac{1}{3}$.

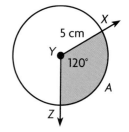

$$A = \frac{120}{360} \times \pi r^2$$

$$\approx \frac{1}{3} \times 3.14 \times 5^2 \approx 26.2$$

So, the area of sector *XYZA* is about 26 cm².

## Try It

**Find the area of sector *XYAZ* to the nearest whole number. Use 3.14 for π.**

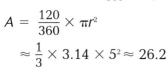

1.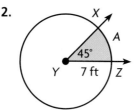

2. 

3. 

4.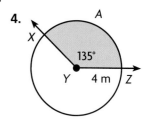

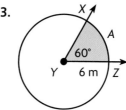

**WRITE Math** Explain how to find the area of a sector of a circle with a central angle of 150° and a radius of 3 cm.

# Unit Review/Test
## Chapters 15–17

## Multiple Choice

**1.** Mr. Greene has a ranch in the shape of a quadrilateral. The sides of the ranch form angles measuring 55°, 90°, and 110°. What is the measure of the unknown angle?
(MG 2.0, p. 400)

A 15°

B 60°

C 95°

D 105°

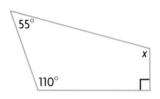

**2.** Which angle measure is complementary to an angle that measures 47°?
(O—∎ MG 2.2, p. 374)

A 43°

B 53°

C 123°

D 133°

**3.** The angle at each vertex of a regular hexagon is 120°. Which *best* describes this type of angle? (MG 2.0, p. 370)

A acute

B obtuse

C right

D straight

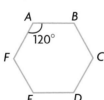

**4.** Two angles of a triangle have measures 46° and 57°. What is the measure of the third angle? (O—∎ MG 2.2, p. 392)

A 77°

B 87°

C 257°

D 267°

**5.** Which angle measure is supplementary to an angle that measures 76°? (O—∎ MG 2.2, p. 376)

A 14°

B 90°

C 104°

D 114°

**6.** Two lines intersect to form a set of four angles. If one of the angles measures 78°, what are the measures of the other angles?
(O—∎ MG 2.2, p. 378)

A 12°, 12°, 102°

B 12°, 12°, 78°

C 78°, 102°, 102°

D 78°, 12°, 180°

**7.** Which equation could be used to find the area in square inches of a circle with a radius of 9 inches? (O—∎ MG 1.1, p. 420)

A $A = 4.5 \times \pi$    C $A = 9 \times \pi$

B $A = \pi \times (4.5)^2$    D $A = \pi \times 9^2$

**8.** Which is a true statement about angles 1 and 2 shown below? (MG 2.1, p. 376)

A ∠1 is complementary to ∠2.

B ∠1 is supplementary to ∠2.

C Both angles are obtuse.

D Both angles are acute.

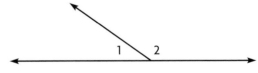
**Technology** Use *Online Assessment.*

9. In the figure below, $\overrightarrow{VY}$ intersects $\overleftrightarrow{ZX}$ at $U$. If m$\angle XUY = 45°$ and $\angle WUV \cong \angle VUZ$, what is m$\angle WUX$? (○━ MG 2.2, p. 378)

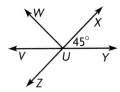

A 45°

C 90°

B 55°

D 135°

10. Which figure is an acute triangle? (MG 2.0, p. 392)

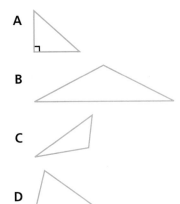

A

B

C

D

11. A circle has a diameter of 56 m. Which expression could be used to find the circumference? (○━ MG 1.1, p. 424)

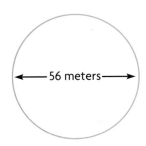

← 56 meters →

A $2 \times 28 \times \pi$

B $2 \times 56 \times \pi$

C $56 \times 56 \times \pi$

D $28 \times 28 \times \pi$

## Short Response

12. A bicycle wheel has an inside radius of 12 inches Find the inside circumference of the wheel. (○━ MG 1.1, MG 1.2, p. 424)

13. The circumference of a hat band is 21.98 inches. Find the diameter of the hat band. Round to the nearest inch. (○━ MG 1.1, MG 1.2, p. 424)

14. Draw a parallelogram. (MG 2.3, p. 400)

15. Draw a scalene right triangle with one side measuring 8 units. (MG 2.3, p. 392)

16. Tell whether the following statement is *always*, *sometimes*, or *never* true: (MG 2.0, p. 392)

An acute triangle has only one acute angle.

17. Find the area of a circle with a radius of 20 inches. (○━ MG 1.1, MG 1.2, p. 420)

18. Find the area of the semicircle below. (○━ MG 1.1, MG 1.2, p. 420)

12 yd

## Extended Response ▐WRITE Math▷

19. Dana knows the area of a circle. **Explain** the steps she could take to find the circumference of the circle. (MG 1.2, p. 424)

20. Katie says that complementary angles are always adjacent. Leah disagrees. Do you agree with Katie or Leah? **Explain** your answer and draw a diagram. (MG 2.1, p. 374)

21. Van says the circumference of a circle with a diameter of 4 inches is approximately 25.12 inches. Do you agree with his answer? **Explain** (○━ MG 1.1, MG 1.2, p. 424)

22. **Explain** how to find the area of $\frac{1}{3}$ of a circle when the radius is known. (○━ MG 1.1, p. 420)

23. Can an isosceles triangle also be a right triangle? **Explain.** (MG 2.0, p. 392)

from THE WORLD ALMANAC FOR KIDS

# California Architecture

## ROMAN INFLUENCE

California's famous missions reflect the architecture of other cultures, including ancient Rome. The Romans were the first to use arches and domes in their buildings. The builders of the California missions used the decorative styles of Spain; however, many of the buildings have arches and domes that are typical of Roman buildings.

One of the most famous Roman buildings is the Pantheon, which has a huge dome. It is often said that architecture is surrounded by geometry. Look at the Pantheon below; can you see the angles, lines, rays, and shapes that make up this amazing building?

**The Mission Santa Barbara has arched windows and domes.**

## FACT·ACTIVITY

**Use the diagram to help answer some of the questions.**

❶ What is the measure of a straight angle?

❷ What is the sum of angles 1, 2, and 3?

❸ $\overrightarrow{AC}$ bisects ∠BAD. What angle is congruent to ∠3?

❹ If ∠3 measures 30°, what are the measures of ∠1 and ∠2 together?

❺ Identify at least two different polygons in the diagram of the Pantheon. List the characteristics of each polygon.

❻ **WRITE Math** The diagram shows half of the Pantheon. **Explain** what type of symmetry would be used to draw the other half of the building. Now draw the other half of the building.

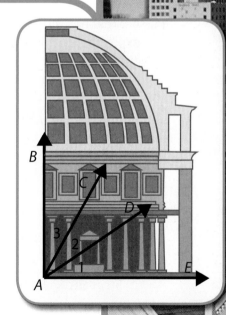

# FAMOUS BUILDINGS

California is home to many types of architecture. Some influences go back to ancient times. Some other styles are more modern, all combining different geometric shapes. For instance, in San Francisco, the Transamerica Pyramid resembles an Egyptian pyramid. Look at other buildings in California. Do you see an ancient influence, or the ideas of a modernist?

**US Bank Tower**

**Venice Beach House**

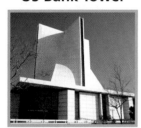

**St. Mary's Cathedral**

**Transamerica Pyramid**

# FACT·ACTIVITY

Design a building for your town or city in California. Research ideas for your building before you begin.

❶ Sketch your idea. What shape or shapes will it have? What dimensions will it have?

❷ Draw your final plan.

▶ Label all of the polygons that can be found in your building. Explain why polygons are important in architecture. Which polygon is used most often in architecture?

▶ Identify the types of angles that can be found in your building. Highlight the angles and find the measurements.

❸ What architectural influences does your building have? Explain why you chose that style, and why it works for your town or city.

# 6 Ratio, Proportion, and Percent

# Math on Location

▲Ratios and statistics are used to understand the target market of a product before work on a commercial begins.

▲Storyboards that define the actors' movements, expressions, and messages are drawn before filming begins.

▲When background, acting, voice, and music are combined, the specifications of message, time, and cost are reviewed.

# VOCABULARY POWER

### TALK Math

What math do you see in the **Math on Location** photographs? How can you use ratios in advertising?

### READ Math

**REVIEW VOCABULARY**   You learned the words below when you learned the basic facts on ratio, proportion, and percent. How do these words relate to **Math on Location**?

**percent** the ratio of a number to 100

**proportion** an equation that shows two ratios are equal

**rate** a ratio that compares two quantities having different units of measure

### WRITE Math ▶

Copy and complete bridge maps like the ones below. Use what you know about rate, ratio, proportion, and percent to complete them.

---

## Ratio, Proportion, and Percent

Use the analogy to complete the bridge map.

Rate — as —

a ratio that compares two quantities having different units of measure     a comparison of two numbers

— as — Percent

an equation that shows two ratios are equal

---

**Technology**
Multimedia Math Glossary link at
www.harcourtschool.com/hspmath

# 18 Ratios and Rates

**The Big Idea** A ratio is a comparison of part to whole, part to part, or whole to part.

## Investigate

Suppose you are studying cheetahs in Africa. The chart below shows data you have collected on several cheetahs. Show how you could compare the rate of speed of two different animals.

### Cheetah Field Notes

| Specimen | Distance Run (yds) | Time (sec) |
|----------|--------------------|------------|
| Large Female | 150 | 5.0 |
| Small Female #1 | 175 | 6.25 |
| Small Female #2 | 250 | 9.25 |
| Large Male | 100 | 4.0 |

**CALIFORNIA FAST FACT**

Cheetahs, like this one at the San Diego Zoo, can sprint at speeds of 70 mi per hr and can accelerate from 0 to 45 mi per hr in 2 seconds!

**GO ONLINE**

**Technology**
Student pages are available in the Student eBook.

Check your understanding of important skills
needed for success in Chapter 18.

▶ **Simplest Form**

Write each fraction in simplest form.

1. $\frac{6}{9}$   2. $\frac{5}{10}$   3. $\frac{6}{18}$   4. $\frac{3}{15}$

5. $\frac{3}{27}$   6. $\frac{4}{32}$   7. $\frac{4}{6}$   8. $\frac{5}{35}$

9. $\frac{2}{10}$   10. $\frac{6}{8}$   11. $\frac{5}{20}$   12. $\frac{9}{12}$

13. $\frac{10}{15}$   14. $\frac{3}{18}$   15. $\frac{3}{9}$   16. $\frac{8}{20}$

17. $\frac{2}{6}$   18. $\frac{4}{16}$   19. $\frac{9}{18}$   20. $\frac{12}{15}$

▶ **Solve Multiplication Equations**

Solve.

21. $6x = 24$   22. $3p = 12$   23. $36 = 9k$

24. $\frac{2}{3}d = 8$   25. $72 = 8b$   26. $12 = \frac{3}{4}a$

27. $0.04n = 8$   28. $176 = 11y$   29. $\frac{1}{3}h = 21$

30. $6.4 = 0.08m$   31. $55 = 2.5d$   32. $23h = 23$

33. $9 = \frac{3}{4}z$   34. $8.1 = 0.09c$   35. $45 = 5m$

# VOCABULARY POWER

**CHAPTER VOCABULARY**

equivalent ratios
rate
unit rate

**WARM-UP WORDS**

**equivalent ratios** ratios that name the same comparison

**rate** a ratio that compares two quantities having different units of measure

**unit rate** a rate that has 1 unit as its second term

# 1 Ratios

**OBJECTIVE:** Identify ratios and write equivalent ratios.

## Quick Review

**Tell whether the two fractions are equivalent.**

1. $\frac{2}{5}, \frac{3}{5}$    2. $\frac{5}{8}, \frac{10}{16}$

3. $\frac{7}{21}, \frac{1}{3}$    4. $\frac{10}{11}, \frac{5}{6}$

5. $\frac{12}{36}, \frac{3}{9}$

## Vocabulary

**equivalent ratios**

## Learn

**PROBLEM** On Career Day, Erica's father visits her class to discuss the parts of a microchip. He has a microchip and a diagram of it. The ratio of the size of the actual microchip to the diagram is 1 to 60. This means that the size of the microchip is $\frac{1}{60}$ of the size of the diagram. You can write a ratio three ways.

| with the word "to" | with a colon | as a fraction |
|---|---|---|
| 1 to 60 | 1:60 | $\frac{1}{60}$ $\leftarrow$ first term $\leftarrow$ second term |

Each of these is read as one to sixty.

Ratios compare amounts: a part to a part, a part to the whole, the whole to a part.

**Remember**

A ratio is a comparison of two numbers, $a$ and $b$, written as a fraction $\frac{a}{b}$.

**Example 1** Tyler's computer keyboard has 104 keys. There are 20 number keys and 26 letter keys. Write the following ratios.

a. number keys to letter keys $\rightarrow \frac{20}{26}$, or $\frac{10}{13}$    part to part

b. letter keys to total number of keys $\rightarrow \frac{26}{104}$, or $\frac{1}{4}$    part to whole

c. total number of keys to number keys $\rightarrow \frac{104}{20}$, or $\frac{26}{5}$    whole to part

**Equivalent ratios** are ratios that name the same comparison. You can write equivalent ratios by multiplying both terms by the same number or dividing both terms by a common factor.

**Example 2** Write three equivalent ratios that compare the **red counters** to the **yellow counters**.

$\dfrac{\text{red counters} \rightarrow 2}{\text{yellow counters} \rightarrow 4}$

$\frac{2}{4} \rightarrow \frac{2 \div 2}{4 \div 2} = \frac{1}{2}$   Divide both terms by a common factor.

$\frac{2}{4} \rightarrow \frac{2 \times 3}{4 \times 3} = \frac{6}{12}$   Multiply both terms by the same number.

So, $\frac{1}{2}, \frac{2}{4}$, and $\frac{6}{12}$ are equivalent ratios.

**NS 1.2** Interpret and use ratios in different contexts (e.g. batting averages, miles per hour) to show the relative sizes of two quantities, using appropriate notations (a/b, a to b, a:b). *also* **NS 1.0, MR 2.2, MR 2.4, MR 2.5, MR 3.0, MR 3.1, MR 3.2, MR 3.3**

1. Write the ratio of stars to stripes on the American flag. $\frac{\blacksquare}{13}$

2. Write the ratio of stripes to stars on the American flag. $\frac{13}{\blacksquare}$

**Write two equivalent ratios.**

3. $\frac{6}{14}$

4. $\frac{15}{21}$

✅ 5. $\frac{3}{4}$

✅ 6. $\frac{7}{8}$

7. **TALK Math** Explain how you can write equivalent ratios.

## Independent Practice and Problem Solving

**Write two equivalent ratios.**

8. $\frac{15}{35}$

9. $\frac{8}{12}$

10. $\frac{16}{40}$

11. $\frac{22}{20}$

12. $\frac{3}{5}$

13. $\frac{2}{9}$

**Write the ratios in fraction form.**

14. 72 mi on 4 gal

15. 90 cards in 6 packs

16. 108 items in 12 boxes

17. 288 pages in 15 days

⭐ **Algebra** Find the value of *m* that makes the ratios equivalent.

18. 5 to 3; *m* to 9

19. 3:10; 21:*m*

20. $\frac{5}{m}$; $\frac{15}{21}$

21. 3 to 8; *m* to 32

**For 22–25, use the diagram at the right.**

22. Write the ratio of the width of the monitor to its total height in three ways.

23. Write the ratio of the total height of the monitor to its length.

24. There are 23 students who use the computer, and 12 of the students are girls. Write the ratios of boys to girls and then girls to total number of students.

25. **WRITE Math** What's the Error? Elaine writes the ratio of length to width as $\frac{28}{34}$. Describe her error and give the correct ratio.

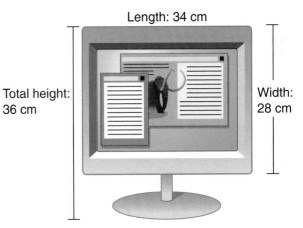

Length: 34 cm

Total height: 36 cm

Width: 28 cm

## Achieving the Standards

26. Order the values from least to greatest: 2.35, 2.03, 2.3. (⊙━┓ NS 1.1, p. 122 )

27. An extra–large drink lid has a diameter of 10.5 cm. To the nearest cm, what is the circumference of the lid? (MG 1.2, p. 420)

28. What is the ratio 55 to 15 written in simplest form? (⊙━┓ NS 1.2, p. 442)

29. **Test Prep** Which of the following is equivalent to 2:3?

   **A** 4:5　　**B** 8:10　　**C** 12:13　　**D** 14:21

## Quick Review

Write in simplest form.

1. $\frac{42}{7}$    2. $\frac{26}{13}$

3. $\frac{18}{2}$    4. $\frac{15}{5}$

5. $\frac{24}{8}$

## Vocabulary

rate          unit rate

## Learn

A **rate** is a ratio that compares two quantities that have different units of measure.

$$\text{rate: } \frac{\text{price}}{\text{weight}} \rightarrow \frac{\$12.70}{2 \text{ lb}}, \text{ or } \$12.70 \text{ for 2 lb}$$

A **unit rate** is a rate that has 1 unit as its second term.

Given any rate, you can divide by the second term to find the unit rate.

$$\frac{\$12.70}{2 \text{ lb}} \rightarrow \frac{12.70}{2} = \frac{12.70 \div 2}{2 \div 2} = \frac{6.35}{1}, \text{ or } \$6.35 \text{ per pound}$$

**PROBLEM** Kiera and her mother enjoy hiking through Yosemite National Park. If Kiera spends 45 min hiking, she burns 225 calories. At what unit rate is Kiera burning calories?

### Example 1  Find the unit rate.

**Step 1**

rate: $\frac{\text{calories}}{\text{minutes}} \rightarrow \frac{225}{45}$      Write a rate to compare calories burned to minutes.

**Step 2**

unit rate: $\frac{225}{45} = \frac{225 \div 45}{45 \div 45} = \frac{5}{1}$      Divide both terms by the second term.

So, Kiera burns calories at a unit rate of 5 calories per minute while hiking.

Average speed is average distance traveled per unit of time. So average speed is a unit rate.

### Example 2

The Franklins are driving up the coast from Oceanside, CA, to Santa Rosa, CA, which is a distance of 500 mi. They travel 300 mi in 6 hr. At this rate, how long will it take them to make the whole trip?

| Step 1 | Step 2 | Step 3 |
|---|---|---|
| Write a rate showing distance over time. $\frac{\text{miles}}{\text{hours}} \rightarrow \frac{300}{6}$ | Find the unit rate or average speed. $\frac{300 \div 6}{6 \div 6} = \frac{50}{1}$, or 50 mi per hr | THINK: $50 \times 10 = 500$. Multiply each term by 10 to find the number of hours for 500 mi. $\frac{50}{1} = \frac{50 \times 10}{1 \times 10} = \frac{500}{10} \begin{array}{l}\leftarrow \text{miles} \\ \leftarrow \text{hours}\end{array}$ |

So, it will take the Franklins 10 hr to complete the trip.

AF 2.2 Demonstrate an understanding that *rate* is a measure of one quantity per unit value of another quantity. *also* NS 1.0, NS 1.2, AF 2.0, AF 2.3, MR 2.2, MR 2.4, MR 2.5, MR 3.0, MR 3.2, MR 3.3

1. Find the unit rate. $\frac{\$15}{5 \text{ oz}} \rightarrow \frac{15 \div 5}{5 \div 5} = \frac{\blacksquare}{\blacksquare}$, or $\blacksquare$ per ounce

**Write the ratio in fraction form. Then find the unit rate.**

2. 16 servings for 8 people
3. 280 calories in 4 hr
4. $20.88 for 9 gal

5. 45 volunteers for 15 events
✓6. 54 revolutions in 12 min
✓7. $32.20 for 7 lb

8. **TALK Math** Explain how you can find a unit rate when given any rate.

## Independent Practice and Problem Solving

**Write the ratio in fraction form. Then find the unit rate.**

9. 288 pages in 12 days
10. 72 mi on 4 gal
11. $14.28 for 4 tickets

12. 108 items in 12 boxes
13. 112 students to 14 teachers
14. 90 cards in 6 packs

**Algebra** Write the rate in fraction form. Then find the value of *x*.

15. Joe spends $8.05 for 7 oz of cologne, so the unit rate is *x* dollars per ounce.

16. Casper eats 18 crackers in 3 min, so he can eat *x* crackers in 1 min.

**USE DATA** For 17–19, use the table at the right.

17. On which day was Hope's average speed 4 mi per hr?

18. Name the days during which Hope traveled at the same average speed.

19. On which day was Hope hiking the fastest?

20. **Reasoning** Estes bikes along a 54-mile mountain trail. He travels 18 mi in 2 hr. At this rate, how long will it take him to ride the whole trail?

21. Wesley kayaks along the Carson River at an average speed of 9 km per hr. At this rate, how long will it take him to kayak 27 km?

22. **Pose a Problem** Look back at Problem 21. Write a similar problem so that the answer is 7 km per hr.

23. **WRITE Math** Explain how you solved problem 19.

Hope's Hiking Log

| Day | Miles | Hours |
|-----|-------|-------|
| 1 | 15 | 5 |
| 2 | 12 | 6 |
| 3 | 16 | 4 |
| 4 | 10 | 5 |

## Achieving the Standards

24. Angles *A* and *B* are complementary. Find m∠B if m∠A = 23°. (○━ MG 2.2. p. 374)

25. Write an equation for the sentence, "The quotient of 52 and a number is 2." (AF 1.0, p.300)

26. Write two equivalent ratios for 2:3. (○━ NS 1.2. p. 442)

27. **Test Prep** Larry is on a train that is moving at 60 miles per hour. How far will he travel in 4.5 hours?

A  3 miles        C  160 miles

B  34.5 miles     D  270 miles

# Apply Ratios and Rates

OBJECTIVE: Apply ratios and rates to solve problems.

## Learn

You can use ratios and rates to help solve different kinds of problems. Finding an equivalent ratio can help find an unknown value.

**PROBLEM** When Mrs. Esparza makes guacamole, she mixes 2 tbsp of lime juice with 5 avocados. How many tablespoons of lime juice does she need with 15 avocados?

### Example 1 Find an equivalent ratio.

**Step 1**

$$\frac{\text{tbsp of lime juice} \rightarrow 2}{\text{avocados} \rightarrow 5}$$

Write the given ratio.

**Step 2**

$$\frac{2 \times ?}{5 \times ?} = \frac{?}{15}$$

Find the factor used to get 15 avocados. THINK: $5 \times ? = 15$

**Step 3**

$$\frac{2 \times 3}{5 \times 3} = \frac{6}{15} \leftarrow \frac{\text{tbsp of lime juice}}{\text{avocados}}$$

Multiply both terms by the factor, 3.

So, Mrs. Esparza needs 6 tbsp of lime juice.

• How much lime juice would Mrs. Esparza need with 10 avocados?

Unit rates can be used for comparing costs.

**ERROR ALERT**

When you want to compare the unit costs, be sure that the cost is the first term of each ratio.

### Example 2

Hailey spends $3.52 for a 1-lb jar of jalapeños. Sonny spends $3.78 for an 18-oz jar of jalapeños. Who got the better deal?

**Step 1**

Write the rates in ounces (1 lb = 16 oz)

Hailey's 1-lb jar: $\frac{\text{cost}}{\text{ounces}} \rightarrow \frac{\$3.52}{16}$

Sonny's 18-oz jar: $\frac{\text{cost}}{\text{ounces}} \rightarrow \frac{\$3.78}{18}$

**Step 2**

Find unit rates for both jars.

16-oz jar: $\frac{3.52 \div 16}{16 \div 16} = \frac{0.22}{1}$, or $0.22 per ounce

18-oz jar: $\frac{3.78 \div 18}{18 \div 18} = \frac{0.21}{1}$, or $0.21 per ounce

**Step 3**

Compare the unit rates.

$0.21 per oz < $0.22 per oz

So, Sonny got the better deal.

O—¬ **AF 2.2** Demonstrate an understanding that *rate* is a measure of one quantity per unit value of another quantity. *also* O—¬ NS 1.0, O—¬ NS 1.2, AF 2.0, AF 2.3, MR 2.4, MR 2.5, MR 3.2

1. Six copies of a book weigh 14 kg. How many copies of the same book weigh 56 kg?

$$\frac{\text{books} \rightarrow}{\text{kilograms} \rightarrow} \frac{6 \times \blacksquare}{14 \times \blacksquare} = \frac{\blacksquare}{56}$$

**Solve.**

2. A company ships 16 packages in 2 boxes. How many boxes would it take to ship 32 packages?

3. Three windows have 24 panes. How many of the same windows would have 96 panes?

4. **TALK Math** **Explain** the difference between a ratio and a rate.

## Independent Practice and Problem Solving

**Solve.**

5. The ratio of white marbles to blue marbles in a bag is 4:5. How many white marbles are there if there are 15 blue marbles in the bag?

6. Quinn gets 54 pencils after buying 3 pencil packs. How many pencils would Quinn have if he bought 9 packs?

7. Emma uses 7 cans of gray paint to every 4 cans of red paint. If she buys 16 cans of red paint, how many cans of gray paint should she buy?

8. At the local market, strawberries cost $1.98 for 1 lb. How much will 48-oz of strawberries cost?

**Tell which is the better deal.**

9. A: $4.50 for 9 in. of fabric
   B: $5.40 for 1 ft of fabric

10. A: $5.10 for 6 pairs
    B: $7.36 for 8 pairs

11. A: $12.24 for 12 party favors
    B: $15.75 for 15 party favors

**USE DATA For 12–13, use the data in the table.**

12. Which two fruits have the same unit rate?

13. **FAST FACT** Fallbrook, CA, is known as the avocado capital of the world. Suppose 30 avocados cost $27.90 at Fallbrook's annual Avocado Festival. Is this a better deal than the avocados in the table? **Explain.**

14. **WRITE Math** A basket holds peppers and ears of corn. If the ratio of peppers to corn is 7 to 5, what is the ratio of peppers to vegetables in the basket? **Explain.**

**Cost of Produce**

| Type | Number | Cost |
|------|--------|------|
| Avocados | 5 | $4.90 |
| Limes | 5 | $1.90 |
| Mangos | 4 | $3.92 |
| Pears | 3 | $2.49 |

## Achieving the Standards

15. Evaluate $12m$ for $m = 4$. (AF 1.2, p. 284)

16. Draw a triangle that has 2 equal sides and an obtuse angle. (MG 2.3, p. 398)

17. Solve $5m = 85$ for $m$. (AF 1.1, p. 336)

18. **Test Prep** Mel uses 3 mushrooms with 2 onions to make a soup. When she uses 8 onions, how many mushrooms does she need?

   **A** 6    **B** 9    **C** 8    **D** 12

# 4 Distance, Rate, and Time

**OBJECTIVE:** Solve problems involving distance, rate, and time.

## Learn

**PROBLEM** Maggie takes 45 min to walk the length of a trail that is 3,285 yd long. How fast was she walking?

You can use the formula *distance = rate × time,* or $d = rt$. When you know two parts of this formula, you can solve for the third part.

**Example 1 Find the rate.**

| | |
|---|---|
| $d = rt$ | Write the formula. |
| $3{,}285 = r \times 45$ | Replace *d* with 3,285 and *t* with 45. |
| $\dfrac{3{,}285}{45} = \dfrac{45r}{45}$ | Solve the equation. |
| $73 = r$ | |

So, Maggie walks 73 yd per min.

**Example 2 Find the time.**

Helen drives 221 mi to visit relatives in Sacramento, CA. She drives at an average speed of 52 mi per hr. How long does the trip take?

| | |
|---|---|
| $d = rt$ | Write the formula. |
| $221 = 52 \times t$ | Replace *d* with 221 and *r* with 52. |
| $\dfrac{221}{52} = \dfrac{52t}{52}$ | Solve the equation. |
| $4.25 = t$ | |

So, the trip took 4.25 hr, or 4 hr and 15 min.

**Example 3 Find the distance.**

Paul's class is going on an overnight field trip. To reach their destination, the bus travels at a speed of 65 mi per hr. The bus travels for 2 hr. How far did the bus travel?

| | |
|---|---|
| $d = rt$ | Write the formula. |
| $d = 65 \times 2$ | Replace *r* with 65, and *t* with 2. Multiply. |
| $d = 130$ | |

So, Paul's class traveled 130 mi.

AF 2.3 Solve problems involving rates, average speed, distance, and time. *also* NS 1.2, AF 1.0, AF 1.1, AF 2.0, AF 2.2, MR 2.4, MR 2.5, MR 3.1, MR 3.2

## Example 4

Two different planes leave the airport at the same time. Plane A travels an average speed of 540 mi per hr for 3 hr. Plane B travels an average speed of 280 mi per hr for 5.8 hr. Which plane flies the greatest distance?

**Step 1**    **Find the distance Plane A flies.**

$d = rt$             Write the formula.

$d = 540 \times 3$     Replace $r$ with 540 and $t$ with 3. Multiply.

$d = 1,620$

**Step 2**    **Find the distance Plane B flies.**

$d = rt$             Write the formula.

$d = 280 \times 5.8$     Replace $r$ with 280 and $t$ with 5.8. Multiply.

$d = 1,624$

**Step 3**    **Compare the distances.**

Plane A flies 1,620 mi. Plane B flies 1,624 mi.

$1,624 > 1620$

So, plane B flies the greatest distance.

- **What if** plane A traveled at an average speed of 545 mi per hr for 3 hr. Would plane A have traveled farther than plane B?

## Guided Practice

1. A jogger runs at a rate of 3 m per sec. How far has she run after 50 sec?

$$d = rt$$

You need to find distance, $d$. Replace the rate, $r$, with 3 and the time, $t$, with 50.

2. A car travels 130 mi in 2 hr. How fast did the car travel?

$$d = rt$$

You need to find rate, $r$. Replace the distance, $d$, with 130 and the time, $t$, with 2.

**Use the formula $d = rt$ to complete.**

3. $d = 25$ cm
$r = 4$ cm per sec
$t = \blacksquare$

4. $d = 18$ yd
$r = \blacksquare$
$t = 2$ min

5. $d = \blacksquare$
$r = 46$ km per hr
$t = 3.8$ hr

6. $d = 30\frac{1}{4}$ mi
$r = 11$ mi per day
$t = \blacksquare$

7. **TALK Math** Describe how to find distance if you are given the rate and the time.

**Use the formula** $d = rt$ **to complete.**

**8.** $d = 6.4$ cm
$r = 2$ cm per sec
$t = $ ▨

**9.** $d = 10.4$ yd
$r = $ ▨
$t = 4$ min

**10.** $d = $ ▨
$r = 12$ km per hr
$t = 40$ hr

**11.** $d = 100$ cm
$r = $ ▨
$t = \frac{1}{4}$ min

**12.** $d = 0.75$ mi
$r = 60$ mi per hr
$t = $ ▨

**13.** $d = \frac{7}{8}$ in.
$r = $ ▨
$t = \frac{7}{8}$ min

**14.** $d = $ ▨
$r = 250.5$ mi
$t = 9.25$ hr

**15.** $d = 14\frac{4}{10}$
$r = 8$ mi per hr
$t = $ ▨

**Find the distance, rate, or time.**

**16.** A cyclist travels 5 mi in 20 min. How far will he travel in 32 min?

**17.** A train travels at a rate of 75 mi per hr. How far does it travel in 3.5 hr?

**USE DATA For 18–20, use the table.**

**18.** How fast does Ferry A travel in feet per minute?

**19.** Which ferry travels at the fastest rate of speed: Ferry B or Ferry C?

**20.** Ferry C departs on schedule and travels at an average rate of 2,915 ft per min. Will it arrive on time?

**21. Reasoning** Jeremy and Cynthia leave at the same time to travel 75 mi to an area attraction. Jeremy drives 15 mi in 12 min. Cynthia drives 26 mi in 20 min. If they continue at the same rates, who will arrive at the attraction first? **Explain.**

**22.** **WRITE Math** **Sense or Nonsense** Bonnie says that if she drives at an average rate of 40 mi per hr, she can drive 45 mi across town in about 2 hr. Does Bonnie's statement make sense? **Explain.**

| Ferry Schedule | | | |
|---|---|---|---|
| | **Depart** | **Arrive** | **Distance** |
| **Ferry A (Pier 1)** | 10:15 A.M. | 11:15 A.M. | 148,500 ft |
| **Ferry B (Pier 2)** | 10:30 A.M. | 11:10 A.M. | 141,720 ft |
| **Ferry C (Pier 3)** | 1:30 P.M. | 2:25 P.M. | 182,187.5 ft |
| **Ferry D (Pier 4)** | 3:00 P.M. | 3:45 P.M. | 101,640 ft |

## Achieving the Standards

**23.** Order the numbers 10.98, 11.02, 11.2, 10.89, and 11.021 from least to greatest.
(O━┓ NS 1.1, p. 122]

**24.** Marcus took a survey on whether fruit juice vending machines or soda vending machines should be placed in middle schools. He surveyed an organization of fruit growers. Is this a biased or unbiased survey?
(O━┓ SDAP 2.4, p 208)

**25.** Write a ratio equivalent to $\frac{2}{5}$. (O━┓ NS 1.2, p 442)

**26. Test Prep** Shane goes down to the river for some rowing exercise. He rows 18 kilometers at a rate of 9 kilometers per hour. How long did it take Shane to row 18 kilometers?

**A** $\frac{1}{2}$ hour

**B** 2 hours

**C** 20 hours

**D** 162 hours

# Write a Conclusion

Tanner cycles around a track at a constant rate of 7 m per sec. His trainer records Tanner's progress in a log. Tanner studies the table his trainer made. He asks himself this question:

What conclusion can I make about how a change in time affects the distance I travel?

Tanner wrote this explanation and conclusion to answer his question.

| Rate | Time | Distance |
|------|------|----------|
| 7 m/s | 15 sec | 105 m |
| 7 m/s | 30 sec | 210 m |
| 7 m/s | 60 sec | 420 m |
| 7 m/s | 120 sec | 840 m |

First, I noticed a pattern in how the time changes in the table. Each time is twice the previous time. So, the time doubles from one row to the next.

Then, I studied how the distance is affected by the time. I noticed that when the time doubles, its corresponding distance also doubles. I wrote this to check my explanation;

Change in Time:    15    30    60    120
                      ×2    ×2    ×2

Change in Distance: 105   210   420   840
                      ×2    ×2    ×2

Finally, I wrote my conclusion. If you travel at a constant rate and the time you are traveling doubles, then the distance you travel also doubles.

## Tips

To write a conclusion:

- Study the data and write explanations of any patterns you notice.

- Use words such as *first, then*, and *next* to state your explanation in a logical order.

- Write your conclusion using the words *if* and *then* to describe how one thing affects another.

- State your conclusion in the last sentence of your answer.

**Problem Solving** Use each entry from Tanner's log book to write an explanation and a conclusion for each question.

1. If the rate changes but the time stays the same, then what effect does this have on the distance traveled?

| Rate | Time | Distance |
|------|------|----------|
| 3 m/s | 120 sec | 360 m |
| 6 m/s | 120 sec | 720 m |
| 12 m/s | 120 sec | 1,440 m |
| 24 m/s | 120 sec | 2,880 m |

2. If the time changes but the rate stays the same, then what effect does this have on the distance traveled?

| Rate | Time | Distance |
|------|------|----------|
| 8 m/s | 20 sec | 160 m |
| 8 m/s | 30 sec | 240 m |
| 8 m/s | 40 sec | 320 m |
| 8 m/s | 50 sec | 400 m |

# Problem Solving Workshop
## Skill: Relevant or Irrelevant Information

**LESSON 5**

**Read to Understand**
**Plan**
**Solve**
**Check**

**OBJECTIVE:** Solve problems by using the skill *relevant or irrelevant information*.

**PROBLEM** Tamika is making crafts that measure 3 in. by 4 in. She has finished 12 of the 36 crafts that she is planning to make for the Art & Craft Festival in South Lake Tahoe, CA. She can make 8 crafts in 2 hr. How long will it take for her to finish the rest of her crafts?

Carefully, reread the paragraph above and determine what information is relevant and what is irrelevant.

| RELEVANT | IRRELEVANT |
|---|---|
| • She has finished 12 of 36 crafts. | • The crafts measure 3 in. by 4 in. |
| • She can make 8 crafts in 2 hr. | • She is planning to display her crafts at the Art and Craft Festival in South Lake Tahoe, CA. |

Use the relevant information to solve the problem.

$36 - 12 = 24$

Subtract to find the number of crafts she still has to make.

$\dfrac{\text{crafts} \to 8}{\text{hours} \to 2}$

Write a ratio of crafts to hours.

$\dfrac{8 \times 3}{2 \times 3} = \dfrac{24}{6} \begin{matrix} \leftarrow \text{crafts} \\ \leftarrow \text{hours} \end{matrix}$

Use equivalent ratios to find the number of hours.

So, it will take Tamika 6 hr to finish the rest of her crafts.

## Think and Discuss
**Tell which information is relevant or irrelevant. Then solve the problem.**

a. Juanita stands in line for 10 min at the register and then spends $18.55 for 7 ft of molding. She returns the next day to buy 4 more feet of the same molding. How much does she spend for 4 more feet of molding?

b. Mike finds a 4-oz bottle of glue for $1.93 and an 8-oz bottle of glue for $3.12. He has a $5 bill and a $10 bill in his pocket. Which bottle of glue is the better deal?

**452**

NS 1.2 Interpret and use ratios in different contexts (e.g. batting averages, miles per hour) to show the relative sizeds of two quantities, using appropriate notations (*a/b*, *a* to *b*, *a:b*). *also* NS 1.0, MR 1.0, MR 1.1, MR 2.0, MR 2.4, MR 2.5, MR 3.0, MR 3.1, MR 3.2, MR 3.3

**Identify the relevant and irrelevant information. Then use the relevant information to solve the problem.**

1. Debbie makes floral arrangements that are 42 cm tall. In 3 hr, she can make 9 arrangements. How long will it take her to make 54 arrangements for the Lompoc Flower Festival?

   **First,** identify the relevant and irrelevant information.
   
   Relevant: In 3 hr, she can make 9 arrangements.
   She will make 54 arrangements.
   Irrelevant: The arrangements are 42 cm tall.
   Arrangements are for a festival.

   **Then,** use the relevant information to write equivalent ratios.

   $$\frac{\text{arrangements} \rightarrow}{\text{hours} \rightarrow} \frac{9 \times ?}{3 \times ?} = \frac{54}{?}$$

   **Finally,** write the number of hours in the equivalent ratio.

2. **What if** Debbie makes arrangements that are 36 cm tall, and it takes her 4 hr to make 15 of these arrangements. How long would it take her to make 45 of them?

3. Max spends $148 for 3 prints at the La Jolla Festival of the Arts. He then drives 240 mi to his home in Bakersfield. If he drives at an average rate of 40 mi in 45 min, how long does it take him to get home?

## Mixed Applications

4. Joshua drives 260 mi to attend the Kings Mountain Art Fair, where he plans to spend $500 on paintings. For the first 3 hr of his trip, he averages 52 mi per hr. How many miles has he traveled?

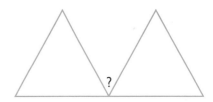

5. Bella is purchasing a handcrafted jewelry box at the Tuolumne Lumber Jubilee. She can select a cherry, oak, or maple finish, and there are four styles to choose from. How many choices does she have?

6. Rob is making a sculpture with triangles of cut glass. If he uses congruent equilateral triangles and places them side by side, what is the angle measure between them?

7. Holly is making a craft that uses 1 sticker and 1 colored piece of paper. The stickers come in packages of 8, and the paper comes in packages of 12. What is the least number of packages of stickers and colored paper Holly needs to use all the packages?

8. Caitlyn uses 36 in. of lace to make a washcloth and 24 in. of lace to make a hand towel. She is making 18 sets of each. How much lace will she need?

9. **WRITE Math** ▶ Look back at Problem 6. **Explain** how you solved the problem.

# Extra Practice

## Set A  Write two equivalent ratios. (O—n NS 1.2, pp. 442–443)

1. $\frac{5}{6}$  2. $\frac{16}{20}$  3. $\frac{2}{3}$  4. $\frac{8}{26}$  5. $\frac{30}{12}$  6. $\frac{7}{8}$

7. $\frac{15}{25}$  8. $\frac{1}{9}$  9. $\frac{2}{7}$  10. $\frac{28}{16}$  11. $\frac{12}{18}$  12. $\frac{7}{35}$

13. A fruit stand has 10 oranges and 16 apples. Write the ratio of oranges to apples and the ratio of apples to total pieces of fruit.

14. Mariana competed in 12 tennis matches this year. She won 8 of the matches. Write the ratio of losses to total matches played.

15. Emily made sun tea for a club picnic. She used 3 large tea bags for every 4 quarts of water. How many tea bags did she use to make 20 quarts of tea?

16. Jack and Kevin are reading a book over summer vacation. Jack reads 90 pages in 4 days. Kevin reads 105 pages in 5 days. Who is getting through the book faster?

## Set B  Write a ratio in fraction form. Then find the unit rate. (O—n AF 2.2, pp. 444–445)

1. 80 cards in 5 packs
2. $15.36 for 3 tickets
3. 175 calories in 2 hours
4. 168 pages in 14 days
5. 96 oz in 12 bottles
6. 45 marbles in 3 bags
7. 90 pencils in 6 boxes
8. 224 bottles on 7 shelves
9. 196 people in 7 buses

## Set C  Tell which is the better deal. (O—n AF 2.2, pp. 446–447)

1. A: $5.53 for 7 oranges
   B: $6.56 for 8 oranges
2. A: $4.50 for 18 packs
   B: $5.20 for 20 packs
3. A: $21.00 for 3 T-shirts
   B: $27.60 for 4 T-shirts

4. A: $25.25 for 5 comic books
   B: $29.70 for 6 comic books
5. A: $12.50 for 10 tomatoes
   B: $15.48 for 12 tomatoes
6. A: $7.75 for 5 grapefruit
   B: $10.50 for 7 grapefruit

## Set D  Use the formula $d = rt$ to complete. (AF 2.3, pp. 448–451)

1. $d = \blacksquare$
   $r = 3$ cm per sec
   $t = 4$ sec
2. $d = 81$ ft
   $r = \blacksquare$
   $t = 45$ min
3. $d = 63$ km
   $r = \blacksquare$
   $t = 6$ hr
4. $d = \blacksquare$
   $r = 7$ in. per min
   $t = 4$ min

5. $d = 120$ in.
   $r = 12$ in. per min
   $t = \blacksquare$
6. $d = 288$ mm
   $r = 12$ mm per sec
   $t = \blacksquare$
7. $d = \blacksquare$
   $r = 15$ km per hr
   $t = 4$ hr
8. $d = 120$ mi
   $r = 15$ mi per hr
   $t = \blacksquare$

9. $d = 192$ cm
   $r = \blacksquare$
   $t = 12$ sec
10. $d = \blacksquare$
    $r = 52$ mi per hr
    $t = 4$ hr
11. $d = 94.5$ m
    $r = \blacksquare$
    $t = 3.5$ hr
12. $d = 512$ in.
    $r = 12.8$ in. per min
    $t = \blacksquare$

13. An airplane traveled at a rate of 610 mi per hr. How far did the plane travel in 5 hr?

14. Carla ran a 10-km race in 50 min. At that rate, how far did she run in 10 min?

# THE PERFECT DEAL!

### Get Ready
2–4 players

### Get Set
- Number cube labeled 1, 1, 2, 2, 3, 3
- 2 different coins
- Deal cards

**FINISH LINE**

Go back 3 spaces

Move ahead 1 space

**START**

Move ahead 1 space

Lose a turn

Go back 1 space

Take another turn

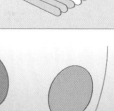

### Play

- Each player selects a different coin and places it on START.
- Shuffle the deal cards, and place them facedown in a pile. Decide who will go first.
- Player 1 draws a deal card from the pile.
- Player 1 chooses the better deal from the deal card.

- The other players check the answer. If it is correct, Player 1 tosses the number cube and advances that number of spaces on the gameboard and play passes to the next player.
- If the answer is incorrect, play passes to the next player and play continues.
- The first player to reach or cross the FINISH LINE wins.

#  Chapter 18 Review/Test

## Check Vocabulary and Concepts

Choose the best term from the box.

**VOCABULARY**

equivalent ratios

rate

ratio

unit rate

1. A __?__ is a comparison of two numbers. (O⊸▥ NS 1.2, p. 442)

2. A __?__ is a rate that has a 1 unit as its second term. (O⊸▥ AF 2.2, p. 444)

3. Ratios that name the same comparison are called __?__. (O⊸▥ NS 1.2, p. 442)

4. Explain how to find the distance traveled when given the rate and time.
   (AF 2.3, p. 446)

## Check Skills

Write two equivalent ratios. (O⊸▥ NS 1.2, pp. 442-443)

5. $\frac{7}{15}$    6. $\frac{24}{30}$    7. $\frac{9}{24}$    8. $\frac{10}{6}$    9. $\frac{5}{12}$

10. $\frac{20}{8}$    11. $\frac{14}{22}$    12. $\frac{3}{8}$    13. $\frac{9}{45}$    14. $\frac{16}{18}$

Write a ratio in fraction form. Then find the unit rate. (O⊸▥ AF 2.2, pp. 444-445)

15. 135 feet in 45 steps    16. 25 plates in 5 boxes    17. $12.42 for 3 tickets

18. 36 bananas in 6 bunches    19. $34.65 for 9 pounds    20. $121 for 11 pounds

Tell which is the better deal. (O⊸▥ AF 2.2, pp. 446-447)

21. A: $4.12 for 4 oranges
    B: $4.95 for 5 oranges

22. A: $12.10 for 2 belts
    B: $30.50 for 5 belts

23. A: $12.45 for 3 tickets
    B: $20.60 for 5 tickets

24. A: $44.15 for 6 hats
    B: $29.05 for 4 hats

25. A: $16.25 for 10 melons
    B: $26.24 for 16 melons

26. A: $18.60 for 3 meals
    B: $56.25 for 9 meals

Use the formula $d = rt$ to complete. (AF 2.3, pp. 448-451)

27. $d = $ ▤
    $r = 6$ cm per sec
    $t = 7$ sec

28. $d = 320$ mi
    $r = $ ▤
    $t = 4$ h

29. $d = 72$ m
    $r = 3$ m per sec
    $t = $ ▤

30. $d = $ ▤
    $r = 56$ ft per min
    $t = 9$ min

## Check Problem Solving

Solve. (O⊸▥ NS 1.2, MR 1.1, pp. 452-453)

31. Jason spent $12.50 for 5 ft of 6-in. copper pipe. He returned after 2 days to buy 3 more feet of the same pipe. How much did he spend in all for the pipe?

32. Mr. Michaels bought $45 worth of gas and then drove 205 mi to his home in Middletown. If he drove at an average rate of 55 mi per hr, how far did he get in 2 hr?

33. **WRITE Math** ▸ Sarah counted 36 of her heart beats in half a minute. **Explain** how she can find how many times her heart beats in 2 min.

**GO** **Technology** Use *Online Assessment.*

# Enrich • Golden Ratio
# APPEALING TO THE EYE

Any ratio equivalent to approximately 1.6:1 is called the **Golden Ratio**. When the ratio of a rectangle's dimensions is about 1.6 to 1, the rectangle is called a **Golden Rectangle**. Many people feel that a Golden Rectangle is more appealing to the human eye than any other rectangle. Many works of art and architecture, from ancient through modern times, are based on the Golden Rectangle.

## Look

Tell which window at the right is a Golden Rectangle.

Compare ratios.

| | Window **A** | Window **B** |
|---|---|---|
| Write the ratio of length to width for each window. | $\frac{l}{w} = \frac{72}{45}$ | $\frac{l}{w} = \frac{66}{55}$ |
| Divide each term by the second term of the ratio. Identify the Golden Rectangle. | $\frac{72 \div 45}{45 \div 45} = \frac{1.6}{1}$ | $\frac{66 \div 55}{55 \div 55} = \frac{1.2}{1}$ |

So, window A is a Golden Rectangle.

## Try It

**Identify the rectangle that is a Golden Rectangle.**

1.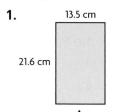
   13.5 cm
   21.6 cm
   A
   11 cm
   12 cm
   B

2.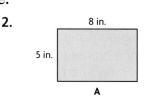
   8 in.
   5 in.
   A
   6 in.
   4 in.
   B

3.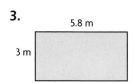
   5.8 m
   3 m
   A
   4 m
   2.5 m
   B

4.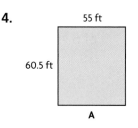
   55 ft
   60.5 ft
   A
   20 ft
   32 ft
   B

**WRITE Math** ▸ **Explain** how you can use equivalent ratios to determine whether a sheet of 8.5-in. × 11-in. paper is a Golden Rectangle.

## Number Sense

**1.** The weekly juice order for Camp Arrowhead includes 25 gallons of apple juice and 15 gallons of orange juice. What is the ratio of the number of gallons of apple juice to orange juice in the camp's weekly juice order? (O—n NS 1.2)

  **A** 3:1        **C** 5:3

  **B** 5:1        **D** 8:3

**2.** Which point shows the location of $\frac{7}{2}$ on the number line? (O—n NS 1.1)

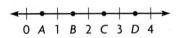

    0 A 1 B 2 C 3 D 4

  **A** point $A$        **C** point $C$

  **B** point $B$        **D** point $D$

**Test Tip** Decide on a plan.

See item 3. First find the number of windows the group can paint in 1 minute. Next, calculate how many minutes are in 3 hours, and then multiply.

**3.** Joseph's group was responsible for painting windows on the set of a community play. The group painted 16 windows in 80 minutes. If they continued painting at this rate, how many windows could they paint in 3 hours? (O—n NS 1.2)

  **A** 24

  **B** 36

  **C** 54

  **D** 72

**4.** ⊟WRITE Math▶ **Explain** how to add the fractions $\frac{1}{6}$ and $\frac{3}{4}$. (O—n NS 2.0)

## Algebra and Functions

**5.** $6 + 9 \times (2 + 3)^2 =$    (AF 1.4)

  **A** 33        **C** 231

  **B** 51        **D** 375

**6.** Which algebraic equation best describes the total growth in height, $T$, of redwood trees over a 4-year period, if $g$ equals the rate of growth in centimeters per year? (O—n AF 1.1)

  **A** $T = 4g$

  **B** $T = 4 + g$

  **C** $T = \frac{g}{4}$

  **D** $T = \frac{4}{g}$

**7.** Which of the following is the missing $y$-value for the function table below? (O—n AF 1.1)

| $x$ | $^-3$ | $^-1$ | 0 | 1 | 3 |
|---|---|---|---|---|---|
| $y$ | 9 | 3 | 0 | $^-3$ | ■ |

  **A** $^-13$        **C** $^-5$

  **B** $^-9$        **D** 0

**8.** What value of $c$ makes the following equation true? (O—n AF 1.1)

$$c \div 3 = 42$$

  **A** 14

  **B** 45

  **C** 96

  **D** 126

**9.** ⊟WRITE Math▶ **Explain** how to find how fast Roberto was running if it took him 30 minutes to run a path that was 21,120 feet long. (AF 2.3)

## Measurement and Geometry

**10.** Devon knows the diameter of his bicycle tire, but he needs to find the circumference.

Which method can Devon use to find the circumference? (O━┓ MG 1.1)

**A** Multiply the circumference by 2 and divide the result by $\pi$.

**B** Divide the circumference by 2 and multiply the result by $\pi$.

**C** Multiply the diameter by $\pi$.

**D** Divide the diameter by $\pi$.

**11.** In the figure below, $\overleftrightarrow{AF}$ intersects $\overleftrightarrow{CD}$ at $E$, $m\angle AEC = 55°$, and $m\angle BED = m\angle DEF$. What is $m\angle AEB$? (O━┓ MG 2.2)

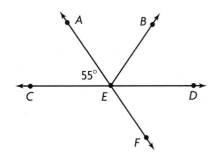

**A** 35°      **C** 70°

**B** 55°      **D** 80°

**12.** $\angle A$ and $\angle B$ are complementary. If $m\angle A$ is 65°, what is $m\angle B$? (O━┓ MG 2.2)

**A** 5°      **C** 105°

**B** 25°      **D** 115°

**13.** **WRITE Math** **Sense or Nonsense** Frank says that two triangles are similar because their corresponding angles are congruent. Is he correct? **Explain.** (O━┓ MG 2.2)

## Statistics, Data Analysis, and Probability

**14.** The table shows the temperatures outside for six consecutive days in May.

| Date (May) | 1 | 2 | 3 | 4 | 5 | 6 |
|---|---|---|---|---|---|---|
| Temperature (°F) | 65 | 72 | 70 | 68 | 63 | 70 |

Which of the following represents the mode of the data set? (SDAP 1.1)

**A** 72°F

**B** 70°F

**C** 68°F

**D** 65°F

**15.** Carly recorded the colors of the first 36 cars that drove by her house on Sunday afternoon. The table shows how many of each color car Carly saw.

| Car Colors | | | | | | |
|---|---|---|---|---|---|---|
| Color | White | Black | Red | Blue | Green | Other |
| Number of Cars | 6 | 8 | 4 | 7 | 6 | 5 |

Which fraction represents the number of green cars that she counted? (O━┓ SDAP 3.1)

**A** $\frac{1}{9}$

**B** $\frac{1}{6}$

**C** $\frac{2}{9}$

**D** $\frac{1}{4}$

**16.** **WRITE Math** Mr. Barrows recorded these English test scores for his sixth-grade students.

68, 69, 71, 73, 73, 74, 75, 79, 81, 83, 86, 88, 88, 88, 88, 90, 90, 93, 94, 96, 98, 99

**Explain** how to find the median of these test scores. (SDAP 1.1)

**CHAPTER**

# 19 Proportions

**The Big Idea** A proportion expresses an equivalent relationship between two ratios.

## Investigate

Draw a model of the Stratosphere Giant redwood tree that is between 2 feet and 5 feet tall. Write a ratio to represent the height of the model to the height of the actual tree. Then use proportions to find how tall models of the other trees in the table would be if the same proportion were used.

### Giant Trees in California

| Tree Name | Height (in ft) |
|---|---|
| Stratosphere Giant redwood | 370.1 |
| National Geographic Society redwood | 365.5 |
| Paradox redwood | 366.3 |
| General Sherman sequoia | 274.9 |
| General Grant sequoia | 268.1 |
| Chief Sequoyah sequoia | 228.2 |

**CALIFORNIA FAST FACT**

The "General Sherman" sequoia tree, in Sequoia National Park is the largest tree by volume in the world. "General Sherman" stands 274.9 ft tall and measures 36.5 ft in diameter at its base.

**GO ONLINE** Technology
Student pages are available in the Student eBook.

# Show What You Know

Check your understanding of important skills
needed for success in Chapter 19.

▶ **Write Equivalent Fractions**

Complete each number sentence.

1. $\frac{5}{6} = \frac{\blacksquare}{24}$

2. $\frac{4}{9} = \frac{12}{\blacksquare}$

3. $\frac{\blacksquare}{4} = \frac{30}{24}$

4. $\frac{3}{4} = \frac{\blacksquare}{24}$

5. $\frac{5}{\blacksquare} = \frac{25}{35}$

6. $\frac{\blacksquare}{6} = \frac{45}{54}$

7. $\frac{4}{\blacksquare} = \frac{28}{49}$

8. $\frac{24}{64} = \frac{\blacksquare}{32}$

▶ **Solve Multiplication Equations**

Solve.

9. $6x = 21$

10. $3p = 15$

11. $64 = 4k$

12. $42 = 7m$

13. $81 = 3b$

14. $51 = 1.5d$

15. $0.2n = 8$

16. $143 = 13y$

17. $\frac{2}{3}h = 21$

18. $6.3 = 0.07m$

19. $18 = \frac{3}{4}a$

20. $65h = 65$

▶ **Congruent and Similar Figures**

Write *similar* or *congruent* to compare the figures. If the figures
appear not to be similar or congruent, write *neither*.

21.

22.

23.

24.

25.

26.

27.

28.

# VOCABULARY POWER

**CHAPTER VOCABULARY**

corresponding angles
corresponding sides
indirect measurement
proportion
similar figures

**WARM-UP WORDS**

**proportion** an equation that shows that two ratios are
equal

**similar figures** figures with the same shape but not
necessarily the same size

**corresponding sides** sides that are in the same position in
different plane figures

# 1 Explore Proportions

OBJECTIVE: Find equivalent ratios to form a proportion.

## Investigate

**Materials** ■ two-color counters

The ratio of length to width of a window in John's house is $\frac{3}{2}$. If the length of the window is 27 in., the width is 18 in. These form the ratio $\frac{27}{18}$, which is equivalent to $\frac{3}{2}$.

These ratios can be used to write a proportion. A **proportion** is an equation that shows two equivalent ratios.

| Equivalent Ratios | | Proportion |
|---|---|---|
| $\frac{3}{2}$ and $\frac{27}{18}$ | $\longrightarrow$ | $\frac{3}{2} = \frac{27}{18}$ |

You can use counters to model proportions.

**A** Use red and yellow counters to model the ratio 8:12.

**B** Separate the red and yellow counters into two equal groups. Write a ratio to represent red counters to yellow counters in each group.

**C** Separate the red and yellow counters into four equal groups. Write a ratio to represent red counters to yellow counters in each group.

**D** Use the ratios you found in B and C to write a proportion.

## Draw Conclusions

1. Explain how you used counters to find equivalent ratios.

2. **Application** How can you use counters to find a ratio that is equivalent to $\frac{10}{15}$ and then to write a proportion?

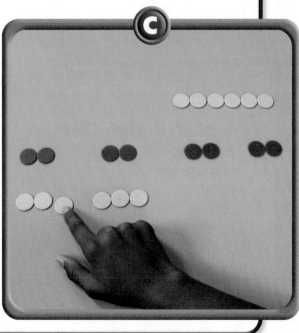

⌐ NS 1.3 Use proportions to solve problems (e.g., determine the value of N if $\frac{4}{7} = \frac{N}{21}$, find the length of a side of a polygon similar to a known polygon). Use cross-multiplication as a method for solving such problems, understanding it as the multiplication of both sides of an equation by a multiplicative inverse. *also* ⌐ NS 1.1, MR 1.1, MR 2.0, MR 2.4, MR 2.5, MR 3.2

## Connect

You can determine whether two ratios form a proportion by finding a common denominator.

**Example** Find whether the ratios $\frac{3}{4}$ and $\frac{12}{16}$ form a proportion.

Two ratios form a proportion if the ratios are equal.

$$\frac{3}{4} \overset{?}{=} \frac{12}{16}$$  Determine a common denominator.

$$\frac{3 \times 4}{4 \times 4} \overset{?}{=} \frac{12}{16}$$  Rewrite the ratios using a common denominator.

$$\frac{12}{16} = \frac{12}{16}$$  Compare the ratios to see if they are equivalent.

So, the ratios $\frac{3}{4}$ and $\frac{12}{16}$ do form a proportion, since they are equivalent ratios.

**TALK Math**

Can the ratios $\frac{3}{4}$ and $\frac{12}{18}$ be used to form a proportion? **Explain.**

## Practice

**Use counters to find equivalent ratios and then write a proportion.**

1.

2.

3.

✓4.

**Use common denominators to determine whether the ratios can be used to form a proportion.**

5. $\frac{3}{5}$ and $\frac{9}{15}$

6. $\frac{3}{4}$ and $\frac{8}{12}$

7. $\frac{2}{3}$ and $\frac{6}{10}$

8. $\frac{6}{7}$ and $\frac{12}{14}$

9. $\frac{3}{12}$ and $\frac{2}{3}$

10. $\frac{3}{6}$ and $\frac{6}{9}$

11. $\frac{5}{16}$ and $\frac{15}{48}$

12. $\frac{12}{24}$ and $\frac{10}{20}$

13. $\frac{4}{18}$ and $\frac{18}{72}$

14. $\frac{10}{16}$ and $\frac{15}{24}$

15. $\frac{9}{21}$ and $\frac{27}{63}$

✓16. $\frac{16}{20}$ and $\frac{24}{40}$

17. **WRITE Math** ▸ **Explain** how to tell whether the ratios $\frac{8}{10}$ and $\frac{20}{25}$ can be used to form a proportion.

## ALGEBRA
# Write Proportions

OBJECTIVE: Write proportions that model problem situations.

**Quick Review**

Write as a ratio.

1. $3.99 for 1 lb
2. 60 mi on 3 gal
3. 25 tickets for 4 people
4. $4.00 for 10 cans
5. 100 pages in 5 chapters

## Learn

**PROBLEM** Lavonne handpicks 18 lb of grapes and places them outside on paper trays to dry. In a few weeks, she will have 4 lb of raisins. How many pounds of raisins can she expect from 45 lb of grapes? Write a proportion that represents this situation.

### Example 1

**Step 1**

Identify the categories and write the ratios.

categories: grapes and raisins

ratios: 18 lb of grapes to 4 lb of raisins $\rightarrow \dfrac{18}{4}$

45 lb of grapes to ■ pounds of raisins $\rightarrow \dfrac{45}{\blacksquare}$

Let $r$ represent the unknown amount of raisins.

**Step 2**

**ERROR ALERT**

Write a proportion. Write the categories for each ratio in the same order.

$$\dfrac{\text{grapes}}{\text{raisins}} \rightarrow \dfrac{18}{4} = \dfrac{45}{r} \leftarrow \dfrac{\text{grapes}}{\text{raisins}}$$

Be sure that the first terms of the proportion are the same category and that the second terms are the same category.

So, the proportion $\dfrac{18}{4} = \dfrac{45}{r}$ represents the situation.

• Can the proportion be written in a different way? Explain.

### Example 2 Use two of the ratios $\dfrac{4}{5}$, $\dfrac{8}{15}$, and $\dfrac{16}{20}$, to write a proportion.

Find equivalent ratios using common denominators.

$$\dfrac{4 \times 12}{5 \times 12} \overset{?}{=} \dfrac{8 \times 4}{15 \times 4} \qquad\qquad \dfrac{8 \times 4}{15 \times 4} \overset{?}{=} \dfrac{16 \times 3}{20 \times 3} \qquad\qquad \dfrac{4 \times 4}{5 \times 4} \overset{?}{=} \dfrac{16}{20}$$

$$\dfrac{48}{60} \neq \dfrac{32}{60} \qquad\qquad\qquad \dfrac{32}{60} \neq \dfrac{48}{60} \qquad\qquad\qquad \dfrac{16}{20} = \dfrac{16}{20}$$

The ratios are not equivalent.   The ratios are not equivalent.   The ratios are equivalent.

So, $\dfrac{4}{5} = \dfrac{16}{20}$ is a proportion.

**○━┓ NS 1.3** Use proportions to solve problems (e.g., determine the value of N if $\frac{4}{7} = \frac{N}{21}$, find the length of a side of a polygon similar to a known polygon). Use cross-multiplication as a method for solving such problems, understanding it as the multiplication of both sides of an equation by a multiplicative inverse. *also*, **MR 1.1, MR 2.0, MR 2.2, MR 2.4, MR 2.5, MR 3.2**

1. Sheila makes oatmeal-raisin cookies with 2 cups of oats and 3 boxes of raisins. How many boxes of raisins will she use with 6 cups of oats? Write a proportion to represent this situation.

$$\frac{\text{oats}}{\text{raisins}} \rightarrow \frac{2}{3} = \frac{\blacksquare}{\blacksquare} \leftarrow \frac{\text{oats}}{\text{raisins}}$$

**Write one proportion using two of the ratios.**

2. $\frac{4}{8}, \frac{14}{18}, \frac{3}{6}$

3. 5 to 9, 6 to 15, 18 to 45

☑4. 2:12, 4:16, 3:18

☑5. $\frac{8}{10}, \frac{10}{14}, \frac{4}{5}, \frac{16}{25}$

6. **TALK Math** Explain why you can use $\frac{7}{10}$ and $\frac{21}{30}$ to write a proportion, but you cannot use $\frac{7}{10}$ and $\frac{30}{21}$ to write a proportion.

**Independent Practice and Problem Solving**

**Write a proportion to represent the situation.**

7. Garner plants 2 rows of grapes in 16 min. How many rows can he plant in 24 min?

8. Bette cuts 3 pears into 36 slices. How many slices can she cut from 5 pears?

**Write one proportion using two of the ratios.**

9. 1:3, 6:12, 21:63

10. $\frac{3}{4}, \frac{16}{12}, \frac{18}{24}$

11. 24 to 45, 10 to 15, 16 to 30

12. $\frac{20}{10}, \frac{16}{32}, \frac{4}{8}$

13. 3:21, 14:28, 2:14

14. $\frac{9}{24}, \frac{12}{18}, \frac{30}{80}$

15. 38 to 57, 9 to 12, 54 to 81

16. $\frac{5}{12}, \frac{16}{36}, \frac{20}{28}, \frac{60}{84}$

**USE DATA** For 17, use the circle graph.

17. The owner of a healthfood store wants to know how many boxes of dried cranberries and pineapples she should order if she plans on ordering 80 boxes of dried raisins. Write proportions to represent these situations.

18. **WRITE Math** It takes 12 oranges to make 3 glasses of juice. Can you use the proportion $\frac{3}{12} = \frac{x}{18}$ to find how many oranges are needed to make 18 glasses of juice? Explain.

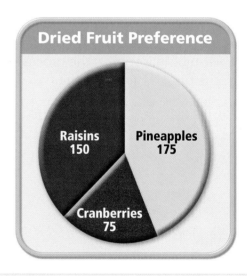

**Dried Fruit Preference**

Raisins 150

Pineapples 175

Cranberries 75

 **Achieving the Standards**

19. Classify the triangle by its angles. (MG 2.3, p. 398)

145°
15°
20°

20. Use $<$, $>$, or $=$ to compare the decimals 3.582 and 3.497. (O— NS 1.1, p. 19)

21. Solve $3x = 27$. (O— AF 1.1, p. 336)

22. **Test Prep** Which pair of ratios can be written as a proportion?

A 9:24 and 6:16

B 6:8 and 12:24

C 6:16 and 12:24

D 12:24 and 4:12

## ALGEBRA
# Solve Proportions

OBJECTIVE: Solve proportions.

### Quick Review

Solve.

**1.** $2s = 22$    **2.** $76 = 4f$

**3.** $5d = 64$    **4.** $6 = 18p$

**5.** $2 = 50j$

## Learn

**PROBLEM** Dennis takes 14 min to read a 7-page short story. At this rate, how long will it take him to read a 30-page short story?

**ONE WAY**   Use the multiplicative inverse.

$$\frac{14}{7} = \frac{t}{30}$$    Write a proportion. Let $t$ represent the unknown amount of time.

$$\frac{\overset{1}{\cancel{7}}}{1} \times \frac{30}{1} \times \frac{14}{\underset{1}{\cancel{7}}} = \frac{7}{1} \times \frac{\overset{1}{\cancel{30}}}{1} \times \frac{t}{\underset{1}{\cancel{30}}}$$    Multiply by the multiplicative inverses of $\frac{1}{7}$ and $\frac{1}{30}$. Simplify.

$$\frac{30 \times 14}{1} = \frac{7 \times t}{1}$$    Multiply.

$$420 = 7t$$

$$\frac{420}{7} = \frac{7t}{7}$$    Divide.

$$60 = t$$

**Remember**
When you multiply a number by its reciprocal, or multiplicative inverse, the result is 1.

You can also use cross-multiplication to solve proportions. Cross-multiplication is the process of multiplying by the reciprocals of the denominators of the two sides of the equation.

**ANOTHER WAY**   Use cross-multiplication.

$$\frac{14}{7} = \frac{t}{30}$$    Write a proportion. Let $t$ represent the unknown amount of time.

$$\frac{14}{7} \xleftarrow{} = \xrightarrow{} \frac{t}{30}$$    Use cross-multiplication.

$$14 \times 30 = 7 \times t$$    Multiply.

$$420 = 7t$$

$$\frac{420}{7} = \frac{7t}{7}$$    Divide.

$$60 = t$$

So, it will take Dennis 60 min to read a 30-page short story.

Notice that the last four steps in both methods are the same. This is because using cross-multiplication is another way of using the multiplicative inverses.

**O━┓ NS 1.3** Use proportions to solve problems (e.g., determine the value of N if $\frac{4}{7} = \frac{N}{21}$, find the length of a side of a polygon similar to a known polygon). Use cross-multiplication as a method for solving such problems, understanding it as the multiplication of both sides of an equation by a multiplicative inverse. *also,* MR 1.1, MR 2.0, MR 2.2, MR 2.4, MR 2.5, MR 3.2

Solve the proportion.

**1.** $\frac{8}{3} = \frac{a}{6}$     $\frac{3}{1} \times \frac{6}{1} \times \frac{8}{3} = \frac{3}{1} \times \frac{6}{1} \times \frac{a}{6}$

$6 \times 8 = 3 \times a$

$48 = 3a$

$\frac{48}{3} = \frac{3a}{3}$

▨ $= a$

**2.** $\frac{4}{8} = \frac{a}{10}$     $8 \times a = 10 \times 4$

$8a = 40$

$\frac{8a}{8} = \frac{40}{8}$

$a = $ ▨

Solve the proportion.

**3.** $\frac{3}{6} = \frac{x}{4}$     **4.** $\frac{4}{b} = \frac{14}{63}$     **5.** $\frac{w}{7} = \frac{8}{14}$     ✓**6.** $\frac{3}{15} = \frac{5}{c}$     ✓**7.** $\frac{6}{12} = \frac{g}{16}$

**8.** ⎡TALK Math⎤ **Explain** how to solve a proportion using cross-multiplication.

Solve the proportion.

**9.** $\frac{5}{10} = \frac{11}{n}$     **10.** $\frac{k}{6} = \frac{25}{10}$     **11.** $\frac{d}{24} = \frac{3}{9}$     **12.** $\frac{v}{18} = \frac{7}{21}$     **13.** $\frac{2}{z} = \frac{5}{30}$

**14.** $\frac{16}{24} = \frac{w}{6}$     **15.** $\frac{18}{15} = \frac{6}{t}$     **16.** $\frac{6}{b} = \frac{36}{27}$     **17.** $\frac{14}{d} = \frac{6.25}{9}$     **18.** $\frac{40}{12.5} = \frac{8}{k}$

Write and solve a proportion.

**19.** Mei does 6 homework problems in 18 min. How many can she complete in 12 min?

**20.** A pack of 6 juice boxes cost $5.34. How much would 30 juice boxes cost?

**USE DATA** For 21-22, use the table.

**21.** The fourth period class is participating in a school improvement day. During the work day, 5 students can paint 2 walls. If the entire class participates, how many walls can be painted?

**22.** **Reasoning** The ratio of girls to boys is the same for second and sixth periods. If there are 12 girls in sixth period, how many boys are in second period?

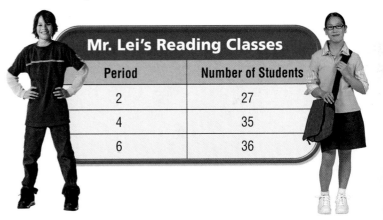

**Mr. Lei's Reading Classes**

| Period | Number of Students |
|--------|--------------------|
| 2 | 27 |
| 4 | 35 |
| 6 | 36 |

**23.** ⎡WRITE Math⎤ **What's the Error?** Greg uses these steps to solve a proportion. **Describe** and correct his error.

$$\frac{k}{12} = \frac{2}{3} \rightarrow 2k = 36 \rightarrow k = 18$$

### Achieving the Standards

**24.** Find the product $^-8 \times {}^-7$. (○━┓ NS 2.3, p. 172)

**25.** Evaluate $2x - 7$ for $x = {}^-5$. (AF 1.2, p. 254)

**26.** Solve $\frac{x}{24} = \frac{2}{3}$. (○━┓ NS 1.3, p. 466 )

**27. Test Prep** Burt makes 12 baskets in 18 tries. How many baskets can he expect to make in 6 more tries?

**A** 2          **B** 4          **C** 9          **D** 12

# Customary and Metric

**OBJECTIVE:** Use proportions to convert one unit of measurement to another.

## Learn

**PROBLEM** The General Sherman Tree in Sequoia National Park is the largest known living tree in the world. Its trunk has a circumference of about 102.6 ft. About how many inches is this?

You can use proportions to convert customary and metric units.

### Example 1  Use a proportion to convert customary length.

$$\frac{\text{feet} \rightarrow}{\text{inches} \rightarrow} \frac{1}{12} = \frac{102.6}{y} \frac{\leftarrow \text{feet}}{\leftarrow \text{inches}}$$

Write a proportion using 1 ft = 12 in. Let $y$ represent the circumference of the tree.

$$\frac{1}{12} \longleftrightarrow = \longleftrightarrow \frac{102.6}{y}$$

Use cross-multiplication.

$$1 \times y = 12 \times 102.6$$

Multiply.

$$y = 1,231.2$$

So, the circumference of the tree is about 1,231.2 in.

### Example 2  Use a proportion to convert metric length.

The length of a branch is about 15 dm. How many centimeters is this?

$$\frac{\text{decimeters} \rightarrow}{\text{centimeters} \rightarrow} \frac{1}{10} = \frac{15}{b}$$

Write a proportion using 1 dm = 10 cm. Let $b$ represent the length of the branch.

$$\frac{1}{10} \longleftrightarrow = \longleftrightarrow \frac{15}{b}$$

Use cross-multiplication.

$$1 \times b = 10 \times 15$$

Multiply.

$$b = 150$$

So, the length of the branch is about 150 cm.

GENERAL SHERMAN

**Remember**

**Metric**
kilo = 1,000
hecto = 100
deka = 10
m/g/L = 1
deci = 0.1
centi = 0.01
milli = 0.001

**Customary**
1 gal = 4 qt
1 qt = 2 pt
1 pt = 2 c
1 c = 8 fl oz

### More Examples  Find the unknown measurement.

**A  Capacity**

$$45 \text{ c} = \blacksquare \text{ pt}$$

$$\frac{\text{pint} \rightarrow}{\text{cup} \rightarrow} \frac{1}{2} = \frac{x}{45}$$  Write a proportion using 1 pt = 2 c.

$$2x = 45$$  Use cross-multiplication.

$$x = 22\frac{1}{2}$$  Divide by 2.

So, $45 \text{ c} = 22\frac{1}{2}$ pt.

**B  Mass**

$$4,800 \text{ g} = \blacksquare \text{ kg}$$

$$\frac{\text{kilograms} \rightarrow}{\text{grams} \rightarrow} \frac{1}{1,000} = \frac{x}{4,800}$$  Write a proportion using 1 kg = 1,000 g.

$$1,000x = 4,800$$  Use cross-multiplication.

$$x = 4.8$$  Divide by 1,000.

So, $4,800 \text{ g} = 4.8$ kg.

 **AF 2.1** Convert one unit of measure to another (e.g., from feet to miles, from centimeters to inches).  *also* AF 2.0, ⊙━┓ NS 1.3, MR 1.1, MR 2.2, MR 2.4, MR 2.5, MR 3.2

# Convert between systems

The table shows some common relationships between the customary and metric measurement systems. You can use proportions to convert between the systems.

| Approximate Customary and Metric Conversions | | | |
|---|---|---|---|
| 1 m ≈ 3.28 ft | 1 qt ≈ 0.95 L | 1 lb ≈ 0.454 kg | 1 in. ≈ 2.5 cm |
| 1 mi ≈ 1.6 km | 1 oz ≈ 28.35 g | 1 ft ≈ 30.48 cm | 1 gal ≈ 3.79 L |

**Example 3** The General Sherman Tree stands 279.4 ft high. About how many meters is this?

$$\frac{\text{meters} \rightarrow}{\text{feet} \rightarrow} \frac{1}{3.28} = \frac{h}{279.4}$$

Write a proportion using 1 m ≈ 3.28 ft. Let $h$ represent the height of the tree.

$$\frac{1}{3.28} \underset{\rightarrow}{\overset{\leftarrow}{=}} \frac{h}{279.4}$$

Use cross-multiplication.

$$1 \times 279.4 = 3.28 \times h$$

Multiply.

$$\frac{279.4}{3.28} = \frac{3.28h}{3.28}$$

Divide.

$$85.2 \approx h$$

Round to the nearest tenth.

> **Remember**
> The symbol ≈ means "is approximately equal to."

So, the tree stands about 85.2 m high.

- **What if** you convert the height of the tree from feet to centimeters? About how many centimeters high is the tree?

## More Examples

**A** 2 L ≈ ■ qt

$$\frac{\text{quarts} \rightarrow}{\text{liters} \rightarrow} \frac{1}{0.95} = \frac{z}{2}$$

Write a proportion using 1 qt ≈ 0.95 L.

$$\frac{1}{0.95} \underset{\rightarrow}{\overset{\leftarrow}{=}} \frac{z}{2}$$

Use cross-multiplication.

$$1 \times 2 = 0.95 \times z$$ Multiply.

$$\frac{2}{0.95} = \frac{0.95z}{0.95}$$ Divide.

$$2.1 \approx z$$ Round to the nearest tenth.

So, 2 L is about 2.1 qt.

**B** 4 lb ≈ ■ kg

$$\frac{\text{pounds} \rightarrow}{\text{kilograms} \rightarrow} \frac{1}{0.454} = \frac{4}{a}$$

Write a proportion using 1 lb ≈ 0.454 kg.

$$\frac{1}{0.454} = \frac{4}{a}$$

Use cross-multiplication.

$$1 \times a = 0.454 \times 4$$ Multiply.

$$a \approx 1.8$$ Round to the nearest tenth.

So, 4 lb is about 1.8 kg.

## Guided Practice

Convert to the given unit.

**1.** 45 lb = ■ oz

$$\frac{\text{pounds} \rightarrow}{\text{ounces} \rightarrow} \frac{1}{16} = \frac{45}{n}$$

$$1 \times n = 16 \times 45$$

**2.** 4 mi ≈ ■ km

$$\frac{\text{kilometers} \rightarrow}{\text{miles} \rightarrow} \frac{1.6}{1} = \frac{n}{4}$$

$$1.6 \times 4 = 1 \times n$$

**Convert to the given unit.**

**3.** 8 qt = ■ gal  **4.** 1.4 m = ■ cm  **5.** 240 fl oz = ■ c  **6.** 450 hm = ■ dm

**7.** 168 in. = ■ ft  **8.** 6 gal = ■ qt  ✓**9.** 78 hg = ■ g  ✓**10.** 60,000 mL = ■ L

**11.** (**TALK Math**) **Explain** how to write a proportion to find how many kilograms there are in 68 lb.

## Independent Practice and Problem Solving

**Convert to the given unit.**

**12.** 25 c = ■ fl oz  **13.** 60 ft = ■ yd  **14.** 8 kg = ■ g  **15.** 970 mm = ■ cm

**16.** 1,500 lb = ■ T  **17.** 2.3 L = ■ mL  **18.** 9.5 hm = ■ m  **19.** 0.25 gal = ■ pt

**Estimate the conversion. Round to the nearest tenth if necessary.**

**20.** 59 ft ≈ ■ m  **21.** 242 cm ≈ ■ in.  **22.** 31 gal ≈ ■ L  **23.** 14 kg ≈ ■ lb

**24.** 300 oz ≈ ■ g  **25.** 55 in. ≈ ■ cm  **26.** 12 L ≈ ■ qt  **27.** 34 km ≈ ■ mi

**Compare. Write <, > or =.**

**28.** 108 in. ● 9 ft  **29.** 12 dm ● 1.2 cm  **30.** 7 oz ● 450 g  **31.** 5.5 L ● 5.5 qt

**32.** 16 in. ● 42 cm  **33.** 22 L ● 6 gal  **34.** 2.5 mi ● 4 km  **35.** 140 mm ● 1.4 cm

**Find the unknown measure.**

**36.** An average lead pencil can draw a line that is 35 mi long. If there are 1,760 yd in a mile, how many yards is this?

**37.** A milk container holds 2 qt. How much milk does the container hold in liters?

**USE DATA** For 38–40, use the table.

**38.** The average crown spread is the average width of a tree's foliage. What is the average crown spread of the General Sherman Tree in centimeters?

**39.** About what is the diameter of the largest branch in inches?

**40.** **Reasoning** Drew uses 1 m ≈ 3.28 ft and finds that the height of the first large branch is about 129.88 ft. Jan uses 1 m = 100 cm and 1 ft ≈ 30.48 cm and finds that the height of the first large branch is about 129.92 ft. **Explain** why their answers are slightly different.

**42.** Amy has a pair of wooden chopsticks that measure 34 cm in length. Are these longer or shorter than a pair of chopsticks measuring $12\frac{3}{4}$ in. in length?

| General Sherman Tree Statistics | |
| --- | --- |
| Diameter of Largest Branch | 210 cm |
| Average Crown Spread | 32.5 m |
| Maximum Diameter at Base | 1,110 cm |
| Height of First Large Branch Above the Base | 39.6 m |

**41.** **≡FAST FACT** A typical tree can clean 330 lb of carbon dioxide a year from Earth's atmosphere. There are 2,000 lb in 1 ton. How many years would it take a typical tree to clean 3.3 T of carbon dioxide from the atmosphere?

**43.** (**WRITE Math**) **What's the Question?** Greg writes the proportion $\frac{1 \text{ gal}}{3.79 \text{ L}} = \frac{x \text{ gal}}{65 \text{ L}}$. The answer is $x \approx 17.2$.

**Technology**
Use Harcourt Mega Math, Ice Station Exploration, *Linear Lab*, Levels C–J.

(**Extra Practice** on page 484, Set C)

**44.** Solve $\frac{45}{112.5} = \frac{8}{b}$. (○━┓ NS 1.3, p. 466)

**45.** Find the area of a circle with diameter 48 m. Use 3.14 for $\pi$. (○━┓ MG 1.1, pg. 426)

**46. Test Prep** About how many miles are in 24 kilometers?

    **A** 0.1         **C** 25

    **B** 15         **D** 38.6

**47.** Order from greatest to least:

    $^-0.214$, $^-0.242$, $^-0.222$. (○━┓ NS 1.1, p.122 )

**48. Test Prep** Mark's change jar weighs 45 pounds. Which proportion could be used to find the weight of his jar in ounces?

    **A** $\frac{1}{16} = \frac{m}{45}$     **C** $\frac{16}{45} = \frac{1}{m}$

    **B** $\frac{1}{16} = \frac{45}{m}$     **D** $\frac{45}{16} = \frac{1}{m}$

## Problem Solving [ connects to ] Science

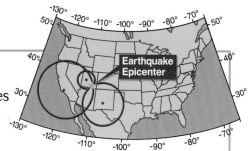

The epicenter of an earthquake is a location on Earth's surface directly above where an earthquake begins. On a map, scientists mark three sites that have reported the earthquake. Around each site they draw a circle, whose radius represents the distance from the site to the earthquake. The intersection of the circles is the epicenter of the earthquake.

An earthquake is reported 22 km from Lakeport, CA; 16 mi from Kelseyville, CA; and 23 km from Ukiah, CA. A scientist converts the 16 mi from Kelseyville to kilometers.

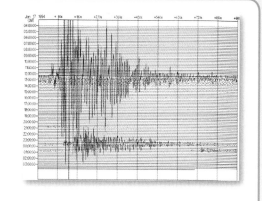

$\frac{\text{miles}}{\text{kilometers}} \rightarrow \frac{1}{1.6} = \frac{16}{n}$    Write a proportion.

$1 \times n = 1.6 \times 16$    Use cross-multiplication.

$n = 25.6$

$n \approx 25.6$

So, the earthquake is about 25.6 km from Kelseyville.

**Use the table to solve. Round to the nearest tenth, if necessary.**

1. Convert Eureka's reported distance to kilometers.

2. Convert Banning's reported distance to miles.

3. Did Beaumont or Banning have an epicenter with a greater reported distance?

| Reported Distances from Epicenter | |
|---|---|
| **April 25, 2006** | **May 1, 2006** |
| Petrolia, CA–20 km | Banning, CA–13 km |
| Ferndale, CA–37 km | Beaumont, CA–7 mi |
| Eureka, CA–39 mi | Yucaipa, CA–5 mi |

OBJECTIVE: Convert units of money and temperature using proportions, rates, and formulas.

## Learn

Currencies, or money, of different countries usually do not have the same value. So when exchanging currencies, a conversion needs to be made. Ratios, called exchange rates, are used to help find the equivalent values. These exchange rates can change daily.

You can use a proportion to convert currencies.

### Example 1  Use a proportion.

Before her trip to Germany, Mrs. DeMarco needs to exchange $175 for euros. If 1 euro is worth $1.27, how many euros should she receive?

$$\frac{\text{dollar} \rightarrow}{\text{euro} \rightarrow} \frac{1.27}{1} = \frac{175}{e}$$    Write a proportion. Use the exchange rate.

$1.27 \times e = 175 \times 1$    Use cross-multiplication.

$\frac{1.27e}{1.27} = \frac{175}{1.27}$    Divide.

$e = 137.79527$

$e \approx 137.80$    Round to the nearest hundredth.

So, she should receive 137.80 euros.

• Mr. Diago wants to exchange $48 for British pounds. If 1 pound is worth $1.82, how many pounds will he receive?

You can also use formulas to convert currency.

| Dollars and Pounds | Dollars and Euros |
|---|---|
| $d = r \times p$ | $d = r \times e$ |
| $d$ = dollars, $r$ = rate, $p$ = pounds | $d$ = dollars, $r$ = rate, $e$ = euros |

### Example 2  Use a formula.

A raincoat costs 35 pounds in Newcastle, England, and $62.75 in Sacramento, CA. If 1 British pound is worth $1.82, in which city is the raincoat less expensive?

$d = r \times p$    Write the formula.

$d = 1.82 \times 35$    Replace $r$ with 1.82 and $p$ with 35. Multiply.

$d = 63.70$

$\$63.70 > \$62.75$    Compare.

So, the raincoat is less expensive in Sacramento, CA.

AF 2.1 Convert one unit of measurement to another (e.g., from feet to miles, from centimeters to inches). *also,* NS 1.3, AF 2.0, MR 1.1, MR 2.2, MR 2.4, MR 2.5, MR 3.0, MR 3.1, MR 3.2, MR 3.3.

# Converting Temperatures

To convert from degrees Celsius to degrees Fahrenheit, you can use the formula $F = (\frac{9}{5} \times C) + 32$.

### Example 3 Convert Celsius to Fahrenheit.

Mrs. DeMarco will be participating in a seminar that is being held in Frankfurt, Germany. A weather report shows that the temperature will be 23°C on the day of the seminar. What is this temperature in degrees Fahrenheit?

| | |
|---|---|
| $F = (\frac{9}{5} \times C) + 32$ | Write the formula. |
| $F = (\frac{9}{5} \times 23) + 32$ | Replace C with 23. Multiply. |
| $F = 41\frac{2}{5} + 32$ | Add. |
| $F = 73\frac{2}{5} = 73.4$ | |

So, the temperature will be 73.4, or about 73°F, on the day of the seminar.

- Suppose the temperature on the day of the seminar is 25°C. How many degrees Fahrenheit is this?

You can use the formula $C = \frac{5}{9} \times (F - 32)$ to convert from degrees Fahrenheit to degrees Celsius.

### Example 4 Convert Fahrenheit to Celsius.

Upon arrival at Frankfurt Airport, in Germany, the pilot of Mrs. DeMarco's plane reports a temperature of 68°F. What is the temperature in degrees Celsius?

| | |
|---|---|
| $C = \frac{5}{9} \times (F - 32)$ | Write the formula. |
| $C = \frac{5}{9} \times (68 - 32)$ | Replace F with 68. Subtract. |
| $C = \frac{5}{9} \times 36$ | Multiply. |
| $C = 20$ | |

So, the temperature at Frankfurt Airport is 20°C.

**Math Idea**

Either formula can be used to convert Fahrenheit to Celsius or Celsius to Fahrenheit.

## Guided Practice

1. Suppose 1 British pound is worth $1.82. Convert $320 to pounds.

$\frac{\text{pounds}}{\text{dollars}} \rightarrow \frac{1}{1.82} = \frac{x}{320}$

2. Convert 16°C to degrees Fahrenheit.

$F = (\frac{9}{5} \times C) + 32$

$F = (\frac{9}{5} \times 16) + 32$

$F = \blacksquare$

**Suppose 1 pound is worth $1.78, and 1 euro is worth $1.30. Convert the following.**

3. $50 = ■ pounds    4. $240 = ■ euros    ✓5. 380 euros = $ ■    ✓6. 21 pounds = $ ■

7. **TALK Math** Explain how to use a formula to convert 30°C to degrees Fahrenheit.

## Independent Practice and Problem Solving

**Suppose 1 pound is worth $1.92, and 1 euro is worth $1.33. Convert the following.**

8. $77 = ■ pounds    9. $16 = ■ euros    10. 19.50 euros = $ ■    11. 150 pounds = $ ■

12. $36.40 = ■ pounds    13. $535 = ■ euros    14. 10 euros = ■ pounds    15. 34.80 pounds = ■ euros

**Convert the temperature. Round to the nearest degree.**

16. 15°F = ■°C    17. 101°F = ■°C    18. 20°C = ■°F    19. 62°C = ■°F

20. 48°F = ■°C    21. 91°C = ■°F    22. ⁻56°C = ■°F    23. ⁻12°F = ■°C

**USE DATA** For 24–27, use the table.

24. How many euros would Mrs. DeMarco receive if she is exchanging $400?

25. Chris wants to purchase a hat in London for 11 pounds. He has $20 to exchange. Does he have enough to purchase the hat? **Explain.**

| Average Exchange Rates (2005) | |
|---|---|
| US Dollar | $1 |
| British Pound | $1.82 per 1 pound |
| Euro | $1.24 per 1 euro |

26. In 2005, Molly had a book that cost $16.99 in the United States. She then saw the same book in Britain for 8.25 pounds. In which country was the book less expensive?

27. Karen paid 55 pounds to rent a car in London. Monique paid 80 euros to rent the same model car in Germany. Whose rental was more expensive?

28. **≡FAST FACT** On July 10, 1913, a record high temperature of 134°F was recorded at the Greenland Ranch in California. What is this temperature in degrees Celsius?

29. **WRITE Math** Look at the formula for converting Celsius to Fahrenheit. Will 35°C convert to a whole number in degrees Fahrenheit? **Explain** without calculating.

## Achieving the Standards

30. Find the sum $7\frac{1}{4} + 1\frac{5}{9}$. (O─┓ NS 2.1, p. 42)

31. Write 3 equivalent ratios for 5:8.
(O─┓ NS 1.2 p. 442)

32. Find the mean and median of the data set 12, 15, 15, 16, 14, 17, 14, 14, 11, 13.
(SDAP 1.1, p. 224)

33. **Test Prep** A necklace advertised on a British website costs 22 pounds. Suppose $1 is worth 1.85 British pounds. How much does the necklace cost in U.S. dollars?

A $10.25     C $32.86

B $11.89     D $40.70

# At Sea

**Reading Skill** **Use the Details**

Fathoms and leagues are nautical units of measure. Leagues are used to measure distance between points on a body of water. One league is equivalent to 3 mi.

The deepest dive ever recorded for a bottlenose dolphin was 990 ft. Suppose a band of bottlenose dolphins is swimming 45 leagues from the coast of Santa Maria, CA. How many miles are the dolphins from land?

To begin to solve the problem, identify the details and decide which details you can use to help solve the problem.

| Detail | Use to Solve Problem? |
|---|---|
| • Fathoms and leagues are nautical units of measure. | No |
| • One league equals 3 mi. | Yes |
| • Deepest recorded dive for a bottle nose dolphin is 990 ft. | No |
| • A band of dolphins is swimming 45 leagues from the coast. | Yes |

▲ Before measurement tools were widely used to measure ocean depths, sailors would attach a heavy object to a rope and toss it into the ocean. After the object hit the bottom, the sailor would pull it up and measure the rope by holding it between his outstretched arms and counting the number of lengths from fingertip to fingertip. The length of a sailor's arm span was about 6 ft, which was called a fathom.

**Problem Solving** **Use the details to solve the problems.**

1. Use the details that are identified to solve the problem above.

2. Two ships set sail from San Francisco Bay. At one point, the ships are 648 mi apart. How many leagues is this?

3. **≡FAST FACT** The average depth of the Pacific Ocean is 12,900 ft. The average depth of the Atlantic Ocean is 12,100 ft. There are 6 ft in 1 fathom. To the nearest fathom, what is the difference between the average depths of the Atlantic and Pacific Oceans?

4. **WRITE Math** Write a problem about dolphins and leagues. Include several details. Have a classmate identify all the details, decide which details to use to solve the problem, and then solve the problem.

## Learn

**PROBLEM** Willis makes decorative crafts using similar triangles of colored glass. How can you tell if the red triangle and the orange triangles are similar?

Figures that have the same shape but not necessarily the same size are called **similar figures**. Matching sides and angles of similar figures are called **corresponding sides** and **corresponding angles**.

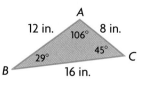

## Vocabulary

similar figures

corresponding sides

corresponding angles

Corresponding Angles:　∠A and ∠X　Corresponding Sides:　$\overline{AB}$ and $\overline{XY}$
　　　　　　　　　　　　∠B and ∠Y　　　　　　　　　　　　　　　$\overline{BC}$ and $\overline{YZ}$
　　　　　　　　　　　　∠C and ∠Z　　　　　　　　　　　　　　　$\overline{CA}$ and $\overline{ZX}$

Two triangles are similar if their corresponding angles are congruent or if the ratios of the lengths of their corresponding sides are equal. Only one needs to be tested.

### Example 1 Tell if △ABC is similar to △XYZ.

Check the corresponding angles or the ratios of the lengths of the corresponding sides.

$m\angle A = m\angle X = 106°$, so $\angle A \cong \angle X$　　All the corresponding angles

$m\angle B = m\angle Y = 29°$, so $\angle B \cong \angle Y$　　are congruent.

$m\angle C = m\angle Z = 45°$, so $\angle C \cong \angle Z$

**Remember**

Congruent means having the same size and shape. The symbol for congruent is $\cong$.

So, △ABC and △XYZ are similar.

Other polygons are similar only if both their corresponding angles are congruent and the ratios of their corresponding sides are equal.

### Example 2 Tell if ABCD is similar to JKLM.

Check the corresponding angles.

$m\angle A = m\angle J = 126°$, so $\angle A \cong \angle J$;　$m\angle B = m\angle K = 54°$, so $\angle B \cong \angle K$

$m\angle C = m\angle L = 126°$, so $\angle C \cong \angle L$;　$m\angle D = m\angle M = 54°$, so $\angle D \cong \angle M$

Check the ratios of the lengths of the corresponding sides.

$\frac{AB}{JK} = \frac{14}{7} = \frac{2}{1}$, $\frac{BC}{KL} = \frac{5}{4}$, $\frac{CD}{LM} = \frac{14}{7} = \frac{2}{1}$, $\frac{DA}{MJ} = \frac{5}{4} \rightarrow \frac{2}{1} \neq \frac{5}{4}$

The corresponding angles are congruent, but the ratios of corresponding sides are not equal.

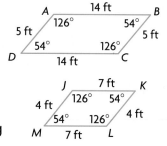

So, ABCD is not similar to JKLM.

 MG 2.0 Students identify and describe the properties of two-dimensional figures: *also* O━┑ NS 1.2, MR 1.1, MR 2.4, MR 2.5, MR 3.0, MR 3.2, MR 3.3.

1. Tell whether the triangles are similar. Write *yes* or *no*.

$\frac{GH}{MN} = \frac{14}{28} = \frac{1}{2}$, $\frac{HJ}{NP} = \frac{15}{30} = \blacksquare$, $\frac{JG}{PM} = \frac{21}{42} = \blacksquare$

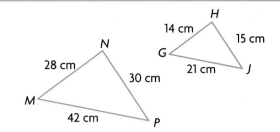

**Tell whether the figures are similar. Write yes or no. Explain why or why not.**

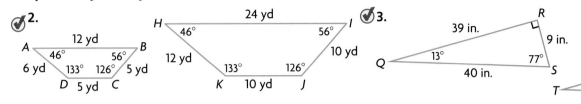

2. 

3. 

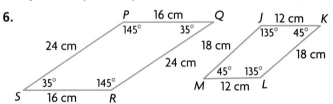

4. **TALK Math** Explain how to use ratios to tell whether two triangles are similar.

**Tell whether the figures are similar. Write *yes* or *no*. Explain why or why not.**

5. 

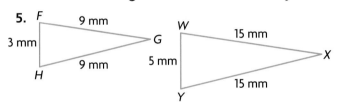

6. 

**For 7–9, use the design at the right.**

7. What are the angle measures of the rectangles?

8. Are the labeled rectangles similar? **Explain.**

9. Suppose a 9-in. by 24-in. rectangle and a 3-in. by 8-in. rectangle are added to the design. Which labeled rectangle would the new rectangles be similar to?

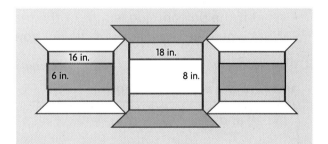

10. **WRITE Math** Can two rectangles of different length and equal width ever be similar? **Explain.**

11. Evaluate: $^-2 \times {}^-8 + 7 - 4$. (AF 1.3 p. 276)

12. For a school survey, would it make sense to survey all 4,192 students or to survey a sample? (SDAP 2.1, p. 200)

13. Solve $6 \times a = 14 \times 3$. (AF 1.1, p. 336)

14. **Test Prep** △HJK has side lengths of 24 m, 32 m, and 36 m. △NMP is similar to △HJK. Which could be the side lengths of △NMP?

    **A** 6 m, 8 m, 10 m          **C** 28 m, 40 m, 45 m

    **B** 20 m, 24 m, 30 m       **D** 36 m, 48 m, 54 m

## ALGEBRA
# Proportions and Similar Figures

OBJECTIVE: Use proportions to find unknown lengths of sides of similar figures.

## Quick Review

The triangles are similar. Find the ratio of the lengths of the corresponding sides.

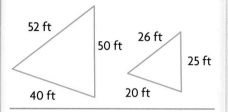

## Vocabulary
indirect measurement

## Learn

**PROBLEM** Brett uses two sizes of garden stones to border his flower beds. The faces of the stones are similar hexagons. Find the unknown length.

If two figures are similar and you know the lengths of two corresponding sides, as well as one other side, you can use proportions to find the length of the other corresponding side.

### Example 1 Use a proportion to find the unknown length.

$\frac{15}{25}$ and $\frac{y}{10}$    Write the ratios of the corresponding sides. Let $y$ represent the unknown length.

$\frac{15}{25} = \frac{y}{10}$    Use the ratios to write a proportion.

$25 \times y = 10 \times 15$    Use cross-multiplication.

$25y = 150$

$\frac{25y}{25} = \frac{150}{25}$    Divide.

$y = 6$

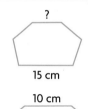
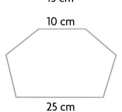

? 

15 cm

10 cm

25 cm

So, the unknown length of the garden stone is 6 cm.

• **What if** the bottom side length of the smaller stone is 10 cm? What would be the length of the unknown side?

### Example 2 The triangles are similar. Write a proportion and find the unknown length.

$\frac{6}{a}$ and $\frac{9}{12}$    Write the ratios of the corresponding sides. Let $a$ represent the unknown length.

$\frac{6}{a} = \frac{9}{12}$    Use the ratios to write a proportion.

$9 \times a = 6 \times 12$    Use cross-multiplication.

$9a = 72$

$\frac{9a}{9} = \frac{72}{9}$    Divide.

$a = 8$

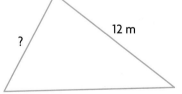

6 m      9 m

12 m

?

So, the unknown length is 8 m.

**NS 1.3** Use proportions to solve problems (e.g., determine the value of N if $\frac{4}{7} = \frac{N}{21}$, find the length of a side of a polygon similar to a known polygon). Use cross-multiplication as a method for solving such problems, understanding it as the multiplication of both sides of an equation by a multiplicative inverse.
*also* AF 2.0, MR 1.1, MR 2.2, MR 2.4, MR 2.5, MR 3.2

# Indirect Measurement

When you use similar figures and a proportion to find an unknown length, you are using a method called indirect measurement. You can use indirect measurement to find lengths that are difficult to measure with a ruler. This method can be used when similar right triangles can be identified.

## Example 3

Selena is 6 ft tall. On a sunny day, she casts a shadow that is 3 ft long. At the same time, a gazebo on her property casts a shadow that is 5 ft long. Find the height of the gazebo.

$\dfrac{h}{6}$ and $\dfrac{5}{3}$    Write the ratios of the corresponding sides

$\dfrac{h}{6} = \dfrac{5}{3}$    Use the ratios to write a proportion.

$3 \times h = 6 \times 5$    Use cross-multiplication

$3h = 30$

$\dfrac{3h}{3} = \dfrac{30}{3}$    Divide.

$h = 10$

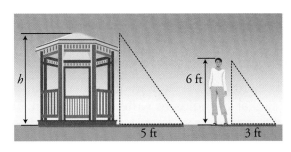

So, the height of the gazebo is 10 ft.

## Guided Practice

1. The parallelograms are similar. Find the unknown length.

$$\frac{4}{w} = \frac{7}{14}$$

**The figures are similar. Write a proportion. Then find the unknown length.**

2.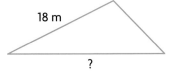

✓3.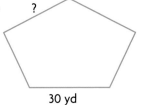

**Use similar triangles to write a proportion. Then find the unknown length.**

4.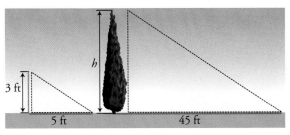

✓5.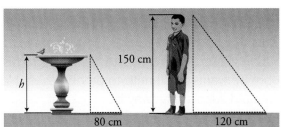

6. **TALK Math** Explain how to write a proportion to find unknown lengths of similar figures.

**The figures are similar. Write a proportion. Then find the unknown length.**

**7.**

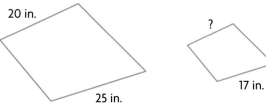
20 in.
25 in.
?
17 in.

**8.**

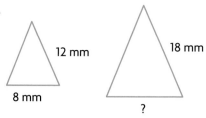
12 mm
8 mm
18 mm
?

**9.**

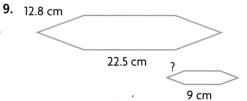
12.8 cm
22.5 cm
?
9 cm

**10.**

7 yd
4 yd
?
5 yd

**Use similar triangles to write a proportion. Then find the unknown length.**

**11.**

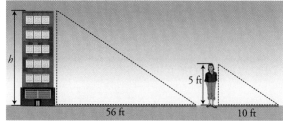
*h*
5 ft
56 ft
10 ft

**12.**

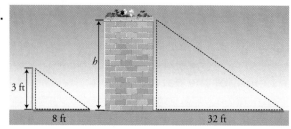
*h*
3 ft
8 ft
32 ft

**For 13–15, use the quadrilaterals at the right.**

**13.** Quadrilateral *ABCD* is similar to quadrilateral *LMNP*. If $\overline{LM} = 27$ m, find the other side lengths of quadrilateral *LMNP*.

**14.** Suppose that *MN* is 4 less than 3 times *BC*. If quadrilateral *ABCD* is similar to quadrilateral *LMNP*, how long is $\overline{NP}$?

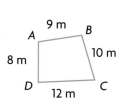
9 m
A
B
8 m
10 m
D
12 m
C

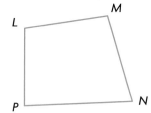
L
M
P
N

**15. Pose a Problem** Look back at Problem 13. Write a similar problem, but change the side lengths of quadrilateral *ABCD*.

**16.** A man who is 7 ft tall casts a 15-ft shadow. At the same time of day, his house casts a 75-ft shadow. Draw a diagram with similar right triangles. Then find the height of the house.

**17.** The figures at the right are similar quadrilaterals. Find the unknown lengths.

**18.** Juan wants a rectangular driveway for his new home. His neighbor's driveway is 30 ft long and 18 ft wide. Juan wants his driveway to be similar to his neighbor's, but he wants the length to be only 25 ft. How wide should Juan's driveway be?

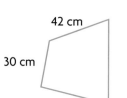
42 cm
30 cm
32 cm

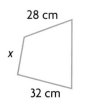
28 cm
*x*

*y*
24 cm

**19.** **WRITE Math** **Explain** how you can use similar figures to measure the height of a tall lamp post.

**20.** In $\triangle ABC$, $m\angle A = 42°$, and $m\angle B$ is 3° greater than half the $m\angle A$. Find $m\angle B$ and $m\angle C$.

(○━┐ MG 2.2, p. 392)

**21.** Find the range: 22.1, 22.3, 22.5, 22.7, 22.9, 22.1, 22.5. (SDAP 1.1, p. 224)

**22. Test Prep** The rectangles are similar. Which is the unknown side length?

48 ft

?

28 ft ▭

42 ft ▭

**A** 2 feet

**B** 24 feet

**C** 72 feet

**D** 96 feet

**23.** Write three ratios that are equivalent to the number of red counters compared to the number of yellow counters.

(○━┐ NS 1.2, p. 442)

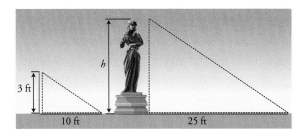

**24. Test Prep** Which is the height of the statue?

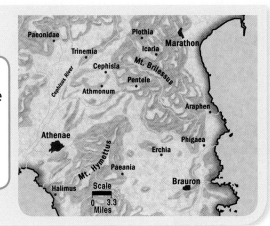

**A** 7.5 feet

**C** 75 feet

**B** 9 feet

**D** 83.3 feet

# Problem Solving connects to Social Studies

When you learn about ancient civilizations, your social studies teacher might provide you with a map that shows the locations of various cities. The measurements on a map are proportional to the actual distance between these locations. You can use the scale of a map to write a proportion.

**Example** Find the actual distance between Athmonum and Araphen.

Use a ruler to measure the distance from Athmonum to Araphen. The map distance is 3.1 cm.

$$\dfrac{cm \rightarrow}{mi \rightarrow} \dfrac{1}{3.3} = \dfrac{3.1}{d}$$

The scale on the map is 1 cm = 3.3 mi. Write a proportion. Let $d$ represent the actual distance.

$1 \times d = 3.1 \times 3.3$ Use cross-multiplication.

$d = 10.23$

So, it was about 10.2 mi from Athmonum to Araphen.

**Find the actual distance between the two cities.**

**1.** Trinemia to Plothia

**2.** Paeania to Phigaea

**3.** Paeonidae to Pentele

# Problem Solving Workshop
# Strategy: Compare Strategies

OBJECTIVE: Compare different strategies used to solve problems.

**PROBLEM** Bald eagles make nests that are an average of 2 ft deep and 5 ft across. Ranger Lewis counts 3 active bald eagle nests along 8 mi of the border of a wildlife refuge. If this pattern continues, how many nests can the ranger expect to find along the 72-mi border of the refuge?

## Read to Understand

Reading Skill

- Classify and categorize the given information to determine what you are asked to find.

## Plan

- **What strategies can you use to solve the problem?**

  You can write an equation or draw a diagram to solve the problem.

## Solve

- **How can you use the strategies to solve the problem?**

| ONE WAY | Write an equation. |
| --- | --- |

Use like categories of information to write a proportion equation.

$$\frac{3}{8} = \frac{n}{72}$$  Write a proportion.

$8 \times n = 3 \times 72$  Use cross-multiplication

$8n = 216$

$\dfrac{8n}{8} = \dfrac{216}{8}$  Divide.

$n = 27$

| ANOTHER WAY | Draw a diagram. |
| --- | --- |

Model the given information in a diagram.

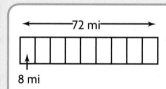
← 72 mi →

8 mi

Draw a rectangle to represent the 72-mi border. Divide the rectangle into 8-mi sections. There are 9 sections.

72 mi

| 3 | 3 | 3 | 3 | 3 | 3 | 3 | 3 | 3 |

$9 \times 3 = 27$

There are 3 nests in every 8-mi section.

Multiply to find the total number of nests in 72 mi.

So, Ranger Lewis can expect to find 27 nests along the 72-mi border.

## Check

- **How do you know the answer is correct?**

**NS 1.3** Use proportions to solve problems (e.g., determine the value of *N* if $\frac{4}{7} = \frac{N}{21}$, find the length of a side of a polygon similar to a known polygon). Use cross-multiplication as a method for solving such problems, understanding it as the multiplication of both sides of an equation by a multiplicative inverse. *also* MR 1.0, MR 2.0, MR 2.4, MR 2.5, MR 2.7, MR 3.0, MR 3.1, MR 3.2, MR 3.3

**Write an equation or draw a diagram to solve.**

1. Anita measures the height and wingspan of a young male bald eagle. The bird stands 7 in. tall and has a wingspan of 16 in. If it grows to a height of 35 in., how long could Anita expect its wingspan to be?

   **First,** write a proportion. $\dfrac{7}{16} = \dfrac{35}{w}$

   **Then,** use cross-multiplication. $16 \times 35 = w \times 7$

   $$560 = 7w$$

   **Finally,** divide to solve for $w$. $\dfrac{560}{7} = \dfrac{7w}{7}$

2. **What if** the young male is 21 in. tall and has a wingspan of 51 in.? What can Anita expect its wingspan to be if it grows to a height of 35 in.?

3. A golden eagle flies 8 mi in 14 min. If it continues at this rate, how long will it take to fly 24 mi?

Draw a Diagram or Picture
Make a Model or Act It Out
Make an Organized List
Find a Pattern
Make a Table or Graph
Predict and Test
Work Backward
Solve a Simpler Problem
Write an Equation
Use Logical Reasoning

## Mixed Strategy Practice

4. In a protected area, the ratio of falcons to pelicans is 3 to 10. If there are 40 pelicans in the area, how many falcons would you expect to find?

5. Jarret, Rehanna, Abby, and Marcus each purchase a souvenir at the zoo's aviary gift shop. The amounts they spend are $18, $25, $20, and $12. Abby spends $2 more than Jarret, and Rehanna purchases the least expensive item. Who pays what amount?

**USE DATA** For 6–7, use the double bar-graph.

6. A banded red-tailed hawk lives about 2 yr longer than the hawk in sample group 1 and 6 yr less than the hawk in sample group 2. About how long does the banded red-tailed hawk live?

7. **WRITE Math** Which strategies would you use to find the greatest average life span of the birds? Explain how you would use it.

8. At a wildlife refuge, discounts are given to encourage patrons to revisit and support the refuge. The first family in line at the refuge gates has visited the refuge 2 times, and every family that follows has revisited 2 more times than the family before it. How many times has the sixth family revisited the refuge?

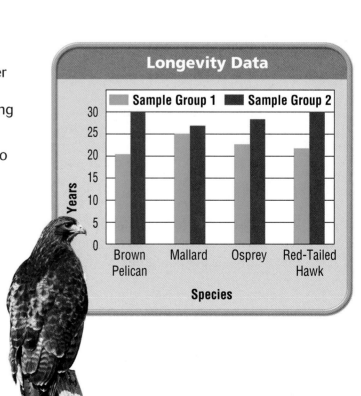

**Longevity Data**

# Extra Practice

## Set A  Write one proportion using two of the ratios. (pp. 464–465)

1. $\frac{3}{6}, \frac{6}{16}, \frac{9}{18}$

2. 4 to 5, 6 to 10, 16 to 20

3. 2:10, 3:12, 12:60

4. 4:12, 10:20, 21:42

5. 3 to 6, 7 to 14, 2 to 5

6. 2 to 10, 9 to 12, 7 to 35

7. $\frac{4}{5}, \frac{8}{9}, \frac{12}{15}, \frac{24}{27}$

8. 3:5, 5:8, 12:20

9. $\frac{7}{21}, \frac{11}{15}, \frac{33}{45}, \frac{40}{50}$

10. $\frac{3}{7}, \frac{10}{16}, \frac{30}{48}$

11. 7:14, 6:18, 8:24

12. 1 to 3, 2 to 6, 5 to 9

## Set B  Solve the proportion. (pp. 466–467)

1. $\frac{3}{5} = \frac{12}{x}$

2. $\frac{k}{14} = \frac{6}{7}$

3. $\frac{8}{r} = \frac{12}{24}$

4. $\frac{10}{20} = \frac{p}{24}$

5. $\frac{y}{15} = \frac{3}{18}$

6. $\frac{8}{20} = \frac{t}{15}$

7. $\frac{10}{16} = \frac{15}{z}$

8. $\frac{8}{m} = \frac{20}{25}$

9. $\frac{12}{32} = \frac{a}{16}$

10. $\frac{b}{21} = \frac{6}{42}$

11. $\frac{d}{4} = \frac{8}{10}$

12. $\frac{1.2}{6} = \frac{12}{h}$

13. A long-distance telephone company charges $3 for an 8-minute call to Germany. If Mr. Hagen makes a 24-minute call to Germany, how much will the phone call cost?

14. At a restaurant, 4 out of 7 diners prefer sweetened tea to unsweetened tea. Out of 56 diners, how many would you expect to order sweetened tea?

15. The Oakmont Middle School basketball team won 18 out of their first 24 games. How many games would you expect the basketball team to win during a 40-game season?

16. Coach Jackson bought 18 volleyballs for $288. If you bought 6 volleyballs for the same price per volleyball, what would be the total cost of the 6 volleyballs?

## Set C  Convert to the given unit. (pp. 468–471)

1. 15 yd = ▇ ft

2. 16 fl oz = ▇ c

3. 11 cm = ▇ mm

4. 900 g = ▇ kg

5. 2 T = ▇ lb

6. 5 gal = ▇ qt

7. 4.7 L = ▇ mL

8. 10 m = ▇ cm

9. 144 in. = ▇ ft

10. 4,500 mL = ▇ L

11. 39 g = ▇ kg

12. 16 qt = ▇ gal

13. A pine tree in a local park stands 62.4 feet high. If 1 meter equals 3.28 feet, how many meters high is the pine tree?

14. A bag of sugar weighs 2.6 pounds. If 1 pound equals 0.454 kilograms, what is the mass of the bag in kilograms?

15. Sarah builds a wooden birdhouse with a width of 6 inches. If 1 inch equals 2.54 centimeters, how many centimeters wide is the birdhouse?

16. A cake recipe calls for 2 cups of milk. If 1 cup equals 237 milliliters, how many milliliters of milk does the recipe require?

**Technology**
Use Harcourt Mega Math, Ice Station Exploration, *Polar Planes*, Level I.

**Set D** Suppose 1 pound is worth $1.92, and 1 euro is worth $1.33. Convert the following. (pp. 472–475)

1. $45 = ▦ pounds

2. 4.75 euros = $ ▦

3. 10 pounds = $ ▦

4. 200 euros = $ ▦

5. 135 pounds = $ ▦

6. $120 = ▦ euros

7. $375 = ▦ euros

8. 15 euros = ▦ pounds

9. 74.15 euros = $ ▦

10. $64.10 = ▦ pounds

11. 100 pounds = ▦ euros

12. 86 euros = ▦ pounds

13. A CD that cost $12.75 in the United States sold for 10 euros in France. In which country was the CD less expensive?

14. How many pounds would you receive if you were exchanging $100?

**Set E** Tell whether the figures are similar. Write *yes* or *no*. **Explain why or why not.** (pp. 476–477)

1.
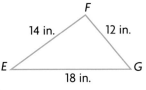

2.
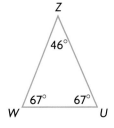
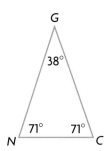

3.
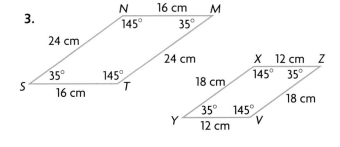

4.
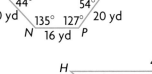
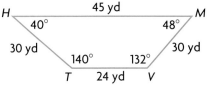

**Set F** The figures are similar. Write a proportion. **Then find the unknown length.** (pp. 478–481)

1.
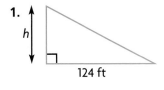

2.
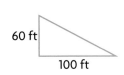

3. A woman who is 5 ft tall casts an 8-ft shadow. At the same time of day, a stop sign on a pole casts a 12-ft shadow. Draw a diagram with similar right triangles. Then find the height of the stop sign.

4. Ty is adding a bay window to the front of his house. His neighbor's bay window is 8 ft wide and 6 ft tall. He wants his window to be the same shape as his neighbor's, but its width to be only 6 ft. How tall should Ty's window be?

## Check Vocabulary and Concepts

For 1–2, choose the best term from the box.

1. Sides of two figures that are in the same position in the figures are called ___?___. (O━ᴨ NS 1.2, p. 476)

2. When you use similar figures and a proportion to find an unknown length, you are using a method called ___?___. (O━ᴨ NS 1.3, p. 478)

3. Explain how you can use counters to find a ratio that is equivalent to $\frac{3}{5}$ and then write a proportion. (O━ᴨ NS 1.2, pp. 462-463)

## Check Skills

Write one proportion using two of the ratios. (O━ᴨ NS 1.3, pp. 464-465)

4. 4:6, 8:16, 24:36

5. $\frac{4}{9}, \frac{16}{36}, \frac{21}{30}, \frac{63}{90}$

6. $\frac{6}{14}, \frac{8}{18}, \frac{36}{84}$

7. 3 to 9, 9 to 15, 27 to 45

Solve the proportion. (O━ᴨ NS 1.3, pp. 466-467)

8. $\frac{7}{10} = \frac{21}{x}$

9. $\frac{k}{5} = \frac{12}{30}$

10. $\frac{3}{11} = \frac{m}{33}$

11. $\frac{48}{h} = \frac{16}{5}$

12. $\frac{3}{18} = \frac{5}{x}$

Convert to the given unit. (O━ᴨ NS 1.3, pp. 468-471)

13. 36 yd = ■ ft

14. 4.6 L = ■ mL

15. 3 gal = ■ qt

16. 840 mm = ■ cm

Suppose 1 pound is worth \$1.92, and 1 euro is worth \$1.33. Convert the following. (O━ᴨ NS 1.0, pp. 472-475)

17. \$24 = ■ pounds

18. \$104 = ■ euros

19. 125 pounds = \$ ■

20. 103.5 euros = \$ ■

Tell whether the figures are similar. Write *yes* or *no*. Explain why or why not. (O━ᴨ NS 1.2, pp. 476-477)

21.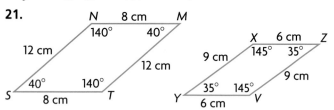

22.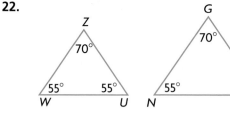

## Check Problem Solving

Solve. (O━ᴨ NS 1.3, pp. 482-483)

23. Emily ran 1 mi in 12 min. If she continues at this rate, how long will it take to run 5 mi?

24. Mr. Gavin plants 3 trees per hr. How long will it take him to plant 48 trees?

25. **◖WRITE Math◗** Explain how you would solve $\frac{x}{9} = \frac{10}{3}$.

**GO** ONLINE **Technology** Use *Online Assessment.*

# Enrich • Proportional Reasoning
## Carnival Time

Maisy and Mackenzie are enjoying the school carnival. Maisy pays $9 for 20 tickets. Mackenzie plans to buy 15 tickets. How much should she expect to spend?

You can use proportional reasoning to solve this problem.

## Arrive

**Make a table that relates the cost to the number of tickets.**

### One Way

| Cost | Tickets | |
|------|---------|---|
| $9 | 20 | For 20 tickets, the cost is $9. |
| $2.25 | 5 | Divide both columns by 4 to find the cost of 5 tickets. |
| $6.75 | 15 | Multiply both columns by 3 to find the cost of 15 tickets. |

### Another Way

| Cost | Tickets | |
|------|---------|---|
| $9 | 20 | For 20 tickets, the cost is $9. |
| $4.50 | 10 | Divide by 2 to find the cost of 10 tickets. |
| $2.25 | 5 | Divide by 2 to find the cost of 5 tickets. |
| $6.75 | 15 | Add the two previous rows. |

So, Mackenzie should expect to spend $6.75 for 15 tickets.

## Have Fun

**Use proportional reasoning to find the unknown amount.**

1. Ken runs the swing ride 2 times in 5 min. If he continues at this rate, how many times will he run this ride in 40 min?

2. Sherri buys 24 oz of roasted peanuts for $5.76. How much should she expect to pay for 8 oz of roasted peanuts?

3. It takes 18 tickets for 6 students to go through the fun house. How many tickets will this attraction take in from 48 students?

4. Fun 'N' Games rents a dunking booth at $128 for 4 hr. How much will it cost for Mr. Barlow to rent the booth for 1.5 hr?

## Go Home

**WRITE Math** Compare and Contrast proportional reasoning with writing and solving proportion equations.

# Achieving the Standards
## Chapters 1 – 19

## Number Sense

1. During basketball season, Katrina missed the basket on 1 out of every 4 free throws. How many missed free throws can she expect in her next 12 attempts? (O—ᴨ NS 1.3)

   **A** 1          **C** 4

   **B** 3          **D** 9

**Test Tip** **Decide on a plan.**

See item 2. You can solve this problem several different ways. One way is to set up a proportion. Another way is to find the unit rate.

2. Carl's group of volunteers was responsible for planting flowers around a new youth center building. The group planted 34 flowers in 40 minutes. If they continued planting at this rate, how many flowers did they plant in 3 hours? (O—ᴨ NS 1.2)

   **A** 65          **C** 102

   **B** 82          **D** 153

3. Which list of numbers is ordered from *greatest* to *least*? (O—ᴨ NS 1.1)

   **A** $1\frac{1}{8}$, $\frac{3}{4}$, 0.70, 0.80

   **B** 0.80, $\frac{3}{4}$, $1\frac{1}{8}$, 0.70

   **C** 0.70, $\frac{3}{4}$, 0.80, $1\frac{1}{8}$

   **D** $1\frac{1}{8}$, 0.80, $\frac{3}{4}$, 0.70

4. **WRITE Math** **Explain** how to add the fractions $\frac{5}{6}$ and $\frac{1}{5}$. (O—ᴨ NS 2.0)

## Algebra and Functions

5. Which point on the graph represents (⁻2,4)? (Grade 5 O—ᴨ AF 1.4)

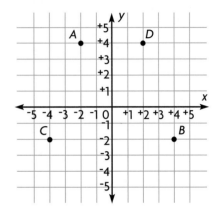

   **A** point *A*          **C** point *C*

   **B** point *B*          **D** point *D*

6. Sam had some change in his pocket. After he gave a friend $0.64, Sam had $2.25. Which equation can he use to find the original amount of money, *m*, he had in his pocket? (O—ᴨ AF 1.1)

   **A** $m + 0.64 = 2.25$

   **B** $2.25 = m - 0.64$

   **C** $m = 2.25 \times 0.64$

   **D** $m + 2.25 = 0.64$

7. What value of *z* makes the following equation true? (O—ᴨ AF 1.1)

   $$z \div 7 = 14$$

   **A** 2          **C** 88

   **B** 21          **D** 98

8. **WRITE Math** **Explain** the steps you would take to evaluate the expression $4k - 4 \div 4$ when $k = 6$. (AF 1.3)

## Measurement and Geometry

**9.** Triangle *RST* is a right triangle. Angle *R* measures 30°. What is the measure of angle *T*? (O━┓ MG 2.2)

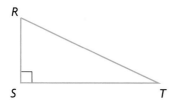

**A** 15°

**B** 30°

**C** 60°

**D** 90°

**10.** A Ferris wheel at the local carnival has a diameter of 44 meters. Which expression can be used to find its circumference, *C*, in meters? (O━┓ MG 1.1)

**A** $C = 22 \times \pi$

**B** $C = 2 \times 44 \times \pi$

**C** $C = 22^2\pi$

**D** $C = 44 \times \pi$

**11.** The angles below are complementary. What is the unknown angle measure? (O━┓ MG 2.2)

**A** 31°

**B** 59°

**C** 90°

**D** 149°

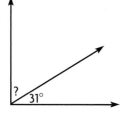

**12.** **WRITE Math** ▸ Sense or Nonsense Alexandra says that a triangle can have no more than one right angle. Is she correct? **Explain.** (O━┓ MG 2.2)

## Statistics, Data Analysis, and Probability

**13.** There are 5 Little League baseball teams in the town of Jackson Heights.

| **Number of Players Per Team** | | | | | |
|---|---|---|---|---|---|
| **Team** | 1 | 2 | 3 | 4 | 5 |
| **Number** | 19 | 26 | 21 | 24 | 25 |

Which shows the median number of players on the teams? (SDAP 1.1)

**A** 19        **C** 24

**B** 23        **D** 26

**14.** Marcus scored 88, 79, 93, 89, and 91 on his science tests during the past year. What is the mean of his test scores? (SDAP 1.1)

**A** 91        **C** 88

**B** 89        **D** 79

**15.** Debra recorded the colors of the first 24 bicycles that passed her on the bike path on Saturday morning. The table below shows the data she collected.

| **Bicycle Colors** | | | | | | |
|---|---|---|---|---|---|---|
| **Color** | **Silver** | **Red** | **Black** | **Gold** | **Yellow** | **Other** |
| **Bicycles** | 3 | 4 | 5 | 2 | 4 | 6 |

Which fraction represents the number of yellow bicycles that she counted?
(Grade 5 SDAP 1.3)

**A** $\frac{1}{9}$   **B** $\frac{1}{6}$   **C** $\frac{1}{5}$   **D** $\frac{1}{4}$

**16.** **WRITE Math** ▸ Steven randomly surveyed 50 boys from his school to find out what type of music is most popular among students at his school. **Explain** whether his sample is biased or unbiased. (O━┓ SDAP 2.2)

# 20 Percent and Change

**The Big Idea** Percents can be expressed as fractions and decimals.

**CALIFORNIA FAST FACT**

California is the largest producer of fruits and vegetables in the country, accounting annually for 49 percent of the total U.S. value.

## Investigate

Suppose you are visiting the local farmer's market to buy vegetables for a salad you would like to prepare for some friends. If you were to choose three or four vegetables for the salad, how much would you have to pay?

### Farmer's Market Price List

| Item | Regular Price | Today's Discount |
|------|--------------|------------------|
| Arugula | $2.49 per bag | 25% |
| Avocado | $1.99 for two | 15% |
| Broccoli | $1.99 per head | None |
| Carrots | $0.89 per bag | 10% |
| Cucumber | $1.29 for three | 25% |
| Red leaf lettuce | $1.99 per head | 15% |
| Red pepper | $1.29 each | 20% |

**Technology**
Student pages are available in the Student eBook.

Check your understanding of important skills
needed for success in Chapter 20.

## ▶ Relate Decimals and Percents

Write the corresponding decimal or percent.

| | | | | |
|---|---|---|---|---|
| **1.** 23% | **2.** 0.6 | **3.** 0.27 | **4.** 99% | **5.** 0.45 |
| **6.** 2% | **7.** 0.9 | **8.** 0.13 | **9.** 6% | **10.** 10% |
| **11.** 0.925 | **12.** 12.5% | **13.** 44.6% | **14.** 0.127 | **15.** 0.999 |

## ▶ Write Decimals as Fractions

Write each decimal as a fraction.

| | | | | |
|---|---|---|---|---|
| **16.** 0.2 | **17.** 0.35 | **18.** 0.06 | **19.** 0.85 | **20.** 0.41 |
| **21.** 0.092 | **22.** 0.07 | **23.** 0.625 | **24.** 0.15 | **25.** 0.015 |
| **26.** 0.12 | **27.** 0.01 | **28.** 0.99 | **29.** 0.255 | **30.** 0.199 |

## ▶ Multiply with Decimals

Find the product.

| | | | | |
|---|---|---|---|---|
| **31.** 0.1 $\times 0.1$ | **32.** 0.1 $\times 5$ | **33.** 0.9 $\times 0.2$ | **34.** 0.25 $\times 16$ | **35.** 0.9 $\times 0.5$ |
| **36.** 0.2 $\times 6$ | **37.** 0.35 $\times 0.5$ | **38.** 0.25 $\times 5$ | **39.** 0.125 $\times 0.2$ | **40.** 0.1 $\times 15$ |

# VOCABULARY POWER

| CHAPTER VOCABULARY | WARM-UP WORDS |
|---|---|
| discount<br>principal<br>sales tax<br>simple interest | **discount** an amount that is subtracted from the regular price of an item<br><br>**sales tax** a percent of the cost of an item, added onto the item's cost<br><br>**principal** the amount of money borrowed or saved |

# Percent

OBJECTIVE: Write, compare, and order percents.

## Learn

**PROBLEM** Diego has designed a mosaic wall mural. Twenty-five of the 100 tiles are blue. Write this relationship as a percent.

The ratio 25 out of 100 can be expressed as a percent. A percent is the ratio of a number to 100. *Percent*, %, means "per hundred."

$$\frac{\text{blue tiles}}{100} \rightarrow \frac{25}{100} = 25\%$$

So, 25% of Diego's mural is blue.

A percent can be between 0% and 100% or greater than 100%.

### Example 1 Write the percent that is shaded.

**Ⓐ**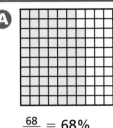

68 of the 100 squares are shaded.

$$\frac{68}{100} = 68\%$$

**Ⓑ**

$\frac{1}{4}$ square of the 100 squares is shaded.

$$\frac{\frac{1}{4}}{100} = \frac{1}{4}\% \text{ or } 0.25\%$$

> **Math Idea**
> Percents can be modeled on a 10 x 10 grid. The whole square is 100%. One small square is 1%.
>
> 1%

• How would you model 125%?

You can compare and order percents just as you do other numbers.

### Example 2 Order 0.2%, 40%, 6%, and 300% from least to greatest.

Compare every possible pair of percents.

| | | |
|---|---|---|
| 0.2% < 40% | 0.2% < 6% | 0.2% < 300% |
| 40% > 6% | 40% < 300% | 6% < 300% |

So, from least to greatest, the percents are 0.2%, 6%, 40%, and 300%.

**NS 1.0** Students compare and order positive and negative fractions, decimals, and mixed numbers. Students solve problems involving fractions, ratios, proportions, and percentages: *also* MR 2.4, MR 2.5, MR 3.2

## Guided Practice

**Write the percent that is shaded.**

**1.**   26 out of 100 = $\frac{26}{100}$ = ▦

**2.** 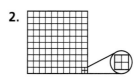  $\frac{1}{2}$ square of the 100 squares

$\frac{\frac{1}{2}}{100}$ = ▦

**3.**

**4.**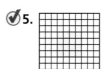

**✓5.**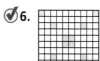

**✓6.**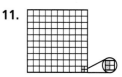

**7.** **TALK Math** Explain how $\frac{39}{100}$ can be written as a percent.

## Independent Practice and Problem Solving

**Write the percent that is shaded.**

**8.**

**9.**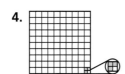

**10.**

**11.**

**Order from least to greatest.**

**12.** 14%, 16%, 11%, 13%

**13.** 16%, 25%, 21%, 20%

**14.** 0.5%, 50%, 5%, 55%

**15.** 37%, 3.7%, 77%, 0.37%

**16.** 0.4%, 140%, 14%, 4.3%

**17.** 217%, 0.72%, 72%, 17%

**For 18–20, use the mural.**

**18.** Kendra used 100 tiles to design the mural shown. What percent of the mural is white?

**19.** Compare the percent of the mural that is red to the percent that is yellow. Use <, >, or =.

**20.** **WRITE Math** What must all the percents of the various colors of tile total? **Explain.**

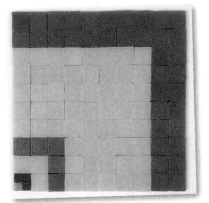

## Achieving the Standards

**21.** A pollster surveyed every tenth person who passed on the street. What kind of sampling was used? (O━n SDAP 2.2, p. 202)

**22.** Convert. 350 meters = ▦ centimeters

(AF 2.1, p.468)

**23.** Order 0.45, 0.34, and 0.54, from least to greatest. (O━n NS 1.1, p. 122)

**24.** **Test Prep** Chris got 7 out of 100 questions on his test wrong. What percent did he get right?

# 2 Percent, Decimals, and Fractions

**OBJECTIVE:** Convert among percents, decimals, and fractions.

## Learn

**PROBLEM** In a survey of sixth graders in an after-school theater program, $\frac{3}{5}$ said they attend a theater class and $\frac{5}{8}$ said they attend a dance class. What percent of students surveyed attend a theater class? What percent attend a dance class?

### Example 1

**ONE WAY** Write $\frac{3}{5}$ as an equivalent fraction with a denominator of 100.

$\frac{3}{5} = \frac{3 \times 20}{5 \times 20} = \frac{60}{100}$    Write an equivalent fraction with a denominator of 100.

$= 60\%$    Since percent is the ratio of a number to 100, write the ratio as a percent.

**ANOTHER WAY** Use division to write $\frac{5}{8}$ as a decimal.

$\frac{5}{8} \rightarrow \begin{array}{r} 0.625 \\ 8\overline{)5.000} \end{array}$    Divide the numerator by the denominator.

$0.625 = 62.5\%$    Multiply by 100 by moving the decimal point two places to the right.

So, 60% of students are enrolled in a theater class and 62.5% in a dance class.

You can also convert decimals to percents.

### Example 2  Write 0.7 as a percent.

**ONE WAY**    Use place value.

$0.7 = \frac{7}{10}$    Use place value to express the decimal as a ratio in fraction form.

$= \frac{7 \times 10}{10 \times 10} = \frac{70}{100}$    Write an equivalent fraction with a denominator of 100.

$= 70\%$    Since percent is the ratio of a number to 100, write the ratio as a percent.

**Remember**
When you multiply decimal numbers by powers of 10, you move the decimal point one place to the right for each factor of 10.

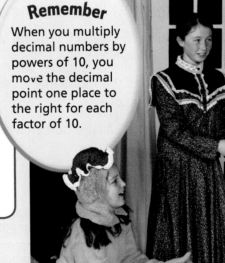

**ANOTHER WAY**    Multiply by 100.

$0.7 = 0.70$    Multiply by 100 by moving the decimal point two places to the right.

$= 70\%$    Add a percent sign.

NS 1.0 Students compare and order positive and negative fractions, decimals, and mixed numbers. Students solve problems involving fractions, ratios, proportions, and percentages: *also* MR 2.4, MR 2.5, MR 3.1, MR 3.2

# Percents to Fractions and Decimals

**Example 3** About 35% of the students in acting signed up for voice and speech during the next session. Write 35% as a fraction.

$35\% = \dfrac{35}{100}$     Write the percent as a fraction with a denominator of 100.

$\dfrac{35}{100} = \dfrac{35 \div 5}{100 \div 5} = \dfrac{7}{20}$     Write the fraction in simplest form.

So, 35% written as a fraction is $\dfrac{7}{20}$.

You can also convert percents to decimals.

**Example 4** Compared to last year, the number of students who said they took singing increased 228%. Write 228% as a decimal.

$228\% = \dfrac{228}{100}$     Write the percent as a fraction with a denominator of 100.

$\phantom{228\%} = 2.28$     Write the fraction as a decimal.

So, 228% written as a decimal is 2.28.

• How can you write 28% as a decimal?

**ERROR ALERT**

When writing a decimal greater than 1 as a percent, remember to multiply by 100. Recall that 100% is equal to 1.00, or 1. So, any number greater than 1 will convert to a percent greater than 100%.

Sometimes it takes several steps to convert a percent less than 1% to a fraction or a decimal.

**Example 5** About 0.5% of middle school students said they had never seen a local theater production. Write 0.5% as a fraction and as a decimal.

To write 0.5% as a fraction, recall that percent means "per hundred."

$0.5\% = \dfrac{0.5}{100}$     Write the percent as a fraction with a denominator of 100.

$\dfrac{0.5}{100} = \dfrac{0.5 \times 10}{100 \times 10} = \dfrac{5}{1{,}000}$     Multiply the numerator and denominator by 10 to remove the decimal from the fraction.

$\dfrac{5}{1{,}000} = \dfrac{5 \div 5}{1{,}000 \div 5} = \dfrac{1}{200}$     Write the fraction in simplest form.

To write 0.5% as a decimal, divide by 100.

When you divide decimal numbers by powers of 10, you move the decimal point one place to the left for each factor of 10.

$0.5\% = 00.5\%$     Divide by 100. Move the decimal point two places to the left.

$\phantom{0.5\%} = 0.005$     Remove the percent sign.

So, 0.5% can be written as $\dfrac{1}{200}$ or 0.005.

• How can you write 5.8% as a fraction and as a decimal? **Explain.**

1. Write 0.4 as a percent.    $0.4 = \frac{4}{10} = \frac{4 \times 10}{10 \times 10} = \frac{40}{100} = \blacksquare\%$

**Write each decimal or fraction as a percent.**

2. 0.1          3. 0.25          4. 3.4          5 $\frac{4}{5}$          ✓6. $\frac{1}{4}$

**Write each percent as a decimal and as a fraction in simplest form.**

7. 20%          8. 50%          9. 24%          10. 0.6%          ✓11. 140%

12. **TALK Math** Explain how to write 1.0 as a percent.

**Independent Practice and Problem Solving**

**Write each decimal or fraction as a percent.**

13. 0.04          14. 0.9          15. 1.6          16. $\frac{3}{10}$          17. $\frac{1}{2}$

18. 0.625          19. $\frac{2}{5}$          20. $\frac{7}{8}$          21. 2.08          22. $1\frac{1}{5}$

**Write each percent as a decimal and as a fraction in simplest form.**

23. 1%          24. 10%          25. 76%          26. 355%          27. 0.5%

**Write each percent as a decimal.**

28. 89%          29. 30%          30. 9%          31. 0.2%          32. 150%

**Compare. Write <, >, or = for each ●.**

33. 37% ● $\frac{3}{8}$          34. $\frac{1}{2}$ ● 50%          35. 0.35 ● 3.5%          36. 120% ● 12.0          37. $\frac{1}{3}$ ● 30%

**USE DATA** For 38–43, use the table.

38. What fraction of class offerings are for students in middle school?

39. For which group are $\frac{3}{25}$ of the classes offered?

| Theater Classes Offered by Grade | |
| --- | --- |
| Elementary School | 12% |
| Middle School | 36% |
| High School | 52% |

40. **Pose a Problem** Look back at Problem 39. Write a similar question by changing the fraction so that it is for a different group.

41. **Reasoning** What percent of theater classes are not offered to elementary students? **Explain** how you found your answer.

42. For which group of students are there the greatest percent of class offerings?

43. What percent of classes are not for high school students? Write that percent as a decimal.

44. A negative percent can refer to a loss. In 2003 total ticket income was ⁻10.7% compared to the previous year. Write the percent as a decimal and a fraction.

45. In 2004, the change in ticket income from the previous year was ⁻4.7%. In 2003, the change in ticket income was ⁻10.7%. By how much did the percent of change decrease from 2003 to 2004? Write your answer as a decimal and a fraction.

**Solve.**

**46.** The enrollment in the theater program in 2004 was 109% of the number of students enrolled in the theater program in 2003. What decimal can you write for this percent?

**47.** **WRITE Math** ▶ **What's the Error?** About 8.4% of the students enrolled are new to the theater program this season. Joe says 0.84 of the students were new this season. Is he correct? **Explain.**

 **Achieving the Standards**

**48.** Evaluate $^-4 \div {}^-2 - 3 \times {}^-52 - ({}^-10)$.
(AF 1.3, p. 276)

**49.** Is $2\frac{1}{8}$ greater or less than $\pi$? (MG 1.2, p. 18)

**50.** **Test Prep** Sarah answered 85% of the trivia questions correctly. What fraction describes this percent?

**51.** Write the fraction $\frac{3}{5}$ as a decimal. (Grade 5 NS 1.0)

**52.** **Test Prep** Morton made 36 out of 48 free throws last season. What percent of his free throws did Morton make?

**A** 36%    **C** 48%

**B** 40%    **D** 75%

# Problem Solving connects to Theater

Nearly 2,500 years ago, the city of Athens experienced its Golden Age of drama. Twice a year, Athens held the *Dionysia*, which was a competition among three playwrights. Each submitted 3 tragedies, 1 mythological comedy, and 1 other comedy. Most plays had only 2 actors, along with 4 to 8 people who made up the chorus.

**Dionysia Performers**

| Playwright | Actors | Chorus |
|---|---|---|
| A | 10 | 30 |
| B | 26% | 74% |
| C | 0.24 | 0.76 |

The table shows the numbers of performers that three playwrights might have used in their plays. For which playwright was the percent of actors the greatest?

**Convert to percents as needed. Then order *from greatest to least*.**

| Playwright A | $\frac{10}{10+30} = \frac{10}{40} = 0.25 = 25\%$ |
|---|---|
| Playwright B | 26% |
| Playwright C | $0.24 = \frac{24}{100} = 24\%$ |

24% < 25% < 26%

So, Playwright B used the greatest percent of actors.

**Solve.**

**1.** For which playwright was the percent of chorus performers the least?

**2.** Playwright D joins the competition with 20 performers, 6 of whom are actors. How does Playwright D's percent of actors compare to those of the other playwrights?

# 3 Percent of a Number

OBJECTIVE: Find a percent of a number.

## Quick Review

Write the percent as a fraction.

1. 25%    2. 90%

3. 50%    4. 80%

5. $62\frac{1}{2}\%$

## Learn

**PROBLEM** In Maria's postcard collection there are 48 postcards from California. Of these postcards, 25% are from Hollywood. How many postcards are from Hollywood?

### Example 1 Find 25% of 48.

**ONE WAY** Write the percent as a fraction and multiply.

$25\% = \frac{25}{100}$   Write the percent as a ratio in fraction form.

$= \frac{1}{4}$   Write the ratio in simplest form.

$\frac{1}{4} \times \frac{48}{1} = \frac{48}{4} = 12$   Multiply the ratio by the number.

**ANOTHER WAY** Write the percent as a decimal and multiply.

$25\% = 0.25$   Write the percent as a decimal.

$0.25 \times 48 = 12$   Multiply the decimal by the number.

So, 12 postcards are from Hollywood.

• What percent of the postcards are not from Hollywood? Explain.

You can write and solve a proportion to find a percent of a number.

**Remember**

To change a percent to a ratio in fraction form, write the percent over 100. Then simplify.

### Example 2 Raul collects coins. Of the 120 coins in his collection, 35% are pennies. How many coins are pennies?

Find 35% of 120.

$35\% = \frac{35}{100}$   Write the percent as a ratio in fraction form.

$\frac{p}{120} = \frac{35}{100}$   Write a proportion.

$100 \times p = 35 \times 120$   Use cross-multiplication.

$100p = 4200$

$\frac{100p}{100} = \frac{4,200}{100}$   Divide.

$p = 42$

So, 42 coins are pennies.

• Of the 120 coins, 7.5% are nickels. How many coins are nickels?

NS 1.4 Calculate given percentages of quantities and solve problems involving discounts at sales, interest earned, and tips. also NS 1.0, MR 2.2, MR 2.4, MR 2.5, MR 3.0, MR 3.2, MR 3.3

**Use a fraction or a decimal to find the percent of the number.**

**1.** 40% of 35     $40\% = \frac{40}{100} = \frac{2}{5}$       **2.** 27% of 80     $27\% = 0.27$

$\frac{2}{5} \times \frac{35}{1} = \blacksquare$                                            $0.27 \times 80 = \blacksquare$

**3.** 50% of 70     **4.** 15% of 40     **5.** 120% of 50     ✓**6.** 0.5% of 2,400     ✓**7.** 90% of 30

**8.** **TALK Math** **Explain** how to use a proportion to find the percent of a number.

**Independent Practice and Problem Solving**

**Use a fraction or a decimal to find the percent of the number.**

**9.** 25% of 36     **10.** 30% of 90     **11.** 0.2% of 600     **12.** 150% of 84     **13.** 10% of 47

**14.** 0.8% of 100     **15.** 45% of 250     **16.** 210% of 180     **17.** 98% of 480     **18.** 26.5% of 240

**Algebra** **Use a proportion to find the percent of the number.**

**19.** 30% of 80     **20.** 22% of 15     **21.** 75% of 48     **22.** 4% of 320     **23.** 36% of 80

**USE DATA** For 24–27, use the table.

**24.** The Golden Gate Bridge appears in 20% of the photos Alex took in San Francisco. How many photos show the Golden Gate Bridge?

**25.** Alex took 45% of the San Diego photos at the zoo and 20% at the Natural History Museum. What is the total number of photos taken at the zoo and Natural History Museum?

**26.** **Reasoning** Alex used black and white film for 36% of the photos he took in Palm Springs. The rest of the Palm Springs photos are in color. How many of the Palm Springs photos are in color?

**27.** **WRITE Math** **What's the Question?** Alex took 80% of the photos at night. This was 28 of the photos taken in this city.

**Alex's Photo Collection**

| Location | Number of Photos |
|---|---|
| Los Angeles | 35 |
| Oakland | 30 |
| Palm Springs | 50 |
| Santa Barbara | 20 |
| San Diego | 60 |
| San Francisco | 45 |

 **Achieving the Standards**

**28.** Solve $6 = \frac{3}{8} y$. (○━ AF 1.1, p. 340)

**29.** Find the area of a circle with a radius of 8 meters. Round to the nearest square meter. Use 3.14 for $\pi$. (○━ MG 1.1, p. 426)

**30.** Write 60% as a fraction. (○━ NS 1.4, p. 494)

**31.** **Test Prep** Jake's basketball team won 70% of the 30 games played. Which shows the number of games Jake's team won?

    **A** 7 games          **C** 21 games

    **B** 14 games        **D** 70 games

# Discount and Sales Tax

**OBJECTIVE:** Solve problems involving **discounts** and sales tax.

## Learn

When an item is on sale, it has a discount. A **discount** is an amount that is subtracted from the regular price of an item. To find the discount, multiply the regular price of the item by the discount rate.

$$\boxed{\text{discount} = \text{regular price} \times \text{discount rate}}$$

To find the sale price of an item, subtract the discount from the regular price.

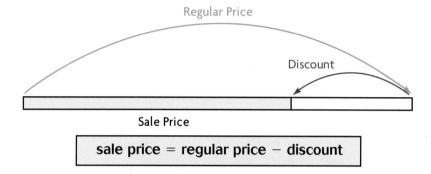

Regular Price

Discount

Sale Price

$$\boxed{\text{sale price} = \text{regular price} - \text{discount}}$$

SNOWBOARD SALE

Regular Price $120

Now 25% off!

### Example 1  Find the sale price.

Tim wants to buy a snowboard for his vacation to Mount Shasta. He saw the newspaper ad shown. How much will the snowboard cost with a 25% discount?

**Step 1**

**Find the discount.**

discount = regular price × discount rate
       = $120 × 25%
       = $120 × 0.25    Write the percent as a decimal. Multiply
       = $30.00

So, the discount is $30.00.

**Step 2**

**Find the sale price.**

sale price = regular price − discount
        = $120.00 − $30.00
        = $90.00

So, the sale price is $90.00.

- **What if** Tim waits until the following week to purchase the snowboard and gets a discount of 35%? How much will the snowboard cost with a 35% discount?

**NS 1.4** Calculate given percentages of quantities and solve problems involving discounts at sales, interest earned, and tips. *also* **NS 1.0, MR 2.2, MR 2.4, MR 2.5, MR 3.0, MR 3.2, MR 3.3**

**Example 2** Use the advertisement to find the regular price.

You can find the regular price if you know the sale price and the discount rate. The regular price has been discounted 40%. That means the sale price must be 60% of the regular price, since $100\% - 40\% = 60\%$.

**Think:** sale price = 60% × regular price

Let $n$ = the regular price.

$48 = 60\% \times n$    Write an equation.

$48 = 0.6 \times n$    Write the percent as a decimal.

$\dfrac{48}{0.6} = \dfrac{0.6n}{0.6}$    Divide.

$80 = n$

Regular Price

| ←————100%————→ |
| 60% | 40% |
| Sale Price | Discount |

So, the regular price of the ice skates is $80.

**All Ice Skates on Sale!**
**40% Off!**
*Now only $48!!*

**ERROR ALERT**

When writing percents as decimals, be sure to divide by 100 by moving the decimal point two places to the left.

A **sales tax** is calculated using a rate that is a percent of the price. To find the amount of the sales tax, multiply the price of the item by the sales tax rate.

**Example 3** Dennis purchased a pair of skis for $425. The sales tax rate was 8%. What was the total cost of the purchase?

**ONE WAY** Find the sales tax and add it to the price.

sales tax = price of item × sales tax rate
= $425 × 8%
= $425 × 0.08 = $34

total cost = price of item + sales tax
= $425 + $34 = $459

**ANOTHER WAY** Multiply the price by 108% since 8% is added to the cost.

total cost = price of item × (sales tax rate + 100%)
= $425 × 108%
= $425 × 1.08 = $459

So, the total cost of the purchase was $459.

You also can find the price of an item before sales tax is added.

**Example 4** Kate paid $68.64 for a toboggan that included the 7.25% sales tax. What was the price of the toboggan before tax?

Divide to find the price of the item.

price of item = total cost ÷ (sales tax rate + 100%)
= $68.64 ÷ (7.25% + 100%)
= $68.64 ÷ 107.25%    Change the percent to a decimal.
= $68.64 ÷ 1.0725 = $64    Divide.

So, the price before tax was $64.

**1.** Find the discount and the sale price of a $45 parka discounted 20%.

discount = $45 × 20%        sale price = $45 − discount

**Find the sale price.**

**2.** regular price: $44
discount rate: 25%

**3.** regular price: $150
discount rate: 30%

**4.** regular price: $27
discount rate: 10%

✓**5.** regular price: $65
discount rate: 20%

**Find the regular price.**

**6.** sale price: $120
discount rate: 25%

**7.** sale price: $99
discount rate: 10%

**8.** sale price: $78.50
discount rate: 50%

✓**9.** sale price: $231
discount rate: 30%

**10.** ( TALK Math ) **Explain** how you can find the regular price of a snow tube when the sale price is $18 and the discount rate is 25%.

## Independent Practice and Problem Solving

**Find the sale price.**

**11.** regular price: $30
discount rate: 15%

**12.** regular price: $215
discount rate: 20%

**13.** regular price: $75
discount rate: 50%

**14.** regular price: $342
discount rate: 25%

★**Algebra** **Find the regular price.**

**15.** sale price: $65
discount rate: 35%

**16.** sale price: $108
discount rate: 10%

**17.** sale price: $36.50
discount rate: 50%

**18.** sale price: $315
discount rate: 30%

**Find the total cost of the purchase. Round to the nearest cent.**

**19.** price: $129
sales tax rate: 6%

**20.** price: $14.95
sales tax rate: 4.5%

**21.** price: $1,029
sales tax rate: 5%

**22.** price: $89.95
sales tax rate: 6.25%

**Find the price of the item before sales tax. Round to the nearest cent.**

**23.** total cost: $84.40
sales tax rate: 5.5%

**24.** total cost: $16.48
sales tax rate: 3%

**25.** total cost: $2,652
sales tax rate: 4%

**26.** total cost: $214.50
sales tax rate: 7.25%

**USE DATA** For 27–29, use the table.

**27.** Snowboard wax is on sale. The discount rate is 20%. What is the sale price?

**28.** Jim buys a helmet. The sales tax rate is 8%. What is the amount of the sales tax?

**29.** Keisha buys snow goggles and ski gloves. The sales tax rate is 8%. What is the total cost of Keisha's purchase?

**30.** ≡**FAST FACT** The first snowboards, called snurfers, were sold in 1965 for $15 each. Suppose sales tax at the time was 5.5%, find the cost of purchasing a snurfer.

| Winter Sports Accessories | |
|---|---|
| **Item** | **Regular Price** |
| Snow Goggles | $42 |
| Ski Gloves | $30 |
| Snowboard Wax | $15 |
| Helmet | $65 |

**Technology**
Use Harcourt Mega Math, The Number Games, *Buggy Bargains,* Levels Q&S.

**Solve.**

31. Ski lift tickets are on sale at a 25% discount. The sale price of a ticket is $24. What is the regular price of a ski lift ticket?

32. **Pose a Problem** Look at Problem 31. Write a new problem that is open-ended.

33. The cost of a sled including 8.25% sales tax was $43.30. What was the price of the sled before the sales tax was added?

34. **WRITE Math** ▸ **Explain** two different ways of finding the amount of the discount for an item on sale for 30% off a regular price of $20.

 **Achieving the Standards**

35. Evaluate $q \div 0.4$ for $q = 8$. (AF 1.2 , p. 284)

36. Find the circumference of a circle with a radius of 3 feet. Use 3.14 for $\pi$. (○━┓ MG 1.1, p. 420)

37. **Test Prep** The sale price of a bike is $252. The discount is 20 percent. Which is the original cost of the bike?

 **A** $200  **B** $275  **C** $302  **D** $315

38. If 10% of a number is 6, what is 5% of the number? (○━┓ NS 1.3 p. 498)

39. **Test Prep** Ed paid $17.28 for a shirt. This amount included an 8% sales tax. What was the price of the shirt without tax?

 **A** $15.90  **C** $18.66
 **B** $16.00  **D** $31.10

## Problem Solving | connects to | Science

At 14,163 ft high, Mount Shasta is the second-highest volcano in the United States and a popular mountain-climbing destination.

Lin will be climbing the Casaval Ridge route, a winter trail. She wants to buy mountaineering boots, ropes, an ice axe, and an avalanche transceiver. The California sales tax is 7.25%. What will be the total cost of Lin's purchase? Round to the nearest cent.

| Mountain-Climbing Gear | |
| --- | --- |
| **Item** | **Cost** |
| Ice Axe | $249 |
| Avalanche Transceiver | $309 |
| Avalanche Beacon | $299 |
| Mountaineering Boots | $420 |
| Ropes | $195 |
| Carabiner | $9 |

Amount of purchase = $420 + $195 + $249 + $309 = $1,173

Find the sales tax and add it to the amount of purchase.

sales tax = amount of purchase × sales tax rate
 = $1,173 × 7.25%
 = $1,173 × 0.0725
 = $85.0425 = $85.04

total cost = amount of purchase + sales tax
 = $1,173 + $85.04 = $1,258.04

So, the total cost is $1,258.04.

**Find the total cost of each purchase, including 7.25% sales tax. Round to the nearest cent.**

1. avalanche beacon, ropes, and ice axe

2. mountaineering boots, ropes, and 3 carabiners

3. avalanche transceiver and avalanche beacon

## Quick Review

**Estimate the sum to the nearest whole number.**

1. 1.25 + 3.89
2. 4.27 + 9
3. 24.87 + 3.12
4. 6.95 + 0.85
5. 9.75 + 63.19

## Learn

Leaving a tip for service is customary when you eat at a restaurant.

**PROBLEM** Casey had quesadillas at the restaurant. About how much should she leave if she wants to add a 15% tip for a dinner bill of $11.89?

### Example 1 Estimate the amount of the tip.

Estimate $11.89 as about $12.

**Think:**   15% = 10% + 5%

10% of $12 = $1.20

5% of $12 is half of $1.20, or $0.60

Add: $1.20 + $0.60 = $1.80

So, 15% of $11.89 is about $1.80.

You can use a proportion to find the amount of a tip.

### Example 2 The Marshalls went out to lunch. Their meals cost $24.16, and they left a 15% tip. How much did they spend on lunch in all?

**ONE WAY** Use a proportion.

$$15\% = \frac{15}{100}$$ — Write the percent as a ratio.

$$\frac{t}{24.16} = \frac{15}{100}$$ — Write a proportion. Let $t$ represent the amount of the tip.

$100 \times t = 15 \times 24.16$ — Use cross-multiplication.
$100t = 362.4$

$$\frac{100t}{100} = \frac{362.4}{100}$$ — Divide.

$t = 3.624$, or
    about 3.62 — Round to the nearest cent.

$24.16 + $3.62 = $27.78 — Add the tip to the cost.

**ANOTHER WAY** Use an equation.

$15\% = 0.15$ — Write the percent as a decimal.

$t = 0.15 \times 24.16$ — Write an equation. Let $t$ represent the tip. Multiply.

$t = 3.624$, or
    about 3.62 — Round to the nearest cent.

$24.16 + $3.62 = $27.78 — Add the tip to the cost.

So, the Marshalls spent $27.78 on lunch.

NS 1.4 Calculate given percentages of quantities and solve problems involving discounts at sales, interest earned, and tips. *also* NS 1.0, MR 2.2, MR 2.4, MR 2.5, MR 3.0, MR 3.2

## Guided Practice

**Estimate a 15% tip for each amount.**

1. $16.25

$16.25 \approx $16

10% of $16 = $1.60

5% of $16 = $0.80

$1.60 + $0.80 = ■

2. $4.95 3. $18.20 4. $22.15 ✓5. $11.85 ✓6. $39.50

7. **TALK Math** Explain how you could estimate the amount of a 20% tip for a dinner bill of $22.95.

## Independent Practice and Problem Solving

**Estimate a 15% tip for each amount.**

8. $14.00 9. $5.76 10. $24.85 11. $48.90 12. $7.89

13. $12.29 14. $33.65 15. $8.33 16. $54.83 17. $79.12

**Algebra** Use a proportion to find a 15% tip to the nearest cent.

18. $16.75 19. $55.00 20. $3.20 21. $26.30 22. $12.67

**Algebra** Find the total amount for the meal and the tip.

23. $28.00 with a 15% tip 24. $79.48 with a 20% tip 25. $18.77 with a 25% tip

26. Nell and her 3 friends spent a total of $75 for their dinner meal. They decided to leave a 15% tip and to divide the total cost of the dinner evenly among themselves. What was Nell's share of the dinner to the nearest cent?

27. Ed ordered 2 tacos and a raspberry lemonade for lunch. Each taco cost $3.15, and the raspberry lemonade cost $1.25. Ed left a 20% tip. How much money did Ed spend on lunch?

28. **Reasoning** How would you use multiplication by 10% to find a 15% tip for a meal that costs $40?

29. **WRITE Math** Explain how you would calculate a 20% tip on a restaurant bill of $32.50.

## Achieving the Standards

30. What is 5.25% written as a decimal? (O━ NS 1.1, p.24)

31. Robert gave Jess $5 and she now has $12. Write an equation to find the amount of money Jess had originally. (O━ AF 1.1, p.300)

32. What is the range of the list of numbers? 16, 5, 18, 12, 27, 8 (SDAP 1.1, p.224)

33. **Test Prep** About how much would you leave for a 20% tip with a dinner bill of $62.50?

A $3 C $12

B $6 D $20

## ALGEBRA
# Simple Interest

OBJECTIVE: Find simple interest.

## Learn

**PROBLEM** John received a $100 reward for finding a lost wallet. He put the money in a savings account at a simple interest rate of 4% per year for 3 years. How much interest will he earn?

The original amount you put in a bank account is called the **principal.** The bank regularly adds money to the account. The amount the bank adds is called interest.

**Simple interest** is a fixed percent of the principal and is paid yearly. Use the formula $I = p \times r \times t$, or $I = prt$, to calculate simple interest, where $I$ = interest, $p$ = principal, $r$ = interest rate per year, and $t$ = time in years.

**Remember**

To convert a percent to a decimal, divide by 100. You can do this by moving the decimal point two places to the left.

### Example 1  Find John's simple interest.

| | |
|---|---|
| $I = prt$ | Write the formula. |
| $I = \$100 \times 0.04 \times 3$ | $p = \$100$, $r = 4\%$, $t = 3$ years |
| $I = \$12$ | |

So, the simple interest is $12.

• Suppose the savings account pays interest after 6 months. How much interest will John's account earn after 6 months?

You may be charged simple interest on money that you borrow. The original amount you borrow is the principal. The amount charged is the interest.

### Example 2 Rosalie borrows $2,000 to help pay her college tuition. She will repay the money in 2 years at a simple interest rate of 7.5%. How much will she have to repay at the end of 2 years?

| | |
|---|---|
| $I = prt$ | Write the formula. |
| $I = \$2,000 \times 0.075 \times 2$ | $p = \$2,000$, $r = 7.5\%$, $t = 2$ years. |
| $I = \$300$ | |
| $\$300 + \$2,000 = \$2,300$ | Add the interest to the principal. |

So, Rosalie will have to repay $2,300.

• **What if** Rosalie borrows $2,000 for 10 years at a simple interest rate of 7.5%? How much will she have to repay at the end of 10 years?

O—π **NS 1.4** Calculate given percentages of quantities and solve problems involving discounts at sales, interest earned, and tips. *also* **MR 2.4, MR 2.5, MR 3.2**

## Guided Practice

1. How much interest will Celinda earn if she puts $500 in a savings account at a simple interest rate of 6% for 5 years?

$I = prt$
$= 500 \times 0.06 \times 5$
$= \blacksquare$

**Find the simple interest.**

2. principal: $200
   rate: 5%
   time: 1 year

3. principal: $750
   rate: 10.5%
   time: 3 years

4. principal: $125,000
   rate: 6%
   time 20 years

5. principal: $1,000
   rate: 8%
   time: 6 months

6. **TALK Math** Explain how you could find the interest earned on $10,000 in a savings account for 18 months with a simple interest rate of 8.5%.

## Independent Practice and Problem Solving

**Find the simple interest earned.**

7. principal: $900
   rate: 3%
   time: 3 years

8. principal: $8,000
   rate: 5.25%
   time: 10 years

9. principal: $100
   rate: 10%
   time: 2 years

10. principal: $100,000
    rate: 4.5%
    time: 15 years

**Find the total amount to be repaid for the loan.**

11. principal: $5,000
    rate: 5%
    time: 1 year

12. principal: $700
    rate: 6.25%
    time: 2 years

13. principal: $89,000
    rate: 4%
    time: 18 months

14. principal: $25,000
    rate: 7.5%
    time: 20 years

15. You want to borrow $30,000 for 10 years. How much more will you have to repay if the simple interest rate is 6.25% instead of 6%?

16. Jarvis put $2,000 in a savings account for 6 years at a simple interest rate of 6%. Melody put $2,400 in an account for 5 years at a rate of 5.5%. Who earned more interest? How much more?

17. **WRITE Math** What's the Error? Fiona calculated that she will earn $648 in 3 years with a principal of $360 and an interest rate of 6%. Find and correct her error.

## Achieving the Standards

18. $\angle A$ and $\angle B$ are complementary. If $m\angle A = 35°$, what is $m\angle B$? (O━┓ MG 2.2 p. 374 )

19. What is 7.25 written as a percent?
    (O━┓ NS 1.0, p. 24)

20. What is the median of the data set 37, 19, 42, 54, 42, 61? (SDAP 1.1, p. 224)

21. **Test Prep** How much simple interest is earned with a principal of $400 at a rate of 7% for 3 years?

    A $84          C $28

    B $56          D $7

**Extra Practice** on page 510, Set F

# LESSON 7

# Problem Solving Workshop
## Skill: Use a Formula

OBJECTIVE: Solve problems by using the skill *use a formula*.

Read to Understand
Plan
Solve
Check

## Read to Understand

**PROBLEM** The Harrises borrowed $5,000 at a simple interest rate to buy a swimming pool for their backyard. After 2 years, they repaid a total of $5,600, including $600 in interest. What was the simple interest rate?

If you know three of the four parts of the formula $I = prt$, you can solve for the fourth part.

You can solve for the simple interest rate since you know the amount of interest paid, the principal, and the time in years.

**Identify each detail.**

| amount of interest paid | principal | time in years |
|---|---|---|
| $600 | $5,000 | 2 |

**Determine how the details are related and what method can be used to solve the problem.**

$I = prt$      Write the formula.

$600 = 5,000 \times r \times 2$      Replace $I$ with 600, $p$ with 5,000, and $t$ with 2. Multiply 5,000 by 2.

$600 = 10,000r$

$\dfrac{600}{10,000} = \dfrac{10,000r}{10,000}$      Divide.

$0.06 = r$

So, the simple interest rate was 6% per year.

## Think and Discuss

**Use the formula $I = prt$.**

**a.** Brian borrowed $300 at a simple interest rate to buy a barbecue grill. After 2 years, he repaid a total of $318. What was the simple interest rate per year?

**b.** Shaniqua put some money in a savings account at a simple interest rate of 4.5% for 3 years. At the end of the 3 years, she had earned $81 in interest. How much money did Shaniqua originally put in the savings account?

**c.** Amber invests $2,000 in a savings account at a simple interest rate of 10%. For how many years will Amber have to keep her money in the savings account to earn $1,000 in interest?

**508**

NS 1.4 Calculate given percentages of quantities and solve problems involving discounts at sales, interest earned, and tips. *also* NS 1.0, AF 1.2, AF 2.3, MR 1.0, MR 2.0, MR 2.4, MR 2.5, MR 3.0, MR 3.1, MR 3.2, MR 3.3

1. The Chans borrowed $3,500 at a simple interest rate to build a new patio. After 5 years, they repaid a total of $4,025. What was the simple interest rate per year?

   **First,** identify the amount of interest paid, the principal, and the time in years.

   **Then,** replace variables in the formula $I = prt$ with the correct amount.

   **Finally,** solve the equation to find the simple interest rate per year.

✓ 2. What if the Chan family repaid a total of $4,375, including $875 interest, after 5 years? What would be the interest rate per year?

✓ 3. Bill swam a distance of 198 yards in 5.5 minutes. What was his rate in yards per minute? Use the formula $d = rt$.

## Mixed Applications

**USE DATA For 4–6, use the table.**

4. Lina uses the formula $F = \left(\frac{9}{5} \times C\right) + 32$ to convert degrees Celsius, C, to degrees Fahrenheit, F. What is the average July temperature for Las Vegas in degrees Fahrenheit? Round the answer to the nearest tenth degree.

5. Tomi plans to make a wall-size version of the temperature conversion chart for her classroom. She wants to arrange the five cities in order from least average July temperature to greatest average July temperature. In what order should she list the cities?

| Average Temperature July Conversion Chart | | |
|---|---|---|
| City | Fahrenheit | Ceisius |
| Boston | ? | 23.3°C |
| Los Angeles | 69.3°F | ? |
| Las Vegas | ? | 32.9°C |
| Portland, OR | 68.1°F | ? |
| San Francisco | 62.8°F | ? |

6. Al compares the average July temperatures for Boston and Los Angeles using the formula $C = \frac{5}{9} \times (F - 32)$. Which city has the higher average temperature and by how much? Write the answer in degrees Celsius, and round to the nearest tenth degree.

7. A train that is scheduled to arrive at 5:15 P.M. arrives 20 minutes late. If the train left at 9:30 A.M., how long was the trip?

8. A total of 51 students and teachers are using cars to go on a field trip. Six people can ride in each car. How many cars are needed for the trip?

9. In a survey, 35% of the students in a school said they had swimming pools. There are 420 students in the school. How many students said they had swimming pools in their backyards?

10. Rosalita ordered ten pizzas for her pool party. The cost of the pizzas was $79. Rosalita gave the delivery person a 20% tip. To the nearest cent, what was the total cost, including the tip?

11. In one week, Michael practices twice as long as Mya. Mya and Allison practice a total of 19 hr, but Allison practices 5 hr longer than Mya. How long does Michael practice?

12. **WRITE Math** Thirty-six students come for baseball and basketball tryouts. Twenty students try out only for baseball, and 8 try out for both sports. **Explain** how to find the number of students who try out for basketball only.

# Extra Practice

## Set A  Write the percent that is shaded. (pp. 492–493)

**1.**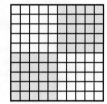

**2.**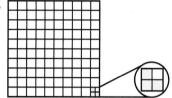

**3.**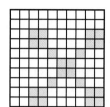

### Order from least to greatest.

**4.** 0.3%, 3%, 33%, 30%

**5.** 27%, 19%, 17%, 20%

**6.** 10%, 1%, 0.1%, 1.1%

**7.** 98%, 89%, 76%, 67%

**8.** 11%, 0.11%, 1.1%, 111%

**9.** 62%, 71%, 59%, 60%

**10.** 9%, 8.9%, 9.8%, 8.8%

**11.** 22%, 13%, 24%, 15%

**12.** 70%, 7%, 0.7%, 700%

## Set B  Write each decimal or fraction as a percent. (pp. 494–497)

**1.** $1\frac{1}{2}$

**2.** 0.7

**3.** 0.03

**4.** $\frac{1}{5}$

**5.** 2.9

**6.** 0.225

**7.** $\frac{3}{5}$

**8.** $\frac{5}{8}$

**9.** 0.15

**10.** 1.85

**11.** $\frac{3}{4}$

**12.** 0.957

**13.** 1.35

**14.** $2\frac{7}{10}$

**15.** 0.005

**16.** A local bakery baked apple pies to sell at the annual fair. Each apple pie required 10 apples and $\frac{3}{4}$ cup of sugar. What percent of a cup of sugar is being used for each apple pie?

**17.** A congressman conducted a survey. Of the constituents who responded, 0.85 said they planned to vote in the next election. What percent of the constituents plan to vote in the next election?

## Set C  Use a fraction or a decimal to find the percent of the number. (pp. 498–499)

**1.** 25% of 64

**2.** 40% of 45

**3.** 0.5% of 500

**4.** 200% of 22

**5.** 10% of 23

**6.** 150% of 46

**7.** 20% of 120

**8.** 300% of 2

**9.** 1% of 800

**10.** 20% of 82

**11.** 100% of 112

**12.** 25% of 256

**13.** 0.1% of 12

**14.** 250% of 34

**15.** 37.5% of 240

**16.** A photographer discovered that 20% of the 35 photographs he took during a photo shoot had to be retaken. How many photographs had to be retaken?

**17.** Miriam's volleyball team won 80% of the 25 games they played during the season. How many games did Miriam's volleyball team win?

 **Technology**
Use Harcourt Mega Math, Fraction Action, *Fraction Flare Up,* Level N.

## Set D  Find the sale price. (pp. 500–503)

1. regular price: $25
   discount rate: 15%

2. regular price: $185
   discount rate: 15%

3. regular price: $65
   discount rate: 10%

4. regular price: $325
   discount rate: 25%

5. regular price: $99
   discount rate: 20%

6. regular price: $62
   discount rate: 15%

7. regular price: $23
   discount rate: 50%

8. regular price: $5
   discount rate: 35%

### Find the total cost of the purchase. Round to the nearest cent.

9. price: $28.75
   sales tax rate: 6%

10. price: $110.95
    sales tax rate: 4.5%

11. price: $365.10
    sales tax rate: 5.5%

12. price: $1,265
    sales tax rate: 7.5%

13. price: $98.12
    sales tax rate: 6.5%

14. price: $45.86
    sales tax rate: 7%

15. price: $775.09
    sales tax rate: 5%

16. price: $3,596.62
    sales tax rate: 6.5%

## Set E  Estimate a 15% tip for each amount. (pp. 504–505)

1. $10.00
2. $5.66
3. $32.15
4. $43.25
5. $4.57

6. $22.31
7. $110.00
8. $26.23
9. $12.71
10. $18.65

11. Russ and his 2 friends spend a total of $66 for lunch. They divide the cost of the lunch and a 15% tip evenly among them. What is Russ's share of the tip and the meal to the nearest cent?

12. Karen orders a ham and cheese sandwich and an iced tea for dinner. The sandwich costs $4.95, and the iced tea costs $1.35. Karen gives a 20% tip. How much money does Karen spend on dinner?

## Set F  Find the simple interest earned. (pp. 506–507)

1. principal: $600
   rate: 5.25%
   time: 2 years

2. principal: $8,000
   rate: 3%
   time: 8 years

3. principal: $200
   rate: 8%
   time: 3 years

4. principal: $10,000
   rate: 3.5%
   time: 10 years

5. principal: $4,000
   rate: 6%
   time: 1 year

6. principal: $8,600
   rate: 12.25%
   time: 3 years

7. principal: $85,000
   rate: 4%
   time: 18 months

8. principal: $20,000
   rate: 6.25%
   time: 15 years

9. Shanna borrowed $4,000 to help pay her college tuition. She will repay the money in 4 years at a simple interest rate of 6.25%. How much will she have to repay at the end of 4 years?

10. Kim received a $200 prize for her work with disabled senior citizens. She put the money in a savings account at a simple interest rate of 4.95% for 2 years. How much interest will she earn?

11. Rick borrowed $4,250 to buy a motorcycle at a simple interest rate of 8%. How much did he pay back at the end of 3 years?

12. Elizabeth put $1,000 in a share certificate at a simple interest rate of 2%. In how many years will her principal double?

# Chapter 20 Review/Test

## Check Vocabulary and Concepts

**Choose the best term from the box.**

| VOCABULARY |
|---|
| discount |
| percent |
| principal |
| sales tax |

1. A __?__ is an amount that is subtracted from the regular price of an item. (NS 1.4, p. 500)
2. The __?__ is a percent of the cost of an item, added onto the item's cost. (NS 1.4, p. 501)
3. The original amount you put in an account is called the __?__. (NS 1.0, p. 506)

## Check Skills

**Order from least to greatest.** (NS 1.0, pp. 492-493)

4. 15%, 20%, 8%, 10.1%
5. 45%, 4.5%, 4%, 5%
6. 30%, 25%, 15%, 52%
7. 225%, 125%, 13.5%, 215%

**Write each decimal or fraction as a percent.** (NS 1.0, pp. 494-497)

8. 0.55
9. 0.3
10. $\frac{5}{8}$
11. $1\frac{3}{4}$
12. 1.06

**Use a fraction or decimal to find the percent of the number.** (NS 1.4, pp. 498-499)

13. 0.6% of 400
14. 135% of 14
15. 35% of 80
16. 15% of 110
17. 5% of 135

**Find the sale price.** (NS 1.4, pp. 500-503)

18. regular price: $124
    discount rate: 25%
19. regular price: $35
    discount rate: 15%
20. regular price: $7.50
    discount rate: 30%
21. regular price: $235
    discount rate: 45%

**Estimate a 15% tip for each amount.** (NS 1.4, pp. 504-505)

22. $12.34
23. $76.12
24. $6.75
25. $26.00
26. $43.06

**Find the simple interest earned.** (NS 1.4, pp. 506-507)

27. principal: $500
    rate: 5%
    time: 2 years
28. principal: $3,000
    rate: 4.25%
    time: 6 years
29. principal: $850
    rate: 8.5%
    time: 3 years
30. principal: $12,000
    rate: 3.5%
    time: 10 years

## Check Problem Solving

**Solve.** (NS 1.4, MR 2.0, pp. 508-509)

31. Nel invests $4,000 at a simple interest rate of 8%. How many years will it take Nel to earn $1,280 in interest?
32. Ron borrowed $400 at a simple interest rate. After 1 year, he repaid a total of $421 including $21 interest. What was the interest rate?
33. WRITE Math **Explain** how you would calculate a 20% tip on a restaurant bill of $18.50.

GO ONLINE **Technology** Use *Online Assessment.*

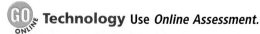

# Enrich • Percent of Increase and Decrease
## ⚓ Sea of Change! ⚓

Jorge counted 24 sea lions at Seal Rock this week. Last week, he counted 30 sea lions at Seal Rock. What is the percent of decrease?

**Percent of decrease** equals the amount of decrease divided by the original amount. You divide by the original amount because you are comparing the decrease to the original amount.

Find the percent of decrease.

$$\% \text{ decrease} = \frac{\text{amount of decrease}}{\text{original amount}}$$     Write the formula.

$$= \frac{30 - 24}{30} = \frac{6}{30} = \frac{1}{5}$$     Amount of decrease: 30 – 24 = 6
Original amount: 30

$$= \frac{1}{5} = 0.20, \text{ or } 20\%$$     Write the fraction as a percent.

So, the percent of decrease is 20%.

**Percent of increase** equals the amount of increase divided by the original amount. You divide by the original amount because you are comparing the increase to the original amount.

## All Aboard!

Tickets for a harbor cruise cost **$5 each during the day** and **$7 each at sunset. What is the percent of increase in price?**

$$\% \text{ increase} = \frac{\text{amount of increase}}{\text{original amount}}$$     Write the formula.

$$= \frac{7 - 5}{5} = \frac{2}{5}$$     Amount of increase: 7 – 5 = 2
Original amount: 5

$$= \frac{2}{5} = 0.40, \text{ or } 40\%$$     Write the fraction as a percent.

So, the percent of increase is 40%.

## Set Sail

**Find the percent of increase or decrease.**

1. 48 increased to 60
2. 30 decreased to 21
3. 8 increased to 9
4. $220 decreased to $33
5. 6 increased to 9
6. $1,500 increased to $3,000

## Go Home

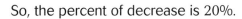 **WRITE Math** Is it possible to have a percent of increase greater than 100% or a percent of decrease greater than 100%? **Explain.**

# Unit Review/Test
## Chapters 18–20

## Multiple Choice

1. Coach Jim mixes sports drink for his players before each game. He mixes 4 gallons of water with 2 packs of drink mix. What is the ratio of gallons of water to packs of drink mix? (O—¬ NS 1.2, p. 442)

   **A** 3:1          **C** 5:3

   **B** 2:1          **D** 10:7

2. If 50% of a number is 40, what is 75% of the number? (O—¬ NS 1.4, p. 498)

   **A** 15          **C** 60

   **B** 30          **D** 75

3. How many inches are in $1\frac{3}{4}$ feet? (AF 2.1, p. 468)

   **A** 12 inches

   **B** 19 inches

   **C** 21 inches

   **D** 22 inches

4. Monique read a 150-page book in 10 hours. At that rate, how long will it take her to read a 225-page book? (O—¬ NS 1.3, p. 466)

   **A** 15 hours          **C** 20 hours

   **B** 17 hours          **D** 30 hours

5. A certain map uses a scale of 1 inch equals 30 miles. How many miles are represented by 4 inches on this map? (O—¬ NS 1.3, p. 466)

   **A** 4 miles

   **B** 30 miles

   **C** 40 miles

   **D** 120 miles

6. It takes a machine 14 minutes to fill 160 boxes of cereal. At this rate, how many boxes will the machine fill in 42 minutes? (O—¬ AF 2.2, p. 446)

   **A** 188 boxes          **C** 480 boxes

   **B** 320 boxes          **D** 588 boxes

7. $\triangle DEF$ is similar to $\triangle XYZ$. What is the length of $\overline{XZ}$? (O—¬ NS 1.3, p. 478)

   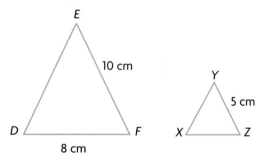

   **A** 3 centimeters          **C** 5 centimeters

   **B** 4 centimeters          **D** 12 centimeters

8. The chairman of the board took her staff out to lunch. If the lunch was $125 and she gave a 15% tip, how much money did she spend on lunch? (O—¬ NS 1.4, p. 504)

   **A** $18.75          **C** $143.75

   **B** $106.25          **D** $152.75

9. How many centimeters are in $2\frac{3}{4}$ meters? (AF 2.1, p. 468)

   **A** 75 centimeters

   **B** 225 centimeters

   **C** 255 centimeters

   **D** 275 centimeters

**GO ONLINE Technology** Use *Online Assessment.*

10. A farmer harvested 9,600 pounds of cotton from a 12-acre field. Which proportion could be solved to find y, the expected harvest from a 40-acre field? (O—¬ NS 1.3, p. 464)

A $\frac{12}{9,600} = \frac{y}{40}$

B $\frac{12}{9,600} = \frac{40}{y}$

C $\frac{40}{9,600} = \frac{y}{12}$

D $\frac{40}{9,600} = \frac{12}{y}$

11. Jon spent $4.25 to wash his car. If one quarter operates the car wash for 60 seconds, how long did it take him to wash his car? (O—¬ AF 2.2, p. 446)

A  10 minutes     C  17 minutes

B  16 minutes     D  42.5 minutes

12. Which is equivalent to 3:4? (O—¬ NS 1.2, p. 442)

A  6:9     C  13:14

B  8 to 10     D  15 to 20

13. Lucy's chess team won 60% of the 30 tournaments they entered. How many tournaments did they win? (O—¬ NS 1.4, p. 498)

A  6     C  18

B  12     D  60

14. The sale price of a car is $6,500. The discount is 20%. What was the original price of the car? (O—¬ NS 1.4, p. 500)

A  $5,500     C  $7,125

B  $6,500     D  $8,125

## Short Response

15. The Chen family is driving from San Francisco to Los Angeles, a distance of 380 miles. They have traveled 95 miles in 2 hours. At this rate, how long will it take them to make the complete trip? (AF 2.3, p. 448)

16. Seventeen out of 85 families living in town have high-speed Internet access. What fraction of families living in town do not have high-speed Internet access? (O—¬ NS 1.2, p. 442)

17. Nancy's team won 3 out of the first 7 games. How many of the next 28 games should her team expect to win? (O—¬ NS 1.3, p. 466)

18. When wheel B turns 4 revolutions, wheel A turns 1 revolution. When wheel B turns 24 revolutions, how many revolutions does wheel A turn? (O—¬ NS 1.3, p. 466)

19. James harvests 30 apples in 5 minutes. Write a proportion that could be used to find how many apples James can harvest in 2 hours. (O—¬ NS 1.3, p. 464)

20. The ratio of white cars to blue cars on a city street is 3:5. If there are 15 blue cars, how many white cars are there? (O—¬ NS 1.2, p. 446)

## Extended Response ⟨WRITE Math⟩▸

21. Rafael purchased a new snowboard for $375. The sales tax was 6%. What was the total cost of the purchase? **Explain** how you found your answer. (O—¬ NS 1.4, p. 500)

22. A pickup truck can travel 15 miles on 1 gallon of diesel fuel. How many gallons of diesel fuel would the pickup truck need to travel 225 miles? **Explain** how you found your answer. (O—¬ NS 1.3, p. 466)

23. Kim canoes along the Eel River at an average rate of 8 kilometers per hour. How long will it take her to canoe 32 kilometers? **Explain** how you found your answer. (AF 2.3, p. 448)

# Solar Power–Energy for the future?

## SOLAR POWER

**S**ome houses and buildings obtain energy from the sun to generate electricity. California is a leading state in solar power use. However, less than 1% of the energy produced in the U.S. comes from solar power. One reason solar power is not used more often is due to the cost of the panels used to collect solar energy. Another reason is not all areas receive enough sunlight to make the use of solar energy practical.

Solar powered house in California

## FACT·ACTIVITY

**Use the diagram to answer the questions.**

❶ The diagram of the solar panels shows a 5 x 8 array of modules and the percentages of energy needed for each use. Write the ratio of home heating and cooling.

❷ In the diagram, nine panels are needed for water heating, compared to 15 panels for home heating. If a larger house has solar panels in a 20 x 32 array, how many panels would the larger house need for water heating and home heating? Write a proportion.

❸ Suppose lights and appliances make up 25% of your home's energy consumption. In the month of August, your energy bill was $216. What was the cost of running your lights and appliances?

❹ **Pose a Problem** Write a problem like problem 2, but change the size of the larger array.

Water Heating 22.5%

Home Heating 37.5%

Cooling 15%

Appliances 25%

# SOLAR POWERED RIDES

Other objects can also use solar power. In Santa Monica, there is a Ferris wheel that lights up the night sky by using solar energy. The 130-foot ride generates more than 71,000 kilowatt hours of energy from the sun. Another solar-powered ride is a carousel at the Solar Living Institute, in Hopland, California. The carousel was built in 2005 by William Henry Dentzel III, whose family has been making carousels for five generations.

## FACT·ACTIVITY

**Design an everyday item to be solar powered.**

❶ What is the item you chose? How will you modify your item so that it is solar powered? Draw a diagram to show the modifications.

❷ Suppose your item requires 2 kilowatts of energy per hour. If the cost of energy is 30 cents per kilowatt hour, how much does it cost to run your item for 1 hour? 24 hours?

❸ Los Angeles has an average of 5.62 hours of direct sunlight a day. Each hour the sun generates about 1 kilowatt of energy to a square yard on Earth. Write a ratio to show how many kilowatts would be generated in a square yard in Los Angeles in one day. Now write a ratio showing how many kilowatts would be generated in a week.

❹ Since your modified item will be using solar energy, explain the importance of knowing the average amount of sunlight in your city.

# Probability

# Math on Location

**①**

▲ The engineering of the software that operates a robot reduces the likelihood or probability of failure.

**②**

▲ Many interacting elements are put together to build a robotic system with a high probability of success.

**③**

▲ The robot has more than enough backup systems or redundancies for each action to reduce chances of failure.

# VOCABULARY POWER

## TALK Math

What math is used in the **Math on Location**? How can you use probability when designing robots?

## READ Math

**REVIEW VOCABULARY** You learned the words below when you learned the basics about probability. How do these words relate to **Math on Location**?

**experimental probability** the ratio of the number of times an event occurs to the total number of trials, or times the activity is performed

**outcome** a possible result of an experiment

## WRITE Math

Copy and complete the Frayer model below. Use what you learn about probability to make another model for dependent events.

### Independent Events

| Definition | Characteristics |
|---|---|
|  | Two or more events Events independent of each other Multiply probability of each event |
| **Examples** | **Non-examples** |
| Rolling two number cubes | Choosing two cards from a deck without |
| Flipping three coins Choosing a ball in a bag, replacing it, and choosing another ball | replacement Choosing a ball in a bag, and then choosing another ball without replacement |

(center label: Independent events)

**Technology**
Multimedia Math Glossary link at
www.harcourtschool.com/hspmath

# 21 Probability of Simple Events

**The Big Idea** Probability measures the likelihood of simple events and provides the basis for making predictions.

## Investigate

Suppose you are at Six Flags Magic Mountain for the day. The table below lists various rides available at the park. You have time for only one more ride, so you choose one at random from a list. How can you find the probability of choosing a particular ride? Of choosing a specific type of ride?

### Magic Mountain Rides

| Ride Name | Ride Type |
|---|---|
| Log Jammer | Water ride |
| Psyclone | Wooden roller coaster |
| Revolution | Steel roller coaster |
| Roaring Rapids | Water ride |
| Viper | Steel roller coaster |

**CALIFORNIA FAST FACT**

Six Flags Magic Mountain, located in Valencia, California, is home to Viper. The largest looping roller coaster in the world, it towers 188 feet high.

**GO ONLINE**

**Technology**
Student pages are available in the Student eBook.

# Show What You Know

Check your understanding of important skills
needed for success in Chapter 21.

▶ **Simplest Form of Fractions**

Write each fraction in simplest form.

1. $\frac{3}{12}$    2. $\frac{6}{9}$    3. $\frac{24}{40}$    4. $\frac{15}{40}$    5. $\frac{42}{56}$

6. $\frac{36}{78}$    7. $\frac{18}{75}$    8. $\frac{33}{55}$    9. $\frac{60}{96}$    10. $\frac{72}{120}$

11. $\frac{39}{90}$    12. $\frac{60}{72}$    13. $\frac{70}{130}$    14. $\frac{55}{200}$    15. $\frac{200}{600}$

▶ **Fractions, Decimals, and Percents**

Write each fraction as a decimal and percent.

16. $\frac{3}{5}$    17. $\frac{1}{8}$    18. $\frac{9}{10}$    19. $\frac{3}{4}$    20. $\frac{7}{20}$

21. $\frac{14}{25}$    22. $\frac{1}{4}$    23. $\frac{7}{25}$    24. $\frac{4}{5}$    25. $\frac{9}{25}$

26. $\frac{3}{10}$    27. $\frac{7}{8}$    28. $\frac{3}{20}$    29. $\frac{1}{25}$    30. $\frac{4}{50}$

▶ **Certain, Impossible, Likely, Unlikely**

Tell if the event is certain, impossible, likely, or unlikely.

31. Next week having more than 7 days
32. Talking on the phone to a friend tomorrow

33. October following September
34. Watching 7 movies in one day

35. Walking 100 mi in one day
36. Four quarters equaling one dollar

37. Rain falling in the desert
38. Draw a blue tile from a bag of green tiles

# VOCABULARY POWER

**CHAPTER VOCABULARY**

disjoint events
experimental probability
outcome
probability
sample space
theoretical probability

**WARM-UP WORDS**

**outcome** a possible result of a probability experiment

**sample space** the set of all possible outcomes

**probability** a measure of the likelihood that an event will occur

# Theoretical Probability

OBJECTIVE: Find the probability of a simple event.

## Learn

When you perform an experiment, a possible result of that experiment is called an **outcome**. The **sample space** of an experiment is the set of all possible outcomes.

The **theoretical probability** of an event, written P(event), is the ratio of the number of favorable outcomes to the number of possible, equally likely outcomes. This ratio can be written in fraction form.

$$P(event) = \frac{\text{number of favorable outcomes}}{\text{number of possible, equally likely outcomes}}$$

The probability of an event is a measure of the likelihood that the event will occur. Numerically, this measure ranges from 0, or impossible, to 1, or certain. The closer the probability is to 1, the more likely the event is to occur.

impossible  unlikely          likely    certain

0          $\frac{1}{2}$, 0.5          1

**PROBLEM** Brenda and 7 other students are in the Agriculture Club. Each student's name is written on equally-sized cards and placed in a bag. The person whose name is randomly drawn runs the meeting. What is the probability that Brenda's name will be drawn? Write the answer as a fraction, a decimal, and a percent.

## Example 1

| | |
|---|---|
| 1 favorable outcome: Brenda | Count the favorable outcomes. |
| 8 possible outcomes: 8 different names in the bag | Count the possible outcomes. |
| $P(Brenda) = \frac{1}{8}$ ← favorable ← possible | Write the ratio of favorable outcomes to possible outcomes. |

So, the probability of drawing Brenda's name is $\frac{1}{8}$, 0.125, or 12.5%.

• Is drawing Brenda's name impossible, unlikely, likely, or certain?

## Example 2

Each letter of the word CHALLENGES is written on equally-sized cards and placed in a bag. Find the probability of randomly drawing the given letter. Write the answer as a fraction, a decimal, and a percent.

**A** $P(H) = \frac{1}{10}$, 0.1, or 10%  ← 1 choice out of 10 is the letter H

**B** $P(L) = \frac{2}{10}$  ← 2 choices out of 10 are the letter L

$= \frac{1}{5}$, 0.2, or 20%

○━⊓ SDAP 3.3 Represent probabilities as ratios, proportions, decimals between 0 and 1, and percentages between 0 and 100 and verify that the probabilities computed are reasonable; know that if P is the probability of an event, 1-P is the probability of the event not occurring. *also* SDAP 3.0, MR 2.4, MR 2.5, MR 3.0, MR 3.2, MR 3.3

# Probability of an Event Not Occurring

The probability that an event will not occur is written P(not event).

**Example 3** Marc is one of 10 students at an Agriculture Club meeting. Each student's name is written on equally-sized cards and placed in a bag. One card is randomly drawn. What is the probability that Marc's name will not be drawn? Write each answer as a fraction, a decimal, and a percent.

| 9 favorable outcomes: | 9 names other than Marc | Count the favorable outcomes. |
|---|---|---|
| 10 possible outcomes: | 10 different names | Count the possible outcomes. |
| P(not Marc) = $\frac{9}{10}$ ← favorable ← possible | | Write the ratio of favorable outcomes to possible outcomes. |

So, the probability of not drawing Marc's name is $\frac{9}{10}$, 0.9, or 90%.

- What is the result when you add the probability of drawing Marc's name to the probability of not drawing Marc's name?

The sum of P(event) and P(not event) is always 1. So, if P is the probability of an event occurring, then $1 - P$ is the probability of an event not occurring.

$$P(\text{event}) + P(\text{not event}) = 1$$

$$P(\text{not event}) = 1 - P(\text{event})$$

**Example 4** Use the spinner at the right to find each probability. Write each answer as a fraction, a decimal, and a percent.

**A** P(not red) = 1 − P(red)
$= 1 - \frac{3}{8} = \frac{5}{8}$

**B** P(not yellow) = 1 − P(yellow)
$= 1 - \frac{1}{4} = \frac{3}{4}$

So, P(not red) is $\frac{5}{8}$, 0.625, or $62\frac{1}{2}$%.

So, P(not yellow) is $\frac{3}{4}$, 0.75, or 75%.

## Guided Practice

1. Equally-sized cards labeled 1 to 8 are placed in a bag. A card is randomly drawn. What is the probability of drawing a number greater than 2?

   P(greater than 2) = $\frac{\blacksquare}{8}$ = $\frac{\blacksquare}{4}$

For 2–4, use the spinner at the right to find each probability. Write each answer as a fraction, a decimal, and a percent.

2. P(yellow)  **✓3.** P(brown)  4. P(not brown)  **✓5.** P(not yellow)

6. **TALK Math** Explain how to find the probability of rolling a 4 using a number cube labeled 1 to 6?

**For 7–15, use the spinner at the right to find each probability. Write each answer as a fraction, a decimal, and a percent.**

**7.** P(purple)  **8.** P(yellow)  **9.** P(green)  **10.** P(not blue)

**11.** P(white)  **12.** P(not brown)  **13.** P(not purple)  **14.** P(not orange)  **15.** P(red)

**Equally-sized cards labeled 1, 1, 2, 3, 3, 4, 5, 7, 8, and 9 are placed in a box. A card is randomly drawn. Find each probability. Express the answer as a fraction, a decimal, and a percent.**

**16.** P(1)  **17.** P(not 4)  **18.** P(not even)

**19.** P(not divisible by 3)  **20.** P(3)  **21.** P(divisible by 1)

**22.** P(12)  **23.** P(less than 3)  **24.** P(not greater than 5)

**USE DATA** **For 25–27, use the table at the right.**

**25.** What is the probability that a club member chosen at random is not 12 years old?

**26.** One member is randomly chosen to attend a national competition for young chess players. Find the probability that the member chosen is 13 years old.

**27.** A member is chosen at random. Find the probability that the member's first name begins with the letter T. Then find the probability that the member's first name does not begin with T.

**28.** **Reasoning** Can a probability ever be greater than 1? **Explain.**

**29.** **WRITE Math** **What's the Question?** Equally-sized cards labeled 2, 2, 2, 4, 4, and 5 are placed in a bag. The answer is 50%.

| Chess Club | |
|---|---|
| **Member** | **Age** |
| Franz | 12 |
| Kim | 11 |
| Travis | 12 |
| Andrea | 13 |
| Ned | 13 |
| Guy | 12 |
| Trent | 12 |
| Nathan | 12 |

## Achieving the Standards

**30.** Find the value of x. (○━┓ NS 1.3, p. 466)

$$\frac{15}{x} = \frac{3}{13}$$

**31.** A vacuum cleaner that regularly sells for $240 is on sale at a 15% discount. Find the sale price of the vacuum. (○━┓ NS 1.4, p. 500)

**32.** Write $\frac{32}{48}$ in simplest form. (○━┓ NS 2.4, p.8)

**33.** **Test Prep** Josh chooses from equally-sized flower seed packs without looking. What is the probability that he will choose zinnia seeds?

| | Cosmos | Pansy | Zinnia | Daisy |
|---|---|---|---|---|
| **Seed Packs** | 4 | 8 | 12 | 6 |

**A** 13%  **B** 20%  **C** 27%  **D** 40%

**Technology**
Use Harcourt Mega Math, Fraction
Action, *Last Chance Canyon*, Level H.

# Write to Prove or Disprove

**WRITE Math WORKSHOP**

**S**ometimes you must evaluate whether a statement is true or false. You can use math ideas and logical reasoning to prove or disprove your answer.

Sam reads the word problem below on a math test.

The table shows the contents of a bag of equally-sized marbles. Clark says the probability of randomly choosing red is higher than the probability of randomly choosing any other color. Is his claim correct?

| Red | Blue | Green | Yellow |
|-----|------|-------|--------|
| 16  | 12   | 10    | 12     |

Read how Sam evaluated Clark's claim.

> To prove or disprove Clark's claim, first find the probability of selecting each color.
>
> $P(red) = 32\%$, $P(blue) = 24\%$
> $P(green) = 20\%$, $P(yellow) = 24\%$
>
> Next, compare the probabilities.
>
> $32\% > 24\%$ and $32\% > 20\%$
>
> $P(red)$ has the greatest percent.
>
> Finally, write a logical explanation.
>
> It is true that $32\%$ is greater than $20\%$ and $24\%$. So, the probability of choosing red is greater than the probability of choosing any of the other three colors. Therefore, Clark's claim is true.

## Tips

**To prove or disprove a claim:**

- Do the math computations that will support your explanation.

- Explain the steps you took and the reasoning you used.

- Summarize your paragraph using words such as *so* and *therefore*.

- State whether the claim is *true* or *not true*.

---

**Problem Solving** The tiles and beads are placed in different bags.

**Prove or disprove each claim.**

1. The probability of randomly choosing a white tile is twice that of randomly choosing a brown tile.

2. The probability of randomly choosing a maroon tile is 30%.

3. The probability of randomly selecting a silver bead is the same as the probability of tossing heads on a coin.

| Equally-Sized Tiles | | | | |
|--------|--------|-------|--------|-------|
| Orange | Purple | Brown | Maroon | White |
| 8 | 8 | 5 | 9 | 10 |

| Equally-Sized Beads | | |
|--------|------|-----------|
| Silver | Gold | Turquoise |
| 10 | 6 | 4 |

**Chapter 21 525**

# 2 Disjoint Events

**OBJECTIVE:** Tell whether events are disjoint or not and find the probability of disjoint events.

## Learn

Two or more events that cannot happen at the same time are called **disjoint events**. When events are disjoint, you can add their probabilities to find the probability that either event will occur: $P(A \text{ or } B) = P(A) + P(B)$.

**PROBLEM** A spinner has 8 equal sections. The blue sections have even numbers, and the yellow sections have odd numbers. What is the probability that the pointer will land on either a 1 or a 4?

### Example 1 Find P(1 or 4).

The pointer cannot land on a 1 and a 4 at the same time, so these are disjoint events.

$P(1) = \frac{1}{8} \leftarrow \frac{\text{favorable outcomes}}{\text{possible outcomes}}$

$P(4) = \frac{1}{8} \leftarrow \frac{\text{favorable outcomes}}{\text{possible outcomes}}$

$P(1 \text{ or } 4) = P(1) + P(4)$

$= \frac{1}{8} + \frac{1}{8} = \frac{2}{8}, \text{ or } \frac{1}{4}$

*Determine whether the events are disjoint.*

*Find P(1).*

*Find P(4).*

*P(A or B) = P(A) + P(B)*

So, P(1 or 4) is $\frac{1}{4}$, 0.25, or 25%.

### Example 2 A regular 10-sided polyhedron is labeled 1 to 10. Find P(even or 3). Are the events disjoint?

You cannot roll an even number and a 3 at the same time, so they are disjoint events.

$P(\text{even}) = \frac{5}{10} \leftarrow \frac{\text{favorable outcomes}}{\text{possible outcomes}}$    $P(3) = \frac{1}{10} \leftarrow \frac{\text{favorable outcomes}}{\text{possible outcomes}}$

$P(\text{even or 3}) = P(\text{even}) + P(3)$

$= \frac{5}{10} + \frac{1}{10} = \frac{6}{10}, \text{ or } \frac{3}{5}$

*Determine whether the events are disjoint.*

*Find P(even) and P(3).*

*P(A or B) = P(A) + P(B)*

So, rolling an even number and rolling a 3 are disjoint events, and P(even or 3) is $\frac{3}{5}$, 0.6, or 60%.

- Tell whether spinning a yellow or a 5 on the spinner above are disjoint events. Explain.

## Guided Practice

1. Use the spinner at the right. Tell whether spinning a B and spinning a vowel are disjoint events . If so, find P(B or vowel).

   Spinning a B or a vowel are disjoint events. P(B or vowel) = P(B) + P(vowel).

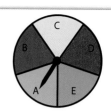

**The contents of a jar are shown. Cards are randomly drawn. Tell whether the events are disjoint. If so, find the probability.**

2. P(K or B)    ✓3. P(B or consonant)    ✓4. P(L or vowel)

5. **TALK Math** Explain how you can tell whether or not two events are disjoint.

## Independent Practice and Problem Solving

**The contents of a jar are shown. Cards are randomly drawn. Tell whether the events are disjoint. If so, find the probability.**

6. P(2 or 3)

7. P(5 or odd number)

8. P(4 or number divisible by 2)

9. P(8 or number less than 8)

10. P(7 or even number)

11. P(2, 4, or 7)

**Opal tosses a regular 8-sided polyhedron labeled 1 to 8. Find the probability.**

12. P(1 or 3)    13. P(odd or 4)    14. P(2, 4, or 6)    15. P(even, 1, or 5)

**For 16–19, use the spinner at the right.**

16. Find the probability of spinning an H or spinning orange.

17. Find the probability of Hannah spinning one of the letters from her name.

18. Find P(green or purple) and find P(vowel or G). Which set of disjoint events is more likely?

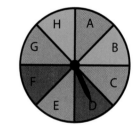

19. **Pose a Problem** Look back at problem 18. Change the events so that they are disjoint and their probabilities add up to 1.

20. **WRITE Math** Geena tosses a number cube labeled 1 to 6. Describe a set of disjoint events and a set of events that are not disjoint.

## Achieving the Standards

21. Verne walks 14 meters in 7 seconds. At what rate is he traveling? (○━┓ AF 2.2, p. 448)

22. Draw a quadrilateral that has no congruent angles or sides. (MG 2.3, p. 404)

23. Mona tosses a number cube labeled 1 to 6. Find P(odd). (○━┓ SDAP 3.3, p.522)

24. **Test Prep** The table shows the contents of a bag of marbles. Find P(red or green).

| Red | Green | Blue | White |
|-----|-------|------|-------|
| 5 | 7 | 18 | 10 |

   **A** 0.05    **B** 0.125    **C** 0.175    **D** 0.3

# Problem Solving Workshop
## Skill: Evaluate Answers for Reasonableness

**OBJECTIVE:** Solve problems by using the skill evaluate answers for reasonableness.

## Use the Skill

**PROBLEM** A clothing rack has 8 denim skirts in sizes 2, 5, 6, 8, 9, 10, 12, and 14. Tina assumes that if you randomly select a skirt off the rack, the probability that it is an even size is $\frac{1}{4}$. Is her assumption reasonable?

When you evaluate an answer for reasonableness, you must read and understand the problem.

Reread the paragraph and use logical reasoning.

The probability must be between 0 and 1. Tina's answer checks out.

$$0 \le \frac{1}{4} \le 1$$

Examine the favorable outcomes and the sample space.

| favorable outcomes: | sample space: |
|---|---|
| 2, 6, 8, 10, 12, 14 | 2, 5, 6, 8, 9, 10, 12, 14 |
| 6 total | 8 total |

You can see that more than $\frac{1}{2}$ of the skirts are even sizes, so the probability should be greater than $\frac{1}{2}$. Since $\frac{1}{4} < \frac{1}{2}$, Tina's answer does not check out.

So, in this situation a probability of $\frac{1}{4}$ is not reasonable.

## Think and Discuss
**Tell whether the statement is reasonable. Explain your reasoning.**

a. An employee at a store brings out a box of brown leather belts. The sizes in the box are 8, 8, 10, 12, 12, 12, 14, and 16. A manager asks the employee to hand him a belt in size 9. The employee tells the manager that since the box contains only even sizes, the probability that he will randomly select a size 9 is ⁻0.25.

b. The table shows the contents of a container of equally-sized key chains in a department store. The cashier says that if you randomly select one, the probability that it is silver is $\frac{1}{4}$.

| Gold | Silver | Bronze | Pewter |
|---|---|---|---|
| 6 | 10 | 12 | 12 |

SDAP 3.3 Represent probabilities as ratios, proportions, decimals between 0 and 1, and percentages between 0 and 100 and verify that the probabilities computed are reasonable. *also* MR 1.0, MR 2.0, MR 2.4, MR 2.5, MR 2.7, MR 3.0, MR 3.1, MR 3.2, MR 3.3

**Tell whether the statement is reasonable. Explain your reasoning.**

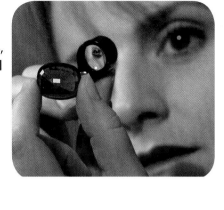

1. A new shipment of jewelry sets arrived. The clerk needs to locate one of each type for display. The shipment contains 8 ruby pendants, 8 turquoise pendants, 5 silver pendants, and 3 emerald pendants. All the pendants are the same size. The clerk says the probability of randomly choosing a ruby pendant is 50%.

   **First,** use logical reasoning to determine boundaries for the answer. A probability as a percent must be between 0% and 100%.

   $0\% \leq 50\% \leq 100\%$

   **Then,** examine the favorable outcomes and the sample space.

   |favorable outcomes: | sample space: |
   |---|---|
   |(8 ruby pendants) | $(8 + 8 + 5 + 3) = 24$ total pendants |

   **Finally,** explain whether or not the answer is reasonable.

2. **What if** there are 16 jewelry sets on the display table and 8 of them have ruby pendants? Would it be reasonable to say that the probability of choosing a jewelry set with a ruby pendant is $\frac{1}{2}$?

3. Lisa spins the pointer at the right to win a discount coupon through a promotion offered at a popular shoe store. The owner tells her that the probability of winning a $10 or a $2 discount is 25%.

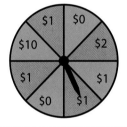

## Mixed Applications

4. The sum of Kyle's and Scott's ages is 40 yr. Kyle is 6 yr. older than Scott. How old is Kyle?

5. Emma is thinking of two powers of 3. Their difference is 72. What are the two powers of 3?

6. Christopher spent a total of $48.95 at a department store. He bought shorts for $19.75, a T-shirt for $16.25, and socks for $2.59 per pair. How many pairs of socks did he buy?

7. Each week, Josephine has to fill one shelf of Hal's Grocery Store's cooler with 16 bottles of fresh fruit juice. How many bottles of fruit juice will she put on the shelf in one year?

8. Janna exercises each morning by walking in the local shopping mall. It takes Janna $20\frac{3}{4}$ min to walk the perimeter of the shopping mall. She decreases her time by $\frac{3}{4}$ min each day. In how many days will she be able to walk the perimeter of the mall in 17 min?

9. The table shows the cost, $c$, for several quantities of spools of thread, $t$. How much should 14 spools of thread cost?

   | $t$ | 2 | 4 | 6 | 8 |
   |---|---|---|---|---|
   | $c$ | $1.50 | $3.00 | $4.50 | $6.00 |

10. Mr. Hanks has $14,353.14 to spend on advertising for his store. Each half-page ad costs $1,500. How many full pages of advertising can he buy?

11. Look back at Problem 10. How much more money would Mr. Hanks need in his budget to pay for 13 full pages?

12. **WRITE Math** The table shows the contents of a box of randomly mixed cotton shorts. Virginia says the probability of randomly selecting blue shorts from the box is $\frac{3}{4}$. **Explain** whether her statement is reasonable.

    | Black | Blue | Tan | White |
    |---|---|---|---|
    | 10 | 8 | 14 | 18 |

# 4 Experimental Probability

OBJECTIVE: Find the experimental probability of an event.

## Quick Review

Simplify.

1. $\frac{6}{18}$    2. $\frac{9}{24}$

3. $\frac{10}{25}$    4. $\frac{3}{12}$

5. $\frac{14}{16}$

## Vocabulary

experimental probability

## Learn

The **experimental probability** of an event is the number of times the outcome occurs compared to the total number of trials, or the total number of times you do the experiment. This can be expressed as a ratio in fraction form.

$$P(event) = \frac{\text{number of favorable outcomes that occur}}{\text{total number of trials}}$$

**PROBLEM** Keisha has a container of congruent square tiles that are either red, orange, yellow, or green. She randomly selects a tile, records its color, and replaces the tile. She does this activity 20 times and records her results in a table. What is the experimental probability of randomly selecting each color?

| Color | Red | Orange | Yellow | Green |
|---|---|---|---|---|
| Times Selected | 2 | 11 | 4 | 3 |

## Example Find the experimental probability.

Use the results in the table to write the probability of selecting each color.

$P(red) = \frac{favorable}{total\ trials} \rightarrow \frac{2}{20}$ or $\frac{1}{10}$, 0.1, 10%        $P(orange) = \frac{favorable}{total\ trials} \rightarrow \frac{11}{20}$, 0.55, 55%

$P(yellow) = \frac{favorable}{total\ trials} \rightarrow \frac{4}{20}$ or $\frac{1}{5}$, 0.2, 20%        $P(green) = \frac{favorable}{total\ trials} \rightarrow \frac{3}{20}$, 0.15, 15%

So, the experimental probabilities are $P(red) = \frac{1}{10}$, $P(orange) = \frac{11}{20}$, $P(yellow) = \frac{1}{5}$, and $P(green) = \frac{3}{20}$.

- Which tiles do you think are the most and least common in the container? Explain.

### Math Idea

Notice that you do not know how many of each color of tile Keisha has in the container. Experimental probability is calculated only on the results of the experimental trials.

## Guided Practice

1. Lydia tosses a coin 40 times and records her results in the table. Find the experimental probability of tossing each side of the coin.

| Heads | Tails |
|---|---|
| 28 | 12 |

$P(heads) = \frac{\blacksquare}{40}$ or $\frac{\blacksquare}{10}$, 0.7, 70%        $P(tails) = \frac{\blacksquare}{40}$ or $\frac{\blacksquare}{10}$, 0.3, 30%

SDAP 3.0 Students determine theoretical and experimental probabilities and use them to make predictions about events. *also* O—🔑 SDAP 3.3, MR 2.4, MR 2.5, MR 3.2

Equally-sized marbles are in a bag. Ed randomly selects a marble from the bag and then replaces it 50 times. For 2–5, use his results to find the experimental probability.

| Color | Red | Blue | Green | White |
|---|---|---|---|---|
| Times Selected | 9 | 18 | 8 | 15 |

**2.** P(red)  **3.** P(blue)  ✓**4.** P(green)  ✓**5.** P(white)

**6.** (TALK Math) **Explain** how you can use experimental results to find the experimental probability of an event.

## Independent Practice and Problem Solving

Equally-sized numbered tiles labeled 1 to 4 are in a bag. Emily randomly selects a tile from the bag 16 times and replaces her tile each time. For 7–10, use her results to find experimental probability.

| Number | 1 | 2 | 3 | 4 |
|---|---|---|---|---|
| Times Selected | 2 | 4 | 6 | 4 |

**7.** P(1)  **8.** P(2)  **9.** P(3)  **10.** P(4)

Louise and Mark each toss a number cube and record their results. Find the experimental probability of tossing each number.

**11.**

| Louise | | | | | | | |
|---|---|---|---|---|---|---|---|
| Number | 1 | 2 | 3 | 4 | 5 | 6 | Total Trials |
| Tosses | 3 | 4 | 3 | 6 | 5 | 4 | 25 |

**12.**

| Mark | | | | | | | |
|---|---|---|---|---|---|---|---|
| Number | 1 | 2 | 3 | 4 | 5 | 6 | Total Trials |
| Tosses | 9 | 8 | 7 | 10 | 9 | 7 | 50 |

**13.** Colleen and Bill each have 2 cards labeled A and B. They each lay a card down at the same time and record the outcome. They do this 70 times and record their results in the table at the right. Find the experimental probability that Colleen will lay down B and Bill will lay down A.

| Outcome | Times Recorded |
|---|---|
| Both A | 19 |
| Colleen–A, Bill–B | 16 |
| Colleen–B, Bill–A | 14 |
| Both B | 21 |

**14.** Make a bag of 4 index cards labeled 1, 2, 3, or 4. Draw a card, record its number, and replace the card. Repeat this 30 times. Combine your results with 3 other students to find the experimental probability of drawing each number. Then compare the experimental probabilities with the theoretical probabilities of drawing each number.

**15.** **Reasoning** Can experimental probability be negative? **Explain.**

**16.** (WRITE Math) Compare and contrast the methods for finding experimental and theoretical probabilities.

## Achieving the Standards

**17.** Draw a right isosceles triangle.
(O—¬ MG 2.3, p. 392)

**18.** Solve $3x = 36$. (O—¬ AF 1.1, p. 336)

**19.** Find the theoretical probability of tossing heads on a coin. (O—¬ SDAP 3.3, p. 522)

**20.** **Test Prep** Cagle tosses a coin 80 times and records 34 heads and 46 tails. What is his experimental probability of tossing tails?

**A** 25%  **C** 57.5%

**B** 42.5%  **D** 77%

# Estimate Probability

OBJECTIVE: Estimate the probability of future events.

## Learn

**PROBLEM** John made 12 baskets out of his last 30 attempts of shooting a basketball. Based on that record, estimate the probability that John will make a basket on his next attempt.

You can use experimental probabilities to estimate the probability of a future event.

**Example 1** Based on John's performance, estimate how many baskets he will make on his next 40 attempts.

$P(\text{basket}) = \frac{12}{30} = \frac{2}{5}, 0.4, 40\%$     Find the experimental probability of making a basket.

$0.4 \times 40 = 16$     Multiply 0.4 by 40

So, John will make about 16 baskets out of his next 40 attempts.

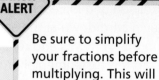

**ERROR ALERT**

Be sure to simplify your fractions before multiplying. This will help keep calculations simple.

**Example 2**

John is shooting 3-point baskets and makes 3 baskets out of 30 attempts. Based on his performance so far, about how many baskets can John expect to make on his next 40 attempts at shooting a 3-point basket?

$P(\text{3-point basket}) = \frac{3}{30} = \frac{1}{10}, 0.1, 10\%$     Find the experimental probability of making a 3-point basket.

$\frac{1}{10} \times 40 = \frac{40}{10} = 4$     Multiply $\frac{1}{10}$ by 40.

So, John will make about four 3-point baskets out of his next 40 attempts.

- **What if** John made 6 out of 30 3-point baskets? About how many 3-point baskets can John expect to make on his next 40 attempts?

## Guided Practice

1. Danielle made 3 soccer goals in 8 tries. Based on her experience, estimate how many goals she can expect to make in her next 24 tries.

$P(\text{goal}) = \frac{3}{8}, 0.375, 37.5\%$

$\frac{3}{8} \times 24 = \blacksquare$

 SDAP 3.2 Use data to estimate the probability of future events (e.g. batting averages or number of accidents per mile driven). *also* SDAP 3.0, ⊶ SDAP 3.3, MR 2.4, MR 2.5, MR 3.2

A box contains equally-sized colored buttons. Meg randomly selects a button and replaces it. She does this 40 times. For 2–3, use her table of results.

| Color | Red | Yellow | Orange | White |
|---|---|---|---|---|
| Times Selected | 6 | 4 | 14 | 16 |

2. Estimate how many times Meg can expect to select a yellow button on her next 50 tries?

3. Estimate how many times Meg can expect to select a white button on her next 30 tries?

4. **TALK Math** Explain how you can use experimental results to estimate the number of times a future event will take place.

## Independent Practice and Problem Solving

A bag contains equally-sized colored tiles. Logan randomly selects a tile and replaces it. He does this 25 times. For 5–8, use his table of results.

| Color | Purple | Black | Green | Blue |
|---|---|---|---|---|
| Times Selected | 5 | 3 | 8 | 9 |

5. Estimate how many times Logan can expect to select a black tile on his next 50 tries.

6. Estimate how many times Logan can expect to select a blue tile on his next 50 tries?

7. Estimate how many times Logan can expect to select a green or purple tile on his next 75 attempts.

8. Estimate how many times Logan can expect to select a black or blue tile on his next 75 tries?

Brian spins a pointer on a spinner with 6 equally sized regions 50 times. For 9–10, use his table of results.

| Section | A | B | C | D | E | F |
|---|---|---|---|---|---|---|
| Spin | 5 | 6 | 9 | 12 | 10 | 8 |

9. Estimate how many times Brian can expect the pointer to land on C or D in the next 100 spins.

10. Estimate how many times Brian can expect the pointer to land on a vowel in the next 200 spins?

11. **≡FAST FACT** Basketball player Elton Brand made 57 free throws in 76 attempts for the L.A. Clippers during the 2006 playoffs. Based on that performance, estimate how many free throws he can expect to make in a game where he gets 12 free throw attempts.

USE DATA For 12–13, use the table.

12. Estimate the number of hits William can expect to get in his next 120 times at bat?

13. **WRITE Math** What's the Error? Bryce multiplies $\frac{12}{25}$ by 100 and says Aaron can expect to make about 60 hits in his next 100 times at bat. Describe and correct his error.

| Baseball Statistics | Hits | Times at Bat |
|---|---|---|
| Charlie | 65 | 150 |
| Aaron | 84 | 175 |
| William | 100 | 200 |

## Achieving the Standards

14. Draw a parallelogram. (MG 2.3, p. 404)

15. Find the product of ⁻3 and 6. (O─┓ NS 2.0, p. 180)

16. Solve: $\frac{4}{5} = \frac{12}{x}$. (O─┓ NS 1.3, p. 466)

17. **Test Prep** Tim completes 9 football passes in 15 attempts. Estimate how many completed passes he can expect in his next 25 attempts.

   **A** about 4  **B** about 6  **C** about 9  **D** about 15

Extra Practice on page 536, Set D

# 6 Make Predictions

OBJECTIVE: Use probabilities to make predictions.

## Quick Review

Solve the proportion.

1. $\frac{8}{a} = \frac{12}{15}$    2. $\frac{4}{9} = \frac{x}{36}$

3. $\frac{r}{14} = \frac{24}{56}$    4. $\frac{3}{5} = \frac{42}{b}$

5. $\frac{5}{y} = \frac{8}{160}$

## Learn

**PROBLEM** A southwestern company creates polished gems from rocks. In a random sample of 200 rocks, 30 were properly shaped to be cut and polished. Predict the number of rocks that would be properly shaped from a truckload of 800 rocks.

You can use the results from a sample and write a proportion to make predictions about outcomes.

### Example 1

Use the sample to find the probability that a randomly selected rock is shaped properly to be cut and polished.

$\frac{3}{20} = \frac{n}{800}$    Write a proportion. $\frac{30}{200}$ simplifies to $\frac{3}{20}$. Use cross-multiplication.

$3 \times 800 = 20 \times n$    Multiply.

$2{,}400 = 20n$

$\frac{2{,}400}{20} = \frac{20n}{20}$    Divide.

$120 = n$

So, about 120 rocks from a truckload of 800 would be properly shaped.

You can also use a table or graph to make predictions about outcomes.

### Example 2

The graph shows the favorite gemstone of 210 randomly selected students from Woodruff Middle School. If there are 1,800 students at the school, about how many of them prefer emeralds?

P(prefers emeralds) $= \frac{28}{210} = \frac{2}{15}$    Find the probability that a randomly selected student prefers emeralds.

$\frac{2}{15} = \frac{n}{1{,}800}$    Write a proportion. Use cross-multiplication.

$2 \times 1{,}800 = 15 \times n$    Multiply.

$\frac{3{,}600}{15} = \frac{15n}{15}$    Divide.

$240 = n$

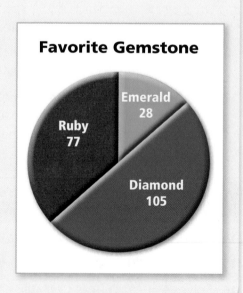

**Favorite Gemstone**

Emerald 28
Ruby 77
Diamond 105

So, about 240 students would prefer emeralds.

**SDAP 3.0** Students determine theoretical and experimental probabilities and use these to make predictions about events: *also* **SDAP 3.3, MR 2.4, MR 2.5, MR 3.2**

## Guided Practice

1. A jewelry vendor showcases 750 rings. Sandy browses through a random sample of 25 rings and finds that 8 of them are made with diamonds. Predict the number of rings in the showcase that are made with diamonds.

$$\frac{8}{25} = \frac{n}{750}$$
$$\blacksquare = n$$

The table shows the results of a survey of 240 randomly selected students at a middle school. For 2–7, predict how many of the school's 2,100 students have the indicated preference.

| Preferred Necklace Length | | | | | | |
|---|---|---|---|---|---|---|
| Length | 15 | 16 | 18 | 20 | 22 | 24 |
| Number of Students | 64 | 52 | 44 | 36 | 25 | 19 |

2. 15 in.  3. 16 in.  4. 18 in.  5. 20 in.  ✓6. 22 in.  ✓7. 24 in.

8. [TALK Math] **Explain** why you need to round to the nearest whole number when you are making predictions about student preferences.

## Independent Practice and Problem Solving

The graph shows the results of a random survey of 320 students at a middle school. For 9–14, predict how many of the school's 2,000 students have the indicated favorite.

9. Oval  10. Square  11. Other

12. Raindrop  13. Circle  14. Rectangle

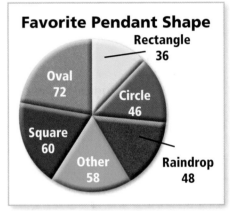

**Favorite Pendant Shape**
Rectangle 36
Oval 72
Circle 46
Square 60
Other 58
Raindrop 48

There are 600 gems of 5 types in a bag. In a random sample of 25 gems from the bag, there are 2 sapphires, 3 opals, 5 garnets, 7 jades, and 8 peridots. For 15–19, predict the number of each type of gem in the bag.

15. sapphires  16. opals  17. garnets  18. jades  19. peridots

For 20–21, use the survey results of the 200 students surveyed.

20. The survey reported that 12 more students collect pins than would collect rocks. About how many of the school's 1,350 students would collect pins?

21. [WRITE Math] **Sense or Nonsense** Owen uses the survey to predict that about 40 of the 120 students in his after-school class would collect rocks. Does his prediction make sense? **Explain.**

| What Students Collect | |
|---|---|
| Rocks | 60 |
| Coins | ? |
| Pins | ? |
| Other | 20 |

##  Achieving the Standards

22. Find P(heads) when flipping a coin.
(O—∏ SDAP 3.3, p. 522)

23. Find the sum $24 + {}^-18 + {}^-2$. (O—∏ NS 2.3, p. 154)

24. Three books cost $15.90. How much will 8 books cost? (O—∏ NS 1.3, p. 466)

25. **Test Prep** In a random sample of 80 earring posts, 4 were found to be defective. About how many posts in 5,000 would you predict would be defective?

A 16  B 250  C 1,250  D 4,750

[Extra Practice] on page 536, Set E

# Extra Practice

**Set A** Equally-sized cards numbered 1, 1, 2, 3, 4, 5, 6, and 8 are placed in a box. You choose one card without looking. Find the probability. Express your answers as fractions, decimals, and percents. (pp. 522-525)

1. P(4)
2. P(not 5)
3. P(not odd)
4. P(odd)

5. Carlton has a bag with 5 red, 6 orange, and 4 purple marbles, all the same size. Find the probability that he will randomly choose a marble that is not orange.

6. Jeffery has a box that contains slips of paper with a letter written on each. There are 6 L's, 4 E's, 7 T's, 3 X's, and 5 S's. Find the probability that the letter chosen is *not* an X.

**Set B** The contents of a jar are shown. Tell whether the events are disjoint. If so, find the probability that one event or the other will occur. (pp. 526-527)

1. P(3 or 5)
2. P(7 or number less than 4)
3. P(7 or odd number)
4. P(1 or number greater than 1)
5. P(4 or even number)
6. P(1, 2, or 8)

**Set C** Paul randomly selects a marble from a bag, containing equally-sized marbles and then replaces it. He does this 40 times. Use his results shown in the table to find each experimental probability. (pp. 530-531)

| Color | Purple | Orange | Blue | Brown |
|---|---|---|---|---|
| Times Selected | 12 | 5 | 8 | 15 |

1. P(purple)
2. P(orange)
3. P(blue)
4. P(brown)

**Set D** A box contains several equally-sized colored buttons. Amy randomly selects a button and then replaces it. She does this 20 times. Use her table of results. (pp. 532-533)

| Color | Yellow | Black | Green | White |
|---|---|---|---|---|
| Times Selected | 5 | 4 | 8 | 3 |

1. Estimate how many times Amy can expect to select a black button on her next 60 tries.

2. Estimate how many times Amy can expect to select a yellow button on her next 40 tries.

3. Estimate how many times Amy can expect to select a green or white button on her next 120 tries.

4. Estimate how many times Amy can expect to select a black or white button on her next 80 tries.

**Set E** The table shows the result of a random survey about favorite music types given to 400 students at a middle school. Predict how many of the school's 2,200 students have the indicated preference. (pp. 534-535)

| Rock | Classical | Country | Jazz | Blues | Other |
|---|---|---|---|---|---|
| 160 | 20 | 120 | 40 | 24 | 36 |

1. Country
2. Classical
3 Rock
4. Blues

**Technology**
Use Harcourt Mega Math, Fraction Action, *Last Chance Canyon*, Levels D, E, and J.

# PRACTICE GAME

# What are the Chances?

● **Get Ready**
2–4 players

○ **Get Set**
- Game cards
- Number cube labeled 1–6
- Different coins

FINISH

START

## Let's Roll

■ Each player selects a coin and places it on START. Decide who will go first.

■ Shuffle the game cards, and place them facedown in a pile.

■ A player draw a game card from the pile.

■ The player finds the probability of the event shown on the card.

■ The other players check the answer. If it is correct, the player tosses the number cube, advances the number of spaces shown, and play passes to the next player.

■ If the answer is incorrect, the player does not advance. Play passes to the next player.

■ The first player to reach FINISH wins.

**Chapter 21 Review/Test**

## Check Vocabulary and Concepts

Choose the best term from the box.

1. The __?__ of an experiment is the set of all possible outcomes. (O—∏ SDAP 3.3, p. 522)

2. Two or more events that cannot happen at the same time are called __?__. (SDAP 3.4, p. 526)

## Check Skills

The cards numbered 1, 1, 2, 3, 3, 4, 6, and 7 are placed in a box. You choose one card without looking. Find the probability. Express your answers as fractions, decimals, and percents. (O—∏ SDAP 3.3, SDAP 3.4, pp. 522-527)

3. P(6)
4. P(not 1)
5. P(8)
6. P(less than 4)

7. P(greater than 5)
8. P(1 or 5)
9. P(3 or even)
10. P(2, 3, or 7)

Trey randomly selects a marble from a bag and then replaces it. He does this 50 times. Use his results shown in the table to find each experimental probability. (SDAP 3.0, pp. 530-531)

| Color | Purple | Orange | Blue | Brown |
|---|---|---|---|---|
| Times Selected | 12 | 5 | 8 | 15 |

11. P(orange)
12. P(yellow)
13. P(blue)
14. P(green)

A box contains several colored buttons. Beth randomly selects a button and then replaces it. She does this 40 times. Use her table of results. (SDAP 3.2, pp. 532-533)

| Color | Red | White | Blue | Green |
|---|---|---|---|---|
| Times Selected | 12 | 6 | 7 | 15 |

15. Estimate how many times Beth can expect to select a green button on her next 80 tries.

16. Estimate how many times Beth can expect to select a white or a blue button on her next 120 tries?

The table shows the result of a random survey of 140 students in a middle school. Predict how many of the school's 2,100 students have the indicated favorite. (SDAP 3.0, pp. 534-535)

17. Science
18. Reading

| Favorite Subject | | | |
|---|---|---|---|
| **Subject** | Math | Science | History | Reading |
| **Times Chosen** | 30 | 40 | 34 | 36 |

## Check Problem Solving

Solve. (O—∏ SDAP 3.3, MR 3.1, pp. 528-529)

19. Gus is tossing a coin. He states, "I flipped heads 3 times in a row, so the next flip has to be tails." Is his assumption reasonable?

20. **WRITE Math** John has 5 caps that are sizes M, M, S, L, and XL. He says that he has a 50% chance of randomly selecting a size M. Explain how you know his answer is not reasonable.

**GO ONLINE Technology** Use *Online Assessment.*

# Enrich • Geometric Probability
# THE COIN TOSS

The theoretical probability of an event compares favorable outcomes to all possible outcomes. **Geometric probability** compares the favorable areas of a figure with the total area of the figure.

If Roberto tosses a coin onto this target, what is the probability that the coin will land on blue?

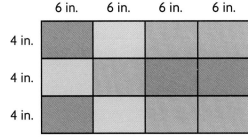

## Toss It

Assume that the center point of Roberto's coin lands at some random point on the target, and that all points are equally likely.

> **Remember**
> The formula for the area of a rectangle is $A = l \times w$.

| | |
|---|---|
| **Area of Blue Sections** | |
| $A = l \times w = 6$ in. $\times$ 4 in. $= 24$ in.$^2$ | Find the area of one blue section. |
| 24 in.$^2$ $\times$ 5 sections $= 120$ in.$^2$ | There are 5 congruent blue sections, so multiply the area of one section by 5 to get the total area of the blue sections. |
| **Total Area of Target** | |
| $A = l \times w = 12$ in. $\times$ 24 in. $= 288$ in.$^2$ | Find the area of the target. |
| $P(\text{blue}) = \dfrac{\text{area of blue sections}}{\text{area of target}} = \dfrac{120}{288} = \dfrac{5}{12}$ | Find the probability that the coin randomly will land on blue. |

So, the probability that Roberto's coin will land on blue is $\frac{5}{12}$.

## Observe It

**For 1–4, use the target above.**

1. P(red)

2. P(green)

3. P(red or blue)

4. **Reasoning** How can you change the target so that the probability of landing on blue is 50%, and the probability of landing on red is the same as the probability of landing on green?

5. In the 18th century, the Comte de Buffon investigated the probability of dropping a needle onto a section of a wooden floor similar to the one at the right. Find the probability that the needle would land on a part labeled D or E.

6. Draw and color a geometric figure so that the probability of a coin's landing on blue is less than the probability of its landing on orange. Write the probability for each as a fraction and as a decimal.

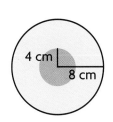

## Record It

**WRITE Math** **What's the Error?** Deborah says that the probability of a token's landing on the red circle is 50%. Find and correct her error.

## Number Sense

**1.** Which point shows the location of $\frac{13}{2}$ on the number line? (O⟍ NS 1.1)

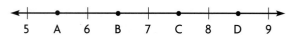

**A** point A

**B** point B

**C** point C

**D** point D

**2.** The weekly order for the school cafeteria includes 32 cases of frozen pizza and 12 cases of hot dogs. What is the ratio of the number of cases of frozen pizza to cases of hot dogs in the weekly order? (O⟍ NS 1.2)

**A** 3:1

**B** 4:1

**C** 4:3

**D** 8:3

**3.** A paper clip company can make 15,000 paper clips in 8 minutes. Which proportion could be solved to find $x$, the expected number of paper clips made in 30 minutes? (O⟍ NS 1.3)

**A** $\dfrac{30}{15,000} = \dfrac{8}{x}$

**B** $\dfrac{30}{15,000} = \dfrac{x}{8}$

**C** $\dfrac{8}{15,000} = \dfrac{30}{x}$

**D** $\dfrac{8}{15,000} = \dfrac{x}{30}$

**4.** **WRITE Math** **Explain** how to write $\frac{1}{8}$ as a decimal and as a percent. (O⟍ NS 1.0)

## Algebra and Functions

**5.** What value of $h$ makes the following equation true? (O⟍ AF 1.1)

$$h \div 4 = 28$$

**A** 7

**C** 102

**B** 32

**D** 112

**6.** A telephone company charges $0.07 per minute for local calls and $0.15 per minute for long-distance calls. Which expression gives the total cost in dollars for $m$ minutes of local calls and $x$ minutes of long-distance calls? (AF 1.2)

**A** $0.07m + 0.15x$

**B** $0.07m - 0.15x$

**C** $0.22(m + x)$

**D** $0.22mx$

**7.** The rectangle shown below has length 18 inches and width 6 inches.

18 inches

6 inches

Which equation could be used to find the area of the rectangle? (O⟍ AF 1.1)

**A** $A = 18 + 6$

**B** $A = 18 + 6 + 18 + 6$

**C** $A = 18 \times 6$

**D** $A = 18 \times 6 \times 18 \times 6$

**8.** **WRITE Math** **Explain** how to solve and check $x - 12 = 41$. (O⟍ AF 1.1)

## Statistics, Data Analysis, and Probability

9. Mandy has 2 navy, 10 white, and 8 black pairs of socks in a drawer. If Mandy grabs a pair of socks without looking, what is the probability that she will grab a navy pair from the drawer? (O─ᴨ SDAP 3.3)

   **A** 10%          **C** 50%

   **B** 40%          **D** 80%

**Test Tip** **Look for important words.**

See item 9. The question asks you to find the probability. The probability of an event is the number of favorable outcomes divided by the number of possible outcomes.

10. The table shows the result of a random survey of 100 students at a middle school.

| Color | Number of Shirts |
|-------|-----------------|
| Purple | 15 |
| Pink | 28 |
| White | 14 |
| Blue | 23 |
| Black | 20 |

   How many shirts in 2,000 would you predict to be white? (O─ᴨ SDAP 3.3)

   **A** about 100          **C** about 200

   **B** about 140          **D** about 280

11. **WRITE Math** Matt wants to know how many sixth-grade students in California use email. **Explain** which sampling method Matt should use. (O─ᴨ SDAP 2.2)

## Measurement and Geometry

12. This rectangular prism has a length of 12 inches, a height of 8 inches, and a width of 2 inches. What is the volume? (Grade 5 O─ᴨ MG 1.3)

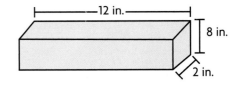

   **A** 22 cu in.

   **B** 96 cu in.

   **C** 192 cu in.

   **D** 212 cu in.

13. Which equation could be used to find the area in square inches of a circle with a radius of 6 inches? (O─ᴨ MG 1.1)

   **A** $A = 3 \times \pi$          **C** $A = 6 \times \pi$

   **B** $A = \pi \times 3^2$          **D** $A = \pi \times 36$

14. Which is a true statement about angles $A$ and $B$ shown below? (MG 2.1)

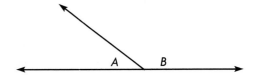

   **A** $\angle A$ is complementary to $\angle B$.

   **B** $\angle A$ is supplementary to $\angle B$.

   **C** Both angles are acute.

   **D** Both angles are obtuse.

15. **WRITE Math** A bicycle wheel has a radius of 12 inches. **Explain** how to find the circumference of the bicycle wheel. (O─ᴨ MG 1.1)

# Probability of Compound Events

**The Big Idea** Probability measures the likelihood of compound events and provides the basis for making predictions.

## Investigate

Jenn took a survey of visitors to the state capitol. Her results appear below. Suppose you were to ask three randomly chosen people from Jenn's survey to answer a question regarding their age. Suppose you chose three of those visitors at random to ask about their ages. How would you find the probability that the ages of all three fall within the same range?

### Visitors to State Capitol

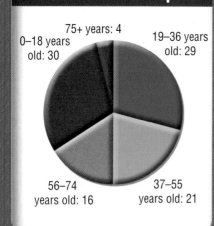

75+ years: 4
0–18 years old: 30
19–36 years old: 29
56–74 years old: 16
37–55 years old: 21

**CALIFORNIA FAST FACT**

The California State Capitol, in Sacramento, has been home to the California State Legislature since 1869. Visitors to the capitol can see exhibits and go on tours.

**GO ONLINE**

**Technology**
Student pages are available in the Student eBook.

**Check your understanding of important skills
needed for success in Chapter 22.**

▶ **Multiply Fractions by Fractions**

**Multiply. Write your answer in simplest form.**

1. $\frac{1}{10} \times \frac{2}{3}$    2. $\frac{3}{5} \times \frac{1}{2}$    3. $\frac{3}{4} \times \frac{1}{3}$    4. $\frac{5}{8} \times \frac{1}{2}$

5. $\frac{4}{7} \times \frac{1}{3}$    6. $\frac{3}{5} \times \frac{1}{8}$    7. $\frac{1}{4} \times \frac{2}{7}$    8. $\frac{1}{6} \times \frac{2}{5}$

9. $\frac{1}{9} \times \frac{4}{5}$    10. $\frac{6}{7} \times \frac{2}{3}$    11. $\frac{3}{4} \times \frac{3}{4}$    12. $\frac{2}{7} \times \frac{4}{5}$

13. $\frac{9}{10} \times \frac{1}{2}$    14. $\frac{2}{5} \times \frac{3}{4}$    15. $\frac{3}{8} \times \frac{1}{4}$    16. $\frac{5}{6} \times \frac{1}{2}$

▶ **Probability of Simple Events**

**Use the spinner at right to find the probability of each event.**

17. P(1)              18. P(even)

19. P(less than 3)    20. P(odd)

21. P(2 or greater)   22. P(less than 5)

23. P(7)              24. P(less than 6)

25. P(more than 3)    26. P(4)

27. P(more than 1)    28. P(5 or less)

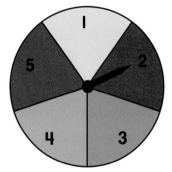

# VOCABULARY POWER

**CHAPTER VOCABULARY**

compound event
dependent events
Fundamental Counting Principle
independent events
tree diagram

**WARM-UP WORDS**

**compound event** an event made of two or more simple events

**tree diagram** an organized diagram that lists all possible outcomes for compound events

**Fundamental Counting Principle** if one event has *m* possible outcomes and a second event has *n* possible outcomes, then there are *m* × *n* possible outcomes for the two events together

# Problem Solving Workshop
# Strategy: Make an Organized List

OBJECTIVE: Solve problems by using the strategy *make an organized list.*

## Learn the Strategy

When you make an organized list, you are organizing the content of a problem into groups, or categories, that are easy to see and use. Then, you can count the items on your list and check to make sure each item is listed and is different from the other items.

### A list can be used to make comparisons.

Connie has cheerleading practice every 4 days, and dance practice every 3 days. She starts both on October 10.

Cheerleading
10/10, 10/14, 10/18, 10/22, 10/26, 10/30

Dance
10/10, 10/13, 10/16, 10/19, 10/22, 10/25, 10/28

### A list can be used to order information.

Five teachers will be recognized as Outstanding Teachers on Awards Day. Mrs. Webb stands between Mr. Williams and Mrs. Todd. Mrs. Smith stands between Mrs. Todd and Mr. Gregg. Mr. Gregg is on the far left.

| 1 | 2 | 3 | 4 | 5 |
|---|---|---|---|---|
| Mr. Gregg | Mrs. Smith | Mrs. Todd | Mrs. Webb | Mr. Williams |

### A list can be used to show possible outcomes.

For a group picture, Bob (B), Ann (A), and Dave (D) can stand in order from left to right in several different ways.

BAD   ADB   DBA

BDA   ABD   DAB

**TALK Math**
For each list, think of a question that can be answered by using the list.

# Use the Strategy

**PROBLEM** Kari and her friends eat dinner at a restaurant that offers Swiss, cheddar, or Appenzeller cheese fondues. For the main course, Kari can choose beef or chicken. For dessert, she can select a white, dark, or milk chocolate fondue. How many different meals are possible if she selects a cheese fondue, a main course, and a dessert?

## Read to Understand

Reading Skill

• Classify and categorize the given information.
• Is there any information that is not needed?

## Plan

• **What strategy can you use to solve the problem?**

You can make an organized list to help you solve the problem.

## Solve

• **How can you use the strategy to solve the problem?**

List all possible combinations of a cheese fondue, main course, and dessert. First, list all possible dinner combinations that have Swiss cheese followed by cheddar and Appenzeller.

| | | |
|---|---|---|
| Swiss, beef, white | cheddar, beef, white | Appenzeller, beef, white |
| Swiss, beef, dark | cheddar, beef, dark | Appenzeller, beef, dark |
| Swiss, beef, milk | cheddar, beef, milk | Appenzeller, beef, milk |
| | | |
| Swiss, chicken, white | cheddar, chicken, white | Appenzeller, chicken, white |
| Swiss, chicken, dark | cheddar, chicken, dark | Appenzeller, chicken, dark |
| Swiss, chicken, milk | cheddar, chicken, milk | Appenzeller, chicken, milk |

So, 18 different meals are possible.

## Check

• **How can you check your results?**
• **What other strategy could you use to solve the problem?**

**Make an organized list to solve.**

1. Warren and his father are trying a new restaurant. The appetizers are stuffed mushrooms (m) or zucchini wedges (z). The specials are catfish (c) or grouper (g). The desserts are a brownie (b) or a slice of apple pie (p). How many meals are possible if Warren selects an appetizer, a special, and a dessert?

**First,** list all the possible dinner combinations that have a mushroom appetizer.

| | |
|---|---|
| m, c , b | m, g, b |
| m, c, p | m, g, p |

**Then,** list all the possible dinner combinations that have a zucchini appetizer.

**Finally,** count all the combinations in both lists.

2. **What if** the restaurant sells out of the grouper before Warren and his father order? How many meal choices would they have then?

3. Chris manages a grocery store with cash registers A, B, C, and D. If he needs to make sure that 2 registers out of 4 are open, how many possible combinations of 2 open registers are there?

## Problem Solving Strategy Practice

**Make an organized list to solve.**

4. The available pizza choices at Joe's Pizza Shop are shown on the menu at the right. How many ways can Lucy make a pizza with one crust, one sauce, and one topping?

5. Kiana's parents are treating her to 3 scoops of her favorite ice cream. Her favorite flavors are butter pecan, mint chip, and rocky road. In how many different orders can one scoop of each flavor be arranged on a cone?

6. **Reasoning** A box of 30 assorted recipe cards is set up so that every 4th card is a vegetarian meal and every 6th card is a garlic-based meal. The top card is a garlic-based vegetarian meal. Which other cards in the stack are garlic-based vegetarian meals?

**Joe's Pizza Shop**

| Crusts | Sauces | Toppings |
|---|---|---|
| Thin | Red | Extra Cheese |
| Pan | White | Pepperoni |
| Original | | Anchovies |
| | | Mushrooms |

**USE DATA** For 7–8, use the table at the right.

7. Jane and Benson each order a meal from the menu. How many different dollar amounts are possible for the total cost of their meals?

8. **WRITE Math** Look back at Problem 7. How would the answer change if Jane and Benson agreed not to order the same meal? **Explain.**

**Fish Meals**

| Fish | Price |
|---|---|
| Trout | $12 |
| Albacore Tuna | $13 |
| Halibut | $10 |

## Mixed Strategy Practice

**9.** While on vacation, Kelly and Thom want to try a Chinese restaurant, an Indian restaurant, and a German restaurant, but they will be free only 2 nights to eat at a restaurant. Thom writes the 3 types of restaurants on cards, shuffles them, and asks Kelly to choose 2 cards. How many possible combinations of restaurants are there?

**10. Pose a Problem** Look back at Problem 9. Write a similar problem where Kelly and Thom also choose the order in which they visit the restaurants.

**USE DATA** For 11–14, use the diagram at the right.

**11.** Lizzie is the last person on the wait staff to leave for lunch. One after another, each person takes 45 min for lunch. If Lizzie leaves at 2:00 P.M. what time does the staff start leaving for lunch?

**12.** Two customers, Carol and Jane, enter the restaurant at the same time. Carol sits in Casey's section and Jane sits in Jack's section. If no one else is seated in either section, how many seating arrangements are possible?

**13.** Parties with the last names Bolt, Hair, Peevey, Edwards, and Allen are seated in Frank's section. The Hair party is seated at one end of the section. The Bolt party is next to the Edwards and Peevey parties. The Edwards party is at booth 11. Who is seated at booth 14?

**14. Open-Ended** The restaurant can currently seat 120 people, up to 4 people in each booth and up to 8 people at each table. Plan a new seating arrangement with no more than 12 sections that will hold a total of 250 people. Each section should have no more than 6 tables or 6 booths and no section may have both. Draw a diagram of your plan.

## Problem-Solving STRATEGIES

**Make an Organized List**

Draw a Diagram or Picture

Make a Model or Act It Out

Find a Pattern

Make a Table or Graph

Predict and Test

Work Backward

Solve a Simpler Problem

Write an Equation

Use Logical Reasoning

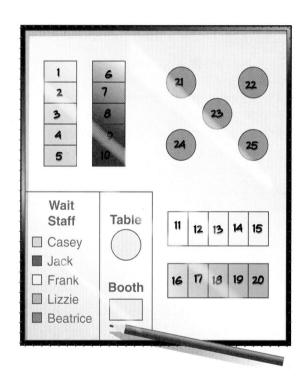

## CHALLENGE YOURSELF

**A restaurant offers 5 different, equally popular meal options at an average price of $19.95 per meal.**

**15.** Three of the meals sell at prices of $24.85, $9.95, and $16.99. If one of the two remaining meals sells for $2.00 more than the other remaining meal, what are the prices of the remaining two meals?

**16.** The restaurant is open seven days a week and records a total income of about $25,935 during a 3-week period. About how many meals does the restaurant sell per day during that period?

# 2 Outcomes of Compound Events

OBJECTIVE: Find all possible outcomes of compound events.

## Quick Review

Multiply.

1. $2 \times 5 \times 6$    2. $3 \times 3 \times 4$

3. $2 \times 4 \times 4$    4. $3 \times 5 \times 9$

5. $5 \times 5 \times 7$

## Vocabulary

compound event

tree diagram

Fundamental Counting Principle

## Learn

**PROBLEM** At camp, each camper gets one sandwich for lunch. The meat choices are turkey, roast beef, and ham. The bread choices are white, wheat, and multigrain. If one of each type of sandwich is on every table, how many sandwich choices are on each table?

A **compound event** occurs when you combine two or more simple events. You can make a list or use a grid to make a table to find the sample space of compound events.

**menu**

| Meats | Breads |
|-------|--------|
| Turkey | White |
| Roast Beef | Wheat |
| Ham | Multigrain |

### Example 1

**ONE WAY** Make a list.

List each meat with each type of bread. Then count the items in the list.

| | | |
|---|---|---|
| turkey, white | roast beef, white | ham, white |
| turkey, wheat | roast beef, wheat | ham, wheat |
| turkey, multigrain | roast beef, multigrain | ham, multigrain |

**ERROR ALERT**

Check your list to be sure that all outcomes have been listed and there are no duplicates.

**ANOTHER WAY** Use a grid to make a table.

| | | Bread | | |
|---|---|---|---|---|
| | | **White (A)** | **Wheat (B)** | **Multigrain (C)** |
| **Meat** | **Turkey (T)** | T, A | T, B | T, C |
| | **Roast Beef (R)** | R, A | R, B | R, C |
| | **Ham (H)** | H, A | H, B | H, C |

List the types of bread in a row and the types of meat in a column.

Count the number of choices.

So, there are 9 sandwich choices on each table.

• **What if** pumpernickel is added to the bread choices? How many sandwich choices would there be?

### Example 2 Tomás chooses a sandwich at random. What is the probability that he chooses ham on wheat bread?

Look at the table above.

$P(\text{ham, wheat}) = \frac{1}{9}$    There are 9 possible outcomes in the sample space.

So, the probability of choosing ham on wheat bread is $\frac{1}{9}$.

**SDAP 3.1** Represent all possible outcomes for compound events in an organized way (e.g., tables, grids, tree diagrams) and express the theoretical probability of each outcome. *also* MR 2.4, MR 2.5, MR 3.0, MR 3.1, MR 3.2, MR 3.3

# Compound Events

A **tree diagram** is an organized diagram that lists all possible outcomes for compound events.

## Example 3 Find the number of possible outcomes when tossing 3 coins.

**ONE WAY** Draw a tree diagram.

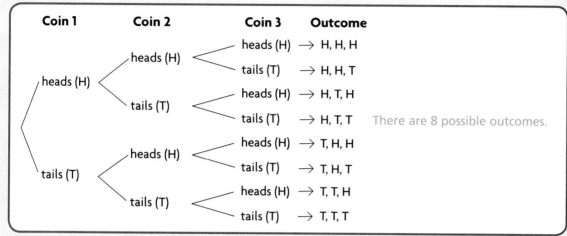

So, there are 8 possible outcomes when tossing 3 coins.

You can also use the Fundamental Counting Principle to find the number of possible outcomes of compound events.

The **Fundamental Counting Principle** states that if one event has *m* possible outcomes and a second event has *n* possible outcomes, then there are $m \times n$ possible outcomes for the two events together.

**ANOTHER WAY** Use the Fundamental Counting Principle.

| Coin 1 | Coin 2 | Coin 3 | |
|---|---|---|---|
| 2 | × 2 | × 2 | = 8 |

There are 2 possible outcomes for each coin, heads or tails.

So, there are 8 possible outcomes when tossing 3 coins.

- You have a choice of 4 pizza crusts and 6 toppings. Use the Fundamental Counting Principle to find the number of possible outcomes.

## Example 4 Find the probability that all 3 coins land heads up.

There is 1 possible outcome for all 3 coins landing heads up. There are 8 possible outcomes when tossing 3 coins.

Look at all the outcomes on the tree diagram.

$$P(\text{heads, heads, heads}) = \frac{1}{8}$$

Write the probability.

So, the probability of tossing 3 heads when tossing 3 coins is $\frac{1}{8}$.

- What is the probability that all 3 coins land tails up?

1. Copy and complete the table to find the number of possible outcomes when spinning the pointers on these 2 spinners.

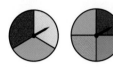

|  |  | Spinner 2 | | | |
|---|---|---|---|---|---|
|  |  | Red (R) | Green (G) | Blue (B) | Pink (P) |
| Spinner | Red (R) | R, R | R, G |  |  |
|  | Yellow (W) | Y, R | Y, G |  |  |
|  | Green (G) | G, R | G,G |  |  |

**Use a grid to make a table, make a list, or draw a tree diagram to show the number of possible outcomes for each situation.**

2. a red, blue, or green shirt with jeans or shorts

✅ 3. a dance pairing of Ron, Paul, Jason, or Zack with Jill, Kara, Breanna, or Susie

**Use the Fundamental Counting Principle to find the number of possible outcomes for each situation.**

4. selecting a colored marble and colored tile from the colors blue, red, and black

✅ 5. a choice of 2 bagels, 3 fruits, and 2 drinks

6. **TALK Math** **Explain** how to use the Fundamental Counting Principle to find the number of possible outcomes when rolling 4 number cubes labeled 1 to 6.

## Independent Practice and Problem Solving

**Use a grid to make a table, make a list, or draw a tree diagram to show the number of possible outcomes for each situation.**

7. a choice of yellow gold, white gold, or silver for a 16 in., 18 in., 20 in., or 22 in. chain.

8. rolling a number cube labeled 1 to 6 and spinning the pointer of a spinner with 3 sections

9. a choice of 5 salads and 4 dressings

10. rolling a number cube labeled 1 to 6 and tossing a coin

**Use the Fundamental Counting Principle to find the number of possible outcomes for each situation.**

11. typing a letter to Tiera, Gwen, or Alice with a font size of 12 or 14 points

12. having a beach party or pool party this weekend or next weekend and inviting 8 or 10 guests

**Find the probability.**

13. Sean rolls 2 number cubes labeled 1 to 6. Find the probability that he rolls a 6 on the first cube and a 2 on the second cube.

14. Eva rolls a number cube labeled 1 to 6 and tosses a coin twice. Find the probability of rolling a 3, tossing heads, and then tossing tails.

⭐ **Algebra** **Use the Fundamental Counting Principle to write an expression that represents the number of possible outcomes for each situation.**

15. toss a coin and spin the pointer of a spinner with $x$ equally-sized sections

16. spin the pointers of 2 spinners, each with $y$ equally-sized sections

**USE DATA** For 17–18, use the breakfast menu at the right. A breakfast plate consists of 1 main dish, 1 side item, and 1 fruit.

**Bailey's Breakfast Bar**

| Main Dish | Side Items | Fruit |
|---|---|---|
| Eggs | Hash Browns | Pineapple |
| Pancakes | Grits | Bananas |
| French Toast | Sausage | |

**17.** Use the Fundamental Counting Principle to find the number of possible breakfast plates.

**18.** Draw a tree diagram of all possible breakfast plates. Find the probability of randomly choosing French toast, pineapple, and sausage.

**19.**  **What's the Error?** Describe the error Jan made at the right in listing all possible outcomes of choosing vanilla, chocolate, or strawberry ice cream in a cup, sugar cone, or waffle cone.

| | |
|---|---|
| vanilla, cup | vanilla, sugar cone |
| chocolate, cup | chocolate, sugar cone |
| strawberry, cup | strawberry, sugar cone |

## Achieving the Standards

**20.** Find the area, to the nearest whole number, of a circle with a radius of 5 centimeters.
(O➡ MG 1.1, p. 420)

**21.** Ryan drinks 4 cups of juice every 6 days. How many days will it take him to drink 10 cups of juice? (O➡ NS 1.3, p. 466)

**22.** What is the product of $\frac{2}{5}$ and $\frac{3}{8}$?
(O➡ NS 2.0, p. 72)

**23. Test Prep** What is the probability that the pointers of the three spinners will all stop on yellow?

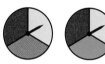  

**A** $\frac{1}{36}$   **B** $\frac{1}{12}$   **C** $\frac{1}{4}$   **D** $\frac{1}{3}$

## Problem Solving connects to Social Studies

Senet is the oldest known board game. Ancient Egyptians used a 3 × 10 playing board and four 2-sided sticks to play. The sticks were tossed to find how many spaces to move, similar to rolling number cubes in popular board games today. Each stick was painted on one side and unpainted on the other side.

**Answer each question about tossing 4 Senet sticks.**

**1.** Draw a tree diagram to show all the possible outcomes when tossing four 2-sided sticks. Use P for painted and U for unpainted.

**2.** Compare the probability of tossing 4 painted sticks with the probability of tossing a 2 on a number cube labeled 1 to 6.

**3.** What is the probability of tossing 3 painted sticks and 1 unpainted stick or 2 painted sticks and 2 unpainted sticks?

# 3 Explore Independent and Dependent Events

**OBJECTIVE:** Explore the difference between independent and dependent events.

## Quick Review

List the possible outcomes for tossing 2 coins?

## Vocabulary

independent events

dependent events

## Investigate

**Materials** ■ 10 index cards ■ box ■ 5-section spinner
■ 5 blue and 5 red marbles

Events for which the outcome of the first event does not affect the outcomes of the second event are **independent events**. Events for which the outcome of the first event does affect the outcomes of the second event are **dependent events**.

**A** **Start the first experiment.** Number the index cards from 1 to 10 and place them in the box. Draw a card from the box without looking and record its number. Set the card aside.

**B** What are the possible numbers that you can still draw from the box? Draw a second card without looking and record its number.

**C** **Start the second experiment.** Replace all the cards in the box. Draw a card from the box without looking and record its number. Then replace this card in the box.

**D** What are the possible numbers that you can still draw from the box? Draw a second card without looking and record its number.

## Draw Conclusions

**1.** In the first experiment, how did drawing the first number without replacing it affect the choices for drawing the second number? Are the events independent or dependent? Explain.

**2.** In the second experiment, how did drawing the first number and replacing it affect the choices for drawing the second number? Explain.

**3.** **Synthesis** What is the difference between independent and dependent events?

SDAP 3.5 Understand the difference between independent and dependent events. *also* **MR 2.0, MR 2.4, MR 2.5, MR 3.2**

## Connect

You can compare the possible outcomes of two events to determine
if the events are independent or dependent.

**A** Color one section of the spinner red, one blue, one green, one
yellow, and one purple. Spin the pointer of the 5-section spinner
twice and determine whether the events are independent
or dependent.

There are 5 possible outcomes, red, blue, green, yellow, and purple,
for the second spin regardless of the outcome of the first spin. The
choices remain unchanged. The first spin does not affect the possible
outcomes of the second spin.

So, the events are independent.

**B** Select a marble from a bag containing 5 blue and 5 red marbles, do
not replace it, and then select a second marble from the same bag.
Determine whether the selections are independent or dependent.

Only 9 of the 10 choices are available for the second selection since
one marble was removed on the first selection. So the first choice
does affect the possible choices on the second selection.

So, the events are dependent.

**TALK Math**

**Describe** a situation
that models independent
events and another
situation that models
dependent events.

## Practice

**Write _independent_ or _dependent_ to describe the events. Then explain
your choice.**

**1.** Draw a marble from a bag of 20 marbles,
don't replace it, and draw a second marble.

**2.** Select a card from a box containing cards,
labeled 1 to 10, do not replace it, and select a
second card from the same box.

**3.** Toss a coin and then roll a number cube
labeled 1 to 6.

**4.** Spin the pointers on two spinners each
divided equally into yellow, red, and blue.

**5.** A number cube labeled 1 to 6 is rolled twice.

**6.** Toss a coin three times.

**7.** **WRITE Math** A jar contains cards labeled 1, 2, 2, 3, 4. **Explain** whether
it is possible to select 2, do not replace it, and select 2 again.

## Learn

**PROBLEM** Roger writes 4 science words and definitions on index cards and shuffles the cards. He randomly draws a card, studies its definition, and then replaces the card and reshuffles the stack. He then randomly draws a card again. What is the probability that he will draw the definition for *mass* twice in a row?

To find the probability of two independent events, use the formula below to multiply their probabilities.

If A and B are independent events, then
$$P(A, B) = P(A) \times P(B).$$

### Example  Find P(mass, mass).

$P(\text{mass}) = \frac{1}{4}$    Find the probability of drawing the card for *mass*.

$P(\text{mass, mass}) = P(\text{mass}) \times P(\text{mass})$

$\qquad = \frac{1}{4} \times \frac{1}{4} = \frac{1}{16}$    Multiply the probabilities.

So, the probability is $\frac{1}{16}$, 0.0625, or 6.25%.

### More Examples  Independent Events

**A** Bev spins the pointers on the spinners, one time each. Find P(yellow, not red).

$P(\text{yellow, not red}) = P(\text{yellow}) \times P(\text{not red})$

$\qquad = \frac{1}{5} \times \frac{3}{4} = \frac{3}{20}$

So, the probability is $\frac{3}{20}$, 0.15, or 15%.

**B** Equally-sized marbles are placed in a bag. Find P(orange, blue) when the first marble randomly drawn is replaced.

| Orange | Black | Blue |
|--------|-------|------|
| 12 | 18 | 10 |

$P(\text{orange, blue}) = P(\text{orange}) \times P(\text{blue})$

$\qquad = \frac{3}{10} \times \frac{1}{4} = \frac{3}{40}$

So, the probability is $\frac{3}{40}$, 0.075, or 7.5%.

## Guided Practice

1. Maddie rolls a number cube labeled 1 to 6 twice. Find the probability that she rolls an even number on the first roll and an odd number on the second roll.

First roll:

$P(\text{even}) = \frac{3}{6} = \frac{1}{2}$

Second roll:

$P(\text{odd}) = \frac{3}{6} = \frac{1}{2}$

$P(\text{even, odd}) = \frac{1}{2} \times \frac{1}{2} = \blacksquare\blacksquare$

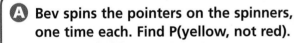 SDAP 3.4 Understand that the probability of either of two disjoint events occurring is the sum of the two individual probabilities and that the probability of one event following another, in independent trials, is the product of the two probabilities. *also* SDAP 3.0, ○━┓ SDAP 3.3, ○━┓ SDAP 3.5, MR 2.4, MR 2.5, MR 3.2

Delilah spins the pointers, one time each, on the spinners at the right.
For 2–4, find the probability of each event.

**2.** P(green, blue)    ✓**3.** P(orange, not red)    ✓**4.** P(green, blue or red)

**5.** [ TALK Math ]  **Explain** how to find the probability of two independent events.

## Independent Practice and Problem Solving

Juan spins the pointers, one time each, on the spinners at the right.
For 6–11, find the probability of each event.

**6.** P(purple, green)    **7.** P(yellow, not orange)    **8.** P(not red, not green)

**9.** P(not purple, orange)  **10.** P(red or purple, green)  **11.** P(yellow or red, not green)

The table shows the contents of a bag of equally-sized colored
buttons. Peter randomly selects a button from the bag, replaces it,
and selects again. For 12–19, find the probability of each event.

| Red | Blue | Green | White |
|-----|------|-------|-------|
| 4 | 3 | 2 | 3 |

**12.** P(red, blue)    **13.** P(red, not blue)    **14.** P(not green, not white)  **15.** P(white, white)

**16.** P(not red, red)    **17.** P(white, blue, red)    **18.** P(green, not red, blue)  **19.** P(blue, blue, blue)

**USE DATA** For 20–23, use the table. Ashton has to study
facts about people, plants, and animals for her test. She
writes each fact on an index card and shuffles the cards.

| People | Plants | Animals |
|--------|--------|---------|
| 8 | 2 | 10 |

**20.** If Ashton removes the animals from her stack
of cards, what is the probability that she will
randomly draw a plant, replace it, and then
draw a person? Is this event more likely with,
or without, the animals included? **Explain.**

**21.** Ashton randomly draws a person, replaces the
card, and randomly draws another card. What
is the probability that the second card she drew
was the same person?

**22.** What is the probability that Ashton randomly
draws 3 animals in a row if she replaces each
card that she draws?

**23.** **Reasoning** Suppose Ashton draws a card,
replaces it, and draws another card. Are
P(people, plants) and P(plants, people) equal?
**Explain.**

**24.** [ WRITE Math ] ▶ **What's the Question?** Mia has a quarter and a nickel.
She flips each coin. The answer is 25%.

## Achieving the Standards

**25.** Find the area of a triangle with base 3 inches
and height 18 inches. (Grade 5 O⊓ MG 1.1)

**26.** A 10-section spinner with equally-sized
sections has 3 blue sections. The pointer on
the spinner is spun. Find P(blue). Write your
answer as a fraction, decimal and percent.
(O⊓ SDAP 3.3, p. 522)

**27.** What is $\frac{2}{5} \times \frac{1}{2}$? (O⊓ NS 2.0, p. 70)

**28.** **Test Prep** What is the probability of tossing
a coin that lands heads up and then rolling an
odd number on a cube labeled 1 to 6?

**A** 10%      **C** 20%

**B** 15%      **D** 25%

# Dependent Events

OBJECTIVE: Find probabilities of dependent events.

## Quick Review

Multiply.

1. $\frac{1}{4} \times \frac{2}{5}$      2. $\frac{1}{9} \times \frac{3}{8}$

3. $\frac{1}{5} \times \frac{1}{6}$      4. $\frac{3}{4} \times \frac{7}{10}$

5. $\frac{5}{6} \times \frac{5}{12}$

## Learn

**PROBLEM** Michelle is selecting music for a dance recital. She has a collection of 16 CDs in a case. She randomly selects a CD from the case, does not replace it, and then randomly selects another. The contents of the case are shown in the table. What is the probability that Michelle will select a soft rock CD and then a classical CD?

| Soft Rock | Classical | Movie Soundtrack | Hip Hop |
|-----------|-----------|------------------|---------|
| 4 | 3 | 3 | 6 |

To find the probability of two dependent events, use the formula below.

> If A and B are dependent events, then
> P(A, B) = P(A) × P(B after A).

## Example Find P(soft rock, classical).

P(soft rock, classical) = P(soft rock) × P(classical after soft rock)

Michelle's first selection:

$P(\text{soft rock}) = \frac{4}{16} = \frac{1}{4}$     There are 4 soft rock CDs in a case of 16 CDs.

Michelle's second selection:

$P(\text{classical after soft rock}) = \frac{3}{15} = \frac{1}{5}$     There are 3 classical CDs in a case that now has 15 CDs.

$P(\text{soft rock, classical}) = \frac{1}{4} \times \frac{1}{5} = \frac{1}{20}$     Multiply the probabilities.

> **Math Idea**
> When 2 events are dependent, calculate the probability of the second event after the first event has taken place.

So, the probability that Michelle will select a soft rock CD and then a classical CD is $\frac{1}{20}$.

• Find P(hip hop, movie soundtrack).

## Guided Practice

1. Twelve index cards labeled 1–12 are placed in a jar. Find the probability of randomly drawing an even number and then an odd number if the first card is not replaced.

First draw:

$P(\text{even}) = \frac{6}{12} = \frac{1}{2}$

$P(\text{even, odd}) = \frac{1}{2} \times \frac{6}{11} = \blacksquare\blacksquare$

Second draw:

$P(\text{odd after even}) = \frac{6}{11}$

**SDAP 3.5** Understand the difference between independent and dependent events. *also* **SDAP 3.0,**
**SDAP 3.3, SDAP 3.4, MR 2.4, MR 2.5, MR 3.0, MR 3.2, MR 3.3**

Without looking, Sid draws a card from the jar, does not replace it, and selects another card. For 2–7, find the probability of each event.

2. P(S, S)  3. P(R, L or A)  4. P(not O, O)

5. P(not C, not C)  ✓6. P(M, O, O)  ✓7. P(L, M)

8. **TALK Math** Explain how to find the probability of dependent events.

## Independent Practice and Problem Solving

Without looking, Linda draws a card from the jar, does not replace it, and selects another card. For 9–17, find the probability of each event.

9. P(H, E)  10. P(C, R)  11. P(not C, C)

12. P(E, not H)  13. P(not E, not E)  14. P(C or R, H)

15. P(R, C or E)  16. P(H, C or R)  17. P(E, E, C)

**Algebra** A bag contains 100 equally-sized tiles. There are $x$ red tiles and $y$ blue tiles. If tiles are chosen without replacement, write an algebraic expression for each probability.

18. P(red, blue)  19. P(blue, red)  20. P(blue, blue)

21. ≡**FAST FACT** The 3,400 seat Kodak Theatre in Hollywood, CA, is home to the Academy Awards®. Look at the table at the right. If two tickets are randomly selected and not replaced, what is P(D, F)?

| Kodak Theatre Seating | | | | | | |
|---|---|---|---|---|---|---|
| Section | A | B | C | D | E | F |
| Seats | 586 | 813 | 638 | 525 | 757 | 81 |

**USE DATA** For 22–25, use the table. For a dance recital, students at a dance school randomly draw dance styles written on index cards from a bag until the bag is empty.

| Ballet | Swing | Tap | Ballroom |
|---|---|---|---|
| 3 | 6 | 9 | 6 |

22. Suppose 1 of each dance type was selected. For the next 2 selections, find P(ballroom, tap).

23. **Reasoning** For the first 2 selections, show how P(swing, not swing) and P(not swing, swing) are calculated differently.

24. **Pose a Problem** Look back at Problem 22. Write a similar problem by changing the dances that have already been selected. Then solve.

25. **WRITE Math** What's the Error? Wanda uses $\frac{3}{24} \times \frac{6}{24}$ to find P(ballet, swing) for the two cards selected. Describe and correct her error.

## Achieving the Standards

26. Solve $82 = 24 + x$. (O─╖ AF 1.1, p. 304)

27. If P(event) = $x$, write an expression for P(not event). (O─╖ SDAP 3.3, p. 522)

28. Find the sum: $\frac{1}{2} + \frac{4}{5} + \frac{3}{4} + \frac{3}{5}$ (O─╖ NS 2.0, p. 38)

29. **Test Prep** A bag contains 4 red, 3 blue, and 2 green equally-sized marbles. Jim randomly selects 3 marbles, one at a time without replacement. What is P(red, green, blue)?

A $\frac{1}{21}$  B $\frac{1}{6}$  C $\frac{1}{4}$  D $\frac{1}{3}$

**Extra Practice** on page 558, Set C

 **Extra Practice**

**Set A** For 1-4, use the Fundamental Counting Principle to find the number of possible outcomes for each situation. (O⊓ SDAP 3.1, pp. 548-551)

1. a choice of cheddar, Swiss, or American cheese with white, wheat, or rye bread

2. rolling a number cube and spinning the point of a spinner with 3 sections

3. a choice of white, navy, or yellow shirts with khaki or brown pants

4. tossing two coins and spinning the point of a spinner with 4 sections

5. Marina tosses 2 number cubes. Find the probability that she tosses a 5 on the first cube and a 1 on the second cube.

6. Barrett tosses two coins and rolls a number cube. Find the probability that both tosses are heads and he rolls an even number.

**Set B** The table shows the contents of a bag of colored buttons. Paul randomly selects a button from the bag, replaces it, and selects again. Find the probability of each set of events. (SDAP 3.4, pp. 554-555)

| Red | Blue | Green | White |
|---|---|---|---|
| 6 | 4 | 6 | 8 |

1. P(red, blue)

2. P(red, not blue)

3. P(not green, not white)

4. P(blue, blue)

5. P(not blue, blue)

6. P(white, blue, red)

7. P(green, not red, blue)

8. P(red, red, red)

9. Lyman tosses a coin. Out of 30 tosses he records 12 heads and 18 tails. What is the experimental probability of tossing heads?

10. Candy records the colors of cars that pass her house. Out of 26 cars, 12 are silver. What is the probability that the next car will be silver?

**Set C** Without looking, Bailey draws a card from the jar, does not replace it, and selects another card. For 1–9, find the probability of each set of events. (O⊓ SDAP 3.5, pp. 556-557)

1. P(P, N)

2. P(P, P)

3. P(A, N)

4. P(not N, not N)

5. P(L, not L)

6. P(P or L, not A)

7. P(I, E or L)

8. P(A, P or N)

9. P(I, A)

10. P(not P, A or E)

11. Liz has a bag containing 5 blue marbles and 5 white marbles. What is the probability that she will randomly choose 3 white marbles in a row without replacing any of the marbles?

12. Devlin fills a jar with slips of paper. Each slip of paper has a letter of his name written on it. He draws a letter and replaces it. Find the probability that the next letter he draws is the same letter.

 **Technology**
Use Harcourt Mega Math, Fraction Action, *Last Chance Canyon*, Level M.

# Independently Dependent

**On Your Mark**

2–4 players

**Get Set**
- Game cards
- Number cube labeled 1–6
- Coins

UNCERTAIN

CERTAIN

## Go

- Shuffle the game cards, and place them facedown in a pile.

- Each player selects a coin and places it on UNCERTAIN. Decide who will go first.

- A player draws a game card from the pile.

- The player finds the probability of the independent events shown on the card.

- The objects for the events are a number cube labeled 1 to 6 and a 5-section spinner with equal-sized sections—2 red, 1 blue, 1 green, and 1 yellow.

- The other players check the answer. If it is correct, the player tosses the number cube, advances the number of spaces shown, and play passes to the next player.

- If the answer is incorrect, the player does not advance. Play passes to the next player and play continues.

- The first player to reach CERTAIN wins.

#  Chapter 22 Review/Test

## Check Vocabulary and Concepts

Choose the best term from the box.

1. The __?__ states that if one event has *m* possible outcomes and a second event has n possible outcomes, then there are *m* × *n* possible outcomes for the two events together. (O—¬ SDAP 3.1, p. 549)

2. Events for which the outcome of the second event depends on the outcome of the first event are __?__. (O—¬ SDAP 3.5, p. 552)

## Check Skills

Use the Fundamental Counting Principle to find the number of possible outcomes for each situation. (O—¬ SDAP 3.1, pp. 548-551)

3. rolling one number cube and tossing one coin

4. having lunch or dinner with Li, Mark, or Jose

5. rolling a number cube and spinning the point of a spinner with 5 sections

6. a choice of small, medium, or large sizes of frozen yogurt, ice cream, or sherbet

The table shows the contents of a bag of equally-sized colored buttons. Caleb randomly selects a button from the bag, replaces it, and selects again. For 7–14, find the probability of each set of events. (pp. 554-555)

| Purple | Red | Blue | White |
|--------|-----|------|-------|
| 8      | 2   | 6    | 4     |

7. P(purple)

8. P(red, red)

9. P(purple, not purple)

10. P(purple, not red)

11. P(purple, white)

12. P(red, white, blue)

13. P(red, not blue, purple)

14. P(not red, not red)

Without looking, Elizabeth draws a card from the jar, does not replace it, and selects another card. For 15–23, find the probability of each set of events. (O—¬ SDAP 3.3, pp. 556-557)

15. P(A, P)

16. P(P, S)

17. P(L, S)

18. P(E, not E)

19. P(L, L)

20. P(L, E, S)

21. P(A, not P)

22. P(not A, not A)

23. P(not P, E)

## Check Problem Solving

Solve. (O—¬ SDAP 3.1, MR 1.0, pp. 544-547)

24. At an ice cream shop, you can choose from whipped cream, nuts, or sprinkles. In how many ways can you choose 2 different toppings?

25. **WRITE Math** Susie has a bag of equally-sized marbles on her desk. She randomly pulls a marble from the bag, places it on her desk, and then pulls another marble from the bag. **Explain** what Susie could have done to make the events independent.

**GO ONLINE Technology** Use *Online Assessment.*

# Enrich • Compare Probabilities
## Coins and Marbles

Alexis and Norberto performed experiments by tossing a coin, and pulling a marble without looking, from a bag containing 3 blue, 4 red, 2 green, and 1 yellow marble. During their first experiment, Alexis tossed tails and pulled a blue marble out of the bag. Norberto tossed tails and pulled a red marble out of the bag. Use what you know about probability to determine how their events compare.

**Is the probability of Alexis's event *greater than*, *less than*, or *equal to* the probability of Norberto's event?**

---

**Step 1**  Find the probability of each compound event.

**Alexis's Event**

$P(\text{tails, blue}) = P(\text{tails}) \times P(\text{blue})$

$P(\text{tails}) \times P(\text{blue}) = \frac{1}{2} \times \frac{3}{10} = \frac{3}{20}$, or 15%

**Norberto's Event**

$P(\text{tails, red}) = P(\text{tails}) \times P(\text{red})$

$P(\text{tails}) \times P(\text{red}) = \frac{1}{2} \times \frac{4}{10} = \frac{1}{2} \times \frac{2}{5} = \frac{2}{10} = \frac{1}{5}$, or 20%

**Step 2**  Compare the probabilities.

$$15\% < 20\%$$

---

So, the probability of Alexis's event is less than the probability of Norberto's event.

## Dare to Compare
Use mental math to determine if the probability of Alexis's event is *greater than*, *less than*, or *equal to* the probability of Norberto's event.

1. **Alexis's Event**
   P(heads, red or blue)

   **Norberto's Event**
   P(tails, green)

2. **Alexis's Event**
   P(tails, yellow)

   **Norberto's Event**
   P(tails, blue or green)

3. **Alexis's Event**
   P(heads, white)

   **Norberto's Event**
   P(tails, orange or brown)

## Think About It

**WRITE Math** How many green marbles would you need to add to the bag to make the probability of tossing tails and pulling a green marble greater than the probability of tossing heads and pulling a marble that is not green? **Explain** your thinking.

# Unit Review/Test
## Chapters 21–22

## Multiple Choice

1. Mrs. Stirman has 10 floral, 3 plaid, and 8 solid color scarves in one drawer. What is the probability that, without looking, Mrs. Stirman will pick a plaid scarf from the drawer? (O—⊓ SDAP 3.3, p. 522)

   A $\frac{1}{7}$

   B $\frac{8}{21}$

   C $\frac{3}{7}$

   D $\frac{4}{7}$

2. In her pocket, Bailey has 8 green marbles, 5 red marbles, 6 purple marbles, and 2 blue marbles that are all the same size. If Bailey picks one marble out of her pocket without looking, what is the probability that it will be either green or purple? (O—⊓ SDAP 3.3, p. 522)

   A $\frac{3}{4}$

   B $\frac{1}{4}$

   C $\frac{7}{12}$

   D $\frac{2}{3}$

3. What is the probability of spinning two blues when spinning the pointers of both spinners? (SDAP 3.4, p. 256)

   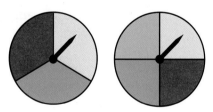

   A $\frac{1}{12}$

   B $\frac{1}{4}$

   C $\frac{7}{12}$

   D $\frac{2}{3}$

4. The table shows how many pairs of socks of each color Hal has in a drawer.

   | Color | Blue | White | Brown |
   |---|---|---|---|
   | Number of Pairs | 5 | 12 | 8 |

   Hal chooses a pair of socks without looking. What is the probability that it will be blue? (O—⊓ SDAP 3.3, p. 522)

   A 5%          C 25%

   B 20%         D 50%

5. Leah is going to choose one sandwich and one soup for lunch.

   | Sandwich | Soup |
   |---|---|
   | tuna<br>turkey<br>cheese | tomato<br>lentil |

   Which set lists all the possible choices for Leah's lunch? (O—⊓ SDAP 3.1, p. 548)

   A (tuna, turkey), (tuna, cheese)

   B (tuna, tomato), (tuna, lentil)

   C (tuna, tomato), (turkey, lentil), (cheese, tomato), (cheese, lentil)

   D (tuna, tomato), (tuna, lentil), (turkey, tomato), (turkey, lentil), (cheese, tomato), (cheese, lentil)

6. What is the probability of rolling heads on a coin and then rolling an even number on a number cube labeled 1 to 6? (O—⊓ SDAP 3.4, p. 554)

   A $\frac{1}{12}$          C $\frac{3}{8}$

   B $\frac{1}{4}$          D $\frac{1}{3}$

Technology Use *Online Assessment.*

7. The table shows the contents of a bag of equally-sized marbles. Josiah takes 2 marbles without replacing them. What is P(red, green)? (⊙━┓ SDAP 3.5, p. 556)

| Red | Green | Blue |
|-----|-------|------|
| 5 | 3 | 2 |

**A** $\frac{1}{12}$      **C** $\frac{1}{6}$

**B** $\frac{1}{10}$      **D** $\frac{1}{2}$

8. Jack missed his target on 6 out of 15 dart throws. Based on his performance so far, how many times can he expect to miss in his next 25 attempts? (SDAP 3.2, p. 532)

**A** 5      **C** 15

**B** 10      **D** 17

9. Eva can go to camp in June, July, or August. She can go to volleyball or tennis camp. How many choices does she have? (⊙━┓ SDAP 3.1, p. 548)

**A** 2      **C** 5

**B** 3      **D** 6

10. In a random sample of 120 pennies, 6 were found to be made before 1960. How many pennies in 6,000 would you predict to be made before 1960? (SDAP 3.0, p. 534)

**A** about 150

**B** about 300

**C** about 1,500

**D** about 3,000

11. Cameron tosses a number cube 3 times. What is the probability that she tosses an odd number on her first, second, and third tosses? (⊙━┓ SDAP 3.4, p. 554)

**A** 0      **C** $\frac{1}{6}$

**B** $\frac{1}{8}$      **D** $\frac{1}{2}$

## Short Response

12. A jar contains 7 slips of paper each with a letter from Martina's name on it. Tell whether choosing an A and a consonant are disjoint events. If so, find the probability that one or the other event will occur. (SDAP 3.4, p. 526)

13. Jacob is arranging 3 books on a shelf. In how many different orders can he arrange the books? (⊙━┓ SDAP 3.1, p. 548)

14. Use the Fundamental Counting Principle to find the number of possible outcomes of choosing between vanilla, mint chip, or rocky road ice cream, served in a cup, sugar cone, or plain cone. (⊙━┓ SDAP 3.1, p. 548)

## Extended Response ▐WRITE Math▐▶

15. In a random sample of 90 bolts, 5 were found to be defective. Explain how you could predict the number of defective bolts in a sample of 2,000. (SDAP 3.0, p. 534)

16. Alexander randomly draws a 10 from a group of index cards labeled 1 to 10. He replaces it and draws a 5. Are these two events independent or dependent? Explain. (⊙━┓ SDAP 3.5, p. 552)

17. A box contains 5 blue, 4 black, 7 white, and 9 tan pairs of gloves. Katrina says that the probability of randomly choosing a black pair is 16%. Explain if her answer is reasonable. (⊙━┓ SDAP 3.3, p. 552)

18. A bag contains 100 tiles of equal size and shape. There are x white tiles and y green tiles. Explain how to write an algebraic expression to find the probability of randomly choosing 3 white tiles in a row without replacing them. (⊙━┓ SDAP 3.5, p. 556)

# Board Games

## HOW MANY SIDES?

**M**illions of people enjoy playing board games with their families and friends. Many popular board games are played by rolling game pieces with numbers. Name some of the games you have played that use number pieces. The number game pieces used in board games might have 6, 8, 10, or 20 sides. There is an equal chance that each side of the game piece will come up. That is what makes playing the game fair.

Which of these pieces have you seen or used before?

## F·A·C·T·A·C·T·I·V·I·T·Y

**For 1–3, use a 10-sided polyhedron with sides labeled 1 to 10.**

❶ What is the theoretical probability of rolling an even number?

❷ What is the theoretical probability of rolling a 7?

❸ What is the theoretical probability of rolling a multiple of 3?

**For 4–5, copy and use the net of an 8-sided polyhedron.**

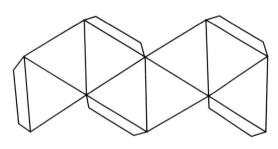

❹ Color the faces of the 8-sided polyhedron so that $\frac{3}{8}$ is red, $\frac{1}{4}$ is blue, and $\frac{3}{8}$ is green.

❺ Write numbers on the sides of the number piece so that the probability of rolling an even number is 3 times greater than rolling an odd number.

❻ **WRITE Math** Compare the probability of rolling an odd number on an 8-sided polyhedron with sides labeled 1 to 8 and on a 6-sided number cube with sides labeled 1 to 6. **Explain** your answer.

## SOCIAL GAMES DAY

The Board Gaming Association in Southern California hosts Games Days. These events encourage people to bring their favorite board games to play. People can choose to play simple games such as Mancala, or they can play harder strategy games that take hours to play. The events last all day.

# FACT·ACTIVITY

❶ Suppose you are at a Games Day event. You can play 3 different games. These are your choices.

| | |
|---|---|
| First round: | Mancala or checkers |
| Second round: | chess or backgammon |
| Third round: | historical game or trivia game |

Make a tree diagram to show all the possible outcomes for the 3 games you can play. How many different outcomes are there?

❷ In the trivia game, these are the possible categories you can roll for each of your first 3 rolls.

| | |
|---|---|
| First roll: | history or current news |
| Second roll: | music or sports |
| Third roll: | science, math, or literature |

Make a tree diagram to show all the possible outcomes for your first three rolls. How many different outcomes are there?

# 8 Perimeter, Area, and Volume

# Math on Location

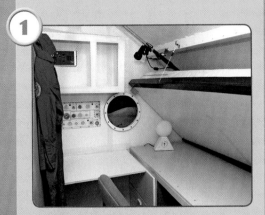

**1**

▲Designing spaces where humans can live and work on the moon or Mars is the job of these architects.

**2**

▲Recycling water for human use and maintaining a greenhouse require complicated shapes and spaces.

**3**

▲The perimeter, area, and volume of structures like these determine how many humans can live there.

# VOCABULARY POWER

### TALK Math

What math do you see in the **Math on Location** photographs? What math is used to create the astronauts' living areas?

### READ Math

**REVIEW VOCABULARY**  You learned the words below when you learned about perimeter, area, and volume. How do these words relate to **Math on Location**?

**perimeter** the distance around a figure

**surface area** the sum of the areas of the surfaces of a solid figure

**volume** the number of cubic units needed to occupy a given space

### WRITE Math

Copy and complete a word definition map like the one below. Use what you know about perimeter, area, and volume to answer the questions.

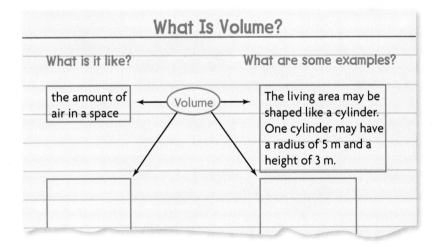

## What Is Volume?

| What is it like? | | What are some examples? |
|---|---|---|
| the amount of air in a space | ← Volume → | The living area may be shaped like a cylinder. One cylinder may have a radius of 5 m and a height of 3 m. |

**Technology**
Multimedia Math Glossary link at
www.harcourtschool.com/hspmath

# 23 Perimeter and Area

**The Big Idea** Attributes of two-dimensional figures can be measured and computed using appropriate formulas.

## CALIFORNIA FAST FACT

In 1831, George Yount, the first American settler in the Napa Valley, was given a grant of 11,000 acres of land. On the land, he planted the first grapevines in the valley.

## Investigate

Suppose you are planning to plant grapevines in the Napa Valley. You draw a diagram of a rectangular field measuring 100 yd by 25 yd. Describe two other plane figures with approximately the same area.

| Plane Figures | |
| --- | --- |
| Square | Triangle |
| Parallelogram | Trapezoid |

**Technology**
Student pages are available in the Student eBook.

Check your understanding of important skills
needed for success in Chapter 23.

▶ **Addition of Fractions and Decimals**

**Find the sum.**

1. $\frac{3}{4} + \frac{1}{2}$

2. $\frac{4}{11} + \frac{2}{3}$

3. $\frac{5}{8} + \frac{4}{9}$

4. $6\frac{3}{5} + 4\frac{1}{6}$

5. $5\frac{1}{3} + 3\frac{2}{3}$

6. $2\frac{1}{4} + 3\frac{1}{8}$

7. $\frac{3}{4} + \frac{5}{8}$

8. $7\frac{3}{4} + 5\frac{1}{5}$

9. $9.11 + 7.06$

10. $16.1 + 54.78$

11. $1.908 + 22.5$

12. $762.1 + 229.43$

▶ **Multiply Fractions and Whole Numbers**

**Find the product.**

13. $2 \times \frac{1}{2}$

14. $\frac{2}{7} \times 21$

15. $\frac{4}{5} \times 35$

16. $18 \times \frac{1}{2}$

17. $4 \times \frac{7}{8}$

18. $45 \times \frac{5}{9}$

19. $\frac{1}{2} \times 36$

20. $56 \times \frac{22}{7}$

21. $5 \times \frac{1}{4}$

22. $12 \times \frac{5}{6}$

23. $\frac{22}{7} \times 42$

24. $\frac{3}{5} \times 25$

▶ **Evaluate Algebraic Expressions**

**Evaluate for the given value of the variable.**

25. $\frac{4a}{7}$ for $a = 21$

26. $2m + 12$ for $m = 6$

27. $4f$ for $f = 12$

28. $\frac{1}{2} \times 12(b + 14)$ for $b = 7$

29. $15a$ for $a = 15$

30. $\frac{1}{2}r \times 5$ for $r = 8$

31. $p^2$ for $p = 13$

32. $s + s + s + s$ for $s = 11$

33. $5x$ for $x = 7$

34. $y^2 + 7$ for $y = 5$

35. $r + r + r$ for $r = 12$

36. $17p + 9$ for $p = 12$

# VOCABULARY POWER

**CHAPTER VOCABULARY**

area
rectangle
parallelogram
square
trapezoid

**WARM-UP WORDS**

**area** the number of square units needed to cover a given surface

**perimeter** the distance around a figure

**square** a rectangle with four congruent sides

 **LESSON 1**

**ALGEBRA**

# Find Perimeter

OBJECTIVE: Find the perimeter of polygons.

## Learn

**PROBLEM** Mr. Xander is building a frame for a large, trapezoid-shaped window which will go in an office building. The shape and dimensions of the window are shown below. He needs to know the perimeter of the window in order to know how much wood he needs for the frame. What is the perimeter?

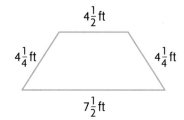

The perimeter, *P*, of a polygon is the distance around it. You can use a formula to find the perimeter of a polygon.

**Quick Review**

Evaluate.

**1.** $2(12.5) + 2(3.2)$

**2.** $3\frac{1}{4} + 5\frac{1}{2} + 2\frac{3}{4}$

**3.** $4(9.8)$

**4.** $2(7\frac{5}{8} + 1\frac{7}{8})$

**5.** $4(5\frac{1}{6})$

### Example 1 Find the perimeter.

Use the formula $P = a + b + c + d$.

| | |
|---|---|
| $P = a + b + c + d$ | Write a formula. |
| $P = 7\frac{1}{2} + 4\frac{1}{4} + 4\frac{1}{2} + 4\frac{1}{4}$ | Replace the variables with the lengths. |
| $P = 7\frac{1}{2} + 13$ | Use mental math to add. |
| $P = 20\frac{1}{2}$ | |

So, the perimeter is $20\frac{1}{2}$ ft.

**Math Idea**
The perimeter of a polygon is equal to the sum of the lengths of its sides.

A regular polygon has sides that are equal in length. To find the perimeter of a regular polygon, multiply the length of one side by the total number of sides.

### Example 2 A patio in the shape of a regular hexagon measures 9.3 m on each side. Find the perimeter of the patio.

| | |
|---|---|
| $P = 6s$ | Write a formula. Let *s* equal the length |
| $P = 6 \times 9.3$ | of one side. Replace *s* with 9.3. Multiply. |
| $P = 55.8$ | |

9.3 m

So, the perimeter is 55.8 meters.

## Rectangles

Since the opposite sides of a rectangle are equal in length, you can find the perimeter by adding the products (2 × length) and (2 × width). This gives the formula $P = 2l + 2w$.

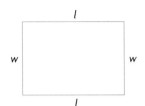

### Example 3 Find the perimeter of the rectangle.

$P = 2l + 2w$ — Write the formula.

$P = (2 \times 5) + (2 \times 3\frac{1}{2})$ — Replace $l$ with 5 and $w$ with $3\frac{1}{2}$.

$P = 10 + 7$ — Add the products.

$P = 17$

5 ft

$3\frac{1}{2}$ ft

So, the perimeter of the rectangle is 17 ft.

**ERROR ALERT**

When using the formula $P = 2l + 2w$, be sure to follow the order of operations and multiply before you add.

### Example 4 A rectangle has a width of $w$. Its length is 3 more than twice its width. Find the perimeter of the rectangle in terms of $w$.

Draw a diagram. Label the width $w$. The length is 3 more than twice $w$ so label the length $2w + 3$.

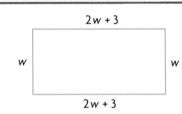

$2w + 3$

$w$

$w$

$2w + 3$

To find the perimeter, add the lengths of all the sides.

$P = w + 2w + 3 + w + 2w + 3$ — Write the sum of the sides.

$P = w + 2w + w + 2w + 3 + 3$ — Use the Commutative Property.

$P = 6w + 6$ — Add the like terms.

So, the perimeter in terms of $w$ is $6w + 6$.

• What if the length of the rectangle was 5 more than twice its width? What would be the perimeter of the rectangle in terms of $w$?

### Example 5 The rectangle shown below has length 12 in. and perimeter $P$ inches. Write an equation that can be used to find the width, $w$, of the rectangle.

$P = 2l + 2w$ — Write the formula.

$P = 2 \times 12 + 2w$ — Replace $l$ with 12. Multiply.

$P = 24 + 2w$

12 in.

$w$

So, an equation that can be used to find the width of the rectangle is $P = 24 + 2w$.

## Guided Practice

**Find the perimeter.**

**1.**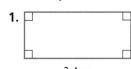
$$P = 2l + 2w$$
$$P = 2 \times 3.4 + 2 \times 1.5$$
$$P = \blacksquare$$

1.5 m

3.4 m

**2.**
9 in.   12 in.
14 in.
$$P = a + b + c$$
$$P = 9 + 12 + 14$$
$$P = \blacksquare$$

**3.**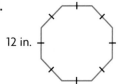
7 in.

10 in.

**✓4.**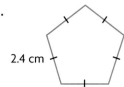
6.8 m
5.4 m   3.7 m
4.2 m

**✓5.**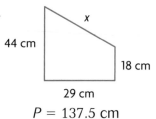
$3\frac{1}{2}$ yd

$3\frac{1}{2}$ yd

**6.** **TALK Math** **Explain** how you can find the perimeter of a regular pentagon with sides of length 5 in.

## Independent Practice and Problem Solving

**Find the perimeter.**

**7.**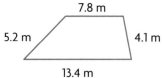
7.8 m
5.2 m      4.1 m
13.4 m

**8.**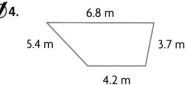
19.5 mm      7.5 mm
8 mm

**9.**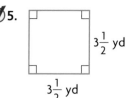
2 ft
9.5 ft

**10.**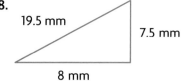
12 in.

**11.**
2.4 cm

**12.**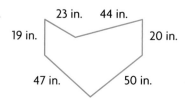
23 in.   44 in.
19 in.              20 in.
47 in.        50 in.

**13.** square 9.9 cm on a side

**14.** rectangle $4\frac{1}{8}$ in. long and $2\frac{3}{8}$ in. wide

★**Algebra** Solve.

**15.** Find the perimeter of the rectangle below in terms of *w*.

3w + 1
w        w
3w + 1

**16.** The rectangle below has a length of 6 cm and perimeter *P* cm. Write an equation that could be used to find the width, *w*, of the rectangle.

6 cm
w

★**Algebra** The perimeter is given. Find the unknown measure.

**17.**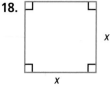
x
44 cm
18 cm
29 cm
$$P = 137.5 \text{ cm}$$

**18.**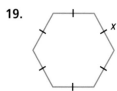
x
x
$$P = 40 \text{ ft}$$

**19.**
x
$$P = 73.8 \text{ cm}$$

**Extra Practice** on page 588, Set A

**20.** Elise uses $45\frac{1}{2}$ ft of border paper to trim the four walls of her rectangular bedroom. The longer walls each measure $12\frac{1}{4}$ ft. What is the length of each of the shorter walls?

**21. Algebra** A rectangle has a length of 8.5 m and perimeter $P$ meters. Write an equation that could be used to find the width, $w$, of the rectangle.

**22. Pose a Problem** Write and solve a problem similar to Problem 20 by making the problem more open-ended.

**23. Algebra** A rectangle has a width of $w$. Its length is 2 less than 3 times its width. Find the perimeter of the rectangle in terms of $w$.

**24. Reasoning** A square piece of fabric measures $6\frac{1}{2}$ ft on each side. It is cut in half to make two congruent rectangular banners. What is the perimeter of each banner?

**25.** **⬛WRITE Math** ▸ **Sense or Nonsense** Wendy says the length of her rectangular mirror is $5\frac{4}{5}$ ft. The perimeter is $11\frac{3}{5}$ ft. Does Wendy's statement make sense? **Explain.**

## Achieving the Standards

**26.** A bag contains 4 red, 5 blue, and 6 yellow marbles. Find the probability of randomly drawing a red marble, not replacing it, and then drawing a yellow marble.
(O━┓ SDAP 3.5, p. 556)

**27.** Find the product $3\frac{1}{2} \times 7$. (NS 2.1, p. 74)

**28. Test Prep** What is the perimeter of a rectangle with a length of 10 feet and a width of 5 feet?

    **A** 5 feet  **B** 10 feet  **C** 15 feet  **D** 30 feet

**29.** A $25.00 jacket is on sale for 15% off. What is the sale price of the jacket? (O━┓ NS 1.4, p. 500)

**30. Test Prep** A rectangle has a length of 10 inches and perimeter $P$. Which equation could be used to find the width, $w$, of the rectangle?

    **A** $P = 10 + \frac{w}{2}$    **C** $P = 20 + 2w$

    **B** $P = 15 - w$    **D** $P = 20 - 2w$

## MATH POWER — Problem Solving and Reasoning

**GEOMETRY** You can use geometric relationships to find unknown measures.

**Example** Find the unknown measures. Then find the perimeter.

The height of the figure is 12 units, so, $x + 7 = 12$. So, $x = 5$.

The width of the figure is 16 units, so $y + 6 = 16$. So, $y = 10$.

$12 + 6 + 5 + 10 + 7 + 16 = 56$

So, $x = 5$, $y = 10$, and the perimeter is 56 units.

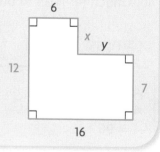

**Find the unknown measures. Then find the perimeter.**

**1.**

**2.**
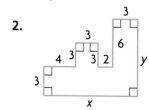

**3.**
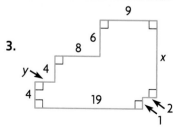

**ALGEBRA**

# Area of Squares and Rectangles

OBJECTIVE: Find the area of squares and rectangles.

**Quick Review**

Evaluate.

1. $13 \times 7$
2. $4.5^2$
3. $0.6 \times 0.8$
4. $8^2$
5. $2\frac{1}{2} \times 16$

## Learn

The area of a figure is the number of square units needed to cover it. You can use square tiles to learn how the area of a rectangle is related to its length and width.

**HANDS ON**

### Activity

**Materials** ■ ruler ■ square tiles

• Use a ruler to draw a rectangle with a length of 5 in. and a width of 3 in.

• Use square tiles to completely cover the rectangle.

• Count the number of tiles needed to cover the rectangle. This gives the area of the rectangle.

• Count the number of tiles along the length and the width of your rectangle. Find the product of these two measurements.

• How does the product compare with the area?

• Write a formula to use to find the area of a rectangle.

To find the area of a rectangle you can use the formula $A = lw$ where $A$ is the area, $l$ is the length and $w$ is the width.

**PROBLEM** Sonia has a rectangular garden, with a length of 12 ft and a width of 8 ft. She needs to know the area of the garden so she knows how much fertilizer to buy. What is the area of Sonia's garden?

### Example 1  Use the formula $A = lw$ to find the area.

| | |
|---|---|
| $A = lw$ | Write the formula. |
| $A = 12 \times 8$ | Replace $l$ with 12 and $w$ with 8. Multiply. |
| $A = 96$ | |

8 ft

12 ft

So, the area of Sonia's garden is 96 ft$^2$.

• What if Sonia increases the width of her garden by 3 ft and decreases the length by 4 ft? What would be the new area of the garden?

AF 3.1 Use variables in expressions describing geometric quantities (e.g., $P = 2w + 2l$, $A = \frac{1}{2}bh$, $C = \pi d$–the formulas for the perimeter of a rectangle, the area of a triangle, and the circumference of a circle, respectively). *also* **AF 3.2, MG 1.0, MR 2.2, MR 2.4, MR 2.5, MR 3.2**

# Squares

A square is a rectangle whose length and width are the same. To write a formula for the area of a square, use the formula for the area of a rectangle, $A = lw$, and let $s$ represent the length of a side of the square.

$A = lw$     Replace both $l$ and $w$ with $s$.
$A = s \times s$     Multiply. $(s \times s = s^2)$
$A = s^2$

So, a formula for the area of a square is $A = s^2$ where $s$ represents the length of a side of the square.

**Example 2** Raphael is tiling his bathroom floor. If each square tile measures 9.5 cm on a side, what is the area of each tile?

Use the formula $A = s^2$.

$A = s^2$     Write the formula.
$A = 9.5^2$     Replace $s$ with 9.5.
$A = 90.25$

9.5 cm

9.5 cm

So, the area of each tile is 90.25 cm².

Sometimes you may need to use variables to represent area.

**Example 3** A square with a side of $x$ is inside a square with a side of 10 as shown below. Write an expression that represents the area of the shaded region in terms of $x$.

**Step 1**

Find the area of the large square.

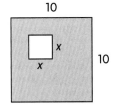

10

$x$

$x$

10

$A = s^2$     Write the formula.
$A = 10^2$     Replace $s$ with 10.
$A = 100$

The area of the large square is 100.

**Step 2**

Find the area of the small square.

$A = s^2$     Write the formula.
$A = x^2$     Replace $s$ with $x$.

The area of the small square is $x^2$.

**Step 3**

The area of the shaded region is the difference between the area of the large square and the area of the small square, or $100 - x^2$.

So, the area of the shaded region is $100 - x^2$.

- What is the area of the shaded region if $x = 4$?

**Find the area.**

**1.**   4.1 m  8.3 m

$A = lw$
$A = \blacksquare \times \blacksquare$
$A = \blacksquare$

**2.** 12.5 ft  12.5 ft

$A = s^2$
$A = \blacksquare^2$
$A = \blacksquare$

**3.**  7 in.  18 in.

**✓4.** 2.5 mm  2.5 mm

**✓5.** 2 yd  $5\frac{1}{2}$ yd

**6.** **TALK Math** Explain how the number of square units that cover a rectangle is related to the length and the width of the rectangle.

## Independent Practice **and Problem Solving**

**Find the area.**

**7.** 6.4 m  9.1 m

**8.** 15 ft  15 ft

**9.** 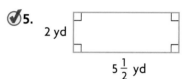 $9\frac{1}{2}$ in.  $1\frac{3}{4}$ in.

**10.** 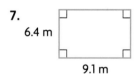 5.7 m  5.7 m

**11.** 8 yd  7 yd  3 yd  11 yd

**12.** 10.3 cm  11.3 cm  5.2 cm  19.1 cm

**The area is given. Find the unknown measure.**

**13.** 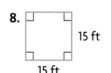 5 in.  $A = 30$ in.$^2$  $x$

**14.** 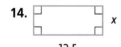 $x$  12.5  $A = 50$ cm$^2$

**15.** $x$  $A = 81$ m$^2$  $x$

**16. Reasoning** A square with a side of 9 is inside a square with a side of $x$ as shown at the right. Write an expression that represents the area of the shaded region in terms of $x$.

9
9
$x$
$x$

**17. ≡FAST FACT** The largest rectangular photograph ever printed in California had an area of 3,024 ft$^2$ and a width of 28 ft. Find the length of the photograph.

**18.** Sonia plans to have zucchini plants cover a large part of her garden. She stakes off a rectangle 5 ft long by $4\frac{1}{2}$ ft wide. What is the area of this part of her garden?

**19.** Jeremy fertilizes his rectangular 7-by-18-ft garden with compost. The recommended amount is 2 lb of compost for every square yard of the garden. How many pounds of compost will he need?

**20. Reasoning** Joan plans to surround her garden with a gravel walkway as shown at the right. The final dimensions of the garden and walkway together will be 14 ft by 10 ft. What will be the area of the walkway?

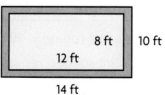
8 ft    10 ft
12 ft
14 ft

**21.** Harriet puts a 9-by-9-ft piece of landscape fabric over her garden to keep weeds out. She cuts a 2.5-by-2.5-ft square piece from the center of the sheet. How much area will be covered by the remaining fabric?

**22.** **WRITE Math** ▶ What's the Question? A rectangle has a length of 12 m and a width of 10 m. The answer is 120 m².

**23.** Two angles are supplementary. One of the angles measures 37°. What is the measure of the other angle? (○━┓ MG 2.2, p. 376)

**24.** Evaluate $\frac{1}{2}bh$ if $b = 10$ and $h = 7$. (AF 1.2, p.284)

**25.** **Test Prep** A rectangular rug measures 13 feet by 8 feet. What is the area of the rug?

   **A** 21 feet²     **C** 42 feet²

   **B** 52 feet²     **D** 104 feet²

**26.** Find the probability of rolling an odd number on a number cube labeled 1–6. Write the probability as a fraction, a decimal, and a percent. (○━┓ SDAP, 3.3, p. 522)

**27.** **Test Prep** Which expression represents the area of the shaded region in terms of $x$?

   **A** $24 - 2x$

   **B** $48 - 4x$

   **C** $144 - x^2$

   **D** $x^2 - 144$

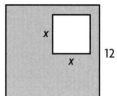

 **Problem Solving and Reasoning**

**MEASUREMENT** Caroline plants a rectangular garden that measures 5 ft by 3 ft. She then decides to plant a rectangular garden that has dimensions twice the size as the original garden. How does the area of the new garden compare to the area of the original garden?

**Original Garden**

3 ft
5 ft

$A = lw$
$A = 5 \times 3$
$A = 15$, or 15 ft²

**New Garden**

6 ft
10 ft

$A = lw$
$A = 10 \times 6$
$A = 60$, or 60 ft²

The areas are 60 ft² and 15 ft². So, the area of the new garden is 4 times as great as the area of the original garden.

**Compare the area of the new rectangle to that of the original rectangle.**

**1.** A rectangle with dimensions of 4 m by 6 m has its dimensions tripled.

**2.** A rectangle with dimensions 10 ft by 14 ft has its dimensions halved.

**ALGEBRA**

# Area of Triangles

OBJECTIVE: Find the areas of triangles.

## Quick Review

**Multiply.**

1. $\frac{1}{2}(6)(3)$   2. $\frac{1}{2}(5)(4)$

3. $\frac{1}{2}(4)(7)$   4. $\frac{1}{2}(8)(9)$

5. $\frac{1}{2}(2)(15)$

## Learn

You can use rectangles to find a formula for the area of right triangles. The figure at the right shows how two congruent right triangles can be used to model a rectangle. The area of each triangle is half that of the rectangle. The area of each right triangle is $\frac{1}{2}lw$. In a right triangle, the dimensions of the two legs are the base, $b$, and the height, $h$. So, the formula for the area of a right triangle is written as $A = \frac{1}{2}bh$.

(height, $h$, or width, $w$)

(base, $b$, or length, $l$)

### Example 1 Find the area of the right triangle.

| | |
|---|---|
| $A = \frac{1}{2}bh$ | Write the formula. |
| $A = \frac{1}{2} \times 6 \times 2.5$ | Replace $b$ with 6 and $h$ with 2.5. |
| $A = 3 \times 2.5$ | Multiply. |
| $A = 7.5$ | |

2.5 m

6 m

So, the area of the right triangle is 7.5 m².

You can use what you know about right triangles to find the area of other triangles. Look at triangle $XYZ$ at the right.

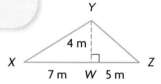

$Y$

4 m

$X$   7 m   $W$   5 m   $Z$

Area of right triangle $YWX$

⟶

$A = \frac{1}{2}bh = \frac{1}{2} \times 7 \times 4 = 14$

Area of right triangle $YWZ$

⟶

$A = \frac{1}{2}bh = \frac{1}{2} \times 5 \times 4 = 10$

The area of triangle $XYZ$ equals the sum of the areas of right triangles $YWX$ and $YWZ$.

So, the area of triangle $XYZ$ is $14 + 10$, or 24 m².

• Find the area of triangle $XYZ$ by using 7 m + 5 m, or 12 m, as the base and 4 m as the height. Compare your answer to 24 m².

As you have just seen, the formula $A = \frac{1}{2}bh$ works for all triangles.

> **Math Idea**
> The height, or altitude, of a triangle is perpendicular to its base. The height can be a leg, or a line drawn inside or outside the triangle

### Example 2 Find the area.

**A** The triangle has a base of 10 in. and a height of 6.5 in.

6.5 in.

10 in.

$A = \frac{1}{2}bh$   Write the formula.

$A = \frac{1}{2} \times 10 \times 6.5$   Replace $b$ with 10 and $h$ with 6.5. Multiply.

$A = 32.5$ or 32.5 in.²

**B** The triangle has a base of $b$ and a height of $2b$. Find the area in terms of $b$.

$A = \frac{1}{2}bh$   Write the formula.

$A = \frac{1}{2} \times b \times 2b$   Replace $h$ with $2b$. Use the Commutative

$A = \frac{1}{2} \times 2 \times b \times b$   Property. Multiply. ($b \times b = b^2$)

$A = b^2$

$2b$

$b$

**578**

**AF 3.1** Use variables in expressions describing geometric quantities (e.g., $P = 2w + 2l$, $A = \frac{1}{2}bh$, $C = \pi d$–the formulas for the perimeter of a rectangle, the area of a triangle, and the circumference of a circle, respectively). *also* ○━┑ NS 2.0, NS 2.1, AF 3.0, AF 3.2, MG 1.0, MR 2.2, MR 2.4, MR 2.5, MR 3.2

**Find the Area.**

**1.** 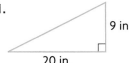 9 in.
20 in.

$A = \frac{1}{2}bh$
$A = \frac{1}{2} \times 20 \times 9$
$A = \blacksquare$

**2.** 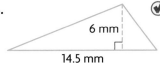 1.5 cm
14 cm

$A = \frac{1}{2}bh$
$A = \frac{1}{2} \times 14 \times 1.5$
$A = \blacksquare$

**3.**
8 ft
6 ft

**4.** 6 mm
14.5 mm

**✓5.** 52 m    31 m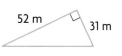

**✓6.**  10 cm
17 cm

**7.** **TALK Math** Explain how the areas of a rectangle and a triangle with the same base and height are related.

**Find the area.**

**8.** 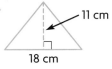 11 cm
18 cm

**9.** 1.2 m    0.5 m

**10.** $1\frac{1}{3}$ in.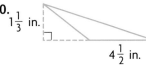
$4\frac{1}{2}$ in.

**11.** 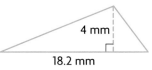 4 mm
18.2 mm

**12.** a triangle with a base of $\frac{1}{2}$ in. and a height of $\frac{1}{2}$ in.

**13.** a triangle with a height of 10.8 cm and a base of 48 cm

**14.** Find the measure of the base of a triangle if the height is 24 mm and the area is 180 mm$^2$.

**15.** Triangular supports for a bookshelf are in the shape of congruent isosceles right triangles as shown in the figure. If the shelf is 14 in. deep, how many square inches of wood were used to construct the two supports?

**16.** A triangle has a base, $b$, and a height that is 4 times as great as the base, or $4b$. Find the area of the triangle in terms of $b$.

**17.** **WRITE Math** What's the Error? Clay said the area of a triangle with a base of 12 cm and a height of 8 cm is 96 cm$^2$. Find and correct his error.

**18.** Find the sum $3\frac{1}{6} + 5\frac{2}{3}$. (NS 2.1, p. 42)

**19.** Evaluate $\frac{1}{2}(a + b)$ if $a = 11$ and $b = 5$.
(AF 1.2, p. 284)

**20.** Draw a quadrilateral that has exactly one pair of parallel sides and two right angles. What is the name of the shape you drew? (MG 2.3, p. 404)

**21. Test Prep** What is the area of the triangle?

**A** 9 cm$^2$

**B** 10 cm$^2$

**C** 16 cm$^2$

**D** 20 cm$^2$

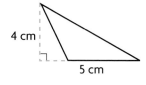
4 cm
5 cm

**Extra Practice** on page 588, Set C

ALGEBRA

# Area of Parallelograms and Trapezoids

**OBJECTIVE:** Derive formulas to find the areas of parallelograms and trapezoids.

## Learn

The area of a parallelogram is related to the area of a rectangle.

**HANDS ON**

### Activity 1

**Materials** ■ graph paper ■ scissors

• Draw the parallelogram at the right on graph paper and cut it out.

• Cut along the dotted line. Move the triangle to the right side of the figure to form a rectangle.

• What is the area of the rectangle? What is the area of the parallelogram?

• How are the dimensions and area of the parallelogram related to those of the rectangle?

• What formula can you write for the area of a parallelogram?

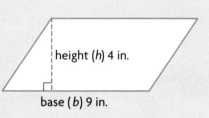

height (*h*) 4 in.

base (*b*) 9 in.

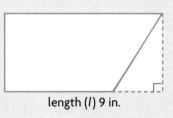

width (*w*) 4 in.

length (*l*) 9 in.

You can use the formula for the area of a rectangle to write a formula for the area of a parallelogram.

$A = lw$     The length of the rectangle is the base of the parallelogram. The width of the rectangle is
  ↓       the height of the parallelogram.
$A = bh$

### Example 1 Find the area.

$A = bh$       Write the formula.
$A = 23 \times 12$   Replace *b* with 23 and *h* with 12. Multiply.
$A = 276$

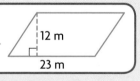

12 m

23 m

So, the area is 276 m².

### Example 2

The base of a parallelogram is three times the height, *h*. Find the area of the parallelogram in terms of *h*.

$A = bh$       Write the formula.
$A = 3h \times h$   Replace *b* with 3*h*. Multiply. ($h \times h = h^2$)
$A = 3h^2$

*h*

3*h*

So, the area of the parallelogram in terms of *h* is $3h^2$.

**AF 3.1** Use variables in expressions describing geometric quantities (e.g., $P = 2w + 2l$, $A = \frac{1}{2}bh$, $C = \pi d$–the formulas for the perimeter of a rectangle, the area of a triangle, and the circumference of a circle, respectively). *also* **AF 3.2, MG 1.0, MR 1.2, MR 1.3, MR 2.2, MR 2.4, MR 2.5, MR 3.2**

## Activity 2

**Materials** ■ graph paper ■ scissors

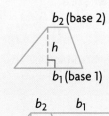

- Trace two copies of the trapezoid shown at the right on a piece of graph paper. Label both trapezoids using $h$, $b_1$, and $b_2$ as shown. Cut them out.

- Arrange the trapezoids to form a parallelogram. The length of the parallelogram is $b_1 + b_2$. The height is $h$.

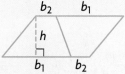

- Write a formula for the area of the parallelogram. Use $(b_1 + b_2)$ for the base and $h$ for the height in the formula $A = bh$.

- How does the area of one trapezoid relate to the area of the parallelogram?

Since the area of each trapezoid is half the area of the parallelogram, a formula for the area of a trapezoid is $A = \frac{1}{2} \times (b_1 + b_2) \times h$, or $A = \frac{1}{2}h(b_1 + b_2)$.

---

### Example 3   Find the area of the trapezoid.

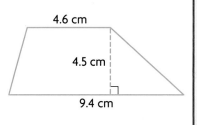

$A = \frac{1}{2}h(b_1 + b_2)$     Write the formula.

$A = \frac{1}{2} \times 4.5 \times (9.4 + 4.6)$     Replace $h$ with 4.5, $b_1$ with 9.4, and $b_2$ with 4.6. Add.

$A = \frac{1}{2} \times 4.5 \times 14$

$A = \frac{1}{2} \times 14 \times 4.5$     Use the Commutative Property to simplify the calculation.

$A = 7 \times 4.5$     Multiply.

$A = 31.5$

So, the area of the trapezoid is 31.5 cm².

---

## Guided Practice

1. Find the area of the parallelogram.

   $A = bh$

   $A = 12 \times 7$

   $A = \blacksquare$

   7 ft

   12 ft

2. Find the area of the trapezoid.

   $A = \frac{1}{2}h(b_1 + b_2)$

   $A = \frac{1}{2} \times 18 \times (43 + 17)$

   $A = \blacksquare$

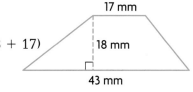
   17 mm

   18 mm

   43 mm

**Find the area.**

3.

9 yd

4 yd

✓ 4.
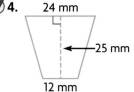
24 mm

25 mm

12 mm

✓ 5.
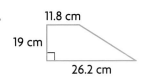
11.8 cm

19 cm

26.2 cm

6. **TALK Math** **Explain** how the areas of some parallelograms and rectangles are related.

**Find the area.**

**7.**

8 ft
21 ft

**8.**

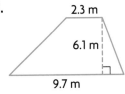

2.3 m
6.1 m
9.7 m

**9.**

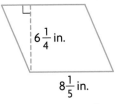

$6\frac{1}{4}$ in.

$8\frac{1}{5}$ in.

**10.**

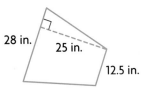

28 in.
25 in.
12.5 in.

**11.**

3 cm
2.5 cm
7.5 cm

**12.**

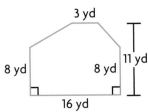

3 yd
8 yd    8 yd
11 yd
16 yd

**13.** The height of a parallelogram is four times the base, *b*. Find the area of the parallelogram in terms of *b*.

**14.** The area of a parallelogram is 32 cm². The base of the parallelogram measures 8 cm. What is the measure of the height?

**15.** Draw a parallelogram on a piece of paper. Measure the base and height of your parallelogram to the nearest inch. Use your measurements to estimate the area of your parallelogram.

**16.** Draw a trapezoid on a piece of paper. Measure both bases and the height of the trapezoid to the nearest inch. Use your measurements to estimate the area of your parallelogram.

**17.** A pattern used for tile floors is shown at the right. A side of the inner square measures 10 cm, and a side of the outer square measures 30 cm. What is the area of one of the equally-sized trapezoid tiles?

**18. Reasoning** A large tile is cut into three smaller tiles as shown. The measures of the bases of the triangles are equal. What is the area of each of the three new tiles?

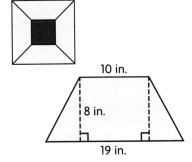

10 in.
8 in.
19 in.

**19.** [WRITE Math] **What's the Error?** A trapezoid has a height of 12 cm and bases with lengths of 14 cm and 10 cm. Tina says the area of the trapezoid is 288 cm². Find her error and the correct area.

## Achieving the Standards

**20.** Find the difference. 200 − ⁻6. (O—π NS 2.3, p. 182)

**21.** If it keeps the same proportions as a photo 6 inches long and 4 inches wide, how wide is an enlargement that is 27 inches longer? (O—π NS 1.3, p. 478)

**22.** Find the area. (MG 1.0, p. 578)

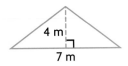

4 m
7 m

**23. Test Prep** Find the area.

  **A** 13.5 square inches  **C** 27 square inches

  **B** 40.5 square inches  **D** 50.5 square inches

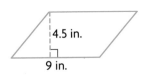

4.5 in.
9 in.

Extra Practice on page 588, Set D

**Technology**
Use Harcourt Mega Math, Ice Station
ROM Exploration, *Polar Planes,* Levels Q & R.

# How Does Your Garden Grow?

 **Reading Skill** Cause and Effect

▲ The scientific name for the California poppy is Eschscholzia californica.

Eric wants to reduce the size of his 10-ft by 6-ft rectangular California poppy garden by cutting either the length or the width of the garden in half. How will cutting the width in half affect the area and perimeter of the garden? How does this compare to cutting the length in half?

**Cause:** changing dimensions
**Effect:** change in area and perimeter

Calculate the area and perimeter of Eric's garden.

| Area | Perimeter |
|---|---|
| $A = lw$ | $P = 2l + 2w$ |
| $A = 10 \times 6$ | $P = 2 \times 10 + 2 \times 6$ |
| $A = 60$ ft$^2$ | $P = 32$ ft |

Now examine what happens to the perimeter and area when the width is halved.

| Area | Perimeter |
|---|---|
| $A = lw$ | $P = 2l + 2w$ |
| $A = 10 \times 3$ | $P = 2 \times 10 + 2 \times 3$ |
| $A = 30$ ft$^2$ | $P = 26$ ft |

The area of the new rectangle is half the area of the original.

The perimeter of the new rectangle is 6 feet less than the original, which is a difference equal to the original width.

Repeat the process to see how the area and perimeter would be affected by cutting the length of the original rectangle in half.

**Problem Solving** Analyze cause and effect to solve.

1. How does halving the length of Eric's garden affect the area and perimeter? How does this compare to halving the width? **Explain.**

2. The length and the width of a rectangle are both halved. How does this affect the area? How does this affect the perimeter? **Explain.**

# Problem Solving Workshop
## Strategy: Solve a Simpler Problem

**OBJECTIVE:** Solve problems using the strategy *solve a simpler problem.*

## Learn the Strategy

You can use the strategy solve a simpler problem to make difficult problems easier to solve.

*A simpler problem helps to find the area of a complex figure.*

Find the area of the figure.

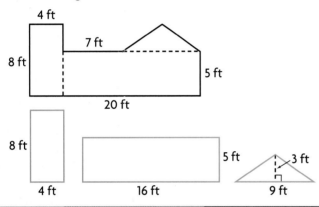

4 ft

7 ft

8 ft

5 ft

20 ft

8 ft

5 ft  3 ft

4 ft        16 ft        9 ft

*A simpler problem helps find a pattern.*

How many edges and vertices are there in a prism with a 12-sided base?

| Sides on a Base | 3 | 4 | 5 |
|---|---|---|---|
| Vertices | 3+3=6 | 4+4=8 | 5+5=10 |
| Edges | 3+3+3=9 | 4+4+4=12 | 5+5+5=15 |

The number of vertices is 2 times the number of sides on the base.
The number of edges is 3 times the number of sides on the base.

> **TALK Math**
>
> How does solving a simpler problem help you solve the original problem?

**MG 1.0** Students deepen their understanding of the measurement of plane and solid shapes and use this understanding to solve problems. *also* AF 3.1, MR 1.0, MR 1.3, MR 2.0, MR 2.1, MR 2.2, MR 2.4, MR 2.5, MR 2.7, MR 3.0, MR 3.1, MR 3.2, MR 3.3

# Use the Strategy

**PROBLEM** The new entryway to the fun house at Happy World Amusement Park is made from rectangles, parallelograms, and triangles, as shown in the diagram. It will be painted bright green. The painter needs to know the area of the entryway so she knows how much paint to buy. What is the area of the entryway?

## Read to Understand

- **Summarize the details of the problem.**
- **What information will you use?**

*Diagram labels: 3.8 ft, 4.5 ft, 9 ft, 5 ft, 5 ft*

## Plan

- **What strategy can you use to solve the problem?**
  You can solve a simpler problem to help you solve the main problem.

## Solve

- **How can you use the strategy to solve the problem?**

  Think of the entryway as a collection of smaller shapes: two rectangles, two parallelograms, and one triangle. Find the area of each shape. Then find the sum of the areas to get the total area.

Two rectangles

9 ft
5 ft

$A = lw$
$A = 9 \times 5$
$A = 45$

Area of 2 rectangles:
$2 \times 45 = 90$
Area: $= 90$ ft$^2$

Two parallelograms

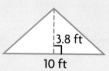
4.5 ft
5 ft

$A = bh$
$A = 5 \times 4.5$
$A = 22.5$

Area of 2 parallelograms:
$2 \times 22.5 = 45$
Area: $= 45$ ft$^2$

One triangle

3.8 ft
10 ft

$A = \frac{1}{2}bh$
$A = \frac{1}{2} \times 10 \times 3.8$
$A = 5 \times 3.8$
$A = 19$

Area of 1 triangle:
Area: $= 19$ ft$^2$

Total area: $90$ ft$^2 + 45$ ft$^2 + 19$ ft$^2 = 154$ ft$^2$

So, the area of the entryway is $154$ ft$^2$.

## Check

- **Is the answer reasonable? Explain.**

## Guided Problem Solving

1. One of the walls in the fun house is covered with mirrors. The mirrors are shaped like rectangles and a trapezoid, as shown. What is the area of the mirrors on the wall?

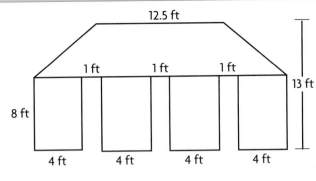

   **First,** identify the shapes and their dimensions.

   four rectangles                one trapezoid

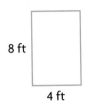 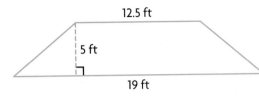

   **Then,** find the area of each shape.

   $A = lw$           $A = \frac{1}{2}h(b_1 + b_2)$

   $A = 8 \times 4$     $A = \frac{1}{2} \times 5 \times (19 + 12.5)$

   $A = \blacksquare$         $A = \blacksquare$

   Area of 4 rectangles:

   $4 \times \blacksquare = \blacksquare$

   **Finally,** add the areas to find the total area of the mirrors.

2. **What if** the top mirror is replaced by a triangular mirror with the same bottom base and height measurements as the trapezoid? What will be the new area of the mirrors?

3. At the ball-toss booth, players try to throw a ball through one of the openings in the rectangular wall pictured at the right. There are 4 of these walls. All the walls need to be painted. If the sides of each square opening and the base and height of each triangular opening is $\frac{1}{2}$ ft, how many square feet of walls must be painted?

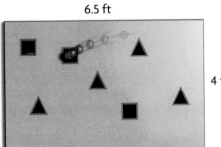

## Problem Solving Strategy Practice

**Solve by solving a simpler problem.**

4. Rex is playing a number game in the game tent. He has to find the sum of the first 20 odd numbers. Find the sum of the first 20 odd numbers.

5. In the craft tent, Maggie is making a model of a prism. The prism will have bases with 10 sides each. She will use balls of clay for the vertices and straws for the edges. How many balls of clay will Maggie need?

6. How many straws will Maggie need to build the prism in Problem 5?

## Mixed Strategy Practice

7. Ashton wants to go on 6 different rides before lunch time. If he wants to go on the roller coaster first and the log flume last, in how many different orders can he go on the 6 rides?

8. Ravi went on twice as many rides as Dan. Sam went on 3 more rides than Ravi. If Sam went on 9 rides, how many rides did Dan go on?

9. **Pose a Problem** Look back at problem 7. Write a similar problem by changing known and unknown information. Then solve your problem.

**USE DATA** For 10–12, use the table.

10. Mr. Sherman, who is an adult, plans to take his son, who is 14, and his daughter, who is 10, with him to the amusement park. How much will they save if they go on Monday instead of on Sunday?

11. Six members of the Mulligan family visited the amusement park last Thursday. Mrs. Mulligan paid for the tickets with a $100 bill. If she received $2.75 change, how many of each type of ticket did she buy?

12. **Open-Ended** Plan a trip for a family of 6 to Happy World Amusement Park. Decide on the ages of each family member and the number of times the family will visit the park in one year. Then tell which kind of tickets would be the least expensive for the family.

13. **WRITE Math** ▶ Look back at one of the problems you solved using the strategy solve a simpler problem. Describe how the solution to the simpler problem helps you find the solution to the main problem.

**Problem-Solving STRATEGIES**

Draw a Diagram or Picture

Make a Model or Act It Out

Make an Organized List

Find a Pattern

Make a Table or Graph

Predict and Test

Work Backward

Solve a Simpler Problem

Write an Equation

Use Logical Reasoning

### Happy World Amusement Park

**Ticket Prices**

| | Weekday Tickets | Weekend Tickets | Yearly Passes |
|---|---|---|---|
| **Adults** | $18.75 | $23.95 | $99.00 |
| **Children (12 and under)** | $15.75 | $19.95 | $79.00 |
| **Senior Citizens** | $12.50 | $15.50 | $65.00 |

## CHALLENGE YOURSELF

**Each week, about 2,000 more people visit the amusement park the entire weekend than on Monday through Friday combined.**

14. Last week, half as many people visited the park on Tuesday as on Monday. A total of 9,900 people visited on Wednesday, Thursday, and Friday. If 4,680 people visited on Monday, about how many visitors did the park have on the weekend?

15. This week, a total of 2,130 people attended the park on Monday, 3,152 people on Tuesday, and 1,966 people on Wednesday. A total of 15,149 people attended the park on the weekend. About the same number of people attended on Thursday as on Friday. About how many people attended on Thursday?

# Extra Practice

## Set A Find the perimeter. (pp. 570–573)

**1.**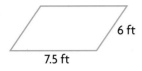
7.5 ft, 6 ft

**2.**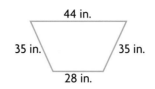
44 in., 35 in., 35 in., 28 in.

**3.**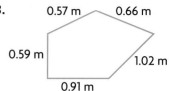
0.57 m, 0.66 m, 0.59 m, 1.02 m, 0.91 m

**4.** Elaina made a rectangular quilt that is 8 ft long by 6 ft wide. She wants to sew decorative ribbon around the edges to finish it. How much ribbon will she need?

**5.** A rectangular field measures 12 m wide by 18 m long. How many meters of fence should be ordered to completely enclose the field?

## Set B Find the area. (pp. 574–577)

**1.**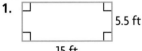
5.5 ft, 15 ft

**2.**
5 m, 2 m

**3.**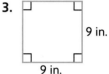
9 in., 9 in.

**4.** Martina is building a rectangular deck in her backyard that measures 8 yd long by 6 yd wide. What is the area of the deck?

**5.** The area of a square is 256 square feet. What is the length of each side?

## Set C Find the area. (pp. 578–579)

**1.**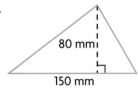
80 mm, 150 mm

**2.**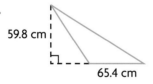
59.8 cm, 65.4 cm

**3.**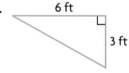
6 ft, 3 ft

**4.**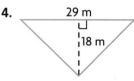
29 m, 18 m

**5.** The area of a triangle is 1,500 ft². The height of the triangle measures 20 ft. What is the measure of the base of the triangle?

## Set D Find the area. (pp. 580–583)

**1.**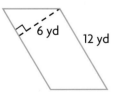
6 yd, 12 yd

**2.**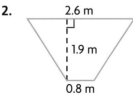
2.6 m, 1.9 m, 0.8 m

**3.**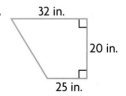
32 in., 20 in., 25 in.

**4.** The area of a parallelogram is 96 cm². The height of the parallelogram measures 6 cm. What is the measure of the length of the parallelogram?

**Technology**
Use Harcourt Mega Math, Ice Station Exploration, *Arctic Algebra*, Level CC.

# PRACTICE GAME

# WHAT'S MY AREA?

**Players**
2 players

**Materials**
- Game cards
- 2 different coins

FINISH

START

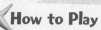

## How to Play

- Each player selects a coin and places it on START. Decide who will go first.

- Separate the cards into Easy, Difficult, and Finish piles.

- Shuffle each pile of game cards and place it facedown.

- A player can draw a game card from either the Easy pile or the Difficult pile.

- The player finds the area of the figure shown on the card.

- The other player checks the answer. If the answer is correct, the player moves his or her coin the number of spaces shown on the game card and play passes to the other player.

- If the answer is incorrect, play passes to the next player.

- When a player lands in the FINISH circle, he or she selects a Finish card and finds the area of the figure on it.

- The first player to correctly answer a FINISH card wins.

  **Chapter 23 Review/Test**

## Check Vocabulary and Concepts

1. Explain how to find the perimeter of a regular octagon. (AF 3.1, p. 570)

## Check Skills

**Find the perimeter.** (AF 3.1, pp. 570–573)

2.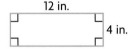
12 in.
4 in.

3.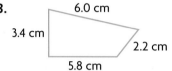
6.0 cm
3.4 cm
5.8 cm
2.2 cm

4.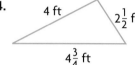
4 ft
$2\frac{1}{2}$ ft
$4\frac{3}{4}$ ft

5. a square with sides 5.2 cm in length

6. a rectangle with length 7 in. and width $5\frac{1}{3}$ in.

7. a regular hexagon with sides 17.3 mm in length

**The perimeter is given. Find the unknown length.** (AF 3.1, pp. 570–573)

8.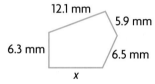
12.1 mm
5.9 mm
6.3 mm
6.5 mm
$x$
perimeter = 41.8 mm

9.
9 ft
4 ft
$x$
9 ft
perimeter = 27 ft

10.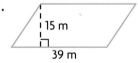
$x$
$x$
perimeter = 67.6 cm

**Find the area.** (AF 3.1, pp. 574–577, 578–579, 580–583)

11.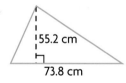
15 m
39 m

12.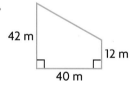
55.2 cm
73.8 cm

13.
42 m
12 m
40 m

14.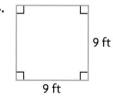
9 ft
9 ft

15. a rectangle with length 13 ft and width 11.5 ft

16. a triangle with a base of length 10 in. and height 5 in.

17. a trapezoid with bases of length 12 m and 10 m and a height of 5.2 m

## Check Problem Solving

**Solve.** (MG 1.0, MR 1.1, MR 2.0, pp. 584–587)

18. For a project at school, Ray taped four pieces of square construction paper together to form a larger square. If each original square had an area of 100 in.², what is the perimeter of the larger square?

19. Each morning, Martha's mother walks around a 90-ft by 150-ft rectangular building. If she walks around the building 10 times each day, how far does she walk?

20. **WRITE Math** ▶ **Explain** how to find the area of a trapezoid.

**GO ONLINE Technology** Use *Online Assessment.*

# Enrich • Area of Kites

**PROBLEM** Liam has drawn a diagram showing the dimensions of the kite he is building for the annual kite-flying contest. What is the area of Liam's kite?

A **kite** is a quadrilateral that has two pairs of congruent, adjacent sides and one pair of congruent, opposite angles. In a kite, diagonals intersect at right angles, and one of the diagonals is bisected by the other diagonal.

The area of kite $ABCD$ can be found by adding the areas of triangles $ABC$ and $ADC$. Remember that the area of a triangle is given by $A = \frac{1}{2}bh$. Let $d_1$ represent the length of the longer diagonal in the kite and $d_2$ represent the length of the shorter diagonal.

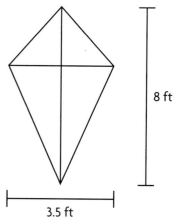

Area of kite $ABCD$ = Area of triangle $ABC$ + Area of triangle $ADC$

$$\text{Area of kite } ABCD = \frac{1}{2}d_1 \times \frac{1}{2}d_2 + \frac{1}{2}d_1 \times \frac{1}{2}d_2 \qquad A = \frac{1}{2}bh; b = d_1; h = \frac{1}{2}d_2$$

$$= \frac{1}{4}d_1d_2 + \frac{1}{4}d_1d_2 \qquad \text{Multiply.}$$

$$= \frac{2}{4}d_1d_2 \qquad \text{Add by combining like terms.}$$

$$= \frac{1}{2}d_1d_2 \qquad \text{Simplify.}$$

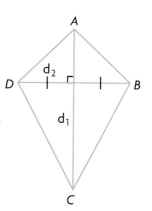

So, the area of a kite is given by the formula $A = \frac{1}{2}d_1d_2$.

## Run With It

**Find the area of Liam's kite.**

$$A = \frac{1}{2}d_1d_2 \qquad \text{Write the formula.}$$

$$A = \frac{1}{2} \times 8 \times 3.5 \qquad \text{Replace } d_1 \text{ with 8 and } d_2 \text{ with 3.5.}$$

$$A = 4 \times 3.5 \qquad \text{Multiply.}$$

$$A = 14$$

So, the area of Liam's kite is 14 ft².

## Hold On

**Find the area of the kite.**

**1.** $d_1 = 28$ cm, $d_2 = 10$ cm     **2.** $d_1 = 12.5$ m, $d_2 = 8$ m     **3.** $d_1 = 18$ yd, $d_2 = 7.5$ yd

## Reel it In

**WRITE Math** ▸ **Explain** how to find the area of a kite.

# Achieving the Standards
## Chapters 1–23

## Number Sense

**1.** Marta babysat a total of 9 hours last weekend. If she babysat for $4\frac{3}{4}$ hours on Saturday, how many hours did she spend babysitting on Sunday? (**O—** NS 2.0, p. 42)

  **A** $4\frac{1}{4}$ hours

  **B** $5\frac{1}{4}$ hours

  **C** $5\frac{3}{4}$ hours

  **D** $13\frac{3}{4}$ hours

**2.** Which fraction is *not* equivalent to $\frac{5}{8}$?
(**O—** NS 2.4, p. 10)

  **A** $\frac{10}{16}$

  **B** $\frac{15}{24}$

  **C** $\frac{20}{32}$

  **D** $\frac{25}{45}$

**3.** Which is the value of the expression below?
(**O—** NS 2.3, p. 154)

$$^-19 + 37 + 19$$

  **A** 19

  **B** 25

  **C** 37

  **D** 75

**4.** Which of the fractions is closest to 0?
(**O—** NS 1.1, p. 124)

  **A** $\frac{2}{7}$    **C** $\frac{3}{5}$

  **B** $\frac{5}{9}$    **D** $\frac{2}{3}$

**5.** **WRITE Math** Describe two methods that you can use to compare 21%, 0.55, and $\frac{2}{5}$.
(**O—** NS 1.1, p. 24)

## Measurement and Geometry

**6.** Which is the measure of an angle that is complementary to an angle that measures 62°? (**O—** MG 2.2, p. 374)

  **A** 26°

  **B** 28°

  **C** 62°

  **D** 118°

**Test Tip**  **Decide on a plan.**

See item 7. To determine the perimeter, all sides of the trapezoid must be added together. The perimeter is given, so the sum of the given sides must be subtracted from the perimeter.

**7.** The trapezoid shown below has a perimeter of $56\frac{1}{2}$ feet. What is the unknown?
(MG 1.0, p. 570)

  **A** 47 feet

  **B** $38\frac{3}{4}$ feet

  **C** $25\frac{1}{4}$ feet

  **D** $9\frac{1}{2}$ feet

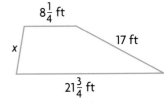

**8.** What is the circumference to the nearest tenth of a circle with a radius of 5.7 millimeters? Use 3.14 for $\pi$. (**O—** MG1.1, p. 424)

  **A** 17.9 millimeters

  **B** 35.8 millimeters

  **C** 102 millimeters

  **D** 326.7 millimeters

**9.** **WRITE Math** **Explain** how to find the area of a circle when the diameter of the circle is given. (MG 1.2, p. 420)

## Algebra and Functions

**10.** What is the value of the expression $3a + b^2 - 1$ when $a = {}^-4$ and $b = 6$?
(AF 1.2, p. 284)

  **A** $^-1$

  **B** 10

  **C** 23

  **D** 34

**11.** What value of $x$ makes the following equation true? (O—∏ AF 1.1, p. 304)

$$x + 10 = 25$$

  **A** 35          **C** $^-15$

  **B** 15          **D** $^-35$

**12.** Which equation could be used to relate $y$ to $x$ in the table below? (O—∏ AF 1.1, p. 344)

| $x$ | $^-2$ | $^-1$ | 0 | 1 | 2 |
|---|---|---|---|---|---|
| $y$ | $^-6$ | $^-3$ | 0 | 3 | 6 |

  **A** $y = x - 7$          **C** $y = 3x - 1$

  **B** $y = 3x$          **D** $y = x - 1$

**13.** Which property is used to help simplify the expression below? (AF 1.3, p. 272)

$$(9 \times 2) \times 5 = 9 \times (2 \times 5) = 9 \times 10 = 90$$

  **A** Commutative Property

  **B** Associative Property

  **C** Identity Property

  **D** Distributive Property

**14.** **WRITE Math** ▸ **Explain** how to solve the equation shown below. (O—∏ AF 1.1, p. 340)

$$\frac{k}{7} = 5$$

## Statistics, Data Analysis, and Probability

**15.** Marco found the median of this list of numbers.

$$2, 6, 9, 3, 7, 9, 1$$

Which shows the median of the data?
(SDAP 1.1, p. 224)

  **A** 3          **C** 6

  **B** 4          **D** 9

**16.** Mr. Bean wants to take a survey to determine which lunch in the cafeteria is most popular with the students. Which is the best way for him to survey a random sample of the students? (O—∏ SDAP 2.2, p. 202)

  **A** Ask the students in his first class today.

  **B** Ask the students that walk past his house in the morning.

  **C** Choose 10 students randomly from each homeroom.

  **D** Survey students who bring their lunch to school.

**17.** Brittany tossed two pennies. What is the probability that both coins will land on heads? (O—∏ SDAP 3.1, p. 554)

  **A** $\frac{1}{8}$

  **B** $\frac{1}{4}$

  **C** $\frac{1}{2}$

  **D** $\frac{3}{4}$

**18.** **WRITE Math** ▸ **Explain** the difference between the mean and median of a set of data. (SDAP 1.1, p. 224)

# 24 Surface Area and Volume

**The Big Idea** Attributes of three-dimensional figures can be measured and computed using appropriate formulas.

## Investigate

Suppose an architect has designed a new university building in the shape of a rectangular prism measuring 75 ft long, 75 ft wide, and 200 ft high. The university has asked for a building with different dimensions but the same space inside. Name two possible sets of dimensions it could have.

### Rectangular Prisms

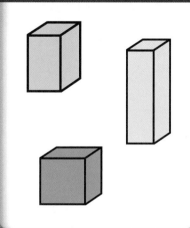

**CALIFORNIA FAST FACT**

The University of Southern California was built from two master plans. The first was prepared in the early 1920s and the second in 1960 by USC alumnus William Pereira.

**Technology**
Student pages are available in the Student eBook.

**Check your understanding of important skills
needed for success in Chapter 24**

▶ **Area of Squares, Rectangles, and Triangles**

Find the area of each figure.

1.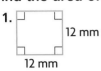
12 mm
12 mm

2.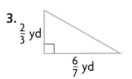
3.5 in.
9.25 in.

3.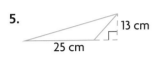
$\frac{2}{3}$ yd
$\frac{6}{7}$ yd

4.
$\frac{4}{5}$ mi
$\frac{3}{4}$ mi

5.
13 cm
25 cm

6.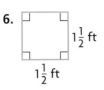
$1\frac{1}{2}$ ft
$1\frac{1}{2}$ ft

7.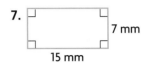
7 mm
15 mm

8.
9 in.
14 in.

▶ **Area of Circles**

Find the area. Round to the nearest whole number. Use 3.14 for π.

9.
34 mm

10.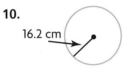
16.2 cm

11.
56 in.

12.
12 yd

▶ **Evaluate Algebraic Expressions**

Evaluate for the given value of the variable.

13. $bc$ for $b = 22$ and $c = 8$

14. $\frac{1}{2}st$ for $s = 6$ and $t = 13$

15. $\frac{1}{2}ab$ for $a = 4.8$ and $b = 7.3$

16. $\pi c^2$ for $c = 10$ (Use 3.14 for π.)

# VOCABULARY POWER

**CHAPTER VOCABULARY**

surface area
cylinder
volume

**WARM-UP WORDS**

**surface area** the sum of the areas of the surfaces of a solid figure

**cylinder** a solid figure that has two congruent, parallel, circular bases

**volume** the number of cubic units needed to occupy a given space

**ALGEBRA**

# Surface Area

OBJECTIVE: Find the surface areas of prisms and cylinders.

## Quick Review

Find the product.

1. $11 \times 4 \times 5$  2. $16 \times 3 \times 4$
3. $12 \times 6 \times 3$  4. $20 \times 10 \times 5$
5. $9 \times 5 \times 2$

## Vocabulary

**surface area**   **cylinder**

## Learn

**PROBLEM** For his design class final project, Daniel used a foam cube measuring 22 in. on each edge to make a footstool. He covered each of the six faces with fabric. How much fabric did Daniel use to completely cover the foam cube?

You can use the formula for the area of a square in finding the surface area of a cube. The **surface area,** $S$, is the sum of the areas of the separate surfaces of a solid figure.

### Example 1  Use a net to help find the surface area.

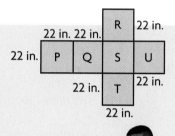

Since each face is a square, use the formula $A = s^2$.

Area of face P: $A = 22^2 = 484$

Since each face of a cube has the same dimensions, faces Q through U have the same area as face P. The surface area of a cube is the sum of the areas of its faces or 6 times the area of one face.

$S = 6 \times 484 = 2{,}904$

So, Daniel used 2,904 in.$^2$ of fabric to cover the foam cube.

- What if Daniel's foam cube measured half the original length on each edge? How much fabric would he have used?

To find the surface area, $S$, of a rectangular prism, remember that opposite faces have the same area.

### Example 2  Find the surface area of the rectangular prism.

Use the formula $A = lw$.

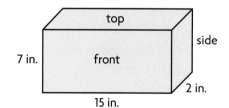

front and back faces: $2 \times l \times w = 2 \times 15 \times 7 = 210$   Multiply by 2 to include opposite faces.

top and bottom faces: $2 \times l \times w = 2 \times 15 \times 2 = 60$

left and right faces: $2 \times l \times w = 2 \times 7 \times 2 = 28$

$S = 210 + 60 + 28 = 298$   Find the sum.

So, the surface area is 298 in.$^2$

**AF 3.1** Use variables in expressions describing geometric quantities (e.g. $P = 2w + 2l$, $A = \frac{1}{2}bh$, $C = \pi d$–the formulas for the perimeter of a rectangle, the area of a triangle, and the circumference of a circle, respectively). *also* **MG 1.0, MR 1.3, MR 2.2, MR 2.4, MR 2.5, MR 3.2**

# Triangular Prisms and Cylinders

To find the surface area, $S$, of a triangular prism, think about the prism's net.

The surface area of a triangular prism equals the sum of the areas of the three rectangular faces and the sum of the areas of the two triangular bases. The triangular bases have the same area.

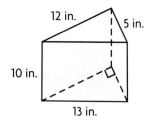

### Example 3 Find the surface area of the triangular prism.

$S = 2 \times$ area of base A + area of face B + area of face C + area of face D

area of bases A and E: $\frac{1}{2} \times 5 \times 12 = \frac{1}{2} \times 60 = 30$

area of face B: $5 \times 10 = 50$

area of face C: $12 \times 10 = 120$

area of face D: $13 \times 10 = 130$

$S = 2 \times 30 + 50 + 120 + 130 = 360$

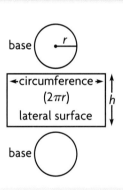

So, the surface area is 360 in.$^2$

- Explain why the area of one triangular base was multiplied by 2.

- Double the dimensions of the triangular prism and find the surface area. Compare the surface area of the new triangular prism with the surface area of the original triangular prism.

A **cylinder** is a solid figure that has two flat, congruent, parallel, circular bases.

To find the surface area of a cylinder, think about the pattern you would use to make a cylinder. The surface area equals the sum of the areas of the lateral surface and two circular bases. When laid flat, the lateral surface is a rectangle. The length of the rectangle is equal to the circumference of the circular base.

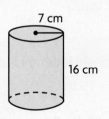

### Example 4 Find the surface area of the cylinder. Use 3.14 for $\pi$.

$S =$ area of lateral surface + $2 \times$ (area of circle)

$S = (l \times h) + 2 \times (\pi r^2)$

$S = (2\pi r \times 16) + 2 \times (\pi r^2)$      Replace $l$ with $2\pi r$ and $h$ with 16.

$S \approx (2 \times 3.14 \times 7 \times 16) + 2 \times (3.14 \times 7^2)$    Replace $\pi$ with 3.14 and $r$ with 7.

$S \approx 703.36 + 2 \times 153.86$

$S \approx 703.36 + 307.72$

$S \approx 1{,}011.08$ cm$^2$

So, the surface area of the cylinder is about 1,011 cm$^2$.

- Double the dimensions of the cylinder and find the surface area.

**1.** Find the surface area of the rectangular prism.

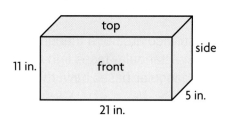

area of front and back              $2 \times \blacksquare \times \blacksquare = \blacksquare$

area of top and bottom           $2 \times \blacksquare \times \blacksquare = \blacksquare$

area of left and right sides     $2 \times \blacksquare \times \blacksquare = \blacksquare$

Add to find the sum of the areas of all faces.

**Find the surface area. Use 3.14 for $\pi$.**

**2.**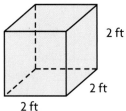

**3.**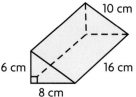

**4.**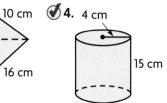

**5.**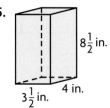

**6.** **TALK Math** **Explain** how to find the surface area of a cylinder with a radius of 3 ft and a height of 8 ft.

## Independent Practice and Problem Solving

**Find the surface area. Use 3.14 for $\pi$.**

**7.**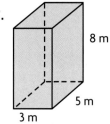

**8.**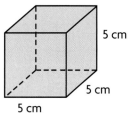

**9.**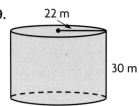

**10.**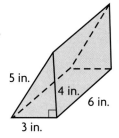

**11.**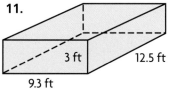

**12.**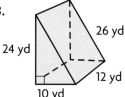

**13.**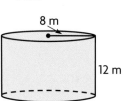

**14.**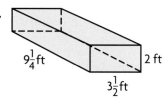

**Find the surface area of each cube with the given side length, s.**

**15.** $s = 15$ ft

**16.** $s = 3.5$ cm

**17.** $s = 4\frac{1}{2}$ yd

**18.** $s = 50$ m

**For 19–20 find the dimensions and surface area of each rectangular prism.**

**19.** The length is 3 times the width. The height is 2 times the length. The width is 5 in.

**20.** The height is 4 times the width. The width is $\frac{1}{4}$ the length. The length is 20 cm.

**21.** Find an object shaped like a rectangular prism. Measure your object to the nearest inch. Estimate the surface area to the nearest square inch.

**22.** Find an object shaped like a cylinder. Measure your object to the nearest centimeter. Estimate the surface area to the nearest square centimeter.

23. For design class, Louisa painted an old rectangular wooden trunk that measures 21 in. long, 11 in. wide, and 5 in. high. How much surface area did she paint?

24. **≡FAST FACT** The Vehicle Assembly Building at Kennedy Space Center is one of the largest buildings in the world, measuring 216 ft long, 518 ft wide, and 525 ft tall. Find its surface area. HINT: The surface area does not include the bottom.

25. **WRITE Math** For a class project, Darlene lines the sides of 5 cylindrical vases with decorative paper. Each vase is 26 in. in diameter and 30 in. high. **Explain** the steps Darlene could follow to find out how much decorative paper she needs.

 **Achieving the Standards**

26. Shoppers were asked, "Do you like the new outstanding taste of Crustingham Biscuits?" Is the question biased? (**O━┓** SDAP 2.3, p. 206)

27. A quadrilateral has opposite sides that are parallel and congruent. What type of quadrilateral could it be? (MG 2.3, p. 400)

28. What is the area of a rectangle with a length of 9 meters and a width of 7 meters?

(AF 3.1, p. 574)

29. **Test Prep** Which is the surface area of a cube measuring 2.4 centimeters on a side?

   **A** 5.76 centimeters²    **C** 23.04 centimeters²

   **B** 13.824 centimeters²    **D** 34.56 centimeters²

30. **Test Prep** Jon will paint the walls, ceiling, and door of a rectangular room with no windows that is 14 ft by 15 ft by 8 ft. What is the total surface area that he will paint?

**MATH POWER** **Problem Solving and Reasoning**

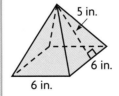

**GEOMETRY** To find the surface area of a complex figure you need to break it into simpler figures and find out the surface area of each figure.

**Example** Find the surface area of the figure on the right.

Find the area of one face.
$6 \times 6 = 36$ in.²

Multiply by 5 since the pyramid covers the top.
$5 \times 36 = 180$

Cube

This surface area of the five faces is 180 in.²

Find the areas of the four triangular faces. Don't find the area of the square base since it sits on top of the cube.

Square Pyramid    $S = 4 \times (\frac{1}{2} \times 6 \times 5) = 60$

This surface area of the four faces is 60 in.²

So, the surface area of the figure is 180 in.² + 60 in.² = 240 in.²

**Find the surface area of the figure.**

1.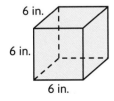

2.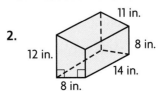

**2**

ALGEBRA

# Volume of Prisms

OBJECTIVE: Estimate and find the volumes of prisms.

## Learn

**Volume** is the number of cubic units needed to occupy a given space. Volume is measured in cubic units. The activity below explores volume.

### Quick Review

How many square yards of tile are needed to cover a square floor measuring 3 yd on each side?

### Vocabulary

**volume**

### HANDS ON

### Activity

**Materials** ■ rectangular prism net ■ tape ■ scissors ■ centimeter cubes

• Cut out the net. Fold it along the dashed lines, and tape the sides to make an open box.

• Estimate how many cubes will fit in the box. Then place as many cubes as you can in the box.

• Do you think the number of cubes you put in the box is the actual volume of the box or an estimate? Explain.

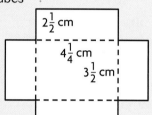

$2\frac{1}{2}$ cm
$4\frac{1}{4}$ cm
$3\frac{1}{2}$ cm

Look at the prism below. A layer of centimeter cubes is placed on the base. It takes 8, or 4 × 2, centimeter cubes to fill the bottom layer. The filled prism has 3 layers of 8 cubes each. It takes 24, or 4 × 2 × 3 cubes to fill the prism.

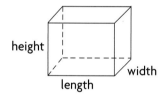

height
length
width

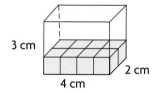

3 cm
4 cm
2 cm

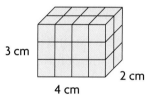

3 cm
4 cm
2 cm

Look at the table. Observe the relationship among the length, width, height, and volume of these three rectangular prisms.

| Length | Width | Height | Volume |
|--------|-------|--------|--------|
| 4 | 3 | 4 | 48 |
| 5 | 3 | 3 | 45 |
| 8 | 4 | 3 | 96 |

The relationship between the dimensions and the volume of a rectangular prism can be written as Volume = length × width × height or $V = lwh$. The formula $V = Bh$ can also be used to find the volume of a rectangular prism. In this formula, $B$ is equal to $l \times w$, since $l \times w$ is equal to the area of the base of a rectangular prism, and $h$ is the height of the prism.

| Rectangular Prism Volume Formulas | |
|---|---|
| $V = lwh$ | $V = Bh$ |

MG 1.3 Know and use the formulas for the volume of triangular prisms and cylinders (area of base × height); compare these formulas and explain the similarity between them and the formula for the volume of a rectangular solid. *also* MG 1.0, MR 2.2, MR 2.4, MR 2.5, MR 3.2

## Example 1 Find the volume.

$V = Bh$, where $B = l \times w$    Write the formula.

$V = (8 \times 3) \times 2$      Replace $B$ with $8 \times 3$ and $h$ with 2. Multiply.

$V = 48$

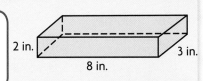

So, the volume of the rectangular prism is 48 in.$^3$

If you cut a rectangular prism in half as shown at the right, you form two congruent triangular prisms.

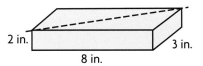

- What do you think the volume of one of the triangular prisms would be compared to the volume of the rectangular prism?

The volume of a triangular prism is one half the volume of a rectangular prism with the same length, width, and height. To find the volume of a right triangular prism, use the formula $V = \frac{1}{2}lwh$. To find the volume of any triangular prism, use the formula $V = Bh$, where $B$ is the area of the triangular base.

| Triangular Prism Volume Formulas | |
|---|---|
| Right Triangular Prism: $V = \frac{1}{2}lwh$ | Any Triangular Prism: $V = Bh$ |

## Example 2 Find the volume.

$V = Bh$      Write the formula.

$V = \left(\frac{1}{2} \times 12 \times 5\right) \times 6$    Replace $B$ with $\frac{1}{2} \times 12 \times 5$ and $h$ with 6. Multiply.

$V = 30 \times 6$

$V = 180$

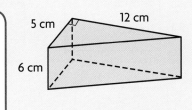

So, the volume of the triangular prism is 180 cm$^3$.

- Explain how the formula for the volume of a rectangular prism is similar to the formula for the volume of a triangular prism?

You can use a calculator to help find volumes of prisms.

## Example 3 Find the volume.

**A** Use these calculator keys to find the volume.

1  2   8

8  5

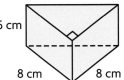

So, the volume of the triangular prism is 160 cm$^3$.

## Guided Practice

**Find the volume.**

**1.**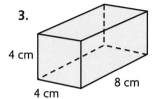

$V = Bh$
$= 15 \times 10 \times 25$
$= \blacksquare$

25 in.
10 in.   15 in.

**2.** 17 m   17 m

$V = Bh$
$= (\frac{1}{2} \times 17 \times 17) \times 28$
$= \blacksquare$

28 m

**3.**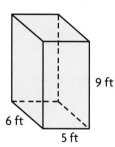

4 cm
4 cm   8 cm

**✓4.**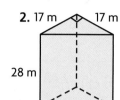

9 ft
6 ft
5 ft

**5.** 7 m   10 m

5 m

**✓6.**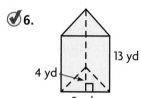

13 yd
4 yd
8 yd

**7.** [ **TALK Math** ]  **Explain** how to find the volume of a triangular prism.

## Independent Practice (and Problem Solving)

**Find the volume.**

**8.**
5 in.   12 in.
9 in.

**9.**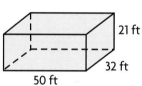
21 ft
32 ft
50 ft

**10.**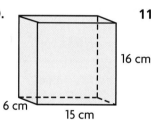
16 cm
6 cm   15 cm

**11.**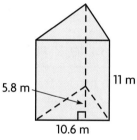
5.8 m
11 m
10.6 m

**12.**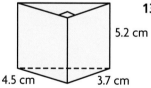
5.2 cm
4.5 cm   3.7 cm

**13.**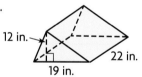
12 in.
22 in.
19 in.

**14.**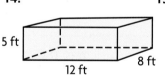
5 ft
12 ft   8 ft

**15.**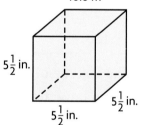
$5\frac{1}{2}$ in.
$5\frac{1}{2}$ in.
$5\frac{1}{2}$ in.

**Find the unknown length.**

**16.**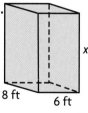
$x$
8 ft   6 ft
$V = 576 \text{ ft}^3$

**17.**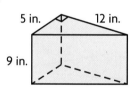
5 m
$x$
7 m
$V = 175 \text{ m}^3$

**18.**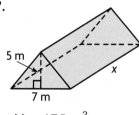
$x$
0.8 cm
0.8 cm
$V = 0.512 \text{ cm}^3$

**19.**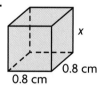
15 cm
$x$   7 cm
$V = 682.5 \text{ cm}^3$

**20.** The youth center has a rectangular children's wading pool that has a length and width of 5 ft and is 1.5 ft deep. How many cubic feet of water are needed to fill the pool?

**21.** The woodworking class needs to build a rectangular gift box that has a volume of 88 in.³ If the length is 8 in. and the width is $5\frac{1}{2}$ in., what should the height of the gift box be?

**CD ROM**  **Technology**
Use Harcourt Mega Math, Ice Station
Exploration, *Arctic Algebra*, Levels AA and DD.

( **Extra Practice** on page 612, Set B )

22. Find an object shaped like a rectangular prism. Measure your object to the nearest centimeter. Estimate the volume to the nearest centimeter.

23. Find the surface area and volume of a cube that measures $1\frac{1}{2}$ ft on a side. Describe the difference between surface area and volume.

24. Find the surface area and volume of the rectangular prism at the right. Then find the surface area and volume if the height is doubled. How do the new surface area and volume compare to the original surface area and volume?

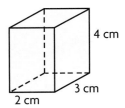

25. **WRITE Math** ▶ **What's the Error?** Students calculated the volume of a sandbox measuring 6 ft long, 5 ft wide, and 3 ft deep to be 30 ft³. Find and correct their error.

## Achieving the Standards

26. Write a word sentence for the following equation: $17 = n + 9$. (○━┓ AF 1.1, p. 300)

27. **Test Prep** What is the volume of a rectangular basket that is 20 centimeters long, 15.6 centimeters wide, and 30.4 centimeters high?

 **A** 9,484.8 centimeters³

 **B** 2,788.48 centimeters³

 **C** 948.48 centimeters³

 **D** 66 centimeters³

28. Order from greatest to least: ⁻3.508, 3.58, ⁻3.08, ⁻3.85. (○━┓ NS 1.1, p. 126)

29. Find the area of a circle with a radius of 9 inches. Use 3.14 for $\pi$. (MG 1.2, p. 420)

30. **Test Prep** What is the volume of the triangular prism?

 **A** 2 feet³

 **B** 3 feet³

 **C** 4 feet³

 **D** 6 feet³

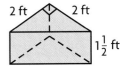

## MATH POWER Problem Solving and Reasoning

**CHANGING DIMENSIONS** The height of the prism at the right is 12 in., the length is 6 in., and the width is 4 in.

1. How would the volume of the rectangular prism change if each dimension were cut in half?

2. How would the volume of the rectangular prism change if the height and length were doubled and the width remained the same?

3. How would the volume of the rectangular prism change if the height were cut in half, the length were doubled, and the width remained the same?

4. Explain how you could change all of the dimensions of the rectangular prism to make a new rectangular prism with the same volume.

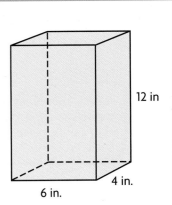

# Problem Solving Workshop
## Strategy: Make a Model

OBJECTIVE: Solve problems by using the strategy *make a model*.

## Learn the Strategy

Making a model can help you visualize a solution to a problem. You can use models to help you solve different types of problems.

### A model can be used to tell if two figures are congruent.

Are the blue and yellow figures congruent?

### A model can be used to solve equations.

Joel stacks 3 books on the top shelf of his bookcase. If this bookshelf holds 7 books, how many more books does Joel need in order to fill it? Solve the equation $x + 3 = 7$ to find the solution.

### A model can be used to help find surface area.

A rectangular prism has a length of 8 cm, a width of 6 cm, and a height of 4 cm. Find the surface area of the prism.

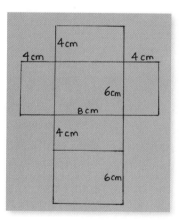

**TALK Math**

What other types of models can you think of that can be used to help solve problems?

MG 1.0 Students deepen their understanding of the measurement of plane and solid shapes and use this understanding to solve problems. *also* MR 1.0, MR 1.1, MR 2.0, MR 2.4, MR 2.5, MR 2.7, MR 3.0, MR 3.1, MR 3.2, MR 3.3

# Use the Strategy

**PROBLEM** Puzzles come in different-sized boxes. For one company, a large puzzle box has a length of 6 in., a width of 4 in., and a height of 2 in. A small puzzle box has dimensions half those of the large puzzle box. How does the volume of the larger box compare to the volume of the smaller box?

## Read to Understand

Reading Skill

- Identify the details of the problem.
- Is there information you will not use? If so, what?

## Plan

- **What strategy can you use to help you solve the problem?**
  You can make a model to help you solve the problem.

## Solve

- **How can you use the strategy to solve the problem?**
  Make a model of each box. Compare the volumes.

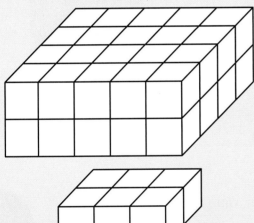

Count the cubes to find the volume of each box. Now compare the volumes.

$$\frac{\text{large box}}{\text{small box}} = \frac{48}{6} = \frac{8}{1}$$

So, the volume of the large box is 48 in.$^3$, or 8 times as great as the volume of the small box.

> **Math Idea**
> Since, $\frac{6}{48} = \frac{1}{8}$ you can also say that the small box has $\frac{1}{8}$ the volume of the large box.

## Check

- **How can you check your answer?**

1. As part of a fundraiser, students sell whole-wheat bread mix in boxes 3 in. wide, 3 in. long, and 5 in. high. Students can also sell the bread mix in a box with dimensions double those of the original box. How does the volume of the smaller box compare to the volume of the larger box?

   **First,** determine the dimensions of the larger box.

   width: $3 \times 2 = $ ▨ in.

   length: $3 \times 2 = $ ▨ in.

   height: $5 \times 2 = $ ▨ in.

   **Then,** use centimeter cubes to make a model of each box.

   **Finally,** compare the volume of the smaller box to that of the larger box.

Bread Mix

5 in.

3 in.

3 in.

✅ 2. **What if** the height and width of the new box of whole-wheat bread mix were double those of the original box? How would the volume of the new box compare to the volume of the original box?

✅ 3. For another fundraiser, students sold oatmeal dog biscuits in boxes like the one shown at the right. If they also sold meat-flavored dog biscuits in boxes that were half the length and width but the same height, what would be the volume of the box of meat-flavored biscuits?

OATMEAL DOG BISCUITS

12 in.

8 in.

6 in.

# Problem Solving Strategy Practice

**Make a model to solve.**

4. For the concession stand, Liam needs to fill with peanuts a rectangular box measuring 3 in. long, 6 in. high, and 1.5 in. wide. How many cubic inches of peanuts does Liam need?

5. Jackie wants to also sell boxes of raisins with Liam's boxes of peanuts. Each box of raisins measures 3 in. long, 3 in. high, and 1.5 in. wide. How does the volume of the peanut box compare to the volume of the raisin box?

6. **Reasoning** Melissa wants to make a spirit ribbon that is 15 in. long. She has ribbons that have lengths of 7 in., 10 in., and 12 in. How can she use these ribbons to measure a length of 15 in.?

7. Andy is building a decorative tower. He is using 4 cubes. He stacks one on top of the other and paints the outside of the stack, but not the bottom. How many faces of the cubes are painted?

8. **WRITE Math** A rectangular box for popcorn measures 6 in. by 4 in. by 2 in. **Explain** how you would use a model to find the volume of the box.

## Mixed Strategy Practice

**For 9–13, use the diagram of the gift boxes. Each of the gift boxes is a cube.**

9. Compare the volume of the fourth gift box to that of the second gift box. What is the relationship?

10. Sherri wants to use the third gift box to hold a birthday gift. She decides to wrap the gift box with decorative wrapping paper. If she has 750 in.$^2$ of wrapping paper, does she have enough to cover the box? **Explain.**

11. **Pose a Problem** Look back at Problem 10. Write and solve a similar problem by using a different box and changing the amount of wrapping paper Sherri has available.

12. Pablo is going to fill the third gift box with flavored popcorn. The flavored popcorn comes in bags that hold 150 in.$^3$ of popcorn and cost $2.75 each. How much will Pablo have to spend to fill the box?

13. Julie wants to stack the gift boxes on top of one another under a table that is 3 ft tall. Will she be able to fit all the boxes under the table?

### Problem-Solving STRATEGIES

Draw a Diagram or Picture

Make a Model or Act It Out

Make an Organized List

Find a Pattern

Make a Table or Graph

Predict and Test

Work Backward

Solve a Simpler Problem

Write an Equation

Use Logical Reasoning

2.5 in.

5 in.

10 in.

20 in.

14. Jackie, Bob, Sally, and Mike open gifts. A girl does not open hers first or last. Mike opens his before Bob. Jackie opens hers right before Bob opens his. In what order did they open their gifts?

15. **Open Ended** Suppose you are in charge of designing a rectangular gift box. Find dimensions of the box that will make its surface area greater than 500 in.$^2$ and its volume less than 900 in.$^3$ Sketch a picture of your gift box.

### CHALLENGE YOURSELF

**As part of a fundraiser, students sell boxes of mixed nuts that measure 3 in. long, 2 in. wide, and 5 in. high.**

16. Rosalie has $50 to spend on wrapping paper to cover the boxes. Wrapping paper costs $3.79 per roll and each roll will cover 2,160 in.$^2$ If the students sell 398 boxes, does Rosalie have enough money to buy the wrapping paper?

17. Students purchased mixed nuts for $0.60 per pound. One of the boxes holds 0.25 lb for every 10 cubic inches. How much should the students charge for each box so they can make a $0.10 profit on each box?

# 4 Volume of a Cylinder

OBJECTIVE: Find the relationship among the area of the base, the height, and the volume of a cylinder

## Quick Review

Find the area of each circle to the nearest whole number. Use 3.14 for $\pi$.
1. $r = 12$ mm    2. $d = 18.2$ m
3. $r = 7$ in.    4. $d = 6$ ft
5. $r = 9$ cm

## Investigate

**Materials** ■ 2 sheets of centimeter graph paper ■ centimeter cubes ■ scissors ■ tape

You can use graph paper and centimeter cubes to estimate the volume of a cylinder.

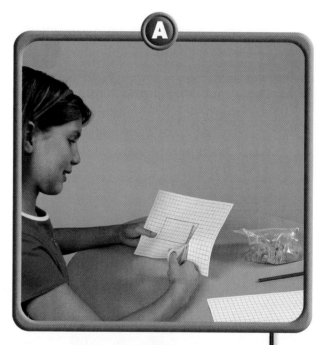

**A** From one sheet of graph paper, cut out a rectangle 12 cm long and 6 cm wide.

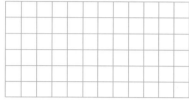

6 cm

12 cm

**B** Without overlapping the edges, roll the rectangle horizontally and tape it to model a cylinder.

**C** Stand the cylinder on the second sheet of graph paper. Trace the circular base of the cylinder.

**D** Count the whole centimeter squares and the parts of centimeter squares inside the tracing.

**E** Estimate how many cubes would fit on the bottom layer of the cylinder.

**F** Estimate how many layers of cubes can fit inside the cylinder.

## Draw Conclusions

1. About how many cubes do you estimate would fit on the bottom layer of the cylinder?

2. About how many layers of cubes do you estimate would fit inside the cylinder?

3. What is the approximate volume of the cylinder?

4. **Analysis** What relationship do you see among the area of the base, the height, and the volume of the cylinder?

MG 1.3 Know and use the formulas for the volume of triangular prisms and cylinders (area of base × height); compare these formulas and explain the similarity between them and the formula for the volume of a rectangular solid. *also* AF 3.0, MG 1.0, MR 2.0, MR 2.4, MR 2.5, MR 3.2

# Connect

Think about the relationship you found in Draw Conclusions. You can further explore the relationship among the area of the base, the height, and the volume of a cylinder.

Look at the cylinder. Suppose it is filled with rice and has a volume of about 402 in.³

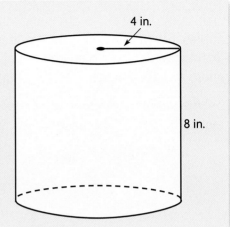

**Step 1**

Calculate the area of the base of the cylinder. Use 3.14 for $\pi$.

$A \approx 3.14 \, (r)^2$      The base is a circle.
$A \approx 3.14 \, (4)^2 \approx 3.14 \, (16) \approx 50.24$ in.²    Use $A = \pi r^2$.

**Step 2**

Multiply the area of the base by the height of the cylinder. Round your result to the nearest whole number.

$50.24 \times 8 = 401.92$, or about 402 in.³

- Compare your result to the given volume of the cylinder. What can you conclude?

- Write a formula that can be used to find the volume of a cylinder. Use $V$ for the volume of a cylinder, $B$ for the area of the base of a cylinder, and $h$ for the height of a cylinder.

**TALK Math**

**Explain** the relationship among the area of the base, the height, and the volume of a cylinder.

# Practice

Draw the following rectangles on centimeter graph paper. Cut out each one, roll it, and tape it to model a cylinder. Estimate the volume of each cylinder.

**1.**
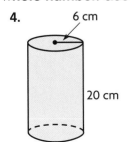
8 cm
20 cm

**2.**

6 cm
15 cm

✓**3.**

4 cm
12 cm

Use your formula to find the volume. Round to the nearest whole number. Use 3.14 for $\pi$.

**4.**
6 cm
20 cm

**5.** 7 cm
18 cm

✓**6.**
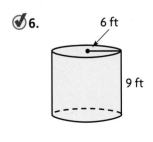
6 ft
9 ft

**7.** **WRITE Math** **Explain** the steps for finding the volume of a cylinder with a radius of 4 cm and a height of 18 cm.

**ALGEBRA**
# Volume of Cylinders

OBJECTIVE: Find the volume of cylinders.

## Quick Review

**Multiply.**

1. $1.25 \times 3 \times 6$
2. $2.34 \times 5 \times 7$
3. $3.14 \times 5 \times 8$
4. $12 \times 4 \times 2.15$
5. $4 \times 5.35 \times 21$

## Learn

**PROBLEM** At a candle company, visitors can make their own candles. Gwen purchased a cylindrical candle mold measuring 6 in. high and 3 in. in diameter. What is the volume of wax the candle mold will hold?

The volume of a cylinder equals the area of base multiplied by the height. The area of the base, which is a circle, is equal to $\pi r^2$.

| Cylinder Volume Formulas | |
|---|---|
| $V = \pi r^2 h$ | $V = Bh$ |

### Example 1 Find the volume to the nearest cubic inch.

$V = Bh = \pi r^2 h$      Write the formula.

$V \approx 3.14 \times 1.5^2 \times 6$     ($r = \frac{1}{2} \times 3 = 1.5$) Replace $\pi$ with 3.14, $r$ with 1.5, and $h$ with 6.

$V \approx 3.14 \times 2.25 \times 6$     Multiply.

$V \approx 42.39$

So, the candle mold will hold about 42 in.³ of wax.

• Explain how the formula for the volume of a cylinder is similar to the formula for the volume of a rectangular prism.

**ERROR ALERT**

The diameter of a circle is twice the radius. In the formula $V = \pi r^2 h$, you need to replace $r$ with the length of the radius.

Sometimes you may have to find the volume of part of a cylinder.

### Example 2 Find the volume of the inside cylinder to the nearest cubic meter.

$3.6\text{ m} - 2.3\text{ m} = 1.3\text{ m}$     Find the radius of the inside cylinder.

Use the radius to find the volume of the inside cylinder.

$V = Bh = \pi r^2 h$     Write the formula.

$V \approx 3.14 \times 1.3^2 \times 9.5$     Replace $\pi$ with 3.14, $r$ with 1.3, and $h$ with 9.5.

$V \approx 3.14 \times 1.69 \times 9.5$     Multiply.

$V \approx 50.4127$

So, the volume of the inside cylinder is about 50 m.³

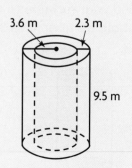

3.6 m    2.3 m

9.5 m

MG 1.3 Know and use the formulas for the volume of triangular prisms and cylinders (area of base x height); compare these formulas and explain the similarity between them and the formula for the volume of a rectangular solid. *also* ○┳ NS 2.0, MG 1.0, MR 2.4, MR 2.5, MR 3.2

## Guided Practice

1. Find the volume of the cylinder to the nearest cubic centimeter. Use 3.14 for $\pi$.

$V = Bh$
$V = \pi r^2 h$
$V \approx 3.14 \times 6^2 \times 10$
$V \approx \blacksquare$

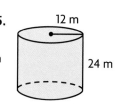
6 cm
10 cm

**Find the volume to the nearest whole number. Use 3.14 for $\pi$.**

2.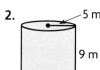
5 m
9 m

3.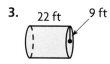
22 ft    9 ft

✅ 4.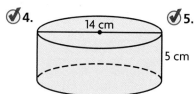
14 cm
5 cm

✅ 5.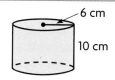
12 m
24 m

6. **TALK Math** Explain which parts of a cylinder are represented by $\pi r^2$ and $h$ in the formula $V = \pi r^2 h$.

## Independent Practice and Problem Solving

**Find the volume to the nearest whole number. Use 3.14 for $\pi$.**

7.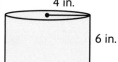
4 in.
6 in.

8.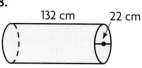
132 cm    22 cm

9.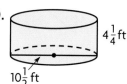
$4\frac{1}{4}$ ft
$10\frac{1}{2}$ ft

10.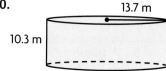
13.7 m
10.3 m

**Find the volume of the inside cylinder to the nearest whole number. Use 3.14 for $\pi$.**

11.
9 in.    4 in.
7 in.

12.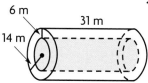
6 m    31 m
14 m

13.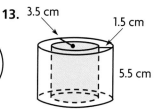
3.5 cm    1.5 cm
5.5 cm

14.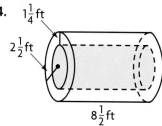
$1\frac{1}{4}$ ft
$2\frac{1}{2}$ ft
$8\frac{1}{2}$ ft

15. Measure to the nearest inch the height and radius of a real cylinder. Estimate the volume to the nearest cubic inch. Use 3.14 for $\pi$.

16. A cylinder has a height of 8 m and a radius of 3 m. What is the ratio of the volume of this cylinder to the volume of a cylinder that has half the height? to the volume of a cylinder that has half the radius? Use 3.14 for $\pi$.

17. **WRITE Math** What's the Question? A cylinder has a height of 12 ft and a diameter of 10 ft. The answer is about 942 ft$^3$.

## Achieving the Standards

18. What is $3\frac{1}{8} \div 2\frac{1}{2}$? (NS 2.2, p. 100)

19. Evaluate $2a - b + 4$ for $a = {}^-3.7$ and $b = {}^-2.6$. (O━m AF 1.2, p. 284)

20. **Test Prep** A cylinder has a diameter of 7 feet and a height of 4 feet. What is the volume to the nearest cubic foot? Use 3.14 for $\pi$.

**Extra Practice** on page 612, Set C

## Extra Practice

### Set A Find the surface area. Use 3.14 for π. (pp. 596–599)

1.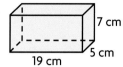
7 cm
5 cm
19 cm

2.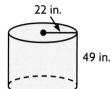
22 in.
49 in.

3.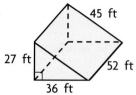
45 ft
27 ft
52 ft
36 ft

4.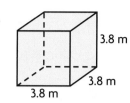
3.8 m
3.8 m
3.8 m

5. The height of a box is four times its length. The length is 5 cm more than its width. The width is 10 cm. Find the surface area.

6. A cube has a surface area of 2,400 m². What is the length of each edge?

### Set B Find the volume. (pp. 600–603)

1.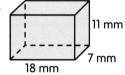
11 mm
7 mm
18 mm

2.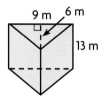
9 m   6 m
13 m

3.
5.7 in.
4.2 in.
3.1 in.

4.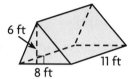
6 ft
11 ft
8 ft

5. A planter box is 3 ft long, 1.5 ft wide, and 0.5 ft high. How many cubic feet of soil are needed to fill the planter box?

6. A box of cereal is 8 in. long, 2.5 in. wide, and 12 in. tall. What is the volume of the box of cereal?

**Find the unknown length.**

7.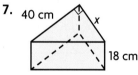
40 cm
x
18 cm

$V = 13,500 \text{ cm}^3$

8.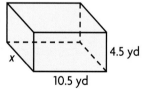
x
4.5 yd
10.5 yd

$V = 292.95 \text{ yd}^3$

9.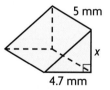
5 mm
x
4.7 mm

$V = 36.425 \text{ mm}^3$

10.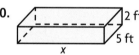
2 ft
5 ft
x

$V = 150 \text{ ft}^3$

### Set C Find the volume to the nearest whole number. Use 3.14 for π. (pp. 610–611)

1.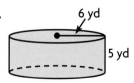
6 yd
5 yd

2.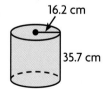
16.2 cm
35.7 cm

3.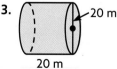
20 m
20 m

4.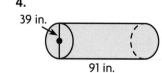
39 in.
91 in.

**Technology**
Use Harcourt Mega Math, Ice Station
Exploration, *Arctic Algebra*, Level DD.

# What's My Volume?

## How

- Each player selects a coin and places it on START.
- The first player tosses three number cubes and sets them in the squares marked *x*, *y*, and *z* below. The number showing on each cube becomes the value for that variable.
- The player uses the values to find the volume of the figure in the gameboard where his or her coin is at. Answers should be rounded to the nearest whole number.

- The other player checks the answer. If it is correct, the player moves his or her coin one space. If the answer is correct or incorrect, play passes to the other player.
- The first player to reach FINISH and find the correct volume of the figure on FINISH wins.

|  |  |  |
|:--:|:--:|:--:|
| *x* | *y* | *z* |

## Check Vocabulary and Concepts

**Choose the best term from the box.**

1. The sum of the areas of the separate surfaces of a solid figure is called the ___?___. (AF 3.1, p. 596)

2. The number of cubic units needed to occupy a given space is called ___?___. (MG 1.3, p. 600)

## Check Skills

**Find the surface area. Use 3.14 for π.** (AF 3.1, pp. 596–599)

3. 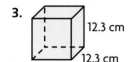 12.3 cm, 12.3 cm, 12.3 cm

4. 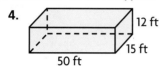 12 ft, 15 ft, 50 ft

5. 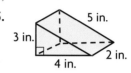 5 in., 3 in., 2 in., 4 in.

6. 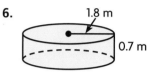 1.8 m, 0.7 m

**Find the volume. Use 3.14 for π.** (MG 1.3, pp. 600–603, 610–611)

7. 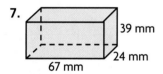 39 mm, 24 mm, 67 mm

8.  6 yd, 17 yd

9. 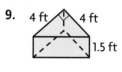 4 ft, 4 ft, 1.5 ft

10. 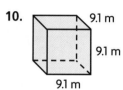 9.1 m, 9.1 m, 9.1 m

11. 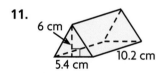 6 cm, 5.4 cm, 10.2 cm

12. 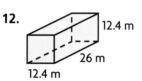 12.4 m, 26 m, 12.4 m

13. 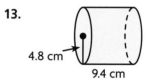 4.8 cm, 9.4 cm

14. 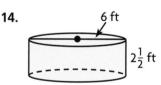 6 ft, $2\frac{1}{2}$ ft

**Find the unknown length.** (MG 1.3, pp. 600–603)

15. 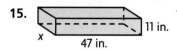 11 in., x, 47 in.
$V = 9{,}823 \text{ in.}^3$

16. 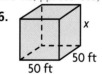 x, 50 ft, 50 ft
$V = 125{,}000 \text{ ft}^3$

17.  25 mm, 22 mm, x
$V = 16{,}500 \text{ mm}^3$

18.  8 cm, 4 cm, x
$V = 160 \text{ cm}^3$

## Check Problem Solving

**Solve.** (MG 1.0, MR 2.0, pp. 604–607)

19. The sandbox at a park measures 5.5 m long, 3 m wide, and 0.75 m deep. How many cubic meters of sand are needed to fill the sandbox?

20. **WRITE Math ▶** **Explain** the similarity among finding the volume of a rectangular prism, triangular prism, and a cylinder.

**GO ONLINE. Technology** Use *Online Assessment.*

# Enrich • Changing Dimensions
## Growing Solid Figures

Paula and Dean wanted to double the amount of nuts they could sell in each box, so they increased the dimensions of the box from 1 in. wide, 3 in. long, and 4 in. high to 2 in. wide, 6 in. long, and 8 in. high. Did Paula and Dean double the volume of the box when they doubled its dimensions?

**Find and compare the volumes of the original and new boxes.**

### Original Box

$$V = Bh \qquad \text{Write the formula.}$$
$$\phantom{V} = 3 \times 1 \times 4 \qquad \text{Replace } B \text{ and } h. \text{ Multiply.}$$
$$V = 12, \text{ or } 12 \text{ in.}^3$$

### New Box

$$V = Bh \qquad \text{Write the formula.}$$
$$\phantom{V} = 6 \times 2 \times 8 \qquad \text{Replace } B \text{ and } h. \text{ Multiply.}$$
$$V = 96, \text{ or } 96 \text{ in.}^3$$

Compare: $\dfrac{\text{new box}}{\text{original box}} = \dfrac{96}{12} = \dfrac{8}{1} = 8$

So, the volume of the new box is 8 times, not double the volume of of the original box.

## Make It Grow

**Find and compare the volumes of the two solid figures. Use 3.14 for π.**

**1.**

**2.**

**3.**

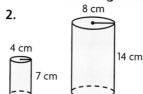

**4. Challenge** Find the volume of the inside cylinder at the right. Double all the dimensions of the figure. Find the volume of the new inside cylinder. How do the two volumes compare? Use 3.14 for π.

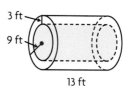

## Think About It

**WRITE Math** How would the volume of a rectangular prism change when its dimensions are tripled? **Explain** your answer, using an example.

## Multiple Choice

**1.** The width of a rectangular prism is 4.5 centimeters. The length is twice as long as the width. The height is three times as long as the width. What is the volume of the rectangular prism? (MG 1.3, p. 600)

  **A** 20.25 cubic centimeters

  **B** 91.125 cubic centimeters

  **C** 121.5 cubic centimeters

  **D** 546.75 cubic centimeters

**2.** The area of a triangle is 24 square inches. If the base measures 6 inches, what is the height? (AF 3.1, p. 578)

  **A** 4 inches      **C** 8 inches

  **B** 6 inches      **D** 10 inches

**3.** What is the area of a trapezoid with a height of 8 feet and bases that measure 12 feet and 27 feet? (AF 3.1, p. 580)

  **A** 47 square feet

  **B** 75 square feet

  **C** 156 square feet

  **D** 210 square feet

**4.** What is the volume of the triangular prism? (MG 1.3, p. 600)

  **A** 1,680 cubic inches

  **B** 840 cubic inches

  **C** 428 cubic inches

  **D** 36 cubic inches

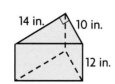

**5.** The perimeter of the pentagon shown below is $6\frac{1}{4}$ feet. What is the unknown length? (AF 3.1, p. 570)

  **A** $1\frac{1}{8}$ feet

  **B** $2\frac{1}{4}$ feet

  **C** $5\frac{1}{8}$ feet

  **D** $6\frac{1}{4}$ feet

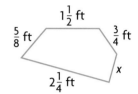

**6.** What is the area of a square that measures 26 meters on each side? (AF 3.1, p. 574)

  **A** 52 square meters

  **B** 104 square meters

  **C** 338 square meters

  **D** 676 square meters

**7.** The perimeter of a rectangle is 320 kilometers. If the width is 100 kilometers, what is the length? (AF 3.1, p. 570)

  **A** 220 kilometers

  **B** 120 kilometers

  **C** 60 kilometers

  **D** 3.2 kilometers

**8.** What is the surface area of the triangular prism shown below? (AF 3.1, p. 596)

  **A** 1,536 square inches

  **B** 1,728 square inches

  **C** 2,688 square inches

  **D** 6,048 square inches

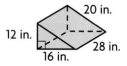

**GO** **Technology** Use *Online Assessment.*

9. What is the volume of a rectangular prism with a width of 12 yards, a length of 30 yards, and a height of 45 yards? (MG 1.3, p. 600)

   A 16,200 cubic yards

   B 8,100 cubic yards

   C 4,500 cubic yards

   D 87 cubic yards

10. A cylindrical can has a diameter of 6 centimeters and a height of 13 centimeters. What is the volume of the can to the nearest whole number? Use 3.14 for π. (MG 1.3, p. 610)

    A about 1,470 cubic centimeters

    B about 367 cubic centimeters

    C about 122 cubic centimeters

    D about 28 cubic centimeters

11. The volume of the prism below is 2,880 cubic feet. What is the unknown length? (MG 1.3, p. 600)

    A 9 feet

    B 32 feet

    C 320 feet

    D 2,844 feet

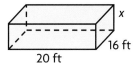

12. A square with a side of $y$ is inside a square with a side of 12. Which is an expression that represents the area of the shaded region in terms of $y$? (AF 1.3, p. 574)

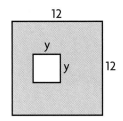

    A 48 − 2$y$        C 144 − 2$y$

    B 48 − $y^2$        D 144 − $y^2$

13. Which figure has the largest area? (AF 3.1, p. 580)

    A a square 20 centimeters on each side

    B a rectangle with base 26 centimeters and height 37 centimeters

    C a parallelogram with base 44 centimeters and height 40 centimeters

    D a triangle with base 59 centimeters and height 49 centimeters

## Short Response

14. What is the perimeter of a rectangular plot of land that has a width of 1.2 miles and a length of 2.5 miles? (MG 1.0)

15. The area of a triangle is 435 square centimeters. If the height is 20 centimeters, what is the base? (MG 1.0)

## Extended Response ⟪WRITE Math⟫

16. The perimeter of a rectangle can be found by using the formulas $P = 2l + 2w$ or $P = l + w + l + w$. Explain why both formulas can be used to find perimeter.
(AF 3.1, p. 570)

17. Explain how you can find the volume of the space between the inside cylinder and the outside cylinder in the figure below. (MG 1.3, p. 610)

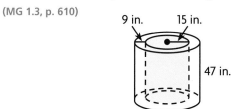

18. Determine the area of each rectangle and each shaded triangle below. Explain any patterns you see. (AF 3.1, p. 578)

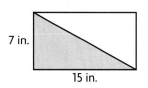

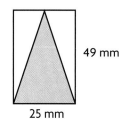

*from* THE WORLD ALMANAC FOR KIDS

# Sand Castles!

## WORKS OF ART

**S**and castle and sand sculpture contests draw thousands of people to check out these works of art. California is a prime area for sand castle contests, since the state has miles of beaches and great sand for building. Each year in Santa Barbara the Santa Barbara Sand Castle festival takes place. The festival includes workshops to teach the basics of sand building. Both novice and expert sand builders can participate.

### FACT·ACTIVITY

Sand castle on the beach at Santa Barbara

**Use the sand castle facts to answer the questions.**

❶ At the Santa Barbara Festival, sand sculpture teams are assigned a square 16-foot by 16-foot marked-off competition plot. What is the area of each plot?

❷ If 12 teams compete at the Festival, how much tape is needed to mark off the competition plots?

❸ Suppose the first place winner of the sand sculpture contest used a cylindrical bucket $1\frac{1}{2}$ feet tall and 2 feet in diameter to make one of the towers. Find the approximate volume of sand in the bucket.

❹ **Pose a Problem** Suppose the towers in a sand sculpture are made in the shape of a rectangular prism. Using this information, write and solve a problem like Problem 3.

# BUILDING SAND CASTLES

**ALMANAC Fact**

Californian Kirk Rademaker designs sand sculptures for contests all over the world. This mechanical-looking sand castle won a first prize.

**Y**ou don't have to be an expert to build a sand castle. For simple sand castles, all you need is a bucket and shovel. Fill the bucket with wet sand and pack it down so the sand is firm. This will allow you to mold it into shapes. Carefully flip the bucket, and then lift the bucket away from the sand. You now have your first sand figure. Stack more figures on top of each other to make walls and towers. Once your castle is built, use a shovel to make details like windows, doors, and other decorations. Professional sand sculptors use special tools that help them to form smooth sides and tiny details.

## FACT·ACTIVITY

**Make a design for a sand sculpture.**

❶ Sketch your design. What solid figures will you use for your sculpture? Write the dimensions for each figure on your sculpture.

❷ Find the area of the base of each figure and the total amount of space your sculpture will cover.

❸ Find the perimeter of the plot that you will need for your sculpture. Remember to leave space around it for building and observing.

❹ Find the volume of sand needed for each section. How much sand will be needed for the entire sculpture?

❺ A reporter from a local newspaper has come to interview you. Write down how you will describe your sculpture, its theme, and why you chose it. Mention its size and the time it took to build it.

# Student Handbook

**Review the Key Standards** . . . . . . . . . . . . . . . . . . . . . . . . . . . . **H1**

These pages provide review of every state standard for your grade. They also help you avoid errors students often make.

# Review the Key Standards

## Compare and Order Fractions, Decimals, and Mixed Numbers

**O—n NS 1.0** Students compare and order positive and negative fractions, decimals, and mixed numbers. Students solve problems involving fractions, ratios, proportions, and percentages.

**O—n NS 1.1** Compare and order positive and negative fractions, decimals, and mixed numbers and place them on a number line.

## Examples

**A** Compare $^-2\frac{2}{5}$ and $^-2\frac{4}{5}$ by using a number line.

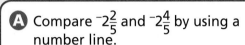

$^-2\frac{2}{5}$ is to the right of $^-2\frac{4}{5}$.

So, $^-2\frac{2}{5} > ^-2\frac{4}{5}$.

**B** Compare $\frac{^-3}{4}$ and $\frac{^-1}{5}$.

$\frac{^-3}{4} = \frac{^-15}{20}$   $\frac{^-1}{5} = \frac{^-4}{20}$   Write equivalent fractions by using the least common denominator, 20.

$^-15 < ^-4$   Compare the numerators.

So, $\frac{^-3}{4} < \frac{^-1}{5}$.

**ERROR ALERT**

When comparing fractions and mixed numbers be sure the denominators are the same before comparing numerators.

**C** Order $\frac{^-1}{5}$, $1\frac{1}{5}$, $^-0.50$, $^-0.05$ from least to greatest.

The only positive number is $1\frac{1}{5}$, so it is the greatest.

$^-0.50 = \frac{^-50}{100}$   $^-0.05 = \frac{^-5}{100}$   Use place value to write the decimals as fractions.

Write equivalent fractions with a denominator of 100.

$\frac{^-1 \times 20}{5 \times 20} = \frac{^-20}{100}$   $\frac{^-50}{100} = \frac{^-50}{100}$   $\frac{^-5}{100} = \frac{^-5}{100}$

$^-50 < ^-20 < ^-5$   Compare the numerators.

So, from least to greatest, the numbers are $^-0.50$, $\frac{^-1}{5}$, $^-0.05$, and $1\frac{1}{5}$.

## Try It

**Compare. Write <, >, or =.**

1. $^-1\frac{1}{8}$ ● $\frac{7}{8}$   2. $\frac{5}{9}$ ● $\frac{5}{6}$   3. $\frac{11}{16}$ ● $\frac{9}{16}$

4. $0.6$ ● $0.06$   5. $0.5$ ● $\frac{1}{2}$   6. $0.3$ ● $0.25$

7. $0.01$ ● $\frac{1}{10}$   8. $12\frac{4}{5}$ ● $12\frac{2}{5}$   9. $5.125$ ● $5\frac{1}{8}$

**Order from least to greatest.**

10. $^-4.0$, $^-0.004$, $^-0.04$, $^-0.4$

11. $\frac{1}{8}$, $\frac{^-1}{8}$, $\frac{^-5}{8}$, $\frac{5}{8}$

12. $\frac{77}{100}$, $0.7$, $7.7$, $\frac{7}{100}$

13. Read the problem below. **Explain** why A cannot be the correct answer. Then choose the correct answer.

**COMMON ERROR**

Which numbers are ordered from least to greatest?

**A** $0.3$, $0.03$, $3\frac{1}{10}$, $\frac{1}{10}$

**B** $0.03$, $\frac{1}{10}$, $0.3$, $3\frac{1}{10}$

**C** $0.3$, $0.03$, $\frac{1}{10}$, $3\frac{1}{10}$

**D** $3\frac{1}{10}$, $0.3$, $0.03$, $\frac{1}{10}$

# Review the Key Standards

## Fractions, Decimals, and Mixed Numbers on a Number Line

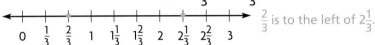

0—n NS 1.0 Students compare and order positive and negative fractions, decimals, and mixed numbers. Students solve problems involving fractions, ratios, proportions, and percentages.

0—n NS 1.1 Compare and order positive and negative fractions, decimals, and mixed numbers and place them on a number line.

## Examples

**A** Use a number line to compare $\frac{2}{3}$ and $2\frac{1}{3}$.

$$0 \quad \frac{1}{3} \quad \frac{2}{3} \quad 1 \quad 1\frac{1}{3} \quad 1\frac{2}{3} \quad 2 \quad 2\frac{1}{3} \quad 2\frac{2}{3} \quad 3$$

$\frac{2}{3}$ is to the left of $2\frac{1}{3}$.

**ERROR ALERT**

On a number line, values increase as you move to the right and values decrease as you move to the left.

So, $\frac{2}{3} < 2\frac{1}{3}$.

**B** Use a number line to order $^-0.3$, 0.7, $\frac{^-1}{2}$, and $\frac{1}{10}$ from least to greatest

$\frac{^-1}{2} = \frac{^-50}{100} = ^-0.50$     Write equivalent fractions with 100 as the denominator. Then use place value to write the fractions as decimals.

$\frac{1}{10} = \frac{10}{100} = 0.1$     Place the numbers on the number line.

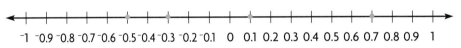

$$^-1 \quad ^-0.9 \quad ^-0.8 \quad ^-0.7 \quad ^-0.6 \quad ^-0.5 \quad ^-0.4 \quad ^-0.3 \quad ^-0.2 \quad ^-0.1 \quad 0 \quad 0.1 \quad 0.2 \quad 0.3 \quad 0.4 \quad 0.5 \quad 0.6 \quad 0.7 \quad 0.8 \quad 0.9 \quad 1$$

$\frac{^-1}{2}$ is to the left of $^-0.3$, $^-0.3$ is to the left of $\frac{1}{10}$, and $\frac{1}{10}$ is to the left of 0.7.

So, the numbers in order from least to greatest are $\frac{^-1}{2}$, $^-0.3$, $\frac{1}{10}$, and 0.7.

## Try It

Compare. Write <, >, or =.

1. $^-0.25 \bigcirc ^-0.27$

2. $\frac{^-3}{4} \bigcirc \frac{^-1}{4}$

3. $\frac{^-17}{100} \bigcirc ^-0.17$

4. $^-0.2 \bigcirc \frac{^-3}{10}$

5. Explain how to use the number line to order $\frac{5}{8}, \frac{3}{4}$, and $\frac{1}{2}$ from greatest to least.

$$0 \quad \frac{1}{8} \quad \frac{2}{8} \quad \frac{3}{8} \quad \frac{4}{8} \quad \frac{5}{8} \quad \frac{6}{8} \quad \frac{7}{8} \quad 1$$

6. Read the problem below.

   **Explain** why D cannot be the correct answer. Then choose the correct answer.

   **COMMON ERROR**

   Which point shows the location of $^-1\frac{2}{3}$ on the number line?

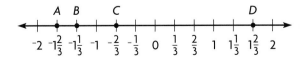

$$\begin{array}{c} A \quad B \qquad C \qquad\qquad\qquad\qquad D \\ ^-2 \quad ^-1\frac{2}{3} \quad ^-1\frac{1}{3} \quad ^-1 \quad ^-\frac{2}{3} \quad ^-\frac{1}{3} \quad 0 \quad \frac{1}{3} \quad \frac{2}{3} \quad 1 \quad 1\frac{1}{3} \quad 1\frac{2}{3} \quad 2 \end{array}$$

   **A** Point A

   **B** Point B

   **C** Point C

   **D** Point D

# Review the Key Standards

## Ratios

NS 1.0 Students compare and order positive and negative fractions, decimals, and mixed numbers. Students solve problems involving fractions, ratios, proportions, and percentages.

NS 1.2 Interpret and use ratios in different contexts (e.g., batting averages, miles per hour) to show the relative sizes of two quantities, using appropriate notations ($\frac{a}{b}$, $a$ to $b$, $a:b$).

A **ratio** is a comparison of two numbers, $a$ and $b$, that can be written as a fraction $\frac{a}{b}$.

$\frac{3}{4}$ ← ratio          $\frac{3 \times 2}{4 \times 2} = \frac{6}{8}$

**Equivalent ratios** are ratios that name the same comparison. You can write equivalent ratios by multiplying both terms by the same number or dividing both terms by a common factor.

$\frac{3}{4}$ and $\frac{6}{8}$ are equivalent ratios.

## Examples

**ERROR ALERT**

When writing ratios, remember to write the ratios in the correct order.

Ex. $3:7 = \frac{3}{7}$, not $\frac{7}{3}$.

**A** For every gallon of gas, Kathy's new hybrid car can travel 45 mi on the highway. Write a ratio, in three ways, comparing gallons of gas to mileage.

| with the word "to" | with a colon | as a fraction |
|:---:|:---:|:---:|
| 1 to 45 | 1:45 | $\frac{1 \leftarrow \text{gal}}{45 \leftarrow \text{miles}}$ |

**B** Pilar is making fruit salad for a party. For every 5 oz of apples she uses in the salad, she uses 1 oz of pears, 1 oz of peaches, and 2 oz of melon. Write each of the following ratios in three ways:

a. ounces of pears to ounces of apples    1 to 5    1:5    $\frac{1}{5}$    part to part

b. ounces of peaches to total ounces    1 to 9    1:9    $\frac{1}{9}$    part to whole

c. total ounces to ounces of melon    9 to 2    9:2    $\frac{9}{2}$    whole to part

**C** Write three equivalent ratios that compare the number of hearts to the number of triangles.

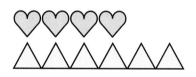

$\dfrac{\text{number of hearts}}{\text{number of triangles}} \rightarrow \dfrac{4}{6}$

$\frac{4}{6} \rightarrow \frac{4 \div 2}{6 \div 2} = \frac{2}{3}$     Divide both terms by a common factor.

$\frac{4}{6} \rightarrow \frac{4 \times 2}{6 \times 2} = \frac{8}{12}$     Multiply both terms by the same number.

So, $\frac{4}{6}$, $\frac{2}{3}$, and $\frac{8}{12}$ are equivalent ratios comparing hearts to triangles.

## Try It

**Write each ratio in three ways.**

1. 20 pages in 2 hr

2. 7 dogs to 5 cats

3. a scale of 1 in. to 10 mi

4. 3 points out of a total of 30 points

5. a width of 24 in. to a length of 40 in.

6. 12 apples to 3 oranges

**Write two equivalent ratios.**

7. $\frac{7}{1}$

8. $\frac{6}{18}$

9. $\frac{3}{2}$

10. $\frac{5}{15}$

11. $\frac{1}{4}$

12. $\frac{10}{12}$

13. $\frac{24}{4}$

14. $\frac{5}{10}$

15. $\frac{2}{14}$

16. $\frac{9}{3}$

17. $\frac{20}{2}$

18. $\frac{1}{6}$

19. Ralph drives 256 mi in 4 hr. Write a ratio relating the number of miles traveled to the number of hours traveled.

20. There are 45 sixth-graders and 65 seventh-graders in the lunchroom. Write a ratio comparing the number of sixth-graders to seventh-graders who are in the lunchroom.

21. In a survey of 200 students, 100 students said they planned to attend a pep rally, 66 said they did not plan to attend, and the rest said they had no opinion. What is the ratio of students who had no opinion to the total number of students surveyed?

22. Jean made a necklace with 35 blue beads, 20 yellow beads, and 65 green beads. Write a ratio comparing the total number of beads in the necklace to the number of yellow beads in the necklace.

23. Write a ratio comparing the number of consonants to the total number of letters in the word MATHEMATICS.

24. Write a ratio comparing the number of vowels to the number of consonants in the word INTELLIGENCE.

25. Sherry struck out 7 times in her last 28 times at bat. The rest of the time, she got a hit. Write a ratio comparing Sherry's strikeouts to Sherry's hits in her last 28 times at bat.

26. The American flag has 7 red stripes and 6 white stripes. Write a ratio comparing the number of red stripes to the total number of stripes on the American flag.

## Solve

27. Read the problem below. **Explain** why A cannot be the correct answer. Then choose the correct answer.

COMMON ERROR

Candace is ordering tiles for her kitchen floor. She orders 75 green tiles and 60 white tiles. What is the ratio of the number of green tiles to the number of white tiles that Candace has ordered?

A 4:5

C 5:4

B 6:7

D 3:2

28. Read the problem below. **Explain** why B cannot be the correct answer. Then choose the correct answer.

COMMON ERROR

In the school homeroom, the ratio of boys to girls is 16 to 12. Which of the following ratios is equivalent to 16 to 12?

A $\frac{1}{2}$

C $\frac{3}{2}$

B $\frac{3}{4}$

D $\frac{4}{3}$

# Review the Key Standards

## Proportions

**O━ NS 1.0** Students compare and order positive and negative fractions, decimals, and mixed numbers. Students solve problems involving fractions, ratios, proportions, and percentages.

**O━ NS 1.3** Use proportions to solve problems. Use cross-multiplication as a method for solving such problems, understanding it as the multiplication of both sides of an equation by a multiplicative inverse.

A **proportion** is an equation that shows two equivalent ratios. Two ratios form a proportion if the ratios are equal.

$$\frac{1}{2} = \frac{2}{4} \leftarrow \text{proportion}$$

## Examples

**A** Determine whether the ratios $\frac{3}{8}$ and $\frac{12}{32}$ form a proportion.

$$\frac{3}{8} \overset{?}{=} \frac{12}{32}$$     Find a common denominator.

$$\frac{3 \times 4}{8 \times 4} \overset{?}{=} \frac{12}{32}$$     Rewrite the ratios using the common denominator.

         Compare the ratios to see if they are equivalent.

$$\frac{12}{32} = \frac{12}{32}$$

So, the ratios $\frac{3}{8}$ and $\frac{12}{32}$ do form a proportion, since they are equivalent ratios.

**ERROR ALERT**

When using cross-multiplication to solve proportions, check to see that both numerators, as well as both denominators, have the same unit.

**Correct**

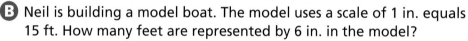

$$\frac{180 \text{ mi}}{9 \text{ gal}} \overset{\leftarrow}{=} \overset{\rightarrow}{\frac{105 \text{ mi}}{7 \text{ gal}}}$$

**Incorrect**

$$\frac{180 \text{ mi}}{9 \text{ gal}} \overset{\leftarrow}{=} \overset{\rightarrow}{\frac{7 \text{ gal}}{105 \text{ mi}}}$$

**B** Neil is building a model boat. The model uses a scale of 1 in. equals 15 ft. How many feet are represented by 6 in. in the model?

$$\frac{1 \text{ in.}}{15 \text{ ft}} = \frac{6 \text{ in.}}{n \text{ ft}}$$     Write a proportion that represents the situation. Let $n$ represent the number of feet represented by 6 inches in the model.

$$\frac{1}{15} = \frac{6}{n}$$

$$\frac{1}{15} \overset{\leftarrow}{=} \overset{\rightarrow}{\frac{6}{n}}$$     Use cross-multiplication to solve the proportion. Multiply the numerator of each fraction by the denominator of the other fraction. Begin with the fraction on the left.

$$1 \times n = 6 \times 15$$     Multiply to solve the equation.

$$n = 90$$

So, 90 ft are represented by 6 in. in Neil's model.

## Try It

**Use common denominators to determine whether the ratios form a proportion.**

1. $\frac{3}{5}$ and $\frac{8}{15}$

2. $\frac{9}{13}$ and $\frac{18}{26}$

3. $\frac{1}{5}$ and $\frac{4}{20}$

4. $\frac{15}{24}$ and $\frac{5}{7}$

5. $\frac{8}{16}$ and $\frac{6}{12}$

6. $\frac{21}{24}$ and $\frac{10}{12}$

**Solve the proportion.**

7. $\frac{n}{12} = \frac{3}{4}$

8. $\frac{9}{4} = \frac{18}{x}$

9. $\frac{10}{x} = \frac{30}{9}$

10. $\frac{x}{2} = \frac{4}{1}$

11. $\frac{9}{7} = \frac{45}{n}$

12. $\frac{3}{16} = \frac{n}{48}$

13. Shelly is buying juice. One bottle contains 12 oz and costs $0.84. Another bottle contains 14 oz and costs $1.12. She writes and solves the proportion below to find the cost per ounce of the 12-oz bottle.

$$\frac{\$0.84}{12} = \frac{\$0.07}{1} = \$0.07 \text{ per oz}$$

Write and solve a proportion to find the cost per ounce of the 14-oz bottle. Which bottle of juice is the better buy?

14. Omar ran 1,760 yd in 8 min. He writes the proportion below to find $n$, the number of yards he ran in 2 min.

$$\frac{1,760}{8} = \frac{n}{2}$$

If Omar set up the proportion correctly, solve the proportion. If he did not, rewrite the proportion correctly and then solve.

15. At her job, Maya gets 1 vacation day for every 35 days she works. How many days will Maya have to work to get 5 vacation days?

16. Janelle typed 90 words in 2 min. Charles typed 400 words in 8 min. Ruth typed 1,200 words in 25 min. Who typed the fastest per minute?

17. Chris and Jacob are reading the same book. Chris has finished reading $\frac{3}{8}$ of the book. Jacob has finished reading $\frac{9}{24}$ of the book. Can the ratios be used to form a proportion? **Explain.**

18. A seamstress can sew 25 pairs of pants in 8 hr. Write and solve a proportion to find $n$, the number of pairs of pants she can be expected to sew in 40 hr.

---

## Solve

19. Read the problem below. **Explain** why A cannot be the correct answer. Then choose the correct answer.

Joe earned $3,750 in 6 weeks. Which proportion can be solved to find $x$, his expected earnings in 14 weeks?

A $\frac{6}{3,750} = \frac{x}{14}$

C $\frac{6}{3,750} = \frac{14}{x}$

B $\frac{14}{3,750} = \frac{x}{6}$

D $\frac{14}{3,750} = \frac{x}{6}$

20. Read the problem below. **Explain** why A cannot be the correct answer. Then choose the correct answer.

A certain map uses a scale of 1 in. = 40 mi. How many miles are represented by 4 in. on this map?

A $\frac{1}{10}$ miles

C 80 miles

B 40 miles

D 160 miles

# Review the Key Standards

## Percentages

**0━** **NS 1.0** Students compare and order positive and negative fractions, decimals, and mixed numbers. Students solve problems involving fractions, ratios, proportions, and percentages.

**0━** **NS 1.4** Calculate given percentages of quantities and solve problems involving discounts at sales, interest earned, and tips.

**Percent** is the ratio of a number to 100; "per hundred." The symbol for percent is %. In the figure at the right, 68 of the 100 squares, or 68% of the squares, are shaded. This amount can be shown as a percent, a decimal, or a fraction.

$$68\% = 0.68 = \frac{68}{100}$$

## Examples

**A** Kim has 300 cards. If 60 are baseball cards, what percent of Kim's cards are baseball cards?

$$\frac{60}{300} = \frac{20}{100} = 20\%$$

**B** What is 5% of 140?

$5\% = 0.05$

$0.05 \times 140 = 7$

So, 5% of 140 = 7.

**ERROR ALERT**

Be sure to move the decimal two places to the left when writing a percent as a decimal.

**C** Kel left a 15% tip for a $24 lunch. How much did Kel spend on lunch?

You can use a proportion to find a percent.

Think: $15\% = \frac{15}{100}$

$\frac{t}{24} = \frac{15}{100}$  Write a proportion. Let $t$ be the amount of the tip.

$100 \times t = 15 \times 24$  Use cross-multiplication.

$100t = 360$

$\frac{100t}{100} = \frac{360}{100}$  Divide.

$t = 3.60$

$\$24.00 + \$3.60 = \$27.60$  Add the tip to the cost.

So, Kel spent $27.60 on lunch.

**D** A $30 hat is on sale with a 10% discount. How much will the hat cost?

**Step 1** Find the discount.

discount = regular price × discount rate
$= \$30 \times 10\%$  Write the percent as a decimal.
$= \$30 \times 0.10$  Multiply.
$= \$3$

So, the discount is $3.

**Step 2** Find the sale price.

sale price = regular price − discount
$= \$30 - \$3$
$= \$27$

So, the hat will cost $27.

**E** How much will Denise earn if she puts $300 in a savings account at a simple interest rate of 5% for 2 years?

The amount of money borrowed or saved is the **principal**. **Simple interest** is a fixed percent of the principal, paid yearly.

Use the formula $I = prt$, where $I$ = interest, $p$ = principal, $r$ = rate per year, and $t$ = time in years.

$p = \$300$, $r = 5\%$, $t = 2$ years
$I = \$300 \times 0.05 \times 2$

$I = \$30$

So, the simple interest is $30.

## Try It

**Find the percent of the number.**

**1.** 20% of 90     **2.** 4% of 225     **3.** 45% of 80     **4.** 77% of 400     **5.** 32% of 50

**Find the sale price.**

**6.** Regular price: $25
   Discount: 20%

**7.** Regular price: $80
   Discount: 5%

**8.** Regular price: $40
   Discount: 10%

**9.** Regular price: $52
   Discount: 25%

**Find the total amount spent on each meal including the tip.**

**10.** $22 with a 15% tip     **11.** $45 with a 20% tip     **12.** $70 with a 20% tip     **13.** $68 with a 15% tip

**Find the simple interest.**

**14.** principal: $1,000
   rate: 5%
   time: 3 years

**15.** principal: $300
   rate: 4%
   time: 1 year

**16.** principal: $800
   rate: 4.5%
   time: 2 years

**17.** principal: $400
   rate: 5%
   time: 5 years

**18.** Aaron put $800 in a savings account for 3 years at a simple interest rate of 5%. Karen put $1,200 in a savings account for 2 years at a simple interest rate of 6%. Who earned more interest? How much more?

**19.** Tricia sold 35 tickets to the school play. Of those tickets, 60% were for the Saturday night performance. How many tickets did Tricia sell to the Saturday night performance of the play?

**20.** Irene orders a burrito for $5.50 and a drink for $1.50. She leaves a 15% tip. What is the total cost of her meal including the tip?

**21.** In a zoo, 40% of the 50 snakes are poisonous. How many poisonous snakes are in the zoo?

**22.** Al made baskets on 25% of the 16 shots he took during a basketball game. How many baskets did Al make?

**23.** Juan took out a $600 loan for one year at a simple interest rate of 9%. What is the total amount Juan will have to repay?

## Solve

**24.** Read the problem below. **Explain** why D cannot be the correct answer. Then choose the correct answer.

What is 6% of 300?

  **A** 6

  **B** 18

  **C** 50

  **D** 180

**25.** Read the problem below. **Explain** why B cannot be the correct answer. Then choose the correct answer.

Mr. and Mrs. Gomez had an anniversary dinner in a restaurant. Their dinner bill was $185. If they left a 20% tip, how much money did they spend on dinner including the tip?

  **A** $37.50      **C** $205.00

  **B** 188.70      **D** $222.00

# Review the Key Standards

## Add and Subtract Integers

○━┓ **NS 2.0** Students calculate and solve problems involving addition, subtraction, multiplication, and division.

○━┓ **NS 2.3** Solve addition, subtraction, multiplication, and division problems, including those arising in concrete situations, that use positive and negative integers and combinations of these operations.

### Integer rules

When adding integers with like signs, add the absolute values of the addends. Use the sign of the addends for the sum.

When adding integers with unlike signs, subtract the lesser absolute value from the greater absolute value. Use the sign of the addend with the greater absolute value for the sum.

When finding the difference between two integers, write the expression as an addition expression. Then use the rules for the addition of integers.

## Examples

**A** Add integers with like signs.

$13 + 5 = 18$

$^-4 + {}^-6 = {}^-10$

Add the absolute values of the integers. Use the sign of the addends for the sum.

**B** Add integers with unlike signs.

$^-9 + 3 = {}^-6$

$7 + {}^-2 = 5$

Subtract the lesser absolute value from the greater absolute value. Use the sign of the addend with the greater absolute value for the sum.

**C** To subtract integers, write the expression as an addition expression and then add.

$8 - 11 = 8 + {}^-11$
$= {}^-3$
$1 - ({}^-3) = 1 + 3$
$= 4$

**ERROR ALERT**

When adding intege with unlike signs, be sure to use the sign the integer with the greater absolute va▶

**D** Lucy has $12. She spends $7 on a book. Then her mother gives her $10. How much money does Lucy have now?

$12 - 7 + 10 = 12 + {}^-7 + 10$    Write an addition expression.
$= 5 + 10 = 15$    Add.

So, Lucy has $15.

## Try It

**Find the value of the expression.**

1. $^-7 + ({}^-6)$    2. $2 - 5$    3. $^-8 + 10$

4. $1 - ({}^-2)$    5. $^-4 - ({}^-22)$    6. $^-50 - 55$

7. At 8 P.M., the temperature was 4°F. By midnight, the temperature dropped 12°F and then rose 7°F by morning. What was the morning temperature?

8. Read the problem below. **Explain** why C cannot be the correct answer. Then choose the correct answer.

**COMMON ERROR**

Find the value of $6 - {}^-3 + 1$.

**A** 2    **C** 8

**B** 4    **D** 10

# 🐻 Review the Key Standards

## Multiply and Divide Integers

🔑 **NS 2.0** Students calculate and solve problems involving addition, subtraction, multiplication, and division.

🔑 **NS 2.3** Solve addition, subtraction, multiplication, and division problems, including those arising in concrete situations, that use positive and negative integers and combinations of these operations.

**Integer rules:**

The product of two integers with like signs is positive.
The product of two integers with unlike signs is negative.
The quotient of two integers with like signs is positive.
The quotient of two integers with unlike signs is negative.

## Examples
**Find the product or quotient.**

**(A)** $^-11 \times ^-5$

$^-11 \times ^-5 = 55$  The product is positive since the integers have like signs.

**(B)** $4 \times ^-6$

$4 \times ^-6 = ^-24$  The product is negative since the integers have unlike signs.

**(C)** $^-18 \div ^-6$

$^-18 \div ^-6 = 3$  The quotient is positive since the integers have like signs.

**(D)** $^-27 \div 9$

$^-27 \div 9 = ^-3$  The quotient is negative since the integers have unlike signs.

**ERROR ALERT**

**(E)** Find $24 \div (3 \times 4)$.

$24 \div (3 \times 4) = 24 \div 12$  First multiply $3 \times 4$.
Then divide $24 \div 12$.

$= 2$

Be sure to show the product or quotient of two negative integers as positive.

## Try It
**Find the value of the expression.**

1. $^-9 \times 5$
2. $7 \times ^-12$
3. $44 \div ^-11$
4. $^-6 \times ^-8$
5. $^-24 \div ^-3$
6. $80 \div ^-10$
7. $8 \div ^-2 \times ^-4$
8. $^-6 \times 6 \div ^-3$

9. Angela typed 90 words. If the words are evenly divided into 5 columns, how many words are in each column?

10. Read the problem below. **Explain** why D cannot be the correct answer. Then choose the correct answer.

COMMON ERROR

Find the value of $^-15 \div ^-5$.

A 10

B 3

C $^-\dfrac{1}{3}$

D $^-3$

# 🐻 Review the Key Standards

## Least Common Multiple and Greatest Common Divisor

**NS 2.0** Students calculate and solve problems involving addition, subtraction, multiplication, and division.

**NS 2.4** Determine the least common multiple and the greatest common divisor of whole numbers; use them to solve problems with fractions (e.g., to find a common denominator to add two fractions or to find the reduced form for a fraction).

The **least common multiple**, or **LCM**, is the smallest number, other than 0, that is a common multiple of two or more given numbers.

The **greatest common factor**, or **GCF**, is the greatest factor that two or more numbers have in common. It is also called the **greatest common divisor**, or **GCD**.

The **prime factorization** of a number is the number written as the product of its prime factors.

The LCM of 6 and 9 is 18.

The GCF, or GCD, of 24 and 32 is 8.

$24 = 2 \times 2 \times 2 \times 3 = 2^3 \times 3$

## Examples

**A** Find the LCM of 8 and 12.

$8 = 2 \times 2 \times 2 = 2^3$

$12 = 2 \times 2 \times 3 = 2^2 \times 3$

Write each factor and use the greater exponent from the two factorizations. Multiply.

$2^3 \times 3 = 24$

So, the LCM of 8 and 12 is 24.

**B** What is the greatest common divisor of 27 and 36?

List the factors of each number.

27: 1, 3, 9, 27

36: 1, 2, 3, 4, 6, 9, 12, 18, 36

So, the greatest common divisor of 27 and 36 is 9.

**ERROR ALERT**

A factor of a number can be no greater than the number itself.

12 is a factor of 24.
24 is not a factor of 12.

## Try It

**Find the least common multiple.**

1. 5, 7
2. 6, 16
3. 9, 15
4. 2, 3, 7
5. 4, 5, 10
6. 6, 8, 9

**Find the greatest common divisor.**

7. 21, 24, 33
8. 8, 20, 28
9. 4, 18, 48

10. Ann uses 63 roses and 81 daisies to make bouquets that are all the same. What is the greatest number of bouquets she can make if each bouquet has the same number of roses and the same number of daisies with none left over?

11. Read the problem below. **Explain** why D cannot be the correct answer. Then choose the correct answer.

    What is the greatest common divisor of 45, 30, and 18?

    **A** 3          **C** 15

    **B** 6          **D** 90

# 🐻 Review the Key Standards

## Solve Problems with Fractions

**○━┓ NS 2.0** Students calculate and solve problems involving addition, subtraction, multiplication, and division.

**○━┓ NS 2.4** Determine the least common multiple and the greatest common divisor of whole numbers; use them to solve problems with fractions (e.g., to find a common denominator to add two fractions or to find the reduced form for a fraction).

**Equivalent fractions** are fractions that name the same amount or part.

A fraction is in **simplest form** if the numerator and denominator of the fraction have no common factors other than 1.

The **least common denominator,** or **LCD,** is the least common multiple of the denominators of two or more fractions.

$\frac{1}{2} = \frac{2}{4}$

$\frac{3}{4}$ is in simplest form.

The LCD of $\frac{1}{3}$ and $\frac{1}{4}$ is 12.

**ERROR ALERT**

Add numerators when adding fractions with the same denominators.

$$\frac{1}{2} + \frac{1}{4} = \frac{2}{4} + \frac{1}{4}$$

$$\frac{2}{4} + \frac{1}{4} = \frac{3}{4}, \text{ not } \frac{3}{8}$$

## Examples

Jack is training for a 10-km race. On Saturday he ran $5\frac{3}{10}$ km. On Sunday, he ran $4\frac{1}{2}$ km. How many kilometers did he run in all on Saturday and Sunday?

Add. $5\frac{3}{10} + 4\frac{1}{2}$

$$
\begin{aligned}
5\frac{3}{10} &= \quad 5\frac{3}{10} \\
+ 4\frac{1}{2} &= +4\frac{5}{10} \\
\hline
&\quad 9\frac{8}{10} = 9\frac{4}{5}
\end{aligned}
$$

Write equivalent fractions, using the LCD, 10.

Add fractions. Add whole numbers.

Divide 8 and 10 by the GCF, 2, to write the answer in simplest form.

So, Jack ran a total of $9\frac{4}{5}$ km on Saturday and Sunday.

## Try It

**Write the sum or difference in simplest form.**

**1.** $\frac{5}{9} + \frac{1}{3}$  **2.** $\frac{1}{8} + \frac{3}{4}$  **3.** $\frac{2}{5} - \frac{1}{6}$

**4.** $4\frac{1}{2} + 2\frac{3}{7}$  **5.** $6\frac{9}{16} - 3\frac{1}{4}$  **6.** $3\frac{11}{12} - 1\frac{3}{4}$

**Write the product or quotient in simplest form.**

**7.** $\frac{1}{5} \times \frac{3}{7}$  **8.** $\frac{4}{9} \times \frac{5}{16}$  **9.** $2\frac{1}{3} \times 1\frac{4}{5}$

**10.** $\frac{5}{6} \div \frac{1}{2}$  **11.** $\frac{3}{8} \div \frac{3}{4}$  **12.** $1\frac{4}{5} \div \frac{8}{15}$

**13.** Chris ran $1\frac{1}{3}$ mile on Monday and $1\frac{1}{6}$ mile on Tuesday. What is the total distance he ran?

**14.** Read the problem below. **Explain** why D cannot be the correct answer. Then choose the correct answer.

$$3\frac{3}{4} + 4\frac{1}{7} =$$

**A** $7\frac{4}{11}$

**B** $7\frac{25}{28}$

**C** $7\frac{4}{28}$

**D** $7\frac{25}{56}$

# Review the Key Standards

## One-Step Linear Equations

AF 1.1 Write and solve one-step linear equations in one variable.

An **equation** is a statement that shows that two quantities are equal. Examples of some equations appear below.

$$x + 5 = 7 \qquad y - 6 = {}^-8 \qquad 3a = 15.3 \qquad \frac{k}{7} = 3\frac{1}{4}$$

To solve one-step equations, you can use inverse operations and either the **Addition, Subtraction, Multiplication,** or **Division Property of Equality.**

### Examples

**A** Kate had some money in her pocket. She spent $5 and had $8 left. How much money, $m$, did she have to start?

$$
\begin{array}{ll}
m - 5 = 8 & \text{Write the equation.} \\
m - 5 + 5 = 8 + 5 & \text{Use the Addition} \\
m + 0 = 13 & \text{Property of Equality.} \\
m = 13 & \\
\\
m - 5 = 8 & \text{Check your solution.} \\
13 - 5 \stackrel{?}{=} 8 & \text{Replace } m \text{ with 13.} \\
8 = 8 ✔ & \text{The solution checks.}
\end{array}
$$

So, Kate had $13.

**B** Solve the equation $7n = 42$.

$$
\begin{array}{ll}
7n = 42 & \\
\dfrac{7n}{7} = \dfrac{42}{7} & \text{Use the Division} \\
 & \text{Property of Equality.} \\
1 \times n = 6 & \\
n = 6 & \\
\\
7n = 42 & \text{Check your solution.} \\
7 \times 6 \stackrel{?}{=} 42 & \text{Replace } n \text{ with 6.} \\
42 = 42 ✔ & \text{The solution checks.}
\end{array}
$$

So, $n = 6$.

**ERROR ALERT** When solving an equation, be sure to add, subtract, multiply by, or divide by the same number on both sides of an equation so that the two sides remain equal.

## Try It

**Solve and check.**

1. $x - 5 = {}^-3$

2. $9x = 63$

3. $4 + n = 8$

4. $c + 9 = 26$

5. $n - 12 = 12$

6. $\frac{x}{3} = 6$

7. $z - 8 = 7$

8. $h + 19 = 37$

9. $i - 72 = 14$

10. ${}^-8 \div 2 = b$

11. ${}^-5x = {}^-15$

12. ${}^-3y = 36$

13. $\frac{x}{6} = 3.5$

14. $4b = 10\frac{4}{5}$

15. $m + 1.8 = 3.2$

16. $c - 2 = {}^-27$

17. $\frac{t}{7} = 8\frac{1}{5}$

18. $15p = 60$

19. Charlie earns $11 for each lawn he mows. In August, he earned $165 mowing lawns. Write and solve an equation to find the number of lawns Charlie mowed.

20. Read the problem below. **Explain** why C cannot be the correct answer. Then choose the correct answer.

    **COMMON ERROR**

    What value of $a$ makes the following equation true? $\frac{a}{8} = 12$.

    **A** 4          **C** 20

    **B** 12         **D** 96

**Review the Key Standards**

## Rate

○━ **AF 2.2** Demonstrate an understanding that rate is a measure of one quantity per unit value of another quantity.

A **rate** is a ratio that compares two quantities that have different units of measure.

$$\frac{\text{miles}}{\text{hours}} \rightarrow \frac{90}{3}, \text{ or 90 mi for 3 hr}$$

A **unit rate** is a rate that has 1 unit as its second term.

$$\frac{90}{3} = \frac{30}{1}, \text{ or 30 mi per hr}$$

## Examples

**A** Yuri typed 360 words in 6 min. What is Yuri's typing rate per min?

rate: $\frac{\text{words}}{\text{min}} \rightarrow \frac{360}{6}$     Write a rate to compare words to minutes.

unit rate: $\frac{360 \div 6}{6 \div 6} = \frac{60}{1}$     Divide both terms by the second term.

So, Yuri types at the unit rate of 60 words per min.

**ERROR ALERT**

Be sure to write the unit rate in the correct order.

Ex. $75 in 5 hr

Correct

$\frac{\$}{\text{hr}} \rightarrow \frac{75}{5}$

Incorrect

$\frac{\$}{\text{hr}} \rightarrow \frac{5}{75}$

**B** Tina runs 15 mi in 3 hr. At this rate, how long will it take her to run 20 mi?

$\frac{15 \div 3}{3 \div 3} = \frac{5}{1}$, or 5 mi per hr     Find the unit rate or average speed.

$\frac{5 \times 4}{1 \times 4} = \frac{20}{4}$, or 20 mi in 4 hr     To find the number of hours for 20 mi, multiply each term by 4.

So, Tina runs 20 mi in 4 hr.

## Try It

**Write the rate in fraction form. Then find the unit rate.**

1. 630 calories in 3 hr
2. $84 for 12 tickets
3. 42 pages in 6 days
4. 220 mi on 4 gal
5. $2.24 for 16 oz
6. 27 ft in 9 min

7. A bus gets 13 mi per gal of gasoline. How many gallons of gasoline would the bus need to travel 221 mi?

8. Stanley's heart beats 288 times in 4 min. At this rate, how many times will Stanley's heart beat in 10 min?

9. A 14-oz bottle of shampoo costs $8.26. What is the price per ounce?  **COMMON ERROR**

10. Read the problem below. **Explain** why D cannot be the correct answer. Then choose the correct answer.

At a quilting bee, Rosa sews 21 quilt squares in 7 hours. At this rate, how long will it take her to sew 63 quilt squares?

  **A** 21 hours       **C** 147 hours

  **B** 63 hours       **D** 189 hours

#  Review the Key Standards

## Circumference and Area of a Circle

⊶ MG 1.1 Understand the concept of a constant such as π; know the formulas for the circumference and area of a circle.

The number **pi**, or $\pi$, can be defined as the area of a unit circle or as the ratio of the circumference to the diameter of any circle. Common estimates of are $\pi$ 3.14 and $\frac{22}{7}$. To find the circumference of a circle, you can use the formula $C = \pi d$ or $C = 2\pi r$. To find the area of a circle, you can use the formula $A = \pi r^2$.

## Examples

**Ⓐ** A circular swimming pool has a diameter of 18 ft. Find the circumference of the swimming pool to the nearest foot. Use 3.14 for $\pi$.

If you know the diameter of a circle, use the formula $C = \pi d$ to find the circumference.

18 ft

$C = \pi d$      Write the formula.

$C = 3.14 \times 18$    Replace $\pi$ with 3.14 and $d$ with 18. Round to the nearest foot.

$C \approx 56.52$

$C \approx 57$

So, the circumference is about 57 ft.

**Ⓑ** Find the circumference of a circle with a radius of 7 m, to the nearest meter. Use $\frac{22}{7}$ for $\pi$.

If you know the radius of a circle, use the formula $C = 2\pi r$ to find the circumference.

$C = 2\pi r$      Write the formula.

$C \approx 2 \times \frac{22}{7} \times 7$    Replace $\pi$ with $\frac{22}{7}$ and $r$ with 7.

$C \approx \frac{2}{1} \times \frac{22}{7} \times \frac{7}{1}$

$C \approx \frac{2}{1} \times \frac{22}{7} \times \frac{\overset{1}{7}}{\underset{1}{1}}$    Simplify and multiply.

$C \approx \frac{44}{1}$, or 44

So, the circumference is about 44 m.

**Ⓒ** Find the diameter of a wheel with a circumference of 157 in.

$C = \pi d$      Write the formula.

$157 \approx 3.14d$     Replace $C$ with 157 and $\pi$ with 3.14.

$\frac{157}{3.14} \approx \frac{3.14d}{3.14}$    Solve.

$50 \approx d$

So, the diameter of the wheel is about 50 in.

**Ⓓ** Find the area of the circle to the nearest foot. Use 3.14 for $\pi$.

$A = \pi r^2.$      Write the formula.

$A \approx 3.14 \times 3^2$    Replace $\pi$ with 3.14. Since $r = \frac{1}{2}d$, replace $r$ with 3. Multiply.

$A \approx 3.14 \times 9$

$A \approx 28.26$, or 28

6 ft

**ERROR ALERT**
Be sure to use the length of the radius, and not the length of the diameter, when using $A = \pi r^2$ to find the area of a circle.

So the area of the circle is about 28 ft².

## Try It

**Find the circumference of the circle to nearest whole number. Use 3.14 or $\frac{22}{7}$ for $\pi$.**

**1.**
5 in.

**2.**
42 m

**3.**
6 ft

**4.**
14 in.

**5.**
2 ft

**6.**
3.5 cm

**7.**
4 m

**8.**
15 in.

**9.** Find the diameter of a circle with a circumference of 44 in. to the nearest inch. Use $\frac{22}{7}$ for $\pi$.

**10.** Find the radius of a circle with a circumference of 18.84 ft to the nearest foot. Use 3.14 for $\pi$.

**Find the area of the circle to nearest whole number. Use 3.14 or $\frac{22}{7}$ for $\pi$.**

**11.**
2 in.

**12.**
7 ft

**13.**
14 cm

**14.**
6 yd

**15.**
1 ft

**16.**
9 in.

**17.**
13 ft

**18.**
4.5 m

**19.** A merry-go-round has a diameter of 42 ft. What is the circumference of the merry-go-round to the nearest foot? Use $\frac{22}{7}$ for $\pi$.

**20.** Martha makes decorative wreaths to sell at craft fairs. She makes a wreath that has a circumference of 37.68 in. What is the diameter of this wreath to the nearest inch?

**21.** A circular pizza has a diameter of 12 in. Find the area of the pizza to the nearest square inch. Use 3.14 for $\pi$.

**22.** A circular mirror has a radius of 13 in. What is the area of the mirror to the nearest square inch? Use 3.14 for $\pi$. **Explain** how you found your answer.

**23.** Mandy put a 22-ft trim around a circular latch hook rug. What is the diameter of Mandy's rug to the nearest foot?

**24.** A circular skating rink has a radius of 21 m. What is the area of the skating rink to the nearest square meter? Use $\frac{22}{7}$ for $\pi$.

## Solve

**25.** Read the problem below. **Explain** why C cannot be the correct answer. Then choose the correct answer.

A hubcap has a diameter of 14 in. Which equation can be used to find its circumference, C, in inches?

**COMMON ERROR**

  **A** $C = 7 \times \pi$      **C** $C = 2 \times 14 \times \pi$

  **B** $C = 14 \times \pi$     **D** $C = 142\pi$

**26.** Read the problem below. **Explain** why B cannot be the correct answer. Then choose the correct answer. Which equation could be used to find the area in square feet of a small circular pool with a radius of 6 ft?

  **A** $A = 3 \times \pi$      **C** $A = 6 \times \pi$

  **B** $A = \pi \times 3^2$     **D** $A = \pi \times 6^2$

# 🐻 Review the Key Standards

## Angles

⊙┳ MG 2.2 Use the properties of complementary and supplementary angles and the sum of the angles of a triangle to solve problems involving an unknown angle.

Two angles are **complementary** if the measures of their angles have a sum of 90°.

Complementary

$$30° + 60° = 90°$$

Two angles are **supplementary** if the measures of their angles have a sum of 180°.

Supplementary

$$125° + 55° = 180°$$

The measures of the angles of a triangle have a sum of 180°.

## Examples

**ERROR ALERT**

> Be sure not to confuse complementary and supplementary angles. Complementary angles sum to 90° and supplementary angles sum to 180°.

**A** Angle $A$ and angle $B$ are complementary angles. Find $m\angle A$.

$m\angle A + m\angle B = 90°$.  The sum of the measures is 90°.

$\underline{\phantom{90}} + 70° = 90°$

$90° - 70° = 20°$  Subtract to find the unknown measure.

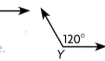

So, $m\angle A$ is 20°.

**B** Angle $X$ and angle $Y$ are supplementary angles. Find $m\angle X$.

$m\angle X + m\angle Y = 180°$.  The sum of the measures is 180°.

$\underline{\phantom{90}} + 120° = 180°$

$180° - 120° = 60°$  Subtract to find the unknown measure.

So, $m\angle X$ is 60°.

**C** Find $m\angle P$.

$x + 26 + 47 = 180$  The sum of the angles in a triangle is 180°.

$x + 73 = 180$  Add.

$x + 73 - 73 = 180 - 73$  Use the Subtraction Property of Equality.

$x + 0 = 107$  Use the Identity Property.

$x = 107$

So, $m\angle P$ is 107°.

## Try It

**Find the unknown angle measure.**

1.
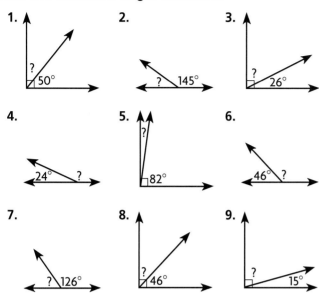
? 50°

2.
? 145°

3.
? 26°

4.
24° ?

5.
? 82°

6.
46° ?

7.
? 126°

8.
? 46°

9.
? 15°

**Find the measure of ∠B.**

10.
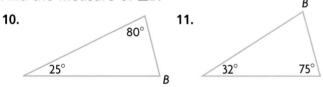
80°
25°
B

11.
B
32° 75°

12.
110°
20°
B

13.
B
55° 35°

14.
B
60° 60°

15. B
90° 27°

16. ∠ABC and ∠JKL are complementary angles. ∠ABC measures 9°. What is the measure of ∠JKL?

17. ∠EFG and ∠MNO are supplementary angles. ∠MNO measures 37°. What is the measure of ∠EFG?

18. Susie draws a triangle. Two of the angles measure 45° each. What is the measure of the third angle?

19. Cara is building a fence around a triangular garden. The measures of two of the three angles formed by her fence are 72° and 32°. What is the measure of the third angle?

## Solve

20. Read the problem below. **Explain** why A cannot be the correct answer. Then choose the correct answer.

**COMMON ERROR**

What is the measure of angle 1 in the figure below?

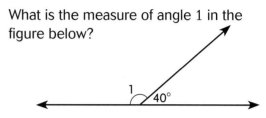
1   40°

**A** 50°

**B** 80°

**C** 140°

**D** 160°

21. What is the measure of angle *B* in the triangle below?

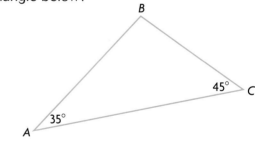
B
45° C
35°
A

**A** 10°

**B** 90°

**C** 100°

**D** 180°

# 🐻 Review the Key Standards

## Samples

○━ **SDAP 2.2** Identify different ways of selecting a sample (e.g., convenience sampling, responses to a survey, random sampling) and which method makes a sample more representative for a population.

A **survey** is a method of gathering information about a population.

A voting survey

The **population** is the entire group of objects or individuals considered for a survey.

Voters in a city with 100,000 residents

When a population in a survey is large, you can survey part of the group, called a **sample**.

1,000 voters in the city

In a **convenience sample**, the most available individuals or objects in the population are selected to obtain results quickly.

1,000 voters selected at a shopping mall

In a **random sample**, every individual or object in the population has an equal chance of being selected. This produces the sample that is most representative of the population.

1,000 voters randomly selected from the city census

## Examples

**A** Ed wants to know the favorite sport of students in his town. He asks students on his school bus. Which sampling method does he use? He obtains results quickly by using a convenience sample.

**B** Li uses a randomly generated list of students at her school for a survey. Which sampling method does she use? She uses a random sample in which each student has an equal chance of being selected.

**ERROR ALERT**

When choosing a sample, the sample should be chosen so it is representative of the population.

## Try It

Which sampling method is used, *convenience, random,* or *responses to a survey*?

1. A cell phone company asks customers to complete a mail-in survey about their cell phone usage.

2. Luan wants to know how many teenagers enjoy surfing. She asks teenagers at the beach.

3. A town manager wants to study the recycling habits of town residents. He surveys every tenth name listed in the phone book.

4. **Explain** why A cannot be the correct answer. Then choose the correct answer.

 **COMMON ERROR**

Bob takes a survey to find out what percent of students in his school own pets. Which of the following methods is the best way for Bob to choose a random sample?

   **A** select 10 students who are his friends

   **B** select 10 students on the baseball team

   **C** randomly select 10 students from each homeroom

   **D** select 10 students from the math club

# Review the Key Standards

## Analyze Data

SDAP 2.3 Analyze data displays and explain why the way in which the question was asked might have influenced the results obtained and why the way in which the results were displayed might have influenced the conclusions reached.

A **biased question** suggests or leads to a specific response, or excludes a certain group.

When a specific response is not suggested in a question, it is an **unbiased question**.

Biased: Is delicous pizza your favorite food?

Unbiased: What is your favorite food?

## Examples

**ERROR ALERT**

Be sure to evaluate the questions used in a survey to gather data. Data obtained from a survey with a biased question may result in a misleading graph.

**A** Sam asked his classmates, "Which color should we use for the school banner: the red, the green, or the beautiful blue?" The graph shows the results of his survey. Is the graph misleading? Explain.

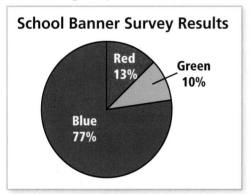

**School Banner Survey Results**

Sam's question is biased since it singles out one color as better than the others. Because of this, more students probably chose blue instead of red or green.

So, Sam's graph is misleading because his question is biased.

**B** Maggie made a graph to display the number of concert tickets she and two classmates sold. Maggie concluded that she sold twice as many tickets as Philip and Neil. Is her conclusion valid? Explain.

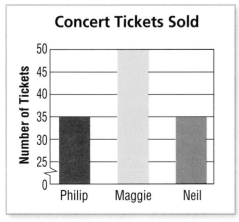

The bar for Maggie's ticket sales appears to be twice the length of Philip's bar and Neil's bar. The numbers show that this is misleading since she sold 50 tickets, while Philip and Neil sold 35 tickets each. The graph is misleading because of the broken scale between 0 and 25.

So, Maggie's conclusion is not valid.

## Try It

1. Ellen surveys 50 randomly selected students about shopping. She asks, "Would you rather enjoy catalog shopping or waste your time at a mall or flea market?" The results are shown in the graph at the right. Ellen concludes that most students prefer shopping by catalog. Is her conclusion valid? Explain.

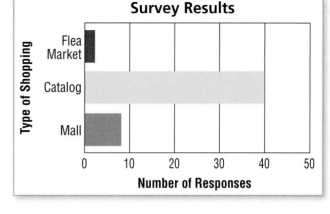

**For 2–3, use the graph at the right.**

2. The graph shows the bank account balances of Carla and her brothers, Mark, Bob, and Ned. Is the graph misleading? Explain.

3. When looking at the graph, Carla concludes that she has twice as much money as her brother Ned. Is her conclusion valid? Explain.

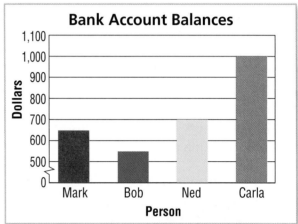

---

## Solve

4. Read the question below. **Explain** why D cannot be the correct answer. Then choose the correct answer.

   Which statement is true about the data shown in the graph below?

   **COMMON ERROR**

   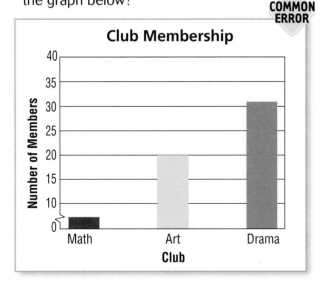

   **A** Less than 10 students are in the math club.

   **B** The art club has fewer than 20 members.

   **C** The drama club has twice as many members as the art club.

   **D** The math club has about one-sixth the number of members as the art club.

5. Read the problem below. **Explain** why A cannot be the correct answer. Then choose the correct answer.

   Which question is *not* biased?       **COMMON ERROR**

   **A** Isn't summer the best season?

   **B** Do you like apples more than pears?

   **C** What is your favorite sport?

   **D** Do you prefer classical music, or loud,

# 🐻 Review the Key Standards

## Sampling Errors

○━ SDAP 2.4 Identify data that represent sampling errors and explain why the sample (and the display) might be biased.

If certain groups from the population are not represented in the sample, then the sample is a **biased sample**.

When all individuals in the population have an equal chance of being selected, the sample is an **unbiased sample**.

**ERROR ALERT**

Be sure to evaluate the sample being used to gather data. Graphs that display data from biased samples are likely to be misleading.

## Examples

**Ⓐ** A library conducts a survey about what type of fiction books citizens in the community enjoy. The graphs below show results from two randomly selected samples. Tell whether each sample is biased or unbiased. Which display better represents the population?

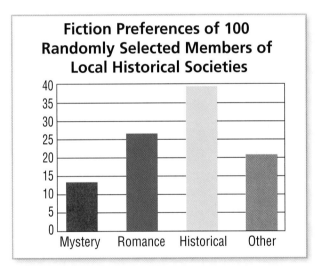

**Fiction Preferences of 100 Randomly Selected Members of Local Historical Societies**

(Mystery, Romance, Historical, Other)

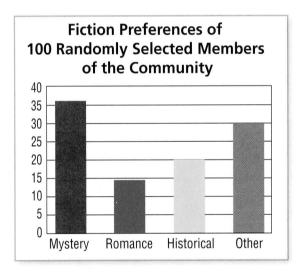

**Fiction Preferences of 100 Randomly Selected Members of the Community**

(Mystery, Romance, Historical, Other)

The sample of 100 historical society members is biased because it excludes people who are not in historical societies.

The sample of 100 community members is unbiased because individuals in the whole community have an equal chance of being selected.

So, the display showing community member preferences better represents the population.

## Try It

**For scenarios A and B, tell whether the sample is biased or unbiased. Explain.**

**Scenario A:** A California college wants to find out the favorite academic subject of California high school students.

1. 1,000 randomly selected tenth-grade students from high schools in California

2. 1,000 randomly selected high school students from all math clubs in California

3. 1,000 randomly selected high school students from all communities in California

4. 1,000 randomly selected boys who are high school students in California

**Scenario B:** A restaurant wants to find the favorite foods of residents of the local community.

5. 50 randomly selected customers at a health food store

6. 50 local residents randomly selected from the census

7. 50 randomly selected students from the local middle school

8. 50 randomly selected residents who are age 25 or older

**Use the graph below to answer question 9.**

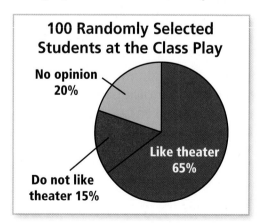

### 100 Randomly Selected Students at the Class Play

No opinion 20%

Like theater 65%

Do not like theater 15%

9. Sean concludes that most students at his school enjoy attending plays. Is his conclusion valid? Explain your answer.

## Solve

10. Read the problem below. **Explain** why D cannot be the correct answer. Then choose the correct answer.  **COMMON ERROR**

Phoebe wants to find out if students in her school like the new lunch menu. She surveys 100 students randomly selected from the entire school population and displays the results in a graph. Which statement below is true?

A The graph should not be misleading because her sample is biased.

B Her conclusion should not be valid because her sample is unbiased.

C The graph should not be misleading because her sample is unbiased.

D Her conclusions should not be valid because her sample is biased.

11. Read the problem below. **Explain** why A cannot be the correct answer. Then choose the correct answer.  **COMMON ERROR**

Dan wants to find out how voters in his town feel about a new highway being built nearby. He designs a survey to be given to an unbiased sample. Which sample below would be *least* biased?

A 80 randomly selected members from various local environmental groups

B 80 randomly selected voters from Dan's neighborhood

C 80 randomly selected middle school students from Dan's town

D 80 voters randomly selected from the voting list in Dan's town

# 🐻 Review the Key Standards

## Claims Based on Data

⌐¬ **SDAP 2.5** Identify claims based on statistical data and, in simple cases, evaluate the validity of the claims.

## Examples

**A** The table shows the annual profit for three companies.

| 2006 Profits | |
|---|---|
| **Company** | **Profit** |
| A | $500,000 |
| B | $100,000 |
| C | $200,000 |

The president of Company A claims that the profit of Company A is twice the profit of Company B and Company C combined. Is the claim valid?
No, the claim is not supported by the given data.

**ERROR ALERT**
Even though survey data may support a claim, the claim may not be valid if the sample or the question is biased.

**B** Lynn asks her friends to name their favorite color. Five friends said blue was their favorite color, 4 said red, 7 said green, and 3 said yellow. Lynn claims that green is the favorite color of all the students at her school. Is her claim valid?
No, her sample is biased.

**C** Bob takes a survey. He asks, "Don't you like beans more than peas?" Based on his results, he claims more people like beans than peas. Is his claim valid? No, his question is biased.

## Try It

**Determine if the claim is valid. Explain your answer.**

1. Inez surveys 50 randomly selected students at her school. She asks, "Is snowboarding your favorite winter sport?" Based on her results, she claims snowboarding is the favorite winter sport of students at her school.

2. School records show that there are 210 students in the sixth grade, 198 students in the seventh grade, and 203 students in the eighth grade. Joseph claims that there are more students in the sixth grade than in the seventh grade or the eighth grade.

3. Wilbur surveys 500 people leaving a movie theater in Los Angeles. One of the questions he asks is, "Do you like action films?" Based on his results, he claims that 80% of the people in California like action films.

4. Read the problem below. **Explain** why D cannot be the correct answer. Then choose the correct answer.

**COMMON ERROR**

| 2004 Population | |
|---|---|
| **City** | **Population** |
| San Jose | 904,522 |
| Anaheim | 333,776 |
| Fresno | 457,719 |

Which claim is valid about the population of these three cities?

**A** Fresno has twice the population of Anaheim.

**B** None of the three cities has a population less than 350,000.

**C** None of the three cities has a population greater than 950,000.

**D** No other city in California has a greater population than these three cities.

# Review the Key Standards

## Compound Events and Probability

SDAP 3.1 Represent all possible outcomes for compound events in an organized way (e.g., tables, grids, tree diagrams) and express the theoretical probability of each outcome.

The **probability** of an event is a measure of the likelihood that the event will occur. The probability of an event can range from 0, or impossible, to 1, or certain.

An **outcome** is a possible result of a probability experiment. A **sample space** is the set of all possible outcomes.

A **compound event** occurs when you combine two or more simple events in an outcome.

The **theoretical probability** of an event, written P(event), is the ratio of the number of favorable outcomes to the number of possible, equally likely outcomes.

## Examples

**A** Zoe is packing for a trip. She packs a green shirt, a red shirt, a blue shirt, a pair of white shorts, and a pair of yellow shorts. How many different outfits will Zoe have to choose from if she wears one shirt and one pair of shorts?

To count the compound events in a sample space, you can:

**make a list.**

Green shirt, white shorts
Green shirt, yellow shorts

Red shirt, white shorts
Red shirt, yellow shorts

Blue shirt, white shorts
Blue shirt, yellow shorts

**make a table.**

| Shirt | Shorts | |
|---|---|---|
| | White (W) | Yellow (Y) |
| Green (G) | G, W | G, Y |
| Red (R) | R, W | R, Y |
| Blue (B) | B, W | B, Y |

**make a tree diagram.**

| Shirt | Shorts | Outcome |
|---|---|---|
| Green (G) | White (W) | G, W |
| | Yellow (Y) | G, Y |
| Red (R) | White (W) | R, W |
| | Yellow (Y) | R, Y |
| Blue (B) | White (W) | B, W |
| | Yellow (Y) | B, Y |

So, Zoe will have 6 different outfits to coose from.

**B** Zoe chooses an outfit at random. Find the theoretical probability that she chooses a blue shirt and white shorts.

The list, table, and tree diagram show 6 outfit choices, so there are 6 possible outcomes in the sample space. There is 1 favorable outcome.

$$P(\text{blue, white}) = \frac{1}{6} \rightarrow \frac{\text{favorable outcomes}}{\text{possible outcomes}}$$

So, the theoretical probability is $\frac{1}{6}$.

**ERROR ALERT**

When counting the compound events in a sample space, make sure all outcomes are identified and any duplicates are eliminated.

## Try It

**Make a list, a table, or a tree diagram to show the number of possible outcomes for each situation.**

1. a pairing of a red or blue tie with a white, blue, pink, or tan shirt

2. a two-member team with one member selected from the group Jan and John and the other member selected from the group Dan, Jeff, and Kelly

3. possible sandwich combinations with one type of bread selected from wheat, pita, or rye and one filler selected from tuna or turkey

4. a two-color bead necklace with one color selected from a box of pink, red, and yellow beads and the other color selected from a box of blue, green, and purple beads

5. tossing a coin three times

6. rolling a number cube labeled 1 to 6 and tossing a coin

**Find the theoretical probability.**

7. Sheena tosses a coin three times. What is the probability that she will toss heads once and tails twice?

8. Lester tosses a coin twice. What is the probability that he will toss heads once and tails once?

9. Esther tosses a coin and rolls a number cube labeled 1 to 6. What is the probability that she will toss heads and roll a 6?

10. Nestor tosses a coin twice and rolls a number cube labeled 1 to 6. What is the probability that he will toss tails twice and roll a 5?

11. Rashid tosses a coin and rolls a number cube labeled 1 to 6 twice. What is the probability that he will toss tails and roll two even numbers?

## Solve

12. Read the problem below. **Explain** why A cannot be the correct answer. Then choose the correct answer.  **COMMON ERROR**

    Howie is going to choose an appetizer from List 1 and a main course from List 2.

    | List 1 | List 2 |
    |--------|--------|
    | Soup | Steak |
    | Salad | Chicken |
    | | Fish |

    Which set shows *all* the possible combinations of appetizer and main course?

    A (Soup, Salad), (Steak, Chicken)

    B (Soup, Steak), (Soup, Chicken), (Soup, Fish)

    C (Soup, Steak), (Salad, Steak), (Salad, Chicken), (Salad, Fish)

    D (Soup, Steak), (Soup, Chicken), (Soup, Fish), (Salad, Steak), (Salad, Chicken), (Salad, Fish)

13. Read the problem below. **Explain** why B cannot be the correct answer. Then choose the correct answer.  **COMMON ERROR**

    Pam is going to choose one person from each of the two lists to be in her reading group.

    | List 1 | List 2 |
    |--------|--------|
    | Duane | Yvette |
    | Ken | Stephen |
    | Pilar | Carla |

    What is the theoretical probability that she will choose Ken and Yvette?

    A $\frac{1}{2}$

    B $\frac{1}{6}$

    C $\frac{1}{9}$

    D $\frac{1}{18}$

# 🐻 Review the Key Standards

## Represent Probabilities

**○━π SDAP 3.3** Represent probabilities as ratios, proportions, decimals between 0 and 1, and percentages between 0 and 100 and verify that the probabilities computed are reasonable; know that if P is the probability of an event, 1 − P is the probability of an event not occurring.

## Examples

**A** The letters in the word CALIFORNIA are printed on equally-sized tiles and put in a bag. Find the probability of randomly drawing the letter A. Write the probability of the event, or P(event), as a fraction, a decimal, and a percent.

2 favorable outcomes: drawing one of the two A tiles

10 possible outcomes: 10 different tiles in the bag

|  | as a fraction | as a decimal | as a percent |
|---|---|---|---|
| favorable outcomes / possible outcomes | $\frac{2}{10} = \frac{1}{5}$ | $\frac{2}{10} = 0.2$ | $\frac{2}{10} = 0.2 = 20\%$ |

So, the probability of drawing the letter A is $\frac{1}{5}$, 0.2, or 20%.

**B** Jacob randomly draws one tile out of the bag. What is the probability that Jacob will *not* draw the letter A?

8 favorable outcomes: drawing a C, L, I, F, O, R, N, or I tile

10 possible outcomes: 10 different tiles in the bag

|  | as a fraction | as a decimal | as a percent |
|---|---|---|---|
| favorable outcomes / possible outcomes | $\frac{8}{10} = \frac{4}{5}$ | $\frac{8}{10} = 0.8$ | $\frac{8}{10} = 0.8 = 80\%$ |

So, the probability of not drawing the letter A is $\frac{4}{5}$, 0.8, or 80%.

If P is the probability of an event occurring, then 1 − P is the probability of an event not occurring: P(not event) = 1 − P(event). The sum of P(event) and P(not event) is always 1.

**ERROR ALERT**

To write a fraction as a percent you can write it as a decimal first. Be sure to multiply by 100 when writing the decimal as a percent.

**C** Verify the reasonableness of the computed probabilities for drawing an A tile and *not* drawing an A tile.

Probability of drawing an A: $\frac{1}{5}$

Probability of *not* drawing an A: $\frac{4}{5}$

P(*not* event) = 1 − P(event)          P(event) + P(*not* event) = 1

$\frac{4}{5} = 1 - \frac{1}{5}$                    $\frac{1}{5} + \frac{4}{5} = 1$

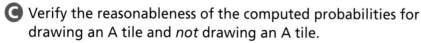

So, the computed probabilities are reasonable.

## Try It

**Find each probability. Write each answer as a fraction, a decimal, and a percent.**

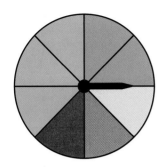

1. P(yellow)
2. P(blue)
3. P(not red)
4. P(not green)
5. P(orange)
6. P(not blue)
7. P(not orange)
8. P(purple)
9. P(green)
10. P(red)

**Equally-sized cards numbered 2, 2, 3, 4, 4, 5, 6, 8, 9, and 10 are placed in a box. A card is randomly drawn. Find the probability. Write your answer as a fraction, a decimal, and a percent.**

11. P(2)
12. P(not divisible by 2)
13. P(not 9)
14. P(divisible by 3)
15. P(less than 5)
16. P(not greater than 4)
17. P(3)
18. P(not 4)
19. P(divisible by 2)
20. P(less than 10)
21. P(less than 2)
22. P(not less than 2)

23. There are 12 identical socks in a drawer. Three of the socks are white, 4 of the socks are black, and 5 of the socks are blue. If Josh picks a sock without looking, what is the probability that he will pick a white sock? Write the answer as a fraction, a decimal, and a percent.

24. A number cube is labeled 1 to 6. If Kate rolls the number cube, what is the probability that she will *not* roll an odd number? Write the answer as a fraction, a decimal, and a percent.

## Solve

25. Read the problem below. **Explain** why A cannot be the correct answer. Then choose the correct answer.

    Marcia is making a necklace. The table shows how many identical beads of each color are in a box.

    | Color | Number of Beads |
    |-------|-----------------|
    | Blue | 3 |
    | Pink | 6 |
    | Purple | 5 |
    | White | 10 |
    | **Total** | **24** |

    If Marcia chooses a bead without looking, what is the probability that it will be pink?

    A 2.5%
    C 25%
    B 12.5%
    D 50%

26. Read the problem below. **Explain** why B cannot be the correct answer. Then choose the correct answer.

    David writes each letter in the word EXCEL on an identical piece of paper and places them in a bag. If he randomly draws 1 piece of paper out of the bag, what is the probability he will *not* draw an E?

    A 2%
    C 40%
    B 6%
    D 60%

# 🐻 Review the Key Standards

## Independent and Dependent Events

⊶ SDAP 3.5 Understand the difference between independent and dependent events.

**Independent events** are events for which the outcome of the first event does not affect the possible outcomes of the second event.

**Dependent events** are events for which the outcome of the first event does affect the possible outcomes of the second event.

## Examples

**A** Equally-sized marbles are placed in a bag. The bag contains a red marble, a blue marble, a green marble, a yellow marble, and an orange marble. Pat randomly draws a marble from the bag, replaces it, and then randomly draws another marble from the bag. Tell if the events are independent or dependent. Then, find the probability that she will draw a red marble twice in a row.

Since the first marble is replaced, it will not affect the number of possible outcomes for the second event. So the events are independent.

P(red) = $\frac{1}{5}$                      Find the probability of drawing a red marble.

P(red, red) = P(red) × P(red)      THINK: P (A, B) = P(A) × P(B)

$= \frac{1}{5} \times \frac{1}{5} = \frac{1}{25}$              Multiply the probabilities

So, the probability is $\frac{1}{25}$.

**ERROR ALERT**

**B** Peter randomly draws a marble from the bag that contains a red marble, a blue marble, a green marble, a yellow marble, and an orange marble. He does not replace the marble. Then he randomly draws another marble. Tell if the events are independent or dependent. Then, find the probability that Peter will draw a blue marble and then an orange marble?

When finding the probability of two dependent events, remember to calculate the probability of the second event based on conditions after the first event has taken place.

Since the first marble is not replaced, it will affect the possible outcomes for the second event. So the events are dependent.

P(blue, orange) = P(blue) × P(orange after blue)

Peter's first selection: P(blue) = $\frac{1}{5}$

Peter's second selection: P(orange) = $\frac{1}{4}$     There is 1 blue marble in the bag of 5 marbles.

P(blue, orange after blue) = $\frac{1}{5} \times \frac{1}{4} = \frac{1}{20}$     There is 1 orange marble in the bag that now contains 4 marbles. Multiply the probabilities.

So, the probability is $\frac{1}{20}$.

## Try It

**For 1–8, find the probability.**

A number cube labeled 1 to 6 is tossed, and then tossed again.

1. P(1, 1)
2. P(5, not 5)
3. P(5, 6)
4. P(2, not 4)
5. P(less than 3, not less than 3)
6. P(4, greater than 4)
7. P(odd number, odd number)
8. P(even number, not even number)

**For 9–16, find the probability.**

A jar contains 5 equally-sized buttons. Two of the buttons are white, one is blue, one is green, and one is red. Without looking, Gail draws a button from the jar and does not replace it. Without looking, she draws another button from the jar.

9. P(white, white)
10. P(red, white)
11. P(green, blue)
12. P(blue, not red)
13. P(not white, not white)
14. P(not green, not green)
15. P(not blue, blue)
16. P(white, green)

**For 17–19, tell if the events are independent or dependent. Then find the probability.**

17. Sarah writes each of the letters in the word NOVEMBER equally-sized index cards. She shuffles the cards and then selects one card at random. Without replacing the card, she shuffles the cards again and randomly selects another card. What is the probability that Sarah will select two vowels?

18. Equally-sized marbles are placed in a container. The container holds 1 white, 3 red, 5 green, and 6 yellow marbles. Matt randomly selects one marble, replaces it, and then randomly selects a second marble. What is the probability that Matt will select a red marble and then a green marble?

19. Robert has ten shirts in his closet. The shirts are identical except for color. Five of the shirts are white and five are blue. The closet is dark and Robert randomly selects a shirt. He does not replace it. Then he randomly selects another shirt. What is the probability that Robert selects a white shirt and then selects a blue shirt?

## Solve

20. Read the problem below. **Explain** why B cannot be the correct answer. Then choose the correct answer.

    A box contains 2 red blocks and 1 blue block. Brandon randomly selects a block, replaces it, and then randomly selects another block. What is the probability that he will select two red blocks?

    A $\frac{1}{2}$      C $\frac{2}{3}$

    B $\frac{1}{3}$      D $\frac{4}{9}$

21. Read the problem below. **Explain** why D cannot be the correct answer. Then choose the correct answer. **COMMON ERROR**

    The letters A, B, C, and D are each written on identical pieces of paper and placed in a box. Shannon randomly draws 1 piece of paper out of the box. She does not replace it. Then she randomly draws another piece of paper out of the box. What is the probability she will draw a C, and then a D?

    A $\frac{1}{2}$

    B $\frac{1}{4}$

    C $\frac{1}{12}$

    D $\frac{1}{16}$

# ![bear] Test-Taking Strategies
## Tips For Taking Math Tests

Being a good test-taker is like being a good problems solver. When you answer test questions, you are solving problems. Remember to **Understand, Plan, Solve,** and **Check.**

## Read to Understand

**Read the problem.**

- Look for math terms and recall their meanings.

- Reread the problem and think about the question.

- Use the details in the problem and the question.

---

**1.** Bob took some friends to dinner. If the dinner cost $52 and he left a 20% tip, what is the total he spent on dinner including tip?

A $10.40

B $41.60

C $52.20

D $62.40

**Test Tip** **Understand the problem.**

The problem is multistep and requires you to find the total amount Bob spent on dinner. Reread the problem to compare the details to the answer choices. You can use estimation instead of calculating the amount of the tip and then adding the tip to the cost. The answer is **D.**

---

- Each word is important. Missing a word or reading it incorrectly could cause you to get the wrong answer.

- Pay attention to words that are in *italics* and words like *round*, *best*, and *least* to *greatest*.

---

**2.** One morning the temperature was 8° Fahrenheit (F) below zero. By 1:00 P.M., the temperature *rose* 18°F and then *dropped* 12°F by evening. What was the evening temperature?

A 10°F below zero

B 2°F below zero

C 12°F above zero

D 38°F above zero

**Test Tip** **Look for important words.**

The words *below*, *rose*, and *dropped* are important. The temperature 8° Fahrenheit *below* zero indicates ⁻8°F. *Rose* indicates increased or addition. *Dropped* indicates decreased or subtraction. Carefully perform the operations to find the correct solution. The answer is **B.**

---

**Think about how you can solve the problem.**

• See if you can solve the problem with the information given.

• Pictures, charts, tables, and graphs may have the information you need.

• Sometimes the answer choices have information to help solve the problem.

---

**3.** Pablo is going to choose one sandwich from the lists below. Which set shows all his possible choices?

> Meat: Tuna, Turkey
>
> Bread: White, Wheat, Oat

A {(white, tuna), (white, turkey)}

B {(wheat, tuna), (wheat turkey)}

C {(oat, tuna), (oat, turkey), (white, tuna), (white, turkey)}

D {(white, tuna), (white, turkey), (wheat, tuna), (wheat, turkey), (oat, tuna), (oat, turkey)}

**Test Tip** **Get the information you need.**

The answer choices give four different sets. Think about each one and the number of choices in each. The problem asks for all the choices so be sure all the breads and all the meats are paired together. The answer is **D**.

---

• You may need to write a number sentence and solve it to answer the question.

• Some problems have two or more steps.

• In some problems you need to look at relationships instead of computing an answer.

• If the path to the solution isn't clear, choose a problem solving strategy and use it to solve the problem.

---

**4.** Sue found the mean and median of the set {9, 9, 12}. If 7 were added to the set, then

A the mean would decrease.

B the mean would increase.

C the median would increase.

D the median would decrease.

**Test Tip** **Decide on a plan.**

From the choices given, you must think of how a number that is less than the others will affect the mean and the median. If you use *logical reasoning*, you can see that the median will remain the same and the mean will decrease. The answer is **A**.

## Solve

**Follow your plan, working logically and carefully.**

- Estimate your answer. Compare it to the answer choices.

- Use reasoning to find the most likely choices.

- Make sure you completed all the steps needed to answer the problem.

- If your answer does not match any of the answer choices, check the numbers you used. Then check your computation.

---

**5.** A cell-phone company charges $0.06 per minute for local calls and $0.08 per minute for long-distance calls. Which expression gives the total cost in dollars for $x$ minutes of local calls and $y$ minutes of long-distance calls?

**A** 0.14xy

**B** 0.14(x + y)

**C** 0.06x + 0.08y

**D** 0.06x − 0.08y

 **Test Tip** **Eliminate choices.**

It is important to understand that $x$ represents minutes of local calls and $y$ represents minutes of long-distance calls. You can eliminate choices *A* and *B* since you would not add $0.06 and $0.08 because they are separate charges. Choice D shows subtraction, so it can be eliminated. The answer is **C**.

---

- If your answer still does not match one of the choices, look for another form of the number, such as a decimal instead of a fraction.

- If answer choices are given as pictures, look at each one by itself while you cover the other three.

- Read answer choices that are statements and relate them to the information in the problem one by one.

---

**6.** Lamar paid $35.10 for a skateboard and the amount includes an 8% sales tax. What is the cost of the skateboard before the tax?

**A** $37.91

**B** $32.50

**C** $8.00

**D** $2.81

**Test Tip** **Choose the answer.**

Since the question asks for the cost of the skateboard before the tax, you need to subtract the tax to find the answer. So, choose the answer that is less than and close to $35.10. The answer is **B**.

---

# Take time to catch your mistakes.

- Be sure you answered the question asked.

- Check for important words you might have missed.

- Be sure you used all the information you needed.
- Check your computation by using a different method.

**7.** △MNO is similar to △PQR. What is the length of $\overline{PQ}$?

A 7.5 feet

B 9 feet

C 10 feet

D 12 feet

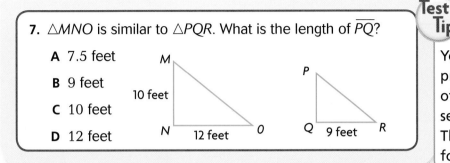

**Test Tip** Check your work.

You need to write and solve a proportion to find the length of $\overline{PQ}$. Check to be sure you have set up the proportion correctly. Then review your computation for any errors. The answer is **A**.

# Don't Forget!

**Before the test...**

- Listen to the teacher's directions and read the instructions.

- Write down the ending time if the test is timed.

- Know where and how to mark your answers.

- Know whether you should write on the test page or use scratch paper.

- Ask any questions you have before the test begins.

**During the test...**

- Work quickly but carefully. If you are unsure how to answer a question, leave it blank and return to it later.

- If you cannot finish on time, look over the questions that are left. Answer the easiest ones first. Then go back to answer the others.

- Fill in each answer space carefully. Erase completely if you change an answer. Erase any stray marks.

- Check that the answer number matches the question number, especially if you skip a question.

# Decimal Computation Review

**Decimal Addition**

## Example 1

**Add. 3.65 + 9.48**

Estimate. $4 + 9 = 13$

### Step 1

$$\begin{array}{r} \overset{1}{3.6\underline{5}} \\ + 9.4\underline{8} \\ \hline 3 \end{array}$$

Line up the decimal points to align place-value positions. Add the hundredths.

### Step 2

$$\begin{array}{r} \overset{1\ 1}{3.65} \\ + 9.48 \\ \hline 13 \end{array}$$

Add the tenths.

### Step 3

$$\begin{array}{r} \overset{1\ 1}{3.65} \\ + 9.48 \\ \hline 13.13 \end{array}$$

Add the ones. Place the decimal point in the sum.

So, 3.65 + 9.48 is 13.13. This is close to the estimate, so the answer is reasonable.

## Example 2

**Add. 21.46 + 5.9**

Estimate. $21 + 6 = 27$

$$\begin{array}{r} \overset{1}{21.46} \\ + 5.90 \\ \hline 27.36 \end{array}$$ ← Place a zero to show an equivalent decimal.

So, 21.46 + 5.9 is 27.36. This is close to the estimate, so the answer is reasonable.

## Try It

**Estimate. Then find the sum.**

1. 56.92 + 14.55
2. 78.4 + 83.25
3. 9.5 + 1.12
4. 7.98 + 45.061
5. 326.9 + 84.3
6. 55.71 + 9.82
7. 23.9 + 74.5
8. 12.113 + 75.649
9. 61.74 + 18.5
10. $9.44 + $1.67
11. 3.9 + 10.557
12. 1,540.7 + 225.98
13. 23.55 + 44.9
14. 3,005.41 + 670.55
15. $7.01 + $5.39

16. Carl spent $12.50 on a ticket to the game and $5.75 for snacks. He had $8.45 left at the end of the day. How much did he have at the beginning of the day?

17. Nancy bought a notebook that costs $5.69, an eraser that costs $1.39, and a pen that costs $2.29. How much did Nancy spend in all?

# 🐻 Decimal Computation Review

## Decimal Subtraction

## Example 1

**Subtract. 5.91 − 2.66**

Estimate. 6 − 3 = 3

> **Step 1**
>
> $\begin{array}{r} \overset{8\ 11}{5.\cancel{9}\cancel{1}} \\ -\ 2.66 \\ \hline 5 \end{array}$  Line up the decimal points to align place-value positions.
> Subtract the hundredths. Regroup if needed.
>
> **Step 2**
>
> $\begin{array}{r} \overset{8\ 11}{5.\cancel{9}\cancel{1}} \\ -\ 2.66 \\ \hline 25 \end{array}$  Subtract the tenths. Regroup if needed.
>
> **Step 3**
>
> $\begin{array}{r} \overset{8\ 11}{5.\cancel{9}\cancel{1}} \\ -\ 2.66 \\ \hline 3.25 \end{array}$  Subtract the ones.
> ↑ Place the decimal point.

So, 5.91 − 2.66 is 3.25. This is close to the estimate, so the answer is reasonable.

## More Examples

**Ⓐ** 39.57 − 10.9

$\begin{array}{r} \overset{8\ 15}{3\cancel{9}.\cancel{5}7} \\ -\ 10.90 \\ \hline 28.67 \end{array}$ ← Place a zero to show an equivalent decimal.

**Ⓑ** 4.5 − 0.116

$\begin{array}{r} \overset{9}{\overset{4\,\cancel{10}10}{4.5\cancel{0}\cancel{0}}} \\ -\ 0.116 \\ \hline 4.384 \end{array}$ ← Place zeros to show an equivalent decimal.

## Try It

**Estimate. Then find the difference.**

1. 73.9 − 25.7
2. 14.98 − 7.6
3. 0.142 − 0.033
4. 39 − 0.74
5. 283 − 155.7
6. 50 − 27.59
7. 560.27 − 400.9
8. 12.491 − 9.662
9. 0.9 − 0.472
10. 62.004 − 14.3
11. 12 − 8.569
12. 1,265.7 − 984.225
13. 0.902 − 0.66
14. 36 − 27.852
15. 1.49 − 1.3

16. Ken has $92.50. Running shoes cost $76.45. How much money will Ken have left after buying the running shoes?

17. Kinsey walked a total of 53 miles during the first two weeks of June. She walked 21.5 miles during the first week of June. How many miles did she walk during the second week?

# 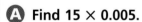Decimal Computation Review

**Decimal Multiplication**

## Example 1

**Multiply. 4.32 × 0.54**

**Step 1**

$$
\begin{array}{r}
4.32 \\
\times\, 0.54 \\
\hline
1728 \\
+\, 21600 \\
\hline
23328
\end{array}
$$

Multiply as with whole numbers.

**Step 2**

Find the total number of decimal places in the factors. Place the decimal point that number of places from the right in the product.

$$
\begin{array}{r}
4.32 \\
\times\, 0.54 \\
\hline
1728 \\
+\, 21600 \\
\hline
2.3328
\end{array}
$$

← 2 decimal places in the factor
← 2 decimal places in the factor

← 2 + 2, or 4 decimal places in the product

So, 4.32 × 0.54 is 2.3328.

## More Examples

**Ⓐ Find 15 × 0.005.**

$$
\begin{array}{r}
15 \\
\times\, 0.005 \\
\hline
0.075
\end{array}
$$

← 0 decimal places in the factor
← 3 decimal places in the factor

↑ Since 3 decimal places are needed in the product, write a zero in this place. Then place the decimal point.

**Ⓑ Find 0.08 × 0.04.**

$$
\begin{array}{r}
0.08 \\
\times\, 0.04 \\
\hline
0.0032
\end{array}
$$

← 2 decimal places in the factor
← 2 decimal places in the factor

↑ Since 4 decimal places are needed in the product, write zeros in these places. Then place the decimal point.

## Try It

**Multiply.**

**1.** 4.2 × 1.6

**2.** 37 × 12.9

**3.** 50.6 × 23.159

**4.** 0.16 × 0.08

**5.** 9 × 105.11

**6.** 6.105 × 9.4

**7.** 52.8 × 44.06

**8.** 0.007 × 0.3

**9.** 98.1 × 44.71

**10.** 6.41 × 7.22

**11.** 38.5 × 22.5

**12.** 4.01 × 13.9

**13.** 44.6 × 22.113

**14.** $135.83 × $6

**15.** 5 × $3.42

**16.** Cliff buys 8 bottles of water at $1.59 each. How much does he spend?

**17.** A pygmy shrew, one of the smallest mammals, measures 6.1 centimeters long. A house mouse is 2.7 times as long as a pygmy shrew. How long is the house mouse?

# 🐻 Decimal Computation Review

## Decimal Division

To divide a decimal by a decimal, first multiply the divisor and the dividend by a power of 10 to change the divisor to a whole number.

$$0.3\overline{)4.11} \quad \rightarrow \quad 3\overline{)41.1}$$

Think: $0.3 \times 10 = 3$

$4.11 \times 10 = 41.1$

## Example 1

**Divide. 19.95 ÷ 21**

Use compatible numbers to estimate. $19.95 \div 21 \rightarrow 20 \div 20 = 1$

$$
\begin{array}{r}
0.95 \\
21\overline{)19.95} \\
-0\phantom{.95} \\
\hline
19\,9\phantom{5} \\
-18\,9\phantom{5} \\
\hline
1\,05 \\
-1\,05 \\
\hline
0
\end{array}
$$

Place a decimal point above the decimal point in the dividend.

Divide. Since 19 is less than 21, place a zero in the ones place in the quotient.

Since the estimate is 1, the answer is reasonable. So, 19.95 ÷ 21 is 0.95.

## Example 2

**Divide. 246.4 ÷ 0.16**

$$0.16\overline{)246.40}$$

Make the divisor a whole number by multiplying the divisor and dividend by 100.

$$
\begin{array}{r}
1,540 \\
16\overline{)24,640} \\
-16\phantom{,640} \\
\hline
86\phantom{40} \\
-80\phantom{40} \\
\hline
64\phantom{0} \\
-64\phantom{0} \\
\hline
00
\end{array}
$$

$0.16 \times 100 = 16 \qquad 246.4 \times 100 = 24,640$
Write a zero in the dividend.
Divide.

Since the remainder is zero, the quotient is a whole number. You do need to put the decimal point in the quotient.

So, 246.4 ÷ 0.16 is 1,540.

## Try It

**Divide.**

1. $303.8 \div 4.9$  
2. $926.28 \div 99.6$  
3. $47.88 \div 0.84$  
4. $408.7 \div 6.1$  

5. $3.36 \div 84$  
6. $0.168 \div 0.14$  
7. $0.848 \div 42.4$  
8. $62.22 \div 3.66$  

9. Diane bought 36 colored pencils for $27.00. How much did each pencil cost?

10. Blueberries are sold in cartons that hold 0.5 qt. How many cartons are needed for 3 qt of blueberries?

# 🐻 Table of Measures

| Metric | Customary |
|---|---|

### Length

| | |
|---|---|
| 1 millimeter (mm) = 0.001 meter (m) | 1 foot (ft) = 12 inches (in.) |
| 1 centimeter (cm) = 0.01 meter | 1 yard (yd) = 36 inches |
| 1 decimeter (dm) = 0.1 meter | 1 yard = 3 feet |
| 1 kilometer (km) = 1,000 meters | 1 mile (mi) = 5,280 feet |
| | 1 mile = 1,760 yards |

### Capacity

| | |
|---|---|
| 1 milliliter (mL) = 0.001 liter (L) | 1 teaspoon (tsp) = $\frac{1}{6}$ fluid ounce (fl oz) |
| 1 centiliter (cL) = 0.01 liter | 1 tablespoon (tbsp) = $\frac{1}{2}$ fluid ounce |
| 1 deciliter (dL) = 0.1 liter | 1 cup (c) = 8 fluid ounces |
| 1 kiloliter (kL) = 1,000 liters | 1 pint (pt) = 2 cups |
| | 1 quart (qt) = 2 pints |
| | 1 gallon (gal) = 4 quarts |

### Mass/Weight

| | |
|---|---|
| 1 milligram (mg) = 0.001 gram (g) | 1 pound (lb) = 16 ounces (oz) |
| 1 centigram (cg) = 0.01 gram | 1 ton (T) = 2,000 pounds |
| 1 decigram (dg) = 0.1 gram | |
| 1 hectogram (hg) = 100 grams | |
| 1 kilogram (kg) = 1,000 grams | |
| 1 metric ton (t) = 1,000 kilograms | |

### Volume/Capacity/Mass for Water

1 cubic centimeter (cm$^3$) $\longrightarrow$ 1 milliliter $\longrightarrow$ 1 gram

1,000 cubic centimeters $\longrightarrow$ 1 liter $\longrightarrow$ 1 kilogram

| Time | |
|---|---|

| | |
|---|---|
| 1 minute (min) = 60 seconds (sec) | 1 year (yr) = 12 months (mo), or about 52 weeks |
| 1 hour (hr) = 60 minutes | |
| 1 day = 24 hours | 1 year = 365 days |
| 1 week (wk) = 7 days | 1 leap year = 366 days |

# Formulas

## Perimeter

| | |
|---|---|
| Polygon | $P = $ sum of the lengths of the sides |
| Rectangle | $P = 2(l + w)$, or $P = 2l + 2w$ |
| Square | $P = 4s$ |

## Circumference

| | |
|---|---|
| Circle | $C = 2\pi r$, or $C = \pi d$ |

## Area

| | |
|---|---|
| Circle | $A = \pi r^2$ |
| Parallelogram | $A = bh$ |
| Rectangle | $A = lw$ |
| Square | $A = s^2$ |
| Trapezoid | $A = \frac{1}{2}h(b_1 + b_2)$ |
| Triangle | $A = \frac{1}{2}bh$ |

## Surface Area

| | |
|---|---|
| Cylinder | $S = 2\pi rh + 2\pi r^2$ |

## Volume

| | |
|---|---|
| Cylinder | $V = Bh$, or $V = \pi r^2 h$ |
| Rectangular Prism | $V = Bh$, or $V = lwh$ |
| Triangular Prism | $V = Bh$ |

## Other

| | |
|---|---|
| Celsius (°C) | $C = \frac{5}{9} \times (F - 32)$ |
| Diameter | $d = 2r$ |
| Fahrenheit (°F) | $F = (\frac{9}{5} \times C) + 32$ |

## Consumer

| | |
|---|---|
| Distance traveled | $d = rt$ |
| Interest (simple) | $I = prt$ |

# Symbols

| | | | |
|---|---|---|---|
| $<$ | is less than | 1:2 | ratio of 1 to 2 |
| $>$ | is greater than | % | percent |
| $\leq$ | is less than or equal to | $\cong$ | is congruent to |
| $\geq$ | is greater than or equal to | $\approx$ | is approximately equal to |
| $=$ | is equal to | $\perp$ | is perpendicular to |
| $\neq$ | is not equal to | $\parallel$ | is parallel to |
| $10^2$ | ten squared | $\overleftrightarrow{AB}$ | line $AB$ |
| $10^3$ | ten cubed | $\overrightarrow{AB}$ | ray $AB$ |
| $10^4$ | the fourth power of 10 | $\overline{AB}$ | line segment $AB$ |
| $2^3$ | the third power of 2 | $\angle ABC$ | angle $ABC$ |
| $^+7$ | positive 7 | $m\angle A$ | measure of $\angle A$ |
| $^-7$ | negative 7 | $\triangle ABC$ | triangle $ABC$ |
| $|^-4|$ | the absolute value of negative 4 | ° | degree |
| (4,7) | ordered pair $(x,y)$ | $\pi$ | pi (about) 3.14, or $\frac{22}{7}$) |
| $5/hr | the rate $5 per hour | P(4) | the probability of the outcome 4 |

By the end of grade six, students have mastered the four arithmetic operations with whole numbers, positive fractions, positive decimals, and positive and negative integers; they accurately compute and solve problems. They apply their knowledge to statistics and probability. Students understand the concepts of mean, median, and mode of data sets and how to calculate the range. They analyze data and sampling processes for possible bias and misleading conclusions; they use addition and multiplication of fractions routinely to calculate the probabilities for compound events. Students conceptually understand and work with ratios and proportions; they compute percentages (e.g., tax, tips, interest). Students know about $\pi$ and the formulas for the circumference and area of a circle. They use letters for numbers in formulas involving geometric shapes and in ratios to represent an unknown part of an expression. They solve one-step linear equations.

## Number Sense

**1.0** **Students compare and order positive and negative fractions, decimals, and mixed numbers. Students solve problems involving fractions, ratios, proportions, and percentages:**

**1.1** Compare and order positive and negative fractions, decimals, and mixed numbers and place them on a number line.

Order the following numbers: $\frac{20}{21}$ $\quad -\frac{4}{9}$ $\quad -4.4$ $\quad 1\frac{1}{12}$ $\quad 1.1$ $\quad \frac{3}{7}$

If you were to place $-\frac{2}{3}$, $-3$ and $-\frac{7}{8}$ on a number line, which number would be closest to $-1$? Use a number line to explain your answer.

Place the following numbers on a number line:

$0.3$ $\quad -\frac{3}{10}$ $\quad 2\frac{1}{2}$ $\quad \frac{4}{5}$ $\quad \frac{7}{8}$ $\quad -2$

**1.2** Interpret and use ratios in different contexts (e.g., batting averages, miles per hour) to show the relative sizes of two quantities, using appropriate notations ($\frac{a}{b}$, $a$ to $b$, $a{:}b$).

**1.3** Use proportions to solve problems (e.g., determine the value of $N$ if $\frac{4}{7} = \frac{N}{21}$, find the length of a side of a polygon similar to a known polygon). Use cross-multiplication as a method for solving such problems, understanding it as the multiplication of both sides of an equation by a multiplicative inverse.

$\triangle ABC$ is similar to $\triangle DEF$. What is the length of $\overline{DF}$?
(*CST* released test question, 2004)

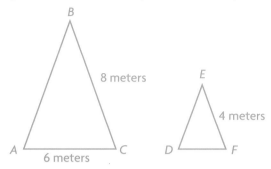

Ballpoint pens are sold in bundles of four. Lee bought 24 pens for $14.40. How much would 56 pens cost? Carefully explain your solution.

Find *n* if:

1. $\frac{49}{21} = \frac{14}{n}$

2. $\frac{28}{n} = \frac{36}{27}$

(This problem also applies to Algebra and Functions Standard 1.1.)

**1.4** Calculate given percentages of quantities and solve problems involving discounts at sales, interest earned, and tips.

Ann paid $70.20 for a dress, and the amount includes an 8% sales tax. What is the cost of the dress before the tax?

**2.0** **Students calculate and solve problems involving addition, subtraction, multiplication, and division:**

**2.1** Solve problems involving addition, subtraction, multiplication, and division of positive fractions and explain why a particular operation was used for a given situation.

Your after-school program is on a hiking trip. You hike $\frac{3}{4}$ of a mile and stop to rest. Your friend hikes $\frac{4}{5}$ of a mile, then turns around and hikes back $\frac{1}{8}$ of a mile. Who is farther ahead on the trail? How much farther? Explain how you solved the problem.

At soccer practice the team has to run around a rectangular field that is $75\frac{1}{2}$ feet by $127\frac{3}{4}$ feet. The coach makes the team run around the field three times. How many total feet does a team member run? Explain how you solved this problem.

Mario wants to make half of his special no-bake cookie recipe. The recipe calls for $1\frac{3}{4}$ cups of white sugar, $\frac{1}{3}$ cup of margarine, $\frac{1}{2}$ cup of peanut butter, and $3\frac{1}{4}$ cups of oats. How much of each ingredient will Mario need? Explain how you solved this problem.

Jim was on a hiking trail and after walking $\frac{3}{4}$ of a mile, he found that he was only $\frac{5}{8}$ of the way to the end of the trail. How long is the trail? Explain.

**2.2** Explain the meaning of multiplication and division of positive fractions and perform the calculations (e.g., $\frac{5}{8} \div \frac{15}{16} = \frac{5}{8} \times \frac{16}{15} = \frac{2}{3}$).

Draw a picture that illustrates each of the following problems and its solution. Explain how your drawings illustrate the problems and the solutions.

1. $\frac{3}{4} \times \frac{1}{2}$

2. $\frac{3}{4} \div \frac{1}{2}$

3. $2 \times \frac{1}{4}$

**2.3** Solve addition, subtraction, multiplication, and division problems, including those arising in concrete situations, that use positive and negative integers and combinations of these operations.

Two friends start out on a daylong hike. They start at an elevation of 526 feet. The morning hike takes them to an altitude 300 feet higher than where they started. In the afternoon the friends descend 117 feet and stop to rest. Then they continue downward and descend another 366 feet. Describe the change in altitude.

Simplify to make the calculation as simple as possible:

1. $-19 + 37 + 19$
2. $(-16)(-28) + (-16)27$
3. $(-8)(-4)(19)(6 + (-6))$

**2.4** Determine the least common multiple and the greatest common divisor of whole numbers; use them to solve problems with fractions (e.g., to find a common denominator to add two fractions or to find the reduced form for a fraction).

$\frac{3}{8} + \frac{1}{2} = ?$ (CST released test question, 2004)

The ⚊ and ⚫ identify the Key Standards for grade six.

**1.0 Students write verbal expressions and sentences as algebraic expressions and equations; they evaluate algebraic expressions, solve simple linear equations, and graph and interpret their results:**

**1.1** Write and solve one-step linear equations in one variable.

What value of $k$ makes the following equation true?
$k \div 3 = 36$ (CST released test question, 2004)
$y - 2 = 10$. What is $y$?
$6y = 12$. What is $y$?

If a number $y$ satisfies $y + 17 = 10$, what is $y$? If a number $x$ satisfies $3x = 25$, what is $x$?

**1.2** Write and evaluate an algebraic expression for a given situation, using up to three variables.

A telephone company charges $0.05 per minute for local calls and $0.12 per minute for long-distance calls. Which expression gives the total cost in dollars for $x$ minutes of local calls and $y$ minutes of long-distance calls? (CST released test question, 2004)

(a) $0.05x + 0.12y$       (c) $0.17(x + y)$
(b) $0.05x - 0.12y$       (d) $0.17xy$

**1.3** Apply algebraic order of operations and the commutative, associative, and distributive properties to evaluate expressions; and justify each step in the process.

Simplify:
1. $(4^3 + 7) - (5 - 8)^3$

2. $11[5(7^2) - 3^2 - 12(20 + 5.4 + 2)]$

3. $-3 \times (3^2 + 3) \div 3^2$

**1.4** Solve problems manually by using the correct order of operations or by using a scientific calculator.

**2.0 Students analyze and use tables, graphs, and rules to solve problems involving rates and proportions:**

**2.1** Convert one unit of measurement to another (e.g., from feet to miles, from centimeters to inches).

Suppose that one British pound is worth $1.50. In London a magazine costs 3 pounds. In San Francisco the same magazine costs $4.25. In which city is the magazine cheaper?

When temperature is measured in both Celsius (C) and Fahrenheit (F), it is known that they are related by the following formula:

$9 \times C = (F - 32) \times 5$. What is 50 degrees Fahrenheit in Celsius?

(Note the explicit use of parentheses.)

How many inches are in $2\frac{1}{2}$ feet? (CST released test question, 2004)

**2.2** Demonstrate an understanding that *rate* is a measure of one quantity per unit value of another quantity.

Joe can type 9 words in 8 seconds. At this rate, how many words can he type in 2 minutes?

**2.3** Solve problems involving rates, average speed, distance, and time.

Marcus took a train from San Francisco to San Jose, a distance of 54 miles. The train took 45 minutes for the trip. What was the average speed of the train?

**3.0 Students investigate geometric patterns and describe them algebraically:**

**3.1** Use variables in expressions describing geometric quantities (e.g., $P = 2w + 2l$, $A = \frac{1}{2}bh$, $C = \pi d$—the formulas for the perimeter of a rectangle, the area of a triangle, and the circumference of a circle, respectively).

A rectangle has width $w$. Its length is one more than 3 times its width. Find the perimeter of the rectangle. (Your answer will be expressed in terms of $w$.)

**3.2** Express in symbolic form simple relationships arising from geometry.

The rectangle shown below has length 15 inches and perimeter $P$ inches.

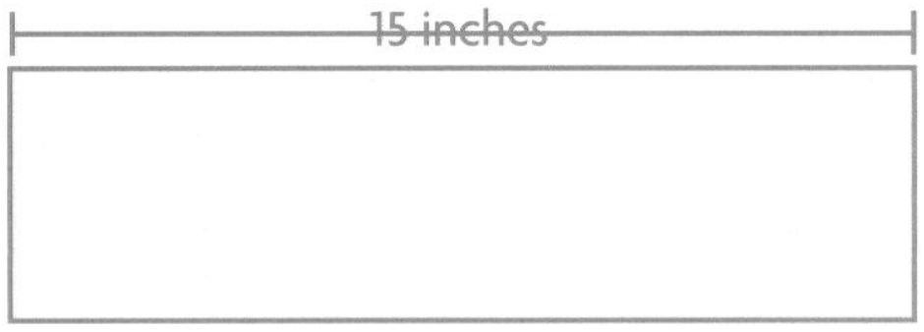

```
|—————— 15 inches ——————|
┌──────────────────────────┐
│                          │
│                          │
│                          │
└──────────────────────────┘
```

Which equation could be used to find the width of the rectangle?

$P = 15 + \frac{w}{2}$    $P = 15 - w$    $P = 30 + 2w$    $P = 30 - 2w$

(CST released test question, 2004)

**1.0 Students deepen their understanding of the measurement of plane and solid shapes and use this understanding to solve problems:**

**1.1** Understand the concept of a constant such as π; know the formulas for the circumference and area of a circle.

Which equation could be used to find the area in square inches of a circle with a radius of 8 inches? (CST released test question, 2004)

(a) $A = 4 \times \pi$     (b) $A = \pi \times 4^2$     (c) $A = 8 \times \pi$     (d) $A = \pi \times 8^2$

**1.2** Know common estimates of π (3.14; $\frac{22}{7}$) and use these values to estimate and calculate the circumference and the area of circles; compare with actual measurements.

What is the circumference of a circle with a radius of 5? (Answer: 10π or approximately 31.4)

The top part of this hat is shaped like a cylinder with a diameter of 7 inches.

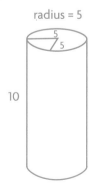

Which measure is *closest* to the length of the band that goes around the outside of the hat? (CST released test question, 2004)

(a) 10.1 inches     (b) 11.0 inches     (c) 22.0 inches     (d) 38.5 inches

**1.3** Know and use the formulas for the volume of triangular prisms and cylinders (area of base × height); compare these formulas and explain the similarity between them and the formula for the volume of a rectangular solid.

Find the volumes (dimensions are in cm).

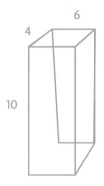
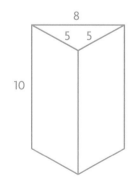
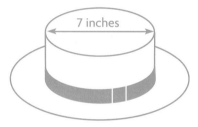

**2.0 Students identify and describe the properties of two-dimensional figures:**

**2.1**    Identify angles as vertical, adjacent, complementary, or supplementary and provide descriptions of these terms.

**2.2**    Use the properties of complementary and supplementary angles and the sum of the angles of a triangle to solve problems involving an unknown angle.

Find the missing angles *a*, *b*, *c*, and *d*.

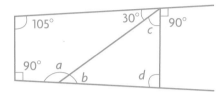

**2.3**    Draw quadrilaterals and triangles from given information about them (e.g., a quadrilateral having equal sides but no right angles, a right isosceles triangle).

---

## Statistics, Data Analysis, and Probability

**1.0 Students compute and analyze statistical measurements for data sets:**

**1.1**    Compute the range, mean, median, and mode of data sets.

**1.2**    Understand how additional data added to data sets may affect these computations.

**1.3**    Understand how the inclusion or exclusion of outliers affects these computations.

**1.4**    Know why a specific measure of central tendency (mean, median) provides the most useful information in a given context.

**2.0 Students use data samples of a population and describe the characteristics and limitations of the samples:**

**2.1**    Compare different samples of a population with the data from the entire population and identify a situation in which it makes sense to use a sample.

**2.2**    Identify different ways of selecting a sample (e.g., convenience sampling, responses to a survey, random sampling) and which method makes a sample more representative for a population.

**2.3** Analyze data displays and explain why the way in which the question was asked might have influenced the results obtained and why the way in which the results were displayed might have influenced the conclusions reached.

**2.4** Identify data that represent sampling errors and explain why the sample (and the display) might be biased.

**2.5** Identify claims based on statistical data and, in simple cases, evaluate the validity of the claims.

Calvin has been identified as the best runner in your school because he won the 50-yard dash at the all-schools track meet. Use the records of the track team in the table shown below to decide if Calvin is the best runner in the school. Explain your decision, using the data in the table.

| Runner | Race 1 | Race 2 | Race 3 | Race 4 |
|--------|--------|--------|--------|--------|
| Brian  | 27.3   | 27.6   | 30.1   | 26.2   |
| Maria  | 26.5   | 26.3   | 26.0   | 27.1   |
| Calvin | 30.2   | 28.1   | 29.4   | 25.0   |
| Alice  | 28.2   | 29.0   | 32.0   | 27.4   |
| Fred   | 32.1   | 32.5   | 29.0   | 30.0   |
| José   | 26.2   | 26.0   | 25.8   | 25.5   |

Soraya has been assigned to do a survey for the student council. However, she forgets to do this task until the morning of the meeting, so she asks three of her best friends what kind of music they would like for a noon-time dance. Their opinions are what Soraya will report to student council.

Do you think Soraya's report is an accurate reflection of the kind of music that students want played for the noon-time dance? Explain your answer.

**3.1 Students determine theoretical and experimental probabilities and use these to make predictions about events:**

**3.1** Represent all possible outcomes for compound events in an organized way (e.g., tables, grids, tree diagrams) and express the theoretical probability of each outcome.

**3.2** Use data to estimate the probability of future events (e.g., batting averages or number of accidents per mile driven).

**3.3** Represent probabilities as ratios, proportions, decimals between 0 and 1, and percentages between 0 and 100 and verify that the probabilities computed are reasonable; know that if $P$ is the probability of an event, $1-P$ is the probability of an event not occurring.

**3.4**    Understand that the probability of either of two disjoint events occurring is the sum of the two individual probabilities and that the probability of one event following another, in independent trials, is the product of the two probabilities.

○━ **3.5**    Understand the difference between independent and dependent events.

---

## Mathematical Reasoning

**1.0 Students make decisions about how to approach problems:**

**1.1**    Analyze problems by identifying relationships, distinguishing relevant from irrelevant information, identifying missing information, sequencing and prioritizing information, and observing patterns.

**1.2**    Formulate and justify mathematical conjectures based on a general description of the mathematical question or problem posed.

**1.3**    Determine when and how to break a problem into simpler parts.

**2.0 Students use strategies, skills, and concepts in finding solutions:**

**2.1**    Use estimation to verify the reasonableness of calculated results.

**2.2**    Apply strategies and results from simpler problems to more complex problems.

**2.3**    Estimate unknown quantities graphically and solve for them by using logical reasoning and arithmetic and algebraic techniques.

**2.4**    Use a variety of methods, such as words, numbers, symbols, charts, graphs, tables, diagrams, and models, to explain mathematical reasoning.

**2.5**    Express the solution clearly and logically by using the appropriate mathematical notation and terms and clear language; support solutions with evidence in both verbal and symbolic work.

**2.6**    Indicate the relative advantages of exact and approximate solutions to problems and give answers to a specified degree of accuracy.

**2.7**    Make precise calculations and check the validity of the results from the context of the problem.

### 3.0 Students move beyond a particular problem by generalizing to other situations:

**3.1** Evaluate the reasonableness of the solution in the context of the original situation.

**3.2** Note the method of deriving the solution and demonstrate a conceptual understanding of the derivation by solving similar problems.

**3.3** Develop generalizations of the results obtained and the strategies used and apply them in new problem situations.

# Glossary

## A

**absolute value** [ab′sə•lōōt val′yōō] **valor absoluto** The distance of an integer from zero (p. 121)

**acute angle** [ə•kyōōt′ ang′gəl] **ángulo agudo** An angle whose measure is greater than 0° and less than 90° (p. 370)

**acute triangle** [ə•kyōōt′ trī′ang•gəl] **triángulo acutángulo** A triangle with all angles less than 90° (p. 392)

**addends** [ad′ endz] **sumandos** Numbers that are added in an addition problem (p. 142)

**Addition Property of Equality** [ə•dish′ən prä′pər•tē əv i•kwol′ə•tē] **propiedad de suma de la igualdad** The property that states that if you add the same number to both sides of an equation, the sides remain equal (p. 320)

**additive inverse** [ad′ə•tiv in′vərs] **inverso aditivo** The opposite of a given number (p. 142)

**adjacent angles** [ə•jā′sənt ang′gəlz] **ángulos adyacentes** Side-by-side pairs of angles that have a common vertex and a common ray (p. 371)
*Example:*

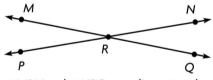

∠MRN and ∠NRQ are adjacent angles.

### Word History

The root for *adjacent* is from the Latin word *jacere,* meaning "to throw." The prefix *ad-* means "near" or "toward." Adjacent angles were thought of as "thrown toward" or beside each other.

**algebraic expression** [al•jə•brā′ik ik•spre′shən] **expresión algebraica** An expression that includes at least one variable (p..280)
*Examples: x + 5, 3a − 4*

**algebraic operating system** [al·jə·brā′ik ä′pə•rā•ting sis′təm] **sistema operativo algebraico** A way for calculators to follow the order of operations when evaluating expressions (p. 277)

**alternate exterior angles** [ôl′tər•nit ek•stir′ē•ər ang′gəlz] **ángulos alternos externos** A pair of exterior angles on opposite sides of the transversal (p. 387)

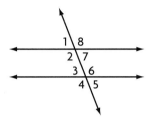

Angles 1 and 5 and angles 4 and 8 are pairs of alternate exterior angles.

**alternate interior angles** [ôl′tər•nit in•tir′ē•ər ang′gəlz] **ángulos alternos internos** A pair of interior angles on opposite sides of the transversal (p. 387)

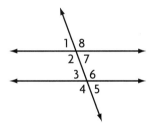

Angles 2 and 6 and angles 3 and 7 are pairs of alternate interior angles.

**angle** [an′gəl] **ángulo** A figure formed by two rays with a common endpoint (p. 370)
*Example:*

**arc** [ärk] **arco** Part of a circle (p. 433)

**area** [âr′ē•ə] **área** The number of square units needed to cover a given surface (p. 418)

**Associative Property** [ə•sō′shē•ā•tiv prä′pər•tē] **propiedad asociativa** The property that states that whatever way addends are grouped or factors are grouped does not change the sum or the product (p. 96)
*Examples:* 12 + (5 + 9) = (12 + 5) + 9
(9 × 8) × 3 = 9 × (8 × 3)

**axes** [ak′sēz] **ejes** The horizontal number line (*x*-axis) and the vertical number line (*y*-axis) on the coordinate plane (p. 348)

**bar graph** [bär′ graf] **gráfica de barras** A graph that displays countable data with horizontal or vertical bars (p. 244)

**base** [bās] **base (arithmetic)** A number used as a repeated factor (p. 14)
*Example:* $8^3 = 8 \times 8 \times 8$; 8 is the base.

**base** [bās] **base (geometry)** In two dimensions, one side of a triangle or parallelogram which is used to help find the area. In three dimensions, a plane figure, usually a polygon or circle, which is used to partially describe a solid figure (pp. 578, 600)
*Examples:*

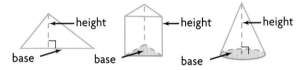

**benchmark** [bench′märk] **punto de referencia** A reference point on a number line that is useful for rounding fractions (p. 34)

**biased question** [bī′əst kwes′chən] **pregunta parcial** A question that suggests or leads to a specific response or excludes a certain group (p. 206)

**biased sample** [bī′əst sam′pəl] **muestra parcial** A sample is biased if certain groups from the population are not adequately represented in the sample. (p. 206)

**Celsius** [səl′sē•əs] **Celsius** A metric scale for measuring temperature (p. 473)

**central angle** [sen′ trəl an′gəl] **ángulo central** An angle in a circle with its vertex at the center of the circle (p. 433)

**central tendency** [sen′ trəl ten′ dən(t)•sē]
**tendencia central** Measure of the location of
or center of a data set (p. 224)

**certain** [sûr′tən] **seguro** Sure to happen (p. 522)

**circle** [sûr′kəl] **círculo** The set of all points a
given distance from a point called the center
(p. 418)
*Example:*

**circle graph** [sûr′kəl graf] **gráfica circular** A
graph that lets you compare parts to the
whole and to other parts (p. 248)
*Example:*

**FAVORITE HOBBIES**

Reading 30%
Crafts 15%
Coin Collecting 10%
Other 7%
Stamp Collecting 8%
Trading Cards 25%
Building Models 5%

**circumference** [sûr•kum′fər•əns] **circunferencia**
The distance around a circle (p. 418)

## Word History

*Circumference* is the combination of the
prefix *circum,* which means "around," and
*ferre,* which means "to carry." Together,
you get "to carry around."

**Commutative Property** [kə•myoo′tə•tiv prä′pər•tē]
**propiedad conmutativa** The property that
states that if the order of addends or factors
is changed, the sum or product stays the same
(p. 170)
*Examples:* 6 + 7 = 7 + 6
7 × 3 = 3 × 7

**complementary angles** [kom•plə•men′tər•ē
ang′gəlz] **ángulos complementarios** Two angles
whose measures have a sum of 90° (p. 374)
*Example:*

**composite number** [käm•pä′zət num′bər] **número
compuesto** A whole number greater than 1 that
has more than two whole-number factors (p. 4)

**compound event** [käm′pound i•vent′] **evento
compuesto** An event made of two or more
simple events (p. 584)

**congruent** [kən•groo′ənt] **congruente** Having the
same size and shape (p. 371)

**conjecture** [kən•jek′chər] **conjetura** A statement,
based on observations, that has been
proposed to be true, but has not yet been
proven true or false (p. 396)

**convenience sample** [kən•vēn′yən(t)s sam′pəl]
**muestra conveniente** The most available
individuals or objects in the population that
are selected to obtain results quickly (p. 202)

**coordinate plane** [kō•ôr′də•nit plān] **plano de
coordenadas** A plane formed by a horizontal
line (*x*-axis) that intersects a vertical line
(*y*-axis) (p. 348)

**corresponding angles** [kôr•ə•spän′ding ang′gəlz]
**ángulos correspondientes** Angles that
appear in the same positions in relation to
a transversal and two lines crossed by the
transversal (p. 387)
*Example:*

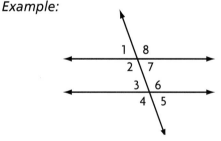

Pairs of Corresponding Angles
∠1 and ∠3          ∠2 and ∠4
∠5 and ∠7          ∠6 and ∠8

**corresponding angles** [kôr•ə•spän′ding ang′gəlz] **ángulos correspondientes** Angles that are in the same position in different plane figures (p. 476)
Example:

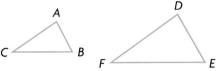

∠A and ∠D are corresponding angles.

**corresponding sides** [kôr•ə•spän′ding sīdz] **lados correspondientes** Sides that are in the same position in different plane figures (p. 476)
*Example:*

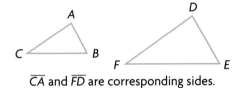

$\overline{CA}$ and $\overline{FD}$ are corresponding sides.

**cube** [kyo͞ob] **cubo** A rectangular solid with six congruent square faces (p. 596)
*Example:*

**cylinder** [si′lən•dər] **cilindro** A solid figure with two parallel bases that are congruent circles. (p. 596)
*Example:*

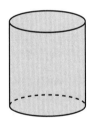

**decimal** [de′sə•məl] **decimal** A number with one or more digits to the right of the decimal point (p. 24)

**denominator** [di•nä′mə•nā•tər] **denominador** The part of a fraction that tells how many equal parts are in the whole (p. 8)
*Example:* $\frac{3}{4}$ ← denominator

**dependent events** [di•pen′dənt i•vənts′] **eventos dependientes** Events for which the outcome of the first event affects the possible outcomes of the second event (p. 552)

**diagonal** [di•a′gə•nəl] **diagonal** A line segment that connects to non-adjacent vertices of a polygon (p. 393)
*Example:*

**diameter** [di•am′ə•tər] **diámetro** A line segment that passes through the center of a circle and has its endpoints on the circle (p. 420)
*Example:*

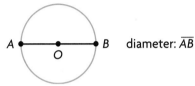

diameter: $\overline{AB}$

**dimension** [di•men′shən] **dimensión** The length, width, or height of a figure

**discount** [dis′kount] **descuento** An amount that is subtracted from the regular price of an item (p. 500)

**disjoint events** [dis•joint′ i•vent′] **sucesos disjuntos** Two or more events that cannot happen at the same time (p. 526)

**Distributive Property** [di•strib′yə•tiv prä′pər•tē] **propiedad distributiva** The property that states that multiplying a sum by a number is the same as multiplying each addend by the number and then adding the products (p. 272)
*Example:* 14 × 21 = 14 × (20 + 1) =
(14 × 20) + (14 × 1)

**dividend** [di′və•dend] **dividendo** The number that is to be divided in a division problem (p. 92)
*Example:* In 56 ÷ 8, 56 is the dividend.

**Division Property of Equality** [di•vi′zhən prä′pər•tē əv i•kwol′ə•tē] **propiedad de división de la igualdad** The property that states that if you divide both sides of an equation by the same nonzero number, the sides remain equal (p. 336)

**divisor** [di•vī′zər] **divisor** The number that divides the dividend (p. 6)
*Example:* In 45 ÷ 9, 9 is the divisor.

**double-bar graph** [də′bəl bar graf] **gráfica de doble barra** A graph that helps to compare two sets of data (p. 244)

**double-line graph** [də′bəl līn graf] **gráfica lineal de doble línea** A graph that helps to compare two sets of data that change over time (p. 246)

**equally likely** [ē′kwə•lē lī′klē] **igualmente probable** Having the same chance of occurring (p. 552)

**equation** [i•kwā′zhən] **ecuación** A statement that shows that two quantities are equal (p. 300)

**equilateral triangle** [ē•kwə•la′tə•rəl trī′ang•gəl] **triángulo equilátero** A triangle with three congruent sides (p. 392)
*Example:*

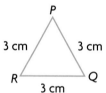

**equivalent fractions** [ē•kwiv′ə•lənt frak′shənz] **fracciones equivalentes** Fractions that name the same amount or part (p. 8)

**equivalent ratios** [ē•kwiv′ə•lənt rā′shē•ōz] **razones equivalentes** Ratios that name the same comparison (p. 442)

**estimate** [es′tə•mit] **estimación** A number close to an exact amount (p. 34)

**evaluate** [i•val′yōō•āt] **evaluar** To find the value of a numerical or algebraic expression (p. 272)

**event** [i•vent′] A set of outcomes **suceso** (p. 522)

**experimental probability** [ik•sper•ə•men′təl prä•bə•bil′ə•tē] **probabilidad experimental** The ratio of the number of favorable outcomes that occur to the total number of trials, or times the activity is performed (p. 530)

**exponent** [ik•spō′nənt] **exponente** A number that tells how many times a base is used as a factor (p. 14)
*Example:* $2^3 = 2 \times 2 \times 2 = 8$;
3 is the exponent.

**expression** [ik•spre′shən] **expresión** A mathematical phrase that combines operations, numerals, and sometimes variables to name a number (pp. 180, 300)

**exterior angles** [ik•stir′ē•ər ang′gəlz] **ángulos exteriores** Angles on the outside of two lines crossed by a transversal (p. 387)

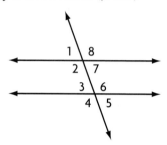

∠1, ∠4, ∠5, and ∠8 are exterior angles.

**face** [fās] **cara** One of the polygons of a solid figure (p. 596)
*Example:*

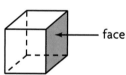

**factor** [fak′tər] **factor** A number that is multiplied by another number to find a product (p. 4)

**Fahrenheit** [fâr′ən•hīt] **Fahrenheit** A customary scale for measuring temperature (p. 473)

**formula** [fôr′myə•lə] **fórmula** A rule that is expressed with symbols (p. 254)
*Example:* $A = lw$

**frequency table** [frē′kwən•sē tā′bəl] **tabla de frecuencia** A table representing totals for individual categories or groups (p. 203)

**function** [funk′shən] **función** A relationship between two quantities in which one quantity depends uniquely on the other (p. 344)

**Fundamental Counting Principle** [fun•də•men′təl koun′ting prin′sə•pəl] **principio fundamental de conteo** If one event has *m* possible outcomes and a second event has *n* possible outcomes, then there are *m* × *n* total possible outcomes. (p. 549)

**greatest common divisor (GCD)** [grā′təst kä′mən də•vī′zər] **máximo común divisor (MCD)** The greatest divisor that two or more numbers have in common (p. 6)

**greatest common factor (GCF)** [grā′təst kä′mən fak′tər] **máximo factor común (MFC)** The greatest factor that two or more numbers have in common (p. 6)

**height** [hīt] **altura** A measure of a polygon or solid figure, taken as the length of a perpendicular from the base of the figure (p. 578)
*Example:*

**hexagon** [heks′ə•gän] **hexágono** A six-sided polygon (p. 570)
*Examples:*

**Identity Property of Addition** [i•den′tə•tē prä′pər•tē əv ə•dish′ən] **propiedad de identidad de la suma** The property that states that the sum of zero and any number is that number (p. 304)
*Example:* 25 + 0 = 25

**Identity Property of Multiplication** [i•den′tə•tē prä′pər•tē əv mul•tə•plə•kā′shən] **propiedad de identidad de la multiplicación** The property that states that the product of any number and 1 is that number (p. 336)
*Example:* 12 × 1 = 12

**impossible** [im•pos′ə•bəl] **imposible** Never able to happen (p. 522)

**independent events** [in•di•pen′dənt i•vents′] **sucesos independientes** Events for which the outcome of the first event does not affect the possible outcomes of the second event (p. 552)

**indirect measurement** [in•di•rekt′ mezh′ər•mənt] **medida indirecta** The technique of using similar figures and a proportion to find a measure (p. 479)

**integers** [in′ti•jərz] **enteros** The set of whole numbers and their opposites (p. 118)

**interior angles** [in•tir′ē•ər ang′gəlz] **ángulos interiores** Angles between two lines crossed by a transversal (p. 387)

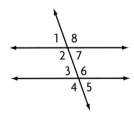

∠2, ∠3, ∠6, and ∠7 are interior angles.

**inverse operation** [in•vərs′ ä•pə•rā′shən] **operación inversa** Operations that undo each other, like addition and subtraction or multiplication and division (p. 94)

**isosceles triangle** [ĭ•sä′sə•lēz trī′ang•gəl] **triángulo isósceles** A triangle with exactly two congruent sides (p. 392)
*Example:*

7 in.  7 in.

5 in.

## L

**lateral faces (or surfaces)** [lat′ər•əl fās′əz] **caras laterales** The faces in a prism or pyramid that are not bases (p. 596)

**least common denominator (LCD)** [lēst kä′mən di•nä′mə•nā•tər] **mínimo común denominador (m.c.d.)** The least common multiple of two or more denominators (p. 39)

**least common multiple (LCM)** [lēst kä′mən mul′tə•pəl] **mínimo común múltiplo (m.c.m.)** The smallest number, other than zero, that is a common multiple of two or more numbers (p. 14)

**leg** [leg] **cateto** In a right triangle, either of the two sides that form the right angle (p. 578)
*Example:*

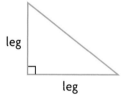

leg

leg

**like terms** [lĭk tûrmz] **términos semejantes** Expressions that have the same variable with the same exponent (p. 284)

**line graph** [lĭn graf] **gráfica lineal** A graph that uses line segments to show how data change over time (p. 246)

**line plot** [lĭn plät] **diagrama de puntos** A graph that shows frequency of data along a number line (p. 226)
*Example:*

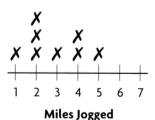

```
    X
    X   X
X   X   X   X   X
+---+---+---+---+---+---+---+
1   2   3   4   5   6   7
```

**Miles Jogged**

**line segment** [lĭn seg′mənt] **segmento** A part of a line with two endpoints (p. 398)
*Example:*

**linear equation** [lĭ′nē•ər ĭ•kwā′zhen] **ecuación lineal** An equation, that when graphed, forms a straight line (p. 350)

## M

**mean** [mēn] **media** The sum of a group of numbers divided by the number of addends (p. 224)

**median** [mē′dē•ən] **mediana** The middle value in a group of numbers arranged in order (p. 224)

### Word History

Some people get the meanings of *mean* and *median* confused. Originally, they both meant the same thing. Both words come from the Indo-European root *medhyo.*

**mixed number** [mĭkst num′bər] **número mixto** A number represented by a whole number and a fraction (p. 12)

**mode** [mōd] **moda** The number or item that occurs most often in a set of data (p. 224)

**multiple** [mul′tə•pəl] **múltiplo** The product of a given whole number and another whole number (p. 4)

**Multiplication Property of Equality** [mul•tə•plə•kā′shən prä′pər•tē əv ĭ•kwol′ə•tē] **propiedad de multiplicación de la igualdad** The property that states that if you multiply both sides of an equation by the same number, the sides remain equal (p. 340)

**multiplicative inverse** [məl•tə•pli′kə•tiv in′vərs] **inverso multiplicativo** A reciprocal of a number that is multiplied to that number resulting in a product of 1 (p. 466)

**natural numbers** [na′chə•rəl nəm′bərz] **números naturales** The set of counting numbers: 1, 2, 3, 4, . . . . (p. 118)

**negative integers** [ne′gə•tiv in′ti•jərz] **enteros negativos** Integers to the left of zero on the number line (p. 142)

**net** [net] **plantilla** An arrangement of two-dimensional figures that folds to form a polyhedron (p. 596)
*Example:*

**numerator** [no͞o′mə•rā•tər] **numerador** The part of a fraction that tells how many parts are being used (p. 8)

*Example:* $\frac{3}{4}$ ← numerator

**numerical expression** [no͞o•mer′i•kəl ik•spre′shən] **expresión numérica** A mathematical phrase that uses only numbers and operation symbols (p. 272)

**obtuse angle** [äb•to͞os′ ang′gəl] **ángulo obtuso** An angle whose measure is greater than 90° and less than 180° (p. 370)

**obtuse triangle** [äb•to͞os′ trī′ang•gəl] **triángulo obtusángulo** A triangle with one angle greater than 90° (p. 392)
*Example:*

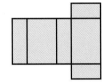

105°

**octagon** [äk′ta•gän] **octágono** A polygon with 8 sides and 8 angles
*Examples:*

**opposites** [ä′pə•zəts] **opuestos** Two numbers that are an equal distance from zero on the number line (p. 118)

**order of operations** [ôr′dər əv ä•pə•rā′shənz] **orden de las operaciones** The process for evaluating expressions: first perform the operations in parentheses, clear the exponents, perform all multiplication and division, and then perform all addition and subtraction (p. 276)

**ordered pair** [ôr′dərd pâr] **par ordenado** A pair of numbers that can be used to locate a point on the coordinate plane (p. 348)
*Examples:* (0,2), (3,4), (⁻4,5)

**outcome** [out′kəm] **resultado** A possible result of a probability experiment (p. 522)

**outlier** [aut′lī•(ə)r] **valor atípico** A value that is very small or very large compared to the majority of the values in a data set (p. 226)

**overestimate** [ō•vər•es′tə•mət] **sobreestimar** An estimate that is greater than the exact answer (p. 35)

**parallel lines** [pâr′ə•lel līnz] **lineas paralelas** Lines in a plane that are always the same distance apart (p. 400)
*Example:*

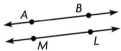

**parallelogram** [pâr′ə•le•lə•gram] **paralelogramo** A quadrilateral where opposite sides are parallel and congruent (p. 400)
*Example:*

**pentagon** [pen′tə•gän] **pentágono** A polygon with five sides and five angles
*Examples:*

**percent (%)** [pər•sent′] **porcentaje** The ratio of a number to 100; *percent* means "per hundred." (pp. 24, 492)

**perimeter** [pə•ri′mə•tər] **perímetro** The distance around a figure (p. 570)

**perpendicular lines** [pər•pen•dik′yə•lər līnz] **lineas perpendiculares** Two lines that intersect to form right, or 90°, angles (pp. 398, 400)
*Example:*

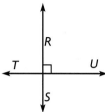

**pi (π)** [pī] **pi (π)** The area of a unit circle; the ratio of the circumference of a circle to its diameter; π ≈ 3.14 or $\frac{22}{7}$ (pp. 418, 424)

**polygon** [pä′lē•gän] **polígono** A closed plane figure formed by three or more straight sides that are connected line segments (p. 407)
*Examples:*

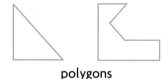

polygons

not polygons

**population** [pä•pyə•lā′shən] **población** The entire group of objects or individuals considered for a survey (p. 200)

**positive integers** [pä′zə•tiv in′ti•jərz] **enteros positivos** Integers to the right of zero on the number line (p. 142)

**prime factorization** [prīm fak•tə•ri•zā′shən] **descomposición en factores primos** A number written as the product of all of its prime factors (p. 6)
*Example:* 24 = $2^3$ × 3

**prime number** [prīm num′bər] **número primo** A whole number greater than 1 whose only factors are 1 and itself (p. 4)

**principal** [prin′sə•pəl] **capital** The amount of money borrowed or saved (p. 506)

**prism** [priz′əm] **prisma** A solid figure that has two congruent, polygon-shaped bases, and other faces that are all rectangles (p. 596)
*Example:*

**probability** [prä•bə•bil′ə•tē] **probabilidad** A measure of the likelihood that an event will occur

**product** [prä′dəkt] **producto** The answer in a multiplication problem (p. 4)

**Property of Zero** [prä′pər•tē əv zē′rō] **propiedad del cero** The property that states that the product of any number and zero is zero (p. 172)

**proportion** [prə•pôr′shən] **proporción** An equation that shows that two ratios are equal (p. 462)
*Example:* $\frac{1}{3} = \frac{3}{9}$

### Word History

*Proportion* comes from the Latin word *proportio*, a translation from the Greek word for *analogy*. Like a proportion in mathematics, an analogy refers to things that share a similar relation.

**Q**

**quadrants** [kwäd′rənts] **cuadrantes** The four regions of the coordinate plane (p. 350)

**quadrilateral** [kwä•drə•lat′ə•rəl] **cuadrilátero** A closed plane figure formed by four straight sides that are connected line segments and has four angles (p. 400)

**quotient** [kwō′shənt] **cociente** The number, not including the remainder, that results from dividing (p. 92)

**radius** [rā′dē•əs] **radio** A line segment with one endpoint at the center of a circle and the other endpoint on the circle (p. 420)
*Example:*

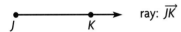

radius: $\overline{OB}$

**random sample** [ran′dəm sam′pəl] **muestra al azar** A sample in which each subject in the overall population has an equal chance of being selected (p. 202)

**range** [rānj] **rango** The difference between the greatest and least numbers in a group (p. 224)

**rate** [rāt] **tasa** A ratio that compares two quantities having different units of measure (p. 444)

**ratio** [rā′shē•ō] **razón** A comparison of two numbers, *a* and *b*, that can be written as a fraction $\frac{a}{b}$ (p. 118)

**rational number** [ra′shə•nəl num′bər] **número racional** Any number that can be written as $\frac{a}{b}$, where *a* and *b* are integers and $b \neq 0$ (p. 118)

**ray** [rā] **rayo** A part of a line with a single endpoint (p. 370)
*Example:*

ray: $\overrightarrow{JK}$

**reciprocal** [ri•sip′rə•kəl] **recíproco** Two numbers are reciprocals of each other if their product equals 1. (p. 94)

**rectangle** [rek′tan•gəl] **rectángulo** A parallelogram with 4 right angles (pp. 400, 574))
*Example:*

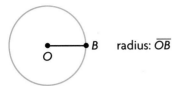

**regular polygon** [reg′yə•lər pä′lē•gän] **polígono regular** A polygon in which all sides are congruent and all angles are congruent (p. 406)
*Example:*

**rhombus** [räm′bəs] **rombo** A parallelogram with four congruent sides (p. 400)
*Example:*

**right angle** [rīt ang′gəl] **ángulo recto** An angle which is half of a straight angle with its measurement being 90° (p. 370)
*Example:*

**right triangle** [rīt trī′ang•gəl] **triángulo rectángulo** A triangle with one right angle (p. 392)
*Example:*

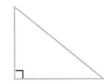

**sales tax** [sālz taks] **impuesto a las ventas** A percent of the cost of an item, added onto the item's cost (p. 501)

**sample** [sam′pəl] **muestra** A representative part of a population (p. 200)

**sample space** [sam′pəl spās] **espacio de muestra** The set of all possible outcomes (pp. 522, 548)

**scalene triangle** [skā′lēn trī′ang•gəl] **triángulo escaleno** A triangle with no congruent sides (p. 392)
*Example:*

**sector** [sek′tər] **sector** A region enclosed by two radii and the arc joining their endpoints (p. 433)
*Example:*

**semicircle** [se′mē•sər•kəl] **semicírculo** One-half of a circle (p. 420)

**similar figures** [si′mə•lər fig′yərz] **figuras semejantes** Figures with the same shape but not necessarily the same size (p. 476)

**simple interest** [sim′pəl in′trəst] **interés simple** A fixed percent of the principal, paid yearly (p. 506)

**simplest form** [sim′pləst fôrm] **mínima expresión** The form in which the numerator and denominator of a fraction have no common factors other than 1 (p. 9)

**solution** [sə•lōō′shən] **solución** A value that, when substituted for a variable in an equation, makes the equation true (p. 302)

**square** [skwâr] **cuadrado** A rectangle with four congruent sides (p. 400)
*Example:*

**square** [skwâr] **cuadrado** The product of a number and itself; a number with an exponent of 2

**straight angle** [strāt ang′gəl] **ángulo llano** An angle whose measure is 180° (p. 370)
*Example:*

**Subtraction Property of Equality** [sub•trak′shən prä′pər•tē əv i•kwol′ə•tē] **propiedad de resta de la igualdad** The property that states that if you subtract the same number from both sides of an equation, the sides remain equal (p. 304)

**sum** [sum] **suma o total** The answer to an addition problem (p. 34)

**Word History**

The ancient Greeks and Romans added columns of numbers from the bottom to the top. They wrote the answer or *sum* at the top. The words *sum* and *summit* are from the Latin root *summus*, which means "highest."

**supplementary angles** [sup•lə•men′tə•rē ang′gəlz] **ángulos suplementarios** Two angles whose measures have a sum of 180° (p. 376)
*Example:*

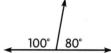

**surface area** [sûr′fəs âr′ē•ə] **área total** The sum of the areas of the faces of a solid figure (p. 596)

**survey** [sûr′vā] **encuesta** A method of gathering information about a population (p. 200)

**T**

**term** [tûrm] **término** Each number in a sequence (p. 284)

**terms** [tûrmz] **términos** The parts of an expression that are separated by an addition or subtraction sign (p. 285)

**theoretical probability** [thē•ə•re′ti•kəl prä•bə•bil′ə•tē] **probabilidad teórica** A comparison of the number of favorable outcomes to the number of possible equally likely outcomes (p. 522)

**transversal** [trans•vûr′səl] **transversal** A line that crosses two or more lines (p. 387)

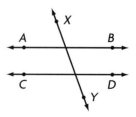

$\overleftrightarrow{XY}$ is a transversal.

**trapezoid** [tra′pə•zoid] **trapecio** A quadrilateral with exactly two parallel sides (p. 400)
*Example:*

**tree diagram** [trē di′ə•gram] **diagrama de árbol** A diagram that shows all possible outcomes of an event (p. 549)

**unbiased question** [un•bi′əst kwes′chən] **pregunta imparcial** A question that does not suggest or lead to a specific response or excludes a certain group (p. 206)

**unbiased sample** [un•bi′əst sam′pəl] **muestra imparcial** A sample is unbiased if every individual in the population has an equal chance of being selected. (p. 206)

**underestimate** [un•dər•es′tə•mət] **subestimar** An estimate that is less than the exact answer (p. 35)

**unit circle** [yü′nət sər′kəl] **círculo unidad** A circle that has a radius of 1 (p. 418)

**unit fraction** [yü′nət frak′shən] **fracción unitaria** A fraction with 1 in the numerator (p. 97)

**unit rate** [yü′nət rāt] **tasa por unidad** A rate that has 1 unit as its second term (p. 444)
*Example:* 55 mi per hr

**unlike fractions** [un′lĭk frak′shənz] **fracciones no semejantes** Fractions with different denominators (p. 38)

**variable** [vâr′ē•ə•bəl] **variable** A letter or symbol that stands for one or more numbers (pp. 280, 300)

**Venn diagram** [ven di′ə•gram] **diagrama de Venn** A diagram that shows relationships among sets of things (p. 118)

**vertex** [vûr′teks] **vértice** The point where two or more rays meet; the point of intersection of two sides of a polygon; the point of intersection of three or more edges of a solid figure; the top point of a cone (p. 370)
*Examples:*

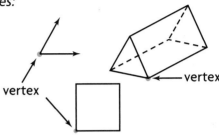

**vertical angles** [vûr′ti•kəl ang•gəlz] **ángulos verticales** A pair of opposite congruent angles formed where two lines intersect (p. 371)
*Example:*

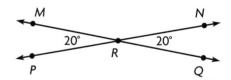

∠MRP and ∠NRQ are vertical angles.

**volume** [väl′yəm] **volumen** The number of cubic units needed to occupy a given space (p. 600)

**whole number** [hōl num′bər] **número entero**
One of the numbers 0, 1, 2, 3, 4, . . . . The set
of whole numbers goes on without end.
(p. 10)

*x*-axis [eks•ak′səs] **eje de la *x*** The horizontal
number line on a coordinate plane (p. 348)

*x*-coordinate [eks•kō•ôr′də•nət] **coordenada *x*** The
first number in an ordered pair; it tells the
distance to move right or left from (0,0).
(p. 348)

*y*-axis [wĭ•ak′səs] **eje de la *y*** The vertical
number line on a coordinate plane (p. 348)

*y*-coordinate [wĭ•kō•ôr′də•nət] **coordenada *y*** The
second number in an ordered pair; it tells the
distance to move up or down from (0,0).
(p. 348)

**Zero Property of Multiplication** [zə′rō prä′pər•te
əv mul•tə•plə•kā′shən] **Propiedad del cero de
la multiplicación** The property that states that
when you multiply by zero, the product is
zero (p. 348)

# Index

## A

**Absolute value,** 115, 121, 137, 145
  equations, 313
**Abundant numbers,** 29
**Achieving the Standards,** 5, 7, 11, 13, 16, 19, 21, 25, 30–31, 37, 41, 44, 49, 62–63, 69, 71, 73, 75, 79, 86–87, 93, 95, 99, 103, 121, 123, 125, 128, 138–139, 147, 153, 157, 166–167, 175, 179, 181, 184, 201, 205, 207, 211, 220–221, 225, 228, 231, 233, 240–241, 245, 247, 249, 253, 256, 275, 279, 282, 287, 289, 296–297, 301, 305, 314–315, 321, 323, 330–331, 338, 341, 343, 347, 349, 353, 372, 375, 377, 381, 388–389, 395, 397, 399, 403, 405, 414–415, 421, 426, 443, 445, 447, 450, 458–459, 465, 471, 474, 477, 481, 488–489, 493, 497, 499, 503, 505, 507, 524, 527, 531, 533, 535, 540–541, 551, 555, 557, 573, 577, 579, 592–593, 599, 603, 611
**Acute angles,** 370, 391
**Acute triangles,** 391, 392
**Addends,** 141
  use an equation to find, 306
**Addition**
  Associative Property, 89, 147, 154, 273
  Commutative Property, 147, 154, 169, 273
  equations, 298, 302–305, 322–323
  estimating sums, 34–37
  of decimals, 317, 569
  of fractions, 32–33, 38–41, 54–57, 317, 569, H13
  Identity Property, 304, 317, 320
  of integers, 140, 144–147, 154, H10
  of mixed numbers, 42–44, 54–57
  models of, 142–144, 302–303
  properties of, 147, 154, 273, 320
  Property of Equality, 317, 320
  of whole numbers, 317
**Additional data**
  effects of, 232–233
**Additive inverse,** 141, 143
**Adjacent angles,** 369, 371
**Algebra**
  absolute value, 121, 145
  coordinate plane
    graphing ordered pairs, 348–353
  equations, 269
    models of, 334–335
    solving, 39, 71, 73, 78
    writing, 324–325, 482–483
  exponents, 14, 276–279
  expressions, 269
    evaluating, 44, 49, 93, 98, 102, 284–289, 569, 595
    simplifying, 175, 285, 286
    with three variables, 288–289
    writing, 280–282

functions
  using to find ordered pairs, 348–349
  writing, 344–347
Fundamental Counting Principle, 550
integer operations, 142–143, 144–147, 148–149, 150–153, 154–157, 170–171, 172–175, 176–179, 180–181, 182–185, H10, H11
missing numbers, 183, 254–256
patterns, 41, 56
properties
  Associative, 175, 272–275
  Commutative, 175, 272–275
  Distributive, 272–275, 287
  of Equality, 304–305, 320–321, 336–339, 340–341
proportions, 462–463, 464–467, 478–481, 499, H6–H7
rates, 444–450
rational numbers, 115–116
simple interest, 506–507
Standardized Test Prep, 30, 62, 86, 139, 167, 221, 241, 296, 314, 330, 388, 414, 458, 488, 540, 593
surface area, 596–599
unknown factors, 5
variables, 11, 280
**Algebra tiles,** 302, 318, 334–335
**Algebraic operating system (AOS),** 271, 277
**Alternate angles,** 437
**Altitude**
  of triangles, 578
**Angles**
  acute, 370, 391
  adjacent, 369, 371
  alternate, 437
  central, 433
  complementary, 374–375
  congruent, 371, 476
  corresponding, 437, 476–477
  exterior, 437
  interior, 437
  measurement of, 369, 376–381, 393–395
  obtuse, 370, 391
  properties of, 437
  relationships among, 368, 379
  right, 367, 370, 391
  straight, 391
  supplementary, 376–377
  triangles, 393–395
  types of, 370–372
  vertex of, 370
  vertical, 369, 371
**Answers**
  evaluating for reasonableness, 528–529

# Photo Credits

KEY: (t) top, (b) bottom, (l) left, (r) right, (c) center, (bg) background, (fg) foreground.

**Front Cover:** (l) Age Fotostock/SuperStock; (r) Pixtal/SuperStock.

**Back Cover:** (l) Pixtal/SuperStock; (r) Greg Probst/Getty Images.

**Front Endsheets:** Page 1 & 2 James Randklev/Photographer's Choice RF/Getty Images; Page 3 Photodisc/Veer.

**Back Endsheets:** Page 1 Phil Schermeister/Corbis;; Page 2 & 3 Bruce Forster/The Image Bank/Getty Images.

**Title Page:** (l) Age Fotostock/SuperStock; (r) Pixtal/SuperStock.

**Copyright Page:** Greg Probst/Getty Images.

**Table of Contents:** iv Carmel Studios/SuperStock; vi Kevin Schafer/Getty Images; viii Gala/SuperStock; x Adam Jones/Getty Images; xii Peter Ginter/Getty Images; xiv Louie Psihoyos/Corbis; xvi Joson/zefa/Corbis; xviii Larry Fisher/Masterfile; xx-xxi Gary Crabbe/Agefoto.

**Unit 1:** 1 (t) The Futures Channel; 1 (c) The Futures Channel; 1 (b) The Futures Channel; 2 Lester Lefkowitz/Getty Images; 4 Larry Caine, Right Light Photography; 7 (cl) Matthew Ward/Dorling Kindersley; 7 (c) Achim Holzem/iStockPhoto; 7 (cr) Konrad Zelazowski/Alamy; 14 Jeff Greenberg/Age Fotostock; 17 ROBYN BECK/AFP/Getty Images; 18 Juan Silva/Getty Images; 19 ASAP Ltd/PictureQuest/Jupiter Images; 20 Stephen Dunn/Getty Images; 21 Masterfile Royalty Free; 23 (b) Tom Pantages/Stock Photos; 25 Neo Vision/Getty Images; 29 (bg) Siede Preis/Photodisc/Getty Images; 32 Carmel Studios/SuperStock; 34 Lawrence Migdale/Photo Researchers, Inc.; 35 Soren Hald/ Getty Images; 36 John Giustina/ Getty Images (Royalty-free); 37 Photodisc/Getty; 41 (tr) Wally Eberhart/Visuals Unlimited; 41 (br) MedioImages/SuperStock; 42 John Foxx/Getty Images (Royalty-free); 43 Stan Honda/AFP/Getty Images; 44 Associated Press; 45 (t) John M. Heller/Getty Images; 45 (inset) AP Photo/Ric Francis; 51 BE&W agencja fotograficzna Sp. z o.o./Alamy; 52 (tr) Roy Gumpel/Getty Images; 52 (br) Ron Kimball Stock/Jupiter Images; 53 Justin Sullivan/Getty Images; 54 Macduff Everton/The Image Works; 57 Ann Ronan Picture Library/Heritage-Images/The Image Works; 61 (tr) The Rhind Mathematical Papyrus, written during the Hyksos Period but claiming to be a copy of a 12th Dynasty work, c.1550 BC (by Egyptian, Second Intermediate Period (c.1750-c.1650 BC). British Museum, London, UK/ The Bridgeman Art Library; 68 Michael Beiriger/Alamy; 69 Greg Vaughn/Alamy; 70 STOCKFOLIO/Alamy; 71 David Young-Wolff/Photo Edit; 72 Myrleen Ferguson Cate/Photo Edit; 73 Pat Doyle/Corbis; 74 Alan King/Alamy; 76 (t) Nordicphotos/Alamy; 76 (b) Jacqui Hurst/Corbis; 77 Michael Newman/Photo Edit; 78 Dorling Kindersley/Getty; 80 Paul Barton/Corbis; 81 (t) Joanne Schmaltz/Stockfood; 81 (b) Mario Lara; 88 Ben Margot/Associated Press; 92 PhotoStockFile/Alamy; 97 (t) Lorne Resnick/age fotostock; 100 David Butow/Corbis SABA; 101 Juliet Butler/Alamy; 102 Tom McHugh/Photo Researchers, Inc.; 105 (b) Corbis/ Harcourt; 112 (tr) Matthew Cavanaugh/epa/Corbis; 112 (cr) The Granger Collection, New York; 112-113 (bg) PhotoLink/Getty Images;

**Unit 2:** 115 (t) NASA/JPL/MSSS; 115 (b) NASA; 115 (c) NASA/JPL; 116 Getty Images/PhotoDisc/Harcourt; 119 Estelle Klawitter/zefa/Corbis; 123 Jean Miele/Corbis; 125 Keith Wood/Getty Images; 126 Brad Wrobleski/Masterfile; 128 CORBIS; 129 Gibson Stock Photography; 137 (bg) PhotoDisc/Getty Images/Harcourt; 140 Kevin Schafer/Getty Images; 144 Duomo/Corbis; 150 Harry Melchert/Newscom; 151 Scott Markewtiz/age fotostock; 155 Getty/Harcourt; 157 Scholastic Studio 10/Index Stock Imagery; 160 Getty Images/PhotoDisc/ Harcourt; 168 Andre Gunther; 172 Bob Grieser/AP Wide World; 173 Alexis Rosenfeld/Science Photo Library; 176 Index Stock Imagery; 177 Greg Ceo/Getty; 178 Jeff Lepore/Photo Researchers; 182 Mike Segar/Reuters/Corbis; 185 Gareth Brown/Corbis; 186 (t) Craig Aurness/Corbis; 186 (b) Bryan Reinhart/Masterfile; 191 (bg) Brand X Pictures/Alamy; 194 (tr) Galen Rowell/Corbis; 194-195 (bg) Ed Freeman/Getty Images; 195 (tr) Arco Images/Alamy.

**Unit 3:** 197 (t) The Futures Channel; 197 (c) United States Department of Agriculture; 197 (b) Public Domain; 198 Gala/SuperStock; 200 SW Production/Index Stock Imagery, Inc.; 201 Getty Images; 202 (cl) Pierre Arsenault/Masterfile; 202 (br) Amos Morgan/Getty; 205 Visual & Written/NewsCom; 206 Richard Hutchings/PhotoEdit; 208 Marji McNeely/Alamy; 209 Purestock/Alamy; 210 Image of Sport Photos/NewsCom; 211 (tr) Jim Zipp/Ardea London Ltd; 211 (tl) Craig K. Lorenz/Photo Researchers; 211 (tcl) Jim Zipp/Photo Researchers; 211 (bcl) Danita Delimont/Alamy; 211 (bl) Phillip Colla Photography Natural History Photography; 213 Glow Images/Alamy; 214 Brian Sytnyk/Masterfile; 215 Chuck Fox/Fox Photography Services; 219 (tr) Royalty-Free/Corbis; 219 (bg) Eddie Linssen/Alamy; 222 Les Walker/NewSport/Corbis; 226 Mike Brinson - Getty Images; 227 Anthony Arendt/California Stock Photo; 228 MIMOTITO/Getty Images; 229 Joel W. Rogers/Corbis; 230 (l) Royalty-Free/Corbis; 230 (r) Aaron Horowitz/Corbis; 231 Getty Images/RubberBall Productions/Harcourt Index; 232 Kevin Summers/Getty; 233 (cr) Peloton Sports; 234 Gary W. Sargent Sargent Stock Image Resource; 235 (tr) ALEXANDRA WINKLER/Reuters/Corbis; 235 (br) ACE STOCK LIMITED/Alamy; 239 (bg) Royalty-Free/Corbis; 242 Andrew McKinney/California Stock Photo; 244 Lawrence Migdale/Getty; 246 Stockdisc/Getty; 247 Getty/Harcourt; 250 Jim Cummins/Getty; 253 age fotostock; 254 Getty Images; 255 (tr) Tony Freeman/PhotoEdit; 255 (br) Mark Gibson Photography; 256 Corbis; 258 Dennis Flaherty/Getty Images; 263 (tr) Michael DeYoung/Corbis; 263 (bg) Chase Jarvis/Corbis; 266 (inset) Mark Downey/California Stock Photo; 266-267 (bg) AP Photo/Paul Sakuma; 267 (inset) Colin Keates/Dorling Kindersley;

**Unit 4:** 269 (t) The Futures Channel; 269 (c) The Futures Channel; 269 (b) The Futures Channel; 270 Tony Roberts/Corbis; 274 Tim Mantoani/Masterfile; 275 Medioimages/Getty Images; 283 Chuck Savage/Corbis; 285 Mike McGill/Corbis; 286 Supermole Collection/Alamy; 288 Gene Lee/iStockPhoto; 289 D. Hurst/Alamy; 298 Jonathan Nourok/PhotoEdit; 300 Richard Levine/Alamy; 301 Iain Masterton/Alamy; 304 AP Photo/Pat Little; 305 Purestock/Alamy; 308 Gary Ombler/Getty Images; 309 (tr) Steve Allen/Alamy; 309 (br) K-PHOTOS/Alamy; 316 Creatas/SuperStock; 320 Dennis MacDonald/Photo Edit; 321 Felicia Martinez/PhotoEdit; 322 M.T.M. Images/Alamy; 324 Jeff Morgan/Alamy; 325 Mark Boulton/Alamy; 329 (bg) Neil Beer/Photodisc Red/Getty Images; 332 Adam Jones/Getty Images; 337 Royalty-Free/Corbis; 339 David M Allen; 340 (tl) Hans Reinhard/Bruce Coleman; 340 (tr) Stephen J. Krasemann/DRK; 340 (cr) Marty Cordano/DRK; 340 (br) Art Wolfe, Inc.; 343 Renee Morris/Alamy; 344 Creatas/age fotostock; 347 BananaStock/Alamy; 350 Glow Images/Alamy; 352 Michael DeYoung/Corbis; 355 Robert Houser/Index Stock Imagery. Inc.; 356 (t) Andre Jenny/Alamy; 356 (b) Gilsdorf/AGE Fotostock; 357 Royalty-Free/Corbis; 364 Bettmann/Corbis; 364-365 (bg) Neema Frederic/GAMMA/NewsCom; 365 NASA.

**Unit 5:** 367 (t) The Futures Channel; 367 (c) The Futures Channel; 367 (b) The Futures Channel; 368 Peter Ginter/Getty Images; 370 Rick Gomez/Masterfile; 371 (br) Farrell Grehan/Corbis/© 2007 Frank Lloyd Wright Foundation/Artists Rights Society (ARS), New York.; 373 Richard Broadwell/Alamy; 374 Gary Moon; 376 Arthur Stern Studios; 378 Pascal Rondeau/Getty; 379 Duomo/Corbis; 381 Sean Justice/Getty Images; 383 AP Photo/Edis Jurcys; 387 (bg) Age Fotostock/SuperStock; 390 Jeremy Woodhouse/Masterfile; 392 Lee Snider/The Image Works; 396 LeighSmithImages/Alamy; 403 (br) Dave G. Houser/Corbis; 404 Douglas Hill/Beateworks/Corbis; 407 John Prior Images/Alamy; 416 Mark Downey/Lucid Images; 421 Corbis; 424

Courtesy of the New York Marriott Marquis; 425 Graham French/Masterfile; 427 WireImageStock/Masterfile; 428 Tim Street-Porter/Beateworks/Corbis; 433 (tl) Corbis/Harcourt; 433 (bg) © Royalty-Free/Corbis; 436 (tr) Enlightened Images/Jupiterimages; 436-427 (bg) Roy Ooms/Masterfile; 437 (tl) AP Photo/Kim D. Johnson; 437 (tc) Virginia Fitzherbert/Alamy; 437 (tr) Peter Bennett/California Stock Photo; 437 (cl) Tom Benoit/SuperStock; 437 (cr) Jupiterimages.

Unit 6: 439 (t) The Futures Channel; 439 (c) The Futures Channel; 439 (b) The Futures Channel; 440 Zoological Society of San Diego; 442 Roger Du Buisson/Corbis; 444 Gibson Stock Photography; 447 (t) Stockdisc/Getty; 447 (tc) Getty/Harcourt; 447 (bc) Corbis; 447 (b) Getty/Harcourt; 449 Robert Harding World Imagery/Corbis; 450 Alamy; 451 Lawrence Migdale; 452 David Young-Wolff/PhotoEdit; 453 LLC, Vstock /Index Stock Imagery; 457 (tr) Free Agents Limited/Corbis; 457 (cr) PhotoDisc/Getty Images/Harcourt; 460 Louie Psihoyos/Corbis; 464 (tr) Noella Ballenger/Alamy; 464 (inset) Zoran Milich- Masterfile; 466 Getty/Harcourt; 467 (l) rubberball/ Getty Images; 467 (r) Getty/Harcourt; 468 Gary Crabbe/Alamy; 470 Ron Niebrugge/Alamy; 471 Science VU/Visuals Unlimited; 472 Carmo Correia/Alamy; 473 Getty/Harcourt; 474 (c) Tif Hunter/Getty Images; 474 (b) Matthias Kulka/Corbis; 475 C&GS Season's Report Karo 1936-88/NOAA; 478 Ulana Switucha/Alamy; 482 Michael Quinton/Minden Pictures; 483 (t) Danita Delimont/Alamy; 483 (b) Konrad Wothe/Minden Pictures; 487 (tr) Amy Eckert/Photonica/Getty Images; 494 Cindy Charles/Photo Edit; 495 (tr) Jeff Greenberg/Photo Edit; 495 (br) Homer Sykes/Alamy; 496 Corbis/Harcourt; 497 Peter M. Wilson/Corbis; 490 Peter Bennett/California Stock Photo; 498 (tr) Steve Allen Travel Photography/Alamy; 498 (cr) Peter Horree/Alamy; 499 (tr) Richard Cummins/Corbis; 499 (br) David R. Frazier/PhotoEdit; 500 Rudi Von Briel/Photo Edit; 501 CLEO Photo/Alamy; 502 Photodisc/Getty Images (Royalty-free); 503 Les David Manevitz/SuperStock; 504 Burke/Triolo Producti/age fotostock; 505 Steve Mason/Getty Images (Royalty-free); 506 (b) David Young-Wolff/Photo Edit; 508 Tom Hussey/JupiterImages; 509 (t) Photodisc/Getty Images; 509 (b) D. Hurst/Alamy; 513 (tr) Chuck Eckert/Alamy; 513 (bg) Corbis; 516 Robert Clay/California Stock Photo; 516-517 (bg) Visions of America, LLC/Alamy; 517 Richard Cummins/SuperStock.

Unit 7: 519 (t) The Futures Channel; 519 (c) The Futures Channel; 519 (b) The Futures Channel; 520 Bill Aron/PhotoEdit; 524 Antonio Ovejero Diaz/ iStockphoto; 526 Nicky Blade/iStockphoto; 528 (t) age fotostock; 528 (b) iStockphoto; 529 Philippe Eranian/Corbis; 532 Getty Images; 533 Getty Images/PhotoDisc/harcourt index; 534 San Rostro/age fotostock; 539 (bg) Corbis/Harcourt; 542 Joson/zefa/Corbis; 548 Acme Food Arts/Jupiter Images; 551 Werner Foreman/Topham/The Image Works; 561 (bg) PhotoDisc/Getty Images/Harcourt; 564 (t) John Still/Getty Images; 564 (b) iStockphoto; 564-565 (bg) Ken Welsh/Alamy; 565 (t) Monopoly in the Park, San Jose; 565 (b) Images of Africa Photobank/Alamy.

Unit 8: 567 (t) The Futures Channel; 567 (c) SISCA; 567 (b) SISCA; 568 George D. Lepp/Corbis; 570 Lance Nelson/Stock Photos/zefa/Corbis; 574 (b) PHONE Labat J.M./Rouqu/Peter Arnold, Inc.; 577 Stephen McBrady/Photo Edit; 583 (bg) Adam Jones/ Getty Images (Royalty-free); 583 (inset) Royalty-Free/Corbis; 587 Haruyoshi Yamaguchi/Corbis; 591 (bg) PhotoDisc/Getty Images/Harcourt; 594 Larry Fisher/Masterfile; 605 Birgid Allig/zefa/Corbis; 610 Kari Erik Marttila Photography/Photographers Direct; 618 Damian P. Gadal/Alamy; 618-619 (bg) Daniel Templeton/Alamy; 619 Kirk Rademaker; Student Handbook: (blind) (bl) Pat Doyle/Corbis.

Student Handbook: H1, (tr) Cyril Laubscher/Getty Images.

All other photos © Harcourt School Publishers. Harcourt photographers; Weronica Ankarorn, Eric Camden, Don, Couch, Doug Dukane, Ken Kinzie, April Riehm, and Steve Williams.

The General Sherman Tree is 275 ft (83 m) high and 36.5 ft (11 m) in diameter at its widest point. It is the largest and one of the oldest living things in the world, estimated to be about 2,500 years old.

Sequoia National Park covers about **405,000 acres.**